P9-ARI-876

SKYSCRAPER

Peter —
Thanks for your
encouragement and
support — read and
enjoy!
— Roger

SKYSCRAPER
The Search for an American Style
1891–1941

Annotated extracts from the first
50 Years of *Architectural Record*

edited by

Roger Shepherd

McGraw-Hill

New York   Chicago   San Francisco   Lisbon   London   Madrid
Mexico City   Milan   New Delhi   San Juan   Seoul
Singapore   Sydney   Toronto

McGraw-Hill

*A Division of The **McGraw·Hill** Companies*

1 2 3 4 5 6 7 8 9 0 DOC/DOC 0 9 8 7 6 5 4 3 2

ISBN 0–07–136970–8

The sponsoring editor for this book was Cary Sullivan; the production supervisor was Sherri Souffrance. This book was designed by Roger Shepherd; associate designer was Susannah Shepherd. Chapters were set in Optima; main articles were set in Bembo; notes and excerpts were set in Univers; dates were set in Goudy Old Style.

Printed and bound by R R Donnelley.

Cataloging-in-Publication Data is on file with the Library of Congress.

This book was printed on acid-free paper.

McGraw-Hill books are available at special quantity discounts to use as premiums and sales promotions, or for use in corporate training programs. For more information, please write to the Director of Special Sales, Professional Publishing, McGraw-Hill, Two Penn Plaza, New York, NY 10121-2298. Or contact your local bookstore.

For my grandfather,
George Arthur Shepherd (1885–1983)

It is an amusing conception to imagine a mind exactly balanced between two equal desires. For it is indubitable that it will never decide, since inclination and choice imply inequality in value; and if we were placed between the bottle and the ham with an equal appetite for drinking and for eating, there would doubtless be no solution but to die of thirst and of hunger. [1]

Montaigne

Beauty rests on necessities. The line of beauty is the result of perfect economy. The cell of the bee is built at that angle which gives the most strength with the least wax; the bone or the quill of the bird gives the most alar strength, with the least weight. "It is the purgation of superfluities," said Michelangelo. There is not a particle to spare in natural structures. There is a compelling reason in the uses of the plant for every novelty of color or form: and our art saves material by more skillful arrangement, and reaches beauty by taking every superfluous ounce that can be spared from a wall, and keeping all its strength in the poetry of columns. In rhetoric, this art of omission is a chief secret of power and, in general, it is proof of high culture to say the greatest matters in the simplest way. [2]

Ralph Waldo Emerson

To be an American is of itself almost a moral condition, an education, and a career. [3]

George Santayana

It is no linguistic accident that "building," "construction, "work," designate both a process and its finished product. Without the meaning of the verb that of the noun remains blank. [4]

John Dewey

Buildings are for a little while, but the idea remains forever. [5]

A. N. Rebori

This is not a history of the skyscraper. It's a compilation of some of the most pungent and effectual criticism written for one of the most influential architecture magazines ever published—*Architectural Record.*[6] Robert A.M. Stern once noted that, "*Architectural Record* was unquestionably the most innovative among the American professional journals…a sounding board for new ideas."[7] This book is a look at how those ideas affect the way we see and think about architecture and ourselves.

Stern's "sounding board" metaphor is a good one. No matter how polemical their ideas, or strident their tone, the editors at *Record* strove always to maintain critical balance in their magazine. And, when it came to ideas about the new, quintessentially American, urban phenomenon called the "sky-scraper," the magazine was particularly balanced, scrupulously weighing the pros and cons of the so-called "problem" in minute detail. A roster of notables wrote for the magazine—architects as well as professional critic/writers—and, they all had strong opinions about the skyscraper.

The pieces chosen for this volume focus on questions of meaning. What is the nature of this new building form? How can it be expressed in architectural terms? How does it express who we are? Is it even capable of expressing who we are? Every question resonates at deeper levels than first meets the eye (or the inner ear). Individually, the articles are often so remarkable that one can still sense the impact they originally had on the search for an American style. Together they form a kind of cultural history.

Readers may be disappointed if their favorite skyscraper doesn't appear in this collection. Some structures now considered important weren't written about at the time, or when they were, the writing was so unimportant as to warrant omitting it here. Others, included here, were once important and have been forgotten. Maybe we'll see them again, and remember them.

The articles in this book have been brought together for the first time. They have been centrally placed on the page and are almost always reprinted in their entirety. Editorial commentary is kept to a bare minimum so that readers may draw their own conclusions. Ideas are more meaningful in

1 From "How Our Mind Hinders Itself," by Montaigne, *Essays*, II:14, p. 462.

2 From "Beauty" in *The Conduct of Life*, essays by Ralph Waldo Emerson, Boston, 1860, p. 253.

3 From "Character and Opinion in the United States," by George Santayana, 1920, p. 32.

4 From "Art and Experience," by John Dewey, 1924, p. 51.

5 From "Louis H. Sullivan (1856-1924)," obituary by A. N. Rebori, [55:6 Jun 1924 p 587].* See page 211.

6 With the June, 1937 issue, *The Architectural Record* became just *Architectural Record*. For the sake of simplicity, the newer name is used in commentary and notes throughout this book.

7 Robert A.M. Stern, *GEORGE HOWE: TOWARD A MODERN ARCHITECTURE*, Yale:New Haven 1975, p. 77.

---

* Citations for articles that appear in *Architectural Record* always take the following form: [volume:number, month year, page(s)].

their original contexts; it's then that these essays are actually thrilling to read. Articles in the margins are there because they shed light on the central ones: these are often excerpts. Notes are given for things that might be otherwise obscure. Unfortunately, some things remain obscure.

Without reproducing the pages as such, an attempt has been made to give the reader a feel for the magazine, particularly the quality of its photographs. Because *Architectural Record* is ostensibly a magazine for the professional, practicing architect, its imagery was and continues to be as influential as its texts (the keen observer can spot where Frank Lloyd Wright picked up many an idea and where, in turn others took a few from him). With all the visual comparisons and connections that can be made, the reader might regard this as a kind of scrapbook.

Wherever possible, photos and graphics have been taken from the articles in which they originally appeared. In cases where a higher quality image accompanies a later article, it has been substituted for an older one. Sometimes articles are without illustrations; so photos, when they appear, have been taken from other articles. In a few of the earliest cases the printed images are of such poor quality, that better, more informative photographs have been substituted; the lenders are given credit on page 297.

Skyscraper histories abound and new ones are published every day. There are far too many to include in a bibliography. The recommended reading list is therefore, comprised of books, both new and classic, that place the skyscraper in some other, larger context.

With a project of this scope, there are many people to thank for their assistance; I sincerely hope I haven't forgotten anyone. I am grateful to my research assistants Caryn Varley and Lara Marrero for their persistent detective work. Without my picture researcher Barbara Hatfield this book would have been far less attractive—thank you. I'm not sure what I would have done without the sharp eyes, talented hands, and indefatigable energy of my associate designer Susannah Shepherd. The editors and staff at *Architectural Record* are generous to a fault, especially Editor-in-Chief Robert Ivy. I thank them for unlimited access to their archives, and I thank Robert Ivy for his personal support. A heartfelt debt of gratitude goes to my agent Faith Hamlin, who always stands up for quality. Thanks to my indexer, Barry Koffler. And, I thank Ann Ledy for her love and emotional support.

*These colored bands represent the height of the
tallest building in the world during each interval
on the time-line at the below. The time-line
spans the period from 1891 to 1941—the first
fifty years of* Architectural Record. *It continues
from here, uninterrupted, through to the end of
the book. By comparing the colored band on any
page to this chart, the reader will see which is
the tallest building at that time.*

1250 feet

Empire State Building, New York City,
Shreve Lamb and Harmon, architects, 1931.

1046 feet

Chrysler Building, New York City
William Van Alen, architect, 1930.

792 feet

Woolworth Building, New York City
Cass Gilbert, architect, 1910–1913.

700 feet

Metropolitan Life Tower, New York City
Napoleon LeBrun & Sons, architects, 1909.

612 feet

Singer Tower, New York City
Ernest Flagg, architect, 1905–08 (demolished 1967).

391 feet

Park Row or **Syndicate Building**, New York City
Robert H. Robertson, architect, 1896–99.

309 feet

World (Pulitzer) Building, New York City
George Browne Post, architect, 1888–90 (demolished).

prologue

The Skyscraper Problem: A Question of Style

January 1899 saw the publication of a critical assessment of the state of the tall building and a suggested "starting point for designers who may insist upon attacking the *problem* instead of evading it." Appearing as it did at the close of one century and the beginning of another, the article intended to influence the future direction of urban architecture, particularly the new building type called the skyscraper. And, it did.

In just the first paragraph we are informed that the elevator doubled the height of office buildings and the steel-frame doubled it again. The result is nearly as distinct an architectural type as the Greek temple or the Gothic cathedral. But, after only 25 years, the treatment is conventional and formulaic. Some "wild work" is expected, but designers have ceased to be experimental. The architect mistakes novelty for originality, when he should be using old forms in new ways. American architects could be better educated, both theoretically and technically. There's less eccentricity and more homogeneity among 20-story buildings than there used to be among 5-story buildings.

After the passage of 100 years, it seems these same concerns, more or less, are still at the heart of things.

The article, "The Sky-scraper Up-To-Date" (page 51), is by Montgomery Schuyler. With a handful of like-minded writers, Schuyler had founded a new kind of magazine just eight years earlier—*Architectural Record*—a publication that almost immediately became one of the most important and influential of its kind.[a]

Already a journalist of some repute, but lacking any architectural training, Schuyler soon became an exponent of a progressive American esthetic and the leading architectural critic of his time. His "point of view" was founded on the critical premise that "the radical defect of modern architecture in general, if not of American architecture in particular, is the estrangement between architecture and building, between the poetry and the

World (Pulitzer) Building, New York City
George Browne Post, architect
1888–90 (demolished) [b]

prose." Schuyler's point of view was essentially the magazine's.

If there were an *estrangement* between architecture and building, then it was evident in all economically advanced, capitalist societies, particularly in the United States, where a struggle between lingering old-world traditions and the forces of industrialization was constantly playing itself out. In just about every endeavor American's sought to find expression of their practical and indomitable national spirit, a spirit caught squarely between the old and the new.

In the 1840s and 50s, the English writer and critic of art and architecture, John Ruskin feared an imminent rift between science and art as a consequence of the industrial revolution. Ruskin admonished the architect to remain clear as to the difference "between mere building and architecture." As a figure whose writings had immense power of persuasion, even more so in America than in England, Ruskin may have arguably contributed to the rift as much as he warned everyone against it.

Montgomery Schuyler disagreed with Ruskin. He believed that architecture *is* building, and he aimed to repair the damage and set the record straight for the sake of the American public. While the intellectual environment at *Architectural Record* invited opposing viewpoints, the writers sympathized with Schuyler's desire to reconcile "the poetry and the prose." When condemning, they were never reactionary; when praising, rarely evangelistic—though they did see themselves as progressive reformers. They were all thoroughly engaged in the here and now, and found effective ways to influence America's architectural and cultural identity. The only thing they mutually abhorred was eclecticism,[c] an architecture of fashion that mixed borrowed forms to pander to every taste.

We initially quoted Schuyler promising to give a "starting point" for architects who want to attack the "problem." What is this starting point? In fact, just what is the *problem*? The reader is welcome to go to the article to find out, but should be warned that there are always more questions to be found in these pages than answers. For our authors, defining the skyscraper was as much a part of the so-called *problem* as finding any particular solution. This is really as it should be, though admittedly one often feels as if one were in an existential morass. The writers weren't unclear nor trying to obfuscate; they were just trying to figure it out. In between defining the problem and attempting a solution is the place where style naturally emerges. Good critics that they were, and many of them were also architects, they knew that proscribed rules could be an even *bigger* problem. As Ada Louise Huxtable wittily points out, "there is more than one way to skin a skyscraper…

> "there are not, and never have been, any immutable rules. … Contrary to accepted opinion and the respected critical texts, there have been many appropriate and legitimate responses to the conflicting cultural forces of our time."

One thing is for certain, the skyscraper is more than a tall building. From its origins in the 1880s until the end of the Great Depression, the skyscraper, along with

a In the 1880s, professional journals began to replace books as principle sources of information about current building practice. In 1891, only two major architectural journals were being published, both established in 1876: *American Architect and Building News* in Boston and *Architecture and Building* in New York. In 1891, four new journals began publication: *Architectural Record* in New York, *Architectural Review* in Boston, *Inland Architect & News Record* and *Western Architect*, both in Chicago. In 1903, *Architecture* began publication and in 1913, the *American Institute of Architects' Journal* was established.

b The 26-story, 309-foot-high structure had three-story entrance and a gold dome reminiscent of Michelangelo's design for St. Peters. Montgomery Schuyler worked for the *New York World* from 1865 to 1868.

c A good example of eclecticism, the Record Building, Philadelphia (above) appeared as the third in a series of *Architectural Aberrations*. The series began with the second issue (1891).

"The 'problem of the skyscraper' indeed! Who is there among our architects that has had courage, we will not say to squarely face it and strive with it, but even to seriously think about it?"

1891

Harry W. Desmond A Rational Skyscraper, *Architectural Record, 1904.*

An ad for iron and steelwork shows the "skin" of a building being applied while the building mounts ever higher.

The four piers that support this structure can be "seen" on its façade. Doll and Sons Building, New York City, Alfred Bossom, architect, 1920.

The first fully glass curtain wall: Hallidie Building, San Francisco, Willis Jefferson Polk, 1918.

the changing city, became a focus of debate over most things architectural and cultural. Feelings were often mixed, but passions always ran high. It's all here.

Hindsight may make it appear so, but life just isn't very neat. Whereas material in a book such this can be put in order (in this case a chronological one), the intentions (or perceived intentions) behind the writings cannot be. We have a group of individuals with extremely different points of view voicing their opinions in an open forum over a fifty-year period of intense change. Regardless, a great deal is to be gained through the diversity. Readers might best regard themselves as *eyewitnesses*. Read the articles as you would a magazine—compare images—make connections and draw your own conclusions.

Certain themes will emerge. One of them is a constantly evolving set of oppositions in an ongoing "battle of the styles," as the early writers often called it. Simply put, these contests occur between things like engineering and architecture; the old world and the new; traditional forms *versus* function and experimentation; commerce and utility *versus* art and beauty, the rational mind *versus* the spirit; the machine *versus* humanity; size *versus* scale. Together, they reflect a kind of collective anxiety, the American struggle with the space between the ideal and the actual. And, *struggle* is the operative term. Americans don't clothe or house themselves with ease, as do the people of Sweden say, or the Ivory Coast. They struggle with culture self-consciously, like Jacob wrestling the angel. In fact, his book might have been called *Skyscraper Agonistes*—much agony, and very little ecstasy. But, then why should this be any different from American politics? Or, education? Or, art? Someday Americans will find out who they are—and be comfortable with it. Meanwhile, the by-products of this process are pretty interesting if we pay attention. It is their *in-betweeness* that is often most American.

> "Our "architectural aberrations" are the slag and scoriæ thrown off in this crystallizing process. Our worthiest performances, whether Romanesque or Renaissance in detail, are strongly American in character, and I cannot help thinking them finger-posts (if I may here change my metaphor) pointing to a still more truly American architecture which in some future time, nearer or more remote, shall be worthy of the age and of the people that gave it existence."

Here A.D.F. Hamlin shares with his fellow critics a desire to peer below the surface and to reconcile extreme terms. These terms change over the decades—taking many forms—but, one thing they have in common, especially when Lewis Mumford joined the magazine, is that architectural expression is bound to *use*—*people* must interact with buildings. What architecture expresses cannot be totally abstract, and it can't be camoflaqued, or hidden. Often forgotten, *people* are the ultimate subject.

Lewis Mumford decried the rupture between public and private life actually caused by the skyscraper. He reminds us that one potential place to resolve this dilemma is right on the street, where the pedestrian is invited into a space, or put off as the case may be. Writing about the newly completed Empire State Building,

Talbot Faulkner Hamlin criticized its architects for not adequately addressing the relationship of the building to the street, and consequently, to the public.

"And the street and avenue façades are a disappointment. As in the case in so many high buildings, a soaring and carefully composed grandeur above disintegrates near the ground level. Great tower scale and pleasant street scale seem difficult to reconcile. The Empire State Building architects recognized this inevitable discrepancy, and by placing the tower as it is, freed it from the building around its base. They created thus a great street façade of pleasing height, a whole block long on Fifth Avenue, and several hundred feet on each of the side streets: apparently, an ideal problem for any architect. And then, apparently the creative drive faded; perhaps speed in designing-the curse of American commercial architecture-prevented adequate study; perhaps the tower absorbed the designers' interest over-much. In any case, there lay the opportunity, and it was lost. Superficial and obvious, its generally merely satisfactory proportions, its rich materials cannot redeem its heavy-handed detail, its basic lack of that creative imagination that distinguishes the tower. To the thousands passing, it brings no lift, no "kick"-it is just another building to walk past-adequate perhaps, but humdrum."

If we return, where we began, to Montgomery Schuyler's article, "The Sky-scraper Up-To-Date," we find one of his observations, in particular, still carries a certain immediate urgency:

"Now, New York has no skyline at all. It is all interruptions, of various heights and shapes and sizes, not even peaks in a mountain range, but scattered or huddled towers which have nothing to do with each other or with what is below."

One of the things that makes a book such as this one important now, and not simply an historical curiosity, is that many of its lessons are *still* waiting to be learned. Just ten short months after the disastrous events surrounding the attack on the World Trade Center, six architectural concepts for the redevelopment of lower Manhattan were put on public display and unveiled in the press. The relative merits of the designs aside, what is most striking about the published presentations is that the newspapers show aerial views of models and schematic plans of land use; none of these show the public what they would encounter on the street.

Let's not be dismayed. The skyscraper may remain a restless object, difficult to define, but there's a treasure trove here waiting to be discovered along the way. Let's accept Harry Desmond's invitation once again, when he says at the end of the very first article,

"A more persistent attempt is needed to build up "a pile of better thoughts" sufficient to be fruitful in great effects, and that is the work which, in really a humble frame of mind, the projectors of THE ARCHITECTURAL RECORD now undertake—not pedantically or after the manner of the pedagogue, but popularly, illustratively, even tentatively, as a traveler sets out for a destination not immediate nor lying at the end of a well-defined, direct and visible route. The road in part has to be discovered, and in the search, which is to be progressive, our readers are asked to accompany us."

(continued on page xiv)

from:
AN "AMERICAN STYLE"
OF ARCHITECTURE
By Barr Ferre
Vol. I, No. 1, July–September 1891,
pp.39–45.

The study of the history of Architecture shows in the most positive manner that the great historical styles—which it is fondly hoped the American will surpass—are the products of natural evolution spread over centuries of time; and are the resultants of the action of very many causes. In one sense their existence is as natural as that of a plant or of an animal. Many attempts have been made to deliberately design an American style of architecture by devising certain ornamental details without undertaking to introduce a principle distinctively American. All, however, rest on the error of supposing that a style of Architecture is something that can be designed or drawn to order on a sheet of paper, much as a client would order his architect to prepare a drawing for a house in some special style. No architectural style originated in such a hypothetical fashion in the past, and amazing as is the fertility of American invention, there is no reason to suppose it can overcome the operation of a law of nature by such a method.

from:
THE BATTLE OF THE STYLES: Part I
By A.D.F. Hamlin
Vol. I, No. 3, January–March 1892,
pp. 265–275.

Architecture has its origin in the material needs of mankind, and these, must necessarily control its development. It has furthermore to deal with the stern laws of gravitation and of the strength of materials, to whose behests all its manifestations must be subordinated. In these aspects, then, it is purely utilitarian, and if it stops here, is not an art, but a science or a trade; it is mere building or engineering.

1891

1 By Harry W. Desmond
[I:3, Jan–Mar 1892 p 277].

2 Philadelphia's commercial architecture, almost always dispar-
aged by RECORD writers, is
described in one article as, "in
the mass, abnormal because the
authors of it do not perceive, or
willfully disregard, the fact that
there is any architectural norma."
[Vol. III, No. 2, October–
December, 1893, p. 207].

3 The "West" refers to Chicago
and "Western Architecture" will
later be called the Chicago
School. The "Westerner" here is
Louis Sullivan or someone very
much like him. The article is
accompanied by a line drawing
(opposite) representing Adler and
Sullivan's second skyscraper
(after their Wainwright Building.
The caption reads, "New German
Opera House." It is actually the
Garrick Theater, 1893, now
known as the Schiller Building.

4 The most famous architect of
Greece, Ictinus flourished in the
second half of the 5th century BC
and was a contemporary of
Pericles and Phidias. He is best
known for the Parthenon and the
temple of Apollo at Bassae.

* John Ruskin (1819–1900) felt
that building technology had
made a farce of the Classic style.

"It is very necessary, in the outset of
all inquiry, to distinguish carefully
between Architecture and
Building....Let us, therefore, at once
confine the name to that art
which...impresses on the building
certain characteristics venerable or
beautiful, but otherwise unnecessary....It may not be always easy to
draw the line sharply and simply;
because there are few buildings
which have not some pretense of
colour or being architectural; neither
can there be any Architecture which
is not based on building; but it
is...very necessary...to understand
fully that Architecture concerns itself
only with those characters of any
edifice which are above and beyond
its common use."

opposite: Schiller Building,
Chicago, Adler & Sullivan, architects, 1891-92 (demolished).

In this urbane mock-Platonic dialogue, the reader will get a sense of the many different schools of architectural thought that existed in 1892 and the constant, even contentious disagreement that constituted what the magazine's editors refer to as the "Battle of the Styles."

MODERN ARCHITECTURE
—A CONVERSATION[1]

ARCHITECT (*perturbed, entering School of Modern Architecture*).—The present condition of our art is most perplexing and unsatisfactory. What comfort, I wonder, is there here?

CLASSICIST, GOTH, ROMANESQUER *look up from their drawing boards and smile pityingly.*

ARCHAEOLOGIST (*greeting him*).— Unsatisfactory? Perplexing? We don't find it so here. My dear Sir, possibly (*smiling with air of superiority*) you are not acquainted with the great work we have accomplished by strict attention to archæology. The imitative…

ARCHITECT.—But the creative…

ARCHÆOLOGIST.—The creative in archaeology! My good sir, what place is there…

ARCHITECT.—Pardon me, but I speak of architecture…

ARCHÆOLOGIST.—And, pray, what is architecture but the strict application of archaeology to modern requirements? If architecture is not applied archaeology, what is…

ECLECTIC (*entering*).—Wouldn't a judicious blending of styles meet the case?

Chorus of dissent from CLASSICIST, GOTH and ROMANESQUER.

ECLECTIC.—That's the trouble with you dry-as-dusts. You have only one idea. You have no conception of how freedom invigorates a design. The Gothic, for instance, is all very well, but it needs broadening and stiffening in the joints, if I may say so. Now, I've used it with great success in an exquisite cast-iron front tenement I turned out the other day for a wealthy New Yorker, but I Romanesqued the entrance somewhat, and with the aid of a

heavy modillioned cornice…

GOTH.
CLASSICIST.   } Vandal!
ROMANESQUER.

ECLECTIC.—Gave quite a modern air to the thing. But in Philadelphia…

ARCHÆOLOGIST (*severely*).—Stop, Sir. The name of that piebald city may not be mentioned within these precincts.[2]

ECLECTIC.—Oh, very well, then. Out West …

WESTERN ARCHITECT[3] (*rising from group of listeners*).—Permit me, sir. In the West, you will be interested to know, several of our brainiest architects are now engaged in the creation of an original "American Style," and what with the Chicago system of construction on one hand, and the inventive genius of our people on the other, this copying of effete forms is about ended.

CLASSICIST.—Effete forms, Sir! Ah, how faint is your appreciation of perfection!

GOTH.   } (*in rapture, each
ROMANESQUER.   } looking in a different direction*).—Perfection!

CLASSICIST.—I maintain that hope for architecture to-day lies in the use of certain forms perfected by the Greeks. The tendency of the time to proceed without precedent is subversive of true art. If we are not grammatical…

ARCHÆOLOGIST.—I beg you, archæological.

CLASSICIST.—Have it so if you will— we are barbarous.

GOTH (*to Classicist*).—But you will admit that Greek architecture is quite undeveloped, one may say is really primitive on the constructive side.

ARCHITECT (*eagerly*).—That's it. How am I to harmonize Grecian precedent and modern requirements, which my clients insist shall be satisfied?

CLASSICIST.—Unreasonable beings; art is not for them.

ECLECTIC.—Nonsense! Harmonize! There is no need to harmonize. Our duty is to select. What do the styles exist for if not for that? I am making a design now for an eleven-story office building for a religious "daily" in what

I call the "classic spirit." That's as near as you can get to antiquity. Doric on the ground floor, you know, with a broken pediment and a bull's-eye to get light; Ionic columns above in brick; then Corinthian, with a mansard roof supporting a spire-like tower surmounted by a forty-foot statue of the Freedom of the Press. Greek elegance with Gothic aspiration. I say, you must break away from precedent a little in these matters. Our effort should be confined to retaining the spirit.

CLASSICIST (in horror).—Shade of Ictinus!

ICTINUS[4] (appearing).—Who called me?

CLASSICIST.—Oh, my master.

ICTINUS (sorrowfully).—Slave, I dreamed that I bequeathed to you a lordly kingdom; but it was only a bondage.

CLASSICIST.—But, master, I have followed in thy footsteps. Thy diameters...

ICTINUS.—Diameters! Poor fool. Think you that we live by a formula?

CLASSICIST.—Master, I have measured every column in thy masterpiece and found...

ICTINUS.—Yes, feet and inches; not our spirit.

CLASSICIST.—But how are we to work?

ICTINUS.—In thy own delight, and with reason, as we did, and as the great ones that followed us did.

CLASSICIST.—But to-day our architecture...

ICTINUS.—Your architecture! Where is it? Show me some work that is really yours—that your soul delights in. Therein will be the hope for your art.

ARCHÆOLOGIST.—But are we to ignore the Past?

ICTINUS (smiling).—No, indeed. You cannot. Useless to try, even. But you question the Past only for its What, not for its How. You seek for the dead matter of Art, not for the living spirit, which is the same yesterday, to-day and forever.

ECLECTIC.—Permit me to suggest. You leave out of view, perhaps, our tenements and office buildings.

ICTINUS (shuddering).—No, great Apollo; no. Believe me I don't. They darken our life yonder. 0! Ilissus, and thy quiet places still haunted by our dreams of beauty, hast thou no message for these barbarians. Ah, friend, I see you are the rash one here. You voyage restlessly among old lands; these your companions abide some, here some there. Those tenements and office buildings of which you speak can–be–made –artistic–I–suppose; but they cannot inspire great art. You cannot clothe the petty things of life with majesty. The hands build greatly only where the feet tread reverently. And, really, it seems to me you modern barbarians have no great architecture because there is so little in your lives that demands—and the demand must be imperious—grand expression. Your office buildings and factories and stores are matters of percentage. Art is not. Your theatres—O shade of Æschuylus!—are also per cent affairs, where the curious and idle make exchanges with...

MODERN ARCHITECT.—The theatrical manager.

ICTINUS (warmly).—Friends, why look for a source of great art there? Your day is not favorable. Perceive that. By and by some vision may come to you as the Vision of Beauty came to us and you may follow it as we did.

GOTH.—And as my masters did that which came to them.

ICTINUS (pointing before him).—Look! Look! O! City of the Purple Crown, again I behold thee, and thy temples and sanctified places. Thy olive groves adorn thee, and the wide blue sea worships at thy feet. And the air is filled with the voices of thy heroes, my city, and of thy poets. The eternal gods are there, and their gift is beauty. Oh, this is life again! Feel it!

CLASSICIST.—What is he talking about?

ARCHÆOLOGIST.—Why, where is he gone to? I wanted to question him about the length of the stadium. ■

from:

WHAT IS ARCHITECTURE?
By Barr Ferre
Vol. I, No. 2, October–December 1891,
pp. 199–210.

It is well that our buildings should be harmonious, beautiful, ornamented, that they contribute to our mental health, power and pleasure, but it is a false limitation to use these terms in telling what architecture really is. It is equally erroneous to raise the distinction between building and architecture, as Mr. Ruskin* and a host of lesser lights do. ... It is a most admirable way of relieving architects of the burden of unsatisfactory structures to represent them as the work of the builder, not of the architect....

"Architecture, therefore, comes to be looked upon as an artificial product, the result of the architect's imagination, a work of beauty, not as the outcome of the application of human resources to human needs and circumstances.

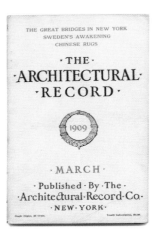

The titles of feature articles, clearly displayed on the magazine's front cover, reveal the scope of its contents and give a clear indication as to the make-up of its readership.

ARCHITECTURAL RECORD was international in scope from the beginning. When it came to the skyscraper, the rise of the tall building was reported in cities across the US as here in "The Architecture of the Pacific Northwest" [XXVI:3 Sept 1909 pp167–175]. The photo shows a "Business Street in Seattle Washington" with its first skyscraper, the Alaska Building.

(continued from page xv)

Though we do it all the time, it is dangerous, to take a series of happenstance events—in this case only those structures deemed worthy to report on in one architecture magazine—and shape them into a coherent story with a beginning, middle, and end. And yet it seems, after all there *is* a beginning, a middle, *and* an end to our story—even a kind of symmetry.

Our tale is sandwiched between two World's Fairs, both held in Chicago; one a tribute to the past, the other a paean to the future. In the middle is the *Tribune* Competition, once more in Chicago; and, of course, Louis Sullivan. We begin with "The Economy of the Office Building," and we end with "The Economic Design of Office Buildings." And, in the latter article is reproduced a note—found in a demolished building's time capsule—written in 1891 just after *Architectural Record* went to press for the first time. So, the circle closes.

The note was written by John M. Carrère of Carrère & Hastings, the architects of the Blair Building (photo page 82). That building, since demolished, was considered a "*tour de force*" in 1904—a near-perfect solution to the skyscraper problem —though few have ever heard of it. The later article (1930) is by Richmond Shreve, an architect few people outside the profession (or academics) know of, a member of the firm responsible for the Empire State Building. Far more than a *tour de force*, the Empire State Building is *the* ultimate skyscraper. So, the Blair Building stands at one end and the Empire State Building at the other.

If this really is a story, it also has a touch of irony, and subsequent tragedy in it. The irony is that the preoccupation with the steel cage, dressing it, undressing it, building higher and more massively, all this has distracted us from some very good, often beautiful buildings—buildings that "lost" the contests—many of them still in our midst. Some of these, at first considered to play important roles in the development of the skyscraper type, were given no further thought once the race for height took hold. As a consequence, the hotels, warehouses, and department stores included in this book are rarely included in the discussions of the skyscraper. Worse, many are just ignored—or forgotten altogether.

The tragedy is that, beginning with the demolition of the Tower Building in 1905 (page 8), only 17 years old at the time of its "passing," skyscrapers began to be replaced as frequently as any other American building. John Ruskin's admonition, "when we build, let us think that we build forever," was understood from the beginning to be an unacceptable motto. In "The Economy of the Office Building," George Hill says, "It sounds very imposing to say 'We are building for all time.' It might be much better business to say, 'We are building for fifteen years.'"

The good news is that, as readers make their way through this book, a remarkably wide array of striking buildings—many still standing, some familiar, others not—will surprise and delight. Perhaps, the familiar will now look different. Maybe we will look at them *all* again with a fresh eye, an open mind, and a deeper insight. ∎

In 1966, Emerson Cole, an editor at Architectural Record, wrote a brief, but fairly thorough history of the first 75 years of the magazine. It is in keeping with the themes of this book to present the article here intact, rather than to summarize its contents.

ARCHITECTURAL RECORD THROUGH 75 YEARS[1]

When I started to review ARCHITECTURAL RECORD through its 75 years of publishing, I must confess, I hoped for a brisk no-nonsense journey, and a quick review of high spots. But the entrancements were not to be denied, and no urge to speed could stand up against the absorbing interest of such a vast store of architectural knowledge and inspiration. The pressure of time yielded to the temptations of riches, and perhaps to the nostalgia of the pace and attitudes of times past.

At any rate I found myself sitting back to read whole articles—long articles they were too—and searching out events and comments and criticisms. Sometimes there was a chuckle over by-gone phases or styles or publishing mannerisms, but the more I read the more my respect grew for the editors, contributors, architects, and commentators—gentlemen, scholars and judges of good architecture. And always ready to leap forward, and to put up a fight when necessary.

The quality of perspicacity is probably what impressed me most. At least there is a consistency about it that goes on through changes in leadership and approach. I have always heard about the famous days of the early RECORD, when some great names in the field of criticism—Montgomery Schuyler, Herbert Croly, Russell Sturgis and others—joined with historians and teachers to educate the public about architecture. They were perceptive, yes indeed, but the perceptiveness of RECORD editors took many other directions, and continued on through many periods when criticism as such gave way to other forms of communication.

This characteristic perspicacity led to many "firsts." Perhaps the most notable one is the early recognition of Frank Lloyd Wright. It is generally believed that his first mention was in the ARCHITECTURAL RECORD for 1908, but in April 1904 a commentator named Arthur C. David had this to say, referring to the new stylistic manifestations of the Chicago spirit: "It really derives its momentum and inspiration chiefly from the work of Mr. Louis Sullivan, and from a very able architect, who issued from Mr. Sullivan's office, Mr. Frank Wright."

The writer went on to remark that it was all too young to have a history, "and probably 10 years must pass before any very intelligent estimate can be placed upon its value." Well, if 10 years didn't prove them right, 62 years certainly have.

So I have been impressed with the fact that for 75 years, good years and bad ones, cocky years and cautious ones, the RECORD has been characterized by a deep perception about architectural currents. That's a long time for such a light of understanding to keep shining.

In the early days a literary periodical

In its original concept, the RECORD was not a "professional" magazine, but a "general" one. While it sought to interest and to serve architects, its primary focus was on the general public. Its purpose avowedly was to educate the public. Its father and first editor, Harry W. Desmond, remarked in its first issue: "The difficulty is that people generally are so ignorant of even the A, B, C of Architecture. The meretricious accidents of the art—mere size, ornateness—the barbaric qualities which dazzle and impose upon the popular mind, are so exclusively appreciated that the essential, lasting and really veracious manifestations of the art are overlooked...a more persistent attempt is needed to build up 'a pile of better thoughts' sufficient to be fruitful in great effects, and that is the work which, in really a humble frame of mind, the projectors of THE ARCHITEC-

MONTGOMERY SCHUYLER and the HISTORY of AMERICAN ARCHITECTURE
by Edward R. Smith
Vol. XXXVI, No. 3, September 1914, pp. 264–267.
[Smith was Reference Librarian of the Avery Architectural Library at Columbia University]

MODERN civilization may be said to lack quality. Many of the broad and generous convictions which characterized the generations immediately preceding our own have been abandoned, and the rich culture of other days seems to be passing.

Perhaps this lack of quality is creeping into architecture. In the rush of modern competition the architect is more or less at the mercy of the financier, and is yielding pre-eminence to the engineer of construction. He finds it difficult to maintain his standing as a scholar and artist.

* * *

The large and genial atmosphere of the older time has persisted in the personality of several men who are well within the field of our friendly recollection.

* * *

Such [a one] was Montgomery Schuyler, of the same generation as [Russell] Sturgis, and intimately associated with him. He had the same large sympathies and the same breadth of knowledge. ▸

1 Photographing 5th Avenue, New York City, while sitting on a slender support 18 stories above the pavement. The photographer, who is using a steroptic camera, is in turn being photographed in 3D.

2 "Suggested color scheme for a bed room" reads the caption under the first color reproduction (chromo-lithograph)—the frontispiece of Vol. III, No. 1, July–September, 1893 (the beginning of year two).

3 Frederick W. Goudy (1865–1947) was a prolific American type- designer and printer. The typeface he designed for ARCHITECTURAL RECORD, displayed on page 231, is very close to Goudy Old Style (1915), which was based on the inscriptions on Trajan's column, Rome, 106–113 A.D.

TURAL RECORD now undertake…"

The "projectors" thought of it as a magazine for the erudite reader, after the manner of *Scribners* or *The Atlantic Monthly*, and the literary orientation shows through. While of course there were illustrations, all kinds of them, the magazine was literary rather than pictorial. It published articles about "the A, B, C," of architecture, history, criticism of trends and styles, but it very rarely published buildings as we do today. There was an article by Dankman Adler on the Chicago auditorium in 1892, and an occasional critique of an individual building, but in general it was at least 10 years before it became the custom to publish current buildings. So what later came to be considered the primary task of an architectural magazine— "publishing" buildings—really got its start quite a few years after the RECORD began its venture of publishing a magazine about architecture.

Actually the magazine went on for almost a quarter of a century before it became a "professional" magazine, directing its content to architects instead of lay readers. One can imagine that this choice was directed by the necessities of earning its keep, not by any wish to give up its communications with the public.

As it happened, the years around 1914 or 15 were a time of self-analysis in the publications world, when determination of objectives—yes, and ethics—were thrust upon magazine publishers. Advertisers were demanding certification of circulation figures (formed a bureau for that purpose), and publishers were asked to define and prove their readership. It became clear (and RECORD publishers have never forgotten it) that a good professional magazine is different from a good general magazine, and that it was time to sharpen the focus. I suppose it was Dr. Michael A. Mikkelsen who made this decision; at least the time coincides with his appointment to the editorship, a post he held with distinction for over 20 years. His change of focus becomes visible, though no doubt the First World War had much to do with the changing magazine.

Now—50 years after this change in course—there is no disposition whatever to quarrel with it, or to alter it. Nevertheless, one can sit on his own side of the fence and wonder about the other. The early RECORD filled a great need—the education of the public about the architect—and this need is perhaps more apparent now than it was then. It is true that architecture now gets gobs of publicity in the general magazines—the picture weeklies, the news weeklies, the newspapers, the "shelter" magazines, the remaining "literary" magazines. But the educational quality of it all is varied (to be kind) or deplorable (to be blunt). The understanding and dedication of the old public-focused RECORD could be very helpful today.

When criticism was rampant in the public arena

And—50 to 75 years later—the old RECORD is still talked about for its fearless and forthright criticism. There was a group of critics whose names are still recalled and whose writings are still quoted. The quality I mentioned before—perception—shines through their writings; that is what made them important. But one suspects that their nerve and combativeness have much to do with their lasting fame, architects being what they are. There are a few "critics" today who understand the impact of sharp words, but generally speaking I should say that they are not in the same class; the sharp words without the equivalent perception don't sting so much.

The same writer who mentioned Mr. Frank Wright in 1904 did not hesitate to publish a house by another architect, and say: it "owes a great deal to the work of Mr. Frank Wright, and this is as it should be." In the same feature he published another house by another architect with this comment: "He is assuredly the 'new architect' in his most garrulous and candid moment. He has not been afraid to design houses which would impress an eye, not merely as extraordinary, but perhaps as grotesque…" He does soften his comment somewhat by suggesting that the architect was one to study and consider.

There was one famous series called "Architectural Aberrations," which ran over several years. A specific building was named and pictured and then verbally reduced to shreds. I don't know that any of the architects so immortalized ever committed hara-kiri, but I can imagine the fun some other architects had. The series was later dropped, and I can't find any stated reason; perhaps the editors were swamped, as editors would be today, by the proliferation of aberrations, or bored by the constant repetition of common faults. Whatever happened, architects were vastly impressed (amused?) by the department, as indeed have been various generations of editors of the RECORD.

In any case, the RECORD, in those early days, made a great deal of noise, and architects, then and ever since, have been happy about it.

Elsewhere in this issue (page 9) I have made some comments about criticism in today's situation. Right here it will have to suffice to say that as the RECORD shifted its aim from the layman to the professional (First World War times) it gradually turned to a calmer, more professional attitude toward the inventions of architects, assuming the sophistication of the audience, and taking up what might more properly be called reporting in depth rather than the more limited idea of "criticism."

But the RECORD was known for charging to the front

If, 50 years ago, the RECORD shifted to a more professional posture, it did not change its charge-forward determination. From an original conviction that architecture deserved the best of publishing techniques and perspicacious if not precocious observations, later regimes of staff management have tended to persist in the tradition. Not always with tremendous rewards, it must be said, but generally with a compulsion to move with the times.

It seems a small thing now, but one of the temptations that brought the gleam to the eyes of its founders was the use of half-tone engravings to reproduce photographs. Our historical notes show that the *Real Estate Record and Guide*, an ARCHITECTURAL RECORD relative now in its 98th year, was the first magazine to take advantage of the half-tone process. That was in 1889. Before that buildings had to be shown in line drawings, or "wood cuts"; the realistic result had to be imagined. Two years later ARCHITECTURAL RECORD made its bow, and it doesn't require imagination to envision the first enthusiasm for showing architecture in actual photographs.[1]

In recent months there has been new enthusiasm around the RECORD for the use of four-color photographs, using a new web offset process of reproduction. Looking back we find the first four-color reproduction of architecture in the July 1893 issue of ARCHITECTURAL RECORD.[2] One presentation in 1894 (Colonial Houses!) had eight full-page, four-color photographs (probably lithographs).

More important, of course, are the "firsts" in recognition of architectural breakthroughs or individual initiative. Louis Sullivan, "Frank Wright," and the "Chicago spirit" have already been mentioned. In 1904 this combination was way in advance of the times. FLW was recognized in Europe after that, and not really accepted in America until later. In 1908 he wrote a famous article for ARCHITECTURAL RECORD, "In the Cause of Architecture," March 1908 —December 1928.

Perhaps it could be considered a "first" when Dr. Mikkelsen re-activated Wright in the twenties. Wright had been through all manner of vicissitudes, was dejected and idle. Mikkelsen made a deal for him to write a series of articles for the RECORD, for a fabulous price, and Wright took new encouragement, got new recognition, and took off again for new victories. In fact he took off so fast that he never wrote the final article; he took great pleasure in his later years in reminding us that he still owed us the summary piece of his famous series.

Still in the area of graphics, the RECORD undertook one of its several redesigns in 1928. The art director was named Charles D. DeVinne, known in the graphics field as the designer of a well-known type face that bore his name. But the type designer for the

He had not the same incisive force, but instead a gentle and temperate quality of mind, which is perhaps quite as valuable. He was not a trained architect, as Sturgis was, but by much study and constant association with active men he became sufficiently conversant with detail. Perhaps the lack of more definite equipment made possible the broad and human point of view which he held better than any American writer on architecture.

* * *

The World's Fair at Chicago was the formal introduction of the new school of architects, who, trained in Paris, have done so much to bring us into sympathy with the Ecole des Beaux-Arts. Most of us have now pinned our faith to classicism in some form, and swear by Piranesi: but to all this Mr. Schuyler was temperamentally antipathetic.

He treats the wonderful Chicago ensemble of 1893 in a characteristic manner; generously conceding the splendid results, but pleasantly suggesting the doubt, whether, after all, the result of this vast experiment will be permanently beneficial. We have gone far enough now with the classic movement to begin to consider whether our kind friend had not some reason for his fears.

The main interest in Mr. Schuyler's work centers in his large grasp of the principles and record of architecture in America. Within the limits of this article it is only possible to show the splendid sketch which he has left, and to express the deep regret that there is no hand with sufficient cunning to raise the pen which he has laid down.

How broad Mr. Schuyler's work really was, how keen his interest in the busy men of his time, may be learned from the bibliography, probably imperfect, which we are able to append. ●

4 See page 199.

*The bridges in question are the Old East River (Brooklyn), the Williamsburg, the Queensboro.

Front of the anchorage of the Manhattan Bridge, New York City, Carrère & Hastings, architects, Leon Moisseiff, engineer. "Where in the world can one see a more impressive effect of sheer power than in the ordered masses of this Manhattan anchorage, which so few of us have thus far taken the trouble to see at all?" —Montgomery Schuyler

new RECORD format then was the famous Frederic W. Goudy,[3] who specified one of his famous types, known as Garamont, for body, and designed new faces for head and caption types.

It is odd, looking backward, that the pictorial aspects of architectural journalism took so long to develop. Naturally all copies of the RECORD used drawings and photographs liberally, but they were used, after the manner of the times, as illustrations for text. In the early issues there are not many plans or sections, maybe because the reader was presumed to be unable to read them. Later they began to appear, as the magazine turned more professional, but somehow their possibilities for communication were unrealized.

Photographs always have dominated the pages; there was a long period, in all architectural magazines, when photographs were "plates," and each took a full page; frequently the page opposite was left blank, doubtless to heighten the pictorial effect. In those days, the text, if any, was isolated from the pictures.

The concept of pictorial journalism that we know today came later (if in fact it has fully come at this date). I mean the consideration of photographs, plans, sections, captions, text as a unified communication effort, in which one element complements, not repeats, the others. Today we study this sort of thing at great length. But this communication science seems to have taken forever to develop, perhaps because there was more time to read, less material to try to encompass, and maybe more enjoyment in the process of digestion.

I doubt if early editors of the RECORD ever considered what we think of today as "double" reading. We consciously arrange many of our "presentations" for two types of reading: scanning and study. A story is designed to give a quick message to the hurried reader, and also to reward the more studious reader—who actually may be the same person at a different time.

At any rate, there is no evidence of this kind of planning effort in any of the magazines until, say, the last 20 years. Slow down

the world; I want to sit down and read a bit!

The greats in architecture in the pages of the RECORD

As one notes, in such a journey through the RECORD's history, the obvious perspicacity in its pages, one notes also a continuous parade of great architects and architectural greats. The institution (the RECORD was that) that first noted the work of "Mr. Frank Wright" kept its pages alive with writings, buildings, battles of the individuals who then (or later) were great in architectural history.

Frank Lloyd Wright wrote for the RECORD in 1908, in the twenties, again in the fifties. Louis Sullivan wrote a long series in the twenties; in fact the articles get shorter as he worked on to his end. Indeed it was an article in the RECORD by Sullivan that pushed Eliel Saarinen to his American fame,[4] the one that blasted the Chicago Tribune competition for giving Saarinen second prize, not first, for his progressive understanding of the skyscraper form. Le Corbusier did some articles; so it seems did everybody else. Looking back, it is in fact difficult to believe the oft-quoted saying that architects would prefer to speak with their work or their drawings, rather than with words. They spoke with words in the RECORD, millions of them.

It is perhaps fitting to comment, also, that the words frequently had more permanent validity than the designs. I don't mean any denigration of the designs of the architects who "made" the history books; what I mean is that as you look back through old magazines you find the words much as they are today; maybe only because words come more easily than works. At any rate architectural objectives have changed but little, while currents of design have continually shifted.

Vitruvius and the pattern of the three-legged stool

Present editors of the RECORD feel the burden, as I have said, of keeping architects informed on many other topics besides visual design, and we think we work pretty hard at it. We keep before us the old line that architecture is a three-legged stool, the three legs being old Vitruvius's "commodity, firmness and delight." Since we do so much more than most magazines on the two legs of "commodity" (Building Types Studies) and "firmness" (Architectural Engineering) we sometimes feel as if we had started the whole business. We didn't: for all its literary approach, the early RECORD started right off with technical articles along with its great concern with the styles. It started a formal technical department in 1895. And it had occasional studies of individual building types and their problems as early as 1892.

The early technical articles tended to be rather elementary, the focus of the magazine being what it was, as did the planning type of article. But they were considered, apparently, an important part of the self-appointed task of educating people on architectural matters.

So what is different today is the depth of the informational material now so necessary for the direct education we publish for the architect. Naturally the intensity developed as decades went by; first as the focus changed to the architect as a reader, later as the technical topics proliferated and became more complicated.

A definite movement to develop more technical material began in the late thirties, when magazines, like other businesses, were fighting their way out of the great depression. Construction was picking up, and things looked promising, but it seemed to require a real effort to re-orient matters to building activity instead of abstract philosophizing, or contemplation of art.

The orientation toward active building was only beginning to make headway when the Second World War upset the architectural world once more. As a magazine formula, however, the three-legged pattern proved well grounded during the war years. Building was all for the war effort—tank plants, airplane plants, factories of all kinds, housing, military encampments and installations. Architectural design theories fell on pretty lean times, but materials and construction techniques were moving fast. Architectural philosophizing became rather academic, or at least futuristic. The "mod-

ern" idea of expressing the world of technology gained great headway, theoretical though it was. And the magazines filled pages and pages with postwar prognostications.

Parenthetically, most of those architectural pronouncements (the extruded plastic house, for example) have not yet come to pass; probably waiting for the mega-structures. This observer joined the RECORD staff just prior to the war, and my beat was Washington and wartime construction. But I read all those dreams of the automated world (assembly line was the phrase then); so few of them came true that I feel not overly impressed with the present glimpses of the coming computerized country.

I should get back (forgive the digression) to the positive effects of the RECORD three-legged image. The war years did bring great technical development, and we undertook to digest and report it for architects. And the RECORD began an upward surge in reader response. The pace now is picking up so fast that we just might have the extruded housing unit in the mega-structure. Very likely it will enlarge our technical reporting operations in the future, exactly as it enlarges the responsibilities of architects and engineers.

A small declaration for a big magazine

The boomtime prosperity of the architectural fraternity, now 75 years after the RECORD bravely moved into it, is undoubtedly beyond anything believable then. If its first editor and founder were flabbergasted by growth (he should see Sweets now—he also founded that), he would probably take a second look and note that the deep understanding of architecture has not come to pass. He might in fact repeat the charge he wrote in the first issue: "Is there a civilization on the face of the earth as uninteresting as ours, as completely material, as lacking in dignity and distinction, as vulgar, commonplace and shabby?"

Well, we can hope that another 75 years will see some of the order the RECORD sought. In any case, Mr. Desmond, we shall keep trying. ■

from:
OUR FOUR BIG BRIDGES*
By Montgomery Schuyler
Vol. XXV, No. 3, March, 1909,
pp. 147-160.

One of the reflections which force themselves upon the New Yorker who has occasion to investigate for himself, and in an amateur way, the way of the lover of beauty and fitness, the two biggest and costliest of the bridges at present under construction by this municipality of Greater New York, is a discouraging reflection. How grievous is the injustice that is done us by our press.

In the matter of public works the press seems to be interested only in the incidental scandals which may arise out of them. All, or almost all, columns are joyously opened to scandals about bridges, as about other costly and important public works. If they turn out to be, or are even plausibly alleged to be, inadequately designed, that is well. If they can plausibly be alleged to be "gigantic jobs," that is immensely better. But if they are simply uncommonly and creditably well done, so as to be among the glories of the city and the country, you will be long in finding out that uninteresting fact from the ordinary newspapers. One who has of his own motion investigated the construction of the newer bridges across the East River, for example, feels himself to have a grievance when he finds a wealth of interest in them, and a just source of local pride, of which his newspaper had given him no hint whatever. Not only has it not told him "the half." It has had nothing at all to say about the matter. Perhaps he ought not repine at having so nearly a virgin field, and ought to be grateful even for his grievance. But what a social symptom the grievance nevertheless is! ●

The cartoon at right,
by Quincy Scott, is from
the September 1904 issue
[XVI:3 Sept. 1904 p 202].

opposite: The cover of the
innaugural issue of
ARCHITECTURAL RECORD,
July–September 1891.

"By Way of Introduction"
is by Harry W. Desmond, one of
the founder/editors. It puts forth
the mission of the magazine in
no uncertain terms.

TIME IS SHORT AND ART IS FLEETING.

The Architectural Record.

VOL. I.   JULY–SEPTEMBER, 1891.   NO. 1.

BY WAY OF INTRODUCTION.

MEN play the hypocrite oftener with their purposes than with their actions. It is in the obscurer field that we keep most jealously not only what friend Nym[1] styled "the behavior of reputation," but most frequently affect reputation itself. There is, perhaps, no occasion—unless we find a parallel in politics—where the temptation to parade purposes, to spread before the world a rich Barmecide[2] feast of virtue and good intention is stronger than in introducing to the public (with interested motives) a new publication. Few publishers can be brought to feel particularly grateful to an editor for even a restrained frankness on such an occasion. No wider candor is permitted than Sganarelle's:[3] "I am not so scrupulous as to tell you the whole truth." We know of no publication started avowedly for the sordid but yet not disreputable purpose of making money. True, in making the venture a measure of financial success may have been hoped for tacitly, as not unwelcome or inconsequential; but, of course, if it came, it was merely because from of old it is not permitted that the righteous shall be forsaken or their seed beg their bread. The printing press always is set in motion to publish some new gospel, to restate some old one unheeded, to vindicate some human right tyrannized over or despised; but for gain—never. The printing press should not have left the precincts of the church; unless, indeed, there came to be too little room for it there; which, if everything stated be exactly true, is plausible.

We hope this frankness has not cut the ground from under our own feet; for we want to say that THE ARCHITECTURAL RECORD is a publication with somewhat of a purpose over and above a purely commercial one. This is due to the very character of the field which the magazine must occupy, as well as to intention. The field is one which must be entered with serious purpose or not at all. To amuse the public with Architecture, obviously is out of the question. Not that the art, as practiced at present, is without a ludicrous side, or is free from rare little bits of humor, grotesqueness and caricature; but unfortunately there are so few who would perceive or appreciate the fun that the publisher will be the only one who will pay for the joke. As to merely recording so often in a blunt, free, indiscriminate way contemporary work popularly classed as architecture, that task already is even too abundantly performed by numerous weekly publications. Only the higher field is unoccupied; but in this country, perhaps more than in any other, entrance into this higher field imposes serious responsibilities; for therein one is brought face to face with the gravest and least assuring facts of our national life. If, as Amiel[4] says, the measure of a civilization is the number of perfected men that it produces, if the test of every religious, political or educational system is the men which it creates, what judgment must we pronounce upon American civilization and the institutions and systems under which we live? It is true that we have judged but from a point of view quite different from Amiel's the civilization of our day and country according to principles which we regard as fundamental and durable

1 *Nym.* One of Falstaff's followers, and an arrant rogue.

2 *Barmecide* n. Insincere benefactor; one who holds out illusory offers, or who promises but does not deliver. The original Barmecide is found in The Arabian Nights. A member of a wealthy Persian family, he decided to amuse himself one night by inviting a starving beggar to a sumptuous meal. Barmecide's prank consisted of presenting the beggar with a succession of grandly served courses, amid all the trappings of luxury—ornate bowls and dishes, magnificent table-settings—the catch being that there was no actual food in any of the receptacles placed before the hapless guest. The name of Barmecide himself has become synonymous with deceit, illusion, hypocrisy, and the offering of bounty only to withhold it until the offerer's terms are met.

3 Sganarelle is a character from the play by Moliere by the same name: Sganarelle, or the Imaginary Cuckold (1660).

4 The swiss critic Henri Frédéric Amiel, 1821–81, was unsuccessful and unnoticed during his life, but the posthumous publication of his *Journal intime* (1883) aroused great interest. It is a document of scrupulous self-observation.

5 Jean-Anthelme Brillat-Savarin, 1755–1826, was among the first to write seriously about eating and the art of the table. In recognition of his accomplishments, a cheese, an omelet, a salmon dish, a garnish, and a consommé all bear his name.

6 In his youth George William Curtis, 1824–92, spent time in Concord, Massachusetts, where he lived among leading literary figures, such as Emerson, Hawthorne, and Thoreau.
In the 1850s, he was critic and travel writer for the New York Tribune, an editor for Putnam's Magazine, and a columnist for Harper's Monthly and Harper's Weekly. Later, as editor of Harper's Weekly (1863) Curtis sought to sway public opinion over a number of political and social reforms, including emancipation; civil rights and social equality for African-Americans, Native Americans, and women; civil service reform; public education; and environmental conservation. He joined forces with illustrator Thomas Nast in the early 1870s to attack the corrupt Democratic political machine in New York City (the Tweed Ring).

7 Sir Thomas Browne, 1605–82, English author and physician, b. London, educated at Oxford and abroad, knighted (1671) by Charles II. His *Religio Medici*, in which Browne attempted to reconcile science and religion, was written about 1635.

8 Charles William Eliot, 1834–1926, American educator and president of Harvard University for 40 years [1869–1909]. Eliot commissioned H.H. Richardson to build Sever Hall (1878), and Austin Hall (1881).

9 The article refers to M. Jourdain a "Prince of the Bourgeoisie" William Shakespeare (1564–1616), British dramatist, poet. Boy, in Henry V, act 3, sc. 2, l. 36-8.

enough; and we find alike complete justification of it, and ample promise for the future in the great gospel which the Census Bureau gives us from time to time; in tables of exports, statistics of manufactures and other arithmetical statements. The danger really is that our judgment may not be as securely founded as we think it is. Perhaps Amiel, dreamer so indifferent to tabulated civilization, idealist so keenly sensitive to the spiritual side of life, may be closer to the truth than we are; and by insisting upon the character of the man produced by a civilization as the test of that civilization's worth and true position in the moral world, which is God's, set up the real abiding standard by which, in the course of things, nations are judged.

But, it may be said, this is merely emotion set to a dithyrambic key; the material facts of life are, after all, the most important, and Brillat-Savarin[5] had hold of a wider truth than Amiel's when he said "the destiny of nations depends upon the manner in which they feed themselves." Besides, is not George William Curtis[6] an apostle of light, and has he not told us that "the railroad is the culmination of civilization?" No doubt there is something of a truth in the Chinese belief that the stomach is the seat of the understanding. We would probably have little philosophy if it accompanied a really empty belly, and without an ample command of material possessions the greatness of no nation would have arisen into the "sunlit heights." But assuredly no nation ever became great solely by reason of its material prosperity, and such mental activity as finds a congenial environment in goods and chattels, and what Sir Thomas Browne[7] called the "vulgar parts of felicity."

No, there are serious reasons for doubting that the railroad is the culmination of civilization. The steam engine has given us a wider touch with life, no doubt; but has it given us a finer? In no country, and at no other time, has mere existence been so full, so abundantly provided for as in this country at the present moment. Ours is no anaemic existence trembling with the fear of

pauperism; but one to which the seasons are husbandmen whose harvest field is a continent. On the other hand, is there a civilization on the face of the earth as uninteresting as ours, as completely material, as lacking in dignity and distinction, as vulgar, commonplace and shabby? President Eliot[8] calls vulgarity our national disgrace, and the saying is sufficient.

All this has been said before repeatedly: it is old enough. The pity is it is so old. We have been unperceptive: we have become indifferent. We can hardly believe that what President Eliot says is true: our self-complaisance is so fat and well fed. With that Prince of the Bourgeoisie, M. Jourdain,[9] we exclaim, "Il n'y a que des sots et des sottes ma femme que se railleront de moi." Of course. Those who laugh at us are fools, and we need not come into contact with other people if they be disagreeable. We have a continent to expand in, and great blaring newspapers that have no doubt about our peculiar admirableness. How fortunate we would be if self-laudation could ever be in the right key. But it is always too high or too low; it never harmonizes exactly with our feelings, and though our newspapers and all who love the popular tone may praise us, though Mr. Curtis may assure us, in the very language of "one of the prophets," "that the railroad is the culmination of civilization; " something akin to that saying of Amiel's will sing through it all: "the test of every religious, political or educational system is the man which it forms," and rob us of the fullness of our satisfaction. Yes, it is better for us to leave the newspapers; go over at once to President Eliot and accept his judgment about ourselves.

The vulgarity of which he speaks—not the vulgarity of table manners, but a spiritual coarseness which in the "familiarity between the mind and things" reveals itself in our social life, in our politics—that malodorous subject in all our activities, wherein we pass aside from the "dignity of humanity—" this vulgarity we believe is the chiefest obstacle in the way of the greater number of the reforms for which pulpit, press and platform are working. For there is no deficiency of intelligence among our people. It is feeling that is lacking right feeling. Upon a certain side of life their sensitiveness is dull. That unfortunate man who spoke the truth probably recognized this fact from his position when he declared the purification of politics to be an iridescent dream. So it is; so it will be until people become keenly sensitive to how dirty, contemptible, vulgar our political life is. Are not the facts of that life known by heart today by everybody? They are not rightly appreciated, that is all. So it is in social matters, commercial life, and even within the field of religion.

Whence, then, shall we look for assistance? That becomes the important question. We have no hesitation in answering that it is to Art we must turn—only in that direction does hope for us lie. If the pressure of life did not make as strongly as it does towards the cities, it might be necessary to give the greater importance in the work of reformation to Religion; for, in the history of the race, Religion, apparently, has found its most favorable environment in rural habitations; as though Nature held a fuller and clearer revelation of Divinity than the works of man. The city, however, has been the favorable environment of Art. There only has it thrived and reached its completest expression. Another consideration there is which makes us regard Art as the ark of salvation—conditions in this country are making more and more strongly than hitherto for Art. Our people are becoming the rich men of the earth, their manner of living more sumptuous and leisurely than ever. At present Art with us means little more than decoration, an appendage and circumstance to tradesmen's prosperity. Nevertheless, it has a vital position, though a degraded one, in the lives of our people. What has to be done is to give it its proper position, to reveal its divinity, to make people feel that Art is not merely decoration, the legitimate function of which is to make a fortune conspicuous; but is the light breaking in upon us from the perfect world beyond our day's circumference; "the fruitful voice of God"

revealing to us "what we are but in hopes and probability."

Art has only one revelation, but many forms. Whether it be Poetry, Music, Sculpture, Architecture, the spirit that speaks is the same, the message to us is the same. They make alike a similar demand upon us for truth, integrity of purpose, seriousness, nobility. They are eminently aristocratic, not with the aristocratic spirit of a regime, with its rise-Sir-Knight formula, but in the loftiness of the higher nobility whose allegiance is given to Truth.

But though the message of Art in all its forms is the same, in some it is more interesting to us than in others; and there are many good reasons why at this moment the people of this country could be more seriously interested to a greater degree in Architecture than in any other of the arts. In the first place it is the most practical, which fact should have much weight with a people so practical as we are. It waits upon, or more properly speaking it accompanies, utility. Compared with Painting, Music, Sculpture, or even Literature, its field is wider than theirs; it touches Life, our common daily Life, at so many more points than they do. It needs no stage, special setting or circumstance. It is content to occupy our streets; bend itself to our commonest circumstances and conditions, dignify the meanest materials, illuminate so many of our ordinary necessities. It is the only art which commerce and trade in a degree foster, necessitate, and even welcome as a graceful auxiliary. Civic pride, commercial prosperity, the ostentation of individuals create an occasion for it. True, Painting, perhaps, has a more popular language than Architecture, and Music none that is more intimate and enticing; but Architecture appeals to the public in a manner so much more frequent, conspicuous and insistent than either that, if it be not, it might easily become the more readily understood.

The difficulty is that people generally are so ignorant of even the A, B, C of Architecture. The meretricious accidents of the art—mere size, ornateness—the barbaric

from:

THE DIFFICULTIES OF MODERN ARCHITECTURE
By A.D.F. Hamlin
*Vol. I, No. 2,
October–December 1891,
pp. 137–150.*

Iron and steel now form a large part of the framework of every important building, and the development of constructive forms in metal has naturally proceeded along the lines of engineering rather than of high art. In the Middle Ages engineering and architecture were practically one, both alike receiving their highest development in religious architecture, whereas modern engineering has busied itself mostly with railroads, bridges and factories, and similar utilitarian problems, to the suppression of any artistic development. Metal construction has followed in its lead, and the architect has to deal with the forms and processes which the market offers alike to the engineer and to him. It is only in rare instances that he is permitted to use these materials in the special shape and manner which his artistic taste would lead him to devise. Furthermore, new materials, building methods and appliances are constantly being invented, all of which the architect must appropriate and use to the best advantage if he would keep up with the times. The building thus becomes a truly mighty problem in construction, requiring an immense amount of scientific and practical knowledge of the most varied kind, and the constant application of elaborate mathematical calculations and geometric processes. It is safe to say that the designing of a great building like the Auditorium at Chicago involves problems of construction fully as serious and difficult as were ever encountered in the most stupendous of mediæval cathedrals. ●

1891

Shot Tower, McCullough Shot Lead
Company, New York City,
James Bogardus, architect, 1855.

Bogardus (1800–1874), an American
architect, was among the first to use
cast iron in the construction of building
façades. He was noted for his commercial building designs in New York
City. Bogardus's success with cast iron
exteriors led eventually to the adoption
of steel-frame construction for entire
buildings.

qualities which dazzle and impose upon the popular mind, are so exclusively appreciated that the essential, lasting and really veracious manifestations of the art are overlooked. With Music and with Painting the daily press does something after its peculiar manner to lead the public and prompt a habit of selection which, while not over nice or too judiciously exclusive, is to some extent educative. But with Architecture no work of the kind is done. Of late the magazines have given some attention to it, but even if continued the effort is too intermittent and cursory to produce results of much importance. A more persistent attempt is needed to build up "a pile of better thoughts" sufficient to be fruitful in great effects, and that is the work which, in really a humble frame of mind, the projectors of THE ARCHITECTURAL RECORD now undertake —not pedantically or after the manner of the pedagogue, but popularly, illustratively, even tentatively, as a traveler sets out for a destination not immediate nor lying at the end of a well-defined, direct and visible route. The road in part has to be discovered, and in the search, which is to be progressive, our readers are asked to accompany us. While keeping close to the invisible presence of the Ideal we must not lose touch with what exists, what each day brings forth, with the unavoidable and limiting conditions of our time. No effective work can be done by cutting adrift from what is. Reformation must be from what is and not against what is. Artificial progress, there is enough of it. We must not forget that the "genius of each race brings forth its best products only when it works in harmony with the laws of its own nature, expressing without affectation the ideas and sympathies excited by immediate contact with the facts of life." The facts of life! How inexorably, how tyrannously even the commonest of them demand recognition, and how many the aspirations and noble efforts which they have broken as glass, leaving only a sound like music to linger in the silences of life. ■

"Cross a step or two of dubious twilight,
Come out on the other side, the novel,
Silent, silver lights and darks undreamt of,
Where I hush and bless myself with silence."

from:

WAS THE HOME INSURANCE BUILDING IN CHICAGO THE FIRST SKYSCRAPER OF SKELETON CONSTRUCTION?

Vol. 76, No. 2, August 1934, pp. 113-118.

Before the 47-year-old Home Insurance Building, located on the northeast corner of LaSalle and Adams Streets in Chicago, was razed to make way for the new Field Building (photo page 100), a committee of architects and others was appointed by the Marshall Field Estate to decide if it was entitled to the distinction of being the world's first skyscraper. This committee, after a thorough investigation, handed down a verdict that it was unquestionably the first building of skeleton construction. Their report follows:

* * *

It has been stated many times and we believe it to be true, that the greatest contribution of America to architecture is the skyscraper. By skyscraper is meant a building that exceeds in height the practical limit of solid masonry construction. The absolute and first essential in the structural creation of the skyscraper is the metal (ferrous) skeleton. The economic essential is the high-speed elevator. It follows, therefore, that the vast number of skyscrapers that have been built and are being built might be derived from and be dependent on the first building of this nature that was erected. If, therefore, it be found that the Home Insurance Building is the first skyscraper as above defined, its importance in architectural history is enormous, for the sequence of skyscrapers from 1884 is very well known and there is no claim that at this time or later was any skyscraper built independently and without knowledge of the peculiar construction of the Home Insurance Building.

The value of skyscrapers built in the United States since 1884 to the present time runs into billions of dollars. Their value in the economic development of the country and in the aesthetic development of architecture is inestimable.

* * *

The other claim for first honors is that of the Tacoma Building. The claim usually takes the form of the first "complete" skeleton skyscraper or the first skyscraper in which the metal skeleton was "completely" developed. This building was built three years after the Home Insurance. The Tacoma Building introduced many important improvements over the construction of the Home Insurance Building and that it marked an advance in the science of skyscraper design there can be no doubt.

* * *

Nevertheless the Tacoma Building still made use of cast iron columns and all shapes other than the beams and girders which were of wrought iron. It also had solid masonry lot line walls, cart and attey watts which could have been made skeleton construction and in our opinion showed a retrograde step in the introduction of the transverse masonry walls which assumed a very large

proportion of the floor loads; whereas the interior of the Home Insurance Building was entirely free from self-supporting masonry. The use of solid masonry party walls were obligatory under the Chicago Building Laws in 1885 and 1887 so it is manifestly unjust to condemn their presence in the Home Insurance Building. The Tacoma Building, however, was not so bound when it elected to use lot line instead of party walls. Probably the first all-skeleton skyscraper in Chicago was not built until 1889, when in the Manhattan Building (Jenney and Mundie, architects) all the inclosing walls were made of skeleton construction.

* * *

Conceding then that wherever the metal skeleton is present it did in fact support all loads, we have then to weigh its importance and position in the evolution of the skyscraper. We believe that the claim of Leroy S. Buffington as the inventor and the father of the skyscraper should be dismissed for the reasons that he never erected a building embodying his patent (issued after the erection of the Home Insurance Building), that his infringement suits were decided in court against him, that he himself stated that his idea of an iron skeleton was suggested by the writings of Viollet-le-Duc, in which case Viollet-le-Duc would have as good or better claim than Buffington.

CONCLUSION

As in the case of every great invention skeleton construction in its completeness was not nor could it have been discovered by any one man nor expressed in any one building. The early buildings for this reason are all more or less transitional and experimental. Each learned from the experience of the preceding and added its contribution in the development of the idea. It is, however, entirely possible, from a consideration of the evidence, to appraise the relative importance of each in terms of its originality and its influence on the work which followed. Acting on this conviction we have no hesitation in stating that the Home Insurance Building was the first high building to utilize as the basic principle of its design the method known as skeleton construction, and that there is convincing evidence that Major Jenney in solving the particular problems of light and loads appearing in this building discovered the true application of skeleton construction to the building of high structures and invented and here utilized for the first time its special forms.

We are also of the opinion that owing to its priority and its immediate success and renown the Home Insurance Building was in fact the primal influence in the acceptance of skeleton construction: the true father of the skyscraper.

Submitted by the Committee, November 24, 1931.
THOMAS E. TALLMADGE, Chairman.

Architect Irving K Pond argues that the Home Insurance Building is **NEITHER A SKYSCRAPER NOR OF SKELETON CONSTRUCTION** on page 279.

top: A special committee, after investigation, has handed down a verdict that the 47-year-old Home Insurance Building, razed to make way for the new Field Building, was unquestionably the first building of skeleton construction and can claim the title of "Father of the Skyscraper." The building was designed by William LeBaron Jenney, who got his idea for skeleton construction from bamboo huts in the Philippines.

Members of the committee who reported the investigation were Thomas E. Tallmadge, chairman; Ernest R. Graham, Alfred Shaw, Earl H. Reed, Andrew Rebori, Benjamin H. Marshall, Richard R. Schmidt, architects; Charles B. Pike, President, Chicago Historical Society; Mark Levy, President, Chicago Real Estate Board; and 0. T. Kreusser, Director, Rosenwald Museum.

bottom: Masonry removed from exterior walls demonstrates that the building was supported by iron columns.

1891

New Conditions/New Forms: The Promise of Function

When *Architectural Record* first began publishing, changing building conditions and new methods of construction had already ushered in a new age that was at once liberating and threatening. Steel-frame construction and the use of reinforced concrete, terra cotta, and glass pointed to a future the writers described as almost redemptive, while traditional values were brought into serious question. Revealing the structure of the new, tall building not only seemed to them the rational thing to do, it seemed to be a moral imperative. Meanwhile, tradition itself began to be regarded everywhere as a veneer of deceit. And, not just in architecture.

In the decades that followed the Civil War, traditions of every kind went by the boards with a rapidity matched only by that of the industrial revolution. Industry dominated the northeastern states particularly, where there was manufacturing and where urban populations concentrated and bourgeoned. As the "American System" fully blossomed, it brought an insatiable capacity to purchase more material luxuries, a passion, fueled by advertising, amongst a population recently enabled to read and write through universal free education. Immense railway stations and bridges, vast factories, tall buildings housing offices for business, all these proliferated aided by ease of communication. In turn, the manufacture of amenities required offices, factories, and railways to carry freight as well as passengers. The system, which continues to this day to feed on itself, demanded a new architecture.

Industrialization provided builders with new materials of revolutionary properties and spawned new types of buildings for industry, transportation, and commerce. It only stood to reason that the new way of building demanded a new appearance—one that wouldn't mask a building's structure, but would reveal it in some way.

Why so? And, what is revealed? In most cases, what is revealed is the viewer's understanding that a steel cage or skeleton now holds up all tall buildings, there-

Tower Building, New York City
Bradford Gilbert, architect,
1888–89 (demolished 1905) [a]

by rendering their walls redundant. If you look at the Gallatin Building on page 29 you'll "see" four piers running from street level to roof. This is where the structure is. What encloses the building is then called a "curtain wall," since it no longer has to bear the load. In his article "Skeleton Construction" (page 13), William J. Fryer, Jr., succinctly defines the curtain wall:

"Within the past three or four years a new method of constructing very high buildings in New York has come into vogue. It is known as the skeleton construction, and consists in the use of iron or steel columns, with thin curtain walls between, in place of solid thick brick walls. The curtain walls themselves are carried on wrought iron or rolled steel girders spanning the distance between the columns, which is usually about 15 feet. In addition, the weight of floors is also transmitted to the columns, so that the latter support the entire building and contents. The columns are encased with brick-work and when the building is plastered and finished on the inside there is no visible evidence of novelty."

It was the steel skeleton that would become the most serious challenge in 20th Century architecture and create a constant paradox—how much of the structure could be revealed and not render the building ugly? And, how much needed to be covered before the building was dishonest? The conundrum taxed all existing definitions of beauty.

The arguments split the profession into *functionalists* and *traditionalists*. Among the older generation of functionalists who were most admired were Karl Friedrich Schinkel in Germany, and Henri Labrouste, and Eugène-Emmanuel Viollet-le-Duc in France. However, none of these were willing to reject ornament out-of-hand. The English critic, John Ruskin, who probably had more influence than any other 19th Century theorist, admonished architects to remember the difference between mere building and architecture. He believed that ornament was a necessary expression of the purpose of a structure. As a result of these powerful influences, many American architects were loathe to expose structure, considering the results unfinished or ungainly. They chose from traditional styles that were deemed appropriate and compatible. But, in purely commercial undertakings these same architects could feel free not to disguise the skeleton entirely. It wasn't long before mere building started to look a lot like architecture.

As a practical consideration, since steel was found to twist and bend in fire, it needed to be encased in fireproof brick (which is previously fired, of course). Terra cotta was recognized early on as the material of choice to clad the new skeleton-framed buildings. Terra cotta could be structural as well as decorative. Pressed in molds, it permitted easy duplication of ornament. And, an extra bonus, in smoke-filled, sooty cities, enameled terra cotta was washable!

In "A White Enameled Building" (pp. 41–47), Charles E. Jenkins described the properties of the steel frame which allowed the architect to raise the remainder of the Reliance Building[b] in the space of six months above the existing two ground stories. Jenkins devotes a great deal of attention to the enameled terra cotta sheathing which he prophesied would be "a conspicuous mark in the history of American Architecture" because it was weather resistant even in Chicago's severe climate, washable, and would eventually be available in lively colors.

"When I define Beauty as the promise of Function; Action as the presence of Function; Character as the record of Function, I arbitrarily divide that which is essentially one....Beauty, being the promise of function, must be mainly present before the phase of action; but so long as there is yet a promise of function there is beauty.
Horatio Greenough The Travels, Observations, and Experiences of a Yankee Stonecutter, *1852.*

[a] The Tower Building was the first skyscraper in New York to employ a skeleton frame. The plot was so narrow (only 21 feet) that conventional bearing-walls would have to have been three feet thick, resulting in only 15-foot width left inside to accommodate stairs, elevators and offices. Gilbert devised an iron frame to support the first six stories of the structure and employed traditional bearing-walls for the upper stories where, due to reduced weight, they could be less thick.

The building's success led to an immediate boom in skeleton construction on lower Broadway—a boom that contributed to it's own obsolescence and demolition after only 17 years.

from:
Notes and Comments
THE PASSING OF A PIONEER
Vol. XVIII, No. 5, October 1905, p. 313.

Even in this hurrying country, it causes some surprise to read reports that "a historic building, seventeen years old," should have to give way before the march of progress. And the phrase loses none of its remarkableness by the fact that the building's historical significance is due to no momentous or interesting events that have taken place within its walls, during their short life, but to their marking of a step in the ancient and usually slow moving history of architecture. The structure referred to is that known as the Tower Building, on lower Broadway, New York City, planned by Bradford L. Gilbert, and claimed to be the first example of steel skeleton construction. It is significant that the seven stories of steel frame, then erected so experimentally, are to give place now to a twenty-story building. A suggestion has been made that it ought to have been kept as much as the pioneer locomotive or steamboat; and it is a pity that the big new sky-scraper could not be constructed around the little cloud scraper, protecting it and showing it off by contrast. ●

1891

A terra-cotta detail from German Bank, Baltimore, Maryland, Baldwin & Pennington, architects. Produced by the Conkling-Armstrong Terra-Cotta Co., this image appeared in one of a series of articles entitled "The Advantages of Terra Cotta,"(1905).

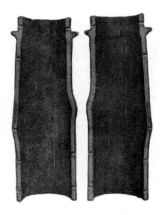

Sections of column from Western Union Telegraph Co. Building showing the action of fire (from "Skeleton Construction," 1891).

b Reliance Building, Chicago, D.H. Burnham & Co., 1894 (photo page 38).

c Architect Henry Rutgers Marshall (1852–1927) lectured on aesthetics at Columbia University in 1894. He lectured at Yale in 1906 and 1907 and at Princeton from 1915 to 1917.

Not everybody was lured by new technology and the science of building. Many felt that utility, thrift, and haste had become the enemies of architecture. And, there was general distrust of the role of engineering. Although trained as an engineer himself, Frank Lloyd Wright would later write, "…music is but sublimated mathematics. And the engineer is no more capable of giving steel structure the life of 'beauty' it should have than a professor of mathematics is capable of a symphony in music."

Charles H. Moore wrote an article in 1921 on "Training for the Practice of Architecture." A staunch defender of masonry construction, and unconvinced about the merits of new materials and methods, he nonetheless arrives at a similar conclusion about the inherent honesty of exposed form:

"In support of the new educational ideas, men speak of a need for meeting new conditions by new methods. But in architecture there are no new conditions, and therefore there is no call for new methods; though new forms may be evolved in the future, as in the past. The only materials suitable for architecture have been long established, and are the same now as in former times. The present use of iron and steel—which indeed requires new methods—comes of no needs of architecture. It is destructive of architecture if not kept apart from it. It comes of the passing excessive industrial and mechanical activities and commercial interests, that demand haste and cheapness in building for purely utilitarian ends. Utilitarian ends are good in their place, but they must not in building be confused with the ends of architecture—with which neither haste nor cheapness are compatible. In the present mixture of the two, the engineering of iron construction destroys the architecture, and the meretricious architecture spoils the good engineering. In the tall office building of New York, for example, the whole structure is a steel frame hidden by a façade of other materials, which is not any part of the structure but only a revetment affixed to it, and dependent on it. True architecture is impossible in such a contrivance. If the building must be a steel frame, let it be frankly shown for what it is. It cannot be a pleasant object to behold, but it will at least have the merit of veracity. Overlaid with foreign materials, simulating architectural forms proper to stone masonry, it is neither true architecture nor honest engineering."

Though the writers at *Architectural Record* didn't always agree, they did share one goal—never to compromise. That would only lead to the eclecticism they all abhorred. They were also always desirous to prod architects to express their time. Defining "Expression in Architecture," in 1900, Henry Rutgers Marshall[c] wrote,

"The architect should aim in all cases to produce a beautiful building; to this end he must avoid obvious constructional untruth which for most intelligent men is ugly. So far as in him lies he should also aim to emphasize the constructional and practical values of the parts of his structure, and he should do this for the simple reason that such emphasis tends to be attractive to the intelligent observer. But he should never emphasize these constructional and practical values at the expense of a loss of beauty; nor need he strive for this emphasis unless it is possible to gain it in a manner which will actually add to the permanent aesthetic value of the building as a whole." [IX:3 Jan 1900 p 263]

Style results from sound relationships between methods, materials, and structure. It also results when choices are collectively meaningful. Style is not merely outer show, it is expressive. The language of architecture was changing, and an architecture that conceals would no longer do. For this group of progressives the styles of Europe were as mendacious as they were ostentatious. ■

In the April 1921 issue Harold Lawson wrote the following which was published under "Notes and Comments:"

Is Steel-Frame Construction Capable of Architectural Treatment?

I have read Mr. Charles H. Moore's article on "Training for the Practice of Architecture," which appeared in the January Architectural Record, with great interest. It is an article which might well be read with profit by any one connected with the architectural profession in any way whatsoever. However, the Architectural Record is also read by a great many laymen who are likely to accept ex cathedra everything written therein, and therefore I feel called upon to take exception to certain opinions expressed by Mr. Moore. The following clauses quoted from his article, I am afraid, cannot help but cause glee among those construction companies who are so rapidly encroaching on the work of architects as practised in the old dignified way.

"In support of the new educational ideas, men speak of a need for meeting new conditions by new methods. But in architecture there are no new conditions, and therefore there is no call for new methods; though new forms may be evolved in the future, as in the past. The only materials suitable for architecture have long been established, and are the same now as in former times. The present use of iron and steel—which indeed requires new methods, comes of no needs of architecture. It is destructive of architecture if not kept apart from it."

If I have drawn the proper conclusions from Mr. Moore's article, briefly put, only architecture that is based on masonry principles is good. The application of this would limit the architect's field to buildings of moderate size and built contrary to modern economic needs. This expression, published in an architectural journal, only tends to confirm the impression already held by the general public that the architect is an expensive luxury. If the architect must design only buildings where art supersedes utility, and he is lucky enough to get a sufficient amount of work of this class to make it worth while keeping an office, it is questionable how long he could afford to keep it up.

Mr. Moore claims the present use of steel and iron comes of no needs of architecture. There is no reason why it should. It is not
architecture which has determined the use of these materials, but modern economic conditions; and if architecture is to live and flourish, it must obey and conform to modern economic needs. Architecture has inherited forms based on materials used by previous civilizations. Must architecture therefore neglect so important a product of this age as steel? Mr. Moore admits new forms may be evolved in the future as in the past, but if steel is divorced from architecture, what agency is going to evolve these forms? Shall the entire designs of buildings containing steel be left to structural engineers or contractors? The steel skeleton must be clothed in some way, for protection if for no other reason, and surely no one is better qualified to do this acceptably and according to the canons of good taste than a well trained architect.

Mr. Moore says, "If the building must be a steel frame, let it frankly be shown for what it is." This is all very well, but buildings are not constructed primarily as exponents of truthful construction but for shelter. The structure must be enclosed in some way, and if the constructive forms are not actually revealed, they can at least be suggested in the enclosing shell. After all there is no great difference between Gothic principles and the present systems of steel construction. In both cases the principal weights of the structure are carried on points. For lateral forces the advantages are all in the favor of steel.

It is quite possible that architecture has not yet thoroughly utilized the great possibilities of steel. It is more than likely that there will be developments of which this age does not dream, but to gain these ends the materials must be used, experiment after experiment must be made until the best possible use is made of the material without sacrificing any of the true principles of architecture. Steel is here to stay. Modern economic needs demand it. Money, time and space are too valuable to neglect it, particularly in our crowded cities. If new forms of architecture result from an intelligent use of the material, it will be the imagination and the resource of the architect that will attain this end.

— HAROLD LAWSON

The preceeding letter was immediately followed by this response from Moore:

The exceptions taken in Mr. Lawson's communication (written in an entirely good spirit) to what I have said in your January issue, on training for the practice of architecture, are based on what appear to me mistaken economic grounds, and not on those considerations of excellence in design and construction which should be the sole concern of the architect. Mr. Lawson thinks that modern economic conditions make the use of what are called modern methods and materials imperative, saying that "if architecture is to live and flourish it must obey and conform to modern economic needs." But if it be true, as he rightly affirms, that "it is not architecture that has determined the use of these materials," it should be obvious that they are not suited to its needs; and to imagine that architecture can live and flourish on unsuitable materials seems to me a mistake. Only mechanical engineering can live and flourish on the modern economic methods of building; and should these methods ultimately prevail, the vocation of the architect would be superseded by that of the engineer. But I do not think this is likely to happen. The architectural faculties of man are not going to be swallowed up in a deluge of utilitarian materialism, however things may look for the moment. Sooner or later it cannot fail to be seen that what are just now called economic methods do not make for good economics. These methods are essentially cheap and ephemeral. For duration, no modern engineering works are likely to last long in comparison with the masonry constructions of the past. There are stone bridges in Europe, some two thousand years old, that are still perfectly sound and serviceable.

I need not discuss Mr. Lawson's minor points, but I may add that he is mistaken in supposing that the application of masonry principles "would limit the architect's field to buildings of moderate size." It has not done so in the past. Hardly any building constructed on the modern lines encloses so many cubic feet of space as Amiens Cathedral—built of stone eight hundred years ago.

— CHARLES H. MOORE

**Woodbridge Building,
New York City,
Clinton & Russell,
architects, 1897.**

The text that accompanies
this image claims that *"the
system known as Skeleton
Construction is without
doubt the greatest innovation that has been made in
the science of building in
recent times, for without it
the modern high building or
'sky-scraper,' which has
already begun to revolu-
tionize the appearance of
American cities, would be
impossible."*
[VII:2 Oct–Dec 1897 p 225]

SKELETON CONSTRUCTION
THE NEW METHOD OF CONSTRUCTING HIGH BUILDINGS
By William J. Fryer, Jr.

WITHIN the past three or four years a new method of constructing very high buildings in New York has come into vogue. It is known as the skeleton construction, and consists in the use of iron or steel columns, with thin curtain walls between, in place of solid thick brick walls. The curtain walls themselves are carried on wrought iron or rolled steel girders spanning the distance between the columns, which is usually about 15 feet. In addition, the weight of floors is also transmitted to the columns, so that the latter support the entire building and contents. The columns are encased with brick-work and when the building is plastered and finished on the inside there is no visible evidence of novelty.

The advantage of using the composite construction is the room space gained in the difference between a thick wall and a thin one. In the ordinary method of building, the higher a brick wall the thicker it must be in its lower parts. The New York building law[1] very properly requires a wall to be built on the principle of a mast of a ship, the off-sets at various stories in the thickness of a wall in heights securing what is in effect a taper from the bottom to the top. The lower story of a building is the most valuable for rental, yet it is in this story, of all the stories above the sidewalk that the greatest area of a valuable lot must, under the old method, be wholly surrendered to enormously thick brick walls. Every inch gained in the width or length of the inside measurements of a costly building increases the availability of the structure, and therefore swells the income derived therefrom by the owner; but when this gain of space is feet instead of inches, in width and length as well, the reasons become obvious why the new method of construction, which takes up less than one-half of the area of plain brick walls, should immediately spring into public favor after an example or two had proved its

strength, safety and probable durability. The great value of favorably located lots, fairly forces owners to build skywards in order to get an adequate return on their investment. The London and Lancashire Insurance Company[2] not long ago erected an office building on a lot which the company purchased on Pine street, New York City, immediately adjoining the U.S. Sub-Treasury property. The lot measures 24.2 front by 74.4 deep, and the price paid for the same was $195,000. The lot is one foot wider on the rear than it is on the front, and one side is one inch deeper than the other side, so that the actual area of the lot is about 1,834 feet, and makes the price figure about $106 per superficial foot. The old building was torn down, and a new building erected of the skeleton construction. The curtain walls between the vertical columns are 12 inches thick, the same thickness in the first story as in the tenth story. Lots on Wall street and lower Broadway are of greater proportionate value than that of the Lancashire Company, which has an area of only three-quarters of the unit of a city lot.

The era of high buildings began with the year 1870. Let any person who has long been a resident of New York draw on his memory and he will find that all high buildings which in the popular and received interpretation of that term are now so styled, are of a date subsequent to the erection of the Post Office building.[3] Prior to that date there was a very limited number of fire-proof buildings within the limits of the United States. Those which did exist were chiefly Government buildings. Only ten years before that the first "I" beams were rolled in this country. Peter Cooper's Trenton, N. J. Mills, and the Phoenix Iron Co., of Pennsylvania, began to manufacture them about the same time. In the early fire-proof buildings—the Cooper Union,[4] Harper's publishing building[5] and the New York Historical Library building[6]—the iron floor beams are of a shape very similar to what are commonly known as deck beams, with brick arches between. It was seen that if buildings were to be built higher than the

1 The New York Building Law of 1887 was in force at the writing of this article. A critique of the law by Wm. J. Fryer, Jr. appears in *RECORD* I:1, Jul–Sept 1891, pp. 69–82.

2 For a photo of the Lancashire Insurance Company Building see page 20.

3 Post Office Building, New York City, Alfred B. Mullett, architect, 1875 (photo page 180).

4 Cooper Union, New York City, 1853–59, Frederick A. Peterson, Architect.

5 Harper & Brothers Publishing Company Building, New York City, John B. Corlies, architect, 1854 (demolished).

6 The New-York Historical Society, founded 1804, housed 75,000 books and 2,700 bound volumes of newspapers in its library.

7 New York Sun Building, unbuilt,
Bruce Price, architect, 1890.

Claude Bragdon wrote, "...I think
it was my old chief, Bruce
Price— conceived of a skyscraper
in the semblance of a classic column or pilaster, consisting of a
base, shaft, and capital. This
resulted in a building with the
first storey or storeys marked off
from those above by a different
material and treatment; the mid-
portion an unadorned stretch of
wall, regularly fenestrated; and
the top again differentiated by
making the windows part of an
ornate crowning feature. In New
York, where it originated, this sort
of thing became almost canoni-
cal, since it fulfilled the fancied
aesthetic requirement of a beginning, a middle, and an end."
[MORE LIVES THAN ONE, pp. 146-
149]

---

* Actually L.S. Buffington.

opposite: Leroy S. Buffington's
"Cloud-scraper"—his sketch of a
twenty-eight story building,1887.
Buffington also sketched a
"Cloud-scraper" that would stand
100-stories tall.

conventional five or six story
limit, to a height beyond the
ability of firemen to successfully cope with a fire, such
buildings must be constructed
with something better for the floors, partitions, stairs and roofs than a mass of wooden
beams, studs, plank, furring and lathing, and
more scientifically arranged than a pile of
kindling wood for burning, each piece
being separated and exposed to the air. With
the incoming of high buildings came a safer
construction. Eight or ten stories in
height—the height always being considered
as above the sidewalk, and not including the
stories below that level nor including towers
nor stories above the level of the main
roof—seemed to be the limit for a long time
that owners could see their interest in going
to. Suddenly a very much higher jump has
been made, and it is a matter of general
knowledge that Mr. Astor's new hotel
(photo page 75), now erecting at 59th street
and 5th avenue, will be seventeen stories in
height. It is quite as generally known that
the proprietors of the Sun[7] are talking of
putting up a new building, to be some
twenty-eight stories in height, on their little
corner which only measures 57 by 72 feet.

The accompanying plan shows the relative space occupied by the walls in the new
system and the old, the dotted lines representing the portion of the area of a lot that
solid brick walls would occupy. High buildings are demanded, and to-day there is simply no limit to the height that a building can
be safely erected. This result has been
reached mainly through three inventions all
of which are distinctively American:

1. The modern passage elevator.
2. The flat-arch system for fire-proof
   floors; and
3. The skeleton construction.

The last enumerated one has only lately
joined the combination in which the first
two were so long inseparable, but it has
come to stay, and the three work in unity for
a common purpose. It is with the third
invention that this article has to deal, but the
other two form so important elements to a

comprehensive understanding of the usefulness of the third, that a brief reference to
them will be necessary.

Up to the year 1870 the elevator was not
used to any great extent for passenger service. Many persons will recollect the old elevator in the Fifth Avenue Hotel, with its vertical iron screw extending the whole height
of the elevator well, and passing through a
sleeve in the centre of the car; very slow in
movement, but safe, although frequently
getting out of order. This was one of the first
passenger   elevators   in   this
city.
Improvements rapidly followed, until now
great speed with absolute safety has been
attained. It was the elevator that taught men
to build higher and higher, for without the
elevator a high building is impracticable. A
story that long ago went the rounds emphasizes this fact. A gentleman had occasion to
make a call upon an architect whose office
was on the top story of a high building. The
elevator service was temporarily stopped on

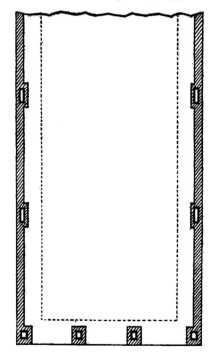

account of repairs being made to the steam boiler, and the caller ascended by the staircase, up flight after flight, towards the clouds until he finally reached his destination in an exhausted condition, when he feebly opened the door and inquired, Is Saint Peter in?

It was in the Post-office building in this city that for the first time in this or any other country was introduced hollow-tile flat arches between iron floor beams. This was the invention of Mr. Kreischer,[8] a well-known manufacturer of fire-brick. His was not the invention of a flat arch in itself, but of a flat arch, whose end sections abut against rolled iron floor beams, and recess around the bottom flanges of the beams, having on top wooden sleepers and wooden flooring, thus forming a level ceiling underneath and a walking surface above. Previous to Mr. Kreischer's invention the method of filling in between iron beams was by means of common brick arches, leveled up on top with concrete, and floored over. On the underside the bottom surfaces of the beams were left exposed and painted. A ceiling of a room then consisted of a series of curved arches between iron beams, which were very unpleasant in their appearance and effect on the eye. If a level ceiling was determined upon, it had to be obtained by wooden or iron furrings and lathing, fastened up to the underside of the beams and then plastered. The flat-arch system provided a level ceiling at once, at less cost and with much less weight of material than before. The iron beams were covered in and protected from fire, and the side walls had a lighter load to carry. A new impulse was given to fire-proof construction, and following the great fires in Chicago and Boston, the Kreischer system came into general use all over the country. In a legal contest that lasted for a number of years, it was finally decided in the U. S. Circuit Court that the Kreischer patent was void for want of originality under the crucial test of publications from all parts of the globe, that a patent must sustain when the law is invoked in its behalf. The decision of Judge Wallace prevented the inventor from realizing the profits of his invention. It did more, it deprived the inventor of the honor of having made the invention which abroad is recognized as an American system of fire-proof floorings.

At a meeting of the Royal Institute of British Architects, held in December, 1882, Mr. A. J. Gale described various things which he had seen during his tour in the United States. Among other things he stated that "In New York at the time of his visit there were many vast building schemes in hand. The floors were mostly of fire-proof construction, consisting of iron beams filled in between with hollow tile flat arches, the iron being protected above and below and joists being laid on the top surface." In connection with this statement, Mr. John Slater said, "It seemed to him that America was the country, par excellence, where suggestions were to be picked up by architects. To put the matter colloquially, it was the great place for 'tips,' and there could be no better place for an architect to visit than the States, after studying on the continent of Europe the artistic and archeological sides of his profession. The Americans were, in fact, so ingenious that their ingenuity was catching, and it appeared to be impossible for any one to visit the States without deriving much instruction. They would be taught the wholesome lesson that everything English was not necessarily the best. It was only in regard to what might be called the constructional part of an architect's profession that he made these remarks." The Chairman, Mr. Ewan Christian, said that "having had the advantage of traveling in America, though only for a short time, he was very much impressed by the go-aheadedness of Americans. If a man in the States brought out a good invention connected with building or anything else, it was straightway adopted all over the country until something better was produced, when that, in its turn was taken up."

The skeleton construction will entitle Americans to as much future praise as have ever been so generously given them for past improvements made in the art of building.

from:

TWENTY-FIVE YEARS OF AMERICAN ARCHITECTURE
By A.D.F. Hamlin
Vol. XL, No. 1, July, 1916

II.
The most noticeable features of our architectural progress during the last twenty-five years have been the development of steel skeleton construction and the influence of several great exhibitions, especially of that at Chicago in 1893. The steel skeleton was born and first developed in Chicago. This statement is made despite the fact that in 1888 the late L. A. Buffington* of Minneapolis patented a system of metallic skeleton construction which embodied many features of the present system. But most of these features were not new; each had been used in varying forms in earlier buildings, and the Buffington column was an unscientific laminated affair of flat plates, wastefully and inefficiently combined. Mr. Buffington failed to induce reputable lawyers to prosecute his suits for infringement against Chicago and New York architects. Whatever may have been the merit of his claims of priority in the conception of the steel skeleton, it was the ►

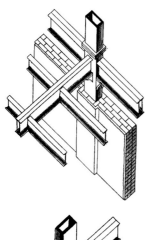

8 Balthazar Kreischer, a Staten Island firebrick manufacturer, developed two types of hollow-tile fireproofing.

The whole history of science is one continuous illustration of the slow progress by which the human mind makes its advance in

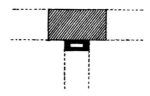

discovery. It is hardly perceptible, so little has been made by any one step in advance of the former state of things, because generally

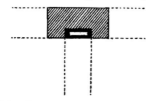

it will be found that just before there was something very nearly the same thing discovered or invented. This is true of the modern Elevator in its steps forward from the

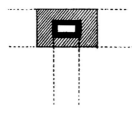

hoisting apparatus of the ancients. It is true of the American flat-arch floor system in the light of earlier publications made in France and other countries. It is true of the skeleton construction.

Without likening the skeleton to a cast iron front buried in a brick wall, its immediate predecessor can be seen in the devise frequently used to provide sufficient bearing strength in brick piers of too small an area to safely bear the load to be imposed without re-enforcement. A brick pier, of a size not larger than required for the safe support of the brick work above, is perhaps also required to carry the end of a line of girders

supporting floor beams. An iron column is therefore placed immediately adjoining the back of the pier. If the projection of the column be undesirable, then the column is embedded within the back line of the pier. In the case of a flank wall on a street front, where the window openings are numerous and the brick piers too small to carry the weight of wall above and floor loads in addition, the piers have been stiffened and strengthened or relieved of load by iron columns entirely concealed within the piers, and iron lintels also concealed above the columns.

Such examples have been used repeatedly for many years, and contain all the essential features of the skeleton construction. The first complete cast-iron front ever erected in the world was put up in New York in 1848, yet that was but a repetition of iron columns and lintels long previously used as a substitute for stone and brick to the extent of a single story. So the skeleton is simply the evolution expansion of the principal so long used in a smaller way. No patent stands in the way of the free use of the skeleton construction. A patent was issued in 1869 to a manufacturer of architectural iron work in New York, which covered the skeleton construction, but that patent expired by limitation five years ago, and the invention is now public property.

There are several variations in the use of iron skeletons. In some cases the frame is carried up to within three or four stories of the roof, and a solid brick wall used for the balance of the height, carried by the skeleton at the top line of the latter. In some cases the columns start from the base course of the foundations; in other cases from the top of the foundation wall, or the top of the basement story. There is still another method, such as was used in the World building, but which is not, strictly speaking, the skeleton construction as the columns are not embedded in the walls but stand clear from the same; the walls are of solid brick and of great thickness, although supporting nothing but their own weight, which indeed is enormous on account of their great height. The floors are carried independently of the walls, and in this respect embodies the same principle as the skeleton construction.

One or the other of two methods is gen-

erally used in the skeleton construction. In one the girders are placed between the columns at each story and carry both the curtain walls and the ends of the floor beams. In the other the girders carry the curtain walls only, and are placed at every second or third story; the floor beams are supported by girders placed at right angles to the columns. In the foregoing cuts the two arrangements are so clearly shown that further description is unnecessary. The small details of bolting, etc., have been omitted, as these would add nothing to the information that the drawings are intended to convey.

The inside four inches of the curtain walls are usually built with hollow bricks, of the dimensions of common brick, so as to allow of the plastering being done directly on the wall, and thus obviates the necessity for the use of furring to prevent dampness from striking through.

At the foot of each of the vertical lines of columns it is the general practice to use a cast-iron flanged base to distribute the imposed load over a greater area of bearing surface.

Crib footings of rolled steel or wrought iron beams are frequently used; and when placed below the water line they should be thoroughly coated with coal tar applied hot. For the skeleton construction the existing building law makes no special provision. At the time when the law was enacted, in 1887,

the use of composite structures was not foreseen. True, under that law, walls may be constructed of stone, brick, iron or other hard incombustible material, and by implication a combination of any of these materials, but the skeleton has been ruled to be one of the kind of cases to which the law does not directly apply, and is therefore subject to the decision of the Board of Examiners whose permission must be obtained before such a structure can be proceeded with. The Board regulates its action in skeleton cases in accordance with one of the amendments contained in the revision of the building law which failed to pass the last Legislature of this State. The columns are required to have a casing of brick work not less than four inches in thickness which must be bonded into the brick work of the curtain walls. The exposed side of the girders are required to be similarly covered in. The thickness of a wall is determined by its height, but where walls are carried upon girders, the heights are. measured from the top of such girders, except that no curtain wall is permitted less than 12 inches in thickness. The metal work is required to be painted before being set up in position.

In the greater number of skeleton buildings erected in New York the columns are of cast iron; in the smaller number rolled steel or wrought iron of various forms of section. Some constructors advocate the use of cast iron only as the material for the columns which are used in the walls. High buildings are erected for permanency, to last for centuries. When columns are built around with brick work they are buried out of sight for all time, so to speak. The oxide of iron paint, so commonly used for coating iron and steel work is largely mixed with fish oil instead of linseed oil, and soon dries out leaving a coating of dry, broken scale or powder. Between the columns and the outer air is only a few inches of brick or stone work, through which dampness or rain finds its way. In wrought iron rust is insidious, and it honeycombs and eats entirely through the metal. Mild steel, such as beams are rolled of, rusts faster than wrought iron at first, then

Chicago architects Jenney and Mundie who first gave the conception practical form and carried it into successful execution: to them belongs the credit for its design in its essential features. Thus it is from the metropolis of the Middle West that the two most potent forces emanated that have transformed modern American architecture.

The steel skeleton was really born in 1889; but the year 1891 saw it accepted as more than a mere experiment, and we may say that from that year dates its definitive adoption in American architecture. It is fair to consider it as the fourth of the great structural advances which have given architecture really new resources. The Roman vault for the first time made vastness of unencumbered space attainable. The Gothic ribbed vault and flying arch and buttress created the masonry skeleton and made possible the majestic loftiness and airy lightness of the medieval cathedral: another new architecture was created. The metallic truss, developed towards the middle of the last century, permitted a wholly new spaciousness and lightness of construction: our vast exhibition halls, train-houses and armories would have been impossible without it; again a new architecture came into existence, hardly recognized as a new architecture. The steel skeleton, the last of the four developments, has brought into being a new loftiness and lightness of construction; it has freed architecture from the limitations of massive walls which had for ages kept it from soaring otherwise than in the frail and beautiful but practically useless form of the spire. We have not yet solved the problem of the ideal artistic treatment of the sky-scraper, but we have gone a long way towards it; and meanwhile our architecture has been endowed with wholly new resources and possibilities. ▸

1891

Preliminary drawing for
Woodbridge Building,
New York City,
Clinton & Russell, architects,
1897 (skeleton on page 12).

Pneumatic caissons being
employed for the first time in the
foundation of the Manhattan Life
Insurance Building, Kimball &
Thompson, architects. Reported
in "Bed-rock Foundations,"
[VII:4 Apr–Jun 1898 pp 478–518]

slower. Cast iron, on the contrary, slowly oxides in damp situations; rust does not scale from it, and the oxidation when formed is of a much less dangerous kind, extending only a little way into that metal, to about the thickness of a knife-blade, and then stops for good. There are other dangers to be apprehended, such as gases and creosote from flues, escaping steam from defective pipes, leaks or an overflow of water, all quite possible and probable to reach the columns. Wrought iron is seriously affected by such mishaps, cast iron practically not at all. Mild steel has come into use so recently that time has not yet enabled men to speak positively how short or how long it can retain integrity in adverse situations. Damp plaster and cement corrode wrought iron and steel; lime is a preservative. If from any cause a column is affected in one place the entire structure above it is affected, but if a girder is affected the trouble is local for any one girder only carries a portion of the floor of one story and the bay or portion of the brick wall which reaches up to the next girder above. While failure in a girder would be far less disastrous than failure in a column, any trouble would be serious enough and fully warrants every precaution being taken in the first instance to avoid possible bad suits. For wrought iron and steel columns a margin in material should be allowed to cover partial deterioration from rust. Instead of a low factor of safety, as 3 to 1, when weight is to be sustained by material that is to remain unimpaired, the factor should be as high as 5, to provide for the loss of a portion of the sectional area of such columns by rust, so that the remainder of the metal may be sufficient to safely carry the load calculated to be imposed. No part of the metal in a wrought iron or rolled steel column should be less than three-eighths of an inch in thickness, nor should such columns have an unsupported length of more than thirty times their least lateral dimension or diameter.

For beams and girders wrought iron has almost entirely superseded cast iron, and latterly rolled steel has crowded out wrought

iron. The facility and promptness with which rolled beams can now be obtained; their admirable and scientific shape by which the greatest strength is obtained with the least weight of metal; the concise and simple tables of the bearing strength for the respective sizes and various lengths beams freely circulated by the manufacturers; their reasonable prices and the preference of architects and engineers to use wrought iron or steel when the load tends to separate or tear the metal asunder; all this has contributed to the extended use of wrought iron and steel for certain purposes. But for durability and lasting qualities under any and all circumstances of time and elements, particularly when buried out of sight in a casing not sufficiently thick to prevent dampness or wet or change of temperature from reaching the metal, as in the case of wall columns and beams for the support of the curtain walls, cast iron is the best material to use. For floor beams and for interior girders, wrought iron or rolled steel is matchless. There was some fear expressed by members of the Board of Examiners when the first plans of the skeleton structures were presented for their approval, that the greater expansion of one material than of another, might work some trouble. The same bugbear had to be overcome when cast iron fronts were first introduced, when predictions of failure were based on the expansion and contraction of the metal. Events proved that the temperature of our climate, from the greatest cold to the greatest heat, exerts upon cast iron appreciable effect, and for use in buildings is practically without expansibility. Cast iron, if of goodly thickness, offers a far better resistance to fire, or fire and water combined than wrought iron or steel. How well even thin plates of good cast iron will bear heat is shown in a familiar way by a common cook stove. Thin sheets of wrought iron will shrivel up almost like paper when brought in contact with flames. A comparatively moderate amount of heat will elongate and twist wrought iron and steel out of shape. When used for girders and floor beams they should be entirely encased in some non-conducting material. Whether columns of these materials should be encased is an open question. The advantage in one direction of a casing for wrought iron or rolled steel columns as a protection against fire, is a disadvantage in another direction, in that it may allow rusting to go on unseen to a dangerous extent. Covered or without covering, cast iron is the superior metal for columns. Cast iron is best for compression, rolled iron or steel for tension. The least thickness for a cast iron column should be three-quarters of an inch, and the greatest unsupported length for such column should not exceed twenty times its average diameter. Usually the box form of cast iron column is employed, but in many respects the H-shape is the best for use in skeleton construction. In order to make allowance for poor quality of cast iron, and for unseen defects in the castings, the factor of safety for cast iron columns should be 6 to 1, the same as the present building law provides for all posts, columns and other vertical supports of every kind of material.

When cast iron is used architects should insist on having the very best kind. Many columns are made in the Pennsylvania iron districts of iron run directly from the blast furnace, thus saving the expense of re-melting pig iron in a foundry cupola. Such columns are almost as brittle as glass, and when so made should be prohibited by law from being used in a building. Pig iron, when melted in a cupola, changes its nature and becomes a different grade of iron, getting rid of a certain amount of impurities, such as combined carbon, which makes iron hard, and phosphorous, which is one of the elements of weakness in iron. The re-melting is not only a purifying process, but it is an annealing process as well. By melting different brands of pig iron together the mixture is given desired qualities which they do not possess separately. This is the practice in all the architectural iron foundries in New York.

The brick work which surrounds the skeleton cannot entirely be depended upon as a protection for the metal against the effects of fire. The covering is thin, and at best brick work is not fire-proof. That bricks resist far better than anything else is beyond question, but a brick wall is quite another thing. The mortar joints compose nearly one-fourth of the whole wall, and lime is no more proof against severe heat than is limestone. Consequently the bond, by burning out, allows the wall to fall, making the damage as complete as though the bricks had been devoured by the flames. The manner in which bricks are hurriedly and carelessly laid up in a wall, not slushed in on all sides with mortar as they should be, but with one inner side of each brick having little or no mortar at all against it, leaves countless air spaces within the wall, and the air within these confined chambers is expanded during a fire. If heated air will run an engine, its expansive force can surely aid in the overthrow and destruction of a brick wall.

The skeleton construction imposes no new conditions on the architect. It calls for no skillful treatment to make appear what it is. The metal frame, like the bones in a human body, is concealed from sight. Indeed, the architect is relieved from many troublesome conditions. He may design his structure without regard to width of piers, so that a front of brick or stone may be made nearly as light and airy in appearance as one of cast iron, and with as large window openings as desired. The building is so tied together laterally and vertically as to resist wind pressure or any other strain with impunity.

Already the architectural appearance of New York is being altered by the skeleton structures. New opportunities are opening up for architects to display their skill in treating problems of height, such as their professional brethren of a few decades ago never dreamed. It remains to be seen whether the aesthetic spirit will keep pace with the mechanical progress in the art of building, and bring forth designs of grace and beauty for the tower-like structures, notwithstanding any pre-conceived notions of disproportion between height and width. ∎

IV.

Our skyscraper architecture hardly requires the mention or comment of my pen. It is omnipresent and insistent, the most conspicuous, revolutionary and American architectural product of the last twenty-five years, from Jenney and Mundie's Home Life Building in Chicago and Bradford Gilbert's Tower Building addition in New York to the 750-foot Woolworth and the vast Equitable in New York, and Boston's much-belauded Custom House. It has been more "cussed and discussed" than any other modern type. It has changed the skyline of New York and of every large American city from Seattle to Bangor, from Los Angeles to Galveston. It has produced a new architectural style, irrespective of that of its varied decorative trimmings; and it speaks so loud for itself as to make further words on this page unnecessary. ●

Father of the skyscraper, William Le Baron Jenney (1832–1907) studied engineering in Paris and worked as a civil engineer in the Union Army. Using that knowledge as a Chicago architect, he designed the landmark iron-and-steel-framed Home Insurance Building, 1885.

1891

**Lancashire Fire Insurance
Building, New York City,
J.C. Cady & Company
1889–90 (demolished).**

This was the City's second
skeleton-framed building, the first
being Bradford Gilbert's Tower
Building, 1888–89 (photo page 8).
J.C. Cady & Co. also built the
Metropolitan Opera House, and
the West 77th Street frontage
and Auditorium of the American
Museum of Natural History,
1887–1901.

opposite: The Metropolitan Opera
House, New York City, J.C. Cady
& Co., architects, 1883 (demol-
ished 1966).

IRON CONSTRUCTION IN NEW YORK CITY:
PAST AND FUTURE

Louis De Coppet Berg

THE writer being recently asked to give an expert opinion as to the best book on the details of modern iron construction, replied that improvements in iron construction were progressing, at so rapid a pace that he could recommend no work, however recent, as being up to the latest standard. Improvements, however, have not progressed with the same strides since New York City began to build in earnest, but nearly all date from a very recent period.

In the days when the wealthy New Yorker's architectural ambitions were satisfied with a three-story brick front, trimmed with sills and lintels of white marble, and crowned with Grecian cornices of painted wood, iron construction proper was practically unknown; it was not even in its infancy. Difficulties in construction were overcome with posts, beams, lintels and trusses of wood, and yet if we look back but half a century we almost touch that period. Since then what a change in our buildings, and what a difference in construction!

The modern successful New York City architect must be not alone an artist, but he must have marked abilities as a civil engineer; he must outrank, if possible, the mechanical engineer in his knowledge of electricity, hydrostatics, heating and ventilation, and the sanitary engineer in the knowledge of plumbing, and withal be an accomplished financier: then, too, it will not do for him to acquire merely a knowledge of these varied sciences, he must keep abreast of the constant improvements in them, and, above all, he must not copy slavishly what his confrères and rivals are doing, but must constantly invent something new.

This state of things is largely brought about by the rapidly developing and changing character of the Metropolis, and its unsuitable shape for rapid expansion. The island is so narrow, and its trade centre, the "Stock Exchange," so near one end, that the tendency of each trade not only to flock to one spot, but to crowd as near to this centre as possible, has made the price of land down-town simply enormous. There are many sales on record where the price was so great that if the property had been covered entirely with silver dollars two layers deep the owner would have scorned the offer. To place low buildings on such property would necessitate the charging of enormous rents to derive income on the ground value; but even if the paying of such rents had been feasible, more room had to be provided to accommodate those clamoring for it. As the old low-priced ground leases expired one by one, owners were called upon to build taller buildings, to give more room and to get more rent. But this was impracticable, for tenants would not mount stairs above four or at most five stories.

It was here that the inventive genius of our race stepped in, and the "elevator" solved the problem.

Daring builders went as high as six, then seven, eight or nine stories, and the climax seemed reached. A few years and the lesson was learned that such buildings were a menace to the city. They could not be controlled in case of fire. Hence the law requiring them to be "fire-proof." This brought about the first great step in the improvement in iron construction. Wood in floors, trusses, stairs, elevator inclosures, in fact every constructive or exposed part had to be replaced by iron, not only to prevent decay and burning of the wood, but because the fire-proof construction in partitions and floors added so greatly to the weights to be borne. Soon, however, nine-storied buildings no longer sufficed; office rents which in the cheapest parts of a building brought at least $2 for each square foot of floor space, no longer made sufficient income. More room was needed and prices continued to rise, therefore buildings had to go higher: hydraulic and electric rapid-running "express" elevators, with a speed of 600 feet a minute or more, solved that part of the problem, and buildings could and did rise to thirteen and fourteen stories.

from:
THE VARIOUS CAUSES FOR BAD ARCHITECTURE
By William Nelson Black
Vol. II, No. 2,
October–December 1892,
pp. 149–163.

But, now, what shall be said with reference to iron as a building material? Were it only a question of the use of iron as a subsidiary material to take the place of wood beams, and the like, very little but good could be said, though we should be forced to deplore the fact that it is such an excellent conductor of heat. Restricted in its use, too, and tastefully moulded, it is not altogether to be condemned for window and door posts where the close grouping of windows and doors is thought architecturally desirable. Then, again, the tornado exposed sections of the West should be able to find in iron something that can be anchored and, held down when the winds blow. Iron may have its uses, certainly, and they are many. But its conceded merits are thus far mainly structural; and as this article deals rather with the aesthetic than with the mechanical or engineering side of architecture the question at the head of the paragraph must be asked differently. What shall be said with reference to the aesthetic utility of iron as a building material? Put in these terms it will be possible to discuss the question in language sufficiently explicit, for if there was ever a building constructed in all its parts of iron that was aesthetically good it was not ▸

1 Old girder.

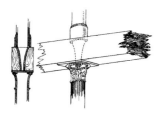

2 Old-fashioned defective dowelled column.

3 Old-fashioned cast-iron lintel.

But here arose a new problem; the brick walls at the base became so enormously thick that their cost was very great, their weight excessive for the poor foundation in many parts of the island, and above all the valuable ground space occupied by them a great loss of income to the owner; so much so that, if a man had a narrow lot, little more than an entrance hall-way would be left between the side walls on the ground floor, and this too on his most valuable renting floor.

It became necessary, therefore, to make the walls thinner; and iron construction was resorted to, culminating, in what are now called "skeleton" constructed buildings. To show how rapid is the progress in such matters, it is but necessary to state that the foundations of the first building of this kind, the Lancashire Insurance Company's building at 25 Pine street, in which all the walls are built with skeleton wrought iron construction, so that though the building is ten full stories high above the ground the brick side walls are only 12 inches thick at the ground level, were laid but little over two years ago, and yet it has already been adopted as the standard of construction for nearly all the new tall buildings, some of which are now rapidly rising towards their proposed seventeen stories.

Where this growth will stop no one can predict. Weight on the foundation may be the limit mark, but aluminium construction in the near future may even overcome that difficulty.

In thus briefly outlining the causes for our recent remarkably rapid progress in iron construction, the writer has hesitated before claiming as modern inventions even the elevator or the New York City "sky-scraper," for as archaeologists rob modern civilization of all that makes life worth living, yielding the palm for luxury to Rome, for art and literature to Greece, for construction and enterprise to Egypt, so he may by such claims arouse a controversy as to whether or no the skeleton constructed "sky-scraper" with its "express" elevators, is not after all but a feeble imitation of the Tower of Babel.

Iron construction in New York City can easily be divided into distinct stages: Infancy, Cast-iron Period, Cast-iron Fronts, Wrought-iron Beams, Riveted Girders and Trusses, Skeleton Construction.

INFANCY

In this period there is nothing of interest to the constructor beyond such interest as is aroused by curious and odd methods of construction discovered in old buildings as they are torn down. The most curious of these contains the incipient idea of the modern riveted girder. This idea of building up I-shaped wrought-iron girders can be found in many old buildings. Their construction is frequently so odd and unnatural that the wonder is not what could be made to stand up, but what failed to fall down. Probably the most curious is where two plates, placed parallel to each other horizontally, are bolted together, being separated by one or two vertical plates, there being no method whatever of attaching the vertical plate or web to its horizontal top and bottom plates or flanges, reliance being placed only on the pressure or squeezing effect due to the bolts.

Illustrations of some curious old girders are given on pages 450 and 451.[1] These were evidently removed by some second-hand dealer, and being only a little too long for his new building, he did not care to stop nor to expend money to cut them off, but built them in as they were, a constant reminder to passers-by of olden times. Such improvised iron girders, and the few curiously-shaped European rolled iron sections, principally channels or deck beams, which found their way at rare intervals into New York buildings, increased spans sufficiently to make iron columns a necessity. These led to the

CAST-IRON PERIOD

The columns were of cast-iron, usually fluted on the shaft, with bell-shaped tops or capitals. Later, the caps frequently were Corinthian in design.

Where wooden girders rested on the columns, the lesson was soon learned that to run the girder over the column and place another column above the girder, meant serious trouble in the building, as the girder began to shrink and thus lowered each column above it. To avoid this the dowel[2] was resorted to, a construction which, though intended to avoid a danger, frequently became of such a curious design itself as to endanger the building more than the danger it aimed to avoid. The dowel is a short column of diminished diameter, a hole being drilled through the girder for Its passage. Thus the load on the column above is transferred to the columns below, for the depth of the girder, through unshrinkable iron. But to have expense frequently the dowel was cast on the upper column, assuming the shape shown in the sketch below. A thin cast-iron plate was laid over the bell-shaped cap and the bottom of the upper column reduced almost to a dull point rested in the centre of this thin plate, over the hollow of the cap below, ready to punch through the plate oil the slightest provocation; an accident which has happened more than once. And yet this construction has been used as recently as within twenty years, and buildings with it stand and are still used with immunity for heavy storage and manufacturing purposes.[*]

From these old columns it is quite a step to the modern wrought iron column, as seen in the foundations of the building at the corner of Broadway and Eighteenth street. (photo at right)

The use of cast-iron further introduced the iron lintel; then, as the daring of con-

structors increased, the span of the opening was lengthened; and the methods of overcoming these new difficulties led to many curiously-shaped lintels, the best known being the "arched" lintel, a good example of which was seen on top of the rubbish caused by the collapse of the buildings after the fire at the corner of Fulton and Nassau Streets.[3] Constructors became so daring at last that the building law took cognizance of these constructions and was largely instrumental in fostering the use of that anomaly, the "bowed girder."

This consisted of an arched rib of cast-iron, with a straight tie rod of wrought iron, the rib being the "bow," the tie rod the "string." These girders, of a kind, can be seen throughout the old Harper & Bros. publishing house. The bowed girder was quite a favorite, until quite a recent period, for lintels, and the writer can remember many a happy hour spent in his early experiences tracing out the various strains due to this mongrel combination of metals. The use of cast-iron finally led to

CAST-IRON FRONTS

Of all periods and styles of architecture

brought to the attention of the writer, and he will hardly be expected to commend what he has not seen.

In the first place the temptation to copy all the vices of wood building is ever present with the workmen in iron, with a further temptation, on account of the greater strength of the material, to magnify those vices. A post that needs to be four or six inches in diameter to sustain its load when constructed of wood might be safely reduced one-half or two-thirds when constructed of iron, and the reduction would be economically a gain to the landlord. Corresponding reflections might be made with reference to every part of a building. The great tensile strength of iron enables the builder to reserve mere figments of wall faces between his apertures. It may be said, indeed, to have almost demolished the wall as an architectural feature in a majority of the examples to be observed along our urban thoroughfares, mere columns and pilasters offering all the support needed for the tallest façades. And such columns and pilasters! The good genius of the designer of stone posterns must have presided at their conception and wrought industriously in their execution. Indeed, to such an excess is this reduction in material carried that men who profess to build of iron, or to build iron fronts, are building mainly of glass and using the iron as a foil to cover their deception. The iron parts of the building are merely an ugly frame work to hold the windows and glass doors in place. The wall, so elaborately and lovingly designed in ancient structures, has disappeared, and in its place we have façades composed chiefly of windows and glass doors.

Now this might be an advantage to architecture were we building ▶

[*]The writer has purposely avoided the discussion of the long mooted question, whether cast or wrought iron columns are preferable in case of fire, and to resist rusting. The former are objected to on the theory that they crack and snap off suddenly when heated and suddenly cooled by water. The latter are supposed to bend and let the load down more gradually, but under less intense heat. As a rule both behave fairly well, though the writer inclines strongly to wrought iron; a fire that will destroy either material would probably destroy the masonry over it anyhow. A curious instance, however, was found in the great Western Union fire, where a cast-iron tower corner column actually partially melted, and settling on itself shortened its length, as shown in the illustration;[4] and still the tower stood intact until torn down by hand. The objection to wrought iron on the score of rusting is perhaps more real, and yet it can be readily answered by the fact that we remove wrought iron anchors from old masonry walls unharmed by rust, though frequently more than 100 years old.

4 Third Avenue Railroad Car
Stables, New York City, Albert
Wagner, architect (photo right).

5 Stage supports, Metropolitan
Opera House (above)

6 Riveted girder and hoisting
engine, new wing, American
Museum of Natural History
(opposite far right)

opposite top left: Roof and
Ceiling, Metropolitan Opera
House.

which New York City has experienced—and she has had them all from Egyptian to the latest fashionable crazes—the cast-iron fronts were the most abhorrent. It was found that the elaborate Renaissance fronts which were being built of stone and chiefly of marble, were very expensive, and instead of abandoning the style and doing something cheaper, cast-iron was used, modeled and painted in imitation of marble or stone, and thus these, to our predecessors beautiful—but to us hideous—designs could be carried out more cheaply than probably any kind of inexpensive style with genuine material. A.T. Stewart's retail store, Ninth street and

ones.

The writer would not, however, wish to be understood that no front should be of iron; on the contrary, he contemplates building at an early opportunity a skeleton construction with an iron front, but the front should be made to express and show the nature of the construction, and of the material, and should not imitate the methods of using a more expensive material.

As already stated, rolled iron beams of European make were at intervals introduced into our buildings, and as the demand for them increased they were rolled in this country. But the protective tariff and the

Broadway, is about the acme of this period. When, however, designers let the cheapness of the material—cast-iron—run away with their good sense and allowed their fancy such play, when we saw great business structures rise in Broadway, with gilded Moorish fronts, the fashion was doomed, and cast-iron fronts were quickly abandoned, to be chiefly replaced by brick and terra cotta

pool arrangement of the mills kept the price of structural shapes so high that rolled iron had to be used sparingly.

In a public building recently destroyed by fire and since rebuilt by the writer's firm, a curious mélange of iron and wooden beams was found, odd bedfellows used in the same floors. Though the old building was erected only about twenty-three years ago, either

the price of iron was too great to use iron throughout for floor beams, so that it was used only here and there with an idea of stiffening the floors, or else the owner's desire to have iron beams used could not be carried out, because they could not be easily obtained in sufficient quantities.

Cooper Union was one of the early structures to have iron beams; but the adoption in such structures as the Post-office, the Western Union Building, and the Tribune Building, in the early "seventies," led rapidly to their more familiar use, as illustrated, for instance, in the Third Avenue car stables (Page 456).[4]

In the Metropolitan Opera House, built in the early "eighties," the use of iron construction undoubtedly made a big stride. As this was the first theatre building probably in the world to introduce fan ventilation, furnishing to every seat a supply of fresh air, so it was also the first absolutely fire-proof theatre in the world. Not only was the ordinary iron construction used, but even the galleries were constructed of iron, though nearly every beam had to be bent to a different shape; the ceiling and stage galleries were iron; and, what at the time was claimed to be an impossibility, iron supports for the stages were invented, to be removable at will, and interchangeable.[5]

RIVETED GIRDERS AND TRUSSES.

The span of the roofs and ceilings in this Opera House, considerably over 100 feet, gave an opportunity to show what could be done in light iron truss construction.

This building, too, was one of the earliest

buildings into which the use of riveted girders of modern design entered. The span of these riveted girders was so great, that their weight was beyond anything that had been hoisted before them, and after they had broken down a successive series of derricks, special derricks had to be devised to get them into place. It should be said that this difficulty had been foreseen; for what were originally designed to be "boxed" or two-web girders, were afterwards built in two halves longitudinally; that is, two single-web girders, of only about half weight each, were substituted, hoisted separately, and afterwards bolted together.

Since then the use of this form of construction has increased so rapidly that now, only a decade later, the claim of these girders to be unusual or very heavy would be ridiculed; and they would be hoisted into place in a few minutes by a steam engine, so small that, as a reporter once put it, "it looked as if the girder could 'yank' that little engine all over the place." This was said of some riveted girders used in the American Museum of Natural History some two years ago, which were some 65 feet long, 3 feet deep, and weighed about 35,000 pounds each.[6]

They supported solid tiled masonry floors, for which no columns were used, the

conservatories; but as we are building nothing of the sort for mercantile uses our iron fronts are constructed in contempt of architecture. As already suggested even the little of iron that they contain is hopelessly tasteless in design, conceived in a spirit on a level with only the lowest of decorative art. Were our iron builders to study utility only, and leave out their imitations of architectural decorations true art would be greatly the gainer. It would no longer be caricatured, and the mischievous influences of caricatures on popular taste would be withdrawn.

What has been said may sound like a complete condemnation of iron as a building material for anything more than structural use in places where it is entirely hidden from view. But it is not intended that the condemnation shall be so sweeping. It may be that the architect for iron buildings has not yet come. It may be that like the architect for wood buildings, he can never come and bring a head full of very grand ideas. Iron is equally with wood unsuitable for the expression of the highest aesthetic sentiment, and this stricture must remain valid even when it is fashioned into a mere imitation of the forms of brick and stone. Conceive of the Equitable Life Insurance Building transformed in its interior from its costly colored marbles and polished stone into an iron finish decorated by the house painter and gilder after this conception, we may have some idea of the hopeless inferiority of iron as a material suitable for the representation of the beautiful. But it is idle to make any conjectures on the possibilities of iron when an attempt is made to fashion it in imitation of brick and stone. No conscientious architect would make the attempt, and were it made only the coarser forms of ▸

7 Truss over Carnegie Music Hall, New York City, William B. Tuthill, architect, year.

8 opposite: Tower Building, New York City, Bradford Gilbert, architect, 1888–89 (photo page 8).

9 Photo page 28.

10 Plan and section, and elevation

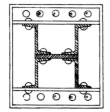

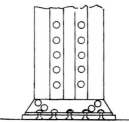

of Zee-bar column and shoe.

unobstructed exhibition space on each floor being about 65 feet by 110 feet. These girders were unparalleled but two years ago; since then they have been surpassed.

In building iron trusses architects copied from the designs of bridge constructors, using the "pin" jointed truss. Good examples are given in the illustrations, showing the great roof trusses over the Metropolitan Opera House; and one of those over the New Music Hall, the latter calculated to carry a load of 678,000 pounds, and weighing 51,000 pounds each.[7]

It was soon found, however, that for the shorter spans used in buildings, a great saving could be made by constructing the roof trusses largely of flat bars and angle irons; as these shapes, not being controlled by the mill pool, are much cheaper; and as the joints of the truss are riveted together, the cost of the "shop-work" is greatly diminished. This form has been largely used in the last five or six years.

SKELETON CONSTRUCTION

As already mentioned, the necessity for economizing space on the lower floors led to skeleton constructions; while its rapid and almost sudden introduction was due to the innovation and successful use of wrought-iron columns and girders in the Lancashire Building, yet for a number of years constructors had been struggling with the problem.

Attempts were made to build thinner walls by stiffening them with iron columns at intervals, a very bad construction, as the wall joints would shrink, while the columns remained or, columns were introduced to remove the weight of floors from the walls, a not much better device.

Several buildings finally were built with cast-iron columns and cast-iron lintels or rolled beams between them at intervals, the Tower Building[8] being probably the pioneer of this class. It was found, however, that such buildings, if narrow and tall, lacked rigidity, as columns of cast-iron can only be bolted together and to the horizontal lintels or beams, and the bolts have to be set by

wrenches and by hand. This construction allowed more or less play at the joints, and such buildings, if very narrow, had to be stiffened laterally that is, sideways, by means of vertical trusses running from side wall to side wall and from top to bottom. These form a very serious drawback in planning, as partitions have to be placed wherever the trusses are, and partitions are frequently not wanted there. The Columbia Building, just completed, uses the cast-iron column with greater success, as the base line of the building is quite broad in comparison with its height. The best-planned modern office building leaves each floor as one great loft, to be subdivided by light interchangeable and easily-moved partitions, to suit the tenants' wishes.

In the Gallatin Bank Building[9] the effort was made to economize space by the use of iron-constructed walls. Both cast and wrought iron were used. The entire rear walls were only 12 inches thick, made of cast-iron columns, of |_|_| shape, the hollows being used to convey air to the offices. The two interior court crosswalls were built of wrought iron and are largely filled with glass, the solid parts being only 6 inches thick over all.

The wrought-iron construction proved so superior in its economy of space and rigidity, that when the Lancashire building was put up cast-iron was eliminated from any consideration whatever. What is known as the Zee-bar column was used, this being four Zee-shaped irons, riveted to a central plate, as shown below.[10]

The Zee bars and plates, where jointed at different points of their height, had wrought-iron plates riveted to the lower column, the next columns above being *riveted* to these plates; in this way the columns, as they grew in height, practically became of one solid, unbroken length. At intervals of from two to three stories, but always immediately at some floor level, horizontal, single-webbed *riveted* girders were riveted to the columns at their ends, and on these the 12-inch brick curtain walls rested; the cross girders carrying the floor beams proper were of course at right angles to the wall girders and were also riveted to the columns at their ends. The floor beams were riveted to the girders, and each floor which came on a level with a wall girder was trussed throughout its entire surface by means of flat-iron diagonal cross bars riveted to beams and girders. Thus every such floor became a truss and gave the building rigidity laterally by transferring any tendency to twist or move laterally to the front and rear walls. The latter had riveted girders at every floor level riveted at their ends to the corner columns, and the corners above and below the girders, thus formed at the columns, were filled as far as the windows would permit with wrought-iron triangular "gusset plates" riveted to columns and to the top and bottom flanges of the girders. It was thus made utterly impossible for the building, though only a little over 20 feet wide, to collapse.

It will readily be seen how well the Zee-bar column and riveted girder adapt themselves to be used in connection with a thin brick wall, as the bricks covering and protecting the columns and girders can readily be bonded with those forming the "curtain walls."

An improvement on the riveted girder, however, was introduced in the Mohawk Building,[*] where the webs of the girders are made up of diagonal flat bars, which readily allow the wall to be carried full thickness past the web, the inner and outer sections being easily bonded together, and the girder consequently much better protected from fire.

With the great weights of our modern buildings, iron and steel are rapidly coming into use to spread the weight at the footings. A curious and most ingenious foundation construction was used in the new Western Union Building.[†] It became necessary to transfer a large part of an enormous load, to be placed on the column at one corner of the lot, to more secure footings. To accomplish this an inverted truss was built into the foundation; its extreme end under the column in question. The vertical column under the column above, for the height of this truss, is so diminished in size that, should the full load attempt to settle on to it, it would be unable to bear it, and bending or giving away, ever so slightly, under the load, would at once transfer it to the truss. This lower column could have been omitted, but is counted on to help spread the load over the footings.

THE FUTURE

With so many ingenious constructors working at the problem of iron construction, as we have in New York, there is no doubt that the rapid strides of the past will be kept up, if not surpassed in the near future. Steel is the material which will probably lead the immediately impending advances.

THE TOWER BUILDING.
Nos. 50 B'way, & 41 & 43 New St. N.Y.
Property of J. Noble Stearns, Esq.

[*] R.H. Robertson, architect.
[†] Dey Street, New York City.

the models could be imitated. But may not iron, after all, have something higher than a merely structural place in the building of the future? It will not be worth while to ask if it can have a higher place in the strictly aesthetic building of the future, because the question has been answered negatively in the context.

There can be little question but that iron could be made an available building material for cottages of the class that are now built of wood, and were it not for the greater cost we should long since have seen it largely made a substitute for wood in this kind of construction. But the day may come when the cost will be more nearly equalized, and then, in the language of the athlete iron may have its inning. The processes of its manufacture are much cheaper than the processes for manufacturing wood, and this would give it an advantage after the lumber forests have disappeared. It is more flexible than wood, too, for moulding into those decorative forms which are thought pretty in cottage architecture.

But, this is a speculation in futures which is hardly fair dealing. Before iron can enter the field as a competitor for cottage building contracts, wood must be abandoned. This only we know for certainty. The use of iron as a material for exteriors in building or for visible interiors has had a mischievous influence on the architectural development of the period. We even observe a disposition among architects who make plans for brick and stone structures to give more space to apertures and less to wall face than was thought either tasteful or prudent a few years ago, and this practice does not represent an architectural advantage. It is a sign rather of corruption and decadence. •

1892

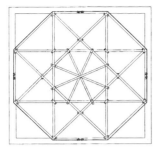

11 Plan of N. Poulsen's floor construction.

12 Ceiling under N. Poulsen's floor construction.

13 Cast-iron stairs—New York Life Insurance Co. Building, Minneapolis, Babb, Cook & Willard, Architects

opposite: Gallatin Bank Building, New York City, J.C. Cady & Co.

Its manufacture is hardly as yet in that state of certainty where it can be used with perfect impunity and without tests, which latter mean increased expense. But it is rapidly assuming a commanding position in architectural construction, and is pushing out of use wrought iron, as the latter has displaced cast-iron.

The great trouble, however, at the present moment, is not so much the material used, as the slavish following of old constructive ideas. At first wooden girders, at larger intervals, supported wooden beams at closer intervals and at right angles to the girders; then iron girders supported wooden beams, at right angles; then iron girders supported iron beams at right angles to them, and now we make steel do the same. Why! the old Egyptians, thousands of years before our era, put stone girders on stone columns, and at right angles to these the stone beams forming the roof coverings!

Can no one invent some new and better method? Does the "Cambered" arch offer no suggestion? The writer believes fully that before long some one will invent some much cheaper and less clumsy arrangement, for the material is now here that will adapt itself to almost any form.

A curiosity, and possibly a strong hint as to future constructive solutions, is afforded by Mr. N. Poulsen's new patent.[11] Flat iron bars are placed across the entire span of the room, these ribs crossing each other at right angles and diagonally across their corners, the whole bent to the "natural arch curve" by being moulded over a rubber bag, inflated with gas. All curves being similar, all parts are interchangeable. The ribs are covered underneath with plain or ornamented plaster ribs,[12] which are moulded to the curve, and cut off in lengths to suit. Above the ribs and at regular intervals between them, concrete partitions are built up to near the floor, these are covered with wire cloth, and a heavy layer of concrete over them forms the floor, ready for any finish. Holes through the ribs allow the hot air to enter under the floor at, say, one corner and to circulate all over, under its entire area, doing away with the objectionable "cold floor," and then the heat enters the room near the point of starting through a floor register.

Whatever may be said as to the artistic effect of this arrangement, or as to its practicability in modern buildings, it certainly has the merit of being a long step, whether forward or not—at least, a long step—far away from our present clumsy methods.

And after steel—our present hope—what next? The writer believes that cast-steel has within it immense constructional possibilities. When it can be made to be as strong, ductile and reliable as wrought steel, then the immense advantage of being able to do away with the expense of hand work, and to introduce the facile and cheaper form of casting, will again supersede the present "wrought" age. When supports for stairs such as those in the New York Life Insurance Company Building, can be done in cast-iron, what may we not hope from the fully-developed and perfect cast-steel.[13]

And after steel, what next? The development of the future will probably come with aluminium, a metal combining with strength, lightness. It is not affected by our trying climate, which requires all steel and wrought iron to be carefully and constantly protected from corrosion.

The writer's hope that this material maybe accessible to constructors in the near future, is largely based on the already rapid reduction in its cost of production since it was first discovered and particularly since the impetus for cheapening its price was started by Napoleon III.

It can now be produced for twenty-five cents a pound, several tons being manufactured daily, for use in household and table goods, military equipments, cartridge shells, in connection with machinery and similar purposes.

When the price has been still further reduced, it will be largely used for covering roofs, for gutters and leaders, and sheet metal-work generally; and, as all alloy, if not in its pure state, it will some day assuredly replace the heavier and corrosive iron and steel constructions of the present day. ■

FIRST SKYSCRAPER DEMOLISHED
*NOTES IN BRIEF, Vol. 64, No. 4,
October 1928, pp.146-147.*

*The Tacoma building, Chicago,
believed to have been the first
true skyscraper, was razed during
the past few months to make
space for a forty-seven story
office building.*

*   *   *

The honor of having the first
William Le Baron Jenney, architect of Chicago, was commissioned in 1883 to design the
Home Insurance Building of that
city. His was the first executed,
metal framed structure. He
described its construction as follows: "A square iron column was
built into each of the piers on the
street fronts and all columns and
mullions were continuous from
the bottom plate to the top of the
building."

There were, however, certain
shortcomings to this design, as
pointed out by H.J. Burt, an
authority on steel construction. It
would have been impossible, he
says, to have erected the superstructure without the additional
support of masonry piers. The
true skyscraper was to become
the accomplishment of the architects Holabird and Roche who
prepared plans in 1887 for the
Tacoma building, a sixteen story
structure on the northeast corner
of Madison and La Salle Streets,
Chicago.

The exterior walls of this building as well as interior frame were
of iron, so designed that the terra
cotta casing served as curtains
suspended from the framework.
Sam Loring, a terra cotta manufacturer, is given credit for the
idea of adapting terra cotta to the
iron frame, but no single person
is recorded as the inventor of the
steel frame. The developments
of a generation were required to
perfect the engineering principles
involved in skyscraper construction, and to this development
many American architects contributed a part. •

1892

2 Brave New World: An Architecture for Our Time

One of the most important events to influence American architecture before the dawn of the 20th Century was the World's Columbian Exposition in Chicago in 1893. Critical reaction was mixed. Some thought that architecture had taken a great leap backwards. Others felt that the "true art of architecture," lost in the recent period of fast-paced invention, had been retrieved for the greater good of a public that recognized the value of such things. Even Daniel H. Burnham, radical proponent of the skyscraper in Chicago, and Chief of Construction for the Fair, spoke of his purposeful "reversion" to classical ideals.[a]

Though many saw this reversion as reactionary, and a form of pandering to public taste, Burnham later traced the beginning of modern city planning to the Exposition. As a result of his innovative work there, he was later called upon to undertake the planning of Cleveland, San Francisco, Manila, Baguio, and eventually Chicago itself.[b]

Montgomery Schuyler was less dismayed by this reversion to the classical as he was by what he saw as an inherent architectural deceit—the contradiction between the use of structural steel and the ornate veneer of plaster and straw that everywhere covered it. In his entry on Architecture of the United States in the *STURGIS DICTIONARY*, Schuyler referred to the Exposition as:

"a pompous architectural display to which no approach had before been made in the United States, and to which, indeed, there is no parallel in real and durable building anywhere. The Greco-Roman architecture was imitated in façades of lath and plaster which had, in the chief and most admired buildings, no relation in their design, either to their own material and actual construction, or to the buildings—which they masked and which were in fact modern engineering constructions in metal. Only in one of the great buildings was an attempt made at an architectural development of the facts of material and construction, and this building was the least admired of any...The grandiose effect of the architectural display was

Concourse, Pennsylvania Station, New York City, McKim, Mead and White, architects, 1906–10 (demolished 1964).

naturally attributed by the public to the style employed, although there were other elements in it of even more importance."

Though nowhere in the pages of *Architectural Record* is there an exact prescription for an American Style, it begins to become clear that it is in part a desire to strip a structure of superfluities and to allow "the building to clearly declare itself." Where did this idea originate? Certainly not with Schuyler himself. When Edward R. Smith wrote Schuyler's obituary in 1914 (page xix) he described the intellectual atmosphere in which the editors worked:

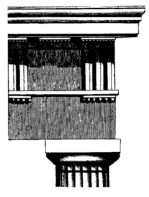

> "In 1892 he published a preliminary book on *American Architecture* which recalls the crisp and formative period of the eighties and early nineties, when American art in all branches began to be conscious of itself and of the art of other people. At this moment Mr. Schuyler was mature, and had a large store of recollections of the past of American architecture. He was dominated, as Mr. Sturgis was, and all serious students of architecture were at the time, by the return which the civilized world was making to the method, the truth and the genuineness of medieval work. Everyone read Ruskin's books, which, with all their faults, had the heart of the matter in them; many passed on to the stronger scholarship of Viollet-le-Duc and the medievalists of France and Germany. [Schuyler's] book of 1892 is full of the pleasant and human phrases of the day, which express the conviction that architecture, after all, is building, and that the verities of construction are fundamental to the normal development of style.

> "The medieval doctrine of that or, rather, of the previous period always tempered Mr. Schuyler's judgment, and made him amiably antagonistic to the results of the teaching of the classic school.

> "Since the publication of Mr. Schuyler's book in 1892, American architecture has expressed itself in a large way. It has been mainly classic, and true to the modern Parisian standards, and seems now to be making a healthy return to the arrested Colonial period."

For an idea of the almost universal fascination with the iron skeleton, it is important to understand something of the impact of the teaching of Viollet-le-Duc on the architecture world. As an architect Viollet-le-Duc had little merit, but as a scholar he developed new and highly influential ideas on the Gothic Style, which he felt was a style of rational construction based on a system of rib vaults, buttresses, and flying buttresses. The ribs are a skeleton and the spaces between, mere infill. All thrusts are conducted from the ribs to the buttresses and flying buttresses, and walls can be replaced by large openings. These ideas were laid down and made universal property in Viollet-le-Duc's *Dictionnaire raisonné de l'architecture française* (1854–68). A comparison between Gothic-skeleton and iron-skeleton building was drawn, or rather implied, in Viollet-le-Duc's *Discourses on Architecture*. Here Viollet-le-Duc appears as a passionate defender of his own age, of engineering, and of new materials and techniques, especially iron for supports, for framework, and for ribs. Though lengthy, the passage is worth quoting in full:

> "Hitherto cast or rolled iron has been employed in large buildings only as an accessory. Where edifices have been erected in which metal plays the principle part, as in the *Halles Centrales* of Paris,—in these buildings masonry ceases to take any but an exceptional part, serving no other purpose than that of partition walls. What has nowhere been attempted with intelligence is the simultaneous employment of metal and masonry. Nevertheless it is this which in many cases architects should endeavor to accomplish. We

a *"The influence of the Exposition on architecture will be to inspire a reversion toward the pure ideal of the ancients. We have been in an inventive period, and have had rather contempt for the classics. Men evolved new ideas and imagined they could start a new school without much reference to the past. But action and reaction are equal, and the exterior and obvious result will be that men will strive to do classic architecture. In this effort there will be many failures. It requires long and fine training to design on classic lines. The simpler the expression of true art the more difficult it is to obtain.*
"The intellectual reflex of the Exposition will be shown in a demand for better architecture, and designers will be obliged to abandon their incoherent originalities and study the ancient masters of building. There is shown so much of fine architecture here that people have seen and appreciated this. It will be unavailing hereafter to say that great classic forms are undesirable. The people have the vision before them here, and words cannot efface it."
—Daniel Burnham [as told to Montgomery Schuyler in "Last Words About the World's Fair," III:3, Jan–Mar, 1894 p 292].

b "Burnham as a Pioneer in City Planning,"William E. Parsons, [XXXVII:1 Jul 1915 pp 13–31].

"...if we would invent that architecture of our own times which is so loudly called for, we must certainly seek it no longer by mingling all the styles of the past, but by relying on novel principles of structure."

1893

Eugène-Emmanuel Viollet-le-Duc Discourses on Architecture, *Lecture XII, p. 59, 1872.*

Ionic capital of the Erechtheum.

c *Discourses on Architecture*, Eugène Emmanuel Viollet-le-Duc, 1872. First English translation, 1877 (Vol. I) and 1881 (Vol. II).

The classical orders represented, either the order of stones in a column, rising from plinth to cornice (right), or the order in which the Greco-Roman capital styles developed from *Doric* (page 31), to *Ionic* (above), to *Corinthian* (right). The Roman architect Vitruvius was regarded as the authority in such matters, as was the Greek philosopher Aristotle before him.

Regarding the rightness and final purpose of things, Aristotle said,

"If, therefore, art imitates nature, it is to nature that the arts owe the fact that all of their productions come into being for an end. For we must surmise that everything that comes into being properly comes into being for an end: that which turns out to be good and beautiful comes into being properly, and everything that comes into being or has come into being, provided it did so according to nature, turns out to be beautiful [and good]..."
—Aristotle, Protrepticus 13

opposite: Classical orders applied to a "tripartite" division of a skyscraper (St. Paul Building, New York City, George B. Post, architect, 1889–90). The lower five stories are the "base," the top three are the "capital;" in between is the "shaft." To limit the impression of the building's overall height, every two stories are made to appear as one.

cannot always erect either railway stations, markets, or other immense buildings entirely of masonry, such buildings being very heavy in appearance, very costly, and not presenting sufficiently ample interior accommodation....The problem to be solved for providing great edifices to be destined to accommodate large assemblages would therefore be this:—To obtain a shell entirely of masonry, walls and vaulting, while diminishing the quantity of material and avoiding obstructive supports by the use of iron; to improve on the system of equilibrium adopted by the mediæval architects, by means of iron, but with due regard to the qualities of that material...some few attempts have been made in this direction, but timidly,—for instance by merely substituting columns of cast iron for stone pillars. Iron, however, is destined to play a more important part in our buildings; it should certainly furnish very strong and slender supports, but it should enable us to adopt vaulting at once novel in plan, light, strong and elastic, and bold constructions forbidden to the mason, such as overhanging projections, corbellings, oblique supports, etc....if we would invent that *architecture of our own times* which is so loudly called for, we must certainly seek it no longer by mingling all the styles of the past, but by relying on novel principles of structure. An architecture is created only by rigorously inflexible compliance with modern requirements, while the knowledge already acquired is made use of, or at least not disregarded." [italics are Viollet-le-Duc's][c]

Opinions of Viollet-le-Duc radically changed by 1926 when Charles H. Moore wrote "The Writings of Viollet-le-Duc." [LIX:2 Feb 1926 pp 128–32] Though Moore admits that Viollet-le-Duc's writings are "a mine of information of unequalled reliability," for the student, he points out that "his architectural enthusiasms were those of the logician rather than the artist," and that "the damage [he] wrought to the world's architectural patrimony [in the form of "so-called restoration"] is incalculable."

To see beneath the surface is always a challenge. The French were no more impressed in 1893, when confronted with the spectacle of the Chicago Fair. They felt the buildings were the exercises of schoolboys—projects the architects might have done while students in Paris. The designers had surely failed by using style as a screen, rather than employing it in the service of the new materials and methods.

A classically trained architect like Thomas Hastings (page 83) believed that architectural problems could still be successfully solved using "modern French" forms as guides and precedents. Hastings, who regarded *Les Halles Centrales* in Paris as the first important complex in which iron was used honestly and artistically, thought the way to design in terms of modern demands was to begin with a thoroughly developed floor plan that would then "determine the entire structure of the building, both external and internal"—a thoroughly Beaux Arts way of going about things.

For Russell Sturgis, meanwhile, the older forms—the classical orders, in particular—would no longer do. Discoursing at length on the "Good Things in Modern Architecture," Sturgis wrote in 1898,

"No form of strictly classic or neo-classic style is of any use to us, because as the orders have no relation to our systems of building, it follows that no architect knows how to handle those orders. No one now holds the orders plastic in his hands as the builders of Roman baths and Herculanean villas held them. No one feels free to deal with intercolumniations and with the proportions and entablatures to columns as the men who invented them and those who re-invented them felt to handle those details." ■

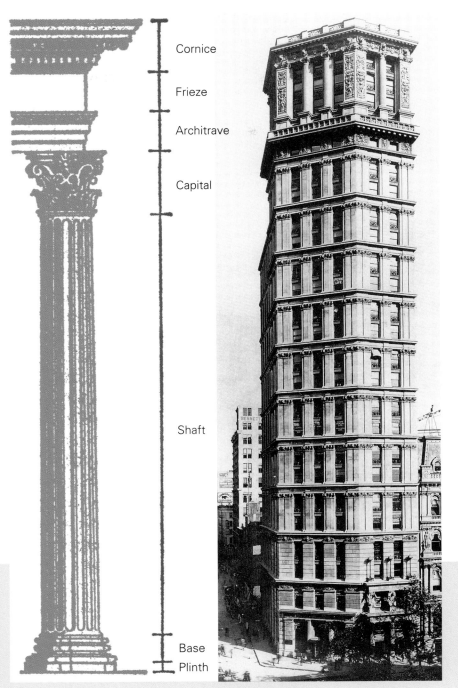

Cornice

Frieze

Architrave

Capital

Shaft

Base

Plinth

from:

LAST WORDS ABOUT
THE WORLD'S FAIR

By Montgomery Schuyler
Vol. III, No. 3, January–March 1894,
pp. 291–301

...the study of classic architecture is a usual, almost an invariable part of the professional training of the architects of our time. It is an indispensable part, wherever that training is administered academically, and most of all at Paris, of which the influence upon our own architecture is manifestly increasing and is at present dominant. Most of the architects of the World's Fair are of Parisian training, and those of them who are not have felt the influence of that contemporary school of architecture which is most highly organized and possesses the longest and the most powerful tradition. Presumably, all of them were familiar with the decorative use of "the orders" and knew what a module meant. What most of them had already practiced in academic exercises and studies, they were now for the first time permitted to project into actual execution....

That would be one good reason for the adoption of a given style—that all the persons concerned knew how to work in it. Another is that the classic forms, although originally developed from the conditions of masonic structure, have long since, and perhaps ever since they became "orders," been losing touch with their origin, until now they have become simply forms, which can be used without a suggestion of any real structure or any particular material. We know them in wood and metal, as well as in stone. They may be used, as they are used in Jackson Park, as a decorative envelope of any construction whatever without exciting in most observers any sense of incongruity, much less any sense of meanness such as is at once aroused by the sight of "carpenter's Gothic." ●

34

Agricultural Building, World's Columbian Exposition, Chicago, McKim, Mead and White, architects 1893.

Like Shakespeare's Prospero who spoke of theatrical illusions, Montgomery Schuyler referred to the Fair as an "insubstantial pageant." He sincerely hoped that the well-trained architect

"...will not be misled by the success of the buildings of the World's Fair into reproducing or imitating them, because he will know too well what are the necessary conditions of their effectiveness, and that these conditions cannot be reproduced except in another World's Fair, and not literally even there. Men bring not back the mastodon, nor we those times. It is, however, the architects who do not know these things with whom we have so largely to reckon, and it is upon such architects that the buildings in Jackson Park are more likely to impose themselves as models for more or less direct imitation in the solution of problems more usual. The results of such an imitation can hardly fail to be pernicious."

opposite: The Central Arch of the Peristyle, Charles B. Atwood, architect.

---

* Bragdon, like Schuyler, quotes Prospero from the Tempest (Act IV, Scene 1), albeit a little faulty:

*And, like the baseless fabric of this vision,
The cloud-capp'd towers, the gorgeous palaces,
The solemn temples, the great globe itself,
Yea, all which it inherit, shall dissolve,
And, like this insubstantial pageant faded,
Leave not a rack behind. We are such stuff
As dreams are made on; and our little life
Is rounded with a sleep.*

LAST WORDS ABOUT THE WORLD'S FAIR[1]

By Montgomery Schuyler

Next after unity, as a source and explanation of the unique impression made by the World's Fair buildings, comes magnitude. It may even be questioned whether it should not come first in an endeavor to account for the impression. If it be put second, it is only because unity, from an artistic point of view, is an achievement, while magnitude from that point of view, is merely an advantage. The buildings are impressive by their size, and this impressiveness is enhanced by their number. Mere bigness is the easiest, speaking aesthetically, though practically it may be the most difficult to attain, of all the means to an effect. It constitutes an opportunity, and one's judgment upon the result, as a work of art, depends upon the skill with which the opportunity has been embraced and employed. But bigness tells all the same, and the critical observer can no more emancipate himself from the effect of it than the uncritical, though he is the better able to allow for it. In this country mere bigness counts for more than anywhere else, and in Chicago, the citadel of the superlative degree, it counts for more, perhaps, than it counts for elsewhere in this country. To say of anything that it is the "greatest" thing of its kind in the world is a very favorite form of advertisement in Chicago. One cannot escape hearing it and seeing it there a dozen times a day, nor from noting the concomitant assumption that the biggest is the best. This assumption was very naively made by the enthusiastic citizen whose proposition we have already noted to occupy the Lake Front, which is one of the few features of the city of Chicago and one of the most attractive of them, with a full-sized reproduction of the Manufactures building.[2] If one ask why Manufactures building, the civic patriot has his answer ready: "Because it is the biggest thing on earth," as indeed it is, having not much less than twice the area of the Great Pyramid, the type of erections that are effective by sheer magnitude. The

Great Pyramid appeals to the imagination by its antiquity and its mystery as well as to the senses by its magnitude, but it would be impossible to erect anything whatever of the size of the Manufactures building or even of the Great Pyramid that would not forbid apathy in its presence. A pile of barrels so big as that would strike the spectator. It would be a monument of human labor, even though the labor had been misdirected, and the evidence of crude labor, if it be on a large enough scale, is effective as well as the evidence of artistic handicraft, though of course neither in the same kind nor in the same degree. "These huge structures and pyramidal immensities" would make their appeal successfully though they were merely huge and immense brute masses quite innocent of art. The art that is shown in this respect is in the development of the magnitude, the carrying further of an inherent and necessary effect and the leading of the spectator to an appreciation of the magnitude by devices that magnify and intensify the impression it makes. That is to say, the art consists in giving it scale. It is a final censure upon the treatment of a piece of architecture which aims at overpowering the spectator by its size that it does not took its size; as is the current and accepted criticism upon St. Peter's. To quote the aestheticians again, succession and uniformity are as essential as magnitude to the "artificial infinite," and it is necessary to it that there should be a repetition, an interminable repetition of the unit, the incessant application of the module. It is an effect quite independent of the style. The bay of a cathedral may furnish the unit as well as the order of a Grecian temple. But it is an effect that depends very greatly upon magnitude. The example of it we have already cited from Gothic architecture, the cloth-hall of Ypres,[3] is perhaps the most striking that mediæval architecture supplies, seeing that the design is a repetition of the unit, in this case a pointed arch, from end to end of an otherwise unbroken expanse of

from:
**ARCHITECTURE IN
THE UNITED STATES II:**
The Growth of Taste
Claude Bragdon
Vol. XXVI, No. 1. July 1909, pp. 38–45.

If the year 1880 marked one period in our architectural evolution, an unobtrusive milestone, as it were, which we passed without noticing, or in our sleep, 1893 marked another, and the flaming posthouse of this stage of the journey was the World's Columbian Exposition, or, in the colloquial phrase, the Chicago Fair. This caused the dullest of its to sit up and take notice, to make inquiry concerning the road we traveled and to speculate about the terminus: that City Beautiful foreshadowed in the spectacle of summer nights when music swelled and softened, while rockets bloomed and faded in the deep blue garden of the sky—of the Court of Honor, vast, pearl-colored, crowded, lighted, with fluttering banners, rippling waves and plashing fountains: still a treasured memory to thousands, who, though reared amid every kind of ugliness, crave beauty as their soul's natural and rightful foot.

> *"The cloud-capped towers, the gorgeous palaces,
> The solemn temples, like an unsubstantial
> Pageant faded, leave not a rack behind."*

All was a simulacrum: the buildings, the statues and the bridges were not of enduring stone, but lath and plaster; the gondolas were imported for the occasion, the civic guards and chair-men were impecunious students, and the crowds were composed not of free citizens of the place, ▸

1 Section II of three sections.

2 See pp. 62n., 63.

3 Cloth Hall, Ypres, Belgium (1299–1304).

4 Administration Building by Richard Morris Hunt (1827–95).

———————————

*Besides the directors there were at least a dozen participating firms:

McKim, Mead and White
Peabody & Stearns
Richard Morris Hunt
Van Brunt and Howe
George B. Post
Solon S. Beman
Adler and Sullivan
Jenney and Mundie
Sophia Hayden
Henry Ives Cobb
Charles B. Atwood
W.J. Edbrooke

**"...The Greco-Roman architecture was imitated in façades of lath and plaster which had,...no relation in their design, either to their own material and actual construction, or to the buildings —which they masked and which were in fact modern engineering constructions in metal...."

*** Transportation Building, Adler and Sullivan. Schuyler observed that"...the famous Golden Doorway suffers from being an isolated fragment, entirely unrelated to the general scheme, and its admirable detail does not for this reason excite the admiration it deserves...."

† Solon S. Beman (1853–1914)

above: The Golden Doorway of Adler and Sullivan's Transportation Building.

right: Exposed steel arches can be seen behind the dynamos of the Westinghouse Exhibit.

opposite page: The Court of Honor with The Republic, statue by Daniel Chester French.

wall 440 feet long. But this extent, impressive as it is, and heightened as its impressiveness is by the skill of the designer, becomes insignificant when it is compared with the flank of the Manufactures building, which is nearly four times as long as the front of Ypres, and of which the arcade in either wing must be quite half as long again as the Belgian arcade. Either of the colonnaded wings of Machinery Hall. Of which, by the way, the treatment is almost literally identical with that of the wings of the Capitol at Washington, must be nearly as long as the whole front of Ypres.

The devices by which these inordinate dimensions are brought home to the comprehension of the spectator are various, but they consist, in most cases, at least of a plinth and a parapet in which the height of a man is recalled, as in an architectural drawing the draughtsman puts in a human figure "to give the scale." While the Fair was in progress the moving crowds supplied the scale, but this was given also by all the architectural appurtenances, the parapets of the bridges and the railings of the wharves, so that the magnitude of the buildings was everywhere forced upon the sense. To give scale is also the chief contribution to the effect of a general survey that is made by the accessory and decorative sculpture of the buildings and of the grounds. In this respect, and without reference to their merits strictly as sculpture, the statuary that surmounts the piers and cupolas of the Agricultural building (see photo page 34) and that with which the angles of

the Administration building[4] bristle are particularly fortunate. On the other hand the figures of the peristyle were unfortunate, being too big and insistent for their architectural function of mere finials.

It would be pleasant to consider in detail the excellencies of the buildings that are most admirable, and the sources of their effectiveness, and to consider, also, the causes of the shortcomings of the less successful buildings. But the success of the architectural group, as a whole, is a success not disturbed by the shortcomings and the consequent success of the associated architects from their own point of view and for their special purpose, is a matter upon which we are all agreed. It is only with the influence of what has been done in Jackson Park upon the architecture of the country that we are now concerned; with the suitableness of it for general reproduction or imitation, and with the results that are likely to follow that process, if pursued in the customary manner of the American architect. The danger is that that designer, failing to analyze the sources of the success of the Fair will miss the point. The most obvious way in which he can miss it is by expecting a reproduction of the success of one of the big buildings by reproducing it in a building of ordinary dimensions. It is necessary, if he is to avoid this, that he should bear in mind how much of the effect of one of the big buildings comes from its very bigness, and would disappear from a reproduction in miniature. ∎

from:
**TWENTY-FIVE YEARS OF
AMERICAN ARCHITECTURE**
A.D.F. Hamlin
Vol. XL, No. 1, July, 1916, pp. 1–14

If the influence of the Columbian Exhibition was less revolutionary than that of the invention of the steel skeleton, it was nevertheless very far-reaching. The ten architects* who collaborated in that remarkable enterprise, in agreeing to adopt a uniform cornice line and a general neo-classic or Renaissance style for the exteriors of the chief buildings, signed the death-warrant of the still lingering Richardsonian Romanesque. The "White City" was scoffed at by many of our French visitors as nothing but "Ecole" projet architecture. In Europe the movement of protest against the academic and traditional had begun; the visitors were surprised and disappointed to find us still in the fetters of the bondage they were trying to throw off. They failed to appreciate the fact that we had never yet been under this bondage; that this was the first time in our history, at least since Thomas Jefferson's modest experiment at Charlottesville, that our architects had had an opportunity to design, or our people to see, a monumental group of buildings planned as an ensemble; the first time that they had seen such buildings set in an environment of gardens and architectural and sculptural adjuncts designed to enhance the total effect. The impression it produced was extraordinary. The grandeur of scale and the intrinsic beauty of the Fair alike elicited universal enthusiasm. There were some, it is true, who deplored the whole scheme and character of the display, as false in principle, un-American, meretricious, and they regretted the imposition upon our people of French ideas and of a "façade architecture" of Renaissance forms as a substitute for thoughtful, original design proceeding logically from American requirements to solutions specially fitted to them. The late Montgomery Schuyler expressed this regret forcefully in his article on "United States, Architecture of" in the STURGIS DICTIONARY OF ARCHITECTURE.** We of today feel that, whatever the justice of this criticism, there was a countervailing benefit in the impression made by the White City that outweighed its drawbacks. It was an object lesson in the possibilities of group-planning, of monumental scale, of public decorative splendor and harmony, and of worthy landscape setting, that was of incalculable value. The detail was neo-classic, and much of it was, as we now recognize, deplorably poor; but the harmony, the general picturesque effect, the union of all the arts in producing it, were merits quite independent of the styles used. Moreover, not all the buildings were in neo-classic styles. Adler and Sullivan's Transportation Building*** and Beman's† Fisheries Building, though in totally diverse styles, somehow fell into place in the general harmony, while uttering their declarations of independence of formal compulsion. ∎

enjoying an accustomed leisure, but the slaves that we all are of the Aladdin's lamp of competitive commerce, snatching a respite, rarely obtained and dearly paid for, from laborious lives.

No matter: we had had at least the vision, and though the actuality were denied us, we perceived that it need not always be denied.

The Science of Cities, that is, the conception of cities as coherent organisms, with many diverse and highly specialized functions, rather than as mere haphazard assemblages of houses, factories and stores, dates from the Chicago Exposition, for in its inception, arrangement and administration that exposition was itself an admirable illustration of the advantages of such a science.

* * *

A record of what has been actually accomplished since the year of the World's Fair, of the greater things assured by the purchase of land, the acquirement of funds, and by the enactment of the necessary legislation, and of the still more considerable improvements planned for and projected, should convince the most skeptical that the civic improvement movement is national in its scope and of preeminent importance. ●

**Reliance Building, Chicago,
D.H. Burnham and Company,
architects, 1894–95**

The epitome of what Schuyler
refers to in this article as
"Chicago construction," these 14
stories of riveted steel were
erected in as many days. The
façade is of "baked clay," or terra
cotta. The building would boast
more glass than any structure
built for many years.

MODERN ARCHITECTURE [1]
Montgomery Schuyler

THE subject that has been assigned to me is that which I should have chosen had I been left free to choose. It is more true, perhaps, of architecture than of any other of the arts that deal with form that the prosperity and advancement of it depend upon the existence of an enlightened public as well as of skillful practitioners. It is true that the public, any public, is enlightened by the efforts of the practitioners and can be enlightened in no other way. The philosophy of art at least is a philosophy teaching by examples. It is only by familiarity with admirable examples that we come to admire rightly. A sense of responsibility for one's admirations may be called the very beginning of culture, nor can a culture be deemed complete that does not include a discriminating judgment of the works of the oldest and the most pervading of all the arts. It is not to be expected, nor perhaps to be desired, that an educated layman shall possess theories of art and standards of judgment either acquired for himself or derived from others. But it is very much to be desired that he shall have a sense so habitual and automatic that it may well seem to be instinctive of the fitness or unfitness, congruity or incongruity, beauty or ugliness of the buildings that he daily passes, and that in any case must exert upon him an influence that is not the less but the more powerful for being unconsciously felt. Such a sense comes most readily and most surely from the habitual contemplation of excellent works. It is the birthright of a man who has been born and reared in a country in which admirable monuments have been familiar to him from childhood. It is a means of education from which we in this country are necessarily to a great degree debarred, for I suppose it will not be denied that there are many American communities in which one may grow up to manhood without once having sight of a respectable specimen of the art of architecture. I remember standing in the square upon which fronts the cathedral

of Rouen, one of the loveliest of the legacies the Middle Ages have bequeathed to modern times, and watching the busy throng of Frenchmen and Frenchwomen, the citizens of a bustling modern town, that passed beneath it. There was scarcely one, of whatever rank in life, that did not pause, in passing, long enough to cast one recognizing and admiring glance at the weatherworn and fretted front. Think what an education the daily sight of such a monument constitutes, how it trains the generations that are reared in its shadow, and how deeply a people so unconsciously trained would fail to admire the very smartest and most ornate edifices of many American towns. It seems to me that something of the same beneficial influence is shed upon the people of New York from the spire of Old Trinity,[2] as it soars serenely above the bustle of Broadway, and stops the vista of Wall Street, or upon the people of Boston by the ordered bulk of the tower of the new Trinity looming so large over the dwellings of the Back Bay.[3]

You may retort upon me that the influence of the cathedral of Rouen is not perceptible in the modern architecture of Rouen; but there is much to be said in behalf of the modern architecture that surrounds Rouen cathedral, as of the modern architecture that surrounds Notre Dame of Paris, in comparison with the current architecture of our American towns. I shall not be charged with underrating the essential differences between the mediaeval and the modern architecture of France and of Europe, or with overrating the modern architecture, because the difference is in a manner the main theme upon which I have to address you. It seems to me one of the most pointed contrasts that the world affords between a living and progressive and a conventional and stationary art. But the modern building, the current building of France, and more or less of Europe in general, is distinguished in this comparison with the current building of American towns—and in either case I am speaking not of the exceptional works of artists, but of the prevailing and vernacular work of journeymen—it is dis-

1 The article was originally delivered by Schuyler as a Butterfield Lecture at Union College, Schenectady, New York, March 9, 1894.

Trinity Building, New York.

2 Trinity Church (on the left, in the above poatcard), New York City, Richard Upjohn, architect, 1839–1846. At 284 feet, the spire of Trinity Church was the tallest structure in New York City until it began to be surrounded by skyscrapers. George B. Post's Pulitzer Building (page xii) would top it at 309 feet in 1892.

3 Trinity Church, Copley Square, Boston, H.H. Richardson, architect, 1873–1877.

4 Matthew Arnold (1822–1888). The essay appears in his Essays in Criticism. Arnold charged the Victorian public with complacent vulgarity. He declared that the aim of all literature is criticism of life. His essay "Emerson" brought the philosopher to a wider American public.

5 Schuyler here alludes to what he felt to be the pernicious influence of the Ecole des Beaux Arts in Paris. His faith in "national characteristics" as opposed to institutions devoted to maintaining formalistic programs roughly parallels that of Viollet-le-Duc.

6 Reference unknown.

7 *Queen Anne:* Term used to describe buildings that were inspired by the transitional architecture of the English pre-Georgian period; classical ornament was applied to buildings that were of medieval form.

8 On the Exposition, see pp. 35–37.

"Scole of Stratford atte Bowe" refers to Chaucer's Canterbury Tales: reference to provincial French spoken after the "Scole of Stratford atte Bowe" instead of the Parisian example.

9 Eugène-Emmanuel Viollet-le-Duc (1814–1879).

opposite, bottom right (pp. 41–47): Reliance Building under construction, Chicago, D.H. Burnham and Company, architects, 1894-95.

tinguished by certain qualities that we must admit to be valuable, by sobriety, by measure, by discretion. Very much of this comes, no doubt, from the learning of the schools, from the learning in particular of the great school that since the time of the great Louis has dominated the official architecture of France, and the influence of which is transmitted as we see to the common workman. You will remember that these qualities of sobriety, measure, discretion are the very qualities which Mr. Matthew Arnold finds to distinguish French literature in the comparison with English literature, and which in that well-known essay of his upon "The Literary Influence of Academies," he attributes so largely to the existence of the French Academy.[4] I cannot help thinking that he exaggerates this influence, and that the undeniable difference is more largely due than he admits to national characteristics and less largely to the machinery of institutions.[5] In the national building, however, the national school of France has without doubt had a great influence. It is an influence which is spreading over the world, and which has already established a distinct cult of its own among American architects that is at present perhaps the dominant influence in our own architecture, an influence the nature of which I shall ask you to consider. But these excellent qualities which French building shows in comparison with American building seem to me to be also due largely to the existence of relics of the great art of the past. In England, where there has never been any official inculcation of architecture, the current building is characterized in comparison with our own, though in a less degree, by the same qualities that characterize the French building. It is less violent, more restrained, more decorous. And England, like France, possesses those monuments the very presence of which seems to temper crudity and to repress eccentricity, to make impossible the architectural freaks that seem to be spontaneously generated in the absence of their restraining influence.

It is not many years since an English trav-

eler, not an architect, but a traveled and cultivated man of the world, delivered the opinion that there was no country in the world in which the art of architecture was at so low a stage as in the United States.[6] He had just traversed the continent and there was certainly no malice in his remarks, the spirit of which was entirely amicable. There can be little doubt that his saying simply reflected the impression that an experience like his would be apt to make upon any cultivated European. It is the impression derived, not from the buildings that are the boast of a few towns, the exceptional and artistic performances, but from a general survey of the building of the country. The building is doubtless more crude and provincial, as a rule, in the newer than in the older parts of the country, and one main reason for this is that the older parts of the country, the towns of the Atlantic seaboard that comprised the colonies, contained examples of colonial building that were as nearly as the builders could make them examples of the current architecture of the old country. They were not very many in number nor very extensive in scale, nor very durable in construction. But every one of the Atlantic towns possessed one or more of them that have lasted to our own time or nearly so, and that gave to the builders who lived and worked in their presence examples of measure and sobriety and discretion that tended to preserve them from the excesses of the pioneer builders who had not the advantage of any models whatever.

It is not to be wondered at that some twenty years ago many of the young architects of this country should have become so revolted by the extravagance and the crudity of the current building as to revert to the colonial building for models. And this accounts for the vogue, short lived as it was, which the so-called Queen Anne fashion of building had in this country.[7] Although the revival of it was imported from England and not developed here, it was connected with this admiration for the colonial work which, though it was commonly tame, was at least never wild. The crudity of much of the work that was done during the Gothic revival set architects to studying the classic detail of the old mansions, although a knowledge of this detail was simply part of the stock in trade of the carpenters and the plasterers who were imported during the eighteenth century, and continued to be part of the stock in trade of their successors during the first quarter at least of the nineteenth. Though Queen Anne, specifically so called, was a very passing fashion, the preference for classic detail, as an orderly and understood assemblage of forms in the use of which it was difficult to attain a positively offensive result, survived Queen Anne, and has been so potent ever since that the present tendency of architecture in this country is a reversion to the Renaissance that has prevailed in Europe for the past three centuries. This tendency has been very powerfully promoted by the increasing influence on this country of the Paris school of fine arts, of which the pupils, filled with its traditions, are every year returning in increased numbers to take part in the building of the United States. Especially has this tendency been stimulated just now by the brilliant success of the architecture of the Columbian Exposition, which was essentially a display, on an imposing scale, of modern French architecture; though it is also true that some of the architecture even of the World's Fair was French not so much after the Ecole de Beaux Arts as "after the Scole of Stratford atte bowe."[8]

The attractiveness of the French ideal in architecture is so great that it has imposed itself all over Europe, insomuch that the new quarters of nearly all European cities are becoming imitations of Paris. It is visibly tending to impose itself upon this country also, under the influences to which I have referred, the revolt against the crudity of our unschooled vernacular building and the zealous propagandism of the pupils of the Beaux Arts, and of the architects whom they have in their turn influenced. It would be folly to dispute that the training of the French school, upon which the architectural training of all Europe is more or less mod-

eled, is a most valuable training in qualities and accomplishments that are common to all architecture and that are needed in all architecture. Founded as it is upon the study of the classic orders, it confers or cultivates a perception of proportion and relation, of adjustment and scale, in other words, of that sobriety, measure and discretion which, in whatever style they may be exhibited, or whether they be exhibited in works not to be classified under any of the historical styles, so plainly distinguish the work of an educated from the work of an uneducated architect, precisely as the literary work of a man who has studied the models of literature is distinguished from that of an uneducated man. One may freely own that the current architecture of Europe is more admirable than the current architecture of America, and that, if that were all, those architects would have reason who urge us to adopt current European methods in the study of architecture and to naturalize, or at least to import current European architecture. But it is not American architecture alone, it is modern architecture in general that leaves a great deal to be desired as the expression in building of modern life. It is not only our own country, but it is the time that is architecturally out of joint. No thoughtful and instructed person who considers what an expression classic architecture was of classic life, or mediaeval architecture of mediæval life, is satisfied with modern architecture, for the reason that no such student can regard it as in the same degree or in the same sense an expression of modern life. The French seem indeed to be very well satisfied with the result of their methods of instruction and practice, but it is worth while to remember that the whole professional and literary life of that French architect whose writings have had the strongest influence upon this generation of readers—I mean Viollet-le-Duc[9]—was a protest against the aims and the methods of the Ecole des Beaux Arts, and the academic architecture which it produced, as unrepresentative of modern French life, as unreasonable and untrue. So inveterate and so radical was his

from:

A WHITE ENAMELED BUILDING
By Charles E. Jenkins
Vol. IV, No. 3, January-March 1895,
pp. 299-306

CHICAGO has been treated to a most novel sight. On one of its crowded thoroughfares a sixteen-story building has been in course of erection, the two lower floors of which are occupied by one of the largest dry-goods establishments in the city, and the daily routine of business goes on without interruption while the fourteen upper stories of steel fireproofing and cream-white enameled terra cotta climb up into the sky to a height of 200 feet. It is the Reliance Building at the southwest corner of Washington and State streets, 55 feet on State street by 85 feet on Washington, and the plans come from the office of D. H. Burnham & Co. Mr. Charles B. Atwood, architect; Mr. Edward C. Shankland, M.A.S.C.E. and M.I.C.E., of London, engineer.

Some five years ago there had been a five-story building on this site of very heavy masonry construction, the lower floor of which was occupied by a National Bank. The leases of the upper floors did not expire until May 1, 1894, but as on the removal of the bank to its own building it was deemed desirable to arrange the first floor for store purposes, plans were made in 1890 for a sixteen-story building by Mr. John Root, and the foundations and first story of this new building were put in, the upper four stories of the old building being held up on screws, while the first story of the new building was slipped in under them. This spring, when the leases ran out and it became possible to proceed with the work, the ▸

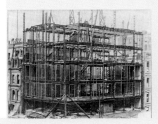

10 Henry Hobson Richardson (1838–1886) attended the Ecole des Beaux Arts in Paris from 1859 to 1865. He was the second American to do so, the first was Richard Morris Hunt.

11 Alfred Lord Tennyson, *Locksley Hall*.

12 John Milton, *Sonnet xi:* "A book was writ of late...."

13 Francis Bacon, *Advancement of Learning*, Book I.

opposition to the manner in which architecture was taught at the French national school, the training of which is held up to us as a completely adequate model, that on his appearance there as a lecturer he was mobbed by the students whom he was invited to address, and to whom his criticisms seemed to be almost in the nature of blasphemy.

The late Mr. Richardson, whose great services to the architecture of this country no one will deny, who was himself a graduate of the Ecole des Beaux Arts and who brought its training to the solution of American architectural problems, bore interesting testimony in the same direction.[10] He told me that, revisiting France many years after his academic experiences in Paris, and when he himself was at the height of his success and celebrity, he had looked up those who had been the most promising of his fellow-students. He found them well-established architects and many of them occupying the position so much coveted in France, of government architects. But he found them—I do not remember that he made any exceptions, but at any rate he found many of them—deeply dissatisfied with the official architecture which was imposed upon them by the necessities of their careers, lamenting that they were not at liberty to transcend the trammels of the official style, and envying him the freedom he enjoyed in this respect as a practitioner in America and not in France. Surely we may very well hesitate before acknowledging that a system which is thus deprecated, by theorists on the one hand and by practitioners on the other, as inadequate to the architectural needs of the country from which it is derived and in which it has been naturalized for two hundred years, and as incompetent to produce the architectural expression of French life, may be transplanted with confidence as promising complete satisfaction of our own needs, and as offering us the expression in architecture of American life.

How are we to explain the anomaly thus presented? While every other art is living and progressive, architecture is by common

consent stationary, if it be not actually retrograde. In every other art the artists have their eyes on the future. They do not doubt that the greatest achievements of their arts are before them and not behind

"That which they have done but earnest of the things that they shall do."[11]

In architecture alone men look back upon the masterpieces of the past not as points of departure but as ultimate attainments, content, for their own part, if by recombining the elements and reproducing the forms of these monuments they can win from an esoteric circle of archaeologists the praise of producing some reflex of their impressiveness. This process has gone so far that architects have expected and received praise for erecting for modern purposes literal copies of ancient buildings, or, where the materials for exact reproduction were wanting, of ingenious restorations of those buildings. In architecture alone does an archaeological study pass for a work of art. The literature of every modern nation is an express image of the mind and spirit of the nation. The architecture of every modern nation, like the dress of every modern nation, is coming more and more to lose its distinctiveness and to reflect the fashion of Paris. It was not always so. The architecture of Greece and Rome tells us as much as antique literature tells of Greek and Roman life. Mediæval architecture tells us so much more of mediæval life than all other documents of that life that they become insignificant in the comparison, and that from their monuments alone the modern man can succeed in penetrating into the spirit of the Middle Ages. Nay, in our own time the architecture of every country outside the pale of European civilization is a perfectly adequate and a perfectly accurate reflex of the life of that country.

I have spoken of the analogy between architecture and literature. It seems to me that it is not fantastic, and that if we follow it it may lead us to a comprehension of the very different state of the two arts to-day. Nobody pretends that modern literature is not an exact reflex of modern civilization. If we find fault with the condition of it in any country we are not regarding it as a separate product which could be improved by the introduction of different methods. We are simply arraigning the civilization of the country, thus completely expressed. If we find one literature pedantic, another frivolous and another dull, we without hesitation impute these defects as the results of national traits. The notion that any modern literature is not a complete expression of the national life no more occurs to us than the notion that any modern architecture is such an expression.

Now, modern architecture, like modern literature, had its origin in the revival of learning. The Italian Renaissance in architecture was inextricably connected with that awakening of the human spirit which was the beginning of modern civilization. It is not that classic models have been discarded or neglected in the one art and retained in the other, for down to our own generation at least a liberal education, a literary education, has been a classical education. Whatever the baccalaureate degree is coming to mean now, for several centuries it has meant a knowledge of the masterpieces of Greek and Roman letters, as the education of an architect has during the same time implied a knowledge of the masterpieces of Greek and Roman building. A main difference has been that in literature the classical models have been used, and in architecture they have been copied. If writers had hesitated, even while Latin was the universal language in Europe, to use locutions "that would have made Quintilian stare and gasp,"[12] it seems to me quite certain that there could have been no literary progress, while it seems to be almost a tenet of the architectural schools, and at any rate it is a fair deduction from modern academic architecture that no architectural progress is possible. There alone in the work of mankind, the great works of the past are not alone useful for doctrine, for reproof, for correction, for instruction, are not even models in the sense in which we use the word in reference to other arts, but

are "orders" to be carried out as literally as the conditions will allow, are fetishes to be ignorantly worshiped and invested with mysterious powers.

At the time of the revival of learning the purists were as strenuous in literature as they are even yet in architecture, and for a time as prevailing. The literary classics were to them what the architectural classics still are to the practitioners of official architecture, and the vocabulary of the ancients as sacred a repertory of words as the orders of the ancients a repertory of forms, to which nothing could be added without offense. To them it was not requisite that a writer should express his mind fully; it was not even necessary that he should have anything to say, but it was necessary that his Latinity should be unimpeachable. So long and so far as it was enforced, the restriction to the ancient vocabulary had as deadening an effect upon literature as the like restriction still has upon architecture. Lord Bacon has given an excellent account in a few sentences of the consequence of this "more exquisite travail in the languages original" upon the progress of literature and the advancement of learning. "Men began to hunt more after words than matter; more after the choiceness of the phrase and the round and clean composition of the sentence, and the sweet falling of the clauses… than after the weight of matter, worth of subject, soundness of argument, life of invention or depth of judgment."[13] The literary purists of the Renaissance were inevitably impatient of men who were preoccupied with what they had to say rather than with their way of saying it, and were especially incensed against the school philosophers "whose writings," to quote Bacon again, "were altogether in a different style and form, taking liberty to coin and frame new terms of art to express their own sense, and to avoid circuit of speech, without regard to the pureness, pleasantness, and, as I may call it, lawfulness of the phrase or word." Substitute "form" for "phrase or word" and you have here an exact statement of the respective positions of the progressive architect and of the architectural purist, and

original plans underwent radical changes, and Mr. Atwood conceived the idea of using cream-white enameled terra cotta for the exterior, with the exception of the first story already completed, which is of polished Scotch granite. The somewhat limited ground space and the great height of the building present difficult problems to the architect who attempts to produce an attractive structure, and with its plate-glass foundations, which the shopkeeper demands, it is hardly to be supposed that even the designer will consider it a masterpiece. Still there is one most important feature which, regardless of the architectural beauties of the structure, must be considered, and which will make this building stand out as a conspicuous mark in the history of architecture in America, namely, the use of enameled terra cotta for the exterior. The question of being able to obtain this material was a serious one…. Should enameled terra cotta prove to be what is claimed for it, if it stands the test of Chicago's severe winters and changeable climate, there can be no possible doubt but what as a material for exterior construction it will be largely used in such cities as are afflicted with a smokey, sooty atmosphere. The idea of being able to wash your building and have it as fresh and clean as the day it was put up, ▸

1894

14 Browning, *Dramatis Personae*, "Rabbi Ben Ezra."

15 Politian (1454-1494), an Italian Humanist, was one of the first who succeeded in rivaling the Greek scholarship of the native-born Hellenes. He translated Plato into Latin.

16 Erasmus, *Ciceronianus*.

17 James Boswell, *The Life of Samuel Johnson*, 1791, under the year l780.

18 Francis Bacon, *Essays*, "Of Studies."

---

* When John Root died in 1891, Charles Atwood replaced him as the chief designer in the firm which then took the name of Root's surviving partner, Daniel H. Burnham. In this capacity, Atwood designed both the firm's contribution to the Chicago Fair, the highly acclaimed Art Building, and the Reliance Building. Although it has not been proven conclusively, it is now thought that Atwood substantially reworked the original 1890 design by Root for the Reliance Building. Root's choice for a dark granite sheathing for the frame, still visible on the first two floors, and completed before his death, is fundamentally different from the white enameled terra cotta sheathing of the upper floors chosen by Atwood.

of the reason why it is out of the question that architecture should advance when the teaching and the practice and the judgment of it are confided to the architectural purists.

In literature the restriction did not last long. If it could have lasted it would have arrested the literature and the civilization of Europe, for a demand that nothing should be expressed in new words was in effect a demand that nothing new should be expressed. Such a restriction, when the human spirit had once been aroused, it could not accept. The instinct of self-preservation forbade its acceptance. Men who had something to say insisted upon saying it, saying it at first in barbarous Latin, to the pain of the purists who had nothing to say and did not see why anybody else should have anything to say that could not be expressed in the classical vocabulary; saying it afterwards in "the noble vulgar speech" which at first, and until it had been developed and chastened and refined by literary use, seemed cruder and more barbarous still. The progress of mankind being at stake, the purists in literature were overwhelmed. Only the progress of architecture being at stake in the other case, the purists have prevailed and architecture has been sacrificed, with only local and sporadic revolts, and these for the most part within our own century, in place of the literary revolution that was triumphantly accomplished four centuries ago.

It was not accomplished without a struggle. The "more exquisite travail in the languages original," when there was no other but classical literature, had induced in scholars the belief that the masterpieces of that literature would never be equaled. It is, I believe, still questioned by scholars whether the classic masterpieces have been equaled even yet; while it is the opinion of scholars that the languages in which they were composed are still the most perfect orders of speech that have existed. It was natural, then, that men who had nothing in particular to say, or at any rate felt no urgent need of expressing themselves, should have deemed that classic literature was complete as well as

impeccable, and that its limitations could not be transcended. Fortunately for us all, there were other men who felt, with Browning, that

"It were better youth
Should strive, through acts uncouth,
Toward making, than repose on aught
    found made,"[14]

and these men were the greatest scholars as well as the greatest thinkers of the age. Politian, of whom it has been said by a critic of our own time that he "showed how the taste and learning of the classical scholar could be grafted on the stock of the vernacular," ridiculed the purists in better Latin than their own. "Unless the book is at hand from which they copy," he said, "they cannot put three words together. I entreat you not to be fettered by that superstition. As nobody can run who is intent upon putting his feet in the footsteps of another, so nobody can write well who does not dare to depart from what is already written.[15] And while the Italian scholar was deriding the Italian pedants, the Dutch scholar, who did not even look forward to a time when the vernacular should supplant Latin, yet protested against the imposition of classic forms as shackles upon modern thought. "Hereafter," said Erasmus, "we must not call bishops reverend fathers, nor date our letters from the birth of Christ, because Cicero never did so. What could be more senseless, when the whole age is new, religion, government, culture, manners, than not to dare to speak otherwise than Cicero spoke. If Cicero himself should come to life, he would laugh at this race of Ciceronians."[16]

It would be as presumptuous in me as it is far from my intention to disparage academic training, in architecture or in literature. The men who have done most towards building up these great literatures that are at once the records and the trophies of modern civilization have for the most part been classical scholars, and classical scholarship stood them in particularly good stead when they worked in the vernacular, especially during the formative periods of these literatures, when there were as yet no standards or models but those of antiquity. Perhaps what seems to us the most autochthonous of our literature owed more to this culture than we are apt to suppose. "I always said," Dr. Johnson observes, "that Shakespeare had enough Latin to grammaticise his English."[17] These writers derived from their classical studies a literary tact that could have been imparted so well in no other way. Certainly the same thing is true of the classically trained architects. Whether they are working in the official style that has been the language of their schools, or have attempted the idiomatic and vernacular treatment of more extended and varied methods of construction than the very simple construction of Greece, which was expressed with consummate art, and the more ambitious and complicated construction of the Romans, which yet is simple compared with our modern constructions and which cannot be said to have attained its artistic expression; in either case there is equally in their work this tact, this measure and propriety that bespeak professional training. It is not the training that I am deprecating, but the resting in the training as not a preparation but an attainment. There is another pregnant saying of Bacon that would well recur to us when we see the attempt to meet modern requirements without departing from antique forms, and to carry out academic exercises in classic architecture into actual buildings: "Studies teach not their own use, but that is a wisdom without them and above them, won by observation."[18] It is as if an educated man in our day should confine his literary efforts to Latin composition. Very curious and admirable essays have been made even in modern Latin and even in our own time. To see how near one can come to expressing modern ideas in classical language is an interesting and useful exercise, by the very force of the extreme difficulty of even suggesting them, and the impossibility of really expressing them. When the modern Latinist has finished this circuitous and approximative progress he has produced what—a

poem? No, but only an ingenious toy for the amusement of scholars, a "classic design." If he devoted his whole literary life to the production of such things we should be entitled to pronounce decisively that he had nothing to say, or he would take the most direct way of saying it. It would be evident that he was preoccupied with the expression and not with the thing to be expressed, not with the idea but "with the pureness, pleasantness and, as I may call it, lawfulness of the phrase or word."

A living and progressive classic poetry, in our day, we all perceive to be merely a contradiction in terms. Classicism is the exclusion of life and progress; and a living and progressive classic architecture is in fact equally a contradiction in terms. Forms are the language of the art of building and architectural forms are the results and the expression of construction. This is true of the architecture of the world before the Renaissance, excepting the Roman imitations of Greek architecture. It is true even now of the architecture of all that part of the world which lies outside the pale of European civilization. It is only since the Renaissance, and in Europe and America, that classic forms have been used as an envelope of constructions not classic, and that the attempt to develop building into architecture has been abandoned in favor of the attempt to cover and to conceal building with architecture. This attempt is beset with difficulties, by reason of the modern requirements that cannot be concealed. I have heard of a classic architect saying that it was impossible to do good work nowadays on account of the windows. This is an extreme instance, doubtless, but the practitioner of classic architecture must often be as much annoyed by the intrusion of his building into his design, and the impossibility of ignoring or of keeping it out altogether, as the modern Latin poet by the number of things of which the classic authors never heard that he has to find words for out of the classic authors. The versifier does not venture to complain in public, because everybody would laugh at him, and ask him

must undoubtedly attract people to the use of this material. No doubt more ambitious conditions will follow with the introduction of extensive color schemes and more elaborate ornamentation. There is certainly no limit to what can be done in this direction, and with a perfect assurance that the material can be produced and that its quality of endurance is assured, why should architects and the public complain of the monotony of the dull greys, browns and reds of the present material used in building. It is to be sincerely hoped that the next enameled building may more extensively introduce color. However, the first step is the important one, and the boldness of the architect* who took the first step is to be commended.

In the Reliance Building the design of ornamentation adapted by Mr. Atwood is quite simple, being of a somewhat French gothic feeling, but as the building is purely a commercial one, there is little elaboration. The accompanying illustration gives a fair idea of the terra cotta work, except that one loses the exquisite color and enameled effect, which is certainly most beautiful. The building being very narrow, compared with its height, especial attention has been given to designing the frame-work, which is of steel and it carries the outer walls as well as the floors of the building. The Z bar column, with ▶

1894

19 A repetition of Erasmus' statement in the original Latin.

20 Reference to the description which the Roman architectural writer of the time of Augustus, Vitruvius, makes in his De Architectura to a basilica, which he built in Fano. Since no illustrations accompanied the ambiguous description, scholars have suggested various reconstructions. One of the best known is that of Viollet-le-Duc in his Discourses, lecture 5, plates 8, 9, and 10.

21 See note 7 page 10.

why he did not write English. But the classic architect is not afraid to make his moan, and to complain of the intractability of modern architectural problems, or to excuse himself from attempting a solution of them upon the ground that they do not fit the classic forms. He is not likely to find sympathy in his complaint of the oppressiveness of shackles which, in this country at least, he has voluntarily assumed. Why should we not laugh at him also? He, too, may be recommended to write English, which in his case means to give the most direct expression possible to his construction in his forms, and to use his training to make this expression forcible, "elegant" and scholarly; poetical, if the gods have made him poetical; at any rate, "to grammaticise his English" instead of confining himself to an expression that is avowedly indirect, circuitous, conventional and classic, a "polite language" like the Latin of modern versifiers. *Si reviviseret ipse Cicero, rideret hoc Ciceronianorum genus.*[19]

The repertory of the architectural forms of the past is the vocabulary of the architect. But there is this difference between his vocabulary and that of the poet, that a word is a conventional symbol, while a true architectural form is the direct expression of a mechanical fact. Any structural arrangement is susceptible, we must believe, of an artistic and effective expression. Historical architecture contains precedents, to be acquainted with which is a part of professional education, for many if not for most of the constructions commonly used in modern building. But classic architecture does not contain them. The Greek construction is the simplest possible. The more complicated Roman construction was not artistically developed and expressed by the Romans themselves and the literary revivalists of classic architecture of the fifteenth century restricted themselves and their successors to the Roman expression without very clearly understanding what it was. They were more royalist than the king, more Ciceronian than Cicero. If we are to accept the statement of Viollet-le-Duc, Vitruvius himself, if he had submitted his own design, as he describes it,

for the basilica of Fano, in a competition of the Ecole des Beaux Arts at the beginning of this century, would have been ruled out of the competition for his ignorance of Roman architecture.[20] But in any case, the classical building embraces but a small part of the range of constructions that are available to the modern builder. To confine one's self to classic forms means therefore to ignore and reject, or else to cloak and dissemble, the constructions of which the classic builders were ignorant, or which they left undeveloped, to be developed by the barbarians. And here comes in another restricting tenet of the schools, that you must not confuse historical styles. No matter how complete an expression of an applicable construction may have been attained, if it does not come within the limits of the historic style that you have proposed to yourself, it is inadmissible. This is not a tenet of the official schools exclusively. It is imposed wherever architecture is practiced archaeologically. In the early days of the Gothic revival in England, Gothic building was divided and classified, more or less arbitrarily, and it would fatally have discredited an architect to mix Early English and Middle Pointed, or to introduce any detail for which he had not historical precedent, and this without regard to the artistic success of his work but only to its historical accuracy. It was not until the architects of the revival outgrew this superstition that their work had much other than an archaeological interest. Any arbitrary restriction upon the freedom of the artist is a hindrance to the life and progress of his art. While it is no doubt more difficult to attain unity by the use of constructions that have been employed and expressed in different ages and countries than by renouncing all but such as have been employed together before, and have been analyzed and classified in the schools, the artist is entitled to be judged by the success of his attempts and not to be prevented from making them. American architects are happy in being freer than the architects of any other country from the pressure of this convention. By the introduction of the elevator,[21] some twenty years ago, an architectural problem absolutely new was imposed upon them, a problem in the solution of which there were no directly available and no directly applicable precedents in the history of the world. That many mistakes should be made, and that much wild work should be done was inevitable. But within these twenty years there has been attained not only a practical but in great part an artistic solution of this problem presented by the modern office building. The efforts of the architects have already resulted in a new architectural type, which in its main outlines imposes itself, by force of merit, upon future designers and upon which future designers can but execute variations. This is really a very considerable achievement, this unique contribution of American architects to their art. While the architects who have had most to do with establishing it have been learned and trained as well as thoughtful designers, it seems to me that they have had advantages here that they could not have enjoyed where conventional and academic restrictions had more force. Certainly, in all the essays that have been made towards the solution of this new problem, none have been less fortunate and less successful than those of academically trained architects, who have undertaken to meet a new requirement by an aggregation of academic forms, and to whom studies had not taught their own use. But the problem is by no means yet completely solved. The real structure of these towering buildings, the "Chicago construction," is a structure of steel and baked clay, and when we look for an architectural expression of it, or for an attempt at an architectural expression of it, we look in vain. No matter what the merits or demerits may be of the architectural envelope of masonry, it is still an envelope, and not the thing itself, which is nowhere, inside or out, permitted to appear. The structure cannot be expressed in terms of historical architecture, and for that reason the attempt to express it has been foregone. The first attempts to express it must necessarily be rude and inchoate. The new forms

that would result from these attempts would be repellent, in the first place because of their novelty, even if they were perfect from the beginning; in the second place, because in the nature of things and according to the experience of mankind, they cannot be perfect from the beginning, for the labors not only of many men but of many generations have been required to give force and refinement to the expression in architectural forms of any system of construction. If the designer, however, is repelled by the strangeness of the forms that result from early attempts to express what has not been expressed before, if "youth" will not "strive through acts uncouth toward making" but takes refuge in "aught found made," that is the abandonment of progress. The Chicago construction doubtless presents a difficult problem. All problems are difficult till they are solved. But the difficulty is no greater than other difficulties that have been encountered in the history of architecture and that have been confronted and triumphantly overcome. Is there anything in modern construction that is a priori more unpromising, as a subject for architectural treatment, than a shore of masonry, built up on the outside of a wall to prevent it from being thrust out by the pressure from within? I do not know what the modern architect would do as an artist if as a constructor he found it necessary to employ such a member. In the absence of applicable precedents he would be apt to conclude that so ugly an appendage to his building would not do to show, and to conceal it behind a screen-wall nicely decorated with pilasters. But the builders upon whom the use of this member was imposed, not having enjoyed the advantage of a classical education, saw nothing for it but to exhibit the shore and to try to make it presentable by making it expressive of its function. Their early efforts were so "uncouth" that the modern architect, if he had seen the work at this stage, would have been confirmed in his conclusion that the shore was architecturally intractable. The mediæval builders kept at work at it, master after master, and genera-

its horizontal cap plates breaking the column in two at every story, was discarded and a new column used composed of eight angles. The ends of this column were planed off and connected by means of vertical splice plates.

As stated in the beginning of the article, the sight of seeing a tremendous building pushing up into the air while one can safely stand at its base and look into shop windows, crowded with the usual display, is, to say the least, rather out of the usual. However, the architect and contractors had the material all ready to go up, and on May 1st, when the building was free—that is, the four upper stories—a protecting platform had been built just above the store front, covering completely the sidewalk. It took only a short time to demolish these upper stories, and the accompanying illustrations show how rapidly the steel frame-work and enameled terra cotta went up. The four illustrations represent conditions July 16th, July 28th, August 1st and Nov 8th, 1894. That the fire-proofing work and finish of the interior will progress with equal speed is suggested by the fact that the building is to be ready for occupancy January 1, 1895, and leases are already signed from that date. That this, the first enameled building erected, should be watched with unusual interest is only natural. ●

1894

22 Emerson, *Essays*
"The Problem."

23 Georges L. C. F. Cuvier,
Recherches sur les ossemens
fossiles (Paris, 1812). It is the
fundamental principle of paleon-
tological reconstruction and articulation.

24 Firth of Forth Bridge at
Queensferry, Scotland, by Sir
John Fowler and Sir Benjamin
Baker,(1881–1890).

25 Viollet-le-Duc, *Discourses on
Architecture*, I, 182.

26 The "Jean Bart," launched in
1889, was among the more formidable French cruisers of its day.

27 John Milton, *Lycidas.*

tion after generation, until at last they made it speak. Made it speak? They made it sing, and there it is, a new architectural form, the flying buttress of a Gothic cathedral, an integral part of the most complicated and most complete organism ever produced by man, one of the organisms so like those of nature that Emerson might well say that

"Nature gladly give them place,
Adopted them into her race,
And granted them an equal date
With Andes and with Ararat."[22]

The analogy is more than poetically true. In art as in nature an organism is an assemblage of interdependent parts of which the structure is determined by the function and of which the form is an expression of the structure. Let us hear Cuvier on natural organisms.

"A claw, a shoulder-blade, a condyle, a leg or arm-bone, or any other bone separately considered, enables us to discover the description of teeth to which they have belonged; so also reciprocally we may determine the form of the other bones from the teeth. Thus, commencing our investigations by a careful survey of any one bone by itself, a person who is sufficiently master of the laws of organic structure may, as it were, reconstruct the whole animal to which that bone had belonged."[23]

This character of the organisms of nature is shared by at least one of the organisms of art. A person sufficiently skilled in the laws of organic structure can reconstruct, from the cross-section of the pier of a Gothic cathedral, the whole structural system of which it is the nucleus and prefigurement. The design of such a building seems to me to be worthy, if any work of man is worthy, to be called a work of creative art. It is an imitation not of the forms of nature but of the processes of nature. Perhaps it was never before carried out so far or so successfully as in the thirteenth century. Certainly it has not been carried out so successfully since. This has not been for lack of constructions

waiting to receive an artistic expression, for mechanical science has been carried far beyond the dreams of the mediaeval builders, and the scientific constructors are constantly pressing upon the artistic constructor, upon the architect, in new structural devices, new problems that the architect is prone to shirk. He is likely to be preoccupied with new arrangements and combinations of historical forms. He asks himself, as it has been said, not what would Phidias have done if he had had this thing to do, but what did Phidias when he had something else to do. An architectural form, being the ultimate expression of a structural arrangement, cannot be foreseen, and the form which the new expression takes comes as a surprise to its author. He cannot more than another tell beforehand with what body it will come. Take one modern instance, the so-called cantilever of modern engineering. Some of you may be familiar with representations of the Forth bridge in Scotland,[24] in which that recent device has been used upon the largest scale thus far and with the most impressive results [opposite]. There is one of the new architectural forms for which we are unthinkingly asking. Is it conceivable that this form could have occurred to a man who sat down to devise a new form, without reference to its basis and motive in the laws of organic structure? And so it is always with real architectural forms. There have been very voluminous discussions within this century upon the "invention" of the pointed arch, discussions which have come to little because they have started from a baseless assumption. Architectural forms are not invented; they are developed, as natural forms are developed, by evolution. A main difference between our times and the mediaeval times is that then the scientific constructor and the artistic constructor were one person, now they are two. The art of architecture is divided against itself. The architect resents the engineer as a barbarian; the engineer makes light of the architect as a dilettante. It is difficult to deny that each is largely in the right. The artistic insensibility of the modern engineer is not more fatal to architectural progress than the artistic irrelevancy of the modern architect. In general, engineering is at least progressive, while architecture is at most stationary. And, indeed, it may be questioned whether, without a thought of art, and, as it were, in spite of himself, the engineer has not produced the most impressive, as certainly he has produced the most characteristic monuments of our time. "A locomotive," says Viollet-le-Duc, "has its peculiar physiognomy, not the result of caprice but of necessity. Some say it is but an ugly machine. But why ugly? Does it not have the true expression of brutal energy?"[25] The modern battleship is purely an engineering construction, developed in accordance with its functions as a fighting machine, and without conscious reference to the expression of these functions. Yet no one who has seen a typical and completely developed example of the modern war ship, such as the Jean Bart,[26] which has been seen in American waters, needs to be told that it is a more moving expression of the horrors of war than has ever been seen in the world before; that no poet's or painter's dream of

> "That fatal and perfidious bark,
> Built in the eclipse and rigged with
>   curses dark"[27]

appeals with anything like so much force to the imagination as this actual, modern and prosaic machine of murder. What may we not hope from the union of modern engineering with modern architecture, when the two callings, so harshly divorced, are again united, and when the artistic constructor employs his cultivated sensibility and his artistic training, not to copying, but to producing, no longer to the compilation of the old forms, but to the solution of the new problems that press upon him; when he shall have learned the use of the studies that teach not their own use. ∎

from:
THE WORK OF BURNHAM & ROOT, D.H. BURNHAM-D.H. BURNHAM & CO. AND GRAHAM, BURNHAM & CO.
By A.N. Rebori
Vol. XXXVIII, No. 1, July, 1915
pp. 9–16

The Reliance Building was the "swan song" to the old traditions, based on independence of design for which were noted the works of Burnham and Root. It stands today a symbol of our inconsistency and an ample proof that no sooner do we approach a common way of working than the promise of a truly expressive style of American architecture is broken by the capricious introduction of a new fashion. Perhaps it is because the design of this building has been rather the statement of a problem than the solution of it, and that the white envelope of terra cotta is confessedly a covering,... [that it] is meant to be judged as such.... as the tall building was constructed with real masonry walls it was still possible to follow the analogy of the three or five story building by making the architectural divisions multiples of the actual stories, but when the actual stories grew into their teens, and the solid masonry walls were replaced by skeleton construction this treatment was no longer feasible. There was no further need of self-carrying walls, for the wall was practically eliminated as far as its structural importance was concerned; therefore it was no longer necessary to cover the cage with irrelevant masonry in an effort to imitate stone architecture. Still it is safe to assume that the architects of that time, confused by the sudden introduction of a new system of construction which in itself was structurally sound and independent of foreign tradition, should turn to their fountain of architectural knowledge and proceed to express tall buildings in terms of historic architecture.... so the Reliance Building, intelligent as it is by its straightforward and unconventional treatment, is not an artistic solution of the problem, but only a statement of it. ●

Sir John Fowler and Sir Benjamin Baker, Firth of Forth Bridge, Queensferry, Scotland, 1881–1890.

1894

Empire Building, New York City, Kimball & Thompson, architects, 1895–98

This ornate, classically inspired façade, overlooking Trinity Churchyard, exhibits the triple division Schuyler describes as "founded upon the analogy of a column, with its division into base, shaft, and capital, and even conforms, as far as may be, to the proportions of the classic column."

opposite: St. Paul Building, New York City, George B. Post, architect, 1895-98 (demolished).

Schuyler's criticism of this building was harsh:

"Not one of them is a freak, though the St. Paul makes that effect by reason of what seems its intractable ground plan. Possibly some other architect might have made us forget the intractability. At all events, the treatment rather aggravated it in one respect, by the doubling of the stories so as to make one architectural out of two actual floors. This was assumed to be done in order to "give scale," but the architect explained that it was to avoid the square opening which resulted from the dispositions. Even so, those who look at the square openings left untreated in the less conspicuous walls will be apt to hold that the more conspicuous would have looked better if they had been left untreated there also."
[XXXV:1 Jan 1914 pp 94–96]

THE "SKY-SCRAPER" UP-TO-DATE

Montgomery Schuyler

It is strange that the solution of a building problem so new as that presented by the steel-framed tall building should have apparently so largely ceased to be experimental. The American architect is a good deal fonder than his co-worker in other countries of proving all things; he is by no means so much inclined to hold fast that which is good. On the contrary, he is still altogether too much disposed rather to vindicate his own "originality" than to essay the task, at once more modest and more difficult, of "shining with new gracefulness through old forms." Of course his originality will be less crude, and more truly original, in proportion to his education, meaning both his knowledge and his discipline. Nothing can be more depressing than the undertaking to do "something new" by a man who is unaware what has already been done, or who has not learned how it is done. When, within a quarter of a century, the practicable height of commercial buildings has been raised, by successive movements and successive inventions, from five stories to twenty-five, we should expect, given the preference for originality that is born in the American architect, and the absolute necessity for originality that has been thrust upon him by these new mechanical devices, some very wild work, indeed, much wilder than we have had. What nobody could have expected, when the elevator came in to double the practicable height of commercial buildings, and even less when the steel-framed construction came in again to double the height made practicable by the elevator alone, is what has actually happened, and that is a consensus upon a new architectural type. The general treatment of the "sky-scraper" is already conventional, in the sense of being agreed upon. It is nearly as distinct an architectural type as the Greek temple or the Gothic cathedral. The fury of experimentation seems already to have subsided, and the designers to be all working upon recognized lines and executing variations within understood limits. All this is the work of twenty-five years, since the vertical extension made possible by the elevator began to be recognized in building. Nay, it is really the work of ten, since the steel frame came in to supplement the elevator. The elevator doubled the height of office buildings, and the steel-frame doubled it again, and yet there is less of eccentricity and freakishness; more of conformity and homogeneousness, among the twenty-story buildings than there used to be among the five-story buildings.

The first business buildings in which the possibilities of the elevator were recognized were the Tribune Building and the Western Union Building[1] in New York, which were concurrently under construction twenty-five years ago. They were much more conspicuous and comment-provoking than even the St. Paul[2] and the Park Row (photo page 60) now are, because they were alone and because lower New York then had a skyline, from which they alone, excepting the church spires, were raised and detached. The skyline was "the purple line of humbler roofs" built to the limit as that limit was set by the power of ascension of the unassisted human leg. Through this line of five stories the new monsters protruded in a portentous fashion, and though really they were but of half as many stories again as the older edifices that formed the skyline, they were more distinctive features than the successors which are four and even five times as high as the old-fashioned edifices. Now, New York has no skyline at all. It is all interruptions, of various heights and shapes and sizes, not even peaks in a mountain range, but scattered or huddled towers which have nothing to do with each other or with what is below. A clever British observer says with truth that New York from either river is "hideous and magnificent," for that it "cries aloud of savage and unregulated energy."

It is true that the first two elevator buildings had visible roofs, the one a lofty mansard with three-story dormers, the other a steep wedge, and that they were, therefore,

1 Tribune Building, New York City, Richard Morris Hunt, architect, 1873–75, (photo page 134).

Western Union Building, New York City, George B. Post, architect, 1874–75.

2 St. Paul Building, New York City, George B. Post, architect, 1895-98 (demolished).

Park Row or Syndicate Building, New York City, Robert H. Robertson, architect, 1897–98. At this article's writing, Park Row was the tallest building in the city at 32 stories.

George Browne Post (1837-1913) had a large reputation as a commercial architect. Among his many designs was an addition to the New York Stock Exchange (pages 82, 139).

3 See page 32.

4 Union Trust Building, New York City, George B. Post, architect, 1889–90 (demolished), pictured opposite left with Empire Building, right foreground.
  Times Building, New York City, also designed by Post, 1888–89, is pictured in the foreground below. American Tract Society Building, Robert H. Robertson, New York City, 1894–95, is in the background.

5 See note 10, page 42.

6 "Architectural Aberrations" were a series of articles begun in 1891. See note note p. xiii.

opposite right: John Wolfe Building, New York City, Henry Janeway Hardenbergh, architect, 1894-95 (demolished).

taller than some of their successors which contained more stories, as well as more shapely. But they were in reality timid beginnings. It came soon to be seen that, even with walls of actual masonry, it was profitable to build full twice as many stories with the elevator as had been practicable without it. Ten or twelve stories became the limit. When the height varied from seven stories to twelve was our period of experimentation in commercial building. There was a great deal of wild work, and some interesting work, but there was no entirely successful work. There was no "convention." Designers were not agreed with each other, and a designer often appeared to be at odds with himself, upon the very data of his artistic problem. They divided their fronts and grouped their stories capriciously and eccentrically. In the face of the new requirements they ignored that primary truths of design were as applicable to ten stories as to three. They would have saved themselves and the people who had to look at their work a grievous trouble by merely reverting to Aristotle and bearing in mind the precept of the father of criticism, that a work of art must have a beginning, a middle, and an end.[3]

The architect who first impressed upon his contemporaries and the public that this precept was applicable to high buildings was a public benefactor. It was from his inculcation of a forgotten truth that the consensus in the design of tall buildings began, of which we everywhere see the result. Confusion became order in his path. I do not undertake to say who it was who first designed a tall front in conformity with this ancient truth, and sharpened Aristotle's wise saw with a modern instance. But I should say that the designer who enforced it most powerfully was the architect of the Union Trust Company's Building on Broadway. He had come from making, in the north front of the Times Building,[4] a success which was only partial by reason of the indistinctness and confusion of the primary divisions, when he perceived, from a contemplation of the executed work, what was the matter

with it, and proceeded, in the design of the Union Trust, to remedy those defects. There is here no confusion about the principal features of the composition nor any doubt about their forming an architectural countenance. The basement is distinctly set off from the superstructure, and this in turn from the crowning feature, the roof and its appendages, and the intermediate stories are plainly intermediate and connecting. The force of the arrangement is independent of the style, a more or less Richardsonian Romanesque,[5] independent of the detail, though this is studied and successful, independent even of the features adopted to carry it out. It does got essentially matter whether the central and chief division be formed by openings running through it, as in the Union Trust, or by rows of small and similar openings, which leave the shaft to assert itself as nearly as may be as an equal and monotonous surface. The essential point is that there should be a triple division, and that the three parts should both assert themselves as parts and combine into a whole.

This is the agreement, the convention, which so many designers of sky-scrapers have adopted that whatever sky-scraper does not conform to it becomes what a contributor of yours is in the habit of calling an "aberration."[6] Let it be noted, however, that aberration is not necessarily a term of reproach. It is, according to the dictionary, "a deviation from the customary structure or type." Such a departure may or may not be justified by its result. If there is less reason in it than in the customary structure, if the deviation seems to come from mere caprice, then the designer has failed to justify it. If, and insofar as it is more reasonable, more expressive, more beautiful, then the designer has justified it and is to be congratulated. Our latest architecture contains in its sky-scrapers examples of both kinds. But let us first consider the more noteworthy of recent tall buildings which conform to the convention. In these the connection is more specific than that of a mere triple division. It is founded upon the analogy of a column, with its division into base, shaft, and capital, and even conforms, as far as may be, to the proportions of the classic column. That is to say, the shaft, the middle division, is much taller and very much plainer than the base or the capital. The plainness of it is as essential to the analogy as the excess. The nearer it comes to being a quite monotonous mass, the more value have the variations and ornaments of the base and the capital to which its plainness is a relief and a foil. It may doubtless be subdivided, so as to be an organic whole within a larger whole. But this subdivision is difficult to manage, for several reasons.

While the inheritance of three thousand years may be taken a warrant for the primary triple division, which thus passes without challenging inquiry, a subsequent subdivision needs an explanation. To be "rhythmical," this subdivision must itself be triple, and to triply subdivide a member of a triple composition, without thereby confusing the primary division and thus the unity of the work is a difficult feat, of which the success

has not been worth the trouble in any example of the tall building known to me. It is, of course, possible to introduce at the bottom and at the top of the shaft a story recalling the transition, in the actual column, to the base and to the capital. This has been done in the Union Trust with success. But the bonding of the shaft itself is recognized in the column as a modern and corrupt interference with classic purity. In the Empire Building,[7] this bonding has been attempted by means of stories intercalated at equal distances, framed in emphatic moldings, and treated with some separateness, in what we may still call the shaft. The principal front of the Empire, the side, is, however, so fortunate in its extent that its altitude is no longer the principal dimension, and that the analogy of the column is not directly recalled. But even here it seems that the decorative top and the decorative base would be more effective, and the composition clearer, if the central mass had been treated with absolute uniformity. The most that can be said for the intercalated stories is that they do not much interfere with the monotony of the central mass. But they interfere enough, it seems to me, to indicate that the architect did not appreciate the high architectural value of the monotony, in conjunction with the more ornamental parts. Any difference in the treatment of the several stories not only is, but must appear, arbitrary and capricious. By this device, one story is made to differ from another story in importance, whereas it is not only true, but it is known to every believer that above the ground floor, or the ground floor and the first floor, the stories are all alike. In the Washington Life,[8] it is true, it is the third story which is the quarters of the corporation that is the builder and owner of the edifice, and this fact is properly enough recognized in signalizing the story in question by a somewhat greater ornateness, which, however, by no means amounts to a separateness of treatment.

Indeed, nothing is to be gained by cloaking or dissembling facts that everybody knows, and such a fact it is that the rentable

from:
A PICTURESQUE SKY-SCRAPER
By Montgomery Schuyler
Vol. V, No. 3, January-March 1896, pp. 299-302.

NOBODY, except owners of land upon which they purpose to erect sky-scrapers, and have not yet effected their purpose, will dispute that it is high time to put a legal limitation upon the height of buildings, and a legal limitation that means something. A single soaring aberration in Washington has sufficed to evoke an ordinance that effectually puts a stop to the repetition of the outrage. Even in Chicago a restriction has been imposed. A limitation of the height of buildings to 120 feet is not, it must be said oppressive, and seems to be nugatory, but nevertheless the enforcement of it would have reduced the height of a considerable number of existing buildings. When an architect contrives to erect a towering building which is not further offensive than its dimensions compel it to be, we are grateful to him, and really the most successful of our recent works in this kind do not go much beyond inoffensiveness, nor does the ambition of the designer seem to extend much beyond this moderate point. When an architect in a commercial building, ten or twelve stories high, produces a structure that is a positive ornament to the city, and that is really picturesque in outline and effect, so that we can imagine an artist ▸

1899

7 Empire Building, New York City, Kimball & Thompson, architects, 1895–97 (photo page 50).

8 Washington Life, New York City, Cyrus L.W. Eidlitz, architect, 1898.

9 "It is necessary to live. . . . I do not see the necessity."

10 The "classical" orders. See page 33.

11 St James Building, New York City, Bruce Price, architect, 1897–1899 (above).

12 John Ruskin, (1819-1900) English art critic and social commentator of the Victorian Age. For a similar idea to that discussed here, in relation to the Empire State Building, see page 271.

13 Refers to the original Singer Building, New York City, Ernest Flagg, architect, 1897–98, before the addition of his Tower in 1908, (photo page 154).

14 Dun Building, New York City, Harding and Gooch, architect, 1896.

opposite: Washington Life. See note 8, above.

stories of an office building are all identical in function and equal in dignity. An attempt to disguise this takes away from the architecture in which it is made the excuse of honest utilitarian necessity. The famous plea of the pickpocket is the best the "sky-scraper" can make for itself: "Il faut vivre." It is ill with that "sky-scraper" upon which the magistrate can retort "Je ne vois pas la necessité."[9] To that crusher the architect exposes his sky-scraper who makes capricious distinctions between stories that everybody knows serve similar purposes. The St. Paul is laid wide open to it by the presentation of its stories as half stories, and the inclusion of two of them in each apparent story, as is done throughout the "architecturesque" part of the work, the three-sided tower faced with limestone, that occupies the truncated angle, and is crowned by the rich order. Doubtless the doubling of the stories "gives scale," and a swaggering aspect to the structure, and avoids the squareness of the openings that would result from leaving the actual arrangement undisguised. But it is plain even from the architecturesque parts that the facts have been suppressed instead of being expressed. A cellular arrangement as equal and monotonous as that of a honeycomb has been overlaid by architectural arrangement which has as little as possible do with it, and deprives it of its one excuse for being, that it is as it must be. "I do not see the necessity," the spectator may and must exclaim. The tall and lanky opening which results from overlaying the real wall with an architectural trellis is no more graceful a form than the nearly square opening which would have ensued if the wall had been let alone. It is true that the orders[10] could not have been applied. But it is very questionable whether the ten orders are as effective as the twenty actual stories would have been. In my case the twenty superposed stories appear alongside, in the parts that are not architecturesque, and put the architecture to an open shame. Not only do we not see the necessity, but we see that there is no necessity, and a caprice like that is fatal to a building which must be justified by its

necessity or not at all.

Upon the whole the most successful of the sky-scrapers are those in which the shaft is made nothing of, in which the necessary openings occur at the necessary places, are justified by their necessity, but draw no attention to themselves. They become impressive not as units, but as a series, and this may be a very fine impressiveness. Rectangular holes are not pretty, but ten stories of them all alike are sure of making their effect. In the St. Paul, the unarchitecturesque fronts which the spectator is requested to ignore, but cannot, in which the square holes stand confessed and nothing is done to them, are to one spectator more impressive than the evidently factitious architecture alongside of them. They would be more impressive still if the cornices which mark the arbitrary architectural division of the truncated front were not continued across them to the impairment of the effect of reality that they would produce if they were left alone, and to the interruption of a monotony so often repeated that it would become almost sublime. The question which Lord Melbourne was in the habit of asking his colleagues, when they asked what ground he meant to take on some new political issue, is one which might property be addressed to a good many designers of sky-scrapers who are solicitous what to do with the main body of their buildings: "Can't you let it alone?"

Of course, a shaft can be effectively variegated without denying either the equality of importance and similarity of purpose between its different stories, or compromising its own importance as an organic part of the building. This may be done, as we shall see hereafter, by the introduction of molded ornament in terra-cotta, which is so plastic that it seems to require ornament, and in which elaborate ornament is so cheap, if it be often repeated, as not to be out of place even in a building of bare utility. It may also be done in color, and that is one of the lessons of the St. James,[11] on many accounts a very interesting building. It is doubtless a good thing that most of the designers of tall buildings have avoided any contrast of color, and have brought their baked clay as nearly as might be to the tint of their stonework. There is safety in monochrome, and who so departs from it does so at his peril. But few critical observers of the St. James will be disposed to deny that its designer has vindicated his right to leave this safe refuge. It is a pity, of course, that the emphasis of color should not go with the emphasis of structure, that the weak tint should cover the frame and the strong tint the filling. It is a mistake to introduce recessed courses in a screen of red brick for the sake of the shadows, and then to nullify the shadows by introducing a course of white brick at the bottom of the recess. But the middle part of the St. James is nevertheless effectively relieved of monotony without denying the identity of purpose in its different stories and without confusing the composition.

This successful exception does not invalidate the rule that the shaft is impressive by its extent and its monotony of repetition, and as an interval of plainness and repose between the more elaborate base and the elaborate capital. It is these features which may properly appeal to attention on their own account, as well as on account of their contribution to the total results. The ornament which is meant to be worthy of the closest inspection is naturally given to the base, though the capital is properly the more ornate member. There is a dictum of Ruskin[12] which is rather exceptional among his dicta as being the expression of mere and obvious good sense. Ornament, he says, may be, or must be, in greater effective quantity at the top of a building, but the most exquisite should be kept at the bottom. Accordingly all the designers make their entrances as well worth looking at as they can, and, indeed, it would be a solecism not to signalize the means by which a population mounting into hundreds gains and leaves its place of daily business. Perhaps the commonest device for giving importance to the entrance is to extend it through two stories. Of course this device in a building of which the primary purpose is to get the maximum of rentable area is illogical as well as wasteful. But it must be owned that the architects who have fined their clients in the rental value of the space in the second story over the entrance, space which might have been rented for a hundred pence and given to the poor owner, get their architectural compensation from the process. The Broadway entrance to the Singer Building[13] has the air of a burrow, and there is an inadequacy bordering on meanness in the actual entrance to the Park Row. Many designers who, although on architecture they are bent, have yet a frugal mind, reconcile their conflicting emotions by confining the actual entrance to the ground floor, and still signalizing it by some special treatment of the opening above it, with which the entrance is supposed to be architecturally incorporated. This is the arrangement adopted in the Dun Building,[14] where, indeed, in the Broadway

desiring to paint it, not in chosen "bits" but as a whole, our gratitude should go out to him freely.

This is clearly the case with the John Wolfe building at the corner of William street and Maiden lane. In this case the architect has observed and applied the conventions which have been arrived at in the course of the experimentation of a quarter of a century, since many-storied buildings began to be erected for commercial purposes, so that his design is an intelligent summation of the architectural progress of these years in this new undertaking. This would suffice to make it respectable and creditable, but there is more in it than that, for it has character, freshness, and charm, and is interesting not as a theorem, with Q-E-D at the end of it, but as an individual work of art.

Let us recapitulate first the conventions of elevator-architecture that have been so well settled that every competent designer of a tall building accepts and observes them. First, the precept that every work must have a beginning, a middle and an end is at once more necessary and more difficult to enforce in very tall buildings than in buildings in which each story is a member of the composition and a term in the proportion. It is more necessary because if it be not enforced the result is more distressing, and it is more difficult because in a serial repetition of stories devoted to like purposes and of equal value and importance a larger division embracing the subdivisions of the stories must be artificial, and in danger of appearing forced and arbitrary, whereas it is essential that it should appear natural and inevitable. Reflection upon these conditions has led thinking architects to the analogy, more and more closely followed as experience accumulates, of the column as the prototype of the tall building. It must have a base, a shaft, a capital. Each of these must be a group of stories. The shaft must be the ▸

15 New York Life Building, New York City, S.D. Hatch & McKim, 1894–96; Mead and White, 1896–98 (above).

16 American Surety Building, New York City, Bruce Price, architect,1894 (see photo page 63).

17 Bayard Building (later Condict Building), New York City, Louis H. Sullivan with Lyndon Smith, architects, 1897–1898. This building still stands, stripped, however, of its original crown and its ornament (see photo page 61).

18 American Tract Society Building, New York City, Robert H. Robertson, architect, 1894 (photo page 58).

19 *Oriel:* A bay window on an upper floor.

front, the "feature" is not even over the entrance, and in the longer front of the Singer Building. In the St. Paul it is the sculptured figures which are represented in the act of carrying twenty stories of wall that emphasize the entrance without sacrificing space. In the Washington Life it is the two-story order at the center of the longer front, which is too nearly an engaged order to constitute or represent a portico, and has the air of having been set up against the building. The same thing is true of the much larger and more conspicuous order in front of the New York Life,[15] an impressive feature in itself which loses much of its impressiveness when it is seen in connection with the building with which it is not architecturally incorporated. The effect of the actually engaged order of the American Surety Building,[16] with the columns in antis behind it is very much better than either of these inadequately projected orders, and is, indeed, about the most successful entrance upon this scheme that any of the tall buildings has to show. Another scheme is that of confining the entrance to the ground story, and surmounting it with a decoration which does not pretend to subserve any other function than that of signalizing it. This is the case with the free-standing circular pediment or panel over the entrance to the Bayard Building,[17] and it may be commended as an example to such architects as are quite sure that they can equal the author of that work in the attractiveness of their surface decoration. To other designers it may be said that the most eligible method of giving importance to their entrances seems to be that of running the opening into the second story if they can gain the consent of their owner to that sacrifice.

The entrance is in most cases the chief feature of the basement, of the architectural base. But it is not the only feature—and, indeed, the most effective treatment is that in which the whole substructure becomes a feature. If one is to forego detailed functional expression in favor of abstract architectonics, the height of a commercial building before the elevator came in suggested a

height of base which is in agreeable proportion to the "sky-scraper." This suggestion has been acted upon by many designers who have underpinned the shafts of their tall buildings with a four- or five-story building, designed as such and fairly complete in itself. The basement of the Dun Building offers a very fairly successful example of this treatment. The crowning member, including all above the eleventh story, seems distinctly infelicitous, both in proportion and treatment, and the variegation of the shaft sufficient to destroy the effect of repetition, which becomes more impressive in proportion to the extent of the series, without substituting any other. But, granting the author his two-story openings, which may at least conceivably light a lofty apartment with a mezzanine floor, the four-story basement seems to me a very well designed building, a composition fairly complete in itself, and at the same time a fitting preparation for the superstructure. In this latter respect the executed work is a distinct improvement upon the original design, which showed the basement as a five-story building with a quite un-meaning trophy to signalize the entrance which it does not designate, and especially with a continuous balcony which emphatically cuts it off from what is above. The restudy the basement has received has done it a great deal of good. The removal of a story from the lofty openings has made them much more tractable. The omission of the huge window frame of the front is a clear gain. But especially the confinement of the balcony to the center of each front, while continuing its line in a belt along the interval of wall, while it still leaves the basement to assert itself as a feature, also allows it to be allied with the superstructure, and substitutes at the angle the effect of continuity for that interruption.

The effect of the triple arcade in the long front of this basement has been very much amplified and extended in the long arcade which is the most striking feature of the flank of the Empire Building. This flank, confronting Trinity churchyard, and thus having as good an assurance of permanent visibility from an effective distance as can be had in New York, offered a very unusual opportunity, of which it will not be disputed, that, so far as this arcade is concerned, the designers have fully availed themselves. Doubtless the tenants of the floor above the springing may consider that they have been sacrificed to architecture. But this arcade of seven openings, on a scale twice that employed elsewhere in the building or in its neighbors, is really architectural, really a stately series, with its effective abutment of a much more solid flank of wall and its effective correspondence in scale with the order, also embracing two stories, at the top of the building. It must be now evident how much these two features, and with them the building, would gain in effect if the interval between them were an interval as nearly as might be of complete repose, a repetition twelve times of an identical design for a story of offices.

But it is the crowning member, the capital, which offers the greatest opportunity for individuality and variety of treatment. It is apt to be the only part which is visible from a distance. Anything like conformity is out of the question. New York has no skyline, and is not likely to have any, so long as the estimates of the most profitable height of commercial buildings vary from ten stories to thirty, and as the law does not intervene to draw the line of altitude. It is impossible for a designer to conform to what exists, much less to what may exist after his building is completed. All that he can do is to make his own building as presentable and shapely as the conditions will permit. It is maintained by some critics that a strict adherence to the conditions compels an architect to stop with the completion of his parallelepiped, and to forbear a visible roof. Doubtless the flat roof enables him to fill his honeycomb level to the top with a row of cells for the working bees. But it does not enable him to give any form or comeliness to the skyline of his building. The parallelepiped is not an architectural form, as anybody will have impressed upon him by looking at the random rows of paral-

lelepipeds in lower New York from across the East or the North River. The practical owner may have had some reason who objected to his architect's design for a steeply roofed ten-story building, upon the ground that "That's all right on the Rhine, but it ain't business." Nevertheless, he was insisting upon a defacement of the city, which is in great part wanton. For a visible roof will obviously supply additional accommodation at a less cost than that of building "to the limit" all the way up. Few sensitive spectators have observed from afar the towering mass of the American Surety Building without feeling that the tall shaft needs the crown that would convert it into a campanile. On other hand, few sensitive spectators can have failed to experience a touch of gratitude to the architect of the American Tract Society[18] for having enclosed part of that edifice in a picturesque hood, even though the hood be avowedly extraneous to the building, which is visibly enclosed and completed without reference to it. The St. Paul has no visible roof, but it has a true crown in the tall order, encrusted with decoration effective from every point from which it can be seen at all, which surmounts the three-fronted tower which the architect has arbitrarily set off as the "architecturesque part" of his building, leaving the architecture of the more shameful parts to take care of itself. This crown is in itself a grateful object, and the more grateful from a point of view from which the edifice it crowns cannot be made out in detail and may be ignored. Of substitutes for a visible roof, in cases where the architect felt bound to build to the limit, vertically and laterally, one of the most successful is the crowning order of the St. James, with an oriel[19] framed in metal in each intercolumniation, and the effect of the whole feature greatly enhanced by its projection from the plane of the wall below. This overhanging of the top is evidently as feasible and legitimate in a steel frame as in a timber frame, in which it has been so often and so effectively employed. It offers an architectural opportunity which it is strange should not have been

tallest of the three. It must also be the plainest and the least varied, because plainness here is needed to give effect to what elaboration there may be elsewhere, and because variety here leads to confusion. The ornament, then, must be concentrated at the base, where it is effective by its nearness to the spectator, but where its delicacy should not be carried far enough to impair the expression of vigor that belongs to a substructure; and at the capital, where it is effective by quantity. A plain, tall middle, which may and almost must be in itself monotonous, with a separate and more enriched treatment of the bottom and the top; this is in general the scheme indicated by the conditions, and carried it out with some strictness in the more successful sky-scrapers.

These conditions are all observed here. There is no doubt about the triple composition, nor about where one subdivision begins and another ends. The first three stories are emphatically set off as the base, the succeeding seven as the shaft, the terminal two in the roof as the capital. But the designer does not stop with this acceptance of the canons of elevator architecture. Contrariwise, he begins where a good many respectable designers of elevator buildings leave off. The mere emphasis of the divisions is apt to entail a stiff, hard and fast, too baldly logical aspect. Here there are transitions and gradations of which the unusual merit is that while they are interesting in themselves, and while they substitute for the sense of something forced and arbitrary the sense of something continuous and growing, they do not in the least compromise the clearness of nor bring into question the lines of demarcation.

In attaining this result the designer has been favored by conditions that many designers would have found obstacles. The site is of moderate dimensions, say eighty feet by thirty, and it is not a parallelogram, but a trapezoid, ▸

1899

20 "The verdict of the world will be conclusive."—St. Augustine in his treatise against the writings of Parmenian III.

American Tract Society Building, New York City, Robert H. Robertson, architect, 1894.

oftener embraced. In the present instance, it has been done rather timidly, as very likely it had to be. But in a free-standing building, or even in a corner building, it seems that it might sometimes be done more boldly and with a corresponding increase of effectiveness.

The same device is employed, though with even less emphasis, although to an excellent result, in the Washington Life Building. This building is acclaimed by everybody as one of the very best of the sky-scrapers, and it owes its whole effectiveness to the treatment of the capital, to the introduction and the treatment of a visible roof. The base is without pretensions, except in the portico of the entrance, where, as has already been remarked, the practicable projection does not suffice to give it the effect of a portico, while on the other hand it is not incorporated with the building. The shaft is reduced to its very simplest expression, a mere repetition of the openings of the tiers of cells, which leaves it as nearly as may be a plain shaft. The detail of the lower stories, successful in scale and careful both in design and execution, offers nothing striking. But the steep wedge-shaped roof seems to have been designed "not laboriously, but luckily." It gives character to the building below it and makes it a picturesque object equally in a near and in a distant view. The projection of the order, slight as it is, is very effective, almost indispensable as a detachment of the capital. The dormers are exceedingly well designed in themselves and most effectively relieved against the greenish bronze of the tiles, the color of which is one of the chief successes of the work, from the pictorial point of view. The widening of the building at the rear gives rise to an unavoidable awkwardness in the roofing, as seen from the south, the quarter from which the illustration of the Broadway front is taken. The awkwardness is mitigated as much as possible, and will disappear when the side comes to be concealed by another tall building. This contingency is contemplated by the evidently provisional treatment of the south wall, a treatment which is an unusual-

ly judicious compromise between the conflicting claims of the owner's pocket and the architect's wish to bestow comeliness upon "the more shameful parts," and to make them presentable so long as they are visible. Meanwhile, however, the most favorable view of the Broadway front is that from the northwest, from which the provisional architecture is not seen, and which the illustrations do not include, our street architecture offers very few glimpses so satisfying as that of this wedge of furrowed bronze, with the single bold dormer, so lucky in scale and in design, relieved against it. Not less good in its way is the broad northern flank with the four dormers, and scarcely less good the west front, which "shines over city and river" standing knee-deep in the lower buildings of the waterfront. If this had been the principal front, the architect would very probably have introduced a single dormer above, to unite and dominate the two, and thus have reproduced the effect so familiar and always so effective in the timberwork of the German Renaissance. The conspicuous roof, with the separate treatment of the upper stories of the wall, emphasized by order, and the slight expansion which it marks, cone the capital of the building, and it is plainly a feature which no equal and uncompromising parallelepiped, built to the limit in all dimensions, can at all compete.

* * * * *

All the buildings thus far mentioned have been designed in general conformity with the convention which enforces not only the Aristotelian triple division, but the more specific analogy of the column. But it should not be forgotten that the assumption of that analogy, convenient as it is, is, after all, only an assumption, and a more or less arbitrary assumption, since it not only does not facilitate, but may even obstruct, the detailed expression in design of structure and of function. That the Aristotelian maxim itself is an assumption, or that the application of it to architecture is arbitrary, not many designers or critics can be prepared to admit. It is not necessary that they should be psychologists, and able to explain in words why a building triply divided should be more "agreeable to the spirit of man" than a building which consists from top to bottom in tiers of similar cells, any more than that they should be able to explain why in fenestration the arithmetical progression 3, 5, and 7 is agreeable. On either point they can safely take an appeal to universal consciousness. *Securus orbis judicabit.*[20] But it is also true that the sky-scraper is in fact a series of equal cells, and that the only suggestions for a triple division that inhere in the conditions are the facts that the ground floor has a different destination from that of the floors above, and suggest a distinctive treatment of the bottom, and the fact that a visible roof or in default of it the necessity for a protective and projecting cornice, compels a distinctive treatment for the top. Almost without exception, the designers of the tall buildings make a further assumption, which is not only arbitrary but manifestly baseless, and that is that in designing them they are designing buildings of masonry, instead of merely wrapping skeletons of metal in fire-resisting material. That basements should be more solid than superstructures; that arches should have visible abutments; that walls should "reveal" their thickness; these and many more of the traditions of masonry have no relevancy at all to the new construction. If architects make and we allow these assumptions, we ought not to forget that they are baseless assumptions, and that the best work done according to them is not a solution, but an evasion of the problem presented by the modern office building. That is why an aberration, a "deviation from the customary structure or type," is not necessarily condemnable, may, on the contrary, be highly laudable. It all depends upon whether the departure is a mere caprice of the designer, or an attempt to come closer to reason and reality than is possible under the conventional treatment.

Decidedly an aberration is the Singer Building in lower Broadway. This scarcely comes within our scope, since the building is not an example of the skeleton construction, and rests at the modest ten stories,

which seems to be the commercially practicable limit of a structure with real walls. Considering the enormous costliness of the land on which it stands, this self-restraint indicates either a very obstinate or a very facile owner, who may well be astonished at his own moderation in contenting himself with half the rentable area he might have had. Commercially, and in spite of the brand-newness and smartness of its modish Parisian detail, the Singer Building is a reversion, advantageous as it might be, on civic grounds, to restrict the height of all commercial buildings to the height to which its owner has voluntarily restricted himself. Moderate as this height is in comparison with the neighbors it has yet seemed excessive to the architect, who has bent his efforts to the task of keeping it down. This he has done by a triple division, accentuated not only by horizontal members emphatic to the verge, if not beyond the verge, of extravagance, but by a change of material in the different divisions, the lower being a monochrome of light stone and the middle a field of red brick relieved with stone. Nay, the principal divisions are so emphasized and the subordinate divisions so slurred that a ten-story building presents the appearance of one of three stories, with a corresponding exaggeration of scale. At least until a legal limit is put upon the height of buildings, this is likely to remain unique. But while it does not invite imitation, one has to own that a thing of which it is questionable whether it was worth doing has been unquestionably well done.

Of another deviation from the customary type, the Park Row Building, it is not easy to discern the motive. This structure has the distinction, which is to be hoped it may retain, of the tallest yet, and confronts the next tallest, the Paul, across the street, which is more properly an alley. It can scarcely be said to be "by merit raised to that bad eminence," although, like its neighbor, it has the salutary effect of a warning rather than of an example. In each case there are inherent awkwardnesses in the problem which were obviously difficult to surmount, and which

with an acute angle at the northern corner. This disposition enforced an unusual treatment, which might have seemed affected for picturesqueness if it had not been so plainly determined by the conditions. The acute angle is truncated, and the bevel is carried through the three-storied base and two stories beyond it where it is merged into a second and deeper chamfer, giving a face equal to that of the remaining wall on the shorter side and admitting a symmetrical treatment of these two. This unusual disposition so evidently and so naturally proceeds from the peculiarity of the site as to relieve it altogether from the sense of something capricious or arbitrary, and, carried out as it has been, makes the architectural fortune of the building. The treatment, indeed, has been singularly happy. While the base is sharply distinguished from the shaft, both by the grouping and separate treatment of its openings and by the emphatic string-course above it, the prolongation of the chamfer through the first two stories of the shaft involves a difference in the treatment of these, and this difference has with notable tact and ingenuity been carried just far enough to relieve the shaft of monotony without impairing its unity. The openings are divided by mullions instead of by piers as above, and in the main walls the doubled openings are united under single arches. The narrower face of wall at the angle is judiciously kept as solid as possible below. It may be from a necessity of the plan that the entrance is placed at the side, and only a narrow window pierces the angle in the lower story, but, it is quite clear how much the architecture gains by this unusual arrangement, in giving mass at the point where mass is most of all needed. The feature formed by the hooded triangular bay of five stories at the angle is as effective and picturesque as it is peculiar, the more effective because its peculiarity ▸

21 Sullivan's arbitrary emphasis on the vertical piers over the horizontal spandrel panels characterizes all his skeletal buildings until the Schlesinger and Mayer (now Carson Pirie Scott) Department Store.

22 Sullivan's classic "The Tall Building Esthetically Considered," originally published in Lippincott's, 57 (Mar. 1896), 403–409; reprinted in the Documents of Modern Art Series as *Kindergarten Chats and Other Writings* (New York, 1947), pp. 202–213.

above: Park Row or Syndicate Building, New York City, Robert H. Robertson, architect, 1896–99.

opposite: Bayard Building, New York City, Louis H. Sullivan with Lyndon Smith, architects, 1897–1898.

have obviously not been surmounted. But the design of the principal front of the Park Row, which in effect comprises the architecture, is noteworthy for its rejection of the convention upon which most of the recent tall buildings have been designed, without substituting for it any scheme that is obviously more rational, or that is even readily apprehensible. Laterally there is an emphatic triple division, into flanking walls kept as plain and solid as the practical requirements will allow, and a more open center, consisting of five superposed orders, not counting the two-story colonnade of the basement. The relation of these orders is by no means felicitous. Some are stilted on pedestals of a story in height, while others stand directly upon the entablatures of those below, without apparent reason. Vertically, there is no clear division. It is apparent whether the first two stories or the first five constitute the architectural base. The upper five pretty clearly constitute the capital, being occupied by an order more developed than those below, although the cornice that marks off them from what is below is no more important than other horizontal lines which can have no such special significance. The sixteen stories below this cornice may be taken as the shaft, and by looking very hard, it is possible to discern that this is meant to be triply subdivided into a beginning of five stories, containing an order furnished with pedestals, a middle of seven, containing two orders directly superposed, an end of four, containing another order, while the intermediate divisions are marked by balconies. But the principal and the subordinate divisions are so nearly equal in emphasis as to produce uncertainty and confusion, and to excuse the cursory observer for declaring that the front shows no composition at all. Without going so far as that, it seems safe to say that the architect would have done better if he had accepted and abided by the current convention.

Very different is the aberration presented by the Bayard Building in Bleecker Street. There is nothing capricious in the general treatment of this structure. It is an attempt,

and a very serious attempt, to found the architecture of a tall building upon the facts of the case. The actual structure is left or, rather, is helped, to tell its own story. This is the thing itself. Nobody who sees the building can help seeing that. Neither the analogy of the column, nor any other tradition or convention, is allowed to interfere with the task of clothing the steel frame in as expressive forms as may be. There is no attempt to simulate the breadth and massiveness proper to masonry in a frame of metal that is merely wrapped in masonry for its own protection. The flanking piers, instead of being broadened to the commercially allowable maximum, are attenuated to the mechanically allowable minimum. Everywhere the drapery of baked clay is a mere wrapping, which clings so closely to the frame as to reveal it, and even to emphasize it. This is true at least of the uprights, for it seems to me a defect in the general design, from the designer's own point of view, that it does not take enough account of the horizontal members.[21] As anybody may see in a steel cage not yet concealed behind its screens of masonry, these are as important to the structure as the uprights. In the Bayard they are largely ignored, for the panels which mark the different floors are apparently mere insertions, answering no structural purpose, and there is no suggestion of any continuous horizontal members, such as, of course, exist and are even necessary to stability. Mr. Sullivan, some years ago, wrote a very interesting paper on the æsthetics of the tall building, of which the fundamental position was that form must follow function, and that "where function does not vary form does not vary."[22] These are propositions from which nobody who believes that architecture is an art of expression will dissent, and with which the present writer heartily agrees. But in applying them to the case in question, Mr. Sullivan declared that the lower two (or possibly three) stories of a tall office building had a destination so different from that of the superstructure, that a distinguishing treatment for them was not only required but demanded, and that the upper-

is so evidently not the result of caprice but of an intelligent consideration of the conditions. The same may be said of the still more picturesque gable that is the crowning feature. It looks so easy and so natural that one forgets how difficult a feat of design it is. Here are two wall faces, made equal, be it noted by art and device, meeting at a very obtuse angle, and carried up a hundred feet in the air. How to unite them by a crowning feature? Architects will agree that it is not easy. Probably most architects would solve it by crowning the two walls with a parapet and rearing a gable behind them, leaving it to be inferred upon what this gable stood. But they will admit the superiority to this obvious and objectionable arrangement of the solution here hit upon by which the two faces are not only carried up to the cornice line, but continued as the sides of the gable, while a third chamfer enables a central wall face, at right angles with the axis of the building to be erected between them, and appropriately to crown the edifice.

The detail, one may say, follows naturally from the irregular disposition that proceeds from the peculiarity of the site. A very free and plastic architecture is needed to follow so irregular a scheme. Fancy an attempt to clothe such a structure in classic forms! Although, as we have seen, the disposition arrived at is not the result of caprice but of necessity, it is characterized at the first glance by oddity, and a style that is quaint to the point of oddity is the most appropriate style in which to express it. The Dutch Renaissance is eminently such a style. It has besides its general appropriateness, a special and local appropriateness to a building erected within the precincts of the ancient Dutch settlement and the very irregularity of which is a consequence of the Dutch street-plan. It is applied here with so much ingenuity and cleverness that it seems to be rather ▶

1899

23 Manufactures Building (1893), World's Columbian Exposition, Chicago, designed by George Post (right). The main roof of iron and glass arched an area 1,400 feet long by 385 feet wide. This exposed structure, an enlargement of Contamin and Dutert's Galerie des Machines of the Paris Exposition of 1889 (photo page 132).The arches of the Hall of Manufactures were clothed on the exterior by the colonnades and triumphal arches in plaster which characterized the entire Court of Honor.

24 Rufus Choate (1799–1859), the famous Boston lawyer, made the remark about Chief justice Lemuel Shaw (1781–1861), who served for thirty years in the Supreme Court of Massachusetts. Schuyler's rendition is a paraphrase of the actual toast.

25 Russell Sturgis, "Good Things in Modern Architecture," [VIII:1 Jul–Sept p 101]. Sturgis criticized the arches and ornament under the projecting eaves as being false to the frame.

opposite: American Surety Building, New York City, Bruce Price, architect, 1894-96.

most story in turn, being in great part devoted to the "circulating system" of the building should also be differentiated. I remember suggesting to him that it was in fact only the ground floor which could be said to differ in function from its successors and that his inclusion of additional stories may have been inspired by an instinctive desire to obtain a base more proportional, according to our inherited notions of proportion, to a lofty superstructure than a single story could furnish. However that may be, in the Bayard it is the ground floor that is treated as the base. Even the second story "counts in" with the superstructure, to which logically it belongs. In spite of the separate treatment of the ground floor, the continuity of the structure is felt and expressed, even in the design of the capitals, which are plainly not real capitals, spreading to carry a weight of greater area, but mere efflorescences of decoration. It is not a question whether two or three stories would not be more effectively proportional to the superstructure than one. It is a question of fact. The result, whatever else one may think of it, is a sense of reality very different from what we get from the sky-scrapers designed on conventional lines. It puts them to the same sort of shame to which the great roof trusses of the Manufactures Building in Chicago[23] put the imitative architecture with which they were associated. Not that the gauntness and attenuation of the resulting architecture are in this case altogether agreeable to an eye accustomed to the factitious massiveness of the conventional treatment. But, at the worst, this front recalls

Rufus Choate's famous toast to the Chief justice: "We look upon him as the East Indian upon his wooden idol. We know that he is ugly, but we feel that he is great."[24] We feel that this front is a true and logical exposition of the structure. If we find it ugly notwithstanding, that may be our own fault. If we can find no failure in expressiveness, the architect may retort upon us that it is no uglier than it ought to be.

Meanwhile the aesthetic, as distinguished from the scientific, attractiveness of the Bayard Building without doubt resides in the decoration which has been lavished upon it, and which is of a quality that no other designer could have commanded. I am unable to agree with Mr. Sturgis's condemnation of the crowning feature of the building, in a recent number of this magazine, as "most unfortunate."[25] In fact, the upper two stories are internally one story, the upper floor being a gallery surrounding a well extending through both, and lighted from above. Doubtless the arches and the rudimentary tracery are not forms of metallic architecture, but they do not belong to metallic architecture.

The arches are in fact of brickwork faced with terra cotta, and the thrust of them is visibly, as well as actually, taken up by the tie-rods at the springing. The intermediate uprights, the mullions, cease at this level, while the prolongation of the principal uprights is clearly denoted by the winged figures under the cornice. A designer who has adhered so strictly to the unpromising facts of the steel cage through eleven stories is scarcely to be severely blamed for "treating resolution" to this extent in the twelfth. If the building, apart from its wealth of decoration, recalls the works of contemporaneous engineering rather than of historical architecture, that also is "as it must be." The Bayard Building is the nearest approach yet made, in New York, at least, to solving the problem of the sky-scraper. It furnishes a most promising starting point for designers who may insist upon attacking that problem instead of evading it, and resting in compromises and conventions. ∎

developed than applied. The old market in Haarlem, that most characteristic Dutch monument of the sixteenth century, has been very freely drawn upon for suggestions of the detail, especially of the crowning member, with its dormers and its gable, but nothing has been used without intelligent adaptation and modification. So free and eclectic, indeed, is the treatment that the Gothic detail of the trefoiled cornice takes its place without jarring. It may be objected that the treatment is not strictly enough utilitarian and commercial, and the objection must be allowed. But whenever, with so perplexing a problem, a designer subjugates its difficulties to the production of a building so picturesque and attractive and individual, we will not attach overmuch weight to the objection. and will not only forgive him freely for bestowing an ornament upon the city, but will be exceedingly obliged to him.

The John Wolf Building, is discussed by Schuyler again in this article on the architect's work.
from:

HENRY JANEWAY HARDENBERGH
by Montgomery Schuyler
Vol. VI No. 3, Jan-Mar 1897,
pp. 335-375.

None of these buildings, however, is a "skyscraper," in the acceptation of that term, which requires a minimum of ten stories. Neither is any an example of the steel-frame construction in which the structure, instead of consisting of visible walls, is only masked by them. The latest of our architect's commercial buildings is a skyscraper, in both these senses, and it is a great encouragement to find it by far the best of all. Not only that, but it is one of the very few examples we can adduce to show that the skyscraper is artistically tractable, if it be intrusted to an artist. I have already, and in these pages (Architectural Record, Vol. V., No. 3), described this work at greater length than is possible under the present limitations. It must suffice here to indicate how unpromising the conditions were for an artistic success, and how such a suc-

cess has been won in spite of them. The site is evidently inadequate in area as the site of a twelve-story building, and it is not only inadequate in size but irregular in shape. This irregularity seems to deal the final blow at any attempt to make a work of art otit of a twelve-story building on such a site. Most architects—even artistic architects— would give it up when the plot of the site was put before them; would content themselves with a "swagger" entrance and an umbrageous and elaborate cornice and a wall between of no pretence of architectural interest. In fact, we have a building which is studied in every story and at every point, and so successfully studied that it becomes a highly picturesque object, as impressive in mass and outline as it is interesting in detail. This is a very rare success. And observe, moreover, that the individuality and picturesqueness of the building come not by ignoring or shirking any of the hard conditions of the problem, but by faithfully grappling with them. It is indeed from these very conditions that the individuality of the work in great part proceeds. Out of this nettle danger the artist has plucked this flower safety. What, at the first view, could be more hopeless than the predicament of an architect required to rear twelve rentable stories at the acute angle of this site and make the result presentable? The difficulties have been so triumphantly overcome that they become factors in the success. Is there anything happier in contemporary work that the art with which the acute angle, bevelled by successive truncations, becomes an equal half of a front which by another truncation gains a central and dominating feature? To appreciate how good it is compare it with the buildings offered by other designers as solutions of somewhat similar problems. Mr. Hardenbergh has here so overcome the difficulties that it is only the critical spectator who infers them, whereas other buildings in similar situations continue, after they are completed, to bristle with the difficulties of the original problem. ●

**Flatiron Building,
New York City,
D.H. Burnham & Company,
architects, 1901–3.**

The building, which faces
Madison Square Park, is clad in
terra cotta from third story up.
Though it originally met with
unfavorable critical reaction, it
has come to be regarded as one
of the most iconic of skyscrapers,
immortalized by Photographers
Alfred Steiglitz (1864–1946),
Edward Steichen (1879–1973),
and Alvin Langdon Coburn
(1882–1966).

opposite: This two-page spread
opens an entire issue of
ARCHITECTURAL RECORD devoted
to D.H. Burnham & Associates.
Burham described himself as "a
business man with a knowledge
of building."

ARCHITECTURAL APPRECIATIONS No. II
The "Flatiron" or Fuller Building

It seemed that there was nothing left to be done in New York, in the way of architectural altitude, which would attract much attention, after the way in which for years we have been piling Pelion upon Ossa. But the architect of the Flatiron, bounded by Broadway, Fifth Avenue and Twenty-third Street, has succeeded in accomplishing that difficult feat. His building is at present quite the most notorious thing in New York, and attracts more attention than all the other buildings now going up put together.

It follows from this extreme conspicuousness and notoriety of the work that it excites more comment, in exciting more attention, than any other recent building. "He who builds by the wayside," says the proverb, "has many judges." And certainly nobody else is building so obviously "by the wayside" as the author of the structure of which the public has thus far refused to accept the official title of "Fuller," preferring the homelier and more graphic designation of the "Flatiron." The corners furnished by the intersection of Broadway with the rectilinear reticulation imposed upon Manhattan island by the Street Commissioners of 1807 are not only the most conspicuous, but really the only conspicuous sites for building, the only sites on which the occupying buildings can be seen all around, can be seen all at once, can be seen from a distance that allows them to be taken in by the eye as wholes. In a civilized municipality these so advantageous spots would have been reserved for public uses, would have been the sites of public and monumental buildings. They are besides so few:

> Oh, it was pitiful
> In a whole cityful,

that those misguided men should have left only half a dozen sites for public buildings, outside, it is true, of those which face public squares. Let us count: This present corner, and the corresponding corner at Twenty-sixth, facing southward, at the intersection of Broadway and Fifth Avenue. At the intersection of Sixth Avenue the truncated triangle, largely spoiled for the purposes of monumental building, by the intrusion of the elevated road, but set back a block by the reservation of Greeley Square, and the corresponding trapezoid on the north, wisely seized upon, years ago, for the uses of the New York Herald, and occupied effectively by the enlarged or at least elongated reproduction of the pretty palazzo of Verona, a building which compels attention by its modest altitude, permitting the owner to stand chronically and increasingly astonished at his own moderation, and has, in addition to its intrinsic attractiveness, the interest of lighting up, on one of the most valuable street corners in Manhattan, the "Lamp of Sacrifice,"[1] no matter at how queer a shrine. At the intersection of Seventh Avenue, the triangle, also truncated by the recession from Forty-third into a trapezoid, of which the base is now occupied by, the new ruin of the Hotel Pabst, (page 78) and the residue by a hole in the ground for the uses of the subway, and the corresponding and broader trapezoid at the north end of Longacre,[2] at Forty-seventh. At the intersection of Eighth Avenue, the highly irregular space formed by the laying out on the gridiron of the street system of the "Circle" now such a scene of chaos,[3] but at some early day, it is to be hoped, to be converted into something cosmical by the adoption of Mr. Lamb's plan,[4] or some equivalent, and at which early date it is to be hoped the buildings which now line the segment and constitute the "improvement" of the Circle may in their turn be improved off the face of the

from:
**DANIEL HUDSON BURNHAM
AND HIS ASSOCIATES**
By Peter B. Wight
Vol. XXXVIII, No. 1, July 1915,
pp. 1–12.

The great Chicago conflagration of the year 1871 was the event which inaugurated a new epoch in the history of that city. Chicago had been a thriving Western city up to that time, and its architecture was essentially "Western," with such exceptions as would naturally be found in a city of 300,000 population. Its best wholesale stores did not exceed five stories in height, though there were two or three of six stories, and one prominently large marble building, of the latter class. Its best dwellings were generally isolated, with garden surroundings, and most of them of wood. Its churches were pretentious and ugly, many of them built of the white lime stone found only fifty miles away, which at that time had been in use not to exceed fifteen years.

* * *

It was in this period that the firm of Burnham and Root was established, and like other beginners they had their struggles. They had both been in the office ▶

1 The "Lamp of Sacrifice" is the first of seven from *Seven Lamps of Architecture*, by John Ruskin (1849). In one of the most influential books of the 19th Century, Ruskin distinguished between architecture and mere building.

2 Longacre Square, 42nd Street and Broadway, New York City, was renamed Times Square in 1904.

3 Columbus Circle, Broadway and 59th Street, New York City.

4 Charles R. Lamb (1860–1942) and his brother Frank Stymentz Lamb (1863–1928) played active roles in the Municipal Arts Society.

5 Paul Bourget (1852-1935), French novelist who was best known for his literary criticism and is associated with the "passive disillusion" of late 19th century décadence. His excitement about the architecture and stockyards of Chicago prompted him to write *OUTRE MER–NOTES SUR L'AMERIQUE*. Schuyler's translation of Bourget's story first appeared in his "Architecture in Chicago," series published in 1885 in *ARCHITECTURAL RECORD*.

This ad for Otis Elevators in a 1905 *RECORD* shows what the company thought of its role in the development of the skyscraper.

earth; and at the north end the very eligible triangle lately occupied by Durland's riding school. Beyond this, westward and northward to the intersection of Ninth Avenue, it is not necessary now to extend our inquiries. Thus far, and in the heart of middle Manhattan, we have found just five sites for noble buildings, for we leave out of view the concave frontage of the circle at Fifty-eighth Street. Just one of these sites is thus far occupied by a modern tall building, which is the Flatiron. The building is thus unique, built not by one wayside alone, but by four waysides, and each of its three frontages far seen from the quarter it respectively confronts, and the Broadway front visible and apprehensible from the east side of Fifth Avenue almost up to the entrance to Central Park. No wonder that the architect should have found "many judges," no wonder that his building should have acted as a challenge, and–goaded to architectural criticism those who never architecturally criticised before, while those who are victims to the habit of architectural criticism criticise all the more. With apologies to Catullus for dislocating his metre, one may say:

Hic judicet qui nunquam judicavit;
Quique judicavit, hic judicet.

It is the first condition of a sane criticism to take account of the conditions. "The sculptor cannot set his own free thought before us, but his thought as he could translate it into the stone that was given, with the tools that were given." And, if this be true of the sculptor, how much truer of the architect, whose work must be "modified at every turn by circumstance and concession." We have been saying that the architect of the Flatiron had a unique opportunity. But also he had to labor with corresponding disadvantages, mainly, of course, the shape of the area he was to cover. This is recognized in the popular name of his building, the long triangle which is called the Flatiron but which has been as graphically described as "a stingy piece of pie." The thoughtless public seems to impute this disadvantage to the architect, by way of criticism as a fault,

instead of condoling with him upon it as a misfortune. In fact, the popular judgment upon buildings as works of art is mostly vitiated by the thoughtless habit of ascribing to the architect his advantages as merits, and correspondingly imputing his disadvantages to him as faults. Criticism must keep clear of this confusion.

The main, indeed, the only advantage the architect of the Flatiron had, was the comparative magnitude, the complete detachment, and the consequent conspicuousness of his work, and that is an advantage or not accordingly as the result is or is not successful enough to justify the conspicuousness. The problem in this case was how to make the most of the advantages of detachment, magnitude, altitude, and conspicuousness, and at the same time to minimize the disadvantages of the awkward shape of the plot, and to do these things without any the least sacrifice of the strictly utilitarian purposes of the structure. For to sacrifice the money getting possibilities of such a site in such a quarter to the monumental aspect of the building would have been as much a mistake in art as in "business." The point was to utilize the site to the very utmost, multiplying as many times as possible, as Paul Bourget[5] has it about the tall buildings of Chicago, "the value of the bit of ground at the base," and yet to make as expressive, harmonious and beautiful a building as the conditions admitted. A candid inquiry into how far such a result has been attained in the actual erection ought to have interest and value.

Foremost among the practical advantages of the site is the fact that the designer did not have to trouble himself in the least about the lighting of his building. Even if we can imagine it confronted on three sides, across Twenty-second Street, across Broadway, and across Fifth Avenue, by buildings as tall as itself, it would be better lighted than many, than most, of the downtown office buildings of comparable altitude. The base is of nearly one hundred feet, but the straight side of the triangle must be nearly, and the hypothenuse on Broadway rather more than two hundred. There is thus no reason why every room on the base of the triangle, or at least of every suite of offices, should not receive light from one of the sides which receives its light from the great area to the north, from which the light cannot be intercepted, the comparatively dark middle of the southern front being backed against an included and counterparting triangle devoted to the service of the building, in which less illumination than in the rentable parts, or even an illumination entirely artificial, is entirely admissible. And then the problem would become, how to get rid of the architectural awkwardness and the practical ineligibility of the thin edge of the wedge, of the apex of the triangle, to get rid, in fact, of the "edge," which, in the expressive language of the street, must "queer" the whole structure if it be allowed to assert itself. We say this edge is practically ineligible, and shall presently point out that fact more in detail. But the architectural intolerableness of it might be expected to appeal first and most powerfully to an architect who was not only a prudent and frugal planner, in the interest of his employer, but also an artist. He would have devoted himself, one would say, to circumventing this awkwardness. Doubtless he would have tried many experimental devices to that end, "proving" them by their practical and their architectural results, and holding fast at last to that which was good, or best. Let us imagine, for example, that, instead of rounding his edge at the bottom, he had truncated the angle to the width of a decent doorway, and had continued this truncation to the top of the architectural basement, including the fourth story, treating his doorway as massively as possible with the dimension he had allowed himself, and, above the doorway, emphasizing the solidity of the truncated wall by leaving a single slit at the centre, which should serve for a lookout to the northward. Then suppose he had terraced the superstructure emphatically back, until the truncation amounted to, say, fifteen or twenty feet, enough to present something that could be called a face of wall, rather than a mere edge, and carried this through the "shaft." Above the shaft,

suppose he had still more boldly and emphatically "refused" the superstructure by another terrace, leaving only a trapezoidal tower of, say, half the length, and two-thirds the area of the whole triangle, and carried this tower high enough to include all the rentable area he had omitted below. If this had been sensitively, that is to say artistically done, would not his building have shown more logic, more organization, more form and comeliness, more variety in a higher unity, than it shows now? And could he have been accused of sacrificing his clients to his architecture, if he had provided them with the same area of rentable apartments of which he had deprived them, at no greater cost, in a more eligible shape, and had even added to the altitude which is the distinction of the existing building, and which he might then, without offense, on such a site, have extended even to "the record," or "the limit," whatever the limit may be.

Of course, this is only a suggestion of one solution. Doubtless there are others, which would commend themselves to an architect buckling down in earnest to such a problem. To convert difficulties into opportunities, out of this nettle, a difficult ground plan, to evoke this flower, architectural beauty, is the work of an architectural artist of high degree. Comparisons are odious. But compare the Flatiron with the John Wolfe Building at William Street and Maiden Lane, (photo page 53) where the area was quite as awkward a base for a skyscraper as this present plot, and which was moreover entirely without the advantages of isolation and conspicuousness which constitute this present opportunity. How have the awkwardnesses there been circumvented and overruled to expressiveness and beauty which here have been left entirely undisguised, and without even an attempt to disguise them, if they have not even been aggravated, by the treatment. That is, in fact, the peculiarity and the misfortune of the present erection, the fact that the problem does not seem to have presented itself to the architect as a problem. It is not his solution which we have to discuss, and with which we have to quarrel, but his

(photo page 53)

of the writer of this article—Mr. Burnham, as student, and Mr. Root, as head draftsman.

...the swarm of architects which the rebuilding of Chicago had attracted, many of them from foreign countries with little or no training, tried to copy our designs, and in most cases made caricatures of them, and the mass of people could see no difference. But a few of the older men, among them the late Dankman Adler, adopted these basic principles in most of their work: and later he formed a partnership with Louis H. Sullivan, who has had more credit than any other man of having been the founder of the progressive school of architecture of the Middle West.

It was through Burnham's great energy and ability to educate his own clients that so much of this work came to his firm, work which included such notably important and interesting buildings as the Chicago Club, first erected for the Art Institute, and sold to the Club, the First Regiment Armory, the Masonic Temple,* the Monadnock Building, the Rookery, and, greatest of all, the Woman's Temple.** With these buildings and the Auditorium,*** the Schiller Building,† the Schlesinger and Mayer store‡ and the K. and M. Temple of Adler and Sullivan, and the Marshall Field Wholesale Store# and McVeagb residence of H. H. Richardson, it may be truly said that architecture had a new birth in Chicago. But it was not the birth of a style. It was rather the birth of independence, of a freedom from the trammels of precedent and the dictum of any school. The first mentioned group is illustrative of the many which Burnham and Root designed during the first period of the well-earned prosperity of the firm from 1880 to 1893, the ▶

1902

failure to offer any solution. Having an awkward triangle as a site, he has not recognized its awkwardness, nor its triangularity, nor the fact that his building was to be seen in perspective and from various points of view. He has simply drawn three elevations of its three fronts, and apparently seen it, certainly studied it, in elevation only. If, architecturally, the "Flatiron" were simply a street front, like so many other skyscrapers, it might very well pass as "ower bad for blessing and ower good for banning." Let us assume that either of the long fronts is the elevation of such a building, visible, or meant to be seen, like the paper elevation, only from a point in front of it. In that case, we should find it respectable but not interesting. Like Dante, we should not speak, but look only and pass, having, in truth, nothing to say. It is the conventional skyscraper, and shows that the architect is aware what he is doing in skyscrapers. We should have to acknowledge that his general dispositions are according to the best authorities, that his three, or four, story basement is in accepted relations to his four-story attic and his twelve-story shaft, and that the eight-story hanging oriels which diversify his front are so spaced as on the one hand not visibly to destroy their own purpose of gaining sidelong views out of certain favored offices, and, on the other, as agreeably to diversify the monotony of the wall without impairing the effect of the repetition of its equable fenestration. Indeed, whether from accident or from design, these oriels have a happy effect in perspective, when the front from which they are projected is seen at a sharp angle, and they take on the appearance of plain piers, bordered above and below by fretted walls. The attic irresistibly recalls that of the Broadway Chambers,[7] from which it seems to be immediately derived. To have improved on the original would have justified the imitation. But it is neither so successful and well adjusted as a crowning member, nor so effectively detailed, nor is it so effective in either respect as the crown of the St. Paul, in which building the architect was no more successful than the architect of the Flatiron

in overcoming or dissembling the difficulties of his site, but of which the crowning feature is in itself most effective and even impressive. The variety of color which makes so much of the charm of the crown of the Broadway Chambers is here expressly renounced.

We have, however, to congratulate the designer upon the effectiveness of his material. "There is safety in monochrome," and monochrome cannot be too monochromatic. In this case, the manufacturer has managed exactly to match the warm yellowgray of the limestone base in the tint of the terra cotta above. Moreover, we have to congratulate the architect upon the success of his detail, especially upon that which answers the purpose, by means of a surface enrichment, of giving appropriate texture to his walls. The frequent failures in this show that it is more of an achievement than the uninitiated might suppose. In a front of hewn stone, this texture is given by means of the various modes of dressing the surface which are employed. In terra cotta it is, or should be, given by ornament. A designer who should confine himself in terra cotta to the limited range of variety available in stone work, and seek appropriate texture simply by roughening the surface according to the distance from the eye, and to the other relevant considerations, would show that he was not alive to the capabilities of his material, to the one point in which terra cotta has an actual advantage over masonry, and that is the facility with which its surface may be moulded into ornament. Systems of ornament, calculated in scale and density to effect the same varieties of texture attained, by cruder means, through the use of the hammer or the chisel, are here imperatively "indicated." And in this respect the architect of the Flatiron has attained a result which is not only satisfactory but exemplary. Whatever its value as ornament, the scale and character of the surface enrichment are throughout such as to make it acceptable as a representation of texture. And, strictly as ornament, none of it is distinctly bad, and some of it is distinctly good. The frieze of the fourth story is effective in itself and particularly effective as denoting and emphasizing a transitional member of the composition. And the detail of the attic, especially of its bounding stories above and below, indeed, the whole feature, even if excessive, and even if inferior to its original, is well adjusted in scale, and the detail well adapted to its altitude.

But this praise, which one can honestly bestow, is all limited to the assumption, which the architect inscrutably chose to make, that he was designing elevations and not a building. Either of the principal elevations, taken in conjunction with the edge upon which they converge, has not the aspect of all enclosing wall, so much as of a huge screen, a vast theatrical "wing," which conceivably rests upon Titanic castors and is meant to be pushed about, instead of being rooted to the spot. Nor, when one takes the point of view from which both fronts call be partly made out at once, the point opposite the thin end of the wedge, is the case at all bettered. To continue the spacing of the fenestration equally whether the space the windows are supposed to light is a hundred feet across, as at the south end of the Flatiron, or five, as at the north, is to invite criticism, even from the utilitarian point of view. The openings which are merely adequate to light an apartment say of thirty feet in depth, would evidently be excessive to light one with an extreme depth of fifteen, even if there were a dead wall opposite them. But to reopen the dead wall with a similar row of windows, and even to carry them across the five-foot end, in a double opening with the minimum of sash frame, is to denote want of thought. It is to provide a mere bird-cage for your tenant. As one looks through the bars of the cage, one pities the poor man. He can, perhaps, find wall space within for one rolltop desk without overlapping the windows, with light close in front of him and close behind him and close on one side of him. But suppose he needed a bookcase? Undoubtedly he has a highly eligible place from which to view processions. Put for the transaction of business? And the

aesthetic effect is even more depressing. The wedge is blunted, by being rounded, to a width of five or six feet—possibly ten. But it might as well have been produced to tile actual point, nay, better, if the angle had been devoted to broadening the piers. For the treatment of the tip is an additional and seems a wanton aggravation of the inherent awkwardness of the situation. The narrowness of the tip and the high lanky columns wherewith the designer has seen fit to flank the entrance, give this feature a meanness of aspect and elongates the columns to an almost intolerable lankiness. And as the eye travels upward, past sash frame after sash frame, which takes away all aspect of massiveness from the point which most of all should seem, as it were, spiked to the ground, the possibility of repose is increasingly removed. And, finally, when, at the very top, one finds the gauntness of the bottom repeated and even enhanced, by the insertion in the narrow tip of another pair of columns running through an attic higher than two average stories of the substructure, he must say to himself that it is a great pity that the architect should have chosen to build on this very odd site an ordinary tall building, "built to the limit" in every dimension, and thus have produced a very commonplace and conventional skyscraper, as the solution of a very unusual and a very interesting problem which clamored for an original and unconventional solution. Such a spectator is bound to admit that Evil is wrought by want of thought As well as want of heart, and that the altitude of this five-foot tip is really a "*productio ad absurdum*." ■

most remarkable building period ever known in Chicago. Their influence upon the other architects of that city was very marked, especially in the design of private residences, before the erection of apartment buildings became the vogue. It was at the beginning of this period that they designed the first high office building, the Montauk Block, only ten stories high, but high enough to be called then a skyscraper. It was of a severe but rational style, in pressed brick, with very little ornamentation.... Near the end of the period just described, in 1890, the Masonic Temple was completed, which long held the record of being the tallest building in the world. Between these dates they designed about a dozen buildings designated as skyscrapers.... About the time of the erection of the Rookery, the all-steel skeleton began to be developed by other architects, though the interior court wall of this building was of skeleton construction, also the south wall of the Phoenix Insurance Building, also by Burnham and Root, now owned by the Western Union Telegraph Company, which was of skeleton construction behind the elevators. The last sixteen-story building designed by Burnham and Root, with solid walls all the way up, was the north half of the Monadnock, which was entirely faced with brick and absolutely without ornament. The massive dignity of this building has not been surpassed. It is also the last skyscraper built in Chicago on spread foundation of steel and concrete, just as the Montauk Block was the first. Thus, building history has been made and an epoch recorded by Mr. Burnham and his coadjutors during his lifetime. The Masonic Temple is among the first buildings attributed to him of all-steel construction. ●

1902

3 Between Two Worlds: The Education of the Architect

"Our National Style of Architecture Will Be Established on Truth Not Tradition" proclaimed the title of a 1908 article in *Architectural Record* by architect J. Stewart Barney. The article is a vitriolic diatribe against the French national school of art and architecture—the Ecole des Beaux Arts. This was no isolated attack; Barney had many American architects on his side. His objections were leveled against moribund ideas that he felt were neither being questioned, nor regularly put to the test by the French faculty.

> "Should we not question any theory which does not seem to be founded on reason and truth, though handed down to us by by those for whom we have the greatest respect? That a professor holding a chair in a great university clings to a theory does not necessarily demonstrate that it is correct. What are the feelings of the thoughtful student before he has been entirely subjugated, bound and fettered by traditions...?"

Clinging to outworn theories, Barney argued, only gives rise to meaningless forms—and the unfortunate desire to be fashionable. He claimed concern for an ignorant American public that he thought desperately needed to "be aroused to the fact that we are importing a commodity without considering the consequences." For their sake "...it will be necessary to show:

> "That there is a most distinct tendency to restrict the development of architecture to certain lines and traditions, which, having filled their places in the history of architecture, are no longer of any value to us except as history.

> "That the Renaissance of Italy and France is the foundation of their theories in composition and their inspiration in design.

> "That the most successful, from their standpoint, are those who have treated with most respect the teachings of the founders of the Renaissance.

> "As it has been stated before, if these evils were entirely confined to the work of the school-boy, it would be a matter of no interest to anyone, but their system of pres-

Times Building, New York City, Eidlitz & McKenzie, architects, 1903–05

entation and judgment, taken with an intense admiration for the French Renaissance, good and bad, is having a greater influence upon the architecture of America than the public realize."

Suffice it to say, there was a hue and cry over this article—no more than one would expect in a culture struggling to apply alien, time-worn vocabularies to its architecture, and whose architects until recently were mostly native trained; Richard Morris Hunt was the first American to receive his training at the Ecole des Beaux Arts between 1845 and 1853.

By the turn of the century, French architects also began being invited to instruct at American schools of architecture. Beaux Arts educated, French architect Paul Philippe Cret was persuaded by the University of Pennsylvania, to teach architecture there in 1903. Cret, particularly incensed by the chauvinism of Barney's article responded with two of his own, and contributed to a heated debate in *Architectural Record*. In his first article entitled, "The Ecole des Beaux Arts: What Its Architectural Teaching Means," Cret points out that the "[Ecole's] function is to give those who ask for it the only thing a school can give—a method of work. It makes no effort to bring people to its classes; it prints no advertisements, no circulars filled with promises. Its purpose is not to defend nor to promulgate any special theories."

When Cret came to the United States the only American architecture schools were the Massachusetts Institute of Technology (founded in 1865), Cornell University (1871), the University of Illinois (1873), Syracuse University (1873), Columbia University (1881), the University of Pennsylvania (1890), George Washington University (1893), Armour Institute of Technology (1895), Harvard University (1895), the University of Notre Dame (1898), Ohio State University (1899), and the University of California (1903).

From then, until the outbreak of World War I, just as many more were founded, but more and more Americans were going to France. What attracted them to the French system, at least in the beginning? They sought there what they wanted to eventually create in America: a well-organized curriculum, a rational design theory, and government patronage. Architects in the United States were being trained in programs that were more technically or "scientifically" oriented. William R. Ware, a student of Hunt's and the founder of the nation's first architecture school (M.I.T), complained that the profession was "in the hands of mechanics." In France one received a Fine Arts education, after all it was called the Ecole des *Beaux Arts*.

A description of the different curricula and a comparison of the philosophies of American and French schools of architecture would be too big a topic for this book; the reader is advised to look at "recommended reading" on page 291.

Just in case we think training at the Ecole des Beaux Arts was a holdover from the 19th Century, we should consider that Ely Jacques Kahn, Raymond Hood, and Ralph Walker met each other there between 1907 and 1911. George Howe was a student at the Ecole and when he returned, he studied first with Charles H. Moore at Harvard, and then with Paul Cret at the University of Pennsylvania. These "family ties" are telling, indeed.

"Wandering between two worlds, one dead,
The other powerless to be born,
With nowhere yet to rest my head,
Like these, on earth I wait forlorn"

Matthew Arnold The Grande Chartreuse *(l. 85–90), 1855.*

College of Architecture, Cornell University—The great drafting room where all classes work together in architectural design. [XXII:1 July 1907].

from:
TRAINING FOR THE PRACTICE OF ARCHITECTURE
By Charles H. Moore
*Vol. XLIX, No. 1, January 1921,
pp. 56-62.*

IN our modern methods of training for the practice of architecture, we are losing sight of the fact that architecture is an art, and not either a learned profession or an applied science; and that a proper equipment for the vocation of an architect cannot be obtained by any purely theoretic education on academic and scientific lines. Our new schools of architecture are proceeding on these lines to the exclusion of nearly every natural mode of training.

* * *

Our present system in Northern Europe and America owes its tangible beginning to the French Ecole des Beaux Arts. This school, which had been established for sculpture and painting, introduced courses of instruction in architecture early in the last century.

* * *

The system is autocratic, and the teaching is based on the principles of design of Classic antiquity and the neo-classic Renaissance, but it allows great freedom in what is considered the adaptation of these principles to modern ideas and conditions.

* * *

When, in the sixties of last century, Mr. Richard Hunt returned from a course of training in France, he opened an atelier in New York, conducted on the Beaux Arts lines. Among the students of this school was Mr. William R. Ware, who, after completing his course with Hunt, ▶

1903

Leopold Eidlitz
(1883)

Not everyone studied in France or the United States. Russell Sturgis studied at the Academy of Fine Arts in Berlin, under Leopold Eidlitz (1823–1908).

Born in Prague, Eidlitz was educated at the Polytechnic in Vienna. He immigrated to New York in 1843, and entered the office of Richard Upjohn. Later he collaborated in Albany with H.H. Richardson and Frederick Law Olmsted.

Eidlitz published THE NATURE AND FUNCTION OF ART, MORE ESPECIALLY OF ARCHITECTURE in London in 1881. It is largely felt that he was more important as a critic and theoretician than as an architect, though his book had little impact on his contemporaries; perhaps through the RECORD he had more of an influence. He wrote two articles for the magazine, the language of both being very close to his book. More important, as Montgomery Schuyler considered himself somewhat of a disciple, Eidlitz's views find their way indirectly, but forcefully into the magazine. Eidlitz's saying, "American architecture is the art of covering one thing with another thing to imitate a third thing which, if genuine, would not be desirable," could well be interpreted as the watch-word of ARCHITECTURAL RECORD.

opposite: Preliminary drawing for New York Times Building, Cyrus L.W. Eidlitz, architect, c. 1902. Cyrus is Leopold's son.

After all is said and done, the best training is of little help to the uninspired. Schuyler in *Modern Architecture* says, "Certainly, in all the essays that have been made towards the solution of this new problem, none have been less fortunate and less successful than those of academically trained architects, who have undertaken to meet a new requirement by an aggregation of academic forms, and to whom studies had not taught their own use." Less politic, Harry Desmond couldn't imagine how French-trained architects could solve American problems:

"The Parisian mode could, no doubt, maintain its native gait easily enough in dealing with problems of the sort presented by American libraries, City Halls, churches and residences. They know of all those things in France, but the skyscraper—that glory and reproach of American architecture—is a very different affair. The expectancy of the native architect as to what would happen when the French method and the American problem met, may perhaps be likened to the curiosity of a crowd of Western cowboys at the approaching attempt of an Eastern horseman to mount a bucking broncho." (page 83)

If Desmond admired anything about the Beaux Arts education it was that it inculcated in the architect "a special trained process of thought"—Cret's "method of work." However, it was only the rare individual, depending on the depth of their understanding and inspiration, who "acquired [the French Modern style] as their vernacular." Desmond felt that Ernest Flagg was just such a rare individual.

"Mr. Flagg's designs are, if one may say so, so thoroughly professional or technical, have been so obviously arrived at by a special trained process of thought, and are expressed in a manner so thoroughly grammatical and educated. His work is indubitably the work of a man who has thoroughly accepted certain, well-defined principles from which he proceeds logically. There is nothing obscure, slipshod, unformulated; no groping, no obvious experimentation. The result is work wherein everything seems definitely and purposely 'placed' and the building, as you study it, clearly 'declares itself.' One may or may not like the building, one may prefer something more structural, or something more picturesque, but there is no denying that the building before one, such as it is, has been deliberately 'done,' is organic and logical and represents a clear process of architectural thought and not a number of loose reminiscences forced together in some way onto paper. And there is something very admirable, and let us add, very French, in this clearness. There is very little work in this country that is so architectural or will stand so well technical analysis as Mr. Flagg's." ["The Works of Ernest Flagg," XI:3 Apr 1902 pp 1–104]

The principles of a Beaux Arts education could certainly be applied, Desmond thought, to the rational problems of the skyscraper, but only in the hands of an architect with this kind of insight into the logic of the problems:

"...Mr. [Ernest] Flagg is one of our notable "Beaux Artists." His activity and indubitable ability have been centered in the effort to import into this country the forms and ideas of current French architecture. Of importers of French modes, we perhaps have enough; but Mr. Flagg's distinction is that he has a clear insight into and a real appreciation of the French mental process of dealing with things architectural, its lucidity and directness. The French forms to which he has hitherto been addicted may perhaps be regarded more as an accident of his French training than as the choice of a reasoned and thoroughly worked-out preference; at any rate, once the problem of the skyscraper was placed before him, he sought its solution directly on logical instead of traditional lines, relying rather upon the "principles" inculcated at the Ecole than upon any established set of patterns." (page 89) ■

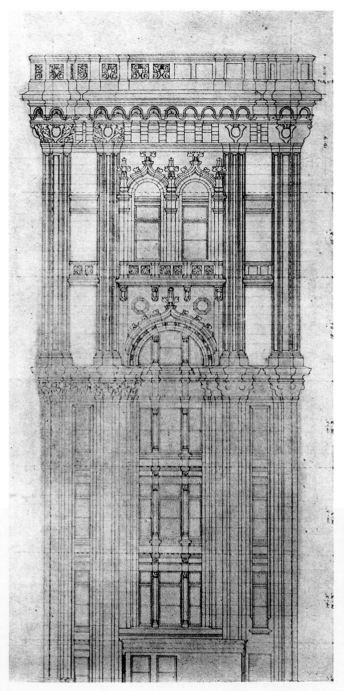

and spending a short time in Europe, was appointed professor of architecture in the Boston Institute of Technology—where he organized, if I am not mistaken, the first professional school of architecture in America. Mr. Ware was a man of scientific bent, and he naturally emphasized the scientific side of the curriculum.

* * *

The courses are substantially the same in all the schools, and consist of lectures on design, on the mathematics of construction, on perspective, on shades and shadows, on stereotomy, and on the history of architectural styles. The practical exercises are in mechanical drawing and designing, and in free-hand drawing, with some practice in modeling. A large amount of time is given to work with the ruling pen, and to elaborate shading of orthographic projections. It will be seen that, save for the free-hand drawing and modelling, the course is mainly theoretical, scientific, and mechanical.

This is no proper training for the practice of architecture—as the history of the art shows. We forget that no architect of the great ages of architectural design had any knowledge of the science of building in the modern sense. Design and construction in architecture are governed by tradition, imagination, artistic aptitude, and practical experience, more than by science, or by any such knowledge as the collegiate schools impart.

The trouble with the schools is, among other things, that by the incorporation in the educational schemes, of engineering science, of the kind required in the modern use of iron, the calling of the architect is confused with that of the mechanical engineer.

In masonry construction, mechanical engineering has no proper part; for in architectural masonry, the eye has to be satisfied; and in order to satisfy the eye, more than the bare needs of stability are required in construction. In architecture these needs cannot, in fact, be exactly determined. To calculate stresses and strains in stone masonry, with mathematical precision, is both unnecessary and impossible. The architect's ability to secure stability comes primarily of that constructive sense which is the first natural qualification for the vocation of an architect. The requisite knowledge of the strength of materials and their proper forms and adjustments, is acquired by observation and experiment, not by scientific theory. The present school system ignores this, and provides no proper exercise of those constructive and artistic faculties on which the right practice of architecture depends. It should, indeed, be obvious that such exercise cannot, in the nature of things, be provided in academic and scientific schools.

* * *

To awaken and discipline the sense of this beauty, there is no means so good as that of drawing from nature itself—an exercise that ought to be constant in the training of an architect....The benefits of drawing are not limited to what concerns the carved ornamentation of buildings; they extend to everything that the architect has to do. The sense of proportion and all the amenities of the art are dependent on the training of mind and eye that drawing tends to give. * * * ●

1903

**Times Building,
New York City,
Eidlitz & McKenzie,
architects,
1903-05**

Pictured under construction
c. 1904, the tower's heavy
steel frame of box columns
and girder beams is com-
plete up to the 17th floor
and the stone cladding is in
place in sections. The triangular lot is very similar to
that of the flatiron building
(photo page 64).

The article, which predates
the commencement of con-
struction, is solely illustrated
with drawings by the architect, Cyrus L.W. Eidlitz.

*"The benefits of drawing
are not limited to what concerns the carved ornamen-
tation of buildings; they
extend to everything that
the architect has to do. The
sense of proportion and all
the amenities of the art are
dependent on the training
of mind and eye that drawing tends to give."*
—Charles H. Moore
[XLIX:3 Jan 1921 p 60]

opposite: In the postcard
circa 1930, the Times
Building is easily recognized
to the left in what is now a
more crowded Times
Square. Looming in the
upper right is the
Paramount Theater Building,
C.W. Rapp & George L.
Rapp, architects, 1926-27,
and in the lower right is the
Astor Hotel, Clinton &
Russell, architects, 1904-08.

THE EVOLUTION OF A SKYSCRAPER[1]

Montgomery Schuyler

THE architectural criticism of a layman is very apt to be warped and vitiated by his failure to make allowances for the difficulties under which the designer labors. In fact, it is almost sure to be defective on this account. To be sure, the layman may say that he does not get very much light in this respect from professional criticism, and that the architects, who ought to know about the difficulties from their experience of the same or the like, do not as a rule make the allowances when they are indulging in private in frank and free remarks about the performances of one another. It is only in the case of a purely monumental building, where the very site is chosen by the architect and he is unlimited in cost, that he does not stand in need of allowances, but is privileged "to set his own free thought before us." And of course such an opportunity as that practically never occurs. The architect's solutions of the ordinary problems of his profession are and must be "modified at every turn by circumstance and concession." Especially, one may say, is the architect of a skyscraper in need of sympathy, having to do a building which must be grimly and strictly utilitarian, to the extent of utilizing every cubic foot of habitable space, by the very same considerations as those which necessitate that it shall be monumental in its magnitude or at least in its altitude and by its necessarily aggressive conspicuousness. What the steel-framed construction tends to become, what is the practical basis of such architecture as can be evolved from it, may be seen as one watches the skeleton arising undraped, or, still better, as one looks at the back or side of a towering structure, with its mere veneer of brickwork, the back or side unregarded by the architect, who concentrates his architecture on the street front that is meant to be seen, and leaves the architecture elsewhere to take care of itself, as it of course fails to do (page 104). One sees that

the ultimate solution of the architecture of the skyscraper must be the recognition that it is a skeleton, and the expression of its articulations, with the protective envelope reduced to its lowest terms and simplest expression. In other words, the skyscraper is a frame building and not a concretion of masonry. There are almost no precedents applicable to the expression of such a structure in the whole of architectural history. The nearest approach that is furnished to a precedent is the half-timbered work of Gothic and Renaissance times in western Europe. For the most part, the historical examples are too modest in scale and too simple in composition to do more than furnish hints for the treatment of detail. But some of the loftier of the German half-timbered erections, the many storied and gabled fronts of Hildesheim or Brunswick, for example, furnish at least suggestion for the architect of the modern "half-steeled" erections. Nobody can look at one of these and at the towering steel skeletons not yet begun to be draped, without perceiving that the old house fronts come much nearer to being an expression of the most modern of constructions than most of the fronts that are applied to these. But in fact, what the architects of skyscrapers are called upon to do is to create a new architecture, an architecture which in its problems has immensely more affinities with modern engineering than with historical architecture. And this task is sprung upon them at a time when, more than at any previous time in human history, architectural education has to do exclusively with reproduction and imitation, and less than at any with invention. Honor to the very few who have tackled this gigantic task, and every allowance for their shortcomings in the fulfillment of it! Every allowance also for the far more numerous architects who have declined it, and have rested in compromises and conventions, or even have contented themselves with concealing the new construction behind such a cento of historical architecture as could be mechanically adjusted to it, without the pretence of architecturally expressing it! "Comprendre tout,

from:
*NEW YORK AS
THE AMERICAN METROPOLIS*
Herbert Croly
Vol. XIII, No.3, March 1903
pp. 193-206

...a city cannot be the metropolis of art, unless it is also a metropolis of industry, commerce and of social and intellectual activity, and in this connection the whole question of its metropolitan quality is worth raising. The majority of New Yorkers will believe the question already settled. During the past fifty years they have made incessant and noisy claims that their city was the metropolis of the United States, but they have rarely understood that the quality of being metropolitan is not merely a matter of population. To be metropolitan a city must possess other claims to superiority. Thirty or forty years ago New York headed the population lists as it does now; yet it was on close scrutiny none the less distinctly provincial; and it was provincial because its place in American industrial and social economy was not distinguished in kind from that of any other city. As the largest city in the country it was, indeed, the best existing mirror of a number of the most ▸

1 Schulyer used this title again, slightly altered, and wrote "The Evolution of the Sky-Scraper" for *Scribner's Magazine*, September 1909.

2 "To understand everything is to forgive everything."

3 The *New York Times* explained that they measured their building's "extreme height of 476 feet" from the floor of the lowest basement to the top of the flagpole. As a consequence, it would seem to top the Park Row Building by at least 85 feet. In point of fact, the Park Row Building is 65 feet taller and remained the world's tallest building until 1908.

4 A simple rectilinear grid was to be extended over all existing rights of way, agricultural holdings, hills, waterways, marshes, and houses. Broadway survived the plan, but little else was allowed to remain.

5 John Henry Muirhead (1855-1940) *America, the Land of Contrasts: A Britain's View of his American Kin* (n.d.).

6 See "Mitgating the 'Gridiron,'" on page 176.

7 In the Jefferson Market Courthouse and Jail, New York City, 1874, (above) Frederick Clarke Withers skilfully incorporated a police court, district court, and fire observatory in a structure many consider his masterpiece. A poll of 1885 considered it to be one of the "ten best buildings in America."

c'est a pardonner tout."[2] And one must see and catch the design for a skyscraper in the making really to "comprehend" the peculiar difficulties it involves.

The present writer has had the advantage of this experience in respect to Mr. Eidlitz's design for an unmistakeable skyscraper, the new building for the New York Times, the tallest skyscraper but one, it turns out, on Manhattan Island, if measured from the ground, and possibly quite the tallest if measured from the beginning of the structure, fifty-five feet below the surface.[3] This very unusual depth of excavation was required on account of the double occupation of the substructure by the tracks of the rapid transit subway, which swings through the basement twenty-two feet below ground, requiring for its own structure a head room of ten feet, which becomes elsewhere the first sub-basement, and by the room required for the presses and other mechanical departments of a modern newspaper, which had to be accommodated in a second sub-basement. It is evident how the necessity of these unusual accommodations complicated the design in the mechanical, in the engineering sense.

But they did not sensibly complicate it at all in the artistic, in the architectural sense. In that sense the problem had its unusual, its well-nigh unique advantage. It had also its corresponding disadvantages, these being, in truth, the sequels and corollaries of its advantages. "The constitution of our nature is such that we buy our blessings at a price." The advantage of the site for the new Times building is that it is one of half a dozen really available sites for tall buildings left in New York—one of the intersections, that is to say, of Broadway with an avenue. Those really astonishingly incompetent citizens, the street commissioners of 1807, who "regularly laid out" New York,[4] without doubt regarded the interruption of the rectangularity, so dear to their narrow souls, which was occasioned by the fact that the property holdings of the diagonal Broadway, or Bloomingdale Road, were too important to be disregarded, as the chief drawback to

their scheme of a "model city" from the New York point of view of 1807, of men who had never seen a real city in their lives, even as cities went then, much less had any data on which to "posit" an ideal city. Doubtless they were most well-meaning burghers, but the extent of their ignorance of city planning was abysmal. As a matter of hard fact, to which they pretended to pay attention, the only salvation of their scheme, and that a very incomplete salvation, was the fact that Broadway was already too important to be disregarded, that they really had to make its intersections exceptions to the rule of rectangularity. Mr. Muirhead, in his delightful book, "America, the Land of Contrasts,"[5] says that the plan of Washington is a "wheel laid upon a gridiron." That is vivid. Put the plan of New York is a gridiron modified only by "force majeure." What a pity that the force was not more "majeure," that there should not have been half a dozen thoroughfares as important as Broadway to hold up those stupid devotees of the unmodified gridiron.[6] As a matter of fact, their dispositions have resulted in this, that the only exceptions in the part that they "regularly laid out" to their Procrustean rule, are these intersections with Broadway. Further down, in the region which grew as it liked and was built as it was wanted, the exceptions are more numerous. When one of them "fell among" an architect, as when the municipality wisely and fortunately chose the late F. C. Withers to fill the irregular polygon at Sixth Avenue and Tenth Street with that picturesque huddle of "Jefferson Market," the result was charming, and made Manhattan to that extent a more eligible place of residence.[7] It is true I cannot recall another instance of a sympathetic treatment of one of these irregular spaces. The Herald Building,[8] which occupies one of the intersections of Broadway, waives picturesque irregularity altogether and pretends that its site is rectangular. That pretence would not have been possible if it had occupied the southern instead of one of the northern trapezoids accruing from the intersection.

The trapezoids, be they northerly or southerly, offer the advantage of a detached site of fair if not of ample area, upon which a building can be set so as to be seen on all sides, and to be seen "all at once," so to speak, enabling the designer, according to his ability, to produce the building "in the round," and not as elsewhere a mere front or at most two fronts at right angles to each other. This is already a considerable architectural opportunity. The drawbacks of it are inherent in its existence, and these are the irregularity of the resulting solid, and the difficulty of securing either formal symmetry on either side of any axis which can be run, or, on the other hand, of securing such a general balance, such a subordination and such a culmination as shall make the spectator forgive and even acclaim the want of formal symmetry. Of course this task becomes more difficult to meet in proportion as the utilitarian demand is more urgent for the utilization of every cubic foot included within the limited periphery of the building. It becomes impossible to meet when it goes the length, as in the "Flatiron," which absolutely refuses to be known to fame under any more formal designation, of a demand that the building shall be built "to the limit" in every dimension. The first thought of the architect of the Times building, his architectural datum, was that this treatment should not be repeated in it, and that the lot should not be built upon at all points to the same height. He had the additional advantage that the "institution" he was to house, the newspaper, might be regarded as a monumental superposition on a purely commercial structure, and not only enabled but demanded a differentiation. At this stage the project contemplated only about two-thirds in length of the plot subsequently acquired, the "Pabst

Hotel"[9] still occupying the broader end of the trapezoid, of which the base was not much more than half that of the "Flatiron." As some compensation, this site was a trapezoid, while that at Twenty-third Street was a triangle. A truncation of twenty feet effected this conversion and enabled something to be done with its face, which in the "Flatiron" is not a face, but only an edge, an "arris."[10] With these data the designer produced his first sketch, which I think will be admitted to be a particularly picturesque and attractive project. While he did not see his way to treating this edifice as a frame building and assumed the convention, which is in fact the current and agreed fiction, that it was a building of masonry, with all that that implies, such as setting it on an apparently massive basement of masonry, yet he did see his way to attenuating the piers of the superstructure into buttresses, with a

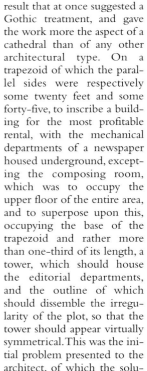

result that at once suggested a Gothic treatment, and gave the work more the aspect of a cathedral than of any other architectural type. On a trapezoid of which the parallel sides were respectively some twenty feet and some forty-five, to inscribe a building for the most profitable rental, with the mechanical departments of a newspaper housed underground, excepting the composing room, which was to occupy the upper floor of the entire area, and to superpose upon this, occupying the base of the trapezoid and rather more than one-third of its length, a tower, which should house the editorial departments, and the outline of which should dissemble the irregularity of the plot, so that the tower should appear virtually symmetrical. This was the initial problem presented to the architect, of which the solu-

1903

8 The Herald Building, New York City, McKim, Mead and White, architects, 1893. At the extreme left is R.H. Macy & Company.

9 Pabst Hotel, New York City, Henry Kilburn and Otto Strack, architects, 1899.

10 *Arris*: a sharp edge produced by the meeting of two surfaces.

11 The quick preliminary sketch is reproduced opposite.

12 The octagonal cupola, seen in the final design on page 80, was never realized in construction.

13 Schuyler uses the plural "lisene," when he means "lisena," a pilaster, or shallow column, which projects only slightly from a wall. The features he describes are best seen in the photo on page 70.

tion was his first sketch, produced in a few hours.[11] The striking picturesqueness of the result was attained not only without doing violence to any of the conditions, but by a strict adherence to them. They were, in fact, the basis of the design. The triple division of the long side proceeded naturally and almost inevitably from the setting off of the most suitable and available space for the base of the tower, and this space became the unit of a division, the span of a "bay." The treatment of the truncation as a single bay thereupon distinctly "imposed" itself and the arching of the large openings that constitute and denote the bay and emphasize the division, could happily be introduced without at all compromising the practicability of the design as that of an office building erected for the most profitable return. For the slight darkening of the stories upon which the arches open does not entail the least inconvenience in a structure so abundantly illuminated, by reason of its detachment. The triple division, vertically, followed, or rather, attended the triple division laterally. Always assuming that the walls are real walls which carry themselves, this vertical division is logical as well as harmonious and artistic, a solid basement of three stories, a middle division of six, itself subdivided into four arched stories and two lintelled, with very good effect when taken in connection with what is below and what above, and an attic of a single story bristling with Gothic pinnacles. Then the crowning member of which the pinnacled angle piers help to dissemble the irregularity of the plan, a result to which the octagonal cupola still more powerfully contributes.[12] Al-together a picturesque and unique skyscraper, distinguished by the lack of the gaunt attenuation which almost inevitably belongs to the extreme commercial skyscraper.

This germinal idea of the building remains and is traceable in the finished design. It was in endeavoring to realize the idea that the designer's troubles began. In the first place, came the requirement that the substructure, the office building for rental, should be raised to the highest rent

paying power, and this limit, what between the probable demand and the difficulties of construction, particularly of wind bracing, on so narrow a base and with so enormous an altitude (430 feet from the foundations, as it has been settled) was set at fifteen stories, exclusive of the attic, which is allotted to the composing room. Doubtless the original limitation to ten stories for the building covering the entire plot was more conducive to graceful and harmonious architecture. The vertical extension eliminated at once the arched openings which were the chief feature of the middle division in the original sketch. The elongation required to make them as conspicuous a feature in a sixteen-story building as they had been in one of ten would have been quite intolerable. There was nothing for it (at least after much experimentation there appeared to be nothing) but to relegate the arcade to the top of the structure, and to conform the span of its bay to the division enforced below by a combined consideration of the exigencies of the structure and the convenience of tenants. With the lengthening of the building made possible by the acquisition of the base of the trapezoid, there accrue four bays in the main structure as against two, with, of course, a corresponding diminution of the effect of each as a feature of the middle wall.

For the same reason, the great arch of the northern narrow front became impossible. The only thing to do was to revert to the conventional treatment of the middle, the shaft, laying no stress upon its openings but simply coupling them between the strips, which in the Italian Romanesque would have been called the "lisenes,"[13] which correspond and indicate the steel framing of the structure. On the northern face, which it was so desirable to keep as solid as possible, the recourse, when the grandiose feature of the single tall arch became impracticable, was to a single plain opening in each story, flanked by the broadest and plainest piers possible in the dimension. Above, in the arcade, by a projection over each supporting "lisene" springing from a corbelled column, and by a subsequent recession from the new plane thus gained, it became possible to give the crowning arcade an effective depth of jamb, and to emphasize this by modeling. The general effect thus perforce becomes, after a start from so different a motive, that which so many skyscrapers exemplify, and which is so successfully done in the

Broadway Chambers (photo page 68) as to make that building in that respect as in some others typical and apparently prototypical. Without the tower, indeed, the Times building would be simply a highly respectable skyscraper of that type, with the addition, which commends itself as an improvement, of the attic which was fortunately indicated and required by the peculiar purpose of the building, and the necessity of providing a tall story, of the maximum area within the site, for the printers.

But all this is comparatively easy and obvious, although, like all successful solutions, it is much more obvious after it has been done than before. The tower was the crux of the whole problem. The first notion naturally was to use this feature so as to dissemble the irregularity of the site, and to do this by reducing it to a parallelopiped, with its central axis the true, or rather the apparent axis of the building, emphasizing this by a steep roof, of which the ridge should denote the axis. The cupola was early abandoned as impracticable for a commercial building. I wish I could show you some of the interminable series of studies that were undertaken to center and to symmetrize this tower, by cutting away, for example, one side of the trapezoid and trimming it down to a rectangle, reducing the pruning to a minimum by restoring, in the form of bays, some of the space that had been retrenched. I am permitted to show one, exhibiting the effect of the Southern front, crowned with a steeply hooded roof, and indicating at the right the excisions that had to be made on the Broadway front on behalf of axiality and symmetry. It is plain how this complicates and difficilitates the construction. This practical difficulty involves an architectural consideration. For to comply with it would be to confuse the spectator's perception that this is in fact a frame building of which the uprights are continuous, and must be, from foundation to roof, and would imply, even to the eye, some awkward structural makeshift, and in all these experiments at fitting a symmetrical top to an unsymmetrical substructure, it was found that, to the eye,

much filled with the offices of corporations, which conduct a business in other parts of the country, as Fifth Avenue is filled with the residences of capitalists who made their money in the West. New York is steadily attracting a large proportion of the best business ability of the country, not only as a matter of business convenience, but quite as much because of the exceptional opportunity it offers to its favored inhabitants of making and spending money.

* * *

The natural heroes of the American are not artists or men of letters: they are politicians and millionaires. The appreciation which the artist, the writer or the thinker receives is chiefly from his own set; and this fact narrows the social basis of disinterested intellectual work. The effect is worse for society than it is for the artist or the thinker; but it is bad for the artist and writer in that it throws them back too much on merely technical or literary or academic motives and disqualifies them for a sufficiently positive and formative influence. The remedy would not or should not come too much from the direct mixture of artists and men of letters in society but rather from the increasing authority of a class of men whose peculiar office it is to mediate between the two. Yet these men, who for lack of a better description may be called critics, can never obtain the authority they ought to exercise, until the popular ideals and traditions have been, in many respects, radically changed.

Insignificant, however, as is the standing of artists and men of letters in vast and quick procession of American life, New York is undoubtedly becoming the centre of an ever-increasing quantity of intellectual work. That city is proving to be quite as attractive to writers and painters as to ▶

1903

14 Many features of the design resemble that of the Campanile of the Cathedral of Florence, Italy, begun by Giotto in 1334 and completed by Francesco Talenti in the 1350s. Here and in a later article (page 184) Schuyler mentions that Cyrus Eidlitz was consciously inspired by this world-famous icon when designing the Times Building.
  The above photo appeared as a full page illustration in *Sturgis' Illustrated Dictionary of Architecture and Building*, 1901–02.

15 New York Produce Exchange, New York City, George B. Post, architect, 1881-41 (demolished).

16 James Fergusson (1808-1886), a Scottish writer on archaeology and architecture whose comprehensive *History of Architecture in All Countries from the Earliest Times to the Present Day* (1867-1876) was the bible of late 19th Century eclecticism.

there was at least one "dead point." While the crowning feature might really come in properly and really crown the edifice from half a dozen points of view, there was sure to be one residuary and overlooked point of view from which it would look lopsided and askew.

Revolted by the results of these experiments, the architect at last threw overboard the whole scheme of which his sketches were notations, and determined to "build to the limit" and let the result take care of itself, or rather to see that it should take care of itself. It was at this juncture that the campanile of Giotto presented itself to him as a model.[14] That famous tower had already been taken for that purpose in New York, in the tower of the Produce Exchange.[15] But that agreeable erection, harmonious in form and proportion and effective in color as it is, and having only the drawback of standing behind the edifice it signalizes, and up an alley, is purely momumental and has no utilitarian exigencies to consider, such as could not be gotten away from in the design of an office building of which every cubic foot must be made practically available. Moreover, that peculiarity of the campanile which does not reappear in the Produce Exchange at all is the very thing which commended it, and almost imposed it, for the present purpose. In his praise of the original Fergusson[16] says: "The octagonal projections at the angles give it considerable relief." For the present purpose they do much more. They indicate a means whereby, through emphasizing and exaggerating them, the irregularity of a trapezoidal tower may be so dissembled that it is reduced virtually to a rectangle without the use of the awkward makeshifts which had been found after all ineffectual. By projecting still more boldly than in the arcade beneath and in turn receding still more deeply, an effect of massiveness, a sense of relief, a play of light and shade are secured which are not only grateful in themselves, but which really and effectively emphasize the framed construction which they reveal while concealing. In all architecture there is a permissible and

artistic exaggeration. The depth of reveal which attracts us in a mass of masonry is very seldom attainable, on the engineering principle of "the least material that will do the work." And, while the framing indicated in this tower is doubtless much more massive than the actual necessities of the case prescribed, the sense of framed construction is more emphatically given in the tower than in the substructure. And it will be observed that the treatment is strictly "practical." There is no sacrifice of room, of light, of any utilitarian consideration. How far the devices of the architect have been successful in their primary purpose of dissembling the

irregularity of the tower it remains for actual execution to show. So far as drawings can show, it may seem to promise a complete success.

To me the most admirable point of design in the projected building is the success with which the huge and lofty tower is at once incorporated in the substructure and detached from it, "belonging" everywhere. It is prefigured in the very base, and in the fenestration of the "shaft," asserts itself more strongly in the "capital," by means of the single three-story opening corresponding in its treatment to the openings of the main arcade and yet differentiated from them with emphasis by the flanking pilasters and the bounding piers kept down to the utmost plainness, until finally, above the cleverly treated feature which at once continues the attic of the lower building and becomes the base of the tower, the monument works itself entirely free of the former conjunction and goes climbing on its way to its dizzy culmination.

Evidently the Times Building is a valuable addition to our short list of artistic skyscrapers, in spite of the failure which has already perhaps been sufficiently dwelt upon, and which it shares with almost all of them, the failure to found the architecture at all points upon the facts of the case. To do that with complete success would be triumphantly to solve the problem of the skyscraper. That it remains to be done does not detract from the interest and value of the partial and tentative solutions propounded by artistic architects. As skyscrapers go, and even as they very exceptionally go, the Times building promises to be worthy of its site, of its conspicuousness and of its isolation. To the writer it has been very interesting to trace the evolution of the design of a typical tall building from the first dream of the architect confronted with a rare opportunity to the finished drawing for what seems so much like a contradiction in terms as a "practical monument." He can only hope that his readers will at least partly partake this interest. ■

millionaires and their families. The authors of American books, except those who are fastened to some particular locality by academic work, are coming to pass more and more of their time in New York; for even when they actually live somewhere else, which is frequent enough, the necessities of their trade take them continually to that city. And if the foregoing is true of the men of letters, it is even more true of the artists. The painter or sculptor is, as a rule, freer to live in the place that pleases him and benefits his work than is the writer, for he has usually been trained by some years of study abroad, and so has become emancipated, both inside and out, from local ties. So that the more eminent American artists, so far as they live in the cities at all, tend strongly to live in or near New York. Boston has almost ceased to be, not only a literary but an art centre. Chicago has no manifest destiny to become either. The good exhibitions in other cities are supplied by pictures of New York painters; and while there are the local art schools all over busily training young painters and sculptors, there seems to be some necessary connection, for these voting people, between knowing their business and leaving their homes.

In the case of the men of letters, this drift is only partly due to the fact that the most important publishing houses are, with a few notable exceptions, situated in New York, and the most important magazines are edited from the same place. Such advantages are undoubtedly extremely influential in attracting the voting writers, who are foot-free, and are seeking the largest and the quickest market for their literary wares. But men of letters have other and better reasons for fastening to New York. They can find in that city more than any other place in the country saltitary and whole clothes and take their pleasures in the city, which in a sense is coming to be the American social metropolis.

In a sense New York is the social metropolis, but in what sense? If in no other sense than as the department store and the playground of people who have more money than they need, then the fact need interest nobody except the keepers of shops and hotels. The metropolis of a great country should, as I have already pointed out, do something to anticipate, to clarify and to realize the best national ideals in politics, society, literature and art. Is New York besides being the metropolis of the rich business man and his wife, is it also the metropolis in any better and deeper sense?

* * *

*That the body of New York life is big with important issues and events, and is somehow suggestive and provocative of a large literary treatment may be admitted, but the large literary treatment will not come in the absence of formative and invigorating intellectual conditions. The stimulus to great works of the imagination derives, not so much from the material offered by life, which always possesses dramatic and salient features, as from the mental attitude of certain gifted and trained people toward that material—an attitude that is formed chiefly by the sweep, intensity, coherence and momentum of the ideas which are currently applied to life. It cannot be said that uneasy and possessing ideas of this kind are at present keeping New York men of letters awake o'nights, but since New York is the most national of American cities, and since the culture basis of a modern literature or art is not municipal, or provincial, but necessarily national, New York is the one American city in which something considerable may happen. At the present moment there is negative if not positive ground for encouragement in that the intellectual ideals of New Yorkers are at least normal and sane. They are holding a proper balance between over-refinement on the one hand and crudity on the other; and, consequently, if they are ever touched by little originality and energy they should not go.   * * *   ●*

Blair Building, New York City, Carrère & Hastings, architects, 1902 (demolished).

Claude Bragdon says of the architects:

"Messrs. Carrère & Hastings' Blair Building if not quite the tallest, is yet the finest flower which has sprung skyward out of the Beaux Arts hotbed. If the so various fruits of this particular training were of a corresponding excellence the value of that training could scarcely be the subject of debate that it is now, for here is living evidence of a mind emancipated by it and not enslaved...If Mr. Sullivan—that militant Goth—had not armed the critical sense with his Excaliber of a formula that form should (everywhere and in all things) follow function, that sense might be tempted to capitulate in the presence of so much excellence, without further ado." (page 159)

To left of the Blair Building is the Johnston Building; to the right is the Commercial Cable Building, Harding & Gooch, architects, 1896–97 (demolished). To the far right, the New York Stock Exchange, by George B. Post, re-opened April 23, 1903.

A BEAUX-ARTS SKYSCRAPER— THE BLAIR BUILDING, NEW YORK CITY

Henry W. Desmond

SINCE the day when the importation of the so-called Beaux Arts influence was first "declared" there has existed among the more strictly "domestic" architects a snickering curiosity to see how the alien tradition and method would fare when brought into working relation with the American office skyscraper. The Parisian mode could, no doubt, maintain its native gait easily enough in dealing with problems of the sort presented by American libraries, City Halls, churches and residences. They know of all those things in France, but the skyscraper— that glory and reproach of American architecture—is a very different affair. The expectancy of the native architect as to what would happen when the French method and the American problem met, may perhaps be likened to the curiosity of a crowd of Western cowboys at the approaching attempt of an Eastern horseman to mount a bucking broncho.

The performance has been extraordinarily tardy in commencing. Acres of "Beaux Arts" residences, much of the work lacking everything deserving the title of Beaux Arts, have been built, and acres of buildings of a more public character including tall hotel and apartment houses, but with the solitary exception of the Singer Building[1] on the corner of Broadway and Liberty street, New York City (and that isn't an exception: as an Irishman would say, being of only ten stories), no office skyscraper has been erected by any one of our architects especially identified with the Beaux Arts movement until the Blair Building, the subject of these remarks, was undertaken. It may be objected, we know, by purists in such matters that the firm of architects[2] responsible for the Blair Building is not to-day strictly what the politician would call "regular." Experience and good sense have led the firm to depart somewhat from the pure tradition. The members of it are no longer *primitifs*, nor are

their designs as distinctly dated from Paris as is the case with the work of some of their younger confreres But, if for this reason the Blair Building is less valid as an illustration of what the unadulterated French tradition would make of our sky-scrapers, it is, on the other hand, more valuable as a demonstration of what might be derived from seasoned French training if called upon for a solution of the only really capital modern problem of design—that of finding a suitable clothing for the steel or skeleton system of construction.

Turning, then, to the Blair Building in this spirit of discovery, the very first fact that strikes the observer is that here, as in so many other attempted solutions, the architects have avoided if not disregarded, the fundamental problem. Such design as the building exhibits is an architectural expression at the surface only. It does not penetrate the plane of the enclosing walls. Structure and architecture remain unrelated facts. The rationalist, we fear, will be disappointed. He does not concede to the architect any right to the joy of pure design. Rather his theory is:

> When joy and duty clash
> Joy must go to smash.

Yet upon a closer study of the Blair Building, even the rationalist, we think, will find that the architects in abandoning the rationalistic method of treatment have taken that deliberate step in so rationalistic a manner that the design unmistakably discloses, if it does not indeed assert, the structural facts. Moreover, although the steel construction of the building is not openly confessed in the architecture, the architecture, at least, does not commit the double sin of simulating solid masonry construction, thus giving expression to a set of totally irrelevant facts. Indeed, one cannot be wrong in saying that the truthful manner in which the architects have avoided the real problem, with which they had to deal, gives the Blair Building something of the value of a *tour de force*, and in conjunction with its other excellencies of detail, places it among the very few highly successful skyscrapers that have been erected

from:
ARCHITECTURE IN THE UNITED STATES I: The Birth of Taste
By Claude Bragdon
Vol. XXV, No. 6, June 1909, pp. 426-434.

The preoccupation of the Chicago architects with the practical and economic aspects of the tall office building to the general exclusion of the aesthetic, had the odd effect of rendering their early essays in that field superior, as a general thing, to those of about the same period in New York. The latter show ornament for the most part misapplied, and an aesthetic preoccupation misdirected. Mr. Root's old Monadnock building, for example, is better architecture than Messrs. Carrère and Hastings' Mail and Express Building, though they stand at opposite extremes in the matter of cost and embellishment. The last-mentioned architects showed later, in their altogether admirable Blair Building, that they had learned from Mr. Sullivan or elsewhere their lesson." ●

from:
THE WORK OF MESSRS. CARRERE & HASTINGS
Vol. XXVII, No. 1, January 1910, pp. 1-120

No doubt American architecture would advance much more rapidly in case the great majority of American architects would accept the authority of one specific style, because in that case their individual experiments would be mutually corroborative and stimulating; and variations, when they intruded, would have to be justified by their real meaning and importance. But this is a counsel of perfection. Americans have a deeply rooted habit of associating individuality with arbitrary personal preferences; and particularly in their relations with the builders of private houses, architects have ▶

1 Singer Building, New York City,
Ernest Flagg, architect, 1908
(photo page 154).

2 Carrère and Hastings, is the
"Beaux Arts" firm in question.
The architects curiously remain
anonymous in this article and the
next.
  John Merven Carrère (1860-
1929) was born of French parents
in Rio de Janeiro and studied in
Switzerland and at the *Ecole des
Beaux Arts*, Paris, where he met
his future partner, Thomas
Hastings (1860-1929). They
formed a partnership in 1886.

opposite: Life Building, New York
City, Carrère & Hastings, 1893
(demolished).

top: Upper stories with cornice;
above: Lower level and entrance,
Blair Building, New York City.

so far.

The reader should turn for a moment to our illustration (page 82), the view looking northward up Broad Street. The standpoint chosen by the photographer was deliberately selected. It does not do justice to the building itself, but the comparisons afforded by the other buildings in the picture will make it easier to perceive both the veracities and the excellencies of the new structure.

For instance, the problems that confronted the designer of the Johnston Building (the building at the extreme left of our illustration), were precisely those that confronted the designers of the Blair Building. In the result, so far as both edifices are concerned, there is only the barest external indication of the steel cage. In the Johnston Building, however, patterned after the common formula of current architectural practice, the design boldly declares the building to be of solid masonry construction. In well-nigh every detail it insists upon this—convention. The extremely heavy basement, the solid-appearing rock-faced piers with their deep reveals, the strong horizontal courses of stone at each third story, the massive cornice—all of these are not merely a front, but an effrontery to the true facts. In comparison, its neighbor, the Blair Building, affords a contrast of a valuable type. Here we find the stone envelope covering the steel cage kept, if we may say so, as close to the surface as possible, so that its veneer-like character is hardly to be overlooked by anyone. The very material selected—marble—and its unaltered use throughout the entire facade emphasizes this face. The evident basement is given a purely architectural as distinct from a strictly structural character. The architects have apparently taken the utmost pains to assure the beholder that he is here dealing entirely with facts of design, not with verities of structure. Even some of the lean steel columns are permitted, as it were, to peer forth through the design as a whole, reveal themselves through the facade, as in the case of the two central stone piers, absolutely flat and smooth without a trace of functional ornament, carried through nine stories. Moreover, that immensely clever third story not only assists the design splen-

didly, but acts admirably in relieving the basement from any suspicion of structural significance. The piers do not rest on the basement, and the treatment of this intermediate floor serves, as it were, to remove from the substructure the slightest idea of the superposition of structural weight.

We are dealing with excellencies of the same order when we turn to the iron balcony, placed with excellent judgment above the thirteenth story, assuming there the function of crown or cornice of the building, when the building is seen from the opposite side of Broad street. From that point, the fourteenth and fifteenth stories are invisible, and the uppermost story shows merely as an attic. A heavy stone cornice would have interjected into the design one of those very falsities which are so very prominent in the Johnston Building. And yet the iron balcony, with its iron brackets, its ample projection, its lightness, its stone panels on the under side ornamented with iron rosettes, terminates the building in a most successful manner not to be imagined from the picture we present.

Something might be said regarding the smaller details of the design, the pleasing proportions, (speaking always within the limitations of the skyscraper), the clear manner in which the banking offices of Blair & Company have been accentuated on the second story, the admirable iron work, here treated in a thoroughly idiomatic manner, and the skilfulness with which the different items of design have been co-ordinated and wrought into a harmonious and consistent architectural design. These will repay scrutiny.   But we prefer for the moment to concentrate attention on the larger fact—on the good qualities of the general scheme of design, on its originality as a method of treating the problem of the skyscraper and on its brilliant success in the Blair Building. If, from the point of view of design, the skyscraper still awaits its creator, if we must for the time being be content in our tall buildings with a denial, or at least a concealment, of the facts of structure, clearly, en attendant, the architects of the Blair Building have shown us a safe intermediate path to follow. ■

to consult personal preferences in the matter of style other than their own.

For the present, American architects will do as much as can be expected of them, in case they will only remain true to the Renaissance, and not allow an intelligent eclecticism to become equivalent to hopeless confusion and anarchy. For the present the platform of the Renaissance should be broad enough to include the largest and best part of American architectural practice, while, at the same time, narrow enough to shut out meaningless and sterile Protestantism.

* * *

The situation which in general confronts the American architectural profession may then be described as follows. Its practitioners should agree, for the most part, to continue the work of establishing an authoritative convention of Renaissance architectural forms in this country, because by so doing they are putting a fruitful limitation upon the range of their individual architectural experimentation, and because Americans are, whether they realize it or not, children of the Renaissance intellectual revival. But in accepting the Renaissance as the source of their architectural forms, they are, as a whole, under no similar obligation to accept any one phase of the Renaissance. Individual architects will most assuredly do very much better to limit their choice to some particular substyle; but there appears to be no unimpeachable reason why they should all limit their choice to the same substyle. It is the Renaissance as a general movement to which they owe their allegiance; and the Renaissance as a general movement is in its architectural expression more a matter of a certain spirit and point of view than it is of specific forms. The Renaissance was itself a revival of Roman architecture; and Roman architecture had borrowed much from the architecture of Greece. Allegiance to the Renaissance means, consequently, more than anything a perpetuation of the spirit resident in Classic architecture—the spirit of repose, of measure without any sacrifice of vivacity, of simplification without attenuation, of style which leaves room for individuality. An architect who can attain to something of this Classic spirit will possess the touchstone, enabling him to give a beautiful and appropriate rendering to any particular set of Renaissance forms best suited to his temperament and purpose. It is just because the Renaissance constitutes our means of historical connection with the Classic ideal that it exercises a peculiar authority over every phase of modern architecture and intellectual life. * * * * ●

1903

Singer Building, New York City, Ernest Flagg, architect, 1902–04.

The "Little" Singer Building, as opposed to the Tower that was demolished in 1970, this "L" shaped structure's curtain wall is a delicate iron-work grille that seems to float in front of each façade.

The "problem," as Desmond describes it, "was to protect a steel frame, provide all the light necessary in a building devoted to strictly commercial purposes, and to let the building tell its own story as agreeably as it might."

opposite: Trinity and US Realty Buildings, New York City, Francis H. Kimball, architect, 1904-05: addition, 1906-07. The structures sit on narrow lots of 67 feet each. A tower was added to the original building, on the left (and on page 39), whose façade otherwise employs the same design.

A RATIONAL SKYSCRAPER

Henry W. Desmond

IN the December number[1] of this magazine, the designers of the new Blair Building,[2] recently completed in New York City, on the northwest corner of Broad street and Exchange place, were praised for an act of deliberate abstention from irrelevancy. In designing their facade they adopted the novel scheme of a palpable decorative screen in place of adhering to the usual semblance of a strictly masonry front. The design itself, no doubt, was managed with skill, even with consummate skill, but then, notable as the building might be from that point of view, excellence of that kind alone would hardly be sufficient to give it preeminence among all skyscrapers recently erected, for no one will say skill of composition, ability to put together on Bristol board[3] tasteful and harmonious arrangements of time-honored architectural forms is so rare with us as it was a few years ago. In literature, the "diffusion of penmanship" has been bewailed by Henry James,[4] but in architecture no one complains because draughtsmanship and "good taste"—the negative discipline—have become general commodities. No! The great deficiency does not lie in that direction! The difficulty is not to get speakers, but to find somebody who has something of import to say.

Many designers, among the number possibly the designers themselves of the very clever Blair Building will disagree with this philosophy, and with its implication that there is anything finer than good design, always meaning by that phrase, design at the surface, the putting of architectural things together—columns, arcades, mouldings and what not—"a string of epithets that improve the sound without carrying on the sense"—in an essentially pictorial way, to please the eye without reference to the reason. That, at any rate, has been the method that has ruled in the past, almost without exception, in the making of the skyscraper, and it is, in the judgment of a few, the very persistent adherence to that method by the entire profession that has vitiated all attempts to deal fundamentally (and in essence that means artistically) with the problem presented by the high building.

The "problem of the skyscraper" indeed! Who is there among our architects that has had courage, we will not say to squarely face it and strive with it, but even to seriously think about it? Is there any wonder that whenever the subject comes uppermost, at convention, or meeting, or elsewhere, among two or among a hundred, there is inevitably in a short time a shrugging of shoulders and finally a dismissal of the matter as one of the impossibilities of life—or shall we say the impertinencies of the client? Throw it out of window! That ends it! And possibly by and by it will be placed in the list of subject tabooed in good professional society like ventilation and acoustics and government architecture Perhaps our architects think as Sancho Panza[5] did, "Recommend the matter to Providence; 'twill be sure to give what is most expedient for thee."

A few have protested, not, indeed, believing that the skyscraper with its bald utilitarian purposes and its fixed 5% "project" afford: the artistic soul the highest empyrean for flight, but nevertheless convinced that Art cannot fail before any problem that may properly be assigned to its beneficence without at the same time losing its ultimate authority in human affairs, and preferring, therefore, to believe that, in the case of the skyscraper, the artist, rather than the Art, is at fault—at least believing so until the architect has applied himself to the problem with great veracity than the scene-painter's, and with more seriousness than the modiste's.

But these were the critics! They preached of function and logic, of reason, veracity and thought. What have these to do with architecture? Why! has not the aim of the architect for four hundred years been to get rid of these *incubi*,[6] to cleanse the Art of its heavier particles, and make it, as it were fit for the emasculated energy of the dilettante, or the quick purposes of the architectural shop?

And if the critics, the protestants, have

Trinity and U. S. Realty Buildings, New York City.

1 Refers to the preceeding article, "A Beaux-Arts Skyscraper—The Blair Building, New York City."

2 Carrère and Hastings, see page 183 for an article on the work of the firm.

3 Bristol board is a smooth, heavy pasteboard of fine quality.

4 Henry James, 1843-1916, American novelist and critic.

5 Don Quixote's companion.

6 *Incubi:* nightmares.

March
1904

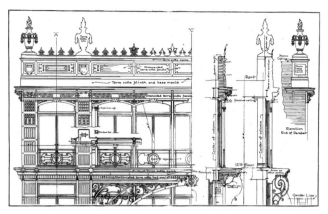

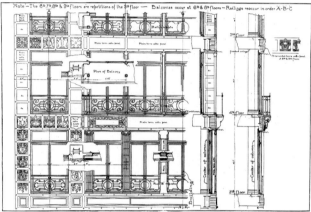

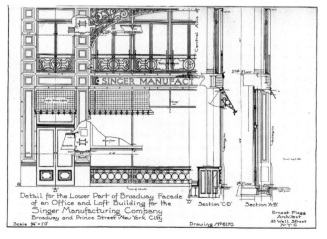

Detail for the Lower Part of Broadway Facade
of an Office and Loft Building for the
Singer Manufacturing Company
Broadway and Prince Street, New York City
Scale ¾"=1'0"

Drawing N° 6170.

Ernest Flagg
Architect
35 Wall Street
N.Y.C.

been few, how much smaller, alas! is the band of those who have labored at the high building problem with any sincerity of soul, sad or otherwise? So far as the skeleton building is concerned, Louis Sullivan is per-haps the only architect of marked ability who has addressed him-self deliberately and sincerely to the discovery of an adequate expression in architectural terms for the metallic frame. The Prudential Building (photo page 212) in Buffalo, N. Y., the Wainwright Building in St. Louis (photo page 210), and the Bayard Building (photo page 61) on Bleecker street, New York City, are the most conspicuous results of his high-ly personal and thoroughly intelligent effort. If we are restrained by a sense of prose from the poetics of one of Mr. Sullivan's ardent admirers regarding the Bayard Building: "Rising thus cream-white, maidenlike and slender, luxuriant in life and joyous as the dawn of wistful spring, this poem of the modern world will ever daily hail the sun on high and the plodder below with its cease-less song of hope, of joy, of the noble labor of man's hands, of the vast dignity and power of men's souls—a song of true democracy and its goal;"[7] we are sure the judgment of the judicious is that Mr. Sullivan's work is very much superior in originality and force to any other productions of the same class. If the lyrics of his admirer are slightly too per-fervid for the case, we trust they will at least faintly indicate the celebration that attends the successful solver of the problem of the skyscraper.

It may well be understood, therefore, that it is not the mere superficial design of the Blair Building, referred to at the outset of these remarks, extremely skilful though that design is, that called primarily for attention. The greater significance of that building lies in the fact that it announces, or at any rate, seems to announce, that one of our highest authorities in architectural practice, a firm particularly addicted to the "school"[8] and the "traditions" have either by a deliberate concession to architectural veracity or from an effort to reduce architecture to a more direct expression—a "lower term," as the mathematicians say—of "pure design," contributed an important step to the task of bringing the tall building back to reason, to the logic of its own facts and functions. For, so long as the steel skeleton building simulates masonry, imitates a construction of strongly differentiated structural parts, progress beyond the limits of draughtsmanship and the copy-books is a sheer impossibility. It is, therefore, a great gain, as in the Blair Building, to get rid, and, moreover, to get rid with conspicuous success, of the masonry fiction. We may be confident that so notable a piece of work so generally acclaimed is bound to be a hint to others, and bring forth imitators, traducers even, and, may be, improvers. And once let us get set up in front of our skyscrapers frank facades, mere decorative front walls that neither express nor conceal the facts of structure, simulate nothing (but a real Art!) and what more natural and easy further step can be taken than to turn up one's artistic shirt-sleeves at last and buckle down to the hard work of making our tall buildings really say, or as Montgomery Schuyler said, sing something veracious about themselves?

And curiously, more than curiously, fortunately, as though to remove this anticipation of ours from the reproach of prophesy, the Blair Building was scarcely finished before the outer walls of a far more revolutionary structure arose to attract attention and, as it were, fulfill the promise of its predecessor, almost its contemporary.

We refer to the Singer Building, situated at Nos. 561 and 563 Broadway, New York City, with a front adjacent on Prince street. Ernest Flagg,[9] the architect of the New Naval Academy at Annapolis, is the designer; and here, again, we are called upon to note the curious and possibly significant fact that it is out of Nazareth that good cometh Mr. Flagg is one of our notable "Beaux Artists." His activity and indubitable ability have been centered in the effort to import into this country the forms and ideas of current French architecture. Of importers of French modes, we perhaps have enough; but Mr. Flagg's distinction is that he has a clear

insight into and a real appreciation of the French mental process of dealing with things architectural, its lucidity and directness. The French forms to which he has hitherto been addicted may perhaps be regarded more as an accident of his French training than as the choice of a reasoned and thoroughly worked-out preference; at any rate, once the problem of the skyscraper was placed before him, he sought its solution directly on logical instead of traditional lines, relying rather upon the "principles" inculcated at the Ecole than upon any established set of patterns. For, in a sense, this Singer Building is Mr. Flagg's first skyscraper. The other Singer Building, lower down on Broadway, for which also he is responsible, is only ten stories high, and, moreover, it is, we believe, of real masonry construction. A story, we remember, was circulated at the time when this building was planned, to the effect that Mr. Flagg was under the bond of a vow, registered somewhere that he would never "commit" a real skyscraper. Ten stories were his limit. Possibly he regarded the crime of designing a tall office building as one impossible to commit with artistic impunity. Certainly he was able to figure out to his own satisfaction that buildings higher than ten stories did not pay financially—they required protection as to light and air by the purchase of abutting property—that is, they became unremunerative as soon as every other pirate of air and sunlight committed similar excesses. It is true, the Bourne Building[10] followed the Singer Building, adjacent to it, and this was carried up many stories beyond the limit of ten. But who can be consistent in a world composed of clients? The skyscraper problem would not "down" even in Mr. Flagg's office. We are afraid it will not be disposed of anywhere until it has either been solved artistically by the architect, or until its very existence has been legally banished by a more sensitive public sense of civic decency.

But if the architect cannot dispense with the skyscraper, the next best thing for him to do is really to grapple with it. Mr. Sullivan pursued that course with success, although

AN EXPERIMENT IN COLOR: THE "WHITEHALL" BUILDING
Russell Sturgis
Vol. XIV, No. 1, July 1903, pp. 70-73.

THE new business building called "Whitehall" which, however, is not built upon a plot facing Whitehall Street, but is of Battery Place, invites notice. It is a perfectly utilitarian building, built inexpensively, without elaborate decorative treatment, without sculpture, without much breaking up whether of sky-line or of plan. In short, it is such an office building as an economical owner of real estate would wish to erect, that his rents might begin to come in speedily and might be as great as reasonably possible in proportion to the amount of investment. The illustration shows how simple a skyscraper it is. Up to the top of the architectural basement, which corresponds to six stories of the interior, besides the half-underground basement-story, the walls are faced outside with grey limestone; above that line, they are everywhere of brick, except as the lines of the cornice and other string-courses cut them. The main front, about two hundred feet wide, faces very nearly south and occupies the whole space between West Street and Washington Street, and on either of these streets, the return, ▸

Front of the "Little" Singer Building under construction.

7 Reference Unknown.

8 Ecole des Beaux Arts.

9 Ernest Flagg (1857-1947), American architect, studied at the École des Beaux-Arts, Paris. The 45-story Singer Building in New York City, became the tallest building in the world in 1908. Flagg's other works include the Scribner Building, New York City, the Corcoran Gallery of Art, Washington, D.C., and numerous residences.

10 Flagg designed the 14-story skeleton-framed Bourne Building (1898-99) for Singer Company President Frederick G. Bourne.

11 Cyma: A type of projecting molding, common in classic architecture and its derivatives.

previous page and opposite top left: Whitehall Building, New York City, Henry Janeway Hardenbergh, architect, 1902-03.

opposite bottom right: This photo c.1912 shows the 416-foot-high extension designed by Clinton & Russell in 1911.

he failed, as we see it, to strictly adhere to his own principle that form should follow function. The functionless arch crept into some of his designs, and some of the members of some of his buildings are only to be accounted for by a reference to "pure architecture." Mr. Flagg has perhaps been more thoroughgoing than Mr. Sullivan, for his design is a much more uncompromising attack upon the structuresque problem of the skyscraper. Traditional forms in the latest Singer Building have given way almost everywhere to structural expression. The architect clearly has endeavored to permit the structure to design itself, confining his own role as much as possible to making the structural features as good looking as lay within his power. His problem, as he understood it, was to protect a steel frame, provide all the light necessary in a building devoted to strictly commercial purposes, and to let the building tell its own story as agreeably as it might.

Our illustrations show clearly the details of how the task was actually performed. The steel frame, it will be seen, is covered with fire-resisting material, held in place by metal bands and straps; the steel columns do not masquerade as stone piers; the steel beams do not conceal themselves behind stone architraves; there are no classic columns, and Renaissance arcades, nor even does the metal itself, where visible, simulate in its proportions or profiles another material. The open spaces are filled with glass where glass is required, and for the rest the encasement consists of small terra cotta panels that reveal themselves between the metal framing or straps. Ornamentation is confined entirely to such expression as rightfully can be imparted to terra cotta and iron. The reader's attention is particularly directed to the isometric drawing, wherein is set forth very plainly the method adopted of filling in the panels of the iron lattice-work which protects the angles with terra cotta slabs; also the plan used for constructing the cornices with angle irons for the angles of the corona, and for the slabs of enriched terra cotta

for its soffits. The drawing also indicates the use of the terra cotta blocks for the cyma[11] and for the bed mouldings, the brickwork which protects the columns and girders, the way in which the upper surfaces .of the cornices and balconies are protected with iron plates, and also the nature of the wrought iron consoles which support the main cornice.

All this is very novel, very ingenious, highly thoughtful. Surely, no other architect has ever so frankly accepted the situation which the skyscraper presents and submitted it to so much real brain work. So much we must all acknowledge. So much is a great gain. So much is immensely creditable to the designer. Apart from Mr. Sullivan's experiments, here we have for the first time, a skyscraper on which a man may ponder, about which he may talk seriously, analyze and judge with the same respect that he may accord to a structure of the days when architecture was not a mere "mode" like the milliner's.

It is not to be expected that a building, the first attempt along such novel lines, should be entirely successful. It is enough for us and for the profession, and it should be immensely gratifying to the designer that his bold attempt must be acclaimed a pronounced success—an innovation which cannot possibly be disregarded in the future by his confreres. Even Roman architecture was not built in a day, and it had no intractable problem to handle like the skyscraper. Experimentation is necessary. Logic may deliver its conclusions in a day, but not so Art. Grace of line and justness of proportion are the result of a long-continued revelation, and of an inspiration persisting with and working through generations. But, one or the other, the revelation or the inspiration cannot be of substantial value unless derived from the actual structure; indeed, neither is a reality so long as its source is merely an academy or a set of copy-books. And this consideration brings us back again to our building and to the value of Mr. Flagg's notable achievement. ■

Whitehall Building, New-York.

the end of the building, has fifty or sixty feet of frontage. The north wall towering high above all the neighboring buildings which are old and belong to a different New York from that of to-day, shows in its plan, rounded convexly in the middle and still leaving room enough for a light court, the purpose to which that part of the building is put. It is clear that the elevators correspond to the curved wall, these being arranged in a sweep according to a plan already accepted in our lofty buildings, and that the two wings are of offices like those which take their light from the front and ends.

That which is attractive about the building is, first, its simplicity and the obvious nature of the design; and secondly, the use of external color to give variety and movement to a large flat front. In other respects, the design is less admirable. The dividing of the building by a pier into two equal parts might be accepted if there were not quite so much of it. What was feasible to do, has been the great doorway of entrance, on the top of which rests the pier, two hundred feet high, as it could never do if this were a masonry building and at the sky-line by the oculus. Eighteen stories of the other system are not to be overcome so readily. This, however, is not an obvious and unmistakable fault. There are times when a design may be halved with propriety. Anything from a sideboard to a chateau may be built in two parts: but it is an admitted difficulty, the overcoming of that rejection of the usual laws of proportion

which say, "a center and subordinate parts, whatever else you do!" In such a case as this, where the external façades have to show themselves for what they are, the slightest and lightest possible shells, built to shut out the weather and protect the steel construction, it would have been easier to make a design out of the south front with a different fenestration and without the noticeable anomaly already alluded to. In like manner, there cannot be anything said in the way of praise, just as there can be nothing felt in the way of pleasurable interest, at sight of the carved stone work. The rounded cushions of the rustication below and the corresponding soft surfaces of the voussoirs which make up the flat arches of several stories, are not redeemed in their uninteresting languor by any crispness of modeling in the slight sculpture which sets them off. There is indeed a somewhat painful lack of vigor about all this stonework of the architectural basement. To one who is not quick to note such details, or who has learned to expect nothing from the carved and wrought stone work of a business building in New York, there still remains a more prominent—a more visible and insistent, a more obvious weakness; and that is the open parapet against the sky, intended, as it seems, to form a part of the design but failing in being very much too small for the proportions of the building and for its own height above the eye. There are flat-roofed buildings in New York in which the large and high pierced parapet, letting the sky into the wall and the wall into the sky, is one of the most attractive features of the exterior; and it seems as if a similar motive of design had been in mind in the present instance. At least it is clear that an opportunity has been lost.

The student is left then to his meditations on the color of the building, and as this cannot be shown by our photograph it is necessary to explain that the red brick of the front is of a rather peculiar hue, pinkish, and as it were, of a subdued crimson, instead of the subdued scarlet which is perhaps the color generally associated with "red brick." This is mentioned neither for blame nor praise, but for record merely. In like manner the yellow bricks are perhaps to be described a dark yellow ochre. One is prepared to have these attributions, these names of colors, disputed by some of those who look at the building, but perhaps students not visiting New York may accept them as partially accurate. The

disposition then is as follows: The whole recessed space above the basement and below the main cornice, enclosing sixty-six pairs of windows, is built, smooth and unbroken, with the pink bricks; and the whole wall of the projecting wing on either side, the whole wall of the attic, the whole of the return or end on either street in which of course the disposition of the wing-wall is carried on, are built with broad stripes of the yellowish-brown brick and narrow, recessed stripes of the pink brick. The stone sills are of neutral color and hardly tell upon the general effect. Now it is evident that a more elaborate design in color might have been carried out without additional cost, or with the very slight additional cost involved in laying up a few hundred bricks with extra care. Feeling an interest in the lovely brickwork of old times and enjoying those flat patterns which were once so common, and which, even in American architecture of the eighteenth century, were employed with surprising effect in even humble buildings, one longs to see the flat red panel in the middle relieved by little crosses, little diamonds, little zigzags—by what you will that will break up its extreme smoothness. Had the brick been less perfect in shape and edge, in short, had the work been in rough brickwork instead of face brickwork, there would have been more play of light which now we can only ask to have allowed us in the way of more inlay of colored details. At the same time it is evident that a designer of such a front might feel that his striped wings and attic required the relief afforded by the flat, red central feature. These are questions which are incapable of solution. The purpose of such a notice as this must be rather to record the facts as they are seen to practiced observers of buildings, old and new, and to note the opportunities given for admiration, on the one side, and of a wish for better things on the other. ●

The Commercial Problem: An Image of the People

4

When the American Institute of Architects posthumously awarded their Gold Medal to Louis Sullivan in 1944, the citation read in part:

"He believed that the dimensions of American architecture are the dimensions of American life, and thus directed us to an art of, by, and for our own people."

It goes on to say:

"He attacked entrenched beliefs. He repudiated false standards. He scorned the stylistic gods of the marketplace.

"He fought almost alone in his generation, lived unhappily, and died in poverty.

"But because he fought, we today have a more valiant conception of our art. He helped to renew for all architects the freedom to originate and the responsibility to create. The standards he set have contributed much to the achievement of today and will augment the promise of tomorrow."

The implications of this citation are worth looking at (without worrying why Sullivan really died in poverty). Once we are told that he was truly democratic and a genuine artist, it's implied that the relationship of the artist/architect to the marketplace and its "stylistic gods" is such that risk of debasement is inevitable, since artistic standards must be lowered. The architect will, by necessity, fall from grace. This is what Lyndon P. Smith alludes to as "the commercial problem." (page 121).

To a great extent this is an American conflict; it lies deep at the heart of an essentially puritanical society. Joseph Stevens Buckminster saw culture, though not a virtue by any means, as an antidote to vice and temptation (love of money and leisure).

"in such a state of society as ours...there is danger lest the love of money, or of merely sensual idleness, should overwhelm the rising generation. To obviate these evils it is much to be desired, that the love of literature and of intellectual pursuits should be greatly encouraged; for though the passion for knowledge is no proof of a principle of virtue, it is often a security against the vices and temptations of the world."[a]

Carson Pirie Scott & Company Building
(formerly Schlesinger & Mayer), Chicago
Louis H. Sullivan, architect, 1899

Comparing America to England, Ralph Waldo Emerson observed, "in America there is a touch of shame when a man exhibits the evidences of large property, as if after all it needed apology."[b] As radical thinkers, both he and Thoreau could at least see the word *economy* as one redolent with virtue. Work was always redemptive, and at least the workplace could reflect its values. The complex relationship between work and consumption is where Americans, before too long, would resolve their conflict, or at least obscure the differences.

Any distinction between culture and commerce was successfully blurred in large-scale stores, such as A.T. Stewart's and Adams & Co. Dry Goods in New York City (page 107), where design contributed to an atmosphere of real spectacle. Shoppers were able to view all the activities in the main gallery, while seeing across and up and down to the various departments that surrounded them. The proliferation of this type of public market made the consumption that is necessary to support industrialization more acceptable. And, women played a vital role in the process. They, in turn, affected design. Lyndon Smith says of the Schlesinger and Mayer store:

> "It is one of many devoted to the retailing of goods, but on an extensive scale and including a large percentage of women among its patrons. This function is unmistakably expressed in the design. The city in which the building is located has the peculiarity of concentrating its commercial district in a comparatively limited area within which there has been erected a large number of buildings of like purpose and character. The one in question is not of colossal type. Its façade is not based on "features," but its individuality is distinct. Its exterior frankly betokens its structural basis and rises in no uncertain fashion from sidewalk to cornice. It is a logical solution of the commercial building, such as a department store, the latest and best achievement produced in this country."

Though Sullivan was naturally disposed towards employing lush arabesques of ornament, it is this building's filagreed decorative elements, especially at street level that he felt would be most attractive to its female clientele (photos pages 120–123). Known to be outspoken against commercial interest, Sullivan was able to find a satisfying balance here in this truly democratic arena. In *Kindergarten Chats*, Sullivan has his young protegé ask the wise architect, "But tell me: When you say; The value of a building, do you really lay more stress on the subjective value than on the Dollar value?" And, the architect answers,

> "On both. For human nature determines that subjective value, sooner or later, becomes money value; and the lack of it, sooner or later, money loss. The subjective value is far the higher, by far the more permanent; but money value is inseparable from the affairs of life; to ignore it would be moonshine."[c]

In all fairness, many builders of commercial structures were less worried by these conflicts, and the attendant guilt, than they were by architects who saw themselves as *artists;* designers who just couldn't grasp the practical demands of commercial planning. Art was now separated from engineering, and art was getting in the way. The architect *cum* artist was a nuisance to George Hill wrote the definition of "Office Building" for the *Sturgis' Dictionary*:

City Investing Company Building, New York City, Francis H. Kimball, architect, 1906-08. The company incorporated in 1904 as what would be called a conglomerate today. With 500,000 square feet (13 acres) of floor space, the 34-story office building was the largest constructed up until that time.

a Joseph Stevens Buckminster, *The Peculiar Blessings of Our Social Condition as Americans,* Boston, 1829.

b Ralph Waldo Emerson, *English Traits,* "X: Wealth," 1856, p. 541.

c Louis Sullivan, *Kindergarten Chats,* "VIII: Values," 1901, pp. 34–35.

"Architecture is not merely an art...it is a social manifestation...we must look to the people; for our buildings as a whole are an image of our people as a whole...the crucial study of architecture becomes...a study of the social conditions producing it."

Louis H. Sullivan Kindergarten Chats, 1901. p. 8

1904

Marshall Field Wholesale Store, Chicago, H.H. Richardson, architect, 1885–87 (demolished 1930). Louis Sullivan sang the praises of this building in his *Kindergarten Chats: "The wonder is that it exists in fact, and not in talk. We hear much of greatness, we see little of it. ...the structure is massive, dignified and simple. But,...it is so much more that I have called it an oasis."*

Wanamaker Building, New York City, D.H. Burnham & Co., architects, 1905. The editors of RECORD praised the building's *"simple unit of design repeated ninefold without accentuation or variation of degree or kind." As a result, they felt "that nothing but...the high price of New York City real estate could possibly have prevented Mr. Wanamaker building on forever once he had got started with his limited unit of design."* [AR XVIII:6, Nov 1905, p 395]

"the design of [office] buildings has gradually become more and more of an engineering problem, until now it may be said that the best results will be obtained by securing the plan from the engineer of special training. He turns over to an artist the bare skeleton, for him to clothe and decorate as well as he can. The former practice of intrusting the design to a man who is primarily an artist, and of permitting him to determine the engineering plan, is commercially bad for everyone but the artist, and is a plain departure from the practice obtaining when the world's most noble edifices were built."

Meanwhile, as projects go, factories, warehouses, and other commercial structures were attracting some of the best architects, since these are building types unencumbered by historical necessity—they pose *pure* challenges. From an early date, the articles in *Architectural Record* on the warehouse number in the dozens; by A.O. Elzner, 1907, Charles H. Patton, 1910, and several by Russell Sturgis 1904 and 1908 (page 151). Peter B. Wight wrote an article, "Studies of Design without Ornament," about fireproof storage facilities! While utility was deemed a good thing by the writers; ornament of any kind became highly suspect. Wight says, "No one has ever discussed the importance [of decorative effects] better than John Ruskin...but, he gave no suggestions applicable to the modern storage warehouse."

In another article, "Utilitarian Architecture," Wight points to a new problem attending commercial projects: convincing the business community of the merits of good design. He saw this as the inevitable outcome of the separation of form from function, if function is solely defined as use (utility).

"The questions that a few years ago agitated the Architectural League of America and at one time came near precipitating a new "battle of the styles" between opposing camps, are beginning to show signs of settlement in the middle west; not as the result of argument, but, as might naturally be expected, of evolution. In the shibboleth of one party 'Function before Precedent'—there now appears to have been a Prophecy. The evolution that is now evident has not been in the gradual modification of preceding styles, though there has also been considerable of this of late, but it has been largely manifest in one class of buildings in which is seen the willingness of investors in utilitarian property to give it a distinctive and attractive character, within the bounds of economy."

A decade and a World War later, the rift between art and utility would there as big as ever. Harvey Wiley Corbett, however, had no problem serving commercial interests. He seemed to regard the American system as the pinnacle of civilization. Singing the praises of Raymond Hood's American Radiator Building in 1924 (page 205), Corbett says, "in the United States where architects have evolved a type of building—the city skyscraper—so daring, so virile that there is nothing else like it in the world...proclaims to all the triumph of industrial efficiency..."

"As an advertisement, I consider the [American Radiator Building] a magnificent success. It is a triumph of commercialism. There is no reason why the term "commercialism" should ever be considered as opposed to art. Perhaps a new type of commercial architecture will be developed. Perhaps architecture will make a great forward step in interpreting commercialism in its new and higher relation to human welfare. There are many civilizations which have left little impress upon humanity and their architecture has faded from human favor. The style at Quirigua, Guatemala, symbolizing the rule of priests of the Sun and kings combined into the one office, over the vanished civilization of the Mayas, have left no trace except a calendar, no other milestone on the road of human welfare. But commercialism in its present significance spells gradual freedom and liberty for the average man." ■

from:

THE SIGNIFICANCE OF ARCHITECTURAL FORM
By H. Toler Booraem
Vol. XXV, No. 3, March 1909, pp. 193-202.

A period of artistic bareness set in throughout Europe during the last century. Political reconstruction and the progress of science and mechanical invention engrossed men's thoughts. Architecture fell back on imitation and reproduction; then the spread of commerce and the rapid development of means of communication destroyed the exclusiveness of nations which had been an essential factor in creating their individuality and in maintaining the character of their art. The commercial idea became dominant in affairs, and architecture had to conform as best it could, with much resultant compromise. Also, the mechanical complexity which distinguishes modern building has forced many inconsistencies upon design.

The typical constructive motive of today—the steel frame—has scarcely a vestige of suggestion of anything worth while to art; it is necessary to do more than ornament or model this skeleton, since it is too rigid, too elementary to allow anything of the kind. What appears to be the building is a mask, a make-believe, in which an imaginary construction has to be more or less resorted to in order to convey even the rudimentary necessities of proportion and the composing of elements, without which there can be no design or architecture whatever, nor any beauty in constructed form, since the latter is not an accidental, not a necessary, thing. In these times, to be sure, we have come to an end of the direct relations that had existed between form and expression; a matter not without a simple explanation.

This is an age in which everything has become specialized. The field of knowledge has become so large that no one mind can command more than a limited range in detail, and must be satisfied with a superficial inkling of the rest. So we are separated in groups, mentally, each group knowing little of the labors of the others, but having full power in its own sphere and buying as it needs of the works of the others. Scientists of many kinds, the great mercantile and financial body, artists in their several branches, and so on. So we may naturally expect much less consistency and less breadth of expression in an art where utility and the aesthetic sense are joined.

Our modern buildings have their significance, but it is one full of contradiction, pretense and irrelevant rise of form. However, the dominant passions of the time are just as much as ever to the front, though expressed between the lines, so to speak, and often in the very limitations and inconsistencies imposed by commercialism and engineering. But in spite of all the confusion of styles and lack of consistent development, if we look beneath the borrowed language to the very different purposes it serves, to the revolutionary construction and planning it is forced to conform to, we may see great changes in the matter expressed, though each individual form may be so little modified. Though we have no modern style, in the complete sense of the word, we give abundance of present-day character to the old styles of which we make use. This is especially true of the French school, withal that the Beaux-Arts is usually supposed to stand for the academic, in form and formula, rather than for a grasp upon new thought of radical innovation. The most important lesson taught by the French, however, though not the most readily learned, is precisely to apply the rudimentary principles of design in a rational manner to the solution of each problem. Of comparatively secondary importance, are the grammar and convention of form.

As a matter of fact, for many classes of building, more especially the commercial, it is a matter of small importance whether the ornamental detail is Italian or French Renaissance, or is Roman in flavor or some other. So long as the selected forms maintain correctness, decorum and scale, one style is often as well as another. What counts more in distinguishing such a design is whether it has secured good proportion and composition, harmony and scale in primary features, and, lastly, whether detail has been managed with the not easily defined intuition of fitness. It conveys little meaning to say that a certain skyscraper is early French Gothic or pseudo Roman, or this or that in style. It is nothing of the kind, except as to some of its detail. Essentially, it is just skyscraper or steel-framed architecture. This is the extreme type, of course, of the new order. •

St. Regis Hotel, New York City, Trowbridge & Livingston, architects, 1901-04.

Hotel McAlpin, New York City, F.M. Andrews & Co., architects, 1911-12. The 25-story Hotel McAlpin was said to be the largest hotel of the time and reportedly had more rooms than any other hotel in the world.

above left: Hotel Knickerbocker, New York City, Warren & Davis and Bruce Price, 1901–06; later annex by Trowbridge & Livingston.

1904

42 Broadway, New York City, Henry Ives Cobb, architect, 1902-03

42 Broadway was a 21-story skyscraper designed by Cobb and constructed by the George A. Fuller Company. The building was unique because of the design of its five-story "Jacobethan" ornament above its entrance.

opposite: Woman's Temple Building, Chicago, Burnham and Root, architects, 1891-92 (demolished 1926). The structure had an exterior light court and a massive entrance.

THE ECONOMY OF THE OFFICE BUILDING

George Hill [1]

from:
**SOME PRACTICAL LIMITING
CONDITIONS IN THE DESIGN OF
THE MODERN OFFICE BUILDING**
By George Hill
Vol. II, No. 4, April–June 1893,
pp. 444-468.

THE writer presented a brief statement of the practical limiting conditions in the design of an office building in a former number of the *Architectural Record* [2] de-scribing it as "the mammoth structure of many stories, that the conditions of our present business life requires us to erect in all centers of population, where the fever of money getting is permitted to have full swing unhampered by any traditions that involve avoidable loss of time." This description still applies to those examples which jump to the mind when office buildings are mentioned: but for the purposes of this article a further definition is needed.

The Duration of Its Economic Life

An office building is a building susceptible of minute subdivision into practically uniform rooms (called office units), all well lighted, heated and ventilated—easy of access both from the street and from its own various floors—and intended for the brain-worker of any type or class, and the clerical force needed to give his work effect. It is the place for housing the executives of all kinds of business and its cost, therefore, is a necessary charge upon business receipts. Generally, the building is too large to be occupied exclusively by one concern, and the renting of the surplus space serves to emphasize its purely commercial aspect. The writer wishes to state once for all, and as strongly as it can be put, that the only measure of the success of an office building is the average net return from rentals for a period of, say, fifteen years. Everything put into the building that is unnecessary, every cubic foot that is used for purely ornamental purposes beyond that needed to express its use and to make it harmonize with others of its class is a waste—is, to put it in plain English perverting someone's money. Of course, in the Wall street district, high rents cannot be obtained from a building with its halls finished in concrete, when the adjoining buildings have a marble finish; but a mansard, or a tower, or a group of statuary does not add to the value of the renting space, and consequently is a waste. For this reason the design of these buildings has gradually become more and more of an engineering problem, until now it may be said that the best results will be obtained by securing the plan from the engineer of special training. He turns over to an artist the bare skeleton, for him to clothe and decorate as well as he can. The former practice of intrusting the design to a man who is primarily an artist, and of permitting him to determine the engineering plan, is commercially bad for every one but the artist, and is a plain departure from the practice obtaining when the world's most noble edifices were built. In a following article this branch of the subject will be elaborated. At present, we will consider the next most important commercial aspect of the skyscraper—its economic life—or the question of how long it will serve its purpose properly.

We know that in manufacturing there are few machines that should not be replaced in from ten to fifteen years, as by that time there are new machines to take their place, doing the work at less cost. In manufacturing plants, as a whole, we know that good business requires a remodeling or re-arrangement at least every ten or fifteen years. In the case of one new plant, for instance, it has earned in three years, over four times its cost, and the point has been reached where a very much larger plant is needed. We frequently hear of such changes, and we occasionally have brought home to us the folly of too much procrastination (such as the ignorant delay in the electric operation of the New York "L" roads [3] for at least six years, and the consequent loss of millions of dollars) and should keep these examples in mind in considering our problem.

It sounds very imposing to say, "We are building for all time." [4] It might be much

THIS term, "modern office building," is used to describe the mammoth structure, of many stories, that the conditions of our present business life require us to erect in all centres of population where the fever of money getting is permitted to have full swing, unhampered by any traditions that involve avoidable loss of time. Whether this building is so high by reason of the desire of men of all callings to come as close to a given centre as possible, to the desire of men of similar callings to be as close together as possible, is due to the superior service that can be rendered for the same outlay, or is due to the necessity to procure enough rentable space to be able to pay interest on the total amount of money invested, might be discussed at considerable length, but is foreign to the present subject except in so far as it furnishes one of the limitations of the problem. The elements that must be combined in the successful building are:
a) ease of access, b) good light, c) good service, d) pleasing environment and approaches, e) the maximum of rentable area consistent with true economy, f) ease of rearrangement to suit tenants, g) minimum of cost consistent with true economy.

* * * *

above: Proposed drawing for 42 Broadway. [AR 1902]

1 New York architect, George Hill, was an associate of the American Society of Civil Engineers, and a member of the American Society of Mechanical Engineers. He was the author of *Office Help for Architects, Modern Office Buildings,* and *Test of Fireproof Floor Arches.*

2 See side-article page 97.

3 "L" road, or "EL," refers to the elevated train lines in New York City.

4 "Therefore, when we build, let us think that we build forever. Let it not be for present delight, nor for present use alone; let it be such work as our descendants will thank us for, and let us think, as we lay stone upon stone, that a time is to come when those stones will be held sacred because our hands have touched them, and that men will say as they look upon the labor and wrought substance of them, 'See! this our fathers did for us.'"
— John Ruskin, *Seven Lamps of Architecture,* chapter VI, "The Lamp of Memory," section X.

better business to say, "We are building for fifteen years." The canvas tent of the traveling circus, the plaster buildings of a World's Fair, the granite and marble of a municipal building, differing as they do, yet each exactly meet the requirements of the particular case. In the case of New York below Chambers street, we may expect to see eventually all the space occupied by office buildings, and so should build for at least fifty years. In other localities, wisdom would limit the probably useful life to twenty years.[5]

Our office buildings of to-day must be of a certain type and plan, slightly varied to suit certain localities and designed in accordance with the definite limiting conditions. What changes are likely to occur in this ever-changing city to make a certain building less remunerative? What changes or improvements will occur in the planning and equipment of office buildings to make our new buildings out of date? How soon may we expect to see these changes? What changes in our business methods might occur which would change business needs so that these buildings would no longer meet them?

Well. the office building has come, because men wish to get closer together and save time in transacting business; and they will not cease to need skyscrapers unless by so doing business can be facilitated. As aids to business, the elevator and the telephone have helped amazingly but the personal interview for really important transactions is still necessary. In fact, the telephone has made it easier to clear the way of preliminaries, and therefore has made more business possible, the personal interview shorter perhaps, but more essential than ever to bring two minds together so that the stenographer and the typewriter may put the conclusion into definite and practicable form. If this reasoning is correct, humanity will continue to press closer together for the purpose of transacting business, until the physical limit is reached in every direction. The only sufficient obstacle to this result would be an invention, whereby two separated rooms are so placed in communication that whatever

goes on in one can be seen and heard in another as readily as if they were one room. Then mankind will perhaps gratify its love of fresh air and sunshine. Our cities will be deserted or will become storehouses for the convenient distribution of manufactured products. Should such an invention be perfected, it would require, however, a generation to work a material change in business methods so that we may continue to build with an easy mind until some such invention comes. While we may, therefore, feel reasonably secure against any complete destruction of the utility of the office building for at least a generation, are there not possible improvements that will change its character or fundamental design?

How Office Buildings May Be Improved

We are accustomed to think and speak of the enormous and steady progress made in modern industrial machinery. While in general this may be true, in the office building it is only true of the details. We are beginning to put into effect improvements suggested years ago, and have made real progress in the direction of carrying out our plans more quickly, and all things considered, more cheaply; but our plans have not changed substantially, and the limiting conditions are the same. We are still aiming to make our buildings attractive, easy to rearrange to suit tenants, well lighted, with convenient internal communication, polite and efficient service, quick elevators, and as accessible as possible to elevated and underground stations. We supply them with every necessity and many luxuries, and do all in our power to get the maximum return for the money invested.

The writer considers it certain that for at least a generation there will be an imperative demand for office buildings, and that the present type will be practically unchanged in its broad outlines.

The improvement made during the past ten years may be briefly stated There has been a very slight increase in net elevator speeds obtained mainly by improved signalling devices. Automatic heat regulation is practically unchanged, but is a little more generally used. Gas has practically been entirely replaced by electricity. The finish of the buildings is a little more luxurious, and the exterior a little more expensive. The average height of a building has increased. There has been the usual number of gold bricks on the market, and as usual they have mostly been connected with the elevator service. One company claimed for a time that it could operate cars at speeds of 700, 800, 1,000 feet per minute, but in the language of the day it did not "make good." The speed was there, but the time lost through missing landings, starting and stopping, was far greater than the time saved in traveling from one landing to another and, besides, poor human nature could not stand the pace. To-day the highest 'practicable speed for a way elevator is 450 feet per minute, and for an express 600 feet to 700 feet per minute, depending on the distance traveled.

We may, therefore, safely say that the future will see but little improvement, except in details, and to show this more plainly, let me state the problem rather more in detail.

We are required to produce on a given lot a building of any number of stories, susceptible of a subdivision into a great number of units, varying in size according to location, but approximately with 16 ft. x 20 ft. of floor space and 10 ft. to 12 ft. high, each one opening into a street or a court of from 18 ft. to 25 ft. in width, which court usually has its long axis north and south, and is as much open to the south as conditions will permit.

The vertical movement of the occupants must be effected by small rooms (elevator cars), moving in vertical shafts at speeds of 600 feet per minute or less. The number of cars is determined by the condition that nobody shall be required to wait at any floor more than 45 seconds in general, and not more than 30 seconds in the financial district and the size of the car by the number of office units per floor and varying from 25 to 40 square feet in area.

The height is to a certain extent unlimit-ed, but probably twenty-five stories is likely to be the average of the high building. The writer may be in error, for there are many influences to be considered: but so far he has been able to discover absolutely no engineering or economic limit of height below about eighty stories, provided the area of the lot be sufficient. Taking into consideration, however, the ethical or sentimental side of human nature, it is the writer's belief that, while many buildings will exceed twenty-five stories, many more, sufficient at least to establish a general practice, will be kept down to sixteen or twenty stories, if left free from municipal interference. On the other hand, the writer believes that the interests of the municipality would be best served by establishing height limits in certain districts, so that the population by day in such areas will not he too large for easy transportation and wholesome living, and so that some regularity of skyline may be secured. The typical plan will naturally tend towards a U-form, open to the south.[6]

Elevator Improvements

It is theoretically possible so to perfect the starting and stopping of elevator cars as to make the higher speeds unobjectionable; but in order to accomplish this the human element in the control of the speed must be almost entirely eliminated. The acceleration must take place in a predetermined number of feet, regardless of the load in the car; the stop must also occur in a predetermined distance, and as a consequence the function of the operator on the car must be to simply push in a starting button and hold it. To stop, either the operator or a person on a landing must push a button corresponding to the proper floor, which will set the stopping device in motion at exactly the right time, without regard to the operator. When a car is at a landing the doors should automatically open and remain open until closed by the operator, and unless closed it should be impossible again to start the car. The mechanical arrangements will not be simple, and will require considerable power. They may cost more than they are worth, when

DO SKYSCRAPERS PAY?
Vol. 12, No. 1, May 1902, pp. 109-111

The economic aspect of the unrestricted construction of skyscrapers is not a matter which has ever received very serious attention. It has been generally assumed that however they may mar the appearance of a city, they are undoubtedly a great business convenience, and a fertile source of real estate values. Howell's some where calls them the "triumph of commerce and the despair of art," or words to that effect. But in the light of certain recent developments of skyscraper economics in New York and elsewhere, we are justified in putting a question mark against this commonly received opinion. The "skyscrapers" undoubtedly pay their owners, just as protection pays the protected manufacturers; but, quite apart from their effect upon the looks of a city, or even upon public health, it is a very doubtful matter, whether their practically unregulated construction, so far as height is concerned, has been of any general economic benefit to New York City.

From the point of view of the majority of the property owners, it can be conclusively shown to be a drawback rather than a benefit. The erection of tall office buildings makes for the concentration of business in small specially favored localities, such as that within a radius of four hundred yards of the Stock Exchange. A limitation on the height of such buildings, on the other hand, would make for the distribution of this business over a larger area, and the consequent distribution of the real estate value created among a larger number of property owners. The effect of the distribution on values would be to diminish the cost of real estate on certain parts of Broadway, Wall St. and Broad St., and to increase it on other streets a little further ▸

5 "The fourth largest office building in the world" at the time of
its construction [76:2 Aug 1934 pp
113–128], the Field Building,
Chicago, (above) Graham,
Anderson Probst and White,
architects, 1931-34, replaced the
Home Insurance Company,
1883–85, reputed to be the
world's first skyscraper. Size outweighed age. See pages 7 and
283.

6 See rear of Woolworth Building
on page 188.

7 Of all the technical innovations
that made skyscrapers possible,
the most important was probably
the safe elevator invented by
Elisha Otis in the early 1850s. His
first model, powered by steam,
featured an automatic safety
device that prevented the car
from falling if the hoisting rope
broke. Otis installed a passenger
elevator in New York in 1857.
Hydraulic elevators, which ran on
water pressure, were first used
commmercially in 1878 and are
still in use today in low buildings.
Not until the advent of electric
elevators in the late 1880s, however, did builders deem elevators
reliable for tall buildings.

compared to the approximation to these
conditions now obtained.

The economy—that is, the relation
between the pounds of coal burned and
work done—by the present appliances is
very low; the work should be done with an
expenditure of not more than one-quarter
of the present amount of energy.

From the nature of the service it is probable that some form of hydraulic apparatus
must continue to be used, since only in the
hydraulic apparatus is there stored up the
large amount of energy necessary to produce the high rate of acceleration absolutely required in an instantly available and convenient form. Electric elevators are
absolutely unrivalled in their field, but office
building service is not their field, nor is
there any sufficient mechanical reason for
the expectation that in any of their present
forms they will ever extend their fields to
include this service.[7] The problem is to
impart a velocity of from 6 to 8 miles per
hour, to a weight of from 175 to 2,000
pounds, in from 1 to 2 seconds, or to bring
this weight to rest when moving at this
velocity, in the same time. The energy stored
up in water under pressure will do the work
perfectly. The work may be stored up in the
water, providing the tanks are large enough,
at the average rate for a day requiring a relatively small amount of power constantly
expended. There are two drawbacks: which
are that the expenditure of energy is not
proportioned to the load, but must be the
same whether the elevator car be full or
empty, and that all forms of pumping
engines suitable for any but the very largest
plants are inefficient. The line of improvement must take the direction of overcoming
these two objections.

The Heating and Ventilating System

The heating of the offices is well enough;
but the ventilation is very largely neglected.
These two are so closely related that they
should be considered together. Present practice is to provide a radiator for heating controlled either by hand or by thermostat for
each office unit, and to provide ventilation
by opening the window, the foul air passing
into the hall. The ideal arrangement would
be to introduce a fixed amount of warmed,
fresh clean air to each office unit at any predetermined temperature automatically, and
all past attempts may be classed as failures for
general use. In fact, there may be said to be
no existing way of properly warming the
bulk of the offices of an office building
without the constant use of a little knowledge, intelligence and trouble. The foul air
can be drawn off into a vent-shaft placed at
any convenient place. For banking and similar large rooms on lower stories, the standard hot-air heating system, with either
exhaust or blast fans, works with entire satisfaction and but little loss of valuable room,
but the air inlets should be always 8 ft. above
the floor and at least 5 ft. from ceiling, and
the outlets for foul air should be near the
floor and large enough to have a very low
velocity (less than 10 ft. per second). Then
the occupants will not feel a draught. The
inlet radiators must be high up, because it is
at times necessary to introduce the fresh air
at a temperature lower than 100° F. when it
feels cold and produces the effect of a
draught. If the fresh air forms a current
flowing always in one direction, surfaces
near it will get very dirty, and we are therefore compelled to keep away from the ceiling.

The expedient of using warmed air furnished to each office through flues in the
walls has been tried, but is objectionable on
account of the large space occupied by the
flues, the transmission of noise from floor to
floor, and the difficulty of maintaining the
desired degree of heat in each office. All
floors and walls might be heated by warmed
air circulating through them, but the necessary air passages are objectionable, because
they afford a harborage for vermin, and in
the case of a fire in the contents of an office
might distribute the smoke through the
building. The necessity of having widely
varying temperatures in the different offices
also complicates the problem.

If ever electricity can be produced commercially at say 1/10 of present minimum

rates, the problem will be solved, for fresh air can be introduced through an opening in the outside wall, all of the dust screened out, warmed to any desired degree by passing over electric heaters and drawn into the office by electric fans, the degree of heat and the speed of the fan being determined by setting a dial hand at the desired temperature, the remaining regulation being automatic and independent of the direction or force of the wind. The windows constitute a serious problem. We want to look out, and at the same time we want fire protection. If we use wire glass we cannot look out, and if we use clear glass it will fly out with the first touch of flame. A three-sash metal window, with one sash glazed with clear glass and two sashes glazed with wire glass, solves the problem and will mark the next step. Cleaning need not present any difficulties or dangers.

Improvements in the Trim

We need either an incombustible wood or a substitute for the trim of the office, the doors, moldings, base and fixtures. It will come—in fact, has probably come, as there are several materials of promise now on the market. The ideal material will be readily worked, wear as well as wood, be a poor conductor of heat and incombustible. It will then be pleasant to sit on, pleasant under foot and absolutely safe.

An improvement will be made by departing from the custom now prevalent of using a cord of wood, more or less, in trimming the office, putting in a high base, chair rail, picture mold and architraves around the doors. There is really needed only the picture mold, and that only to carry wires in a way which permits them to be tapped at any point: and some member to make the joint of the door frame with the partition. With the simplification of design we may expect to see a marked improvement in this latter respect.

Details of Illumination and Construction

We may expect improvements in lighting in the line of luminous surfaces rather than points, the illumination being obtained with a relatively small expenditure of energy. Wires will probably be still used, and our distribution systems will only change in detail. So long as the present conditions obtain, an improvement can be made by using one central chandelier in each office unit; making the picture mold a receptacle for wires and supplying those wires from mains running up column lines. The desk illumination can be obtained by drops from the picture molding and partitions can be easily shifted. If a system should be devised by which the salutary effects of sunlight would be reproduced, we could reduce our courts to simple vent shafts drawing pure air from the roof level and discharging it at a proper temperature in each room. That only means the flooring over of the courts and a shifting of partitions. Nearly all of our buildings could be so changed without difficulty.

Partitions can now be made sufficiently sound and fireproof in a variety of ways. The cost of making them can be decreased under reasonable labor conditions. Any of the solid plaster partitions resting on the floor construction and against the floor construction above are efficient protection against the spread of fire. They are frequently spoiled by the introduction of sashes glazed with plate glass which, in the event of fire, immediately falls out. Only wire glass should be used, and as the sashes interfere with the utilization of the wall, they should be omitted.

Less Steel to be Used in Future

It is probable that the future will see a decreasing amount of structural steel used in the floor framing, and an increasing amount of reinforced concrete, the development progressing until the only structural steel used will be in the columns, in stay beams connecting the columns of sufficient strength to support the centers for the concrete possibly of less strength than that, and in wall beams. This is the writer's opinion. One does not wish to be dogmatic, and it is only fair to say there are other views on the subject, held by well-informed people who would not agree at all with the foregoing.

away. Assuming that the same amount of business would be transacted under a regulated as under an unregulated system, this business would require, of course, a larger number of smaller buildings, and the augmented demand for space all over the city, caused by the purchase of sites for a larger number of buildings would bring about a pretty general increase of values. Moreover, it would not decrease the amount of rentable space within the peculiarly advantageous localities as much as may be supposed, because the owners of eighteen and twenty story buildings have found it necessary in a great many cases to purchase adjoining property, in order to protect their light and air. This is true in the case of the Mutual Life, the Washington Life, the Park Row, the Commercial Cable, the Atlantic Mutual, the Singer, and many other buildings in New York City, and the result is that many very well situated parcels of real estate are withheld from improvement, which in case there had been a limitation of the height of buildings to eight or nine stories, would have been most assuredly improved. The amount of property so withheld varies in different streets, but probably, on the whole, it would amount to as much as a fifth of the space occupied by the tall buildings.

From the point of view of business interests involved, it is not, perhaps, so easy to make out a good case for regulation. The disadvantages of wider distribution of office buildings would in some cases make no difference at all; and in all cases it would be partly neutralized by the constant use of the telephone, and an efficient system of surface transit. But it is probable that a legal restriction as to height would have raised the rents in buildings very favorably situated in the Wall St. district of New York, because the busi- ▸

Writing about the work of
J. Stewart Barney and Henry
Otis Chapman, [AR Sept 1904]
Schuyler lauded this curious
design for "...a proposed building
for the New York 'American' or
'The Journal,' as it is better
known. The site for the building
is quite irregular, the four fronts,
those on Broadway, the Circle,
8th Ave., and 58th Street each
being of a different length. In
order to utilize the area circumscribed by these boundries without the loss of a foot of space
and without producing at the
same time a building that should
emphasize if not exaggerate the
irregularities of the lot, was a
problem that demanded unusually clever handling. It will be seen
even from our illustrations that
the architects succeeded with
conspicuous success and produced a most notable skyseraper,
five hundred and fifty-five feet
high and of forty stories."
Note the similarity between this
building's entrance and that pictured on page 104.

Brick, stone and terra cotta are the materials used at present in constructing the
walls. Concrete is offered as a substitute.
When it is good, it is as good as any other
substance; but for walls it is not likely to be
uniformly good, nor is it likely to be consistent in color or as pleasing in appearance as
stone. Glazed terra cotta is probably the best
substance if properly made and set because
since each rain washes it off, it is less likely
to be injured by fire, and when injured is
more easily replaced. Any material is liable
to serious damage from fire in adjoining
properties. The greatest improvement that
could be made would be a law, requiring all
new structures to be fireproof within certain
limits and making owners of property in
which a fire originated responsible for all of
the damage caused by the fire regardless of
where this damage occurred or how the fire
started.

We are using such large quantities of steel
in our buildings, and in fact, are absolutely
dependent on it for strength, that we need
more knowledge to protect it absolutely
from fire and rust, and should improve our
practice in applying the knowledge we have,
which is certainly sufficient to enable us to
guarantee a life of fifty years.

How Fire Insurance May Be Improved

Fire insurance, as conducted, really places
a premium on bad construction under our
present laws and practice, for it permits the
careless and criminal to avoid the consequences of their acts to a very large degree.
A man can build an inexpensive low building, insure it to the limit—insure its contents to the limit—have a fire from which
he will reap a profit, and damage an adjoining handsome building to a greater amount
than his total loss. Moreover, the adjoining
building cannot be protected fully from this
loss, except by an exorbitant annual pay-
ment. It should be impossible to insure a
really hazardous building. In theory present
practice, expressed generally, is to fix a minimum premium or charge for each building
of a certain class in a certain locality and
increase the premium for each departure

from what is considered good practice and
to force the owner to bear some of the risk.
In practice anything can be insured. The difference in premium between a safe and hazardous building is only a small fraction of
the difference in the interest cost, so that it
is really cheaper to build badly and insure
fully, than to build well and insure reasonably. The increases of premium for departures from good practice, are in some cases
indefinite and in other cases absurd (as when
a charge is made if a fireproof door is omitted between the boiler-room and the rest of
the cellar, even when there are other doors
absolutely shutting off the balance of the
building, and there is positively nothing
combustible in either boiler-room or cellar,
except the coal). The credit for covering the
metal columns of a building, certain to fail if
left bare and exposed to a small, fierce blaze,
certain to cause great damage and loss if
they fail, is so small as to be practically of no
consequence as an offset to the interest on
the cost of covering. The writer knows of
one case where a fire, in itself causing not
more than $500 damage, would endanger
columns, which, if one should fail, would
cause a loss of certainly $20,000, and proba-
bly many lives. Some of our serious losses
have been from so-called exposure fires, and
yet the decrease in insurance cost that comes
from the use of wire glass and metal sashes
and frames, instead of wood sashes and
frames and plain glass, the one affording
complete protection and the other no protection at all, is so little that it is not worth
considering. This whole subject requires
readjustment and reforming, and the data on
which the premium increase is based should
be obtained by a continuing series of experiments conducted by an admittedly impar-
tial, competent director with adequate facilities, and the insurance companies should
absolutely refuse to insure a really dangerous
building or any building, the value of which
was materially less per cubic foot than those
immediately adjoining it. If it were possible
to win a suit for damages, where one building is injured by fire originating in another,
just as it is possible to win a suit for damages

when an owner makes an improper use of his property to the injury of the adjoining property, this liability would quickly force owners of hazardous property so to improve it as to make it safe. It is to be hoped that some of our large corporations will try to establish the precedent. Once established, it would work a wonderful change in the point of view of the owners of many relatively unimproved and really dangerous properties.

The Power Plant

Now let us descend almost literally into the bowels of the earth; let us go far below the surface of the street to the place where heat, light and power are generated, and see what is doing there. We must first of all consider the often discussed and by no means settled question of private plants vs. supply from the street; i.e., from some lighting heating and power company.

An office building is a very large consumer of power. For some years the Public Utility Company has endeavored to supply all the power and heat necessary, and does supply many buildings at a price which often shows a marked economy in the operation of the building by so doing, but the mechanical engineer who is really competent knows that wherever economy is so shown in a large building, the owners of the building have been shamelessly robbed by their employees. The writer knows of many plants in large buildings that could advantageously take all power and light from the street; but for every dollar so saved at least one dollar and fifty cents could be saved by getting a competent superintendent and making a few changes.

To illustrate: Recently the writer changed the fuel of a plant in which he was interested from Pocahontas coal to buckwheat and rice coal. The coal bills were practically cut in two, with no loss in efficiency. In one of our large buildings egg coal is used exclusively—if rice were used the fuel bill for that building would be less than half. Engines are run under improper conditions, using from one and one-half to twice as much fuel as

they need. Pumps are run with their drips open, thus doubling their coal consumption. Compound elevator pumps are run at variable speeds, the maximum being less than one-half what it should be. The consequent coal consumption is from four to eight times that of a decently designed plant. Exhaust steam is wasted and live steam used for beating, thereby increasing the coal consumption from one and one-half to two times.

Architects provide wholly inadequate spaces for machinery, and so necessitate the use of inefficient boilers, insufficient tanks, steam wasting appliances and other bad features that can be put into a design, and make matters still worse by limiting the cost of the plant to an absolute minimum. Contractors are furnished with the merest outlines of requirements; the bids are obtained and contracts awarded to the lowest bidder, who is either careless, ignorant or dishonest enough to talk of an economy (even to guarantee it, sometimes) that a competent man knows he cannot attain. Still it goes; the plant goes in; is a failure, and the New York Edison gets another contract. If, however, the engineer or real architect is familiar with the problem, this very essential part of the building is allowed adequate room. The parts are harmoniously designed to fill the requirements. The superintendent of the building is a competent engineer, who is paid enough to be above the temptation to steal, and knows enough to keep his force up to their work. The plant is relatively simple, easy to handle, and during the first year reports are sent to the designer so that a record of performance is made, by which the owners can judge of competency in the future. When these precautions are taken, the cost of operation is far below the sum which the New York Edison Company will charge. The writer and other engineers have proved this in many plants, but the objectionable conditions obtain in so many more, that general practice is rather in favor of procuring all of the power possible from the Edison Company. Future development will be in the line of better engineering and more independent plants in buildings of 5,000

ness of brokers, bankers, their lawyers and their clients' needs for its transaction a good deal of running about, both by principals and clerks, and an office, which reduced the amount of this traveling to a minimum, would naturally possess an increased value. It may be doubted, however, whether these increased rents would occur in any except the Wall St. district, and in any case a deduction should be made on the score of the enormous bills for electric lighting, which the "skyscrapers" cause the tenants of the lower floors on the narrow streets downtown. On the whole it is questionable whether after all allowances are made, business in Wall St. and elsewhere could not be conducted as economically and conveniently in eight as in eighteen story buildings.

In view of all these considerations which make the economic advantages of "skyscrapers" at least extremely doubtful, except to the owners of very advantageously situated property. Why is it that there has been no more persistent and successful attempt to bring about such regulation? For, if their economic advantages are doubtful, their aesthetic and sanitary disadvantages are manifest and serious, so much so that abroad there is no question about keeping the height of all buildings down to such a level that they will not deprive the street of too much sunlight, or be too much out of scale with its width. The explanation in general seems to be that in this country private and special interests always have more energetic and insistent advocates than the wider public interests. Even Chicago, where a limitation of height to ten stories has prevailed for a good many years could not stick to its guns, but has recently given the favored property owners their own way. It is not easy for a Common Council to resist men who   ▸

In "The Rear View of Skyscrapers," 1905, Russell Sturgis remarks that he has seen the row of buildings in the bottom photograph from another window without realizing they were the plain unadorned backs of the buildings above (including 42 Broadway). He concludes that if the façade had something more interesting at the top, "it would be a little less ponderous at the level of the roof."

8 For some reason there is no (i).

square feet or more.

★ ★ ★

Assuming that these various appliances are properly proportioned and arranged, they require so much room that at least all of the cellar of a building occupying less than two lots is needed. For the building having less than this area, the greater part of the supply must come from the street. Future improvements will be along the line of a more efficient production of electric current, first by improved forms of generating apparatus, engines and boilers; by the introduction of more electrically-operated apparatus; by the use of more economical pumping engines until they can be discarded; possibly by discarding steam and using gas or pulverized coal; and probably filially by the almost direct conversion of the energy stored in the coal into energy in the form of electricity. When electricity is so cheaply produced that it can be used for heating, steam will no longer be needed, and our plants will be practically eliminated. When that time comes the cost of distribution, which is now as great as the cost of generating electricity, will be reduced certainly to ten per cent of its present cost, and so will make it economical to generate the current in the building. With electric current at say 1 per cent per horsepower per hour every plant in New York almost could be economically shut down and taken out.

The field for speculation in this branch of the subject is almost infinite, but really hinges, so far as any radical change is concerned, on the discovery of a new process of producing electricity or power very cheaply.

Two matters remain to be considered—whether as improvements or merely as developments depends on the point of view; they are the question of height and of designing.

Conditions Determining Height

Height is effected by the following considerations: (a) Sixteen stories or less can be carried on piles or grillages, no matter how bad the bottom. More than sixteen stories require caissons, or all equivalent expense if the sub-soil is bad. Therefore, several additional stories must be put in simply to pay interest on the extra cost of the caissons. (b) For lots of 7,500 to 12,500 square feet, five cars will give a satisfactory elevator service up to twelve stories. Higher than that a car should be added for each additional three stories, costing 100 square feet of room on each floor per car. For still greater area the number of cars must be increased, say one car for each 2,000 square feet, and this is because it is impossible to load and unload a large car fast enough—two cars of forty square feet running in a twenty-story building will handle more people in a day than one of eighty square feet, and do it with very much more satisfaction.

(c) In a sixteen-story building, with ordinary foundations, the addition of a seventeenth story will add more than one-sixteenth the cost of the building by 5%; for an eighteenth story 10% must be added to the one-sixteenth, and so on. Thus, if a sixteen-story building costs $480,000, then a seventeenth story will add to the cost $31,500; an eighteenth story, $33,000, etc.

(d) The time necessary to go from a street corner to the twentieth floor of a twenty-story building in front of which a person is standing, is about the same as the time required to walk half a block, and reach the tenth floor of a neighboring building.

(e) The time required to go from the twentieth to the fifth floor of a twenty-story building is about the same as that required to go from the tenth story of a ten-story building to the tenth story of an adjoining ten-story building.

(f) The heating of one upper story (above the tenth) will cost nearly as much as heating two lower stories, unless there is always exhaust steam to waste.

(g) The average temperature of the outside air at any 200 feet above the street and above is from 3° to 5°) less than the average at the street. This is an advantage in the summer and a disadvantage in the winter.

(h) If the elevators could be divided into sections and the shaft-ways for the way elevators stopped, for example, at the tenth floor of a twenty-story building, then a saving of space could be effected. This has not yet been done, and would require a change in the New York building law. The space so saved would not always be available for renting purposes.[8]

(j) No formula can be made to express all the conditions, for it would have to be based on so many assumptions that would have no value when solved; but by averaging a number of cases and making certain assumptions, it may be stated that probably a thirty-two story building would have a gross return of 11% under conditions that would show a gross return of 10% for a sixteen-story building on the same lot. That is, an investment Of $3,420,000 divided into: lot, $1,000,000; building, $2,420,000; would show a return of $376,200; where a total investment Of $2,000,000 divided into lot $1,000,000, building $1,000,000, would show a return of $200,000. That means that an additional expenditure of $1,420,000 would return $176,000. There are many cases in which the smaller amount could be obtained, while the larger could not.

(k) The vibration of very tall buildings (over twenty-five stories) is an unknown quantity. Theory indicates that it would be objectionable. Practice reveals its existence in certain cases, though in a slight degree. It is probable that in buildings exceeding sixteen stories and of a height exceeding five times the least width, there will be objectionable vibration after the buildings have been erected fifteen to twenty years.

If the soil is such as will support a sixteen-story building but no more, the commercial considerations detailed above would limit the height to sixteen stories. If it is doubtful whether more than sixteen stories can be carried and the site is expensive, then we must put in caissons and decide on twenty stories. If the lot is not expensive, we would be content with sixteen stories.

Finally in the design and erection of these buildings we can already see the line of future development. While many owners stick to the old practice of selecting an architect who draws plans and gets gratuitously from contractors the plans for the foundation, heating, lighting, elevators, plumbing and even decorations, who combines them more or less (generally very much less) successfully, and who then jobs out the erection to one or more contractors, other owners have adopted the latest practice of having a corporation make the plans, erect the building, and even for a time operate it; there are even many cases where the owner plans, erects and operates on his or its own account. There can be no question that the best way is to have one concern design, erect and operate, and this will be improved upon only by specializing to the extent of limiting the field of the designing and erecting concern to one class of buildings. Whether this be done by an individual or a corporation makes no difference, since in either case there must be the same organization, the same executive on whom must rest the final responsibility, and from whom is demanded a good general knowledge of the subject, great executive ability and that knowledge of men that will enable him to select his associates successfully. There may be a board of directors, there may be a president to dictate a general policy, but there must be in this work, as in every other work—steel manufacture, railroads, manufacturing—anything else you choose—one head—a calm, constructive, thoughtful, intelligent, self-reliant, honorable man, to direct affairs. It does not follow that necessarily the success of a company will only be coincident with that man's life. In fact, the greatest effort of such a man, after securing the success of the company, would be to develop a worthy successor. Such men, while relatively few, are still to be obtained. The first step in this development will be the combination of promoting, financing and building in one corporation in which the public, as shareholders, will have a part. This final step has, in some cases, been taken, and is destined to be ultimately successful, not by crushing competitors, but by doing so much better work in its chosen field that there will be no competitors. ∎

declare that if case restrictions are removed they are prepared to immediately spend $20,000,000 in new buildings. As for New York, in spite of its claims to metropolitan eminence, it has always been as clay in the hands of the real estate owner and speculator, and the consequences of this let-alone policy, which in another direction has cost the city so much in the way of alienated franchises, are in this matter both irremediable and disastrous. They are irremediable, because to establish a limitation at the present time, after so many "skyscrapers" have been erected, would be an unfair discrimination against other unimproved property in the favored neighborhood and they are disastrous, because the cost of curing the congestion which these "'skyscrapers" will eventually cause is incalculable. This is an aspect of the matter which is too frequent overlooked. If during the next twenty-five years there are continued to be erected an unlimited number of from twelve to twenty story buildings on the narrow streets and infrequent avenues of city, badly planned as they are for the distribution of traffic, the outcome will be a congestion of street traffic and transit, of which the Brooklyn Bridge at present gives some inkling, and when this time comes the remedy for this congestion will be as expensive as its perpetuation will be intolerable. It stands to reason that if very tall buildings are erected in large quantities upon streets that were laid out only for very small ones, and if steps are not early taken to adjust this street system to the increasing demands which are being put upon it, this combination of energetic private building, with negligent public administration, will do more to damage the business interests of the city than any amount of restrictive regulation.●

Corn Exchange Bank Building, New York City, R.H. Robertson, architect 1893–94 (demolished).

Robertson tried to express the structure's height by emphasizing its verticality; Montgomery Schuyler thought the building had far too many horizontal divisions [VI:3 Sept–Jun 1897 p 216].

opposite: Adams Dry Goods Company, New York City, De Lemos & Cordes, architects, 1900. The architects' larger and more elaborate store for R.H. Macy & Company built the following year, established the "Big Store" as a type soon to be emulated everywhere.

THE ART OF THE HIGH BUILDING

Barr Ferree[1]

FEW phrases have included such a miscellaneous collection of facts and statements as this. For much of the phenomena to be classed and discussed under this head has no artistic quality or value whatever. It is sheer ugliness, uncouthness, misunderstanding and absurdity, if judged by artistic standards; and the true artistic elements-so far as they exist-are often of a singularly undeveloped nature. One has but to mentally compare the great high building of to-day-the typical and most noteworthy architectural creation of our time-with the great typical building of the Italian Renaissance or of the French mediaeval period to realize how very different modern standards of art in things architectural are compared with those of more genuinely artistic epochs.

The erection of the high building has been a recognized branch of our architectural industry for some time. For nearly a quarter of a century it has occupied the minds of our architects, given them their most important monuments, on the whole, and lined their pockets with the largest fees ever obtained in general practice. The participants and contemporaries in a movement are not apt to be competent judges of its tendencies and results and yet so much thought and treasure have been poured out on the high building, it has become such an intimate part of the commercial life of our time, that it is by no means impertinent to ask, even at this early day, if some definite steps have been reached in the solution of the artistic problems involved in its construction, or if-and perhaps this is the more rational question-if tendencies have been shown which look anywhere, and whither is the direction towards which they tend.

It is more than right to insist on the artistic conception of the high building Engineers will doubtless maintain that the chief problem is that of engineering. I am not in the least disposed to discount the

importance of the engineering problems in buildings of this description; but I respectfully submit that in a building that covers a considerable area that raises its head as high into the upper strata of the air as the engineers will carry it, which cries aloud for attention and consideration, which invites criticism because of its vast cost, and in which, moreover, the engineering part is carefully hidden and covered up from view-in such a building, surely, the artistic expression, the form, the covering, the outer aspects, are of supreme public importance.

One of the most interesting views in New York may be had from the junction of Liberty street and Maiden lane. Standing there the spectator sees before him a little old brick building, five stories in height, placed at the intersection of Maiden lane and Liberty street. It is a simple little structure, absolutely devoid of ornament and detail, but with a flat, rounded end, a recognition of the site that was as much as its builder cared to consider. The windows are plain, flat-topped openings of the old style; the fifth floor is manifestly an attic floor since it contains fewer windows than the lower stories, and the roof is slightly pointed. How much of this structure may be modern or restored I do not know; but it is distinctly of the old type, and it bears the date "1823." Here, then, is a fair starting point, a building eighty years old, standing in a district long since given up to commercial purposes, and itself used in the same way. And what strange things this little old house has seen grow up around and behind it! The buildings in the foreground are of a later date but still entirely antiquated as commercial buildings go to-day. But behind it, what marvels and miracles of contrast! Directly at the back is the sheer solid brick wall of the John Wolfe Building, (photo page 53) a structure moderate enough in height, as high buildings are built to-day, but colossal compared with the little old house of 1823. To the left, on Liberty street, is the generous facade of the Bishop Building—twelve stories, tier upon tier of windows—a building wholly different in material, in design, in

from:
ALL KINDS OF A STORE
*Vol. XII, No. 3, August 1902,
pp. 287-303.*

THE modern department stores are the results, for the most part, not of combination, but of accretion. There is one combination of stores that is doing business both in New York and elsewhere, but it is exceptional. The other big stores have originated in a small way, and have grown to their present huge dimensions; because they have found, little by little, that, other things being equal, it was cheaper to do business on a big scale than on a small scale. But just because these department stores have grown from the gradual extension, and in the end almost the multiplication of a business, which in the beginning occupied one or two small shops, it was not for many years that their owners erected buildings specially designed to meet the needs and exigencies of their complicated trade. As the demand for more accommodations became pressing, the proprietor of the store would add one neighboring shop after another until he came into possession of the whole block front. Later he would frequently be obliged to lease or purchase additional room across the street, and in this way ▸

above: Looking up Broadway from Bowling Green.

1 Barr Ferrée was a Professor of Architecture at the University of Pennsylvania. He wrote "High Building and Its Art," for Scribner's Magazine in March of 1894. Ten years later he wrote this follow-up article wherein he states his skepticism as to whether much progress had been made toward "the solution of the artistic expression of the high building."

right: The Junction of Liberty Street and Maiden Lane.

below: Land Title and Trust Company Building, Philadelphia, D.H. Burnham & Co., architects, 1900-04.

expression, in use from the old structure with which the neighborhood, as we now know it, started.

Here is effort at architectural treatment, a great building, with a basement in design, a superstructure and a narrow attic a building so different that the barest analysis of its parts shows how tremendously we have moved in eighty years.

But there is more than this; for still further off, and so huge as to almost overwhelm our little brick building, is the mighty tower of the new part of the Mutual Life Building, a building with piers and columns and cornices lifted so high in the air that, we may be very sure, the builders of 1823 could never have conceived of such things or of such possibilities. The entire progress of commercial architecture in seventy-five years is here brought into one view, and one may note the change and advance without moving a step from one's original standpoint.

There is another panorama in New York which is almost as instructive in illustrating progress-not perhaps so picturesque, yet better known-and that is the spectacle that may be viewed from the lower end of Broadway, looking up from Bowling Green. It is a wonderful sight, one of the most astonishing views in the metropolis. Starting with the vast facade of the Produce Exchange, the eye meets just beyond it, looking up the street, with an old brick building, five stories in height—the single antiquated note in this array of splendor as it is understood in commercial New York—then the Wells Building, the Standard Oil Building, with the later addition Mr. Kimball has so cleverly added to it, the Hudson Building, No. 42 Broadway (photo page 96) —the newest of the series—No. 46 Broadway, a brick building of later type than the one at Beaver street, but already so out of date as to be quite comparable to a wedding guest without the wedding clothes in the sumptuous company in which it now finds itself; then an old type four-story building, brick—a veritable derelict—then the Tower Building (photo Page 8) the first structure in this

country, so an inscription tells us, in which the steel cage construction was used-Exchange Court; the Consolidated Exchange, and the vast bulk and height of the Manhattan Life Insurance Company's Building. There is more beyond, but surely there is more than enough here for the philosophic observer, more than even the casual critic can well digest and ponder over on a winter's day.

Surely, then, with these contrasts and this great activity in building, it is time to ask if anything has been accomplished towards the solution of the artistic expression of the high building, or if tendencies have been started which would seem to indicate definite results. Let me frankly admit that I am entirely skeptical on both these points. Progress in architecture does not consist in the multiplication of buildings, but in real artistic achievement; and progress is not

obtained by a hundred individual efforts, each originating separately, each overlooking what has been done by others, each failing to note where others have failed, each ignoring where others have succeeded. Yet a survey of the modern commercial buildings bring out no clearer fact than that this is just what has been done, and, more's the pity, it is just what is being done, and what would seem likely to be done for some time to come.

I am speaking generally, of course, and of high buildings as a whole; for in the case of individual architects very genuine steps of progress may be noted. The Blair Building, (photo page 61) in Broad street, is a much franker and truer expression of the high building than the Mail and Express Building in Fulton street, both by Carrère & Hastings: the Empire Building, (photo page 50) overlooking Trinity churchyard is a much more interesting building than the Manhattan Life across the street, on Broadway, both by Francis H. Kimball. But does the Park Row Building proclaim any note of progress over the building of the American Tract Society? (photo page 55) Or do any of a score of buildings erected in the last two years indicate that their designers have profited by the experiments of other architects or taken the lessons of other buildings to heart? Is the Atlantic Building any more notable contribution to art than the building of the National Bank of Commerce? Does the Broad Street Exchange sum up any nobler thoughts in architecture than the St. Paul Building? (photo page 33)

These are pertinent questions, for the gentlemen who have built these structures have thrust them upon us for all time, so far as living man can see; they have spent huge sums in their architectural doings, and they have given our city—for limits of space in this discussion restrain me to New York—a new and characteristic aspect. It is quite beyond the question to point out the beauty of Manhattan's skyline—that has nothing to do with the case—and a building whose chief merit is that it out-tops its neighbors is necessarily wanting in most of the characteristics we are accustomed to associate with good architecture.

That the commercial building is a commercial enterprise is well known; that it is an architectural enterprise is a circumstance all architects would have us believe. Architectural it is, of course, being concerned with iron and stone, brick and glass; but is it architectural in any other way? Even in its short life of twenty-five years several steps or periods may be noted.

First, the introductory period; the first steps, in which such buildings as the Tribune Building and the Western Union Building were erected. The possibilities of high building design as they were afterwards made known were not at all understood in this remote epoch; but these first efforts were manly and straightforward, and still command respect.

Second, the advertising period. It was suddenly realized that a showy building was a good advertisement for its chief occupant. It attracted attention, it drew tenants, it became a profitable venture. The Pulitzer Building is a fair type, the Broadway front of the Mail and Express an extreme instance; the Manhattan Building a third example. The chief aim of the buildings which may be classed under this head was to be impressive by sumptuousness of parts, by splendor of appointments, by richness of effect. A great financial corporation felt that it might stand better in the community if it had a fine house, and the greater the wealth the more splendid its abiding place—a natural proposition to which no dissent can be taken

It was a type of building that gave architects their greatest opportunities, for they were not merely required to build, but they were commanded to build well and sumptuously, a certain artistic character was required of them; and if the architects failed to rise to their opportunities it was simply and solely because they failed to comprehend the problem presented to them. It is true they have endeavored to proclaim that the fault was not in them, but in the problem; but the bitter fact remains that they gladly accepted these impossible problems, and gleefully signed their names to designs that proclaimed their own incompetency.

Third. Then came the third period, which I take to be the present. A change has certainly come over the designing methods of high buildings within a very few years. The buildings are bigger, higher, broader, more

obtain the larger floor space which his business imperatively demanded. The only two of the large stores doing business in New York which are now in this condition, is that of R. H. Macy & Co. and John Wanamaker. The old store of the former firm, consisting as it does of a scattered collection of heterogeneous buildings—some situated in 13th, some on 14th and some on 15th streets, some twelve and some four stories high—is an excellent example of a department store which has grown without the possibility of any systematic planning. John Wanamaker, also, finds the whole block occupied by the old Stewart store too small for his present business, which has crossed 9th street and occupied the block front on the south side of that street. A few years ago two of the largest Sixth avenue stores, *viz.*, that of Adams & Co. and Simpson, Crawford & Simpson, were in a similar condition, and occupied buildings which had been designed for a number of small businesses, rather than one large one. All kinds of a store were situated in all kinds of a building.

But these casual methods of accommodating a business so complicated and demanding such perfect organization as that of a department store, were manifestly bound to be superseded. Moreover, from the start there were firms who controlled sufficient capital immediately to provide buildings adequate to their needs, The most remark-able instance of this fact in the history of the retail trade of New York was, of course, A. T. Stewart. He began business indeed in a shop 22 x 30 at No. 283 Broadway, and for many years he shifted from place to place, renting ever larger accommodations in much the same neighborhood. But Mr. Stewart soon controlled ▶

First National Bank Building, Chicago, D.H. Burnham & Co., architects, 1903 (demolished).

Store and Office Building, Minneapolis, F.B. & L.L. Long, architects, n.d.

opposite: Railway Exchange Building, Chicago, D.H. Burnham & Co., architects, 1903–04.

costly; but there is less external art, less visible splendor, less effort to create interesting structures; on the contrary, the high building as illustrated in many of its most recent examples in New York, is a frigidly severe edifice, a sheer brick wall, lit with numberless windows, and with the smallest possible efforts to give it architectural form or rhythm.

As an illustration, let me take a group of buildings in lower William street. The Woodbridge Building has a front filling an entire block. Its facade contains no ornamental detail, and yet it is a very excellent effort to treat a commercial front in a dignified and architectural manner. It starts out with a basement of two stories in stone; then an intermediate story, in which the windows are in pairs and round arched; then a superstructure of eight stories, in which the walls are treated as piers carrying round arches; finally an attic story; all above the basement is in warm, yellow brick. The structure, as will now be perceived, is not a "high" building, as such structures are understood; but it is notable for the fact that its architect undertook to treat his front in an architectural way; he discarded ornament, but retained form; and he produced a design of considerable interest and of much architectural merit.

Pass down the street and compare it with the Wyllis Building, the Bishop Building, and No. 68 William street; compare it again with the Kuhn, Loeb & Co. Building, with the Wall Street Exchange, with the new structures in the lower part of Wall street. A basement of one or two stories is still retained; but above there is nothing but wall and windows, windows and wall. There is no effort to group the openings, no wall treatment, no piers; even the attic story fails to emphasize itself, or is so far removed from the street as to be actually out of the design. If these latest buildings are the last word in high design, as it is understood in New York, it is obvious that the artistic architect is but of the effort altogether, and the high building has become a simple box, with openings in it to admit the light.

An economic restraint has, apparently, come over our high buildings, which is most detrimental to them in an artistic manner. Whether the architects have given up the problem in despair, whether clients have despaired of the architects, whether there has come a realizing sense on all sides of the utter commercial character of these structures and therefore, of the apparent folly of making them artistic, I do not know; but here arc the results, and very unpleasant most of them are.

Yet rigidity of treatment is not incompatible with successful and interesting results: huge height is not inconsistent with interesting efforts: a barren wall, the piling of windows one on top of another is not necessarily devoid of merit; all of which is most pleasingly and successfully illustrated in the Whitehall Building. Simplicity of parts could hardly go further than here. The stone basement is as devoid of unconstructional parts as the plainest building in New York; the tremendous superstructure has not a single note of ornament! And the walls are sheer brick fronts. But success here has been obtained by a clever use of color; the central walls are red brick; the end pavilions of light colored brick, with thin lines of red: the stone of the base is gray; the attic is simple and re-strained. In plain words, this elevation was studied, and studied intelligently and well; no one would think, for a moment, that its parts were thrown hastily together and the topmost course of brick laid with the utmost haste, that an unpleasant task could be completed as speedily as possibly and with the smallest effort. Yet New York has not a few such buildings and some of the latest and biggest are distressful examples of such unarchitectural proceedings.

Are we getting anywhere? Apparently we have run the gamut of ornamental structures and settled down-or is it up? -to useful ones, in which there shall be plenty of utility and the smallest possible amount of art. The basic type of design is still adhered to-basement, superstructure and attic-but the basement is hardly more than the protrusion of the foundation above the soil; the superstructure is a shapeless tier of windows; the attic a mere finish. The latter has long been a favorite feature with New York architects. The logic of their proceedings is quite irresistible; the lightest parts cannot be below, and a building must come to an end; let us, they have cried with one voice, adorn our buildings at the top. By this time apparently, they have awakened to the fact that the tops of their structures are so remote from the ground that no one can see them, and it has become absolutely true that the enriched attic story is becoming a feature of the past. But they still remain with us, and as one travels down Wall street quite a series presents itself; the Atlantic Building, the Sampson Building, and the structures below Pearl street, all characterized by a lower severity and enriched crowning, much of which, owing to the low altitude of the adjoining structures, is still visible, but seemingly destined, in the near future to he well hidden from the view of posterity.

The ornamental entrance story has disappeared even more quickly than the decorated attic. The Atlantic Building boasts a crowning member of considerable richness, but the basement story is quite bare in its simplicity. The single feature is a heavy entrance portico, which is in striking contrast with the delicate carving of the United States Trust Company Building labeled immediately adjoining it. The latter is not a high building, although the time is not far past when it was proudly labeled a "modern office building." The contrast is most impressive. The United States Trust is a building of moderate height, treated in an architectural manner, and deco-rated with finely carved capitals and bands. The Atlantic Building is several times its height; has the barest of porticos as its chief lower ornament; has a featureless superstructure, and flares out above with a crowning member of several stories quite elaborately treated, a system of design that has become almost typical in New York.

The change towards simplicity in design, it should be thoroughly understood, is quite for the worst. Mr. Hardenbergh has shown,

in his Whitehall Building, that simplicity is not incompatible with dignity, and that this dignity may have a decided quality of beauty; but the lesson has not been generally learned, nor its possibility appreciated. The featureless high building-the front that is merely, built up, story on story, tier upon tier-until the appropriation gives out-is no embellishment to our thoroughfares. Wealth of ornamentation is not embellishment; the prefixing of unnecessary parts is perhaps needless; but lack of interest is altogether inexcusable, and of this there is still a plenty and to spare.

A plain, wall, however, has merits which the variegated treatment entirely fails in. Our architects are apparently moving away from the repetition of motif illustrated in the American Tract Society Building, the

Park Row Building, the St. Paul Building, in each of which a large feature of several stories is repeated several times. It was an unfortunate system that should never have been tried more than once, for it quite ignored the idea that the high building was a unity, requiring to be designed as a whole, and not treated as a series of buildings piled

sufficient cash to buy any accommodation his business demanded, and in 1848 he astonished New York by building the marble building at Broadway and Chambers street, at present known as the Stewart Building. This was the first example in this country of the dedication of so large a building to retail trade, and the newspapers at the period did not fail to be properly impressed. But Mr. Stewart's marble palace only sufficed for his needs some fourteen years. In 1862 he moved into the store occupying the whole block, bounded by Broadway, Ninth street, Fourth avenue and Tenth street, and this building was the first example, either in the United States or any other country, of the erection of something resembling a modern department store building. When Mr. Stewart died, in 1876, his building was still, so the New York papers stated, the largest of its kind in the world. It was proudly proclaimed to cover eight floors of 2 acres each, to require engines developing 520 horse-power to keel) its machinery going, to accommodate 2,000 employees and to have done a business (although this was an exaggeration) of some $50,000,000 in one year.

At that time, however, none of Mr. Stewart's competitors followed his example, probably because they could not afford to. His resources were immeasurably greater than those of any other storekeeper in New York, and after his death his business was not conducted in a fashion that made competing stores fear the unequal advantages, which his business enjoyed in having a building specially designed for the purpose. It was the appearance, in j896, of a firm, Messrs. Siegel, Cooper & Co., hailing from Chicago, which stirred up the department storekeepers ▸

1904

North American Building, Philadelphia, James H. Windrim, architect, 1900.

opposite: Kean, Van Cortlandt & Co. Building, New York City, Warren & Wetmore, architects, 1903.

one on top of the other. Yet the horizontal line remains in high favor, buildings which are without any other effort at architectural treatment, being erected with each story carefully indicated by bands and string-courses repeated "*ad infinitum.*"

It is strange, this cutting up of buildings into layers. There is a new building going up at Pearl and Beaver streets, unfinished when these words are written; but a building with a sharply rounded end, as befits the site. Each floor of the otherwise unmarked superstructure is indicated by bands of darker brick, as though the breadth was the element to he insisted on in a building whose greatest distinction is its height. The attic member of this structure promises to be a brilliant piece of polychromatic work, one of the most striking novelties in high building design.

The most impressive element in the high building is its height; that is the single feature that distinguishes it from all other structures. Of all the architects who have essayed to solve the problem of high design, Mr. Louis H. Sullivan, of Chicago, has alone frankly expressed the vertical element and given the high building logical as well as genuinely artistic expression. New York is fortunate in possessing in a building in Bleecker street, a fine example of Mr. Sullivan's work. It would be interesting to transplant it to Broad street, set it up before Carrère & Hastings's Blair Building, and ask them to exchange views on each other's aspect.

The architects of both structures studied at the Ecole des Beaux Arts in Paris; the Western architect has long been our most conspicuously individual practitioner; the New York firm is easily one of the most distinguished practitioners in the academic style. Their buildings are as far apart as the poles; both are fine examples of their kind; both well illustrate the characteristics of their designers. And both are vertical buildings. It is a triumph of principles over art; for Mr. Hastings has not previously given us a vertical high building, having contented himself with the repetitive method. Mr. Sullivan can not count Mr. Hastings as a dis-

ciple—they are much too far apart artistically for that—but at least he has pointed the way which Mr. Hastings has gladly taken in this most distinguished design. One has but to compare it with the immediately adjoining Cable Building, to become aware of how much better things can be done to-day than were done a few years since.

The Kean, Van Cortlandt & Co. Building in Cedar street is an-other structure whose chief interest is the frank way in which it displays its Beaux Artism. Here again a vertical design, in so far that the chief part, the superstructure, is treated in great bays of seven stories, that emerge from a base and intermediate story of three floors; the attic is a single story. It is an honest effort to apply Beaux Arts ideas to the high building, although lacking in interest. Like many other new high buildings the ornamental enrichment of the lower stories is heavy and large; more vigorous by far than that which any French architect would produce, and heavier than seems called for in a building of such moderate dimensions.

It is a difficult problem, this of the scale of ornament. The buildings are so huge, the basements necessarily so heavy to seem to carry the weight above them, that the architect who would seek to treat the question logically from the standpoint of the whole, has a sorry task. And his difficulties are not lessened when classic detail is employed, for his capitals and ornaments increase with diameters, and the laws of Vignola were not drawn to solve such problems as the modern Beaux Arts architects set out to illustrate them with.

The sightseer very soon learns to realize that there is little within the high building to see-the more reason, therefore, it would appear to make the outside beautiful and impressive. The problem of the interior is chiefly one of plan and of construction. Yet our great commercial buildings are not entirely without interior interest. The entrance and lobby, the elevator hall and vestibule, are legitimate spaces for the display of the architect's personal taste. Make them as splendid as possible, was once the universal rule; I doubt if this is quite so general now.

Take the Mutual Life Building as an example. The entrance hall on Nassau street–the oldest part of the building–is quite splendid with its columns and arches, its

walls and ceiling, all of polished and carved marble. The entrance is up a flight of steps within an outer porch, and one enters a rectangular vestibule, large enough to give a decided sense of space. The Metropolitan Life has a larger and more sumptuous vestibule than this, but that of the Mutual Life is comparatively large and is by no means recent. It is in striking contrast to the

entrance of the National Bank of Commerce—a later building–just across the street. One stumbles there almost into the elevators, so narrow is the space: but even this shallow entrance is sumptuous with polished marble, as are most of the hallways and corridors of the large buildings.

But the Mutual Life Building has received several successive additions, and it would seem entirely proper to utilize them as types of progress. Around in Liberty street, the first entrance is No. 32. One goes in almost directly from the street level. There is nothing of the splendor of the entrance on Nassau street; only a small, com-pact corridor; marble walls, it is true, but the slightest decoration. Further down, No. 26, is another type. The elevators are in a branch corridor to the right; directly in face is a partly hidden stairway: rich marble again; but restrained. This, then, would seem to be the type of the high building entranceway: rich materials. These materials in older buildings were richly treated: in the newer they are still rich in surface treatment, but the architectural parts have almost completely disappeared. Apparently, no more money is being lavished on these great buildings than can be absolutely avoided.

The outlook is not cheering. There is no standard of artistic excellence. There is no indication of general appreciation of the real problems involved. There is plenty of haphazard effort, a good deal of well-meant effort, an occasional success. We had as much ten years ago: and we have to-day a vast quantity of uninteresting building which harms through its very negativeness. Surely every possible expedient and experiment has been tried. The time for such ventures has passed. The high building problem is not one that will solve itself but it can only be solved by the most painstaking care, by the most thorough study of past efforts and failures, and by a thoroughly artistic meeting of the conditions involved. There never was a type of building evolved yet of which it can be better said, "the more haste the less speed." ∎

of New York to make their buildings as convenient as possible for a class of trade so intricate and so enormous. Before that date, indeed, many important New York stores, such as Altman's, McCreery on 23d street, and Stern's, had provided themselves with improved accommodations. But none of these buildings, while large and interesting examples of store construction, occupied a continuous frontage on three streets, and they were none of them in quite the same class as the building of Siegel, Cooper & Co., which not only covered a block front on Sixth avenue, between 18th and 19th streets, but also included 460 feet on 18th street and 460 feet on 19th street. The example of Messrs. Siegel, Cooper & Co. finally forced other important Sixth avenue firms to follow suit. In recent years Messrs. Adams & Co. and Simpson, Crawford & Simpson have built handsome structures, occupying block frontages and containing all the improvements and conveniences demanded by the peculiar needs of a department store which mechanical ingenuity can suggest. More recently still, Messrs. R. H. Macy & Co. decided to move from the location at 14th street and Sixth avenue, which the firm have so long and so successfully occupied, and build a new and magnificent habitation on Greeley square, between 34th and 35th streets. The plans of this store is the outcome of all the knowledge and experience gained in the planning of the building previously erected, and in describing the kind of building which such a business as that of a modern department store requires, one is obliged inevitably to use this building more than any other as a type. * * * ●

**The Ingalls Building,
Cincinnati, Ohio,
Elzner & Anderson, 1902-1903**

The elegant structure is recognized as the first reinforced-concrete high-rise office building in the world. Although Elzner had designed the city's first fireproof steel-skeleton high-rise office building—the Neave Building, 1890 (demolished)—Cincinnati's financial leaders called upon the Chicago firm of D.H. Burnham & Co. to design a group of steel-skeleton skyscrapers after the turn of the century. The local firm of Elzner & Anderson, however, staked their own—and Cincinnati's—claim to innovation with the Ingalls Building.

opposite: Chamber of Commerce, Cincinnati, H.H. Richardson, architect, 1885–88 (destroyed by fire). The building burned in 1911 and was replaced by a tower designed by Cass Gilbert with Garber & Woodward.

THE FIRST CONCRETE SKYSCRAPER

A.O. Elzner[1]

WHILE it may be some time before all the lessons of the great Baltimore fire[2] will have been learned, one point, at least, appears to have been clearly demonstrated, which is that concrete-steel construction went through the terrible ordeal with remarkable results and has thereby demonstrated its superiority as structural material for buildings. A small four-story building with a cast-iron front located in the heart of the burned district, was originally a brick building with ordinary wooden joist floors. Recently, however, the floors were taken out and the entire interior reconstructed with concrete-steel columns, girders and floors, while the brick walls were retained for the enclosure of the building. The fire demolished a large portion of the walls, but the entire concrete construction, columns, girders and floors, remained standing uninjured by the fire and intact, except some slight bruises inflicted by falling walls. What a pity that the walls, too, had not been of concrete; for in such case the result must surely have been very different.

In view, therefore, of the remarkable test which this wonderful material so successfully withstood, the entire architectural and engineering professions, as well as the builders and the building public, should be interested to know that while concrete-steel is not by any means a new material, or rather combination of materials, and has been seriously taken up only in recent years, it has nevertheless long since passed the experimental stage, and fully demonstrated its general adaptability to the many complex problems of modern building, even to the most exacting of all; the skyscraper-the first example of which is the Ingalls Building, built on the northeast corner of Fourth and Vine Streets, Cincinnati, Ohio. It is, indeed, an accomplished fact—the first concrete skyscraper. It was begun in the fall of 1902 and has just been completed, having required in its erection but very little longer

time than the standard steel cage type would have done, and at probably somewhat less cost. It is but fair to add, also, that in the next building of this kind not only the cost, but also the time required for completion, would undoubtedly be considerably reduced; and without question this process will be carried to a much higher development as the material comes to be more thoroughly studied and understood. The rapidly increasing production of high-grade Portland cement in this country cannot fail to help further in reducing the cost and insuring the popularity of the construction.

The Ingalls Building occupies the entire area of a corner lot, 50 X 100 feet, and is fifteen stories and a full attic, practically sixteen stories, rising to a height of 210 feet above the sidewalks. The one-half of the basement is the usual twelve feet deep; but the other half, containing the power plant, is twenty feet deep. The foundations extend five feet below this, so that the entire height of the structure from the bottom of the foundation is 235 feet, entirely concrete-steel. In fact, it is a concrete box of 8-inch walls, with concrete floors and roof, concrete beams, concrete columns, concrete stairs; the whole entirely devoid of the usual I-beams, Z-bars, angle irons, plates, rivets and bolts. It consists merely of bars embedded in concrete, with the ends interlaced, making actually a complete concrete monolith of the entire building, covered on the exterior with a veneer from four to six inches thick of white marble for the lower three stories, glazed gray brick for the next eleven, and glazed white terra cotta for the top story and cornice.

The principles of concrete-steel are rapidly coming to be fairly well understood, especially so by the structural engineers; for, after all, it is primarily an engineering problem. But without question, a large proportion of the profession, and certainly the great majority of architects have not as yet had actual experience in its use, and perhaps have not given the subject the serious consideration which it deserves.

A brief description, therefore, may not be

from
THE BUILDING OF CINCINNATI
By Montgomery Schuyler
Vol. XXIII, No. 5., May, 1908,
pp. 337-366.

Like every other American town, Cincinnati, after its little futile dalliance with "Queen Anne," submitted to its phase of Richardsonian Romanesque as the next stage of its architectural evolution. To call it evolution were, of course to insult the memory of Darwin, since evolution implies a direction and a progress, which things are incompatible with jumping from one fashion to another without visible motive. We can no more call such changes of fashion evolutionary in architecture than in millinery. But at least Cincinnati was very lucky in its chief example of the Richardsonian Romanesque. It had the advantage of having it done by Richardson himself, and the Cincinnati Chamber of Commerce (above) is one of the most characteristic and most creditable of his works. It is a most instructive example of his talent for simplification.

...The Richardsonian fashion passed away, all the same, and was succeeded as elsewhere, leaving in its wake not only the master's piece, which comes so near being his masterpiece, but such moderate and agreeable and unpretentious examples as the building of the Y.M.C.A. (p. 117). First the elevator building with real walls, and then the skeleton of the skyscraper, were des- ▸

Ingalls Building, under construction, (all photos this page) Cincinnati, Elzner & Anderson, architects, 1903.

1 Alfred O. Elzner (1862-1933) was trained at M.I.T. and in the office of H.H. Richardson near Boston. He returned to Cincinnati in 1886 to supervise construction of Richardson's Cincinnati Chamber of Commerce Building (1885-88). Elzner was joined in 1897 by George M. Anderson (1869-1916), member of a prominent Cincinnati family and brother of an officer of the Ferro Concrete Construction Co., which built the Ingalls Building.
  Melville E. Ingalls was a far-sighted entrepreneur who consolidated the "Big Four" railroad system in Cincinnati.

2 The fire of 1904, which destroyed almost every building in downtown Baltimore, provided impetus for needed revitalization.

out of place at this point. In the first place then, let it be understood that for structural purposes the concrete should be made of strictly high-grade Portland cement, clean sand, containing, if possible, grains of variable size, and crushed stone or gravel. In the superstructure, limestone should not be used, as it would too readily be injured in a fire. Such concrete should be dense, that is to say, the voids should be well filled, and all thoroughly tamped. Enough water should be used to make a soft concrete, so as to insure perfect contact with the steel bars; for concrete-steel, it must be remembered, depends for its strength chiefly upon the adhesion between the concrete and the steel. The concrete itself is figured only in compression, never in tension; and wherever tension occurs, this is to be taken up by the steel bars; as, for instance, in the bottom of a beam or footing, or near the surface of a column where wind or other bending stresses must be considered. The compression in columns is taken up chiefly by the concrete; but where this is not sufficient, vertical steel bars are inserted, which, however, must be thoroughly tied together to prevent spreading. Shearing stresses in beams and columns are taken up first by the concrete, but this must be reinforced by bars placed across the line of shear.

The floors are preferably made in slabs of uniform thickness and reinforced near the underside with bars of steel mesh of various forms. It is of utmost importance, however, that the amount of steel used should be determined by actual calculation, and not by guesswork or rule of thumb, as is apt to be the case. Walls, if used merely as curtain walls, may be as thin as three to four inches, or not more than six to eight inches, as may be required by the depth of the window box. They should, however, be reinforced by a network of bars, placed not over three or four feet apart both vertically and horizontally, to prevent shrinkage cracks.

In the Ingalls Building, described here, a system of cold-twisted square bars was used throughout. This gives excellent results, due to the greatly increased tensile strength of

the bars after twisting, and the mechanical grip of the twisted bar on the concrete.

The floors are continuous slabs 5 inches thick, reinforced with a mesh of 3/4 inch square twisted steel bars from 18 to 20 inches on centers in both directions and strengthened by a beam or rib across the center of the column bay of 16x32 feet, dividing this into two panels, each 16 feet square, without any other supporting beams.

The columns have stiffening bars placed on two opposite sides near the surface to take the wind strains. They are further reinforced near the center by compression bars, which take up all such load as may be required in excess of the carrying capacity of the concrete alone. These bars not being in tension need not be twisted, and accordingly plain round bars were used of various sizes, according to location, from 2 1/2 to 3 1/2 inches in the basement, diminishing in numbers and sizes in succeeding stories until they were reduced to 1-inch and then entirely abandoned at about the tenth floor, from which point on, the concrete was sufficient to do all the work. The interior or compression bars had the ends milled off and were joined just above the floor level by a sleeve of steam pipe, a trifle larger than the

bars and grouted with cement. They were then tied together firmly at three or four points in the height by small bars bent around them. The exterior or wind bars were joined in the center of the story height by splices, which consisted of several smaller bars wired about the joint. The columns were further reinforced by means of hoops of 1/4 inch bars, placed around all the bars near the surface at intervals of from 12 to 18 inches throughout the height. As stated before, these prevent the spreading of the bars and take up the excess of vertical shear.

The question has been asked as to how the girders were connected to the columns. Very simple, indeed; the girder bars merely extend in between the column bars and the concrete of the one being monolithic with that of the other completes and perfects the connection, than which nothing could be more secure. The walls above the piers of the lower two stories are 8 inches thick and afford the best possible system of wind bracing inasmuch as the entire mass between the head of one window and the sill of the one next above is figured as a beam with rods top and bottom.

The method of supporting the exterior facing of marble, brick, or terra cotta, as the case may be, is as simple as it is effective. In the case of the marblework or granite, if such be used, for the lower stories, a concrete ledge or corbel is formed around the piers just below the sidewalk level, and these afford the necessary foundation for such face work.

In the case of the face brick above, the various floor slabs are merely extended out beyond the wall three inches. This forms a ledge for the support of the brick facing, each story being independent of the other, and is afterward covered with 1-inch tile, or whatever may be desired.

All the face work, however, is securely anchored by means of round wrought-iron bars which are built into the concrete by boring holes of proper size through the wood forms and inserting the anchors, which are perfectly straight at the time, but are afterwards bent to suit; they must be straight so that the form work can be drawn over them upon being removed, when the concrete has sufficiently set.

In case of the cornice, which is of terra cotta, the roof slab was simply projected out as a cantilever to the required distance, which in this case was 5 feet. Sleeves of sheet iron were inserted at proper points and remained built into the concrete, and bolts to secure the terra cotta were afterward inserted through them and grouted in place.

In a brief sketch like this, it would be impossible to describe the points of advantage peculiar to this method of construction. There are many, and it might suffice to say that numerous new problems are encountered, and while they are all solved in a satisfactory manner, it must be remembered that this is the first attempt to make a consistent application of the concrete-steel system to the skyscraper problem. It has apparently been eminently satisfactory, yet it is not claimed to be final in all respects, and there will undoubtedly be marked improvements here and there as the system develops.

Let us hope that engineers and architects may apply themselves earnestly to the question, so that little time may be lost in perfecting at last a rational system of construction, which will make impossible such disastrous fires as that of Baltimore.

During the progress of the work on the Ingalls Building, some men of great ability who should have known better, predicted that the structure would never reach the roof, and that even if it did, it would certainly crack all to pieces by shrinkage and that it could not possibly withstand wind pressure. The facts are that it did reach the roof; that there are no shrinkage cracks, and that the building not only has not blown over, but that in the highest winds, there is not even a perceptible tremor, and that too with concrete walls only eight inches thick from bottom to top, and the floors but five inches thick in unbroken slabs sixteen feet square, a portion of which on the second floor carries a bank vault weighing nearly a hundred tons.

Such and other equally absurd arguments

tined to succeed it for commercial purposes. As is apt to be the case, the former is architecturally more attractive than the latter Whatever the fact may be, it is evident that the Sinton Hotel (below) and the Citizens' National Bank (bottom) are susceptible of construction in actual masonry. The widening of the terminal piers, especially great and especially grateful in the case of the latter building is therefore quite plausible, while it would be at least wasteful in the case of a steel skeleton venered with masonry. The hotel looks a good deal like a good many others, but the bank has real distinction. When we come, however, upon ▸

Captions for these building can be found on the following page.

1904

having fallen to the ground. The opponents of this construction pointed first to what they were pleased to call excessively large columns; then they referred to failures of various concrete constructions, and finally discovered that the steel building could be erected more rapidly than the concrete one.

These arguments, which appear to be the only ones left to the opponents of concrete, are really not more substantial than the others. In the first place, the column design, especially in the lower portion of the structure, was almost wholly a new proposition, and was largely controlled by a spirit of conservatism which was but natural in so radical a departure. As a matter of fact the columns might readily be made much smaller, perhaps not much larger than a properly fireproofed steel column. Manifestly the sizes of concrete structural members have not yet been reduced to the most economical basis, and it may, and undoubtedly will, require some little time, for since it is a comparatively new field of engineering, it must have time to grow. But that it will grow and will mature just as steel engineering did, there can be no doubt for we have but to look at the research of such men as Considère and others, to marvel at the possibilities in store for us with this remarkable material.

Regarding the failures of concrete constructions which have occurred and which are much to be deplored it is only fair to say that the popularity of the new method has been so great that anybody and everybody has rushed into it, and as will happen in such events, without stopping to secure experienced foremen or engineers, who, by the way, must naturally be scarce in these first few years of development. But time will correct all this, as it will also the last argument: that of increased facility of erection. If the first concrete skyscraper required only a few months longer in erection than did the most recent one in steel, which has passed through nearly a generation of development, it cannot be difficult to believe that in a few years this slight difference in time will not only disappear, but that in this, as in all

other points, the race will be to the concrete.

Now let us view the question from a purely architectural standpoint. We have been told over and over again that the skyscraper problem still remains unsolved. The critics will have it that there must be no imitation or representation of masonry construction, and that in some way or other still to be discovered or invented, the steel skeleton must find adequate expression through its fireproof casings. Perhaps so; but it will be a difficult thing to do with entire consistency. Again, if the dress is not to be an imitation, even of masonry, then it is clear that we cannot well have a dress at all, and be truthful in our design. And since the building laws very properly require the steel skeleton to be covered, we cannot escape the use of an architectural dress. In other words, as long as the visible architecture of the steel skeleton building will, as it evidently must, remain a mere sham construction, the critics will never be able to accord it a place in true art.

The only way out of the dilemma, therefore, would seem to turn to concrete, and see what solution this construction has to offer. Already it is beginning to assert itself: slowly, of course, but surely. Before long it will enter into friendly rivalry with steel; then will follow sharp competition, and finally a struggle for popularity. Why?

Because, first of all, concrete will form a better investment. Did it not pass through the terrible Baltimore fire better than steel? And this fact carries with it a long story of incidental fire losses, greater endurance, preservation, and what not?

Then, too, it will be considerably cheaper. It requires a great deal of capital these days and always will, to equip and operate a steel plant, and the price of structural steel has been pretty well settled, and is not likely ever to be very much less than it has been. Moreover, it can be produced only in certain limited locations, which involves long hauls and heavy freight bills.

On the other hand, the manufacture of Portland cement involves a comparatively small amount of capital and very small operating expenses. Deposits of suitable material are being discovered everywhere in all parts of the country (and we are only interested in this country at present), and cement plants are springing up in most surprising numbers. This activity is bound to continue in an increasing ratio as the demand for this wonderful material grows. It follows, therefore, that production is not susceptible to the control of combines to such an extent as is the case with steel; the result of which naturally will be relatively lower prices for cement.

Now to turn to the third argument in behalf of concrete. This will appeal to our friends the critics, for it deals with the purely architectural question, which, after all, is the greatest and highest and will endure long after all others have been silenced. Inasmuch as a concrete building is not built up like masonry but is actually poured into a mould in its entirety, it at once becomes a monolithic structure, every particle of which is doing structural duty; and this can be said truthfully and without hesitation. Now then, it is not incumbent upon us to face the concrete with marble, or brick and terra cotta, as was done in the Ingalls Building, for reasons of momentary expediency, for as the state of art advances, the architectural forms, mouldings and what not, will be incorporated with the moulds for the structural work, and upon removing the form work, the surface of the exposed concrete, will be given the desired finish of rubbing or tooling, as the case may be. Thus we will have a truly rational architecture, in which there is no sham, no deception, a solid thing, no joints, every member incorporated with and a part of a living body, living because it is straining every particle of its substance in the performance of a great work, in its own self-preservation; a living architecture, indeed, and a rational one in every sense of the word, which will rise far above criticism and endure as long as the hands of man shall not be raised to its destruction. ∎

such an unmistakable example of the skeleton construction as the Traction building (above) we come upon the pretence of a construction which would manifestly be impracticable. Of course, this is a criticism which "runs at large" and is not to be imputed to the

designers of these particular buildings, although to the designer of the stereotyped pattern of skyscraper we may apply what was said of the mob of gentlemen who wrote with ease pentameter couplets, more or less in the manner of Pope, that one no more admires a man for being able to write them than for being able to write his own name. The Ingalls building is apparently, in the photograph, an exemplification of the same truth. In fact,

however, it is constructed of ferro-concrete, veneered with marble and terra-cotta, and is a pioneer in the application of that made of construction to the skyscraper. The unaffected ugliness and bare utilitarianism, for instance, of the Textile building (below, column two), which is plainly and, so to say, avowedly inconstructible in masonry, become rather dignified in comparison with the pretension of the more "architecturesque" skyscrapers, though to be sure, the cornice projecting above the eighth story of the Textile Building is as manifest as it is a futile sacrifice to the graces. One prefers that straightforward cage, the Pugh Building (below) with which the advertisements plastered

over its flank are not in the least incongruous. But a much more grateful object than any of these skyscrapers is the Baldwin Factory (below), which carries no ornament that can be said to be incongruous with its utilitarian purpose, and yet the design of which, it is quite evident, has received successful architectural consideration. After the skeletons, the wearied eye reposes upon it with much satisfaction. ●

1904

**Schlesinger & Mayer
Department Store,
Chicago,
Louis Henri Sullivan,
architect, 1899.**

This was one of the first
large department stores to
use fireproof steel-frame
construction. As a result of
the lighter supporting members, the interior is spacious, well lit, and has an
ease of access around fixtures and between floors.
Lyndon Smith points out,

*"...window openings are of
maximum size and form a
distinct basis of the exterior
design. The detail of the
decorative treatment
around these openings
enhances the outlook, and
gives additional values to
the exterior effect."*

 Sales levels were joined
by an art gallery, café,
restaurant, and exquisitely-
furnished lounge. The fine-
ly-crafted exterior ornament
at street level is by Sullivan
and George Elmslie.

opposite: A contemplative
portrait of Sullivan from
another article by Lyndon P.
Smith, entitled, "The Home
of an Artist-Architect:Louis
H. Sullivan's Place at Ocean
Springs, Mississippi."
[XVI l:6 June 1905 pp 471-490]

THE SCHLESINGER & MAYER BUILDING

An Attempt to Give Functional Expression to the Architecture of a Department Store

Lyndon P. Smith[1]

THE tide of commerce ebbs and flows along State Street, in Chicago, and as the observer moves with the passing throng, his attention will be drawn toward the corner of Madison Street, and retained there by a building recently completed. It is one of many devoted to the retailing of goods, but on an extensive scale and including a large percentage of women among its patrons. This function is unmistakably expressed in the design. The city in which the building is located has the peculiarity of concentrating its commercial district in a comparatively limited area within which there has been erected a large number of buildings of like purpose and character. The one in question is not of colossal type. Its façade is not based on "features," but its individuality is distinct. Its exterior frankly betokens its structural basis and rises in no uncertain fashion from sidewalk to cornice. It is a logical solution of the commercial building, such as a department store, the latest and best achievement produced in this country.

This result has taken some time to accomplish and is the culmination of a long series of previous efforts, all working toward the better expression of what is regarded as our most unsatisfactory architectural problem. It is the outcome of careful preparation, skillful study and its application, maturity of mind and full sympathy between the maker of ideas and the makers of materials.

The design is thoroughly modern. It shows fully the structural function of the steel frame with the enclosing protection of terra cotta, treated with full knowledge of its plasticity, in its natural state and hardness and durability after treatment in the kiln. The lower portion on the street is equally straightforward in its qualities of "plate glass" architecture. Here are the largest openings possible for display windows and their attractions to feminine eyes are framed by a surrounding of elaborate decoration in cast metal. These forms immediately attract attention. They are full of vitality, of movement, grace and line. They twine and intertwine, divide and subdivide in marvellous fashion, yet they are ever traceable to their parent source and strongly organic.

In the Prudential Building, in Buffalo, which emanated from the same head,[2] the essential element is masculinity.[3] It is an American office building dominated by men and devoted to the transaction, of their business in all its multitudinous forms—the elements of activity, ambition and directness of purpose, are all shown thereby in the architectural forms.

The Schlesinger & Mayer Building is a differentiation of the commercial problem and has been treated entirely on its own merits, both in the general design and in the detail. This is frankly a department store—an establishment where goods of many kinds may be retailed to many people and so displayed over large floor areas, that ease of examination and accessibility to products may be speedily achieved. Hence, throughout its typical floors, the window openings are of maximum size and form a distinct basis of the exterior design. The detail of the decorative treatment around these openings enhances the outlook, and gives additional values to the exterior effect. The building terminates in a cornice based on the projecting roof beams and rationally functional.[4]

There were certain modifications in the structure during its erection based on changes incidental to the growth of the business and project. The first of the sections built was on the less important street and eight stories high. With the erection of the corner section four stories were added in height. This increase showed the integrity of the basic design. The building was simply carried up the additional stories desired, to twelve, and the terminal foliations of the stem-like columns and the cornice detail correspondingly enlarged for their additional distance from normal viewing.

The treatment of the ornamental detail is

review by William L. Steele:
KINDERGARTEN CHATS: ON ARCHITECTURE EDUCTION AND DEMOCRACY, By Louis H. Sullivan. Introduced by Claude Bragdon.
Vol. 78, No. 1, July 1935, pp. 11–12.

Not more than once in a lifetime, it seems to me, may a man expect to be called upon to review a book of such deep and vital significance as this one. As a human document of the utmost sincerity it may not be challenged. Furthermore, the book is dedicated to truth in architecture. A claim to some degree of veracity is therefore implied. To those of us who still cling to the old-fashioned belief in absolute values and who have answered, at least to our own satisfaction, the ancient question of Pilate, the mere idea of such a book suggests an oasis in Sahara. I can promise a thrilling experience to anyone who will read this book in that kind of receptive spirit. The skeptical reader will probably not be converted, but he will enjoy the logical unfolding of Sullivan's philosophy, and the bountiful exuberance of its quality of utterance. It is a rare book, and you are quite likely to be enthralled by it.

* * *

Sullivan was profoundly discouraged by the reception given to "Kindergarten Chats." He loved ▶

1 Little is known about Lyndon P. Smith. A friend of Sullivan's, Smith worked with him on the Bayard Building in New York City (page 61). He owned a house in Palisades, New York, where it seems several of the "Chats" were written. Tear-sheets of the original published *KINDERGARTEN CHATS* were kept in a scrapbook by Smith. Among some letters found in the scrapbook were the following from Sullivan himself:

Dec. 13th 1900
Dear Lyndon:
It may interest you to know that I have arranged to write 52 articles on American architecture for the INTERSTATE ARCHITECT & BUILDER of Cleveland. Publication to begin about March 1st 1901—In reality the 52 articles will constitute one argument and will all be interelated. I have completed two, up to date, and I think the "style" of them will interest you. They will be called "Kindergarten Chats."
Yours,
Louis

Feb. 18 1900
My dear Lyndon:
I should like to have the "Kindergarten Chats" circulated as extensively as possible among the laity. The architects will not understand much of what is in them, but the laity, more open-minded, will.

2 Sullivan's name only appears under photos—never in the article proper. This isn't unusual in the magazine, but it is particularly noticeable with someone of Sullivan's stature.

3 Rarely does one come across writing about Sullivan where the words "virility" or "masculinity" aren't used. These terms originate in Sullivan's own writings.

essentially appealing in its quality to femininity. It is sensitive to a high degree, delicately pleasing to the sympathetic eye and with fine feeling and movement permeating its most incidental ramification.

The entire scheme is one organic whole and is carried out in full harmony and balance. Values are carefully preserved and a consistent motive[5] runs through the ornament. The surfaces, either treated in relief or in one plane indicate careful study with fine appreciation of the natural qualities thereof.

In addition to the cast and moulded ornamental detail of the exterior, this same treatment is preserved to an exceptional degree in the interior work. All of the woodwork has undergone the most careful inspection and valuation before selection in the paneling and careful matching of the wood. There are also effects obtained through the product of modern machines and appliances intelligently used by logical designing. This is

especially achieved in a screen of sawed wood, enclosing a corner of the third floor and making thereof a writing and retiring room. The upper portion of the wainscoting is made with panels of five thicknesses of sawed mahogany. The outer two thicknesses or planes are curved lines, the next two are straight lines, the middle plane a combination of both. These all placed in sequence produce a fine orchestration of ornamental form with a development of light and shade greatly enhancing the values of the successive surfaces. It is, without doubt, the most unique and beautifully elaborate woodwork made in this country, using modern methods in the manufacture.

So, throughout the entire building, inside and out, is carried the integral scheme of functional form and its appropriate expression in terms of material. All this is based on a comprehensive theory of architecture and a carefully developed system of expression. ∎

a good fight, and he received only a shrug of the shoulder. Even the editors of the Interstate Architect and Builder, of Cleveland, Ohio, which published the series, damned with faint praise the whole performance in the issue which carried the closing chapter. They made excuses for Mr. Sullivan, because after all, said they, "For his originality, vigor and boldness in writing who can help liking him? He exhibits a brand of manhood that Americans especially admire." As for his message, it was all a matter of "taste," as was the current "architecture" of the period—a dark period indeed for American Art. In its self-conscious "highly educated" state of mind the times were reactionary, and more hopeless than had been the dark night of twenty-five years further back when Richardson's torch began to shine into the crannies of the architectural caverns. That being so, it is but fair to give those editors credit for real courage in being to publish the essays at all.

* * *

Sullivan's influence, even in his life-time, extended farther than he knew. Certainly he was aware that a medal came to him from France in recognition of his distinguished performance as expressed in his Transportation Building at Chicago's first World's Fair. But he held himself more and more aloof from social intercourse, and could not know the ferment that was going on in the minds of many of the young men. For example, one of the lads who in Pittsburgh had poked fun at the "Chicago Renaissance," later studied in Paris, and wrote me that "these Frenchmen only know one American architect and he is Louis Sullivan."

Now that New York is tired of ▸

4 Ironically, the cornice was removed after the second renovation. The building remains today essentially without a cornice.

5 *motive or motif:* a design that consists of recurring shapes or colors.

below: Schlesinger & Mayer Department Store, as designed by Louis H. Sullivan in 1899.

above: Addition of entrance section and seven window sections, by Louis H. Sullivan in 1903; southward expansion by D.H. Burnham, 1906. Additional work by Holabrid & Root was done in 1960.

opposite: Designed by Sullivan, the office screen is of hand-sawed mahogany.

Another View—What Mr. Louis Sullivan Stands For

By H.W. Desmond

I doubt very much whether Mr. Sullivan's work has yet received the estimation and recognition which unquestionably it merits. In the wilderness of our architectural practice Mr. Sullivan occupies to-day something of the usually isolated position of the prophet, the forerunner, the intensely personal force. It is strange that this should be so in a land where strong individuality is rather prized and applauded than neglected and qualified; and in a profession, too, that is so frequently spurred by a general call for "originality"-a profession, moreover, that is at the same time brought almost daily face to face with new problems in design that really demand by the obvious logic of structure and function, the development of new architectural formulae. For, let it be well understood, Mr. Sullivan 'is really our only Modernist. He is, moreover, strictly of our soil. He has his precedents, no doubt, but his mature work, we might indeed say all but a small residuum of all his work, is not to be dated from elsewhere either as to time or place. Mr. Sullivan himself is the centre of it. He is his own inspiration, and in this sense may be as the first American architect. To say that he has invented a style would, of course, be to say too much, but he has certainly evolved and elaborated a highly artistic form of superficial decorative expression in logical connection with the American steel skeleton building. Richardson is our historical example of American originality in architecture, but Richardson's work, permeated as it is with the author's mighty personality, is not free, is indeed far from free from an archaeological basis. In the presence of Richardson's buildings, we never lose the sense that we are confronted by a colossal importation, buildings lifted, as it were, by giant hands out of some mediaeval locality, of which we fancy we can find the historical reminiscence somewhere in Romanesque France. On the other hand, there is

not a vestige of the past in Sullivan's work. It is as modern as the calendar itself. The artistic ingenuity, nay, the artistic boldness of the attempt is admirable. Here, is L'Art Nouveau indigenous to the United States, nurtured upon American problems, and yet but scantly recognized or considered by a profession that busies itself with the exotic importation of the same principles from an alien source.

The Schlesinger & Mayer Building is the latest result of Mr. Sullivan's personal initiative. We understand from sources not authoritative, but still reliable, that Mr. Sullivan worked for three years on the problem entrusted to him. If this be true it is the only antique element in a design which is almost startlingly bald in its logic and blanched in its complete disregard for any of the traditional architectural tones. The artist has stuck to his own palette, developed from himself; trusted entirely to his own inspiration.

And the result?

Mr. Smith, whose remarks precede these of mine, speaks candidly as an intelligent admirer, as a convinced enthusiast. One's first feelings perhaps is, not to disturb the mellifluous allegro; not even to question the suggested metaphysics by inquiring with too rude an analysis as to what are the essential components of the expression of femininity in architecture. We may have philosophic doubts as to this part of the Sullivan doctrine doubts which, if occasion required, one might even screw up one's courage to state with extreme positiveness; but about Mr. Sullivan's latest architectural achievement itself, one hesitates to say a word off hand or hastily. One's initial impressions of the building have a treacherous elusiveness. At first glance some judges no doubt will be tempted to exclaim: "This will never do! Facility and ingenuity have here out-run themselves—jumped, as it were, on the other side. There is always danger that the mind by excess will parody its own cleverness, and in the Schlesinger & Mayer Building, has not Sullivan himself given us the Sullivanesque?"

There is, I believe, an element in even a rapidly enunciated opinion of this sort which will persist and be a component of a final and mature judgment, but how far will this superficial impression be qualified and in what direction? The immense ability of the ornamental design that like an efflorescence blooms on the Schlesinger & Mayer Building, is not for a moment to be questioned. Its successes are based upon a wonderful inventiveness and ability to handle in a harmonious manner involved surface decoration. Is - there anything at once so original and so capable elsewhere to be found in American work? Where are we even to match its kind abroad? And if much of the decorative design is open to the charge of being vague and inorganic, no little of it possesses a really exquisite definiteness and suitability. The design, moreover, is all very true to its material. One is almost tempted

to the exaggeration of saying it is too true, and in places is rather metalesque than metallic. There is danger in it all no doubt. The singer, we feel, is too much in the lyric strain. The sense of the thing tends to the incoherent. Nevertheless, there is an enthusiasm of inventiveness in the work, a personal reality, a sparkling artistic exuberance which confounds us when we compare it with the dull copybook ornamentation, the repetitions a thousand times repeated that pass in the ordinary category of architectural work for "modern decoration." Under these circumstances it is perhaps the wiser part of judgment to quietly permit this latest production of Mr. Sullivan's to speak to us itself for a time, feeling sure that in the final appraisement we shall find not only that the work possesses great value, and inspiration, but also a lesson-in which Mr. Sullivan himself will need to share. ■

it, the old game of copying ancient buildings, in whole or in part, is pretty definitely played out. Following New York, all the other cities now have examples of "Modernistic Architecture" which they proudly show. Even the revered Treasury of the U.S.A. now occasionally permits an Ishmaelite of an "outside architect" to design a building that is un-classic! France is tired of the old methods, and one wonders what she will use now to give the American students to bring home. Germany has been "stepping out" on her own ever since she became acquainted with Frank Lloyd Wright. The countries of lesser magnitude are doing very interesting things. They are more sure of themselves than we are in America where it all started. It is we who are more or less at a loose end, feeling our way. We have found out that it is one thing to break with the past, or even to assume a pose of so doing. It is decidedly something else again to build up a complete system of philosophy to take the place of the old methods and habits of thought. It does not appear that the schools have had much to do with the change. It does not appear that they are doing much about It. Many a puzzled professor is tolerating an "enfant terrible" in his classes. The ugly ducklings are showing off. Whether or not they will become swans remains to be seen.

At all events Architectural Education is being challenged, and seems to be at a loss as to how to meet the new issues. At least one answer, and I believe the answer may be found in this little book. It may be, and I believe that it is, the book of the hour. For the sake of the future of American Architecture, I pray you gentlemen, let it be read with an open mind. •

"A"t no time has there been anything which might properly be called an American Style of Architecture," proclaimed Ernest Flagg in 1900 in "American Architecture as Opposed to Architecture in America." A bit extreme, perhaps, unless we accept that Americans have always struggled with their cultural identity. Until Ralph Waldo Emerson and Horatio Greenough[1] began to make themselves heard in the 1830s and 40s, there was very little independent examination or criticism of European arts and esthetic theory, let alone recognition of an independent American esthetic. Americans generally accepted European culture reverently and without question, when not ignoring such matters altogether.

When it came to American architecture, the word *vulgar* was frequently used to describe it; "vulgarity is our national disgrace" (page 4). For many Americans, commercial interest was the enemy. When Harry Desmond describes *Architectural Record*'s mission in the first issue, he's so intent on change that his language resonates with something like religious zeal:

> "At present Art with us means little more than decoration, an appendage and circumstance to tradesmen's prosperity. Nevertheless, it has a vital position, though a degraded one, in the lives of our people. What has to be done is to give it its proper position, to reveal its divinity, to make people feel that Art is not merely decoration, the legitimate function of which is to make a fortune conspicuous; but is the light breaking in upon us from the perfect world beyond our day's circumference; "the fruitful voice of God" revealing to us what we are but in hopes and probability."

It's difficult not to wonder how matters spiritual enter into all this. But, we shouldn't forget that questions of ecclesiastical, or even classical style are complicated by the relationship of their forms to their original purposes and, once borrowed, these purposes either no longer pertain or are subverted. The original styles, which were once associated with collective, sacred institutions, sometimes wind up applied to very differ-

*Metropolitan Life Insurance Company
Building and Tower, New York City,
Napoleon LeBrun & Sons, architects, 1892; 1909.*

ent private ones, including warehouses, breweries, and bridges. In England, John Ruskin earnestly tried to sever the link between Catholicism and the love of Gothic—to no avail.

In a paper reprinted in *Architectural Record*, the ever-pious, flamboyant, and powerful Ralph Adams Cram saw the present (1913) as a crisis of faith due to "a crescent individualism. And architecture, like a good art, [has] followed close to heel." His prescription, like that of Henry Adams, was to return, no matter how momentarily, to the middle ages:

> "…we are at the end of an epoch of materialism, rationalism, and intellectualism, and at the beginning of a wonderful new epoch, when once more we shall achieve a just estimate of comparative values,…we are retracing our steps to the great Christian Middle Ages, not that there we may remain, but that we may achieve an adequate point of departure; what follows must take care of itself." (page 173)

This was far too reactionary for either Claude Bragdon or Herbert Croly. They saw the skyscraper as a potentially clean slate just waiting for the right architect to give it national meaning, and consequent beauty. Bragdon says,

> "Our churches, universities and libraries, our capitols and court houses—what are they for the most part but insincere archæological experiments or cut to measure confections from European fashion plates? They involve no unprecedented constructive problems, and contain no potentialities of new beauty. The skyscraper, on the other hand, does both. It affords, for that reason, a magnificent opportunity, and the fact that it has been, for the most part, an opportunity unimproved, reflects less heavily upon the skyscraper than upon the architect thereof." (page 157)

For Herbert Croly, the form of the skyscraper and its commercial requirements was where its style and, ultimately, its liberating power lay:

> "The tall building is the economical building. It renders meaningless all the architectural values upon which the traditional European street architecture has been based. Precisely and exclusively because it was allowed to shoot upwards, American commercial architecture was emancipated from paralyzing restrictions and has become a specific and original type, dominated by novel formative and essentially real, practical requirements." (page 173)

Claude Bragdon caught a glimpse of beauty through a foreigner's eyes:

> "In 1880 this point of view suffered a sea-change. Oscar Wilde, the particular prophet who carried the new gospel of aestheticism to our shores, wrong as he was in matters of morals, was right in matters of taste, and he found, here, a considerable number of men and women who were right, we are bound to believe, in both. Architecture, which is the mirror of man's mind in space, was not slow to reflect this newborn sensitiveness to beauty, but in localities and on a scale commensurate with the restricted character of the movement, which was limited to the towns and cities of the extreme east. Among the ugly and arid crags and crannies of the Boston, New York and Philadelphia streets, there began to appear some rare and delicate flowers of architectural art, the work for the most part, of young Americans whose aesthetic sense had been nourished at the bountiful breast of Italy or France." [XXV:6 Jun 1909 p 427]

Architecture is too often taken for granted or ignored altogether. If beauty is in the eye of the beholder, then of course one must look. ∎

1 Horatio Greenough, *George Washington*, 1832–41. National Collection of Fine Arts, Washington, D.C. Greenough's sculpture was classical by way of Antonio Canova and the French Enlightenment.

Of classical influences he said, "I contend for Greek principles, not Greek things....The men who have reduced locomotion to its simplest elements, in the trotting wagon and the yacht America, are nearer to Athens at this moment than they who would bend the Greek temple to every use."
—*The Travels, Observations, and Experiences of a Yankee Stonecutter*, 1852.

"In the eternal trinity of Truth, Goodness, and Beauty, each in its perfection including the three, [idealists] prefer to make Beauty the sign and the head."

Ralph Waldo Emerson The Transcendentalist, *1842.*

1905

LaSalle Street Station, Chicago, Frost & Granger, architects, 1903 (demolished)

"The American 'way-station' has been until comparatively recently one of our too numerous marks of general æsthetic indifference. It is an excellent and hopeful sign that no inconsiderable part of the new building promoted by our railroads is falling at last into the hands of competent architects with the result that from the comparative standpoint, there has been possibly greater improvement in this class of buildings than in any other."

— Harry W. Desmond
"The Work of Frost and Granger"

opposite: Building of the Chicago & N.W.R.R. Co., Chicago, Frost & Granger, architects.

A PLEA FOR BEAUTY

Alfred Hoyt Granger

The last twenty-five years have witnessed greater changes in thought, manners and general mode of life than any other equal period of time since these United States became a nation. In nothing has the change been more marked than in the appearance of our cities. In the early days of the republic men read the classics, studied the works of the great masters of art and literature, and in building aimed to produce that which was beautiful, and, as far as possible, adapted to their needs. Classic tradition was closely followed, sometimes to the sacrifice of convenience, because it was along those lines beauty was felt to lie. And they were beautiful, those early buildings, as many examples testify. Bullfinch's stately Capitol in Boston, the City Hall in New York, the White House, and above all the National Capitol at Washington, have yet to be surpassed for simple dignity and beauty, the qualities that endure, while many humbler buildings, residences throughout Virginia, Maryland and New England testify to the correct taste of the men of those days. Now all is changed and the practical has taken the place of the beautiful as the thing to be desired.

Our great cities are generally undergoing a process of rebuilding with such rapidity that one wonders what the result will be. What will the men of future years pick out among our mammoth structures to linger o'er and come to again and again, each time with greater love and reverence? To-day our young men go abroad to discover and study over the works of the past, those whose beauty is so alluring that it draws all men of all minds, awes them, subdues them and fills them with reverence and a holy desire to go out and not reproduce, but work in the same spirit as those artists of the past, solve as they did the problems of the day and prove that so long as God reigns life is beautiful and "all's well with the world." All this is true, and yet the fact remains that many of these

same men, who have drunk at the very fountains of art, soon succumb to the spirit of the day and spend their lives in such frantic pursuit of what is practical that they have no time, and eventually no inclination to bring forth that beauty which abides. So potent is this fact that it seems to me wise to consider for a few moments why such things be. Of course the first cause for the rebuilding of our cities is the necessity for larger quarters in which to carry on the great and complex transactions of the day. Another cause is the increased prosperity and the desire to express this fact by means of what is new and striking, so that he who runs may read how prosperous we are. There is yet another cause more potent than the rest, and that is the desire for larger dividends than were possible from the smaller, simpler buildings. For this cause our city streets are turned into canons, deprived of light and air, and millions are lavished upon structures which the passer-by can never see in their entirety. Many of these buildings possess real beauty in themselves, for our millionaires and giant corporations are not niggardly, but such is their size, or more properly speaking, their height, that, to view them en masse one must be so far away he loses all idea of detail or scale. In fact scale is just what they lack, for by their colossal height they are so completely out of harmony with their surroundings or the width of the streets upon which they face that they have destroyed all feeling of dignity or fitness. In the beginning these giant buildings with sides of glass were more or less isolated, and, as they were most carefully planned to offer the possible tenant every creature comfort combined with wonderful light, the returns they gave upon the money invested were enormous. Already, however, a slight change of sentiment is noticeable, because of late years so many lofty buildings have been erected in New York, Chicago and Philadelphia that they have begun to prey upon each other in the matter of light and air. In other words it is no longer quite practical to build solid blocks of twenty-story office or apartment buildings. Thus do we

from:
THE WORK OF FROST & GRANGER
By Henry W. Desmond
Vol. XVIII, No. 2, August, 1905,
pp. 115–145.

* * *

In the La Salle Street Station, …the architects were plunged at once into the double difficulty of producing a railroad terminal of a first magnitude in conjunction with a modern tall office building. From the real estate point of view, this conjunction may be advantageous, if not inevitable, but architectural, the task is an impossible one. In order to achieve a successful result, either the office building must be greatly curtailed in altitude and subordinated to tractable architectural proportions; that is, de commercialized, or the long train shed must be relegated to the rear as a mere appendage of glass and iron screened and overshadowed by the frontal skyscraper, which in that case, becomes itself the sole architectural feature. This latter course, was perforce imposed upon the architects of the La Salle Street Station, and as a result, the building, from our point of view, has to be regarded as an office building, pure and simple, the articulation of the entrances, waiting-rooms and ▸

Staircase, Opéra, Paris, 1854-70, Charles Garnier, architect. Garnier considered his building's major theme to be "the incessant circulation of the crowd going up and down."

Staircase, Metropolitan Life Insurance Company Building, New York City, Napoleon Le Brun & Sons, architects, 1892.

opposite: Interior, LaSalle Street Station, Chicago, Frost & Granger, architects, 1903, (demolished).

come of necessity back to the divine law that beauty and usefulness go hand in hand and are integral parts of each other.

This fact being patent to all let us consider some other essential qualities of beauty. To many, originality is a synonymous term, but originality is a word of great elasticity. In the period of time under discussion we have seen many men appear to dazzle the world for a day and then give place to some newer star among these geniuses, and geniuses they certainly are. I propose to consider only one, and he the greatest.

During the life of Henry Hobson Richardson, (page 42) and for about ten years after his death, his influence overshadowed all others in the American World. The entire country was Romanesque mad. Yet what single architect of note to-day builds in the Romanesque style? Since the decline of the Romanesque we have revived Colonial, Tudor-Gothic, Roman Classic and now are on the top wave of Beaux Arts French Renaissance. This is not because of lack of brains among architects or a weakness of principle. It is because we Americans are still faddists and follow each passing fashion with unholy zeal. The reason for this is very simple if we but recognize the fact that in every human soul there is a haunting love of the beautiful which will not be stifled. Richardson felt it and devoted his life to its pursuit. Because he was a man of an intensely virile type and great poetic feeling, the simple, rugged poetry of the buildings of Southern France appealed to him and satisfied him as no others he had ever seen. He absorbed these types but never copied them as his followers copied him. They copied his tools and details, while he worked from an undying principle, which, had he built in French Gothic, or severest classic, would have made his buildings just as beautiful. And how beautiful they were and are to-day and will be one hundred years from now unless they fall under the ruthless hand of the destroyer.

Among those buildings in America which really satisfy the soul it is hard to surpass Trinity Church, Boston, (photo page 39) or

the little library at Quincy, Massachusetts, or Sever Hall at Cambridge—a monument in brick—or the Chamber of Commerce—in Cincinnati. (photo page 115) I mention these buildings of such different types because they so illustrate the principle I am pleading for in our work to-day. In each of them the main consideration has been their ultimate purpose and how to solve this purpose in the most fitting, I might say, most practical manner; but in so solving the problem the artist has ever kept in mind the fact that if his building is to remain to tell the generations yet to come something of the ideals of to-day it must be beautiful not practical with as much beauty as possible thrown in—but first and always beautiful. It is this principle which makes Richardson's work great and original, and this principle only.

There are but three absolutely essential qualities in a great architect and they are good taste, poetry and common sense, and the measure of his greatness lies in the balancing of these three. Note I say "measure of his greatness," not measure of his success in the modern meaning of that word, for alas, to-day in the public mind success is measured by size of income and little else. In briefly analyzing these qualities I will first consider the last named quality of common sense out of deference to the present demand for the practical. The architect who possesses common sense will first adapt his plan to the actual purposes of the proposed building and its site. Every question upon which depends the comfort and convenience and health of the occupants of the building must be carefully considered and from every standpoint. This is as it should be, for we must build from the bottom upward, but if this be all what have we? All of our modern cities answer this question and none more forcibly than Chicago, where we have scores of great buildings fulfilling every practical want, but from which we turn away with only an ache at the heartstrings, because, in spite of their perfect planning and admirable construction, they leave us with an unquenchable longing for something which they have not, some real beauty. This is not architecture even though it be marvelous building. We can admire the technical skill which produced such results but we can never love it. There we come to the heart of the question, for real architecture always inspires real love, and to create real architecture one must possess good taste

and the poetical instinct which can express itself in stone and brick and steel. That this is perfectly possible a group of men in America to-day are earnestly striving to prove, and they are proving that beauty is essential and possible in every class of building.

Shortness of space will not allow me in any way to show how much is now being done to perpetuate beauty, but I can consider a few buildings which, in my judgment, embody good taste, poetry and common sense. First, I will mention an office building—a skyscraper in other words—as this type of structure is a most common problem for modern solution. At the northwest cor-

ner of Broad St. and Exchange Pl., in New York City, stands a white building, nearly twenty stories high, the Blair building, (photo page 82) designed by Messrs. Carrère & Hastings. This building is essentially modern, carefully planned, scientifically heated and ventilated, absolutely fireproof and supplied with every modern and sanitary convenience. So in fact are the buildings adjoining it on either side, but only thus far are they alike. Over and beyond these common sense qualities the Blair building possesses a beauty which makes the busy passer-by stop and wonder, why? Simply because of its beauty. And this beauty consists in great dignity and simplicity of treatment, in harmony of proportion and accuracy of scale in the relations of the component parts and also an exquisite refinement and grace in the placing and detailing of ornament. All of these qualities make architecture, and without them you have the adjoining buildings and many others in all of our cities.

Farther up town in New York, on the

offices with the train shed being entirely an affair of interior disposition, receiving necessarily only the slightest expression in the exterior design. It must not be understood from these remarks that the La Salle Street Terminal suffers in the slightest degree as a station from this arrangement. Indeed, so far as public convenience, so far as plan and decoration are concerned, the station is to the traveler one of the most admirable that he is likely to encounter anywhere. From the moment he enters the heavy arched portal, he is led easily by the admirable disposition of the plan through each separate department, into the final train shed and cars. Every railroad accommodation that he requires is provided most liberally, and if he be a person of taste, he will hardly refrain from rendering thanks to the architects for having spared him all the cheaper effects of public grandeur. The architects have stuck closely to their construction and have derived from it a great deal of bold and telling effect. In some eyes there may be a certain architectural meanness about these massive undecorated columns, these unsophisticated steel supports, these plain walls of flat marble, but really the result is far more substantial than a lot of cheaper and more highly wrought plaster-work. The eye will not so quickly tire of it and time will not so quickly repudiate it. However, the admiring traveler, for we would like to suppose him a judicious person, in passing through the wide halls up broad flights of steps, and into the spacious waiting-rooms and offices, will have no sense that the accommodation provided for him is over-arched by a skyscraper, and, too, upon the whole a very successful skyscraper. If the design does not on the one hand frankly   ▶

above: Halle des Machines, International Exhibition, Paris, France, Ferdinand Dutert and Contamin, architects, 1889–90.

This incredible feat of engineering struck the architecture world with awe and inspiration. The arches and colonnades of the train shed were soon introduced into the station proper and even the façade of the railway station as a symbolic expression of the daily flow of the multitudes.

1 The Boston firm referred to is Cram, Goodhue & Ferguson, who at the writing of this article were working on the commission they had won for the United States Military Academy at West Point (1903–10).

2 The articles are:"Frank Miles Day & Brother, Architects," [XV:5 May 1904 pp 397–421] and "Cope and Stewardson, Architects," [XVI:5 Nov 1904 pp 407–438], both by Ralph Adams Cram.

right and opposite: LaSalle Street Station, interior—departure and tracks.

southwest corner of Fifth avenue and 36th street, Messrs. McKim, Mead & White are completing a store for the Gorham Manufacturing Company (photo page 172). This is an ordinary, every-day problem, but is not solved in the ordinary manner. Every practical question such as great show windows, plenty of light, elevators, etc., is carefully considered; but beyond formal character and purpose of the three last named and the commercial character of the first two demand a very quiet, conservative handling. That we are not as yet a wholly material people is evidenced by the great development of our educational and philanthropical institutions, but how few, alas, are the temples erected to the worship of God. Except a few most interesting country churches in the suburbs of Boston by Messrs. Cram, Goodhue & Ferguson and some small city parish churches by the same gentlemen, I know of no churches built since Richardson built Trinity in Boston which are filled with the spirit of reverence and spiritual beauty. Other cities contain many large and costly buildings dedicated to worship and called churches, but never to be sought out and

loved and studied over as are the cathedrals, or even the small parish churches of England or France. This same firm of Boston architects[2] are now at work upon the solution of an educational problem which, when completed, must compel the admiration and thankfulness of all lovers of beauty, I mean the new West Point so ably described and illustrated in the *Century* for July, 1904, that I will not dwell upon it here. Among the many educational buildings erected within the last few years none is more to be admired for its great beauty and, at the same time, for its dignity and self-restraint than the groups of buildings at the University of Pennsylvania, at Princeton at Bryn Mawr and at St. Louis by Messrs. Cope & Stewardson. Their merits and charm have been adequately set forth by Mr. Ralph Adams Cram in recent numbers of the *Architectural Record*,[2] but one building in Philadelphia which he described from drawings before its completion, the new gymnasium and athletic field at the University of Pennsylvania by Messrs. Frank Miles Day & Brother, deserves special remark. This building is almost daringly original in its composition, most practical in its plan and construction and wholly satisfying in its beauty except for the unfortunate discoloration of the brick in the towers, while the arrangement of the seating around the wall of the athletic field is unique. It is full of poetry in the harmony of its balance and brings down to us to-day all the charm of the historic tradition of the great English universities in spite of its wholly original and modern handling.

There is one other building, or rather group of buildings, in Philadelphia which I have purposely left until the last. It is the Art Museum connected with the University of Pennsylvania, and it is due to the combined efforts of Messrs. Wilson, Eyre, Cope & Stewardson and Frank Miles Day. Although these buildings have been ofttimes described and illustrated such is their enduring beauty one cannot pass them by. The purist and the practical architect can here unite in criticising the rather exotic, too Italian style of the buildings in this group, but I know no others so full of pregnant lessons of how to use brick beautifully. Almost no stone is in them and the design is consistent throughout in its handling of the medium of expression, common hard burned brick, but only an artist and a poet could produce such results.

In this paper I have only been able to specially mention a very small part of the really beautiful work done in this country in the last quarter of a century, but all of the buildings mentioned are alive and illustrate the power and necessity of beauty to produce any lasting charm. They are of the type which distinguishes the great buildings of Europe and like them will become the inspiration of students and lovers of the beautiful in ages yet to come. All through the country are to be found private homes which embody the essentials of real architecture, and from such homes our people will draw inspiration and strength to ultimately demand beauty as one of the main necessities of life. But until our large city buildings, no matter for what purpose, become beautiful, become real architecture, we cannot hope for a public opinion which will insist upon the things of the spirit in all our work; and until such a public opinion shall be aroused we cannot look to see our cities filled with those things of beauty which abide and make for the enlargement and idealization of life. ∎

acknowledge the skeleton construction, but reverts architecturally to the old formula of a heavy supporting base, a middle section, and a crowning upper member, it is not on the other hand, a mass of quotations or misquotations from other buildings of other times and other purposes. In Chicago they insist upon an architect being a somewhat practical person, and they put a somewhat greater value upon the utilities than upon the mere "features" of a building. Certainly the architects of the La Salle Street Station have not sacrificed any of the real interests of their clients for the sake of superficial effects and yet, the building is thoroughly designed. Here, again, we have to notice how well placed and how well considered are the details, and the result is obtained with a directness and vigor which betoken not only skill and experience but that capacity to rigorously eliminate the superfluous which is one of the most certain signs of the trained designer. An architect in these profuse and eclectic days must be measured possibly even more by what he does not do than by what he does. This positive quality, assuming a negative aspect, is visible more clearly in the design of the La Salle Street Terminus than in the smaller works of Frost & Granger; nevertheless, it distinguishes all the firm's designs in some degree and classes them among the comparatively small amount of thoroughly considered work produced at present. The work is nowhere raw. It does not carry upon it the marks of the effort or the process of thinking. In other words, it is a net result. •

134

Tribune Building, New York City, Richard Morris Hunt, architect, 1873–75 (demolished 1960s).

The first tall building to be built in the an area that would be dubbed "Newspaper Row" after the construction of the New York Times Building seen at right (George B. Post, architect, 1888–89). The tower is loosely based on the Palazzo Vecchio in Florence.

Once the city's tallest commercial structure, the Tribune Building was referred to by Schuyler as one of the first "elevator buildings." Critics generally found the structure's appearance inelegant and overbearing.

opposite: Addition to New York Stock Exchange, New York City, Trowbridge & Livingston, architects, 1923.

SOME RECENT SKYSCRAPERS

Montgomery Schuyler

We are fond of imagining, or of calling upon others to imagine, the sensations of an old New Yorker if he could revisit the glimpses of the metropolitan moon, now represented by Welsbach burners.[1] Manhattan revisited, even by a visitor of an even generation ago, how it would make him stare and gasp. The aspect even of the oldest and longest settled part of the island has changed more since 1874 than it had changed in a century, in two centuries, nay, almost in three centuries before. Hudson[2] himself, sailing into the upper bay even so lately as 1874, would have recognized the island which he sighted in 1609. But he would scarcely recognize it now. For the gentle activity which then would have greeted him, though so builded and peopled as to show that a great city had displaced the woodland, was not so built up as to disguise the lie of the land. But now the aspect is of a city set on a hill. "Surely," the explorer would now say, "there was no such mountain as that when I was here before." He could account for the apparent topographical change only by supposing a seismic upheaval or the advent of a new geological period.

But there is no occasion for going back centuries or even generations, not even one generation. The visitor who remains out of town or even up town for a single year finds down-town transformed in that brief interval and threatening always still stranger transformation. That fabulous time, "When Ilion[3] like a mist rose into towers," is realized now and here. It is a kaleidoscopic, a phantasmagoric change, bewildering and stupefying in the mass, with no ensemble but that of universal strife and struggle. "The very buildings," as our English critic has it, "cry aloud of struggling, almost savage, unregulated strength," unregulated by law, unregulated by custom or comity. The skyscraper remains "ferae naturae,"[4] not only remains, but monthly more becomes. And yet there is so much "ensemble" even of individualism that the individuals are merged in the riot, as in a street in which every shopkeeper tries to make himself conspicuous by his staring sign, and all together frustrate their several intentions. Truly, instead of not being able to see the forest for the trees, you cannot see the trees for the forest. It requires self restraint and willful abstraction and absorption to select and consider an individual among the mob. Still, with the help of a photograph, you may "sit down before" a particular building and try to judge it. And to do this with a certain number of recent and typical instances is the purpose of this paper.

Seniores priores.[5] The "new" Tribune building was the wonder of New York that generation ago of which we were speaking, that and the original Western Union which was under construction at the same time. The wonder mainly by reason of its altitude. Consider that its seven stories and double decked dormers towered over everything. Professor Huxley,[6] visiting these shores three or four years later, took it as an instance of our utilitarian turn of mind. The two edifices, he said, which rose like Sauls[7] above their fellows, as the visitor steamed up the bay, were not castles or cathedrals or fortress towers as they would have been apt to be in an old world port, but a telegraph office and a newspaper office. These were the pioneers in which for the first time the change wrought by the passenger elevator was fully recognized in design, and they were designed on quite different theories. In the Tribune building, Mr. Hunt[8] attempted to make groups of stories take the place as members of his composition of the single stories of the earlier and lower commercial building. In the Western Union, Mr. Post anticipated the present convention by which the basement and the roof were distinguished and the stories between were treated with a similarity amounting in effect to identity. The Tribune building mainly suffered, however, from its

from:

TO CURB THE SKYSCRAPER
Montgomery Schuyler
Vol. XXIV, No. 4, October 1908,
pp. 300-302

It is immensely to the credit of the architects that while as individuals they may seem to have almost the most direct interest in the failure to restrict the height of buildings, as a body they are the only source from which have proceeded any practical measures for restriction. The plan which Mr. Ernest Flagg has worked out in detail, and to which the adhesion has been secured of the New York Chapter of the American Institute of Architects, has been outlined in the daily press. The principle upon which it proceeds, that of penalizing the carrying beyond a certain height of the whole bulk of a building, or of premiating by an allowance of increased height its recession as it rises, is simple enough and was first, we believe, proposed some years ago by Mr. George B. Post. But it has not before been worked out in the same way, or in such detail. Mr. Flagg proposes, in the first place, that no building which covers more than three-quarters of the entire plot on which it stands shall be allowed to exceed 100 feet in ▸

above: The United States Express Company Building, New York City, Clinton & Russell, architects, 1905–07.

1 Welsbach Burners. A trademark used for a lamp consisting of a gas burner and a gauze mantle impregnated with cerium and thorium compounds that becomes incandescent when heated by the burner.

2 English explorer Henry Hudson (d. 1611) sailed up the river later to be named for him in 1609.

3 Ilion is the city also known as Troy. The city was made famous by Homer's account of the Trojan War. Its site is almost universally accepted as the mound now named Hissarlik, in Asian Turkey.

4 *ferae naturae:* Applied in law to animals living in a wild state, as distinguished from animals, which are domesticated.

5 *Seniores Priores*: First and foremost.

opposite: Trinity and US Realty Buildings, New York City, Francis Hatch Kimball, architect, 1904–05: addition, 1906–07.

bichromatic treatment in brick and granite, so applied as almost to give the impression that a building conceived as a monochrome of red had afterwards been patched with gray. The building thus did not do justice to the design. But what would the architect of the original building have said if he had been told at the time of its erection, that, a generation afterwards, and a decade after his own death, it would be found expedient and profitable to double its height, impossible, in fact, to leave it at the old height without falling out of the commercial competition.

Upon the whole, the heightening has been done with tact and discretion. The brick and granite part of the superposition becomes the middle member of the composition. The old building has practically been duplicated in it, and the whole forms a fairly well balanced triple composition. The narrow bay signalized by the entrance at the bottom and the tower at the top, which the original architect introduced as he explained to soften a change of direction in plan, "dissembling thus the irregularity of the front," had a tendency already to spindle and necessarily spindles much more now when the height is doubled. The slender pier, however, which runs from the ninth story to the twelfth, inclusive, seems to spindle unnecessarily and its tenuity becomes rather painful. But the general scheme of the superposition is reasonable and the result effective, and it is very well carried out. The building is architecturally the better for the addition and that is praise that can only in frequently be bestowed. As to the detail, it is all frankly taken from the detail below, excepting the metal work of the dormers which has been substituted, perhaps questionably, for the huge granite frames that were relieved against the former roof. The rebuilder's only care as to the detail was to place it, and this he has succeeded in doing very acceptably.

Doubtless the loudest of the new lions is the United States Realty Building, on the site, more or less, of the Boreel Building. At least, in conjunction with the Trinity Building across the widened alley, down whose dark defile one used to go (eheu,

fugaces)[9] to where the hands of "Old Tom"[10] used to "reach"

To each his perfect pint of stout,
His proper chop to each.

The twin towers (not chronologically twins, for the northernmore is months if not years the younger) together out roar for a moment the architectural rattle of Broadway and arrest the stranger. Each without doubt profits by the juxtaposition of the other, as the elder profits greatly by its confrontation with the yet older Empire Building across Trinity church yard, counterparting frontages to the effect of which nothing in its kind on this side of the Atlantic, at least, is comparable for instantaneous and irresistible effectiveness. Those confronting arcades alone, embracing each three stories, gain immensely by the similarity of treatment and lose nothing by the diversity of detail, one in Gothic and one in classic. It looks lucky that the same architect had the doing of both, since a succeeding architect of the newer would have been in danger of finding his originality compromised by conformity, which in this case is to say by doing the obviously right thing. The two huge white sheets of front seem fittingly, or as fittingly as any skyscrapers could do it, and even tenderly to frame poor dear old Trinity, not so long ago the "landmark of New York" from the Jersey Hills from which it has long been invisible, to frame it as a relic, or rather as a reliquary, a casket, it seems to say containing precious things, or it would not have been left there with its ample setting of greensward, when its site might have been sold for so many hundreds of pence and given to the rich. And the effect of framing and protecting the relic is enhanced by the latest comer, the United States Express Company's new building at the rear of the churchyard, shortly, no doubt, to be adjoined by an other of the same kind, thus completely enclosing on the three sides the open space which enables the construction of the surrounding monsters. The spectacle is an incitement to criticism other than architectural. For, observe that Trinity itself

height. For the remaining quarter of the plot he would impose no restriction in height, excepting that the height mentioned shall not be exceeded within a distance from the front equal to that from the building line to the curb line; that is to say, to the width of the sidewalk. Third (we quote from a published summary of his proposal), "he would allow the purchase and sale between adjoining owners of the right to build high within the limit stated." Finally, he would require absolute incombustibility in all the material and equipment of buildings that went above the first limit, and that all their visible sides should be "treated architecturally."

Without doubt the result would be a great improvement in the aspect of New York. The limitation to 100 feet, or eight stories, say, would automatically restore to our business streets the cornice line which in old times, before the passenger elevator, was automatically imposed by the five stories which were the maximum that a visitor or tenant could be expected to climb. And the new cornice line would be only half as high again as the old. For the rest, as has been promptly foreseen, the regulation would make New York "A City of Towers." It does not follow that it would be "a tiara of proud towers." You may prescribe that all the sides of your tall building shall be "treated architecturally," and the prescription is reasonable. But to make your tall building a sightly or attractive object, this superficial treatment is not sufficient. The aspiring dollar-hunter would continue to protrude stark parallelopipeds into the empyrean, just as he does now. If you were to veneer these with mosaics the amorphous thing would still be amorphous. A collection of these shapelessnesses would not be as sightly; would, in fact, be far less ▸

1907

6 Thomas Henry Huxley (1825–95), English biologist and educator. Huxley gave up his own biological research to become an influential scientific publicist and was the principal exponent of Darwinism in England.

7 *Sauls:* first king of the ancient Hebrews. He was a Benjamite and anointed king by Samuel. The Bible tells his story dramatically, for it is really the story of David, first the protégé, then the rival, and finally the successor, of the king.

8 Richard Morris Hunt, architect, 1873-75 (photo page 134).

9 *Eheu, fugaces:* for the moment, in time.

10 *"Old Tom":* Thomas Norris, one of the men employed in Messrs. Hodges' distillery, opened a gin palace in Great Russell Street, Covent Garden, and called the gin concocted by Thomas Chamberlain, one of the firm of Hodges, "Old Tom," in compliment to his former master.

11 *Sic vos non vobis:* thievery, robbery, pilfering.

opposite: New York Stock Exchange (with columns), New York City, George B. Post, architect, 1903. To the left of the Stock Exchange is the Commercial Cable Building, Harding & Gooch, architects, 1896–97, and the Blair Building, Carrère & Hastings, architects, 1903 (demolished), (photo page 82).

has no part nor lot in the huge profits that its maintenance of the great light wells of Trinity churchyard and St. Paul's churchyard is making and will make for the riparian owners. *Sic vos non vobis,*[11] the remarkable layman who has charge of the "temporalities" of Trinity may well observe as he remarks the great gains the corporation has renounced in favor of extraneous persons. Verily "the children of this world are in their generation wiser than the children of light."

But to return to architecture. The new building gains by comparison with its elder neighbor in that its frontage made a symmetrical disposition practicable, and a central crowning feature. But both gain by the conjunction. The turret of the Trinity building looks better as an intermediate than as a terminal feature, though it seems that it would have been well to avoid the competition with it of the tall canopied opening which is the culmination of the later work and which repeats on a larger scale the like feature in the earlier. In fact, on either scale, this feature cannot be said to be its own excuse for being. In neither case does one "see the necessity," and to say that of a conspicuous feature in so grimly a utilitarian building as the skyscraper is to go near to condemning it. And this stricture applies with still more force to the treatment of the middle part, the "shaft" of the side walls. Not to the north wall of the Realty or even of the Trinity for neither can really be seen, but to the south wall of the Trinity Building as to the north wall of the Empire Building and to the flanking walls of the Manhattan. In each case, it seems to me, Mr. Kimball has taken a mistaken view in undertaking to variegate and diversify the blank monotony of his wall surface, punctured only with "damnable iteration" as he seems to think it of precisely similar openings, and undertaking it to the end that "his uncomely parts have more abundant comeliness." This is particularly, and to me painfully, evident in the south wall of the Trinity Building more than in the north wall of the Empire, which is equally in full evidence, and in which also it seems a blemish. One can imagine the

variegations of the middle wall of Trinity with their Gothic detail, significant and effective, say, in a college building, as distinguishing the staircases from the dormitories. But one cannot imagine any functional differences in the flank of a huge office building, any more than in the cells of a honeycomb. The openings all serve similar purposes, and one cannot make this kind of distinction among them without conveying the sense that it is a factitious and capricious distinction. *Comme il faut,* "as it must be," is the very best impression the architect of a skyscraper can produce with his work. And surely nobody could pretend that these variations make upon him the impression of inevitably. And, moreover, purely as a matter of visual effect preceding any analytic consideration, the mere uniformity and succession, tier after tier, of openings in themselves, or each by itself, insignificant gains by mere repetition conveys an effect of extent and expanse which these interruptions and differences tend to confuse and disturb. Note, in contrast, the effect of the arcade at the base in any one of the three buildings. Note it particularly in the north wall of the newest building, though that wall is always in the dark, or at least in a dusk which is scarcely to be regretted since it adds mystery to the indefinite repetition of the same form from end to end. That long arcade of segment headed openings is bound to make its effect upon any sensitive observer. It is one of the most impressive things not only in the architecture of the skyscraper, but in any architecture one can see. It is the same effect that has been sought and attained by the builders of every building nation from Egypt downward, the simplest and most obvious, but also the surest, and it here testifies anew to the unfailing power in architecture of "uniformity and succession." Upon this, and up on the gorgeous Gothic corridor which corresponds to it in the interior, and in which the architect has succeeded in producing a wonderfully effective piece of architecture without sacrifice or denial of his practical conditions, he is to be congratulated most heartily and without any re

sightly than grove of factory chimneys, which already taper and
have form and so far comeliness.
And, although it would be a very
good and civic thing if the owners
of the parallelopipeds were
required to give them form and
comeliness, and although such a
requirement might be enforced
by the prefecture of the Seine, it
were a fond imagination that the
individualistic New Yorker, whose
rampant individualism is, in fact,
in this matter, the source of all
our woes, would submit to such a
limitation of his right to do what
he will with his own. The parallelopiped is the form which gives
him most space for rental and
which can be most cheaply built.
To prevent him from building it
would seem to him a great outrage. As the American tourist said
of the doctrine of eternal punish-
ment, "Our people wouldn't
stand it."

* * *

But now comes a Philadelphia
architect of standing and repute,
Mr. D. Knickerbocker Boyd,
President of the Philadelphia
Chapter of the American Institute,
with a very different project. He
starts with the same notion of
penalizing projection and premiating recession. But he works it out
to an entirely different result. He
proposes a "norm" of one and a
quarter the width of the street.
But he proposes two methods,
varied according to the character
of the occupation of the street,
by which the public easement in
the air and light at the street level
may be protected.

* * *

"My scheme is in a sense automatic,
and nothing is left to uncertainty. On a
small or medium-sized lot it would be
impossible to erect a high building or
tower, and yet on a lot of ample size
the height would always be in vertical
proportion to the space occupied by
the base of the building. If this
scheme, with such modifications as ▸

1907

above: Royal Insurance Company Building, New York City, Howells & Stokes, architects, 1907.

opposite: One Wall Street, New York City, Barnett, Haynes & Barnett, architects, 1906–07 (demolished 1929).

serve.

As to the background of the church yard or so much of it as is furnished by the new building of the United States Express Company, there is very little to be said. It is so distinctly and exclusively "the regular thing," so palpably, architecturally speaking, neither here nor there. The bottom story, if not more than one, is hidden from view by the elevated railroad. But that concealment was of course allowed for in the design, and one cannot persuade himself that, if it had not been, it would matter. That the architect is a "practical man" serving his client to the best of his ability, and sacrificing no inch of room anywhere to architectural effect, but employing every means of utilizing to the utmost the area and the altitude, all this is not only evident but emphasized. Such a description sounds satirical, but it is not satirically meant. In fact, it is doubtful whether except as the manual of bridge engineering says, "in cases where appearance is imposed as a necessary condition," the designer of skyscrapers could do anything better. Certainly a sacrifice of any practical requirement to "appearance" is not only "bad business," but bad faith and bad architecture. If this building stood where its base was visible, the fettered architect, if he happened to be an artist, might relieve his feelings with a "swagger" entrance, and a piece of sculpture emblematizing the express business. That is, he might do so if he had clearly explained his purpose to his customer, and his customer had consented. as in this case he doubtless would have consented to "stand for" the irrelevant piece of fantasy, and charge the cost of it to the advertising account. But it would be as inartistic as it would be unpractical for the architect of this structure to advise his client to waste his money on an invisible and virtually subterranean piece of architectural pyrotechny. With the exception of the string courses of the lower stories, about which also there is an architectural neither-here-nor-thereness, one cannot accuse him, up to the nineteenth, or as it may be, the twentieth story, of diverting a single dollar from business to

architecture. Above that point, indeed, "a decent respect to the opinions of mankind" has constrained him to follow the fashion and the convention, to set off the upper three stories by themselves by a strong demarcation from what is below, to include them under arches, and to crown the edifice with a crested cornice. This is, in fact, "the thing itself." How much of a denial it really was, the United Express Company gives no real sign. If he be in fact an artist one's sympathies must go out to him. If he be only, as an eminent practitioner of architecture puts it, "a business man with a knowledge of building," he has suffered no pangs, and will be content with the praise which no body can deny him of having done his work in a workmanlike manner.

We were saying that this is "the thing itself," that "unaccommodated" skyscraper, as Shakespeare has it of man, is even as this is. But, if one really thinks that this is the skyscraper reduced to its simplest expression, good gracious, let him look at No. 1 Wall Street. Here, if you like. is "the thing itself." The steel frame here is merely covered with the fire resisting brick it practically needs (very good brick it is, by the way, and a credit to the architect's selection). Not only is there no pretense of a masonry construction in any pretended or apparent adequacy of the visible supports to carry the visible superstructure. Such a pretense is openly scouted. It is made manifest, so to say, and impressed upon you, that the building is not what it seems, and that if it were what it seems, it could not stand up five minutes, that it would come down by the run, beginning with that rood of plate glass framed with a six inch copper moulding, that pretends, or rather does not pretend, to carry eighteen stories of brick work. No humbug of "triple division," of composition, vertical or lateral, in short of architecture, about this man. He has put up a trellis of steel frame and just bricked it over, excepting the square holes he had to leave to light the interior. Truly, this is the simplest expression, if you can bring yourself to call it an expression. For seventeen stories there is not

would develop when more fully worked out, should be adopted and given legislative sanction, the result would not be to restrict high buildings, but the erection of them would certainly be discouraged.

"I would limit the initial height, that is to say, the maximum height at the established building line, to one and a quarter times the width of the street. This would give our principal north and south streets, which are 59 feet in width, a 62 1/2 feet high building if erected at the usual building line, which would be equivalent to a six-story building used for residential or office purposes, or a five-story light manufacturing establishment. On our east and west streets, such as Walnut and Chestnut, which are 60 feet wide, the height of the building, if erected on the normal building line, could be 75 feet, or just about one-story higher.

"Now, if an imaginary line be drawn from the curb of any of these streets to the top of an imaginary building, the limit of height on the normal building line, and continued into space it becomes the line of restriction that I have spoken of. The diagonal thereby becomes the height line and regulates the front building line as well. It thus becomes apparent at once that to go up one must go back, and it can roughly be figured upon for each additional story in height that two feet must be added to the width of the sidewalk."

Without doubt, either scheme has its attractiveness. By the first, an "institution" which is still not enough of an institution to build its own abode by itself, but must perforce combine its own requirements with those of a real estate speculation, and house a numerous tenantry on the same premises, can signalize itself by a street front which would about reach the cornice line assumed as normal, while the cells which lodge "the pig that pays the rint" are withdrawn, and subordinated accordingly. In so far, that would be architecturally as well as hygienically a benefit. And, under the other scheme, an "important" building of which the importance is manifested in its height would automatically withdraw ▶

above: Seligman Building, New York City, Francis H. Kimball & Julian C. Levi, architects, 1907.

opposite: Title Guarantee & Trust Company, New York City, Howells & Stokes, architects, 1905–06.

12 John Wolfe Building, New York City, Henry Janeway Hardenbergh, architect, 1894-95 (demolished). Photo page 53.

a single sign that the designer ever gave a thought to what his work was going to look like. That his intermediate piers were wider than his terminal piers, that his windows were mere square holes cut in the wall, none of these things moved him. But then what a change of heart. Why that shelf above the seventeenth story? That shelf cost money. Why that elaborated and crested frieze? That cost money, too, even though not much, and even though it be, if it be, but of humble sheet metal. And why, oh, why, those amazing obeliscal wreathed pinnacles, making the tower "like a table with all four legs in the air," as Ruskin hath it? It is in vain for him to deny it. That is architecture. At least it is "architecture."

To be sure, some man may say about the Royal Insurance Building what we were just saying about the United States Express Company's Building, that it is the regular thing, the most regular of regular things. But it does not follow that some man would have reason. Here, no doubt, is the convention of the skyscraper recognized, recognized and even emphasized in the difference of material, the brickwork of the nine story shaft marking its difference from the sand stone of the four story base and of the three story capital. Moreover, the building has to endure the very difficult confrontation of the John Wolfe Building[12] on the opposite corner, that remarkable "habitation enforced," in which Mr. Hardenbergh was really driven into a bold picturesqueness as the alternative to an uncouth unsightliness, and in which he acquitted himself so well. This present "Royal" is as strictly utilitarian an edifice as the United States Express Company's building. Nobody can fairly accuse the architect of having blinked his problem or humbugged his client. But he had his advantages, his advantages over the designer of the other. He had for instance, the advantage of showing his building to the bottom, and of exhibiting such special purpose as it derives from its name and proprietorship, in the bit of emblematic sculpture at the en trance. This is not here, as it might have been in the other case, the contest of

the Centaurs and the Lapithae, the Plattites and the Odellites. It resolves itself into the ancient and even matranserine legend of

The Lion and the Unicorn
A fighting for the Crown.

But the heraldic "supporters" of the British Royalty of which the doggerel gives a childish view, do in fact, like most heraldic devices, lend themselves to decorative uses. In the present instance they do relieve what would otherwise be what the irreverent might call the equally childish doggerel of the alternation of metopes and triglyphs below. By design, scale and situation, they do supply a "feature" to the entrance, and do tend to relieve the necessary prosaism of the superstructure. The fact that the superstructure is evidently and avowedly, as evidently and avowedly as in the Express Company's building, "a cold business proposition," does not interfere with the little touch of interest added by this, nor does this interfere with that. Nobody is going to get any artistic thrill in particular out of this "Royal" building. But, on the other hand, nobody is going to dispute that its author has "connaissance des choses," and shows himself aware of the condition under which he is working. The building, upon the whole, is a quite impeccable example of the current fashion in tall buildings, if it be nothing more. And, truly, it is rather more. There has evidently given some consideration to the proportions, to the choice and apportionment of material, to the scale and the design of the detail. It may be, as Baillie Jarvie said about Rob Roy, "ower bad for blessing," but it is surely "ower gude for banning."

No. By the same architects is offered solution of a very different problem. The problem here is not to give respectability, and if possible, distinction, to the common skyscraper, intended to meet the commonest, not to say vulgarest, of human needs, the need of making a living, the only possible purpose for which any human creature would hire quarters in the Royal, or in any other skyscraper. The problem is now to signalize an "institution," as distinguished from

itself to some plane from which it could be better seen, would, in fact, be forced to construct in front of itself the kind of plaza which every such building ought to have and which so few do have.

But you will observe a great difference between the projects of Mr. Flagg and Mr. Boyd, in their aesthetic purpose and their aesthetic results. What Mr. Flagg has evidently in mind is to "citify," to regularize, in a word, to Parisianize the city to which his plan is applied. In spite of his "tiara of proud towers," or collection of blank stark parallelopipeds, as the case may be, he would restore the skyline of the street fronts of New York, the city of which, of course, lie is thinking, and he would retain the plane of that street front, which will automatically preserve itself by reason of the insistence of every builder upon building to the limit of the building line. Mr. Boyd. on the other hand, would apparently welcome diversity and variegation in both these matters. A skyline which is a sierra has no terrors for him, neither has a street front which is a series of ins and outs. He would simply require that every builder should present his "returns" decently clothed and "treated architecturally." Therein, one imagines, he would encounter opposition. The builder who, on one of the streets devoted not to receding terraces, but to fronts in one plane each, but set back according to their respective heights, would apparently, have reason to complain if he chose to build only to the assumed "norm" and his neighbor went back and built higher. Why, he might very plausibly ask, should he be compelled to go to the cost of decorating the return walls of his projecting but humble erection without receiving any benefit therefrom, ▶

1907

above: Evening Post Building, New York City, Robert D. Kohn, architect, 1906.

13 Artemus Ward was a pseudonym of Charles Farrar Browne, 1834–67, American humorist.

14 Cable Building.

15 *Arris:* Two planes that meet in a sharp point.

16 Reference unknown.

17 *Mammon:* The god of this world. The word in Syriac means riches. In Aramaic, the term means worldly riches, retained in the New Testament Greek. "Ye cannot serve God and mammon" is one of the most noted biblical strictures.

a beehive. And it is to distinguish the institution above the flanking beehives which have the advantage of it in actual altitude, and, in the language of Artemus Ward,[12] one of whom it is also which. For it stands to reason that there is a good deal of rentability behind the frontage of the Title Guarantee and Trust Company. All the same, its flankers do overtop it, and something had evidently to be done to enable its eight stories to hold their own against their loftier neighbors. Obviously this something had to be done by "scale." And almost equally obvious, given the necessity of scale, was the expedient of the "colossal order" including five stories of the building itself and equaling five of the flanking buildings. If that, in fact, was the purpose, it has been attained. The institution would not be killed by the beehives if half a dozen more stories were added to each of them. And, although the "institution" by no means expresses and expounds the skeleton construction, and might, perhaps, be quite as it is in appearance if it were a building of masonry, yet it does not deny the construction as many buildings do which are far more representative of the skyscraper. Let us congratulate the architect on a client who "stood astonished at his own moderation" in stopping at eight stories. But let us also congratulate the client upon his architect.

And here is the new Stock Exchange, which has been so much written about that one would not think of writing about it again if the photograph did not happen to be included in one's "list" and to lie before one. But it is of interest in connection with Fig. 7 (page 143) as exemplifying the same problem, likely hereafter to present itself more frequently than heretofore, the problem of giving dignity to a building which by the conditions cannot compete with its neighbors in altitude. The resource which Mr. Post availed himself of so long ago in the Produce Exchange, was to surpass his neighbors in altitude, as well as in other dimensions of magnitude, by adding several stories of rentable offices to the institution he was housing. The effort was not wholly success-

ful even then, when of the two factors of the tall building, only the first, the passenger elevator, had come in, and the second, the steel frame, had not been developed. Even in the Produce Exchange there is a confusion as to what is monument and what is "business," and even whether the big hall or the little office is "the pig that pays the rint," a confusion much to the architectural disadvantage of the edifice. But now that the second factor is operative, the institutional building is evidently taken out of the competition, since one cannot "build to the limit" without hopelessly submerging the institution. Between the rowdy Cable building,[14] which I remember once seeing described in these pages as having the air of having a cigar in its mouth, and the less aggressive in fact the rather platitudinous, but distinctly altitudinous edifice on the north, a very emphatic horizontal extension was needed to enable the "institution" to hold its own, especially since it had been wisely determined that the institution should be the only occupant of its own premises. It must outscale the buildings which overtopped it. Here, too, the obvious and natural means of giving scale was the employment of the colossal order, the order in this case including four of the stories alongside, and, as in the other, really constituting the structure of the building and not a mere applied ornamentation. With this colonnade, and with the sculpture of the pediment, which unfortunately does evidently constitute a mere applied ornament, there is no danger that the Stock Exchange will not continue to hold its own, whatever may come to adjoin or to confront it.

The Seligman Building, corner William and South William streets, is a rather frightful example of the unwisdom of trying to variegate and diversify the accepted type of skyscraper, especially by an architect whose work indicates that his forte lies much rather in conformity than in innovation. Indeed, he could not quite have done the "regular thing" in any case, since the regular thing involves either a parallelopiped or, architecturally, a mere flat front, and he had a site apparently with an "acute" angle, though this one is blunt, so blunt that it may possibly be a right angle. If so, he is to be congratulated so far upon rounding the arris,[15] and giving himself a "feature." Unfortunately he has done nothing with his feature. Up to the eighth story, to the top of the shaft, the treatment of the walls is of distinct neither-here-nor-there-ness, excepting this rounded angle, which it seems that a sensitive designer would have made as solid as possible. Perhaps he could not diminish the size of his openings. But one cannot easily forgive him for having increased that at the bottom, where, precisely, the eye requires the greatest sense of solidity, and where is, in fact, the largest opening on the ground level, the principal entrance alone excepted. And what strange vagaries he wanders into when he comes to the top. From the ground up to the eighth story the form and treatment prefigure a turret or at least a pinnacle. One can imagine a highly effective crowning feature of that kind. But what sort of preparation is it for a lantern or a pinnacle actually to withdraw the wall below it, for two stories, into a reëntrant angle, truncated at that, so as to provide a visible want of support for his solid turret above? This is mere mindless caprice, mere amentia, "Amentia Americana,"[16] too, one is sorry to have to own. It is the rural carpenter's notion of "something fancy" done in durable and costly stone.

Truly, it seems that superfluities and arbitrariness are more explicitly excluded from the skyscraper than from almost any other kind of building. To be sure the caprice we have been noticing is so capricious that one is entitled to call it silly, and is, besides, very ill done. But in cases in which it would be unjust to apply so harsh a criticism as that, cases in which artistic architects are concerned, whom one would not and could not treat otherwise than respectfully, some of the cases, in fact, which we have already passed in review, does it not seem that in the architecture of the skyscraper as Martin Van Buren said about politics, "whatever is entirely superfluous ought to be avoided"? Does not the skyscraper particularly seems

when we come upon a building designed upon these principles, always and primarily given, of course, that it was designed by an artist. Such, eminently, is the new building of the Evening Post, architecturally a mere flat front, but with the great advantage of fronting, not a mere street, still less a mere canyon but the broad greensward of St. Paul's churchyard, which the renouncing corporation of Trinity has gratuitously put at the service of the exploiters of Mammon.[17] This, one may fairly say, is "the thing itself," the "skeleton" hardly draped, but articulated, developed and decorated in accordance with the facts of the case. There is no mistaking what it is or how it is put together. Instead of being concealed and confused, the essential structure is so emphasized that the spectator understands it better than he would have understood the mere steel frame before the architectural treatment of it was begun. The differentiations are not fantastic but, at least in appearance, functional. One supposes, for instance, that the upper most story, with its great openings belongs to the composing room, and that the whole "capital" denotes the abode of the newspaper which is so eminently an "institution," while the architectural base is confined to the single story which alone is really differentiated from the office building that occupies the "shaft." Of course all this might be as logical and yet be ugly, instead of being as it is, highly artistic and effective by reason of the skill of the architect in his emphasis and his subordinates in the successful study he has given to the design and to the placing of his detail, in the artistry of his sparing decoration. But can one imagine an equal architectural success attained by the process of slurring or suppressing the facts instead of bringing them out, by the introduction of features and variations unfounded in fact, as by this strictly "realistic" treatment of the thing he had to do? However that may be, it will not be disputed that the new building of the Evening Post is one of the best things in our recent street architecture, one of the most exemplary and interesting of the skyscrapers. ■

but merely for the adornment of the courtyard of his neighbor who had chosen to build further back and correspondingly higher? And it would be hard to give him a satisfactory answer. It is quite true that the irregularizing of the public streets which the adoption of these two plans would promote might, in the hands of architects of genius, working in irregularly picturesque styles, conceivably result in the beautification of the city to which the plans were applied, and might result in some thing far more attractive than the actual Philadelphia or the actual New York. But, keeping in view the actual race of architectural practitioners and the reasonable probabilities of our street architecture, a regular cornice line and a street front in a single plane seem to offer a better hope of a desirable result than a sawtoothed skyline and a higgledy piggledy of alignment, accompanied by a frontage of sidewalks of varying width, but so far as concerns the convenience of passengers, limited to the width of the narrowest of them.

It is abundantly evident that something must be done about the skyscrapers if our cities are to remain, or to re-become habitable. And it is only from the body of architects that we can expect any promising propositions to issue. ●

1907

**Larkin Building,
Buffalo, New York,
Frank Lloyd Wright, architect,
1903–04 (demolished 1950).**

As the headquarters for a giant
soap manufacturer and mail order
business, Wright's massive structure housed 1,800 workers
charged with processing 5,000
pieces of mail per day. The Larkin
Building is said to be the first
entirely air–conditioned office
building on record. Pictured is the
Central Court.

Sturgis had little sympathy for
what he saw as oppressively
heavy forms:

*"We are left, then, with our
sympathies enlisted in Mr.
Wright's behalf, to consider what
else might have been done, had
the architect felt that he could
not bear to turn out a building so
ungainly, so awkward in grouping, so clumsy in its parts and in
its main mass. Rejecting all that
older styles have to offer us in
the way of construction and in
the way of detail, we may still
ask, How did the designers work
when men knew how to
design?"*

Fig. a

THE LARKIN BUILDING IN BUFFALO

By Russell Sturgis

This business building, the architectural creation of Mr. Frank Lloyd Wright of Chicago, is reproduced in many excellent photographs, some of which will be shown in this article and others in the March[1] number of the Architectural Record. From among them I select Fig. b as the most capable of giving a general idea of the design. The plan given in Fig. g shows the purpose of each member of the building, and the scale can be estimated as to the heights, on the basis afforded by the steps of the entrance doorways, checked by the height of the doorway (seen in Fig. b) themselves, and by comparison with the plan. It is not safe to utilize the courses of brick in this way, because their height is uncertain; the bricks may be of unusual dimension or laid with unusually wide joints. The nearest tower-like mass in Fig. b—that against which the telegraph pole is seen relieved—is about 90 feet high. The broader mass behind it would be, then, about 110 feet high, and this appears to be the highest level of the walls. A perspective draughtsman can easily determine the relative proportions, as width compared to height, etc., but this front may be taken, in the absence of any figure dimensions on the plan, roughly as 90 to 95 feet in width, not, of course, including the north wing seen in Fig. c.

That front shown in Fig. b is called in this paper the east front. The longer side, showing in the same picture seven windowed bays divided by square buttress-piers, is called here the south flank.

It is possible to gain some knowledge of the character of the building by means of photos of the interior. Twenty excellent interior views are found in the collection above mentioned, and Fig. a shows how the building has a nave and aisles—the nave shown in the illustrations having windows at the ends, and a skylight overhead; each aisle is divided up into four lofts or stories of 16 to 17 feet each, in the clear. The broad end

windows, seen in Fig. a at the end of the great hall, are the same windows that show In Figs. b and c between the buttresses, and they correspond with the arrangement of the south front, as in Fig. b—note the four stories of broad windows flanked by narrower ones, which arc seen within and without alike. One relation between exterior and interior is seen in this—the square brick piers which divide what we here call the nave from the galleries at each side—a long double row of them are on the same axes as the buttress-like piers crowned by globes and human sculpture, in Figs. b and c.

In Fig. a there are partly seen the large galleries, at the left and at the right hand of the central skylighted nave. These halls are of only moderate height—one story of windows to each, as seen in Fig. d, which gives the interior of the fourth story, south side. Each one, as well as the floor of the high nave, is filled rather closely, with desk-tables, at which are seen seated clerks fully occupied in their employ. In this view, we are looking, eastward, the window on the left and in face of us, are those seen from outdoors in Fig. b, and the central nave is north of us, on our right.

The western end of the building is very closely like the east front; but the northern side as shown in Fig. c is masked by projecting masses of building which include a great vestibule with entrance doorways to east and west. In the northeast detail view, Fig. e, the doorway at the head of the steps where a young man is standing is one of those two entrances; it has the firm name on the large fan-light, and is probably the working entrance. The plan shows a similar doorway at the west of this one, and opposite to it. The houses of the town and a church crowd the site rather closely on the northern side.

The square towers at either end and flanking the entrance in Fig. e are about 18 feet in horizontal dimension. That one seen in Fig e has the overplus of water very skilfully treated as a cascade with a sculptural setting. The two outer towers, seen in Fig. b, have small doorways, with steps of approach. These are ventilator and stairway towers, and

from:
RUSSELL STURGIS 1836-1909
By Montgomery Schuyler
Vol. XXV, No. 3, March, 1909, p. 1

One of the most frequent, copious and valued of the collaborators of the Architectural Record has just passed over to the majority.

* * *

It has been set forth by the obituaries of the daily press that Mr. Sturgis, though his architectural work entitles him to recognition as one of the practitioners of his early years who practiced architecture with credit and scholarship, was not a born architect. His works, the buildings for Yale, the pretty Gothic Savings Bank in Albany, entitled him to respect, although, with quite characteristic generosity, he assigned the chief measure of credit for this last to his associate in it, Mr. Babb. Richardson, when he was in Albany doing his share of the Capitol, and doing the City Hall, spoke of this building even with enthusiasm. But Sturgis was not a Richardson. Whatever could be attained by study, in an art, which appealed to him, he might quite be relied upon to attain. But he had not that "impulse to create" which results in the manifestation of an artistic individuality. Whereas anybody can pick out the ▸

April
1908

1 The March issue Sturgis refers to is the first in a series of 17 articles Frank Lloyd Wright wrote for *ARCHITECTURAL RECORD* called "In the Cause of Architecture" from March 1908 until May 1952. (An excerpt from the First article appears on page 153).

Fig. b

right: Larkin Building, rear.

opposite: Larkin Building, fourth floor gallery.

below: Larkin Building, front.

Fig. c

that with the fountain contains also a staircase.

In tracing the analysis of this building through all this pile of photographs, and in setting down, as above, its scheme, we have also partly prepared ourselves to judge of it as a work of architecture. The lover of architecture who looks, perhaps for the first time, at building so entirely removed as this one from the traditional styles and schools feels a shock of surprise, and this a surprise which is the reverse of pleasant. Few persons who have seen the great monuments of the past, or adequate photographs of them; who have loved them and have tried to surprise their secret of artistic charm, will fail to pronounce this monument, as seen in Fig. b, an extremely ugly building. It is, in fact, a monster of awkwardness, if we look at its lines and masses alone. It is only capable of interesting that student who is quite aware that the architects of the modern world during fifty years of struggle have failed to make anything of the old system—the system of following the ancient styles with the avowed purpose of developing some one of them and going on to other things.

For such a task, the as yet unperformed duty of making comely a hard working and economical building, the designer might feel that Roman colonnading was out of the question, as extravagant in cost and waste of space, and the frankly arcuated styles of the

Middle Ages unavailable for similar or equally-cogent reasons. He might find his only available suggestion from old times in the seventeenth century Italian, and the eighteenth century French palaces—in styles which depended upon fenestration. And then he might well say that he was tired of seeing imitations of those monuments; that the popular and successful architects of the time have filled our cities with such an array of feeble school studies, based upon plans good in themselves but powerless to suggest an architectural treatment of the whole, that he will have none of that pseudo style.

Admitting, then, that the chase of the Neo-Classic, of the Gothic, of the French Romanesque, has come to nothing, that we are as far as we were in 1850 from a living style of architecture, and even from anything which is worthy to be called architecture at all, when a large mass of the work of a period is taken together, we shall find that the building we are considering puts on a new aspect.

Do we find in this building none of those familiar motives—those accepted details which are architecture for us? It is because the designer of this building was determined to furnish nothing which his practical requirements did not call for. Is there no visible proof? It is because a flat roof is just as easy to make tight and durable, with modern appliances of building, and because a swarm of skylights and other utilitarian openings are better and more easily accommodated in and upon a flat roof. As there are no chimneys, giving an opportunity for an agreeable breaking of the masonry into the sky and the sky into the masonry? It is because there are no separate fires, each fire requiring its own flue, and that flue carried well above all obstructions? There is probably one fire, and one only, in the building; moreover, that one fire is driven by a forced draught and requires no tall chimney shaft to make it burn. Is there no system of fenestration—the windows, and therewith the doors, showing in pretty groups or in long-drawn sequence carefully balancing one another? That is because the building consists of five equal stories, used for similar purposes; divided generally into long, unbroken halls—lofts, in short; and because it seems a feeble thing to do—to break up the arrangement of windows *merely* for the sake of pretty proportions. Are the grouped rooms and closets of utility arranged, even at of the building, by thrusting forward their crude masses to mask and distort, what might have been the effect of the main structure, all as seen in Fig. c? That is because this is to be an economical, working building, the offices of a great business house, and because it was thought well to be resolute in the chosen way and not to pretend to build a monument of architecture when a working structure was desired.

It is, indeed, quite certain that in New York the newly erected business building at the corner of Wall Street and Broadway, is more nearly like what a business building ought to be than the elaborated and delicately detailed skyscrapers around. It is certain that nothing is gained to architecture by trying to make a business building architectural in the good old sense. The fine arts

have nothing to do with the hustle and bustle of daily bread-winning operations. Those are hostile influences, as Ruskin pointed out much more than half a century ago; or it might be urged with still greater force that fine art and active mercantile pursuits are mutually exclusive. If you are to enjoy a work of art you must have leisure and a quiet mind; if you are to produce a work of art you must have peace and a single mind. In neither case will it do to have hanging over you the peremptory calls of the money-making organization—not one paymaster, who might perhaps forget his utilitarian requirements in the light of design and the joy of creation; but the commercial enterprise which can have no enthusiasm and no care for finer things than commerce.

We are left, then, with our sympathies enlisted in Mr. Wright's behalf, to consider what else might have been done, had the architect felt that he could not bear to turn out a building so ungainly, so awkward in grouping, so clumsy in its parts and in its main mass. Rejecting all that older styles have to offer us in the way of construction and in the way of detail, we may still ask,

Fig. d

work of Richardson, and any very sensitive person can discriminate it from that of his imitators, Sturgis's work is simply up to the best level of scholarly attainment of the time and not assignable to an individual. One may say that he would always rather discuss than design. And it was a good thing for him and for the rest of us that he was early withdrawn from design to discussion. The first time I remember hearing his name was in answer to my inquiry, addressed to John Dermett of the Nation, who had written a certain criticism of the then new and now demolished old Park Bank, on the site of the present edifice of the same name, which had appeared in that periodical. From that time until his death, criticism and not creation was evidently the real line of action for Russell Sturgis. His knowledge was so wide, so "encyclopaediacal," it has been called since his death, his anxiety to be right on any point of fact, and to take nothing for granted without proof, was so keen, that his reader might go along with him on any disputed or disputable point with a singular confidence, even though that reader might differ from the artistic judgment that accompanied the erudition. The present writer, in reviewing the "Dictionary of Architecture," took occasion to quote from Samuel Johnson to the effect that Mr. Sturgis never "frolicked in conjecture." When I the editor next met his reviewer, he said: "I am exceedingly obliged to you for pointing that out." This accuracy and secureness in matters of fact are a great source of strength to a critic or an historian. They give his readers the confidence which Mr. Sturgis, among careful readers, never failed to inspire. Readers of the Architectural Record have profited by this care and this circumspection exerted upon a great variety of subjects, historical and contemporaneous, for now these many years. •

1908

The Larkin Building was published along with Wright's domestic architecture as Ausgefuhrte Bauten in Germany in 1911 (cover above), commonly referred to as the *Wasmuth Portfolio*, after its publisher Ernst Wasmuth.

opposite, left: Larkin Building, detail of entrance.

opposite, far right: Cupples Warehouse, St. Louis, Eames & Young, architects, 1894.

How did the designers work when men knew how to design? What, apart at least from the unconscious following of the style accepted during this period was their for light and shade. The interesting treatment of light and shade, the production of graceful and simple combinations of light and shade was their chief aim. A thought in architecture is generally a thought in light and shade.

When the great buildings of the world were designed everything else which was capable of design received it; and all design in pure form, as in sculpture, in relief modeling, in grouping and massing, is design in light and shade. The simple requirements of every-day life were met by the maker of vessels and utensils with as free and as successful a method of designing as the requirements of state and of religion; and he worked in form principally, that is, in light and shade. Earthen vessels and metal utensils were gracefully designed. And all this not because the maker cared greatly to produce a decorative object, for he also was dimly conscious of the fact that it was hardly worth while to waste design on a working tool, but because it was inevitable that a man who did fine things on a Monday would still do comely things on a Tuesday. How can you make a clumsy and an awkward thing if you have made graceful ones for forty-eight hours on end? It is a blessed trait of our nature that good habits as well as bad habits may be formed and will stick. And so the designs of a good time for architectural art are sure to be good designs, that is, to have such forms that the light and shade upon them would be lovely. The design before us could not have been made by any able man at a time when there prevailed a worthy style of design in the world around him.

One may try, comparing these seven or eight views of the exterior—one may try the experiment of familiarity to see whether with longer acquaintance the building is less ugly than it seems at the first look. Ruskin tells the story of his having been led astray by the theory of Use and Wont—by the notion that our liking for certain forms and colors is the result of familiarity, and nothing else, and he says that he kept a skull on his mantelpiece for months, but found it just as ugly when the months had passed. And so it is in all probability with this exterior. If we are to consider it as a piece of abstract form, as a thing which is itself ugly or the reverse, the opinion will remain fixed that nothing uglier could exist among objects that were found perfect in condition, cared for, and showing the signs of human thought and purpose. We should see in a moment that where such qualities as those are found to exist, the building cannot be wholly contemptible. That it is wholly repellant as a work of human artisanship which might have been a work of art and is not—so much is probably the verdict of most persons who care for the fine art of architecture.

Light and shade have been mentioned as the chief elements in our art, and one of the ways in which light and shade are used continually in architectural design is in the way of moldings. What is a molding? What are moldings? It is, they are, a modulation of the surface following continuous lines, straight and curved. Moldings are an abandonment of plane and uniform surface for a broken and generally rounded surface, as along an edge, and a group of moldings consists of all alternation of projecting and retreating forms, mainly of curved surface and of small dimension, although these are broken, interspersed here and there by narrow strips of flat and uniform surface, which we call fillets. Moldings do not weaken the wall where the window jamb, the door jamb, the horizontal cornice or sill course is modified by their interposition. Suppose, for instance, that one who lived opposite this Larkin Building were to have his way for a month, and were to utilize his time in making the building less clumsy in his eyes—would he not begin by molding those square corners which are thrust upon us so sharply in all the exterior views, working those corners into upright beads and coves, developing, perhaps, in an angle shaft with capital and base? This, of course, is not an essential feature. To insert it would be to give, perhaps, too nearly mediæval a look to the design. Suppose that the corners of one of those tower-like masses were molded to such an extent that eight inches on each side of the arris, everywhere, were to be reduced to a series of soft surfaces, concave and convex, parallel one to another, and carried up from a little above the base to a little below the coping? They may be cast in brick, two or three separate patterns of molded brick sufficing for the whole composition. These moldings must either stop or return; and there are very interesting ways of arranging for either. They may stop against the stone coping or belt course itself; or they may have a piece of cast brick or of terracotta or of cut stone, in the mass of which the stop of the groups of moldings may be against a splay or a concave or a convex curved surface.

Moldings are important and valuable, and the designer who rejects them altogether handicaps himself—and yet there are even better things than moldings. The horizontal bands in a building like this would be interesting if they were molded; and yet they would be more interesting still if they were carried out in some greater projection in the face of the building and supported on corbels or on a little arcade. But it is evident that the first principle laid down by the designer for his own guidance was this—to avoid everything that would look like a merely architectural adornment, to add nothing to the building for the sake of architectural effect. He would repel the idea of a projecting cornice as readily as he would the full classical entablature for the top of one of these square towers, which would be no better working elements of the building if they were so adorned. Either you must add to a building something which is unnecessary, and which nothing but existing tradition even suggests to you, or you must have a bare, sharp edged pile of blocks—a group of parallelopipedons like this. The designer seems to have said that even the rounding off of the coping shall be eschewed. He has determined that the square corner, the right angle, the straight

edge, the sharp arris, the firm vertical and horizontal lines, unbroken, unmodified, uncompromising in their geometrical precision—that these and these only shall be the features of his building. But as that characteristic of the building prevents it from having any delicate light and shade, therefore it stands condemned in the eyes of any person who looks at the building asking for beauty of effect.

There is, however, mass. There is the possibility of proportion the proportion of the smaller to the greater, and the possibility of fitting one to another firmly and with grace. There is the proportion obtainable by the horizontal distribution, the alternating of curtain walls with towers, of projecting and receding masses; and there is the possibility of vertically succeeding masses, the parts which serve for a kind of basement at either

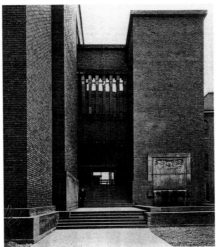

Fig. e

end, and those towers and buttresses which rise above them. There is even a possibility of contrast between walls filled with windows and the massive blank space of the wall which rests upon the piers between the windows.

If, now, we seek to take up a sympathetic position, to consider the building perhaps the architect himself considered it, there are

from:
SOME RECENT WAREHOUSES
By Russell Sturgis
Vol. XXIII, No. 5, May, 1908,
pp. 373-386

Many years ago, when the American Institute of Architects was a New York society, small in membership, without affiliations in other cities, I read a paper before it when my turn had come to entertain the members present at a meeting. I remember that Richard Morris Hunt was in the chair, and that he made sounds and gestures of evident approval when I insisted strongly upon the crying need there was of taking a common veranda, an ordinary shed supported on square posts, a common brick wall resting upon a lintel course which, in its turn, was carried by light iron columns, and making a design of those things. We were to approach design, I thought, not as a study of Roman grandeur, with its essential features taken away or caricatured, but from artistic work upon unpretending structures whose naked utility might be raised into something finer as opportunity might serve. It pleases me, after so many years, to see the truth of that scheme of architectural development—its importance, its need, the obvious common sense of it—recognized, so far as in the twentieth century it is accepted. We have not yet begun to build buildings of high cost and great pretension on those lines, but that will come in its turn. •

above: Schoenhofen Brewery, Chicago, Richard E. Smith, architect—administration Building, 1886; powerhouse,1902.

right: Larkin Building, rear.

opposite: Larkin Building. About the photo on the opposite page, Brendan Gill says, "Wright objected to the descriptiveness of architectural photography except when it happened to serve his purpose. This was his favorite representation of the Larkin Building, which flatteringly distorted its proportions." [*Many Masks: A Life of Frank Lloyd Wright*, p. 169]

Fig. g

to notice the care given to the plan and disposition of the halls and rooms, the care which has evidently resulted in a successful utilitarian building. Construction which is the simplest and most obvious, and which cannot go astray because everything is reduced to the post and lintel; workmanship which is faultless, simple and straight forward brickwork; piers and walls fairly and smoothly built; slabs and beams of stone which have been planed and dressed in the mill and left with sharp arrises; a view down the central hall as seen in Fig. a, which is impressive because of the straightforwardness and simplicity of everything, and because of the clear daylight which fills all parts of the hall; the evidences which the pictures multiply, of a minute prevision in the way of office furniture, safes and cupboards for filing papers, tables and chairs of metal and solid wood, all of the simplest

Fig. f

conceivable forms; the electric bulbs set in racks at a convenient height above tables and counters, which racks, though of inconceivable ugliness, have yet the character of simple utility—all these things unite to make a building which no one can fail to accept. The iron railing which encloses the site comes nearer to being really a design than the larger details, generally; for in this a true economy and a sagacious utility take the place of a sense of form. Our standard is lower, when we consider some hundreds of running feet of fencing.

And so in the exterior it is allowable to the student to feel that a square brick shaft is as fit to contain a winding staircase or an

elevator as a round or octagonal cut stone shaft costing five times the money; that windows are not absolutely necessary when there can be a sky light: and that where there are no windows, and no breaking up for windows without necessity, the result is inevitable—the result that there will be no pierced parapet nor any modifying of the uppermost story to replace in a way the cornice which, of course, such a building does not require. Here is a well-thought-out design, every detail of construction and all the appliances have been studied with care. Here is an excellent arrangement of large windows, raised high toward the ceiling, broad and low and shaped as they ought to be for utilitarian results. It is clear that there is nothing to burn about the building; it is as fireproof as such a building can be made. And while everything has been carried out with a view to practical utility, there has been also some attempt to adorn, to beautify. But we have already seen reason to think that this attempt has failed. See for the attempt and for the failure, in Fig. g, that curious base arranged beneath the brick piers on the right; it is the Attic base reduced to its simplest form, the familiar old Attic base, with its rounded moldings turned back into the square-edged bands which those moldings were in their origin. And those square moldings are put in, the larger below and the smaller above, with the evident purpose of serving as ornament. Accepting this, let the eye now take in the curious square block decoration of the same pier in its upper part, higher than the door and between the great doorway of the entrance where the firm name is painted on the glass, and the small staircase doorway on the right. Is this a serious attempt to create a new system of design? May we assume that the inevitable squareness of the brick-built pier, all molded and specially cast brick being rejected, satisfies the designer so well that he gladly makes everything else, his sculptured ornaments and his bronze fittings, as square as the masses of brickwork? Look, then, at the system of metal frames in which the electric globes are suspended. From this picture go back to Fig. a and study those straight-edged and sharp-cornered groups of ornament at the tops of the great piers, and directly below the skylight see those square ornaments which are clearly nothing but ornaments. Fig. d shows two groups of those extraordinary connections—those terminals of the great supporting piers at the end of the high nave opposite the one shown in Fig. a. It is unnecessary to describe the design of these strange masses of square-edged patterning; no human designer could make anything graceful or even anything effective out of such elements as those. Taking all this accumulation of strange, sharp-edged solids, offering no modulation of surface—nothing but sharp contrast and checkered black and white—and the wonder will grow upon you more and more, how such a costly, careful, thoughtful, well-planned building should be made up of such incongruous parts, leading to such a hopeless result.

One cannot help liking broad surfaces of fair brickwork, and yet those very masses of brickwork may be so much more interesting; they may be invested with color. There is the third chance for the designer! After light and shade have escaped him, or have been rejected, deliberately, and when the artistic use of mass and proportion are out of the question, he has still at his disposal the interest and charm of color, and this exterior calls for it loudly. The careful brickwork, even as it is, has a certain momentary pleasure to offer those of us who feel dissatisfied with the flimsy character and the inappropriate ornament of the buildings around. Such a pleasure lasts but an instant, however. You turn from the florid facade to the plain brick gable wall or rear with a sense of relief, but it is merely an instantaneous pleasure which you feel in escaping from something painful. If we are to look at the building a second time, and that with renewed pleasure, we must have something else; and, where delicate play of light and shade is denied us, as here, variety of color pattern would be an admirable expedient. It is not necessary to expatiate on this view of the case, for any one who has ever made patterns in mosaic or has enjoyed the patterns that others have made for him will see what a pleasure this building might have been to the designer and to the student, had its grimness of aspect been modified by color patterns. Even the simple stripes found in the wall of that New York apartment house which faces on Fourth Avenue and East Sixty-eighth Street, three horizontal courses of dark brown brick, one of scarlet brick, and so on, in alternation, even that is beautiful. More elaborate, more effective combinations might be made where colored bonds pass through—cut across—groups of moldings. ■

from:

IN THE CAUSE OF ARCHITECTURE
By Frank Lloyd Wright
Vol. XXIII, No. 3, March 1908, pp. 155-222.

The Larkin Building is one of a large group of factory buildings situated in the factory district of Buffalo. It was built to house the commercial engine of the Larkin Company in light, wholesome, well-ventilated quarters. The smoke, noise and dirt incident to the locality made it imperative that all exterior surfaces be self cleaning and the interior be created independently of this environment. The building is a simple working out of certain utilitarian conditions, its exterior a simple cliff of brick whose only "ornamental" feature is the exterior expression of the central aisle, fashioned by means of the sculptured piers at either end of the main block. The machinery of the various appurtenance systems, pipe shafts incidental thereto, the heating and ventilating air in-takes, and the stairways which serve also as fire escapes, are quartered in plan and placed outside the main building at the four outer corners, so that the entire area might be free for working purposes. These stair chambers are top-lighted. The interior of the main building thus forms a single large room in which the main floors are galleries open to a large central court, which is also lighted from above. All the windows of the various stories or "galleries" are seven feet above the floor, the space beneath being utilized for steel filing cabinets. The window sashes are double, and the building practically sealed to dirt, odor and noise, fresh air being taken high above the ground in shafts extending above the roof surfaces. The interior is executed throughout in vitreous, cream-colored brick, with floor and trimmings of "magnesite" of the same color. The various features of this trim were all formed within the building itself by means of simple wooden molds, in most cases being worked directly in place. So the decorative forms were necessarily simple, particularly so as this material becomes very hot while setting and expands slightly in the process. The furnishings and fittings are all of steel and were designed with the structure. The entrance vestibules, from either street and the main lobby, together with the toilet accommodations and rest rooms for employees, are all located in an annex which intercepts the light from the main office as little as possible. The fifth floor is given to a restaurant for employees, with conservatories in mezzanines over kitchen and bakery at either end, opening in turn to the main roof, all of which together constitutes the only recreation ground available for employees. The structure, which is completely fireproof, together with its modern heating, ventilating and appurtenance system, but exclusive of metal fixtures and furnishings, cost but little more than the average high class fireproof factory building—18 cts. per cubic foot. Here again most of the critic's "architecture" has been left out. Therefore the work may have the same claim to consideration as a "work of art" as an ocean liner, a locomotive or a battleship. ●

Singer Building and Tower, (left)
New York City, Ernest Flagg, architect, 1899;1905–08 (demolished 1967).

Flagg added the 47-story, 612-foot tower to his earlier Singer Manufacturing Headquarters, making this the tallest building in the world for one year (the title was later claimed by the Metropolitan Life Tower). Although they occupied a single floor, Singer used the tower extensively in its promotional material. The tower now has the distinction of being the tallest building ever razed.

Metropolitan Life Insurance Company Building and Tower, (right) New York City, Napoleon LeBrun & Sons, architects, 1892;1909.

Modeled on the Campanile of the Cathedral of San Marco in Venice (photo 161), the tower was an addition to the earlier building, behind and to the right (since demolished). Nearly completed in this photograph, except for the lantern, the 50-story, 700-foot, white marble structure made this the tallest building in the world. In the lower left foreground is Madison Square Presbyterian Church.

opposite: A postcard proudly displays the proposed Metropolitan Life Tower, "The Light that Never Fails."

Architecture in the United States[1]

III.

The Skyscraper

Claude Bragdon[2]

The various activities noted in the previous articles prove our competence to build, and our desire to build well and beautifully; but however true it may be that the desire for a thing is a necessary condition precedent to its attainment, the desire for fine architecture is impotent when unaccompanied by a certain kind of effort, of taste, of judgment, I may even add of manner of life and mode of feeling. As yet we do not seem to have sufficiently developed that right kind of effort, of taste, of judgment, nor to have learned to live and to feel in just the manner necessary to produce an indigenous architectural art eloquent of our highest intellectual and moral sensibility.

The skyscraper, the only indigenous architectural product to which we can lay claim, is eloquent only of the power of the purse and of the higher turn for business. In it the idea of profit everywhere triumphs over the idea of perfection. The last word of these tall buildings is anything but their address to our sense of formal beauty. As Henry James[3] says, "The attempt to take the æsthetic view is invariably blighted, sooner or later, by their most salient characteristic, the feature that speaks loudest for the economic idea. Window upon window, at any cost, is a condition never to be reconciled with any grace of building, and the logic of the matter here happens to be on a particularly fatal front. If quiet interspaces, always half the architectural battle, exist no more in such a structural scheme than quiet tones, blest breathing spaces occur, for the most part, in New York conversation, so the reason is, demonstrably, that the building can't afford them. The building can only afford lights, each light having a superlative value as an aid to the transaction of business and the conclusion of sharp bargains." In these terms Mr. James registers his final impression: "Such growths, you feel, have confessedly arisen but to be 'picked' in time, with a shears—nipped short off, by waiting fate, as soon as 'science' applied to gain, has put upon the table from far up its sleeve, some more winning card. Crowded not only with no history and consecrated by no uses save the commercial at any cost, they are simply the most piercing notes in that concert of the expensively provisional into which your supreme sense of New York resolves itself. They never begin to speak to you, in the manner of the builded majesties of the world as we have heretofore known such—tower or temples or fortresses or palaces—with the authority of things of permanence, or even of things of long duration. One story is good only till another is told, and skyscrapers are the last word of economic ingenuity only till another word be written."

In very truth these "mercenary monsters" are already menaced through sheer magnitude and multiplication, like some race of giant dinosaurs, threatened with extinction by reason of a productivity in excess of the earth's power to provide them with sustenance. The rentable value, which is the life blood of these tall office buildings, subsisting, as they do, on the light, the air, the sufferance of their undeveloped or underdeveloped neighbors, suffers diminishment in proportion to the extent that these neighbors themselves climb skyward and claim their own.

Already in the business districts of New York and Chicago, there are solid blocks of skyscrapers, and if the building of one of them continues unrestricted the lower sto-

from
THE WORK OF N. LeBRUN & SONS
By Montgomery Schuyler
Vol. XXVII, No. 5, May, 1910,
pp. 365–381

Last January there was a celebration in New York, so far as I know, unprecedented and unique. It was the celebration by a commercial institution of the completion of its great building.

* * *

The occasion was not only to signalize the completion of the tallest and one of the largest office buildings in America, far taller, therefore, than any such edifice in any other country, and very notable anywhere by its magnitude in other dimensions than altitude. For in no capital can an edifice of an area of twenty-five acres be other than very much out of the common. It signalized also the retirement from the practice of their profession of the architects who have lived with the building, so to say, since the beginning of the nucleus on Madison Avenue, almost twenty years ago.

* * *

The huge extent and the unprecedented altitude of the Metropolitan make the beholder prone to forget that quite the ▶

1 Other parts to this article are "Part I: The Birth of Taste," [XXV:6 Jun 1909 pp 426-434] and "Part II: The Growth of Taste," [XXVI:1 Jul 1909 pp 38-45]

2 Claude Fayette Bragdon (1866-1946) was an architect, stage designer, author and theosophist, and was editor of a succession of newspapers.
  Bragdon began his architectural training in 1886 and after moving from firm to firmworked for Bruce Price in New York.In 1891 he returned to Rochester and continued to practice in Rochester until 1923. While actively practicing he wrote for *Architectural Record* from 1908 to 1928. Besides his practical contributions to the field, Bragdon wrote three books on architectural theory, *The Beautiful Necessity*, 1910, *Architecture and Democracy*, 1918, and *The Frozen Fountain*, 1932. He also wrote the forward to Louis Sullivan's *Autobiography of an Idea*, and edited Sullivan's *Kindergarten Chats*.

3 Henry James, page 87, *n*.4.

4 Paul Bourget, page 66, *n*.5.

5 Mammon, page 136, *n*.15.

ries will become (as many of them are today), mere cellars, and the streets deep cañons, dark at noon day, the playground of germ-laden winds. "These leagues of buildings, describable and indescribable, are not beautiful but sinister. One feels depressed by the mere sensation of the enormous life which created them—life without sympathy; of their prodigious manifestation of power—power without pity. They are the architectural utterance of the new industrial age."

And over all broods the horror of a great impending catastrophe—a menace no less real for being unrealized. By reason of the massing of tall buildings on narrow streets, some day a devastating fire will leap from skyscraper to skyscraper, hundreds of feet above the heads of the horror stricken spectators. Such a disaster is not only possible, but inevitable. It is a matter of time and circumstance alone, this springing of the great granite and iron trap. Mr. Babb, the president of the New York Board of Fire Underwriters at a recent meeting of a commission on the limitation of the areas and heights of buildings appointed by the Building Codes Revision Committee of the New York Board of Aldermen, is quoted as having said:

"With our present unlimited height of buildings in the financial centre, where the streets are being converted into narrow cañons by the walls of thirty and forty storied buildings, we are courting a disaster that would outdistance that of any other great fire in the country. The San Francisco fire has taught that so called fireproof buildings cannot withstand the attacks of an uncontrolled wave of flame. How much more dangerous would a fire be when it was sweeping through the top levels of our lines of lofty buildings. Experience has taught that a high building of great area nurses the hottest fires. It is not only not beyond the range of possibility, but the underwriters fear that there is a very strong probability of a fire starting in the nest of skyscrapers and beating across streets from the windows on the top floors to other buildings. All system of sprinklers and all attempts at fireproofing

would not avail in the least in an instance of this kind. The firemen away down below could do nothing. The fire would gain such headway that when the edge of the skyscraper zone was reached, there would be a blaze of such proportions as to imperil the whole city." This is not the scare of a yellow journal, but the mature judgment of an expert. Moreover, engineers have estimated that in case of a sudden shock or other unforeseen incident, calculated to terrify the tenants of the lofty buildings, the narrow streets of the financial district would not be large enough to accommodate the swarm of people from these many storied hives.

The only safeguard against such catastrophes lies, of course, in restrictive legislation, either by the direct curtailment of skyscrapers, to a certain limit of dimension, or by a system of taxation calculated to discourage upward extension. One suggestion is that a builder might be allowed to occupy with his structure a fixed percentage of cubic space, found by multiplying the dimension of his lot by a fixed standard of height. This would make a limit of bulk rather than of height. The best solution, both from a practical and an æsthetic standpoint, might consist in proportioning the height of buildings to the breadth of the interval separating them, permitting skyscrapers, say, only on opposite sides of every alternate street. The effect of a broad avenue, lined by buildings of moderate height, behind and beyond which, on opposite sides of parallel streets rise tiers of tall buildings, facing one another across the wide interval, thus formed between them, besides affording an abundance of light and air, both to the buildings and to the streets, might strike a new and impressive note in the concert of municipal art.

However much our newly acquired power to build with safety to almost any imaginable height is being or may be abused, the growth of cities, the concentration of business within narrow areas, and the consequent high price of land in such areas insures perpetuity, within certain limits, to the type of building made possible by the development of the skeleton frame, and the invention of the elevator. This being so, it is for us to face the problem of the skyscraper squarely, seeking to discover and develop its latent aesthetic potentialities. The more conviction, enthusiasm—love, even—we can bring to the task, the better will the result be. The architect who essays the problem without interest and without sympathy, is foredoomed to failure, and it may be that the consciousness of the "finite—the menaced, the essentially invented state" which Mr. James[3] purports to have detected in "the thousand glassy eyes of these giants of the mere market," was only a reflected gleam from the mercenary and unimaginative minds of the architectural Frankensteins responsible for these monsters.

Mr. James had reference to the skyscrapers of New York. In Chicago, as before explained, the problem has been approached in better faith, with more sincerity and directness. From the tall buildings of that city, Mr. Paul Bourget,[4] an equally competent observer—more competent, in so far as he is more sympathetic—received a very different impression. He says of them:

"The simple force of need is such a principle of beauty, and these buildings so conspicuously manifest that need, that in contemplating them you experience a singular emotion. The sketch appears here of a new kind of art, an art of democracy, made by the crowd and for the crowd, an art of science in which the certainty of natural laws gives to audacities in appearance the most unbridled, the tranquillity of geometrical figures."

"The simple force of need is such a principle of beauty." Here at last, is the particular peg for which we have been looking on which to hang the case for the defendant. These many storied temples to Mammon,[5] whether one thinks them beautiful, as does Mr. Bourget, or, merely revolting, like Mr. James, are the supreme manifestation of our need and our power to build—to build on a gigantic scale, and in an unprecedented manner; and that, say what one may, is architecture—architecture rampant it may be, but at all events alive. Our churches, universities and libraries, our capitols and court houses—what are they for the most part but insincere archaeological experiments or cut to measure confections from European fashion plates? They involve no unprecedented constructive problems, and contain no potentialities of new beauty. The skyscraper, on the other hand, does both. It affords, for that reason, a magnificent opportunity, and the fact that it has been, for the most part, an opportunity unimproved, reflects less heavily upon the skyscraper than upon the architect thereof. Here is a Dark Tower, hedged about with difficulties, and dangers, awaiting its Childe Roland.[6] The imagination of Mr. Sullivan first, and almost alone, has reached up and caught at the possibilities and meaning which are enshrined in those huge office structures, and this, rather than his original and intricate ornamentation, constitutes his chief claim to greatness. As Mr. Caffin says: "to him they are not merely buildings to be deprecated for their negation of all that has been held beautiful in the architecture of the past. They are, or may be made, vital embodiments of the colossal energy and aspiring enterprise of American life. The fact that this piling of story upon story has its origin in the commercial necessities of real estate and in the congestion of population within certain limited areas, does not prevent him from seeing the spiritual possibilities which lurk, undreamed of by most people, in this inert mass of brutal materialism."

The aesthetic problem presented by the tall office building Mr. Sullivan conceives to be "one of the most stupendous, one of the most magnificent opportunities that the Lord of Nature in his beneficence has ever offered to the proud spirit of man." His greatest successes have been in the field of this variety of commercial architecture. The limiting conditions which others accept perforce and compromise with as much as they dare in order the better to conform with traditional ideas of architectural beauty, he accepts willingly, even eagerly, achieving his best effects not in spite of the imposed limitations but by means of them.

In order to understand the quality and the degree of Mr. Sullivan's success in this field,

same artistic qualities displayed in its design were displayed many years before in a mere street front, that of the Home Life, in lower Broadway. The early tall buildings were a series of architectural experiments. It seemed as though the sudden enablement of a greater height than had before been feasible had driven out of the minds of the designers the fact that these new and portentous structures were as amenable to architectural laws as the older and more commonplace, that, in particular the Aristotelian law as completely applied to them, and that every artistic building must have a beginning, a middle and an end.

* * *

Now, the distinction of the Home Life...was in its design an intelligent and artistic summation of what had been ascertained and agreed, at its date, as to the subjection of the new monsters, so long "ferae naturae," to the reign of law....The story above the entrance is signalized in dimensions and in elaboration of ornament as the home of the proprietary institution, and treated to the result of making it an effective and attractive base. The eight stories of the shaft, with a story of connection and transition at top and bottom are treated with absolute uniformity and absolute simplicity, while the openings of the centre are effectively framed between the broad piers with a single opening in each. The capital, the crown, is of a suitable proportion and of a suitable and not excessive richness.

*Most can grow the flowers now,
For all have got the seed;*

but the accepted convention in the treatment of skyscrapers is here so skillfully And tastefully expressed as to make it hard to realize that the building is a pioneer. ▶

6 *Childe Rowland:*
*"Childe Rowland to the
dark tower came;
His word was still 'Fie, foh,
and fum,
I smell the blood of a
Britishman.'"*
Shakespeare: *King Lear*, iii. 4

7 Guaranty Building, Buffalo,
New York, Adler and Sullivan,
architects, 1894 (photo page
212).

8 Charles Follem McKim
(1847–1909) of McKim Mead
and White. Gorham Company
Building, New York City, McKim,
Mead & White, architects, 1905
(photo page 172).

9 Cass Gilbert (1859–1934).

opposite: Home Life Insurance
Building, New York City,
Napoleon Le Brun & Sons, archi-
tects, 1893–94.

below: West Street Building,
New York City, Cass Gilbert,
architect, 1905–07.

the conditions governing the problem of the modern office building must be briefly stated. In its last analysis it is a hive, a system of cells hundreds of similar rooms side by side and superimposed, equally desirable (so far as possible), and equally well lighted. It must be lofty, because while its horizontal dimensions are limited by the size of the lot, and the size of the lot by the cost of land, its vertical height is limited only by its stability, and the stability of one of these steel frame buildings is enormous, for it is, in effect, a truss planted upright in the earth. This steel frame work must be protected from the corroding action of the elements, and especially from fire, which destroys it. The building must have natural light in every part, and (usually) great display windows in the first story.

Let me illustrate now, by means of a typical example, in what manner Mr. Sullivan has translated this thing of utility into a work of architectural art. The Guaranty Building, in Buffalo, affords a good illustration of his method. "What," he demands, "is the chief characteristic of the tall office building? It is lofty. This loftiness is to the artist-nature its thrilling aspect. It must be tall. The force of altitude must be in it. It must be every inch a proud and soaring thing, rising in sheer exultation, that from bottom to top it is a unit without a dissenting line." And he has therefore enhanced the height by art fully emphasizing the vertical dimension, so that when seen in sharp perspective the windows lose themselves behind the piers and the eye is carried irresistibly upward to the beautiful coved cornice which crowns the structure.

"The shape, form, outward expression of the tall office building should, in the very nature of things, follow the function of the building, and when the function does not change the form is not to change." The first two stories, which may be called the "mercantile stories," serve a different purpose from the rest, and so they are treated differently; but above them all of the windows are of the same size and are spaced equally far apart, because they light offices of the same size and equally desirable. This best thing practically, has been made by the skill of the designer the best thing aesthetically, for there is a kind of beauty which comes from the repetition of a few well chosen motives, and, moreover, the building appears what it is—a hive for human bees.

"The materials of a building are but the elements of earth removed from the matrix of Nature, and reorganized and reshaped by force—by force mechanical, muscular, mental, emotional moral and spiritual." The exterior of the building is all of terra cotta, of a salmon-red color, and every square foot, almost every square inch, of this vast surface is "reshaped by force," with beautiful ornament, fine as lace and strong as steel, infinitely various and original. By reason of its flatness and its delicacy, though it charms the eye, it nowhere assumes a prominence sufficient to detract from the simplicity and dignity of the architectural composition. Moreover, the ornament is of a kind exactly suited to the plastic nature of fire-clay; it is clear at a glance that it was modeled, not carved, and the subdivisions of the pattern have been considered in relation to the joints, so that these are nowhere too apparent.

The building is rich in those little felicities which reveal the artist. For example, the strength of the angular corner is emphasized by treating it in the form of a bead rising sheer from base to summit, and this slender, stem-like member flowers out at its far, topmost extremity, into an exquisite foliation, which seems to cling to and lap over the edge of the main cornice, mitigating its geometric severity of line. Even the dirtiness of the atmosphere has been made to serve æsthetic ends, for the terra cotta ornament is of such a nature that particles of dust or soot, lodging in the interstices, bring the pattern into relief, and the building thus grows more beautiful instead of uglier with the lapse of years. Mr. Sullivan has solved the difficult problem of the show window very cleverly. By placing the glass well to the front of the flanking piers he has rendered unto the Cæsar of Trade the things which are that Cæsar's; but, mindful of the claims of art, he has recessed the glass at the transom level, so as to leave revealed beautifully ornamental terra cotta soffits and jambs, together with the caps and the upper portions of the columns, which, visible through the show window, rise boldly through a shallow roof of glass. He attains by these means an effect of solidity usually arrived at by deeply recessing the windows and reducing the glass area in the place of all places where the need for space and light is most imperative.

Of the Guaranty Building,[7] Mr. Montgomery Schuyler says: "I know of no steel framed building in which metallic construction is more palpably felt through the envelope of baked clay." Though it represents perhaps the highest logical and aesthetic development of the steel frame office building, it is scarcely deserving, in the light of recent developments, of the name of skyscraper. It is an insignificant pile of twelve stories and any building under twenty can no longer rightfully lay claim to that title. The new Singer Building tower, and the Metropolitan Life Building rear their proud heads to the height of more than forty stories, affording a glimpse of that unknown and rather terrible generation which is to follow us, unless, as I have already intimated, we read and heed the handwriting on the wall, and curb—before it is too late—this menacing, this mercenary madness.

Although the New York architects have not succeeded in combining, with Mr. Sullivan's success, stern logic in the matter of form, with originality and grace in the matter of ornament, it would be an injustice to deny them the honor of having made substantial contributions towards the aesthetic problem involved in the skyscraper. They have approached that problem more in the Classic than in the Gothic spirit, demanding, in the name of the Classic tradition, a threefold vertical subdivision—a beginning, a middle, and an end—unrelated (or only accidentally related) to any analogous differentiation in the plan. Something they must have corresponding to stylobate, column, and entablature base, shaft and capital. The late Mr. Bruce Price was, I believe, the first

to formulate this into a principle for the tall building, and he applied it with notable success in his American Surety Building, a gigantic pilaster, which has its base, its many windowed, fluted shaft, and its intricately ornamented capital. The success of this essay imposed this principle, and the best of the lately built skyscrapers of New York are for the most part so many embodiments and variants of it. Of these, Mr. McKim's[8] Gorham Building seems to me the most altogether felicitous, perhaps owing to its more manageable proportions. The eye dwells delightedly on its warm grayness, its delicate reliefs, even upon its far spreading fretted and gilded cornice, though the mind, unseduced by beauty, whispers that this feature helps to shut from the low lying street and avenue the antiseptic sun.

Messrs. Carrère & Hastings' Blair Building if not quite the tallest, is yet the finest flower which has sprung skyward out of the Beaux Arts hotbed. If the so various fruits of this particular training were of a corresponding excellence the value of that training could scarcely be the subject of debate that it is now, for here is living evidence of a mind emancipated by it and not enslaved. The façade is a happy blending of audacity in the matter of composition, and restraint in the matter of detail, and the materials are combined with the finest sense of their several qualities. If Mr. Sullivan—that militant Goth—had not armed the critical sense with his Excaliber of a formula that form should (everywhere and in all things) follow function, that sense might be tempted to capitulate in the presence of so much excellence, without further ado.

The promise foreshadowed in Mr. Gilbert's[9] Broadway Chambers of a new Richmond in the architectural field has been amply fulfilled in that architect's West Street Building. The temptation is to render this rather more than justice, so favored is it by its detached, its almost isolated state its background of city and sky against which to display its shapeliness: its foreground of the river and the roaring waterside eliminating the foreshortened perspective and the

The Home Life would be distinguished and noteworthy if the Metropolitan Life had never been built. But, of course, it is the later building that brings the earlier into notice. In several respects the earlier has served as a study for the later. Had the later been kept waiting a few years, it would doubtless have much exceeded the actual limit of ten stories, to which we have reason to be grateful that it was confined. The original building, as it has stood now for seventeen years, would of itself be noteworthy among our commercial structures. The respectable dimensions of the site, roughly 125x150, prevented a ten-story building erected upon it from taking on the similitude ►

10 Caliban was the slave in Shakespeare's *The Tempest.* Rude, uncouth, unknown; as a Caliban style, a Caliban language.

11 Another character from *The Tempest,* Ariel is a spirit of the air and guardian of innocence.

12 Louis XIV (1638-1715) King of France.

13 William Makepeace Thackeray (1811-63) English novelist. He is important not only as a great novelist but also as a brilliant satirist.

right: Broadway Chambers Building, New York City, Cass Gilbert, architect, 1899–1900. Gilbert won a gold medal for the design at the 1900 Paris Exposition.

opposite: Campanile of San Marcos Cathedral, Venice, Italy, architect unknown, c. 912 AD.

painfully bent neck. Discounting all this however, in mass, in outline, in color, in detail, the building is the work of a master mind, the last word in New York skyscraper architecture; in it, the Caliban[10] has become—if not yet Ariel[11]—human, at all events.

The peculiar genius of any given race or any given period incarnates, as it were, in some architectural construction characteristic, and therefore symbolical of it. The iron hand of Roman sovereignty encased within the silken glove of Roman luxury, found its prototype in buildings which were stupendous, crude, brute masses of brick and concrete, encased in coverings of rich marbles and mosaics. The "sad sincerity" of soul, the aspiring mysticism of the Middle Ages, found embodiment in the Gothic cathedral, a thing so delicately adjusted, so almost perilously poised, thrust against counterthrust, that like the overstrained organism of an ascetic it seems ever about to overcome that centripetal force which is nevertheless the law of its being. The arrogant and artificial life of the court of Louis XIV[12] stands as truly imaged in the palace and garden of Versailles as in the wig, the coat, the scepter, and the high heeled shoes of that monarch, used by Thackeray[13] to symbolize his state. In like manner, the tall office building, our most characteristic architectural product, is a symbol of our commercial civilization. Its steel framework, strong, yet economical of metal, held together at all points by thousands of little rivets, finds a parallel in our highly developed industrial and economic system, maintained by the labor of thousands of obscure and commonplace individuals, each one a rivet in the social structure. And just as this steel framework is encased in a shell of masonry, bedecked, for the most part, with the architectural imaginings of alien peoples, meaninglessly employed, so are we still encumbered by a mass of religious, political, and social ideas and ideals, which, if we but knew it, impede our free development and interfere with the frank expression of our essential nature. ∎

of a tower. It would have remained noteworthy by reason of the clearness and the felicity with which the Aristotelian dictum is observed, the skill with which the parts are related and combined into a whole, and the refinement and grace of the detail. "Elegance" is undoubtedly the result. Elegance, indeed, rather than vigor is the result commonly aimed at in the work of these architects, aimed at, as we have seen, in cases in which it was pretty distinctly not the result at which to aim. It is proper to explain that the ornateness of the work is accounted for by the fact that the superstructure, over the rusticated basement, was originally designed for terra cotta, and by an afterthought executed in carved marble. But it is in place, all the same, and, in fact, the elegance of the Metropolitan Life by no means involves feebleness. There is enough of mass and weight and depth in the solids, and enough of skill in their disposition in reference to the voids to preclude that. Again, as in the Home Life, the signalization of the second story as the abode of the "institution" supplies an architectural motive and an architectural feature. The original erection was at once very acceptable as an independent and complete building and available as a nucleus for the huge extension to which it has subsequently been subjected as to suggest that that extension might have been within the contemplation of owners and architects when the original was erected. The character of elegance, which is that of the building in general, is carried furthest in the treatment of the entrance hall, which is of an effective sumptuosity almost without parallel in our interior architecture. But it is saved from any taint of vulgarity or even of ostentation by the clear showing that the richness of material was required by the design. Materiem superat opus. There is nothing which smacks of what the scorner of preciosity describes as "early Pullman or late North German Lloyd." The precious marbles of Pavanazza or Tinos were needed to produce the due effect of the elaborate design and the rich and delicate detail, and they were supplied. Compare this entrance hall with the Philadelphia cathedral, which loses so much of the rightful effectiveness of the design because the due material in which to execute it could not be afforded. The effect is the same in the interminable corridors of the completed and extended building, even in the sumptuosity of the

quarters of the company in the extended second floor. The execution merely corresponds to the intention.

But the tower is, of course, the center of interest, as it has been for these many months, and as it is likely to remain for many more, the cynosure of middle Manhattan. In many respects the design of the Metropolitan tower was dictated by the conditions, by the area, by the intended altitude, by the ultimately utilitarian character of the erection. A parallelopiped of the full area of the site and as high as it could profitably be carried. A "campanile" was imperatively indicated, meaning not a bell tower of many equal stages. The visibility to the bottom, across the square and to the westward, constituted a condition which distinguished this from that other tower with which it is impossible, in discussing either, to avoid comparison. The Singer Tower is merely an emergence, a peak in a mountain chain, and would doubtless have been modified if it also had, from any important point of view, had to be considered from the ground to the sky. In the Metropolitan, the base and the shaft are predetermined, although in the base there may have been a question whether an entrance should be signalized, a question which, if it arose, has been wisely decided in the negative. It is only above the shaft, and in the capital, the crowning member, that the question of general form and general disposition, can have presented itself to the designers as one upon which they had any liberty of choice. This only, therefore, is disputable. It seems highly absurd to say of the highest habitable erection in the world that there are points of view from which it looks too low, looks, not to put too fine a point upon it, squat and in disproportion to its own crowning member. And yet there are, undoubtedly, such points of view which may and must be taken of the Metropolitan tower. It is the case when it is seen from the eastward "above the purple crowd of humbler roofs." In fact, the generous area of the site, 85x75, and the mass of the ten-story building to which it is attached reduce the mass of the tower above the roof of the main building to about a double cube, which is, doubtless, short for a tower.

One wonders if it may not have occurred to the architects, now that the work is irrevocably executed, whether they were not misled by a false analogy in determining upon a triple composition for the crowning member,

as well as for the total structure, whether it would not have been more effective to lengthen the shaft below the loggia, or "belfry-stage," by the height of the member (the "die," shall we call it?) which now appears just above that stage, and to forego the triple division of the top.

But in any case, the tower is a noble and impressive feature, and would be in spite of far more questionable points than those we have been raising. The words with which the New York Chapter of the American Institute of Architects accompanied their award for the most meritorious work of the year 1909 were well measured, well weighed, and well deserved:

"This award is given for the Tower of the Metropolitan Life Insurance Company Building, in consideration of the general excellence of the result attained, and the extremely successful treatment of one of the most difficult problems now presented to American architects.

"And of the lifetime of work of which the tower is the culmination, it may be said that it has never discredited, but has continued and extended the traditions of which the retiring architects are the inheritors. It is a tradition of discretion, of moderation, of decorum—in a word a tradition of 'good taste.'" •

THE CROWN OF THE SKYSCRAPER
by Charles Cressey

Fig. 1. The "skyline" type of cornice, regarded as useless and defective aesthetically.

Fig. 2. A type of cornice placed below the "skyline" and balanced by a visible mass above; suggested as better design (with a cornice) than fig. 1. In this type, the cornice may develop a practical purpose as a balcony and affords scope for new departures in design.

*T*he *problem of the cornice, especially on the buildings in the crowded precincts of the city, where the architecture of the houses is confined to mere embellishment of the visible front, remains in a chaotic condition. While infinite pains have been taken to accommodate features and details of different historic periods to contemporary conditions with some degree of success, the treatment of the crowning member of the tall building remains the bete noir of the designer. Even such progressive architects as Louis H. Sullivan, Cass Gilbert and Robert D. Kohn have done little towards solving the problem.*

Below we print what, in our opinion is a step in the right direction. The author, Mr. Charles Cressey, of Los Angeles, Cal., is an English architect who recently came to this country to establish himself in the practice of his profession. Success to him, if all his ideas are as seriously conceived as his suggestions on cornices. The profession of the architect never stood more in need of conscientious thought of this sort and swift mental action thereon than it does at present. Mr. Cressey's suggestions, which are commended to the attention of architects, should start the architectural ball a rolling in a new direction.

*C*ould it be, that every architectural feature of a tall building, might speak in its own defense, that dominating feature of so many designs, the cornice would probably be the one to find the greatest difficulty, in justifying its existence. So solidly founded in traditional design is this feature that it is with hesitation one dares to question its necessity or propriety in modern design. The skyscraper, however, is an instance where every detail of historic design may legitimately be questioned, and particularly the magnified details from the venerable "Orders."

Though instances do occur, where practical shade and shelter are secured from the use of the classical cornice, it is doubtful whether this aspect has much to do with its general adoption on high buildings. Is there in fact, a single practical advantage which can be urged in favor of the spreading cornice usually found crowning a skyscraper?

On the other hand, there can be no doubt that its practical disadvantages are numerous. What, for instance, could be more unsatisfactory structurally, than the eccentric loads and complicated framing, connected with the support of a heavy overhanging mass, which at its best, DOES NOTHING, is of dubious effect, artistically, and which places purely optional weight where it decreases rather than increases the general stability of the building. That this matter of undesirable load is recognized, is obvious from the use of painted shams, "just like stone," upon buildings where cost has evidently not been the serious question. I would here disclaim any antipathy to the use of metal in the abstract, if it can be presented in honest and seemly guise. Surely, stone detail is an insult to a material capable of good results on its own merits.

Whatever may be the material of the cornice, it is always a more or less troublesome feature, particularly on limited frontages. There must be few architects, who have not, at one time or another, cursed, politely perhaps, the fact that they dare not overhang a neighbor's land. Is not every city full of examples of stunted ends and painful expe-

Fig. 3. Type of cornice which crushes the upper windows and frankly fails to terminate architecturally. An attached feature neither useful or truly decorative.

dients to "stop" the cornice which no ingenuity can make "return." True, many buildings would have less pleasant wall surface next to the boundary lines, were it not for the insistent demand of the cornice terminating above. True, too, it is that much valuable light is lost for this same reason.

American cities are, unfortunately able to show many instances of the unbalanced effects due to prominent cornices appearing on only one or two faces of buildings in full view. Even where conditions permit a continuous cornice, how rarely does the building appear truly plumb—a result not unexpected, when one considers that the eye, traveling upwards from a base thinned to its limit, cannot pass the great cornice overhang to anything above substantial enough to correct the illusion. Probably the best effects occur where the cornices form subordinate features only and tire well below the skyline. The eye, either from custom or by instinct, does not seem aesthetically satisfied without an apparent counterbalance above a projecting cornice, and as this is an ordinary structural requirement, it appears to be logical that the cornice should not form the sky-line.

The habit of using strongly defined cornices is exercising a bad influence on the appearance of cities, as tall buildings of single frontage become more numerous. Usually there is little or no regard for harmony or continuity of level of adjacent cornices. A few years ago the Architectural Record published an article on the value of the curve in street architecture, and the illustrations showed strongly that there is aesthetic value, too, in continuity of street cornices. Continuity is perhaps beyond hoping for in these individualistic days, and the remedy for jerky vanishing lines would seem to be in restraint of the cornice habit. Seen from the street, it cannot be said that the high cornice gives any great amount of pleasure, however carefully detailed it may be, whilst the ponderous members must form a source of wonder, if not of humor, to the spectator who views them from a high level.

Conditions limiting the architect to-day, especially in tall buildings, appear to demand that the custom of projecting architectural features should be restrained and a substitute found in recessing. It would appear, too, that the upper stories of high buildings might more generally be built on receding planes and so express outwardly the gradually reducing weight of the structure. The above thoughts lead the writer to the conclusion that a truer architectural crown to the sky-scraper would be gained if the projecting cornice could be entirely omitted, and the powerful vertical lines allowed to dominate, unaffected by the abrupt and limiting cornice edge. The designer might then find scope for pleasant fancies in pierced parapets and other open-work, expressing protection and enclosure of the roof, and above all, gain a restful merging of the mass of the structure into infinite space. ∎

Fig. 5. Prudential Building, Buffalo, N.Y. An experiment in substituting a receding openwork treatment in place of the overhanging cornice.

Fig. 6. Broadway-Chambers, New York City. A gradually reducing mass and horizontal termination of the upper story.

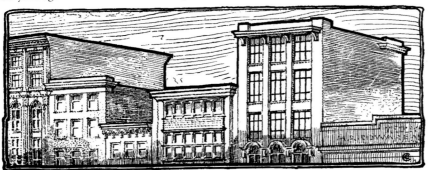

Fig.4. CHAOS IN CORNICETOWN
Many minds may make a cornice, but fail to secure the quiet charm of traditional "horizontal" design. With cornices eliminated and "verticals" the main motive, rugged mass and fretted "skyline" hold infinite possibilities for beauty.

164

**People's Gaslight Company
Building, Chicago,
D.H. Burnham & Company,
architects, 1910–11.**

In this photograph of the building
under construction, its "skin" is
complete along three sides.
When finished, the fourth section
will enclose the central light
court, which will no longer be visible from the street. A later "classicized" skyscraper of the
Burnham firm, the People's
Gaslight Building occupies the
opposite end of the block where
their Railway Exchange Building
also stands (photo page 111).
One of the sculpted lions on the
front steps of the Art Institute
can be seen in the foreground.

opposite: A proposed skyscraper
for Portland, Oregon, B.J. Cahill,
architect. As with World Building
(page xii), the dome is somewhat
reminiscent of St Peter's in
Rome.

ADDITIONS TO CHICAGO'S SKYLINE
A Few Recent Skyscrapers

By Peter B. Wight[1]

Chicago is sometimes spoken of as the birthplace of the skyscraper, but a newspaper correspondent has recently said that he found twelve-story buildings in Genoa one hundred years old—and they were inhabited buildings, not towers. Other newspaper writers are continually speaking of the wonderful height of the Singer Building and the Metropolitan at New York, but neither of them is a genuine "skyscraper." They only happen to have towers of greater height than any before attempted in connection with buildings. The Metropolitan Building has only ten stories above the street grade, counting in a mezzanine floor.

If Chicago is not the birthplace of the "skyscraper," it is the first city in which office buildings for renting purposes, ten, twelve and fourteen stories in height were built. New York was close second, and has long since surpassed Chicago both in height, number and cost of office buildings. And Chicago is not jealous.

After the three-hundred-feet-high Masonic Temple (photo page 192) was built in Chicago, New York commenced to build higher ones, and has been doing so ever since. But they have never been popular at Chicago, except with the promotors [sic] and investors who have been able thereby to get double and treble use of the land they stand upon at the expense of their neighbors' light. I have yet to see a new skyscraper erected between two old ones in that city. It is "first come first served," and "devil take the hindermost," and the hindermost must get what income he can from his little old building, on land supposed to be equally valuable. The general opinion among the best-educated architects of Chicago (not including, of course, the three or four who have linked their fortunes with commercialized promoters) is that the high building is not only a disfigurement of the general design of the city, which it is now hopeless to efface, but that it prevents that diffusion of patronage which would distribute the work into many hands, by which it could be better done; also that it is a deterrent to Urban expansion. Several attempts have been made by municipal ordinances to restrict the heights of buildings in Chicago, and all have resulted in failure. To-day the height is "restricted" to 260 feet above the grade. There have been several previous restrictive ordinances. In one the limit was made 130 feet. Then it was changed to 155 feet at the behest of a politician who wanted to build to that height, after which it was changed back to 130 feet, and several were erected under that restriction. One of these parties wanted to add more stories and secured a change of the limit to 260 feet. The building went up. Since that time three well-known buildings have been built to exceed that height, though the building permits were given for plans showing a height of 260 feet only. Yet no one has protested, and the ordinance is a dead letter. No attempt has ever been made by the building department to enforce the law against these violations, because every good lawyer knows that the court would assert the right of every property holder to build as high as he wants to, as long as he builds safely and does not interfere with the rights of any other person.

Several years ago, when the movement was started to raise the limit of height to 260 feet, interested citizens sought the influence of the Illinois Chapter of the Institute in opposition. But the Chapter, in a formal communication to the City Council, put itself on record as being opposed to skyscrapers on artistic as well as politic grounds but as being also opposed to any restrictions by law, for the reason that it could be changed at any time by the City Council, or would be violated at will without remonstrance.

So, practically, Chicago is in the same position with respect to this matter as New York. The question of safety of foundations

from:
A PACIFIC COAST SKYSCRAPER
Vol. XXIX, No. 5, May 1911, pp. 407–10

ONE learns from the papers of "the Coast" that the construction of by far the tallest building thereon, at Portland, Oregon, is held to be virtually assured. A twenty-six story building, to cost a million, would be noteworthy, that is, worth a "news note," in any American city. A fortiori in one of the cities of the Pacific slope, where the congestion which compels the erection of towering buildings is apprehended rather than felt, and to which to the Easterner or the Middle West- ▸

New City Hall, Chicago, Holabird & Roche, architects, 1911.

1 Architect and inventor, Peter Bonnett Wight (1838–1925) designed furniture and interiors and invented fireproof construction techniques. Wight partnered with Russell Sturgis from 1863 to 1868. In 1868, he won the competition to design the National Academy in New York City. Wight moved from New York to practice architecture in Chicago in December, 1891, the year RECORD started. Along with Schuyler and Sturgis, Wight was a tireless and persuasive champion of the architecture of Chicago.

2 Dwight Heald Perkins (1867–1941) worked for H.H. Richardson, Burnham & Root, and Frank Lloyd Wright. In 1905, Perkins was appointed chief architect for the Chicago Board of Education. During his tenure he designed more than 40 schools for the board, with Carl Schurz High School being the most famous of his Prairie School designs.

3 Dovecote: A compartmented structure with many openings, often raised on a pole, for housing domesticated pigeons.

4 Embrasure: A small opening in the wall or parapet of a fortified building, usually splayed on the inside.

opposite: Hotel Blackstone, Chicago, Marshall & Fox, architects, 1908–10.

has been settled by the use of wells filled with concrete carried down to hard-pan or rock, and the later improvements in fire-proofing have made it possible to make buildings above ground even more safe than before.

In the earlier Chicago skyscrapers the steel skeletons were generally filled in with brick or terra-cotta walls, and carried little ornament. The New York architects tried to give them "style" by piling up the "orders" of architecture and introducing many horizontal bands to try and reduce the effect of height. Some monstrous apparitions, with great overhanging cornices, were the result. Horrid blank brick walls on the backs and sides towered in the air, with little prospect of their being concealed by adjoining structures. The Chicago architects did not fall into this error. They had no money to waste on these elaborate fronts, so they began to study the proper effects. Instead of using strong horizontal lines, except at the top and bottom, they accepted the situation and made the vertical lines more prominent. The first two, three or four stories were treated as a design to be seen from the street only. These, clubbed together, formed a strong base from which the vertical lines of the piers covering the steel uprights started. Then the topmost stories, using generally one less than at the ground for the purpose, were joined together in a unique design. This upper part was given more elaboration than the lower section, and was without a massive cornice, often without any projecting cornice. The treatment was usually called "the base, shaft and capital style," and was accepted all over the country as the best type of design for high buildings yet discovered. The Chicago buildings were also free from any attempt to use the "orders," so-called. But Eastern architects sometimes conceived the idea of using the whole upper section of several stories as a complete architectural order. This gave the effect of a classical building hoisted up into the air on long stilts. Then a few Chicago architects who look to the East for examples brought this fashion back to Chicago, with the result that

several Chicago buildings are thus disfigured.

Another method of treating the exterior design of such buildings has attracted little or no attention from writers who have endeavored to discuss before the public this evolution in design for high buildings. One firm of Chicago architects took advantage of the fact that the vertical steel supports of the exterior are spaced the same as those for the interior to omit intermediate piers in the exterior walls and thus reduce the number of windows. This made the windows much wider than their height. The result was that the windows furnished dark horizontal masses, taking the place of narrow horizontal lines. The effect was remarkable, whether the windows were placed in a smooth wall or between emphasized piers. Of this, the Marquette Building is the best example of the first method, and the Champlain Building of the second, both designed by the same architects—Holabird & Roche. Another example of this effect is in the store of Carson, Pirie, Scott & Company by Sullivan (photo page 92). Yet, notwithstanding the fine effect of these buildings, Chicago has recently erected skyscrapers with windows so multitudinous as to make them resemble dovecotes[3] rather than buildings.

In an article that recently appeared in "Notes and Comments" in this magazine, entitled "The Crown of the Skyscraper" (page 162) the subject of cornices for such buildings was ably discussed. Chicago has all of the kinds referred to and some of the style therein commended. Every fair-minded person, after reading it, must come to the conclusion that no high building ever needs a projecting cornice to shed water free from the walls of the building, and that every narrow street is practically darkened still more by heavy cornices; furthermore, that a projecting cornice on a high building not only darkens the street, but its soffit only can be seen from the street level, and if this cornice is not at the top it cuts off the view of the upper-most stories from the street, and the street from the windows of these stories.

Hence, it has no use. If of no use, how can

it have beauty? What every street and every building needs is a skyline, and the skyscraper, of all buildings, demands and is entitled to a skyline. Attention has already been called in these papers to the value and beauty of the skylines of some of D. H. Perkins'[2] "School Houses" (*Architectural Record* for June), and in all of these cases they have been gained by simple means. A law forbidding projecting cornices could be sustained on constitutional grounds.

The skyscrapers illustrated herewith are the latest creations of Chicago architects, some of them just approaching completion, and all erected within the last year. They are not selected with any motive of appreciation, but as historical records of the present-day condition of the art. They show plainly that there has been little or no progression in the development of design applied to commercial high buildings, or buildings for any purpose in the design of which the architect has had occasion to grapple with this serious problem, which is always before us. They seem to suggest that the lessons that

have been learned in the Schiller, the Marquette, the Champlain and the McClurg, Mandel and the Carson-Pirie, Scott stores are forgotten. As a whole, they are mainly imitations of the work of Eastern architects.

The new City Hall is nearly completed. Some ingenious practicable schemes have been carried out in it, but it does not add anything to the original part erected for the county government, except by its overpowering massiveness. It now even more effectively overpowers and dwarfs all the surrounding buildings, and does not encourage owners of adjoining private property to attempt to compete with it. The new Sherman House, which fronts upon the Court House square (no longer an open square in any sense of the word), and by the same architects, is now about half way up. It will be possible to observe the effect of difference of scale very soon. The main purpose of the design of the city and county buildings has often been expressed in public. It was to erect an eleven-story building, with stories much higher than those recently provided in office buildings and much less in height than those previously and erroneously incorporated in public buildings, so that it would not look like a skyscraper. This has been done by doubling the scale of the exterior mask, and thereby minimizing the fenestration. But this has been done with inconsistency, because the second and third story windows only are clubbed together, and those over them at the corners are made the natural size, which makes them look like embrasures[4] in the bastions of a fortress. This and other inconsistencies mark the failure of the attempt to solve a high-building problem by attempting to conceal its height behind an exaggerated mask. The view given shows the new part facing on La Salle Street.

Only half a block from the City Hall is the new La Salle Hotel, by

erner, the twenty-year old gibe of "a ten-story building in a ten acre lot" seems particularly to apply. The incentive to the construction of such a building may be assumed to be civic as well as commercial. It is in part projected "to advertise the town."

A news note would fit the requirements of the case, however, if the projected structure were to be one of the gaunt altitudinous parallelopipeds we know so well. The perspective sketch which accompanies the newspaper article in question, however, supplemented with some information furnished by the architects, assures us that this is not the case. The design has a Substantive architectural interest quite irrespective of the local interest. It is a contribution towards the solution of the problem of the period in commercial architecture.

First, what is the most advantageous "lay out" of a many-storied building on a corner lot a hundred feet square, the most eligible and economical with respect to facility and security of construction, and to the maximum of capacity, meaning not merely possibility of stowage of occupants, but "accommodation," with reference to abundance and as nearly as possible to equality of air and light"

That is a common enough problem, East or West. Obviously, it is no solution to cover the whole plot with building. The common solution is a fringe of building surrounding an interior court, or two wings of building flanking a court open on one side, In the first case, the value of the court as a light-well diminishes as the height increases. In either case the court marks off the rooms lighted from it as inferior and comparatively undesirable. Some interesting essays have been made towards a ground plan that would obviate the disadvan- ▸

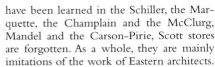

1910

McCormick Office Building, Chicago, Holabird & Roche, architects, 1908–12.

5 *entasis*: The very slight convex curve on Greek or later columns to correct the optical illusion of concavity which would result if the sides were straight.

opposite: La Salle Hotel, Chicago, Holabird & Roche, architects, 1909 (demolished).

opposite, far right: Floorplan for a proposed skyscraper, Portland, Oregon, B.J. Cahill, architect.

the same architects. It is far superior to the City Hall, but so different that no comparison is possible. It is the first building of the kind in which the prevailing "fashion" in hotel building in the Eastern cities has had its introduction at Chicago. Heretofore the Great Northern, the Auditorium and the Congress have been distinctively Chicago buildings, independent in plan, construction and design, adapted to the business requirements of the Middle West and eminently convenient, comfortable and profitable. But in the La Salle, (page 169) the Blackstone (page 167) and the Sherman, now in course of construction, we see the encroachment of those ideas in hotel building and architecture, recently prevalent in New York, as exemplified by the Knickerbocker (page 95) and a few others. This is the tendency to luxury and high life, which, however, does not concern the masses and is of interest mainly to those who are able to pay for it, as well as those others who cannot afford it, but whose aim in life is to ape the habits of the very rich. They are in the domain of fashion, which has no legitimate part in architectural evolution.

The Blackstone Hotel is far superior to the others mentioned, as it is an attempt to localize and introduce some originality in a conventional style. It is no wonder, therefore, that it has been awarded the gold medal of the Illinois Chapter as the most successful architectural undertaking of the last year in the State of Illinois by Illinois architects. As this will be the subject of another article in this magazine,[1] it is entitled here to only the briefest mention.

It has been a subject of regret among Illinois architects that no representation of the new University Club House appeared in the last exhibition of the Architectural Club; otherwise it would have been a close, if not successful, competitor for the medal. But it is a condition of the award that the only buildings eligible are those which are in some way exhibited.

The Blackstone Hotel, on the corner of Peck Court, the McCormick Building, on the corner of Van Buren Street, the People's

Gaslight Building, on the corner of Adams Street and the University Club, on the corner of Monroe Street, all being on northwest corners and facing on Grant Park, may be seen in perspective from one point in the park. They demonstrate that Michigan Boulevard has been the most improved of all the streets of Chicago during the past year. The roadway has been widened, and the sidewalks on the west side of the street are now thirty feet in width. The new McCormick Building at the Van Buren Street corner, opposite the Chicago Club, is a building for renting purposes, and the whole upper part is devoted to offices. Its architecture is not calculated to attract remark. If there is beauty in simplicity, here it is. But there certainly is very little design. The whole building, with its multitude of apparently little windows, reminds one of the Corn Exchange Bank and Office Building erected two years ago. The three lower stories are faced with granite, and all the walls above are of a dull-colored Roman pressed brick.

Continuing northward from this point past a few small and ancient buildings, once considered as prominent ones, and the most ancient of all for Chicago, the Stratford Hotel, which now looks very odd among its tall neighbors, and across Jackson Boulevard past the huge Railway Exchange and the diminutive-looking Thomas Orchestra Hall, we come to the Pullman office building, now twenty-five years old, on the corner of Adams Street. On the opposite corner from the Pullman is the Peoples Gaslight Company's office building, only one-half of which is completed and occupied. This is the largest building erected during the past year, except the City Hall. The new Gas Building and the old Pullman Building have the Alt Institute for nearest neighbors, the center of which is opposite Adams Street. The Institute, as is well known, is located in Grant Park, where it superseded the Exposition Building of ante-World's Fair days, by the grace of Montgomery Ward, the "watchdog of the lake front," and the City Council of Chicago.

Until the Gas Building is completed, we will not be able to judge of its full effect except by the details of the north half. The part now under construction is, however, a duplicate of that which is finished, and when it is completed it will be impossible to secure a photograph of the whole building from any near point of view on account of the interference of the Art Institute. The illustration given is from a photograph taken from the new terrace lately erected around the Art Institute, on the south side of which will be erected Lorado Taft's Fountain of the Great Lakes. Adjoining the Gas Building, on the north, is seen the Municipal Court Building, and next to it the new Illinois Athletic Club. Then across Monroe Street is the corner of the University Club, and beyond it the Chicago Athletic Club. In the distance looms up the Montgomery Ward Tower, from which the "watchdog," can scan the whole lake front when his duty impels him to do so.

When completed, the Adams Street corner of the Gas Building will be a repetition on both streets of the most distant bay shown in the illustration. The whole Adams Street front will be a repetition of the Michigan Boulevard front. There will be ten granite columns on Michigan Boulevard and eight on the Adams Street front. These columns are of polished granite, forty-six inches in diameter, and their shafts are twenty-six feet high, rising through two stories. They are monolithic polished granite, without entasis,[5] and have Ionic capitals and bases. They do not carry either of the front walls of the buildings, but are set up for purely decorative purposes under the walls, after the polished granite third story and all the terra cotta facing above that story has been set. The entire front walls, except about twenty feet at each corner, are supported on steel cantilevers, occupying the height of the third story, connected with the interior steel

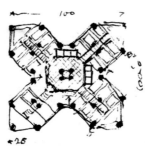

tages of the hollow square for an office building. One of the most interesting of them is that upon which the architects of this projected skyscraper on the Pacific have hit. It will be readily apprehended from the "thumb-nail sketch." The plan, it will be seen, is a square, with a triangle cut out of each face. It is officially described as a "Maltese cross," but lacks the spreading arms of that form. It is rather a St. Andrew's cross, that is, a cross of equal arms, set diagonally, but in this case with arms beveled, or truncated, by the lines of the rectangle within which it is inscribed. A great economy in structural steel is plausibly claimed for a construction in which the main loads are brought near the center, and in which, by the arrangement of the supports, which are twin columns six feet apart, connected by web plates in every story, it is maintained that rigidity of the structure is attained with lighter members than would otherwise be practicable. In any case, it has obvious advantage. At the solid, and, therefore, comparatively dark central "core," or actual junction of the arms, are disposed, and disposed of, the "services" of the building, the elevators and stairways and lavatories, around the "smoke shaft." The corridors seem to be shortened and the corridor area to be reduced to the irreducible minimum. And without doubt the result is attained of an absolute ►

Steger Building, Chicago,
Marshall & Fox, architects,
1909–10.

6 *ashlar:* A squared block of building stone; a thin, dressed rectan-
cle of stone for facing walls.

* Paul Bourget, page 66, *n.* 5.

frame and resting on a row of steel stansions a few feet back of the lines of the exterior walls, which take the weight of the front walls above the second story. To accomplish this the steel uprights and horizontals of the third-story front, which support the granite facing of the story, are hung from the cantilevers at the line of the fourth-story floor. As this suspended steelwork was partly in place before the photograph was taken, the cantilevers, with their bracketing are concealed from view. The granite shafts of the first and second story weigh 26 6/10 tons each. They have a cross-section of 12.04 feet, which, multiplied by 750, which is the average resistance of granite to crushing per square foot in tons, according to Trautwine, shows that their ultimate resistance to crushing is 9,030 tons. With a factor of safety of six, each one should be able to carry safely a weight of 1,505 tons. I do not know whether or not this is the weight of the superstructure over each column, but in the Pullman Building, across the way, a large part of the Adams Street front is carried on polished granite columns which are two feet and four inches in diameter, and by the same rule have an ultimate strength of 3,207 tons and a safe carrying strength of 534 tons each. The walls are of solid brick, and the building is nine to ten stories high. This sets one wondering if these columns under the Gas Building could have carried the wall above them without the use of the expensive cantilevers. There is only one danger in fireproof buildings to be apprehended from the use of granite, and that is fire from a contiguous building. But this building fronts on a park, and the fireproof Art Institute is too far away to do any damage, even if it ever could be burned.

Above the third story the exterior is faced with speckled terra cotta, which is a very good match to the granite used below. In the seventeenth, eighteenth and nineteenth stories the steel stansions of the exterior walls are faced with terra cotta, finished as engaged columns. They are three stories high, while those at the ground level are two stories high. In the twentieth story the plain ashlar[6] wall appears again, being coincident with the ashlar facing of the corner bays; then the terra cotta cornice for the whole building occupies the twenty-first story, and is finished with a serrated cresting. All of this terra cotta is a close match in appearance to the granite.

The effect of the fenestration is shown on the illustration, and from the point of view taken it is not easy to understand that these narrow openings in a low-storied building are windows. But they are windows, coupled together with a small terra cotta pier between.

The apparent uselessness of wasting effort and money in attempting to give architectural effect to skyscrapers in certain localities has been illustrated in the attempt to get a photograph of the new Steger Building, on the northwest corner of Jackson Boulevard and Wabash Avenue, to illustrate this article. If a building cannot be photographed as a whole, it follows that it cannot be seen as a whole. The Steger Building can hardly be said to front on Wabash Avenue. It fronts on the Elevated Railroad structure, which carries the trains of four railroads. The only point of view from which most of it can be seen is the window of any cargoing north on the west track, about three hundred feet away. The photographer was left to his own devices. He secured a lodgment for his camera on the fire-escape of a building on the opposite side of Wabash Avenue. Then he took two negatives with his widest angled lens and tried to match the prints. But he failed. One of them only is here given, with his apologies. This proves that the owners and architects were justified in producing such a plain and unpretending structure. They have given to the passerby some very refined and appropriate shop fronts and a cornice effect that is interesting when seen from the upper windows of buildings a block distant, and that is all. But they have used in every part of the exterior nothing but enameled terra cotta, and have bid for cleanliness, if nothing else.

The Steger Building is used as a piano salesroom and for offices. ∎

equality of desirableness and accommodation among the offices, though some tenants might experience a preference, on the score of the outlook, for the rooms which accrue at the apical ends of the arms of the cross. This equality of accommodation is a capital point in what Paul Bourget,* speaking of the tall buildings of Chicago, calls "an art of democracy, made by the crowd and for the crowd." Manifestly, the design is limited in application to its particular purpose, that is to say, to a square of not very far from 100 x 100, and on a corner. But for such a situation, it may very well seem that the architects of the building in Portland have evolved a typical scheme which will impose itself upon other architects who have to meet essentially the same requirements.

* * *

And now for the actual architectural issue of the "lay out," of the "parti," which, in order to discuss its architectural issue, we have to assume to be the legitimate offspring of the requirements, and which we have seen to be at least plausibly so. The general bulk, the outline, the "silhouette," one has to acknowledge to be expressive and impressive, impressive by dint of being expressive. The detachment from adjoining buildings which in the case of the common skyscraper. is secured by special negotiation with the neighbors, or not secured at all, is here secured by the inherent disposition, so far, at least, as the architectural impression goes. Supposing, even that the neighbors were to build "spite skyscrapers," they could not, on the two inner sides, prevent the functioning of the two triangular light shafts secured by the plan itself, while, on the other two sides, the two open sides, then could not prevent a much more inward reaching illumination than would be secured by the ordinary practice of "building to the limit," which is to say, to the building line. The disposition shown in the perspective sketch could not be infringed. And how much more impressive and expressive a disposition it is than the commoner one of two blank fronts! The light court at the center of each front gives scope and opportunity for the separate architectural treatment of a basement which is now the architectural base of a towering shaft, and now a mere screen wall between two shafts. Thereby

the architectural base gains a motive which is for the most part lacking to it, and no longer appears a capricious and arbitrary variation of stories which have, excepting only the ground story, the same purposes and requirements with those above them. That aphorism upon which Mr. Louis Sullivan insists, "where function does not vary, form does not vary," cannot be quoted against a separate treatment of this base, which does, indeed, in some degree darken the rooms it screens, but, in compensation, supplies additional rooms outside the general scheme. If this present edifice were the project of an institution, instead of an individual, one would almost infallibly infer that the base thus differentiated from its superstructure was the seat of institution and was thus properly signalized in the architecture. Evidently the manner in which the St. Andrew's cross of the ground plan works out furnishes an available motive for the skyscraper, which is primarily the abode of an institution, and only secondarily a "realty investment" of the same. It is, at any rate, this basement, the treatment of its detail quite apart, a logical and natural outcome of the essential scheme.

If one cannot say as much for the capital as for the base, that is because the capital has not the same character of "inevitability" as the base, and what one calls, inevitability, the characteristic of any work of art, is especially a necessary characteristic of these towering utilitarian structures, which must be justified by their logical necessity or not at all. The "capital" proper, the four templar pavilions which occupy the arms of the diagonal cross, inside of the angles formed by their infringement upon the square, and the cupola which dominates and connects them, hooding the emergence of the central "smoke shaft"—all this grows naturally out of the general scheme, and, again in idea, forms an effective crowning feature, in due proportion to the equally natural and logical base. (As to the proportion of either or both to the shaft, that is a matter which, according to the experience of the builders of tall buildings, may safely be left to take care of itself.) One need not trouble, in adjusting his base and his capital, whether the intermediate shaft is of two diameters or of five.) But the two-storied Corinthian order under the main cornice, and abstracted from the shaft,

that is another matter. That has the fatal marks of caprice and arbitrariness. It is a feature the like of which is common enough with architects who do not see their way to making, a real crowning feature. But when, as in this present case, one does see his way, why insert, at the expense of the height and dignity of the shaft, this pseudo capital, and then go on to surmount it with a real capital. It is beginning again after one has solemnly said "Amen."

We imagine that many professional readers considering this scheme, from the various points of view which it invites, will be moved to inquire, "Why not do it in Gothic?" "Papers" have been written and addresses made, as to the superior eligibility of Gothic over classic as the style for the skyscraper. But the practical applications of the theoretical conclusions are few and far between. Truly it is plausible that the historical style which aimed to "skeletonize" masonry, and succeeded in skeletonizing it, should be taken as the model for the quasi-masonic structure which the steel frame, with its protective envelope of masonry, constitutes. Moreover, Gothic has an immense repertory of precedents for the treatment, both structurally and decoratively, of the highly plastic material, terra cotta, of which the skyscraper is so largely composed, inside and out. Take this present case. The ground plan shows a support at each angle of the many-angled figure. The Gothic "angle shaft," a half-rounded moulding, at each of the angles, would express outwardly the member which cannot be shown, and might well be crowned, after the Gothic manner with a niched and sculptured figure. The floor beams could readily be expressed on the exterior so as to relieve the shaft of monotony, without impairing its unity. That basement, filling out the square, would naturally take the semblance of an aisle wall and clerestory, albeit a clerestory in the same plane with the wall below, and divided by buttresses working free above the cornice as pinnacles. For the crowning member, the hood of the central shaft, how many appropriate suggestions does Gothic architecture offer in its central towers or lanterns or flèches. How one would like to see this original and suggestive lay out carried out on the exterior to a result which, however based on precedent in detail, would also be in effect original. ●

Gorham Company Building, New York City, McKim, Mead and White, architects, 1905.

"The Gorham store has been described by a good judge as the best-looking store in the world, and this judgment may be true; but, obviously, it cannot be described as a strictly commercial building. Its customers are people of wealth and refinement; and the management of the Gorham company has, consequently, a good reason for entertaining their stylish customers in a really stylish habitation."

— A.C. David

"A walk up Fifth Avenue from Madison Square to the Park, with one's eyes open, is an experience of some surprises, and equal illumination; and it leaves an indelible impression of that primal chaos that is certainly without form, if it is not wholly void. Here one may see in a scant two miles (scant, but how replete with experiences!), treasure-trove of all peoples and all generations: Roman temples and Parisian shops..."

— Ralph Adams Cram

opposite: Ralph Adams Cram

THE

ARCHITECTURAL

RECORD

VOL. XXVIII.   DECEMBER, 1910   No. 6.

THE NEW ARCHITECTURE

The First American Type of Real Value

A. C. DAVID [1]

from:

STYLE IN AMERICAN ARCHITECTURE
An Address by Ralph Adams Cram
Vol. XXXIV, No.11, September 1913,
pp. 232-39.

This paper is based upon an address
delivered before the Contemporary
Club of Philadelphia, reprinted through
courtesy of the Yale Review, 1913.

NEW YORK is a city in which many things happen, unprecedented in the history of urban humanity. No other city in the world has ever added 500,000 inhabitants to its population every three years. In no other city does such a high level of real estate values prevail over so long a strip of land as the level of prices which are being paid for lots on Fifth Avenue, from Thirtieth Street to Fiftieth Street. In no other city has anything like $200,000,000 been invested in new buildings in any one year. But unprecedented as are these and other evidences of the increases of population, wealth and business in New York, they are less remarkable to a discerning eye than a real estate and building movement which has recently been taking place on a small part of one avenue in the new mercantile district in that city. We refer to the transformation which has been made during the past two years on Fourth Avenue, between Union Square and Thirtieth Street.

The transformation which has been taking place on Fourth Avenue is not remarkable on account of the high level of real estate values which has been thereby established, because real estate on Fourth Avenue is still not worth more than a third of what it is on the best retail section of Fifth Avenue. The peculiarity of the movement on Fourth Avenue has consisted of the large

number of new buildings of a single type erected in a comparatively short time. Within a distance of about a half of a mile, and during an interval of about two years, some fifteen mercantile buildings have been constructed. The largest of them covers a whole block front. The smallest of them a little less than half a block. The lowest of them is twelve stories high. The tallest of them is twenty stories high. The average for the whole group is sixteen stories. They have converted an avenue, which was formerly devoted to small retail stores and old furniture shops, into an avenue given over chiefly to mercantile business of the highest class. They will be used for the offices, the warerooms and the show-rooms of large manufacturing and importing firms and corporations, and they supply more floor space for such purposes than only a short time ago would have been needed during a period of ten years.

The interest of this quick transformation for the readers of the *Architectural Record* does not, however, consist in the evidence it affords of the business growth of New York. It consists, rather, in the opportunity presented on the new Fourth Avenue of appraising the value and effect of the forces which are molding modern American commercial architecture. For this particular purpose, it is much more useful than any other

THE various followings in architecture to-day are so many and so manifest that he who runs may read, and, parenthetically, he who reads very certainly often runs from some of the strange aberrations that beset his path. I am minded therefore, in writing under the above title, to say less about style and styles and half a style, than of the impulse—or the impulses, for they are legion— behind them, and of the goal to which in devious ways they all are tending.

* * *

For chaos is the only word that one can justly apply to the quaint and inconsequent conceits in which we have indulged since that monumental moment in the early nineteenth century when, architecturally, all that had been since the beginning ceased, and that which had never been before on land or sea began. A walk up Fifth Avenue from Madison Square to the Park, with one's eyes open, is an experience of some surprises, and equal illumination; and it leaves an indelible ►

334 Fourth Avenue Building, New York City, George B. Post & Sons, architects.

1 A.C. David is a psudeonym for Herbert David Croly (1869-1930). See page 264.

2 Tiffany & Company, New York City, McKim, Mead & White, architects, 1906.

group of buildings which are concentrated within a similarly small space in another American city or in any other part of New York. In the first place, they are thoroughly contemporary. In the second place, they are strictly commercial. They have not been erected by people who had any money to spend or any reason for spending money on architectural "effects." In the third place, with a few exceptions, they have not been designed by the architectural firms who have been most conspicuously successful in designing other types of buildings. They have usually been issued from the offices of architects who have specialized in commercial work, and who have made their reputation by their ability to plan such structures so that the smallest profitable expenditure of money will bring the largest return in available space, in economy of operation, and in adaptation to use. In certain cases they are owned and have been built by large wholesale firms, who will occupy them as their offices, and who have no reason to advertise their business by any architectural display. In other cases they have been erected by speculative builders, who have constructed them for the purpose of filling them with tenants and then selling them to an investor, and, of course, in all such cases the opportunities for unprofitable expenditure are cut clown to an absolute minimum. These Fourth Avenue buildings have been planned and designed exclusively for the purpose of being made to pay; and on this fact one must insist to the limit, because it is the salient fact concerning them, and because they are distinguished thereby from many other commercial buildings which have been erected in other parts of New York.

Other than strictly commercial reasons have, for instance, dominated the appearance of the great majority of office buildings in the financial district and of many of the new edifices recently erected on Fifth Avenue. A bank, for instance, when it builds an office building, frequently sacrifices a good deal of space and money merely for the purpose of imposing on its customers an impression of its opulent stability; and this expenditure has

its justification, because a big bank, like a big life insurance company, is a financial institution. Moreover, the fact that these financial "institutions" spend money on costly materials and details, and devote rentable space to the purpose of merely creating an "effect," has an influence upon the design and the appearance of competing buildings, the owners of which have no reason connected with their own business for any similar expenditure. A certain standard of ornate decoration is established, which tenants come to demand, and which the builder is obliged to supply at any cost to himself. Similar motives have operated on Fifth Avenue to take many, apparently, commercial buildings out of the exclusively commercial architectural class. The Gorham store (photo page 172) has been described by a good judge as the best-looking store in the world, and this judgment may be true; but, obviously, it cannot be described as a strictly commercial building. Its customers are people of wealth and refinement; and the management of the Gorham company has, consequently, a good reason for entertaining their stylish customers in a really stylish habitation. So it is with the Tiffany store,[2] and so it is to a smaller extent with many other Fifth Avenue commercial buildings. To be sure, certain other commercial buildings have been erected on Fifth Avenue which are veritably and vulgarly commercial; but they are vulgarly commercial not because they are frankly devoted to the transaction of business, but because they are business buildings, which are making an ugly and ostentatious attempt to advertise their importance instead of a comely and a discreet attempt.

This brings us to the gist of the matter. The better Fifth Avenue buildings are either modifications of European residential styles, as in the cases of the Tiffany and Gorham buildings, or they are modifications of European (French) apartment house architecture, as in the case of the Altman's store. They are buildings which are commercial in function, without any pretense of being business-like in appearance; and in this respect they are following in the footsteps of the traditional European methods. Substantially all European buildings which have been used for business purposes have been designed as modifications of urban residential styles. Europe has never had any specifically commercial architecture, and in all probability it never will have. A specifically commercial architecture has no reason for existing unless specifically commercial requirements in a building are allowed full expression. Such can never be the case in cities, which restrict the height of buildings either by ordinance or by any interpretation of rights under the common law, such as the English custom of "ancient lights." If American cities had begun by restricting the height of buildings we should never have had any specifically commercial architecture in this country. The tall building is the economical building. It renders meaningless all the architectural values upon which the traditional European street architecture has been based. Precisely and exclusively because it was allowed to shoot upwards, American commercial architecture was emancipated from paralyzing restrictions and has become a specific and original type, dominated by novel formative and essentially real, practical requirements.

It was, of course, evident from the very beginning of the American skyscraper that some such development was taking place, although the first indications of it appeared in Chicago, rather than in New York. The earliest tall buildings erected in Chicago were dominated by practical requirements, but they were far from being complete expressions of the new American commercial architecture. In the first place, the requirements for such buildings had not at that time been fully defined and standardized, and, in the second place, the buildings were in appearance, unnecessarily uncouth and ugly. The early New York skyscrapers, on the other hand, were designed to a considerable extent independently of practical considerations. From the start the New York architects, supported by their clients, were seeking in their skyscrapers to make some kind of an irrelevant and costly architectural display; and they frequently sacrificed practical advantages and spent an unconscionable amount of money in a kind of architecture that diminished rather than increased the commercial value of the building. It was not until almost ten years later that New Yorkers began to realize that commercial buildings of a certain kind could be made more, rather than less, attractive by a loyal and intelligent attempt to make them serve an exclusively commercial purpose.

It is not our purpose to write a history of the architectural development of the American skyscraper. Many architects have contributed to the process, and it has been helped by many improvements in technical methods. If it had not been for the enterprise and adaptability of manufacturers of front brick, terra cotta, steam-heating plants, elevators and the like, the new commercial architecture would not have been possible; and the earlier architects were hampered by the lack of many materials and devices upon which both the utility and the good looks of the new commercial architecture depends. But a certain result has been reached; and what we wish to call attention to is the fact that this result is summed up better on this half a mile of Fourth Avenue than in any other similarly small neighborhood elsewhere in New York or in the United States. New Yorkers are fully justified in talking very big about these buildings. There is no group of purely commercial structures in the world which do more to earn their living, both in use and in appearance, than does this group on Fourth Avenue. It is American commercial architecture at its best, and American commercial architecture is not only the best, but the only genuine commercial architecture in the world.

By insisting that these Fourth Avenue buildings are, on the whole, the most interesting group of commercial buildings concentrated in one spot, either in this or any other country, we do not mean that they constitute a satisfactory solution of the problem of the design of skyscrapers, or that any one of them is a beautiful and exhilarating piece of architecture. But certain quali-

impression of that primal chaos that is certainly without form, if it is not wholly void. Here one may see in a scant two miles (scant, but how replete with experiences!), treasure-trove of all peoples and all generations: Roman temples and Parisian shops; Gothic of sorts (and out of sorts), from the "Carpenter Gothic" of 1845, through Victorian of that ilk, to the most modern and competent recasting of ancient forms and restored ideals; Venetian palaces, and Louis Seize palaces, and Roman palaces. and more palaces from wherever palaces were ever built; delicate little Georgian ghosts, shrinking in their unpremeditated contact with Babylonian skyscrapers that poise their towering masses of plausible masonry on an unconvincing sub-structure of plate glass. And it is all contemporary —the oldest of it dates back not two generations; while it is all wildly and improbably different.

* * *

We are approaching—in our review—another era in the development of our architecture: let us gather up the many strands in preparation therefore. Here are the "wild and whirling words" of Hunt, Eidlitz, Furness; here is the grave old Gothic of Upjohn's following, Renwick, Congdon, Haight; admirable, much of it, especially in little country churches; here is the Ruskinian fold, Cummings, Sturgis, Cabot— rather Bostonian you will note; here is the old Classical tradition that had slipped very, very far from the standards of Thornton, Bulfinch, McComb, now flaring luridly in the appalling forms of Mullet's Government buildings and the Philadelphia City Hall. Let us pursue the subject no further; there are others, but let them be nameless; we have enough to indicate a condition of some complexity and a certain lack of conviction, or even racial unity. ▶

1910

from:
MITIGATING THE 'GRIDIRON'
STREET PLAN: Some Good Effects
Achieved in New York City
By Franz K. Winkler*
Vol. XXIV, No. 5, May 1911, pp. 379-396

The author bemoans "the monotony" of the gridiron city plan. He
quotes from Frederick Law
Olmstead:

"There is no place in New York
where a stately building can be
looked up to from base to turret,
none where it can even be seen full
in the face and all at once taken in
by the eye, none where it can be
viewed in advantageous perspective. The few tolerable sites for
noble buildings North of Grace
Church and within the built part of
the city remain because Broadway,
laid out curvilinearly, in free adaptation to natural circumstances, had
already become too important a
thoroughfare to be obliterated by
the system. Such distinctive advantage of position as Rome gives St.
Peter's, Paris the Madeleine,
London St. Paul's, New York, under
her system, gives nothing."

He goes on the show how, in
order to relieve an otherwise disastrous situation, good city planners and architects either "Stop
the Street" [top: New York Public
Library, New York City, Carrère &
Hastings, architects, 1897], or
"Round the Corner" [above:
Goelet Building, McKim, Mead
and White, architects].

*Franz K. Winkler is a pseudonym for
Montgomery Schuyler.

ties can be claimed for them as a group, which justify the description. They are real-ly commercial buildings, because they have been built to pay while, at the same time, they have by the use (for the most part) of entirely appropriate means been made measurably attractive. In the course of time the problem of meeting in the most eco-nomical manner the complex group of practical requirements, upon which the earning power of such building are based, will be still more completely solved, and architects will be able to make the resulting design still more appropriate; but even if these Fourth Avenue buildings are still far from completely representing the full devel-opment of their type, they assuredly point in the direction which will lead to the ultimate attainment of the goal.

The mercantile buildings erected on Fourth Avenue differ from the great major-ity of office buildings, in that the rents which can be charged for space therein are smaller than the rents which can be charged in structures used exclusively for office pur-poses. In the latter several dollars a square foot can frequently be obtained. In the for-mer, sixty or seventy cents a square foot is usually the limit. Of course, the difference in the value of the land on which the two types of buildings are erected will account for a large part of the difference in rent. Nevertheless, the architect of a loft building is forced into rigorous economics which the architect of an office building can some-times escape. An additional expenditure of $50,000, which would constitute a small portion of the cost of the office building, would constitute a much larger proportion of the cost of a mercantile building. The expense of the latter must be kept down to somewhere between twenty and twenty-three cents a cubic foot, while, at the same time, the standard of construction, at least in the case of buildings seeking the better class of mercantile tenants, must be very high.

The practical conditions which these buildings are required to meet may be grouped under five heads: (1) those follow-ing from the necessity of obtaining a maxi-mum amount of clear and available floor space, (2) those resulting from the exactions of the insurance companies, (3) those result-ing from the building laws, and (4) those resulting from the necessity of economical operation. Finally, speculative builders have discovered it advisable to pay some attention to design, because, other things being equal, a structure which presents a good appear-ance sells better than one which does not.

Of course, the prime object is to secure the maximum floor space, made properly available by accessibility, the absence of impediments, abundant light and proper dis-tribution. In large lofts, containing 10,000 or more square feet there may be large num-bers of employees, engaged in various kinds of work, all of whom have to be overlooked by a floor manager. The ideal loft, conse-quently, is square in outline; and anything like an L-shaped plot is usually avoided. Among the new Fourth Avenue buildings all except one are built on square or rectangu-lar lots. Starting with a square lot, the great effort of the architect must be to secure the largest possible amount of light for the dif-ferent floors, because on such a supply of light the maximum availability of the floor space will depend. The amount of light which he can get will, of course, depend upon the number of directions from which good light can be secured; and the conse-quence is that the control of a corner is of the greatest practical importance in design-ing an ideal loft. With that advantage more or less light can be secured for three sides of a floor; and the amount will be more, rather than less, when one side fronts on an excep-tionally wide thoroughfare, like Fourth Avenue. As a matter of fact, all but two of the important buildings recently erected on this avenue are built upon one or more corners. Usually the space obtained on any single floor is thrown into one large loft; but some-times such is not the case. In planning the use of his floor space, the architect is obliged to consider the possibility of subsequent subdivision.

The height, no matter how many direc-tions from which it is obtained, is, of course, made available by windows. The great object of the plan is to obtain the maximum area of exterior openings; and these windows must be arranged, if possible, so as to make every square foot of floor space available without the use of artificial illumination. The consequence is that large mullioned windows are used, so as to fill the entire space between the piers with glass. Until recently the height of the windows was determined by the height of the steam radiators from the floor; but more recently the architect has been able to lower his window sills by using a system of indirect steam radiators, which flattened out the space needed for the heating arrangement. The net result has been to leave practically only the pier and the floor lines solid on the exterior, all the rest of the façades being thrown into window space. The dominant consideration of a maximum amount of light has also tended to increase the height of the ceilings to the very limit of economy, because of the aid rendered thereby not only to the lighting, but to the ventilating system. The arrangements for ventilation are very carefully planned and insure good air in all kinds of weather.

Of course, the amount of clear and available floor space is affected by many factors besides the amount of light. The interior columns must be arranged along the fewest possible number of lines, and the various conveniences and services connected with the building must be planned so as to supply an adequate service, without diminishing any more than necessary the rentable floor space. The planning of these services is, perhaps, the most difficult part of the architect's job, because the chance of economy varies with the class of tenants for which the building is prepared, the size of the lot and its shape. The number of elevators needed, for instance, will vary according to the use to which the lofts are put. Two elevators have been considered enough for a building 100 x 100, but of late years such a limitation of the elevator service has been found dangerous. If the floors are used for manufacturing purposes or are subdivided into offices, the number of employees increases;

and as they usually arrive and are dismissed at about the same hour, the elevator service has to be proportioned to the exigencies of emptying the building, if necessary, within a few minutes. A large area has to be devoted, also, to the freight elevators. They have to be provided with a separate entrance, which is situated, if possible, on the side street, where trucks may have less difficulty in unloading and loading. Another difficult matter to arrange economically is the toilet accommodations. Two toilets have to be provided on every floor, one for each sex; and in case the building is used for manufacturing purposes, the factory law requires the furnishing of additional toilets elsewhere in the building.

Second only in importance to the planning of a maximum amount of clear and available floor space is the satisfaction of the exactions of the Board of Fire Underwriters, so that the tenants may obtain the lowest possible rate of insurance. The standard of fireproof construction is thus pretty well fixed, but it tends constantly to become higher on grounds, not only of fire protection, but because of the resulting economics of maintenance. The tenants in such buildings carry large amounts of stock, much larger than the tenants of an office building, and the saving for them is very considerable, in case the building measures up to the highest standard of fire-proofing. Some of the best of Fourth Avenue buildings are models of substantial, safe, economical and at the same time quick construction. In a number of them granolithic or concrete floors have been used. Metal trim of a very simple stock design and painted to represent wood has become almost universal. Ornamental designs are avoided in the plastering, and the plaster corners are protected by metal beading. Speed of construction and necessary quickness of occupancy makes it necessary to standardize all details, and to omit as much paint as possible. Of course, an automatic sprinkler system and full local fire protection have to be provided for every floor.

Floor loads, stairways, fire-escapes and the

Then the Event occurred, and its name was H. H. Richardson. The first great genius in American architecture, he rolled like an aesthetic juggernaut over the prostrate bodies of his peers and the public, and in ten years we did have substantial unity. We were like the village fisherman who didn't care what color they painted the old tub, "so as they painted her red"; we didn't care what our architecture was so long as it was Romanesque. For another ten years we had a love-feast of cavernous arches, quarry-faced ashlar, cyclopean voussoirs, and seaweed decoration; village schools, railway stations, cottages—all, all were of the sacrosanct style of certain rather barbarous peoples in the south of France at the close of the Dark Ages.

And in another ten years Richardson was dead, and his style, which had followed the course of empire to the prairies and the alkali lands and the lands beyond the Sierras; and a few years ago I found some of it in Japan! It was splendid, and it was compelling, as its discoverer handled it; but it was alien, artificial, and impossible, equally with the bad things it displaced. But it did displace them, and Richardson will be remembered, not as the discoverer of a new style, but as the man who made architecture a living art once more.

Eighteen hundred and ninety, and we start again. Two tendencies are clear and explicit. A new and revivified Classic with McKim as its protagonist, and a new Gothic. The first splits up at once into three lines of development: pure Classic, Beaux Arts, and Colonial, each vital, brilliant, and beautiful in varying degrees. The second was, and remains, more or less one, a taking over of the late Gothic of England and prolonging it into new fields, ▸

2 "An office building in New York, 1909." What appears to be the only skyscraper (unbuilt), by Ralph Adams Cram appears in an article called "The Works of Cram, Goodhue and Fergusson," in a section entitled "Ecclesiastical Works," [XXIX:1 Jan 1911 pp 45-86].

opposite: Fourth Avenue Building, New York City, Charles A. Valentine, architect, 1910.

like are all designed so as to conform to the requirements of the local building law. The steel frame has to be of sufficient strength to carry a live load of one hundred and twenty-five pounds to the square foot. A substantial saving can sometimes be brought about by full co-operation between architect and engineer in the design of the frame-work. An economy usually results from combining the stairway and fire-escape provisions of the law. Two stairs are demanded for each 5,000 square feet of space; and in buildings of larger area, the exterior fire-escape, which is also demanded is converted into an outside stairway.

Changes of considerable importance have recently been made in the equipment of these loft buildings. Until recently it was almost the universal custom to install a heating, lighting and power plant in buildings of this character, because the policy of the public utility companies made such private installations profitable. Now, however, contracts can be made to obtain the power from the street, which makes it more economical to buy it; and the consequence is that such plants are now generally omitted. Space is still left for them so that they can be installed at some future time, in case the economical operation of the building should demand it; but the day will probably come when a cheap supply of power from a central plant will be so well assured that such a space will no longer have to be reserved. When this time does come, it will be possible to effect additional economies in interior arrangement.

The foregoing are some of the essential practical requirements, which have to be met by the architects in the design of these buildings, and when they are all met he is not left very much discretion in adapting his interior arrangements to a pleasant exterior effect. The exterior consists of a frame work, usually about sixteen stories high of piers and floors, the lines of both of which are separated by fixed distances, and both of which cannot be disguised by much ornamentation. The use of large detail is forbidden both by the expense and by the knowledge that no detail can be scaled large enough to count effectively at such a great height from the street. There is only one architectural device of importance which they are permitted to use at the expense of practical availability of the building. They have been permitted to place cornices on some of the buildings whose projection is sufficient to hurt the light on the top floor. The consequence has been that the top floor is often used in part for the janitor's quarters, for store-rooms, or for extra toilets, whenever they are needed.

At the same time it must not be inferred that the architect, even if he would, could ignore aesthetic considerations. A certain standard of architectural decency tends to be imposed even on speculative builders. They find that a building which has been made measurably attractive in appearance at some moderate cost will sell better than a building in which such considerations have either been ignored or have been net by clumsy and vulgar methods; and the means whereby some measure of architectural attractiveness can be obtained within the necessary limits of expenditure are now pretty well settled by common consent. Thus the appearance of these buildings, like every other aspect of them, tends to become standardized.

In the effort to render a sixteen-story building attractive at a minimum of expense, the architect has to depend upon a few simple and obvious devices. He can in the first place group his window openings to some slight extent and by these means he can emphasize the corners of the building and give them a certain solidity. In many cases this device has not been used, but in those buildings, such, for instance, as the Braender Building on the southeast corner of 24th St., whose architects have used it, the effect is excellent. In no other way can a structure of this kind be made to look like a tower rather than a cage, and the cost of the arrangement is practically negligible. It gives the building a salient line and direction, from which it can derive some propriety and dignity of appearance.

A tall loft building can do without emphatic lines, but it cannot do without some attractiveness of coloring. The great effort of the architects has been to obtain a good-looking material for the main shaft of the edifice, and in this effort they have been enormously helped by the advances recently made in the manufacture of front brick and glazed terra cotta. In one or two cases stone has been used, and with admirable results, but the cost of stone is usually prohibitive. An architect can now choose between many varieties of brick and terra cotta, all of which give the building a pleasant color and surface, and all of which are susceptible within limits of decorative treatment. It is particularly in this respect that the Fourth Avenue buildings exhibit a considerable average advance over any similar group of their predecessors. A better colored brick or terra cotta has usually been specified; and the material has been treated with discretion and good taste. In some cases decorated patterns have been obtained in the laying up of the brick itself. In other cases white glazed terra cotta decorated with superficial ornamental patterns has been effectively employed. In still other cases a brick building has been trimmed with colored and glazed terra cotta. The variations on the central idea are numerous and ingenious and permit the display of a high degree of aptitude for purely decorative design. What is needed and sought is essentially an attractive and effective arrangement of color and pattern. And in seeking these appropriate and economical means of ornamentation, the architects have abandoned an error, which was very prevalent until recently even among the designers of

strictly commercial buildings—the error of overloading the top stories of a sixteen-story edifice with masses of ugly and bloated terra cotta detail in high relief. Ornamentation of this kind was ineffective from the street, and from the upper windows of an adjacent building it was frankly hideous.

We trust that readers unfamiliar with conditions in New York will now be able to appreciate the importance of this group of mercantile buildings as representing a significant and prominent architectural type. The dominant idea to keep in mind in respect to them is that they are from every point of view essentially a normal and natural growth. In almost all other departments of American architectural design the process of improvement has depended on the somewhat forcible imposition on the American public of European technical standards and traditional forms. But in respect to these commercial buildings this usual source of architectural amelioration has availed nothing. Indeed whenever the attempt has been made to impose these standards and forms on commercial buildings the result has been perverting and in some instances corrupting. Neither has very much progress been made by means of a rigorous application of merely logical ideas. The advance has come about by way of a candid and unpretentious attempt to design buildings, which satisfied every real practical need at the lowest possible cost. The result of this attempt up to date is a group of buildings which really earn their living, and they do so without either any subservience to tradition or any revolutionary departure from it. They are absolutely a case of the survival of the fittest—the fittest, that is, under existing conditions. The conditions will change both aesthetically and practically, but any future advance of American commercial architecture will depend upon a further development of the ideas and the methods which have made these Fourth Avenue buildings what they are. ∎

sometimes into new beauties. So matters run on for another ten years; at the end of that time the pure Classic has won new laurels for its clean and scholarly beauty, the Beaux Arts following has abandoned most of its banality of French bad taste and has become better than the best contemporary work in France, while the neo-Colonial has developed into a living thing of exquisite charm. I feel too near the Gothic development to speak of it without prejudice, but its advance has been no less than that of its Classical rival—or should I say, bedfellow?

And now two new elements enter: steel-frame construction on the one hand, and on the other the Secessionist. The steel frame is the enfant terrible of architecture, but like so many of the genius it may grow up to be a serious-minded citizen and a good father. It isn't that now, it is a menace, not only to architecture, but to society; but it is young and it is having its fling. If we can make it realize that it is a new force, not a substitute, we shall do well. When it contents itself in its own sphere, and the municipality says kindly and firmly, "thus far and no further"—the "thus far" being about one hundred and twenty-five feet above street level, as in the very wise town of Boston—then it may be a good servant. Like all good servants it makes the worst possible master; and when it claims as its chiefest virtue that it enables us to reproduce the Baths of Caracalla, vaults and all, at half the price, or build a second Chartres Cathedral with no danger from thrusting arches, and with flying buttresses that may be content beautifully to exist, since they will have no other work to do, then it is time to call a halt.

* * *

[article continued on page 183]

from left to right:
**Woolworth Building,
New York City,
Cass Gilbert, architect,
1910–13.**

**Post Office Buillding,
New York City,
Alfred B. Mullett,
architect, 1875
(demolished).**

**Municipal Building,
New York City,
McKim, Mead & White,
architects, 1907–14.**

**St. Paul Building, New
York City, George B. Post,
architect, 1895–98
(demolished).**

Though by now, all the
world's tallest buildings
were towers of some kind,
building them was the
exception rather than the
rule. The City Investing and
Equitable Buildings (pages
93 and 205) were a much
more efficient way to manage real estate. Towers
were clearly built for their
height and consequent
corporate prestige.

opposite: View of the
Brooklyn Bridge with the
Woolworth Building.
Montgomery Schuyler
called the bridge, "one of
the greatest...monuments
of the 19th Century." He
believed his essay, "The
Bridge as a Monument"
(1883), was the first
attempt to apply aesthetic
analysis to a work of pure
engineering.

"THE TOWERS OF MANHATTAN"
AND NOTES ON THE WOOLWORTH BVILDING
BY MONTGOMERY SCHVYLER

"RECORDS" IN ALTITUDE are precarious and fleeting, almost ephemeral. Astonishing as it now appears, the Park Row Building (photo page 60), not so very long ago, held the record, and probably held it longer than any subsequent erection. The New York Times (photo page 70) occupied its building in the first year of the new century, and was fain to boast that its edifice "scraped higher clouds" than any other skyscraper in New York. Being interpreted, the boast meant that although the actual altitude of the building from the sidewalk was less than that of the still record-holding Park Row, it stood on so much higher ground as to reach further into the empyrean. And then came the Singer, (photos page 183–86), holding precariously its eminence. And then the Metropolitan, (photo page 182), climbing indisputably "some fathoms further into the ancient region of night" and taking in turn its distinction of being the "tallest inhabited building in the world," and the next in height to the skeleton of the "Tour Eiffel." And now the modern Titan takes another upward shoot in the Woolworth, with the tower a good head and shoulders above that of the Metropolitan, still further overpassing the Singer and, unfortunately and incidentally, "blanketing" that former giant, now reduced, as you may say, almost to moderate stature.

How long will this now new record hold? What next? Truly, what is the limit? It is very clear that the limit is commercial, not technical. In the absence of restraining laws, every projector of a building built for profit will carry it as high as he thinks it will pay him to carry it. And among real estate speculators, among architects, among engineers, you will find a new opinion with every new expert you ask. "Quot homines, tot sententiae." Possibly the Woolworth may retain its preeminence for a decade, possibly it may lose it next year. The sudden upstart of Jonas' gourd or Jack's beanstalk is nothing to the swiftness of these latter uprisings. They shoot up "while you wait."

Meanwhile the competition is not only commercial, but in a measure artistic. No Gradgrind[1] of a projector would dare to attack "the record" without some thought as to how his record beater was going to look. And probably there is no cultivated and ambitious architect, even though as yet "no man hath hired him" to do a skyscraper, who does not carry around in his mind, and in his leisure moments fondle, some idea of the skyscraper he would like to build. When he actually "lands the job" he may find that the necessary concessions to practicality leave the idea hardly recognizable to himself, and not at all recognizable to "the man in the street." The practical requirements in every case issue, as to the body of the building, in an almost identical result, that is to say, a parallelopiped with the minimum of supports or "solids" and the maximum of "voids" or windows. It is only in the skyline, in the upper termination, that he has, as an artist, a real chance. It is at any rate in the towers that the difference between architect and architect most clearly appears, and hence a comparison of the most distinguished and remarkable of these terminal

1 *Gradgrind:* In his novel *Hard Times*, Charles Dickens created a straw man, Thomas Gradgrind, "a creature of mere fact and no humbugging sentiment—a modern, no-nonsense figure of the industrial age."

February
1913

Metropolitan Life Insurance
Company Building and Tower,
New York City, Napoleon Le Brun
& Sons, architects, 1892; 1909.

DIE
or
DADO

2 *Die:* The part of a pedestal
between the plinth and the cornice, also called the dado.

opposite (from right to left):
St. Paul Building, New York City,
George B. Post, architect,
1895–98 (demolished).

City Investing Company Building,
Francis H. Kimball, architect,
1906-08.

Singer Tower (behind City
Investing), Ernest Flagg, architect, 1905–08.

St. Paul's Chapel (foreground),
Thomas McBean, architect, 1766.

features, such as that for which our illustrations supply the material, ought to be
instructive and interesting. The Times tower,
the Singer tower, the Bankers' Trust, the
Municipal Building, the Metropolitan Life,
and now this soaring Woolworth are
undoubtedly among the most interesting of
our experiments in skyscraping.

There is among these all initial and obvious distinction. Our tall building is in fact a
frame building. Some architects endeavor to
express that primary fact and some find it
more convenient to ignore it. The difficulty
in expressing it lies in the circumstance that
the actual structure, the steel skeleton, must
be overlaid, and in part concealed. A writer
who had adduced the Singer Building, not
that of the tower, but the Singer Building in
Broadway near Union Square, as "the logical
skyscraper" was taken sharply to task by
another writer, who insisted that the exposure of the metal frame was not "logical" at
all. It was, all the same, in theory, although in
practice the consensus of architects is that
the frame must be enveloped, or wrapped,
with incombustible material for security
against fire. The writer of the article on
Architecture in the Encyclopaedia Britan-
nica, being unaware of this fact assumes that
the masonry envelope is added "for appearance sake," and thereby goes far to vitiate his
critical comments. The difference is none
the less fundamental between the assumption, that the envelope or screen is a real wall
of masonry which carries itself, and the
acknowledgment in the design that it is only
all envelope and the endeavor to express the
actual structure behind it. Of the towers
which we illustrate, the Metropolitan, the
Bankers' Trust and the Municipal Building
evidently proceed upon the former assumption. The Times tower may be called a compromise. Its substructure assumes the reality
and selfsupport of the visible wall, but in the
tower itself the fact of a frame is unmistakably conveyed and powerfully expressed.
The architect of the Singer tower has also
managed to convey this same sense of the
skeleton behind the padding by artful
devices such as the variation in material and

color, and the lightening and opening of the
fenestration at the centre, in comparison
with the solidity of the outer piers so as to
denote that the central part is not a wall, but
a mere screen quite incapable of supporting
itself. Of all the buildings in our list, the
Woolworth most unmistakably denotes its
skeleton. Nobody could possibly take it for
a masonic structure. The uprights of the steel
frame are felt throughout and everywhere,
while the device of tinting the "transoms"
and of carrying through at intervals the
transverse bands around the building shows
that the uprights are tied together and gives
a grateful sense of a security very different
from that which is obtained by the apparent
immobility of the mass and weight of
masonry.

It will be admitted that all these towers
are shapely, worthy of the attention which
they compel, credits to their designers, ornaments to the city, and the variations in detail
following the several notions of the architects are sources of additional interest.
"There are differences of operation, but the
same law." "The law" is that in a building of
which the utility is the justification, all the
space shall be utilized to the utmost. Of the
towers we are considering, that of the
Metropolitan doubtless comes the nearest to
complying with "the rigor of the game."
Even its steeply sloping roof is divided into
visible and tenantable stories. There is no
superfluity excepting the actual finial of the
crowning member. Even this has its justification as a "belvedere." We believe it has actually made money as an "outlook." If not, it
evidently might do so. What one chiefly
quarrels with, in the design of the Metropolitan tower, is that "die"[2] continuing the
rectangular shaft in a rather shrunken state
through the loggia, with its graceful arcades
and vigorous shadows. Up to that point the
composition is very satisfactory and engaging, but if the shaft had been lifted in its full
dimensions by the number of stories included in what we have called the "die" and the
slanting roof thereon immediately superposed. We think that the dignity of the monument would have been much enhanced.

STYLE IN AMERICAN ARCHITECTURE
continued from (page 179):

* * *

*And there you are: three kinds
of Classic, two kinds of Gothic,
skeleton-frame, and Secessionist—all are operative to-day, each
with its own strong following,
each, one admits, consummately
clever and improving every day;
for there is no architectural retro-
gression in America, there is
steady and startling advance, not
only in facility 'for handling and
developing styles, but in that far
more important affair, recognition
of the fact that styles matter far
less than style. From a purely
professional standpoint the most
encouraging thing is the breadth
of culture, the philosophical
insight into the essence of
things, the liberality of judgment
that mark so many of the architectural profession to-day. Gone
are the old days of the "Battle of
the Styles"; the swords are beat-
en into pruning-hooks, and these
are being used very efficiently in
clearing away the thicket of
superstitions and prejudices that
for so long choked the struggling
flower of sound artistic development. The Goth and the Pagan
can now meet safely in street or
drawing-room without danger of
acute disorder; even the structural engineer and the artist preserve the peace (in public); for all
have found out that architecture
is much bigger than its forms,
that the fundamental laws are the
same for all good styles, and that
the things that count are structural integrity, good taste, restraint,
vision, and significance. No one
now would claim with the clangor
of trumpets that the day of victory was about to dawn for the
Beaux Arts, Gothic, or steel-
frame styles, or for any other,
for that matter; each is contributing something to the mys-* ▸

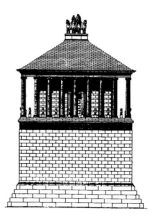

Reconstruction drawing of the Mausoleum at Halicarnassus.

3 Cyrus L.W. Eidlitz loosely based his New York Times Tower, 1903–5, on the Campanile of Giotto (photo page 80).

above (from right to left):
Bankers Trust, New York City, Trowbridge & Livingston, architects, 1912.

Hanover National Bank Building, New York City, James B. Baker, architect, 1901–03.

Equitable Building, New York City, George B. Post, architect, 1870.

opposite: Bankers Trust and Hanover National Bank Building.

Certainly its aspect would have been more commanding in any distant view over the roofs to the eastward. And indeed from any view the "die" does not account for itself. It is either too important or not important enough, and seems to have been injected from an insufficiently discriminating following of precedent or from a misleading analogy of proportion. The plain pyramidal roof of the Bankers' Trust more fittingly "crowns the work." The interior of this pyramid, blinded as it is by the solid sloping walls to outer light and air, may look like a sacrifice of utility to architecture, which in these edifices is not permissible. But in fact one understands that this interior has been found available and profitable as a place of storage, or "archive." An interesting design was shown some years ago in which the pyramidal roof was terraced or stepped," each step being in fact a story furnished with windows and obviously habitable. Perhaps this may be the next development. In the Times tower, which remains one of our best achievements in this kind, the need of a sloping roof by way of protection is frankly disavowed, as indeed with modern construction it is superfluous. The experience of all these centuries has shown it to be superfluous, even in the case of the Campanile of Giotto, the prototype of the Times tower, which the later architect[3] has manipulated to so admirable a result. In the Municipal Building the rigor of the prohibition against the devotion to architectural effect of space which might otherwise be available for occupancy has plausibly been held to be relaxed. This is not only an "office building," which for the most part it very strictly is, and to the conditions of which, for the most part, it very strictly conforms. It is also a civic monument. Hence the designer has held himself free, after he had worked clear of the roof, to produce a purely decorative object. This the tower distinctly is; and moreover, one can imagine that all its stages up to the actual finial are available for occupancy or storage.

The Woolworth Building is in this respect not quite in the same category. For this is a distinctly utilitarian erection, to be justified of its utility, or not justified at all. It may, and indeed almost must, recede as it rises, but the recessions as well as the main mass must be not only "built to the limit" but occupied and made to pay to the limit. Those who remember the design for it as first published will remember how loyally, how almost brutally, this condition was therein fulfilled. Compared with the actual work, the stark mass which resulted from that first consideration was crude and "lumpy." It was the second recession of the upper stages, together with the elaboration and the lightening of the detail, which has converted it into the thing of beauty which we now thankfully recognize. The achievement of this result involved a similar recognition on the part of the client who must have sacrificed some space and added much enrichment of this crowning feature with his eyes wide open. The tower commemorates his sense of civic obligation, as well as the inventiveness and the sensibility of his architect.

DETAILS OF THE WOOLWORTH BUILDING

The introduction into general use in this country of terra cotta as a decorative material is hardly more than a generation old. One of the lessons of the Chicago fire of 1871, reinforced by the Boston fire of the following year was, as everybody interested in the subject knows, that unprotected metal supports could not be trusted to retain their shape, nor their supporting power, in the heat of a fierce conflagration. Soon after the fires in question, experiments began in adjusting to the supports protective envelopes of baked clay. The use of terra cotta, thus began, was extended by the establishment of one or two firms which made a specialty of terra cotta cornices, as a cheaper substitute for stone, as a more efficient and durable substitute for sheet metal. This was by no means the first experiment in the decorative use of terra cotta. Long before the great fires mentioned, in the sixties, even in the fifties, terra cotta had been decoratively employed. It was so employed in the old Trinity Building, designed by the elder Upjohn and facing Trinity Churchyard

terious alembic we are brewing; and all we hope is that out of it may come the philosopher's stone that, touching inert matter, shall turn it into refined gold— which by the way is the proper function of architecture and of all the arts.

* * *

Now I do not feel that we shall be content with an art of the scope of that of the Renaissance; I do not feel that we shall be content with a new epoch of civilization on Renaissance lines. There are better ways of life, and saner. I believe all the wonderful new forces now working hiddenly, or revealing themselves sporadically, will assemble to a new synthesis that will have issue in a great epoch of civilization as unified as ours is disunited, as centripetal as ours is centrifugal, as spiritually efficient as ours is materially efficient; and that then will come, and come naturally and insensibly, the inevitable art that will be glorious and great, because it shows forth a national character, a national life that also is great and glorious.

* * *

This is really all there is to our architectural history, and I have used many words in saying what might have been expressed in a sentence. What lies before us? More pigeon-holes, more personal followings, more individualism, with anarchy at the end? I do not think so, but rather exactly the reverse. Architecture is always expressive; sometimes it reveals metaphysical and biological truth, when in itself there is no truth whatever. If we built Independence Hall in Philadelphia, there was something in us of the same nature, and we glory in the fact. If we built the City Hall in the same town, there was some- ▶

1913

above: Singer Building, New York City, Ernest Flagg, architect, 1905-08.

right & opposite: Woolworth Building, New York City, Cass Gilbert, architect, 1910-13.

in New York. It was so employed at about the same time or perhaps even earlier, in the cornice of the "Tontine Coffee House," near the foot of Wall Street, designed by Renwick. But these experiments remained fruitless. It was in the early eighties, and almost coincidentally with the introduction of the steel frame, that the manufacturers began to offer, and the architects to avail themselves of terra cotta adapted to an extensive system of enrichment. The front of a little brick chapel at the corner of Lexington Avenue and Twenty-third Street, by Messrs. Le Brun, demolished a year or two ago, was noteworthy for the elaborate treatment of its front in terra cotta. This elaboration in effect constituted the entire architectural interest of the front, or of the building. It was further noteworthy as being unmistakably intended for its material, whereas most architects who employed the material in those early days used it as simply a cheaper substitute for stone, and in altogether lithe forms. There was a charming and characteristic use of terra cotta, and of terra cotta admirably executed as well as designed, in a building designed by Mr. Hardenbergh for the Western Union Company, at Broadway and Twenty-third Street, which still stands, but has been so mauled and painted over by subsequent possessors as to have been deprived of much of its interest.

When the steel frame came in, the use of terra cotta instead of stone as the main material of the exterior as well as of the interior was imperatively indicated, not only by the cheapness of the material in the comparison, but by its superior adaptability to the expression of the construction. It is true that not all or most architects of skyscrapers showed much interest in attaining a characteristic and expressive treatment. Perhaps the majority do not show this desire even yet. But for the expression of a frame which must be wrapped to protect it from the elements, it is clear that great advantages are offered by the use of a material originally plastic, which can be moulded so as to conform to the structure which it at once conceals and reveals, and by which the

columns can be tightly "jacketed," over a material which must be painfully and wastefully cut into the desired shapes, and which in fact is not commonly adapted to the actual structure artistically, but only adjusted to it mechanically, purporting to be an actual and self-carrying wall of masonry.

It will not be disputed that the great architectural success of the Woolworth Building is eminently the success of an expressive treatment. Can one imagine an equal success to have been attained, either structurally or decoratively, under any practical conditions, by the use of a material originally non-plastic? It could have been attained in stone at all only by doing violence to the material. Consideration of this violence, and of the waste of material and of labor which it would involve, in truth goes far toward justifying the architect who, having chosen stone for his surfacing, chooses to ignore his essential structure altogether and treat his envelope as a smooth stone wall. And the case is as clear with respect to the decorative features which form the subject of the remarkable series of photographs which we have the pleasure of herewith presenting. The taking of them, from temporary scaffoldings at the levels of the details photographed, scaffoldings now removed, was itself a notable achievement in photography.

thing in us like that, arresting as the thought must be. If we are doing three Classics, and two Gothics. and steel-frame, and Post-impressionism (not to mention the others) at the present moment, then that is because our nature is the same. Now, can we again prove the truth of the saying, "Expede Herculem," and, using our present output as the foot (one admits the connotation is of the centipede), create the Hercules? I mean, can we, from what we are doing to-day, predict anything of the future? Not of our future style that will be what our society makes it; but of society itself. For my own part I think we can; for all that we are doing in architecture indicates the accuracy of the deduction we draw from myriad other manifestations, namely, that we are at the end of an epoch of materialism, rationalism, and intellectualism, and at the beginning of a wonderful new epoch, when once more we shall achieve a just estimate of comparative values, when material achievement becomes the slave again, and no longer the slave driver. when spiritual intuition drives mere intellect back into its proper and very circumscribed sphere, and when religion, at the same time dogmatic, sacramental, and mystic, becomes, in the ancient and sounding phrase, "One, Holy, Catholic, and Apostolic," and assumes again its rightful place as the supreme element in life and action, the golden chain on which are strung, and by which are bound together, the varied jewels of action.

* * *

Shall we rest there? Shall we restore a style, and a way of life, and a mode of thought? Shall we re-create an amorphous mediaevalism and live listlessly in that ▸

1913

above: Woolworth Building details in terra cotta.

right: Rear of Woolworth Building.

oppostie: Municipal Building, New York City, McKim, Mead & White, architects, 1907-14.

"It never can happen again." To get the same effects, the visitor must repeat Tennyson's experience at Milan, an experience which will be vividly recalled to the poetical reader by the contemplation of these photographs:

> I climbed the roofs at break of day:
> Sun-smitten Alps before me lay,
> I stood among the silent statues,
> And statued pinnacles, mute as they.

One of the chief successes of the Woolworth, all will agree, is its success of "scale." This is emphasized and elucidated by these close views of the culminating detail. The "man in the street" can hardly help observing the distinctness and sharpness of the outlines of the canopies and arcades so many hundred feet above him. If a student of architecture, even while admiring the skill with which the scale has been held in mind, and what to him looks like a delicate and elaborate embroidery adjusted to its position, he will be prone to apprehend that when seen close at hand it must become gross and crude in effect. The near view, whether in fact or in these photographs, undeceives him on this point, and shows him that some more subtle process of adjustment than mere magnification has been at work. All this decoration, when looked at from its own level, seems to have been designed to be looked at from that level. Take the flying buttress, take the canopied arcade, take the finials, and you find that the process by which they are made to take their places as properly here as from the sidewalk, has by no means been a process of mere "monstrification." It is much subtler than that. It includes consideration of projections and recessions, of depths and detachments, of lights and shadows. One perceives also the effect of the color applied to the plane surfaces. As color it hardly counts from below, but as a means of detachment and clarification it counts emphatically in the distant view. And in the near view, take such a feature as the doubled window at the angle, with that grotesque gargoyle—from Notre Dame de Paris, is it?—protruding just beyond it. There is nothing in the photograph, nor in fact, to suggest that it would not be perfectly in place, so far as its scale goes, if it were meant to be habitually and exclusively seen on a level with the eye of the passer in the street.

All this is an unusual success. But the artistic quality of this detail is at least as remarkable as its adjustment. One would like to know what a scholarly and academic European Gothicist would have to say to it, or to such of it as does not "give itself away" in the photograph as part of a modern, commercial, many-storied building, considering it merely as "Gothic." One has seen photographic "bits" of famous ministers in comparison with which this brand new American Gothic loses nothing. Far be it from us to use the success of this detail as a means of reopening the Battle of Styles. But one can hardly refrain from asking himself whether a success comparable with that of the latest and greatest of our skyscrapers can be attained within the repertory of our Parisianized architecture. If so, one would delight to see it produced and to celebrate it accordingly. ∎

fool's paradise? On the contrary. When a man finds himself confronting a narrow stream, with no bridge in sight, does he leap convulsively on the very brink and then project himself into space? If he does he is very apt to fail of his immediate object which is to get across. No; he retraces his steps, gains his running start, and clears the obstacle at a bound. This is what we architects are doing when we fall back on the great past for our inspiration; this is what, specifically, the Gothicists are particularly doing. We are getting our running start, we are retracing our steps to the great Christian Middle Ages, not that there we may remain, but that we may achieve an adequate point of departure; what follows must take care of itself.

And in following this course we are not alone; we have life with us; for at last life also is going backward, back to gather up the golden apples lost in the wild race for prizes of another sort, back for its running start, that it may clear the crevasse that startlingly has opened before it. Beyond this chasm lies a new field, and a fair field, and it is ours if we will.

The night has darkened, but lightened towards dawn; there is silver on the edges of the hills and promise of a new day, not only for architects, but for every man. •

1913

6 Subject to Change: The Expanding Stage

The editors of *Architectural Record* maintained a constant and steady course, proclaiming at every turn that to be honest a building must "declare itself," to baldly reveal its structure. And, for years they announced that one individual, and only one, had done just that:

> "The imagination of Mr. Sullivan first, and almost alone, has reached up and caught at the possibilities and meaning which are enshrined in those huge office structures, and this, rather than his original and intricate ornamentation, constitutes his chief claim to greatness." (page 157)

The magazine's critics may have wished to rationally weigh "the facts in the case," but they had essentially fashioned a romance in which every successful solutions was always just out of reach. They were never as pragmatic as they pretended. In fact, as practical as his subject (building with concrete) appears, architect Alfred O. Elzner complained:

> "...as long as the visible architecture of the steel skeleton building will, as it evidently must, remain a mere sham construction, the critics will never be able to accord it a place in true art." (page 118)

Was this all architecture was supposed to do in any case? Ralph Adams Cram was not convinced:

> "The steel frame is the *enfant terrible* of architecture, ... it is a menace, not only to architecture, but to society; ... Like all good servants it makes the worst possible master; and when it claims as its chiefest virtue that it enables us to reproduce the Baths of Caracalla, vaults and all, at half the price, or build a second Chartres Cathedral with no danger from thrusting arches, and with flying buttresses that may be content beautifully to exist, since they will have no other work to do, then it is time to call a halt." (page 179)

For Cram, the cart had been put before the horse, structure was driving everything, and contemporary architecture had lost its meaning.

We've seen a struggle between old world and new, past and present, art and science, beauty and utility,

Design for proposed Burton Memorial Tower,
University of Michigan,
Eliel Saarinen, architect, 1925

and now it would seem between sacred and profane or, as Henry Adams would have it, between "the Virgin and the Dynamo." Everything changed in 1922.

To commemorate its seventy-fifth anniversary the *Chicago Tribune* announced a $100,000 competition for the design of a new tower that would be "an enhancement of civic beauty" and which would "provide…a worthy structure, a home that would be an inspiration to [its] workers as well as a model for generations of newspaper publishers." The competition attracted 263 designs from architects in 23 countries, "a league," as the *Tribune* called it, "for new and bold treatment of the theme of the skyscraper—one that is to make architectural history for generations to come."[a]

The jury gave first prize to Howells and Hood of New York City (see page 221). Second prize went to Eliel Saarinen, whose entry arrived from Finland at the eleventh hour. Third prize went to Holabird and Roche of Chicago. When they were done the jury commented: "One gratifying result of this world competition has been to establish the superiority of American design." They did note Saarinen's design as the one European exception. The majority of the American designs given honorable mention are variations of Woolworth Gothic, as are the two American prize-winners; the majority of the European designs given honorable mention were examples of Beaux Arts classicism.

Of all the entries submitted to the competition, Saarinen's seemed the only one capable of bridging the old world and the new. He enjoyed the distance necessary to understand how the American city had developed the way it did. Subtler and even more unified than the winner itself, his design is clean and very simple, while anything but monotonous. Fine vertical ribs terminate above the roof lines in finial-like projections, some of which carry figural sculptures. Saarinen's design is the only one that suggests a context for the building.

Louis Sullivan responded with considerable indignation over Saarinen's losing. He wrote an article for *Architectural Record* (page 199) in which he said, "The Finnish master-edifice is not a lonely cry in the wilderness, it is a voice, resonant and rich, ringing amidst the wealth and joy of life. In utterance sublime and melodious, it prophesies a time to come, and not so far away, when the wretched and the yearning, the sordid, and the fierce, shall escape the bondage and the mania of fixed ideas." The article had a profound impact on the whole architectural community; it is probably the most incendiary piece of writing to be published by an architecture magazine. Most amazing is the fact that just reproducing Saarinen's drawing made it one of the most influential designs of the next 50 years—for a structure that was never built!

Claude Bragdon describes the influence as if it were a religious experience:

> "Bertram Goodhue, himself a competitor, who had had an advance view of all the drawings, told me that Saarinen's design was in a class by itself and superior to all the others, and such was the consensus of opinion, professional and lay. Observe the workings of poetic justice: though the victory was theirs, and the spoils of victory in good American dollars, the winners themselves were convicted of sin and suffered conversion."[b] ∎

Bullock's Wilshire Department Store, Los Angeles, John and Donald B. Parkinson, architects, 1929. Hailing it as the first suburban department store and the first to cater to the automobile, LA Times critic Alma Whitaker wrote in 1929, "Nowhere in all the world is there such a completely beautiful, aesthetic building as that which opens today on Wilshire Boulevard."
Another critic said, "It is almost a sacrilege to call it a store."
As did Woolworth before him, John G. Bullock referred to his store as a "Cathedral of Commerce."

a From the "Program of the Competition," The Tribune Competition, p. 20. The jury was comprised of four businessmen who were members of the Tribune Building Corporation. The single architect was a member of the Illinois chapter of the American Institute of Architects.

b From Claude Bragdon's "The Frozen Fountain," 1924. The "conversion" refers to Hood's American Radiator Building, page 204.

"[The elements of style are] subject to change just as is the 'vocabulary' of the spoken language—which latter fact the inveterate champion of styles apparently has overlooked…indeed the vocabulary of the spoken language must be subject to changes, as time passes."

Eliel Saarinen Search for Form: A Fundamental Approach to Art, *1948.*

1914

**Masonic Temple, Chicago,
Burnham and Root,
architects,1891-92
(demolished).**

At 302 feet, this structure was
seven feet shorter than New
York's World Building with its
lantern, but it boasted the highest
occupied floor. The building
employed a rigid steel frame with
wrought iron windbracing placed
diagonally between the structural
members above the 10th floor.
The Masonic Temple remained
Chicago's tallest building until the
1920s when the city's new zoning laws permitted towers. In
1939, its offices and stores considered old fashioned, the building was demolished.

opposite: To illustrate the "observations and forecasts" in the article opposite, the author chose "a
design for a Polytechnic School
by J. Beckening Vinckers, a graduate (1923) of the Delft Institute
of Engineering Sciences and
Architecture....he is now working
in the office of William van Alen."

TWENTY-FIVE YEARS
OF AMERICAN ARCHITECTURE
(excerpt)

By A.D.F. Hamlin[1]

★ ★ ★

The most noticeable features of our architectural progress during the last twenty-five years have been the development of steel skeleton construction and the influence of several great exhibitions, especially of that at Chicago in 1893. The steel skeleton was born and first developed in Chicago. This statement is made despite the fact that in 1888 the late L. A. Buffington[2] of Minneapolis patented a system of metallic skeleton construction which embodied many features of the present system. But most of these features were not new; each had been used in varying forms in earlier buildings, and the Buffington column was an unscientific laminated affair of flat plates, wastefully and inefficiently combined. Mr. Buffington failed to induce reputable lawyers to prosecute his suits for infringement against Chicago and New York architects. Whatever may have been the merit of his claims of priority in the conception of the steel skeleton, it was the Chicago architects Jenney and Mundie who first gave the conception practical form and carried it into successful execution: to them belongs the credit for its design in its essential features. Thus it is from the metropolis of the Middle West that the two most potent forces emanated that have transformed modern American architecture.

The steel skeleton was really born in 1889; but the year 1891 saw it accepted as more than a mere experiment, and we may say that from that year dates its definitive adoption in American architecture. It is fair to consider it as the fourth of the great structural advances which have given architecture really new resources. The Roman vault for the first time made vastness of unencumbered space attainable. The Gothic ribbed vault and flying arch and buttress created the masonry skeleton and made possible the majestic loftiness and airy lightness of the medieval cathedral: another new architecture was created. The metallic truss, developed towards the middle of the last century, permitted a wholly new spaciousness and lightness of construction: our vast exhibition halls, train-houses and armories would have been impossible without it; again a new architecture came into existence, hardly recognized as a new architecture. The steel skeleton, the last of the four developments, has brought into being a new loftiness and lightness of construction; it has freed architecture from the limitations of massive walls which had for ages kept it from soaring otherwise than in the frail and beautiful but practically useless form of the spire. We have not yet solved the problem of the ideal artistic treatment of the skyscraper, but we have gone a long way towards it; and meanwhile our architecture has been endowed with wholly new resources and possibilities.

★ ★ ★

Our skyscraper architecture hardly requires the mention or comment of my pen. It is omnipresent and insistent, the most conspicuous, revolutionary and American architectural product of the last twenty-five years, from Jenney and Mundie's Home Life Building in Chicago and Bradford Gilbert's Tower Building addition in New York to the 750-foot Woolworth and the vast Equitable in New York, and Boston's much-belauded Custom House. It has been more "cussed and discussed" than any other modern type. It has changed the skyline of New York and of every large American city from Seattle to Bangor, from Los Angeles to Galveston. It has produced a new architectural style, irrespective of that of its varied decorative trimmings; and it speaks so loud for itself as to make further words on this page unnecessary.

★ ★ ★

In 1891 there were published in the United States, disregarding minor and ephemeral periodicals, two architectural journals: the weekly *American Architect and Building News* in Boston, and the monthly *Architecture and Building* in New York. In that year the ARCHITECTURAL RECORD first made

from:
MODERNISM IN ARCHITECTURE
Leon V. Solon
Vol. 60, No. 3, September 1926,
pp. 193-201.

TECHNIQUE, IN ALL the arts, might be defined as the formulation of convenient methods for manipulating physical vehicles employed for externalizing an aesthetic content. All those unified directions for artistic impulse which we recognize under stylistic designations are identified with techniques. Each so-called style or type has evolved within a distinct imaginative sphere and is the means wherewith some self-contained artistic purpose is stated. The physical media, even when identical, employed in each type of expression, must consequently be endowed with pertinent significance through the manner of their utilization or, in other words, through the formulation of a distinctive technique. A norm in technique is inconceivable, as irrational as a norm in artistic expression. Artistic objective differs in each stylistic type; hence the difference in the manner in which inherent capacities in medium are developed through technique. It is through technique that vital abstract qualities are realized in effect; techniques are not interchangeable in activities directed to unrelated artistic objectives. ▶

1 A.D.F. Hamlin (1855-1926) was an architect and Professor of the History of Architecture at Columbia University. From 1903 to 1912 he was associated with Hamlin and Warren designing buildings for Robert College, Constantinople. He was the author of a number of books on the history of architecture including a standard university text, *The History of Architecture*, 1896.

2 See note *, page 14.

3 A plate from Henry Adams' ever popular classic *MONT–SAINT–MICHEL AND CHARTRES*, 1904. Once considered a must read for all architects "touching on the human side of architecture," by the 1920s the book was considered "a creditable kind of ignorance." [56:2 Aug 1924 p. 123]

opposite: By the 1920s *ARCHITECTURAL RECORD* began putting illustrations its covers; frequently they were urban images with skyscrapers. This February 1925 cover typically uses a German Expressionist style.

* The French sculptor Auguste Rodin (1840–1917) was featured in an extensive, illustrated article in *ARCHITECTURAL RECORD*. [XVIII:5 Nov 1905 pp 327–346]

its appearance, as a quarterly, hailed from the outset as a much-needed addition to our periodical literature, and marked by a seriousness of artistic and literary purpose which has ever since characterized it. Its change in 1903 to monthly issues was a natural result of its high quality, and it has constantly maintained that quality ever since. Meanwhile the Technology Review of Boston has entered the field, and that has developed into the excellent *Architectural Review*, filling a field midway between that of the RECORD and the other periodicals mentioned. *The Inland Architect* of Chicago long served the interests of the Middle West; the *Western Architect* came later, and in 1903 first appeared *Architecture*, another New York monthly, making a specialty of photographic illustrations. Occupying a field of its own, and standing at a very high level of scholarly, literary and artistic excellence, is the *Journal of the American Institute of Architects*, now in its third year; the latest comer in the field of American periodical literature on architecture. Other additional periodicals there is not now space to mention; they are many, and there are still others which, though not primarily architectural, devote a part of their space to architecture or issue special architectural numbers. All this has served to diffuse an interest in architecture among the public, and to provide the architect with information, instruction and suggestion. This periodical literature, much of it excellent, some of it commonplace, some distinctly inferior, is both a cause and a result of the increased general interest in architecture.

Quite as significant is the increase in books on architecture, of which the output has been enormous of late years. These fall into three classes: technical scientific books, among which the successive editions of Kidder's "Pocketbook" have been conspicuous; popular handbooks on house-design, stable-design, bungalows, house-furnishing, etc.; and books of scholarship, history and criticism, among which Sturgis's *Dictionary*, and *European Architecture*, Cummings' *History of Architecture in Italy*, Moore's *The Character of Renaissance Architecture* and *The Mediaeval*

Church Architecture of England, Porter's *Mediaeval Architecture* and *Lombard and Gothic Vaults*, the Sturgis-Frothingham *History of Architecture*, Wallis' *How to Know Architecture*, my *History of Architecture*, Ware's *American Vignola*, Frothingham's *Christian Architecture of Rome*, Adam's *Mont–Saint–Michel and Chartres*,[3] and several books by R. A. Cram may be mentioned among many others, as examples of the wide reach, variety and quality of American scholarship, research and literary skill in this field. They witness to the new position which architecture has reached in the public estimation since 1891. Such books could perhaps have been written before that date; surely but a fraction of them could have been published or could have had any wide sale. Prof. Moore's epoch-making *Development of Gothic Architecture* appeared, it is true, in 1889, but that and W. P. P. Longfellow's *The Arch and Column* were almost the only serious books on architecture by American authors previous to 1891. It augurs hopefully for the future progress of our art that its literature is now firmly established in public favor, and that it has been of such generally high quality.

This brief and hurried survey of a vast subject leaves unsaid much that the writer would have gladly discussed had time and space permitted. The question of style has been left almost untouched. The monuments must speak for themselves; the subject is too big for mere passing mention. The writer hopes that even so inadequate a sketch may inspire its readers with a new respect for the work of our American architects, the veterans and the young men alike; and with a new hope and confidence in the future. Looking back to the architecture of 1865-91, and noting the progress made since then, we have good reason to hope that 1941 will see, throughout our great Republic, an architecture far nobler, purer, more serious and more beautiful than that of to-day, offering to the whole world models of good taste and sound construction, and making our cities and villages fairer and happier places to live in than they are in this year of grace 1916. ∎

When some novel view-point commences to actuate artistic expression, it involves the creation of new attributes in medium, and a revision of proportional relations in constituent elements. The movement passes through an experimental stage, during which every available factor is appraised from a new basis in accordance with its capacity to serve the new purpose, and achieve an unprecedented ideal. This applies to changes of direction for impulse in all the creative arts.

The technique of carving in archaic sculpture was regulated to convey the formal content in idea; at a more mature stage of artistic sensibility, it aimed to transmit those individual and characteristic plastic beauties to which the artist re-acted in living models; at still another period, technique was directed to the externalization of purely aesthetic quantities, such as the crystallization of light upon subtleties of plane and form, as in the work of Rodin.*

A distinct technique was instituted by the Greek potters to express the simple grace of ideal form, the rhythmic balance of mass within a measure of space in a two-dimension species of presentation. In the Middle Ages another technique was developed to meet the dominant leaning towards the precise delineation of form in connection with the decorative massing of sumptuous color areas. Then, subsequent to the seventeenth century, other techniques have evolved; definitions of contour have given place to conditions of chiaroscuro as a main artistic objective.

The Modernist movement in European architecture has already clearly indicated its ultimate objective, and is employing familiar structural systems with an architectonic significance that is foreign to their traditional import in historic modes. This is wholly in accordance with precedent in stylistic evolution. We therefore find a new technique in the utilization of structural means, novel attributes developing, and a new basis for the aesthetic valuation of elements of effect.

One of the most important and interesting features of the movement is the complete disregard of perfunctory significance habitually attached to specific features; we refer to those conventions in decorative treatment intended to convey imaginary properties, such as strength or elegance. Where we find such symbols operative in effect, they have invariably been borrowed from some structural system in which they actually performed ostensible functions of which such attributes were integral factors. For the moment, we are unable to recall a single instance in original examples of a spontaneous or self-contained stylistic type, in which any important feature in composition justifies its presence by reason of symbolic significance. This could hardly be expected, as in such structural types decoration is in subjective relation to function, whereas in the derivative types of design symbolic significance often takes precedence of the statement of actual function.

The Modernist movement cannot be construed as derivative from whatever angle it is considered, and for that reason we may not expect to find recognition of symbolic significance in any of its structural or decorative features. On the other hand, as normal structural means are employed in execution, we may expect to find features of obvious structural purpose invested with novel decorative properties through the manner in which steel, concrete or other physical media are utilized in design: the evolution of a new structural technique is bound to occur.

The ornamental development of the new manner will undoubtedly progress in an unconventional but strictly logical manner; logic is so essential a part of the argument which precedes precise calculation in their structural design, that it is mainly responsible for the elimination of symbolic significance. If the relation of ornamentation to structural mass be studied in the various historic styles, it will generally be found to develop in two main directions, which are typified in the Classic and the Gothic. In the former, the practical purpose of decoration is to accentuate structural articulation and to beautify features which are not performing vital supporting functions. In the Gothic type, ornament performs a totally different function: the articulation of structural mass does not occupy the dominant position it does in the classic; embellishments of the surface and elaboration of silhouette are the designer's fundamental considerations.

The fascination of apparently monolithic mass in the Modernist objective makes articulation of the Classic order incongruous, and the dominant part which plain surfaces play with their rectangular silhouettes renders this Gothic principle equally unacceptable. In the Modernist manner we detect a tendency to regard a major structural area as the unit of space to be decorated. This will necessitate a revision of ornamental technique, departing from those conventions previously identified with architectural decoration.

With towering masses demanding an ornamental scale adjusted to large areas and long range effectiveness, high relief as the formula for visibility cannot be resorted to, because of its disadvantageous reaction upon the dominant characteristic sought in structural mass. It will be necessary to devise a technique in ornament which has the capacity for a new decorative emphasis and for long range visibility. This requirement causes us to feel confident that color will be employed. Color will render low relief capable of any exquisite measure of decorative force.

There seems no doubt that polychromy will prove the logical solution of the decorative problem, and the uncompromising premises which must necessarily control the manner of its application will produce a technique without precedent.

* * * ●

The
ARCHITECTVRAL
RECORD

FEBRVARY 1925

from:
**THE SKYSCRAPER IN
THE SERVICE OF RELIGION**
[from Notes and Comments]
By Herbert D. Croly
Vol. 55, No. 2, February 1924, 203-204.

Recently the New York newspapers published the sketch of a combined church and skyscraper which a Methodist congregation proposed to build on upper Broadway from plans by Mr. Donn Barber. The sketch was, of course, only the preliminary suggestion of a design prepared for purposes of publicity, but it was at least to one reader provocative of some far-reaching and novel speculations. Not that there is anything particularly novel and far-reaching about the idea of housing a church in a few floors of a skyscraper erected as an investment. The Christian Scientists have already practiced this method of demonstrating the unreality, of material things. But the proposed skyscraper on Broadway was designed, not as a business but as an ecclesiastical edifice, and that part of it which was not used for divine service is to be devoted to one or another of the many social and educational activities which an enterprising modern clergyman associates with his church. The writer could not help wondering whether in both these respects Mr. Donn Barber's sketch might not prophesy the advent of a new and extremely promising type of ecclesiastical architecture.

No variety of building ever erected looks less promising as a means of awakening feelings of awe and aspiration with which the architecture of the Christian church is traditionally associated than the rectangular skyscraper built before the Zoning Law went into effect. Its bulk and height might make it imposing, but it was imposing after the manner of a cliff rather than after the manner of a steeple. Its habit of rising straight from the street to a level some hundreds of feet above irritated and fatigued the human eye. The eye demands that when buildings rise as high as hills they shall, like hills, become smaller as they approach their summit. As it happens, however, skyscrapers of this kind, unless you apply the name to modest little twelve or fifteen story buildings, are no longer being erected in New York. The law now requires the upper stories of these towering edifices to occupy an amount of space which diminishes in proportion to their height; and this reform while it was adopted for practical reasons, has, as is already generally recognized, brought with it striking architectural advantages. It has enabled the skyscraper to attain to beauty. What Mr. Barber's sketch suggests is that among these architectural advantages there looms a possibility of erecting a skyscraper which might express for religious minds aspirations analogous to those which they formerly derived from the towers of a lofty cathedral.

Obviously it would be only too easy to overwork the analogy. If a skyscraper church corresponding to Mr. Barber's sketch is ever erected, it will possess many architectural values which are wholly different from those of the loftier members of the French cathedrals. Different, but possibly not inferior. These values will be derived from the varying effects of atmosphere and light which such buildings will produce at different times in the day and on different days in the year. They will find themselves entangled in the clouds and in the mysteries of the upper air just as a hill top does. As darkness draws near, they will gradually loom up as sources and centres of light and murmuring sound in a world which from natural causes is perforce frequently dark and hushed. Vague but strong emotions of this kind lend themselves with the utmost good will to symbolic expression in architecture, and whenever skyscraper churches are actually erected there is no reason why they should not receive such expression from the mind of a sensitive and imaginative architect. The designing of a building which scraped the sky for the greater glory of the Christian God would constitute the most unprecedented, inspiring and generous opportunity afforded by modern architecture to create a noble edifice which might enhance the meaning and dignity of contemporary Christianity. ■

from:

THE CLASSIC IN THE SKYSCRAPER
[from Notes and Comments]
By Fiske Kimball
Vol. 57, No. 2, February, 1925, pp. 189–190.

The classic style is not merely a matter of certain details, like the Orders, as some people seem to think. It is essentially one of geometrical simplicity and clarity of form. The ancient temple, square or circular, was enclosed by a single unbroken bounding line. The primary effect of the Monument of Lysicrates is due, not to its delicacy of detail, but to its orderly variety of simple centralized masses, square below, circular above.

The return to this elementary uniformity and harmony, rather than the reversion to Renaissance or antique details, was the essential characteristic of the movement led by McKim, Mead and White in the 'eighties. In the Boston Library they used that unbroken, uniform façade which Guadet had been saying would have such a great effect, by contrast to, the Beaux Arts system of characteristic—emphasis. In the Columbia Library and many other works they revived the centralized scheme of composition.

They and their followers, in the earlier years, applied the principle chiefly in the public and domestic buildings of ordinary height. When they finally came to the high building, about 1908 to 1912, they brought with them the lesson of clarity and order in surface treatment, in fenestration, and in mass. In the Fifth Avenue apartments they returned to unbroken planes and equalized proportions. In the Municipal Building, under different conditions, they attempted a centralized upbuilding of masses.

When the Zoning Law came, demanding broken masses, the variety of these might readily have taken on a "picturesque" irregularity and a symmetry. It was the force of the classical tradition that, instead, kept them geometrically simple, and subjected them to balance and measure. In the Fisk Building it is a grandiose symmetry, in the Shelton and the Fraternity Clubs it is a centralized grouping of rectangular masses only in one case, of octagonal forms also in the other. To speak of such buildings as different in "style" is to limit style to the most superficial of details. In the lower stories of the Shelton and of the Park Lane, for instance, the motives and disposition are identical. Though the profiles of capitals and mouldings may be suggested by Thiersch's Restoration of antique forms in one, by mediaeval forms in the other, both buildings are alike classic, in the broad sense, and highly modern.

When we think of a tower we somehow tend to think of a Gothic tower. We forget that there was such a thing as a classic tower—one of the greatest of all time, indeed, in the Pharos. Freed from myth, as we see it in Thiersch's restoration, the Pharos might give us inspiration for our own problems. Above a low surrounding structure (it might stand in a "one-and-one-half times district") towers a tall square shaft, diminishing to an octagon and then to a circle. Impractical? Not more so than the Metropolitan, the Municipal, or the Tribune towers. When shall we learn its lesson of variety in utter simplicity? ∎

above: Foshay Tower, Minneapolis, Wilbur Foshay & Magney & Tusler & Hooper & Janusch, architects, 1929.
  Wilbur Foshay, a manufacturer of kitchen utensils, designed his own office building based on the Washington Monument and went bankrupt in the process.

opposite, column one, top: "Cathedral of Entertainment"— Paramount Theater Building, New York City, Rapp & Rapp, architects, 1926–27.

opposite, column one, bottom: "Cathedral of Learning"— University of Pittsburgh, Pittsburgh, Charles Z. Klander, architects, 1926–27.

opposite, column two: Chicago Temple Building, Chicago, Holabird & Roche, architects, 1924.

opposite, column three: "Cathedral of Commerce"— Woolworth Building, New York City, Cass Gilbert, architect, 1910–13.

left: Thiersch's restoration of the Pharos. Built in 270 B.C., the Pharos was a lighthouse on a small island of the same name in the harbor of Alexandria. It stood until about 1300 A.D.

Second prize-winning entry, Chicago Tribune Tower Competition, Eliel Saarinen, architect, 1922.

Hard to believe, Saarinen's design had more impact on structures to follow than almost any other in the century—without ever being built! Publication of this single drawing, and the praise and positive criticism that attended it, was enough to make it a forceful instrument of change.

During photography's first century in the popular press, "paper architecture" was able to obtain this kind of power. Another important example is the photomontage of a glass skyscraper by Mies van der Rohe shown on page 228. Exhibited and circulated in print since 1921, it has inspired imitations ever since.

opposite: Chicago Tribune Tower, Chicago, Howells & Hood, architects, 1925.

THE CHICAGO TRIBUNE COMPETITION

Louis Sullivan

SOME seventy years ago, a philosopher, in the course of his studies of the Ego, separated men into two classes, distinct, yet reciprocally related, to wit: Masters of Ideas, and those governed by ideas. It was upon ideas as powers for good or ill that he laid the heavy hand; upon ideas as a living force obedient to the mastery of vision, springing forth from imagination's depths, from the inexhaustible reservoir of instinct.

Ego, considered solely as free spirit, stands out visibly as Master of Ideas. Ego, examined as a spirit benumbed through lack of action, hence inert and unfree, becomes dim of vision and renounces its will. It thus becomes the slave of imposed ideas whose validity it assumes it has not the strength to test, even were the idea of testing to arise. Hence, in timidity, it evokes the negative idea of Authority as a welcome substitute for its declining volition.

Masters of ideas are masters of courage; the free will of adventure is in them. They stride where others creep. The pride of action is in them. They explore, they test, they seek realities to meet them face to face—knowing well that, realities and illusions exist commingled within and without, but also knowing well that Ego is its own. Hence they walk erect and fearless in the open, with that certitude which vision brings—while slaves are slaves by choice. They seek shelter in the *shadows* of ideas.

Ever such were the great free spirits of the past, and such are those of our own day.

Masters of ideas of the past and now, frequently have sought and seek dominion, and have reached it because the idea of dominion coincides precisely with the idea of submission. Other masters of ideas then and now, mostly those of immense compassion, have been and still are crucified by those so long in the dark that the idea of spiritual freedom is abhorrent.

A consciousness is now growing and widely spreading in our modern world of thought, among masters of truly great ideas, that unless we become free spirits casting off the cruel, and awakening to the constructive power of beneficence, we shall vanish in decay and self destruction.

The simple world idea, now in process of becoming, in the hearts of men, is the idea of freedom from the domination of feudal ideas. Is there a power that can stop this becoming? There is not.

The eyelids of the world are slowly, surely lifting. The vision of the world of men is slowly, surely clearing. A world-idea Is sprouting from its seed in the rich soil of world-sorrow. Beneath the surface of things as they are, everywhere it is germinating unconsciously with the many, consciously with the few.

The old idea that man must ever remain the victim of Fate, will fade as fear fades. The new idea that man may shape his destiny will appear in its place, in a dissolving scene of the world-drama, as Democracy arises through the humus of the age-long feudal idea. For Democracy would remain, as now it is, a senseless word, a vacant shell, a futile sentimentalism, a mere fetish, did it not carry in its heart the loftiest of optimistic aspirations, wholly warranted, spite of all appearance to the contrary, and grasp the mastery of ideas wholly beneficent in power to create a world of joy devoid of fear.

The world is growing more compact every day, and every day the day is shortening, while the fleeting hour becomes thereby so much the fuller. The cold rigidity of frontiers is melting away, unnoted by the blind—every day the world becomes increasingly mobile, every day there is a silent interchange, every day communication is more fleet, and humanity, in response, more fluent. Slowly day by day, with enormous and gathering momentum, the hearts of the world draw together. The process is silent and gentle as the dewfall. There are those who see this; there are those who do not. There are those who see in the lightnings and the raging storms of the feudal idea, reaching now the climacteric of its

The following obituary appeared in *ARCHITECTURAL RECORD* in August 1950, accompanied only by a recent portrait (page 201) and another reproduction of the drawing shown at left.

* * *

The Tribune Competition
Saarinen designs have received awards in innumerable competitions; and it was in fact one of these, the well-remembered Chicago Tribune competition of 1922, that aroused Mr. Saarinen's interest in the United States and a year later brought him here from his native Finland.

* * *

The Tribune's widely-advertised competition to secure a design for "the most beautiful office building in the world" brought Mr. Saarinen the second prize of $20,000 and unloosed a storm of criticism which was reflected in Louis Sullivan's article in the February 1923 issue of the RECORD. ●

State Capital, Lincoln, Nebraska,
Bertram Goodhue, architect,
1921–32.

Boston Avenue Methodist
Episcopal Church, South, Tulsa,
Oklahoma, Bruce Goff, architect,
1924–29.

supreme mania for dominion, the symbol of self-destruction of a race gone wholly mad. But that is not so. The masters of the feudal idea alone have gone mad with hate; the multitudes are sound. They have lost a pathetic faith in the feudal concept of self-preservation which has wooed and betrayed them. They are moving somnambulistically now, upwards towards a faith that is new and real, a constructive idea, common to all, because springing from the hearts of all, of which all shall be masters, and about which shall form for the first time beneath the sun, a sane hope and faith in Life, a faith in Man—an idea which shall banish fear and exalt courage to its seat of power.

This Idea will become the luminous, the central idea of all mankind because it is the offspring of that which is deepest down in all. It is and will continue as long as life lasts in the race, the shining symbol of man's resurrection from the dead past, of man's faith in himself and his power to create anew.

There are those who will decry this hope as they view in despair a world writhing in the depths of pessimism, of mendacity and intrigue. Yet are they those who are without faith in mankind, without faith in themselves. For this is the modern affirmation: Man is not born in sin, but in glory.

All of this has sharply to do with the Tribune Competition, for in that showing was brought into clearest light the deadline that lies between a Master of Ideas and one governed by ideas. There they came, squarely, face to face: the second prize and the first. All the others may be grouped aside, for what is involved here is not a series of distinctions in composition or in detail, but the leading forth into the light of day of the profoundest aspiration that animates the hearts of men. This aspiration has remained articulate too long; its utterance at large has been choked by varied emotions of fear; the splendor of its singleness of purpose has been obscured by the host of shadows generated in bewilderment of thought, in a world that has lost its bearings and submits in distress to the government of dying ideas.

In its preliminary advertising, The Tribune broadcasted the inspiring idea of a new and great adventure, in which pride, magnanimity and its honor were to be inseparably unified and voiced in "the most beautiful office building In the world," to be created for it by any man sufficiently imaginative and solid in competence in whatever spot on the surface of the earth such a man might dwell.

Specifically, on the third page of its formal and official program, these statements were made:

"To erect the most beautiful and distinctive office building in the world is the desire of The Tribune, and in order to obtain the design for such an edifice, this competition has been instituted."

These words are high-minded; they stir imagination.

At the beginning of the paragraph immediately succeeding are found these words:

"The competition will be of international scope, qualified architects of established reputation in all parts of the world being eligible."

These words are magnanimous; they stir not only the world of architectural activity, but as well that of enlightened laity. Never perhaps, in our day, has such interest in architecture been aroused.

Not yet content in its eagerness, and purposing to make assurance of good faith and loyalty to an ideal triply sure, there is to be found on page 13, the final page of the program, the following statement:

"It cannot be reiterated too emphatically that the primary objective of The Chicago Tribune in instituting this Competition is to secure the design for a structure distinctive and imposing—the most beautiful office building in the world."

The intensive use of the word PRIMARY gives to the full clause the imposing promise of a token, of a covenant with the Earth. With that one word, PRIMARY, The Tribune set its bow in the cloud.

The craving for beauty, thus set forth by The Tribune, is imbued with romance; with that high Romance which is the essence, the vital impulse, that inheres in all the great works of man in all places and all times, that vibrates in his loftiest thoughts, his heroic deeds, his otherwise inexplicable sacrifices, and which forms the halo of his great compassions, and of the tragedy within the depths of his sorrows. So deeply seated, so persistent, so perennial in the heart of humanity is this ineffable presence, that, suppressed in us, we decay and die. For man is not born to trouble, as the sparks fly upward; he is born to hope and to achieve.

If a critique of architecture, or any other art, or any activity whatsoever, is to be valid, it must be based upon a reasoned process. It must enter with intelligence into the object or subject at hand, there to seek what signifies, and yet maintain such detachment as to render judgment unconstrained and free. A true critique is not satisfied with the surface of things, it must penetrate that surface to search the animus, the thought; it must go deeply to the roots, it must go to origins, it must seek the elemental, the primitive; it must go to the depths and gauge the status of the work thereby. A true critique must likewise derive of the humanities. It is not its function to deal with cold truths but with living truths.

Viewed in this light, the second and the first prize stand before us side by side. One glance of the trained eye, and instant judgment comes; that judgment which flashes from inner experience, in recognition of a masterpiece. The verdict of the Jury of Award is at once reversed, and the second prize is placed first, where it belongs by virtue of its beautifully controlled and virile power. The first prize is demoted to the level of those works evolved of dying ideas, even as it sends forth a frantic cry to escape from the common bondage of those governed by ideas. The apposition is intensely dramatic to the sensitive mind. Yet it is in this very apposition that we find a key wherewith to unlock and swing open wide a door, and reveal to all the vast and unused power resident in the great architectural art when inspired into motion by a Master of Ideas. The Finnish master-edifice is not a lonely cry in the wilderness, it is a voice, resonant and rich, ringing amidst the wealth and joy of life. In utterance sublime and melodious, it prophesies a time to come, and not so far away, when the wretched and the yearning, the sordid, and the fierce, shall escape the bondage and the mania of fixed ideas.

It is wretched psychology to assume that man is by nature selfish. The clear eye of sympathy sees beyond a doubt that this is not so; that on the contrary, man by nature is a giver; and it is precisely this one discerns in this beauteous edifice; the native quality of manhood giving freely of inherent wealth of power, with hands that overflow, is to say: There is more and more and more in me to give, as also is there in yourselves—if but ye knew—ye of little faith.

Qualifying as it does in every technical regard, and conforming to the mandatory items of the official program of instructions, it goes freely in advance, and, with the steel frame as a thesis, displays a high science of design such as the world up to this day had neither known nor surmised. In its single solidarity of concentrated intension, there is revealed a logic of a new order, the logic of living things; and this inexorable logic of life is most graciously accepted and set forth in fluency of form. Rising from the earth in suspiration as of the earth and as of the universal genius of man, it ascends and ascends in beauty lofty and serene to the full height limit of the Chicago building ordinance, until its lovely crest seems at one with the sky.

This is not all; there remain for some, two surprises; first, that a Finlander who, in his prior experience, had not occasion to design a soaring office building, should, as one to the manner born, have grasped the intricate problem of the lofty steel-framed structure, the significance of its origins, and held the solution unwaveringly in mind, in such wise as no American architect has as yet shown the required depth of thought and steadfastness of purpose to achieve.

Philosophy has been defined by a modern philosopher as the science of substantial grounds. It is the notable absence of substantial grounds, in the ambitious works of

from:
ELIEL SAARINEN
By Donnell Tilghman
Vol. 63, No. 5, May 1928, pp. 393-402.

* * *

Eliel Saarinen was born in Finland in 1873. From the beginning of his career as an architect he was associated with that small but ever increasing group who were struggling to free themselves from the bonds of precedents that were moribund and out of step with modern life. Today we look back, with well justified shudders, at many of those so very earnest efforts of the exponents of "art nouveau" to find the logical path in architecture. But as we look back over Saarinen's work, we find from the very beginning a sanity and restraint, and an unfailing intelligence and good taste that fit him to be looked up to as a great leader of this school.

* * *

The most vital characteristic of Saarinen's work his feeling for material and logical construction. This undoubtedly has its basis in the fact that in his education he worked at times as a practical builder, as a bricklayer and carpenter. He exemplifies the craftsman-architect in his love and understanding of texture. In the Chicago Tribune design, his immediate grasp of the spirit of steel construction for the tall building is little short of astounding. As a writer pointed out at ▶

Rendering by Adolf Loos for the Tribune Tower, Chicago, 1922.

Many of the competition designs attempted in varied, often fanciful ways to fool the eye into seeing the skyscraper as small and intimate in scale. Many were attempts to rationalize the skyscraper as a column or an obelisk; one of the most striking was an Egyptian fantasy. Very few of the designs reflect any awareness of or respect for Chicago and its designs of the 1880's and 1890's, and most of the architects who showed any awareness of Sullivan and Wright were Europeans.

Compare the window designs in the Gropius drawing at far right with those in the Schlesinger and Mayer Store. In turn compare this drawing with the later Battery City design on page 227 and the Majestic Apartments pictured on page 254. Many of the competition drawings influenced future architecture, not just Saarinen's.

opposite: Walter Gropius & Adolf Mayer's sketch for the Tribune Tower, Chicago, 1922.

our American architects, that so largely invalidates such works, and groups them as ephemera. But the design of the Finlander, Master of Ideas, is based upon substantial grounds, and therefore it lives within the domain of the enduring.

Second Surprise: That a "foreigner" should possess the insight required to penetrate to the depths of the sound, strong, kindly and aspiring idealism which lies at the core of the American people: one day to make them truly great sons of Earth; and that he should possess the poet's power to interpret and to proclaim in deep sympathy and understanding, incarnate in edifice rising from Earth in response to this faith, an inspiring symbol to endure.

Why did the men behind The Tribune throw this priceless pearl away?

Would that one might say words of similar nature, if less fervent, for the unfortunate first prize; but it is the business of this review to make a searching psychological analysis and summary of the two designs, as *types*, in order that the heavy of eye may see revealed the architectural art as a vast beneficent power, lying now in continental sleep, ready, ever ready, to be awakened by Masters of Ideas, who shall affirm its reality in eloquence of form.

Then shall we become articulate as a people; for to reveal one art is to reveal all arts, all aspirations, all hopes; and the substantial ground of it all shall arise from out our timid faith in man—a faith patient and long suffering under the superstitious tyranny of insane ideas. But once let the beckoning finger of the Free Spirit be seen in the open, and a voice heard that saith: Arise; come unto me, for I am Life—then will that timorous faith come forth inquiringly, and in the glow of the Free Spirit grow strong. The Ego of our Land shall thus find its own; for Man shall find Man. Why, therefore, deal in trivialities? Why inquire, with spectacles on nose, why this or that dewdad should he thus or so?

Confronted by the limpid eye of analysis, the first prize trembles and falls, self-confessed, crumbling to the ground. Visibly it is

not architecture in the sense herein expounded. Its formula, is literary: words, words, words. It is an imaginary structure—not imaginative. Starting with false premise, it was doomed to false conclusion, and it is clear enough, moreover, that the conclusion was the real premise, the mental process in reverse of appearance. The predetermination of a huge mass of imaginary masonry at the top very naturally required the appearance of huge imaginary masonry piers reaching up from the ground to give imaginary support. Such weird process of reasoning is curious. It savors of the nursery where children bet imaginary millions. Is it possible that its author in his heart of hearts, or his head of heads, really believed that bathos and power are synonyms? It looks that way. It also looks like the output of a mind untrained in the mastery of ideas, in the long discipline of realities and the test of substantial grounds. It looks also like the wandering of a mind unaccustomed to distinguish between architecture and scene painting. This design, this imaginary building, this simulacrum, is so helpless, so defenseless when brought face to face with mastery of ideas and validity of grounds, that it is cruel to go on, for analysis is now becoming vivisection, unless we recognize the palpable effect of self-hypnotism. This is not to say that the individual who made the first-prize design did not believe he had a great idea. Certainly he believed it, otherwise he would not have taken himself so seriously. Such seriousness prevented him from seeing the humor of it, from seeing something funny and confiding. If the monster on top with its great long legs reaching far below to the ground could be gently pried loose, the real building would reveal itself as a rather amiable and delicate affair with a certain grace of fancy. And even so, it could be but as a foundling at the doorstep of the Finn—for it seems they breed strong men in Finland.

So much for the present, concerning the second and the first prize.

Our attention now shall concentrate upon The Tribune. By "The Tribune" is here meant, not alone printed white paper, but incisively the men behind its screen, who stand for ownership and control. These men made a solemn promise to the world. Why did they renege? Individually and jointly they made a triple promise—as set forth above—as members of the Jury of Award. A design setting forth the most beautiful conception of a lofty office building that has been evolved by the fertile mind of man, was presented squarely to them at the last moment. Were they frightened? Why did they welch? Did it come upon them as a ghost, an apparition—a revelation most unwelcome at a time when everything seemed nicely settled? Was this vision as trebly disconcerting as the remembered triple-promise, arising now also as a confronting ghost—the two ghosts standing side by side—likewise the two designs, in material form, standing side by side?

For no choice can exist without motive. Men are both revealed and betrayed by their acts. For men's acts show forth their inmost thoughts—no matter what their speech may be. Man can create solely in the image of his thought; for thoughts are living things—words may dissemble. In men's acts alone is the reality of their thought to be sought and found—there is no hiding place secure against the tracking searcher. In the same sense the two competing drawings are acts. Each clearly reveals the thought of its responsible author. Each sets forth the materials of a drawing, presented as a symbol of an edifice to be, the power or the frailty of the thought within.

No manipulation of words or felicity of phrasing can screen from view the act of the Jury of Award, or the dominating will of one or more of its personnel. The final choice is most obviously an act of dominion—of brutal will. For, to cast aside, with the sop of a money prize, the surpassing work of a "foreigner" of high distinction and thorough discipline in executed works, was an act of savagery in private, regardless of how neatly, how sweetly, thereafter, the man may have been shown the door, as a parting and an honored guest, as one whose presence lit the house had indeed triply honored his host.

Thus vanished from sight The Tribune's bow in the cloud.

Its act has deprived the world of a shining mark, denied it a monument to beauty, to faith, to courage and to hope. Deprived an expectant world of that Romance for which it hungers, and had hoped to receive. "It cannot be reiterated too emphatically that the primary objective of *The Chicago Tribune* in instituting this Competition is to secure the design for a structure distinctive and imposing—the most beautiful office building in the world." ∎

the time, he designed in steel forms covered by masonry, whereas our architects had worked in masonry stiffened by steel.

After the Tribune Building competition, Saarinen came to this country to accept a professorship in the Architectural School of the University of Michigan. His recent connection with the Cranbrook School as architect is giving even wider range to his abilities, and promises still more opportunity to influence American design. The Cranbrook school, magnificently endowed by Mr. George G. Booth of Detroit, gives full play to Saarinen's powers as the craftsman-architect. Established with his family in a studio at Cranbrook, he is assisted by Geza Maroti, the sculptor painter of Budapest, in the creation of buildings for the school. The young men who study under him will eventually contribute to the design. Here we have the prospect of a school which, under Saarinen's influence, will teach a new appreciation for craftsmanship in architecture, a feeling for material, truthful construction, and above all, a real alliance between architecture and the allied arts.

Already Saarinen, through the second prize design for the Tribune tower, has had enormous influence on our architecture. He pointed the way, and gave the most artistic solution to the problem set by modern conditions. It remains to be seen whether the influence of this design and other creative efforts by Saarinen can produce a lasting impression on an age which everywhere is turning to a general adoption of modernist forms. As a brilliant designer who combines a striving for characteristic functional expression with an attitude of independence of historic forms, Eliel Saarinen stands quite alone. In style he belongs to no country but rather to the spirit of the times. •

American Radiator Building, New York City, Hood & Fouilhoux, architects, 1924.

The bold coloration of this design prompted a rare full-color image as a frontispiece to the May 1924 issue (architecture continued to be presented in monochrome for many years to come). Georgia O'Keefe later immortalized the structure in her dramatic painting *American Radiator Building— Night, New York*. The delineator Hugh Ferriss said of the building in 1929, "It has probably provoked more arguments among laymen on the subject of architectural values than any other structure in the country." The design bears a striking similarity to Eliel Saarinen's drawing on page 198.

opposite: Equitable Building, New York City, Ernest R. Graham, architect, 1915–16.
  Though only the fifth largest building in New York at the time, the Equitable was the world's largest in terms of area (1.2 million square feet in slightly under an acre). It is a popularly held belief that the boxy structure prompted the 1916 zoning law. The dates are actually coincidental, since the law had already been years in the planning. The new law limited a building's size as it mounted skywards, so canyons such as the one pictured on page 87 would no longer be possible. The familiar set-back form was a response to the regulations.

The ARCHITECTVRAL RECORD

VOLUME 55   MAY, 1924   NUMBER 5

The AMERICAN RADIATOR BUILDING NEW YORK CITY
RAYMOND M. HOOD, ARCHITECT

By Harvey Wiley Corbett [1]

H AS NOT ARCHITECTURE usually reflected the spirit of its time? The pyramids of Egypt, for example, characterize an age of human toil. Mighty, impressive, vast, enduring throughout the centuries, they are an unchanging memorial to physical debasement. We can almost see the lash curling over the backs of generation after generation of men who built them. No revivified parchments can as vividly reveal the atmosphere of early Egypt, the concentration of supreme power among rulers and the abasement of the many. Yet the pyramids are useless, serving no good purpose to humanity except as relics of departed Pharaohs add new light to historical research. These mountains of stone point to no helpful course in making life easier nor have they advanced the welfare of the human throng.

Beneath the surface of their intellectual accomplishments, and not so far beneath at that, the Romans still possessed the savagery of the semi-civilized man. And we have the arena. They were much given to public debate—and we see the forum.

Mahommed, with visions of a radiant deity so effulgent that his brilliance would have blinded the uncovered eye, inspired millions of the worshippers of Allah with dreams of world conquest and visions of the paradise to come, and the domed mud huts of Arabia became domed palaces of worship, great mosques which were to set their architectural impress upon the Christian world.

It is of course obvious that the architecture of different epochs has been modified by available building materials, by tools, machines, and methods. Granting that, it is proper to inquire whether architecture does not go further and represent the characteristic sentiment and spirit of each age. The answer seems to be supplied by the architecture of the past.

Something more than building methods and materials is revealed in the pyramids, in the forum, in the rugged simplicity of early American colonial architecture whose sturdy quality seems to typify the spirit of the Pilgrim.

THE NEW YORK ZONING RESOLUTION AND ITS INFLUENCE UPON DESIGN
John Taylor Boyd, Jr.
Vol. XLVIII, No. 3, September, 1920, pp. 192-217.

FOUR years' trial has proved the value of the New York Zoning Resolution of 1916. By adopting this measure New York City put into practice principles new to the planning of American cities. Fundamentally, the effects of the law are two: It safeguards the interests of the city and of adjacent property owners in the location and in the design of all buildings; it organizes the city into a coherent, highly developed system of districts or neighborhoods, in which each district unit is clearly defined, and its character maintained by the provisions of the law.

Quite different is this conception of a city from older notions prevailing in America. Both in law, and in fact, our cities are huge, formless masses of streets and blocks, sprawling over areas of geography, none too well accommodated to conditions of topography. Their maps develop haphazardly, without any rational control, in whatever ways irresponsible private interests dictate—usually in deeper confusion as the ▶

1 Harvey Wiley Corbett (1873–1954) was a leading defender of skyscrapers and increased urban density in the 1920s. He wrote extensively on the impact of the zoning law of 1916 and offered futuristic proposals for multilevel traffic separation and pedestrian bridges. Among the many skyscrapers that he designed was the widely acclaimed Bush Tower, which housed his offices in its top two stories. The firm was renamed Corbett, Harrison, and MacMurray after his first partner's retirement in 1928, and later became Harvey Wiley Corbett Associates. (See Rockefeller Center page 272, and Metropolitan Life Insurance Co. page 276).

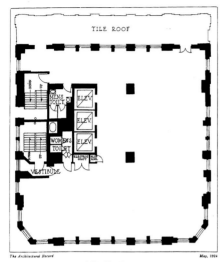

The Architectural Record   May, 1924

Twelfth to Fifteenth Floor Plan
AMERICAN RADIATOR BUILDING, NEW YORK CITY
Raymond M. Hood, Architect

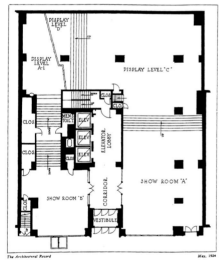

The Architectural Record   May, 1924

First Floor Plan
AMERICAN RADIATOR BUILDING, NEW YORK CITY
Raymond M. Hood, Architect

We pass to the present age in America and we inquire, "What is the prevalent atmosphere? What is the dominant characteristic?" It is my belief that when all answers are exhausted we shall find that most persons will describe our present trend as industrial. We are a commercial people. We have come to the brink of a great mechanical era. Our modern civilization, in contrast with that of the Pharaohs, is founded upon the idea of service to the many. The mainspring of that service is advertising, by which commodities, works and services of all sorts are sold to the many. Advertising, exploitation, publicity, by whatever name you call it, is the force that results in distribution. It is the animating agency behind the commercial age. Only through this dominant force in distribution, whether it be conveyed by printed page, by word of mouth, by radio, or other means do the products of commercialism live.

It would be strange indeed if architecture were not influenced by this spirit, particularly in the United States where architects have evolved a type of building—the city skyscraper—so daring, so virile that there is nothing else like it in the world. It stands unique among edifices. It proclaims to all the triumph of industrial efficiency. It came into being, new, startling, radical, the spontaneous expression of great industry serving the many. Because it is new and spontaneous, free from the indurating touch of blindly followed precedent; because it is away from the orthodox, one may look for its variations in the hope that still new trails will be blazed.

I should like to inquire whether the American Radiator Building does not seem to fall into this class? A great black structure with yellow trimmings, now almost completed, does it not seem to express the spirit of commercialism? It is self advertising. It has been condemned and applauded, talked about and discussed. "What American Radiator Building" is the answer. And by that answer the first principles of commercialism, advertising, has been served.

Comment upon the new building has

been sharply divided. "It is a starling departure in color scheme," says one. "The building as a whole gives the impression of a soft black mass, the windows of which blend with the wall. It looks strong and formidable, throwing out a characteristic atmosphere of endurance and power. It is in keeping with the many sudden changes of modern architecture, I am inclined to believe you will find many who will like it after it is finished, and they have become used to it."

Perhaps it is too early to express an opinion on the American Radiator Building. Present criticism is apt to be either too severe, or to fall short in the direction of according the praise that the building deserves or will deserve. It is true that the artificially treated brick gives a uniform

The Architectural Record   May, 1924
Roof and Pent House Plan
AMERICAN RADIATOR BUILDING, NEW YORK CITY
Raymond M. Hood, Architect

black such as you would probably not find had uncolored black material been selected. The face of a black cliff is not uniformly black. The rocks have been weathered by age. Nature has produced a variation from absolute uniformity. But it is quite possible that the new building may weather with age to produce a most interesting and beautiful effect.

One should be slow to criticize the exercise of the free imagination which soars without restraint of the conventions of the past. We never know whether its outcome may not result in a new form of art. Condemn the new simply because it is new, and you are lost. If commercialism is the guiding spirit of the age, the building which advertises itself is in harmony with that spirit. As an advertisement, I consider the building a magnificent success. It is a triumph of commercialism. There is no reason why the term "commercialism" should ever be considered as opposed to art. Perhaps a new type of commercial architecture will be developed. Perhaps architecture will make a great forward step in interpreting commercialism in its new and higher relation to human welfare. There are many civilizations which have left little impress upon humanity and their architecture has faded from human favor. The style at Quirigua, Guatemala, symbolizing the rule of priests of the Sun and kings combined into the one office, over the vanished civilization of the Mayas, have left no trace except a calendar, no other milestone on the road of human welfare. But commercialism in its present significance spells gradual freedom and liberty for the average man.

After all, why should we not have black buildings? Or red, green, blue, carnation or prismatic? Who knows but that beautiful effects may be achieved by experimenting in color schemes in modern American cities? The Arabs captured the sunrise to color the drab dwellings of Djeddah, Mecca, and Medina, and when they finished the job, the world applauded. We can imagine that the first Arab was criticized. In any event—he started something. ■

complexity of modern life increases, and generating as they grow discomfort, demoralization, and economic loss.

The street system of itself brings no real organization into a city. With its units of blocks, the street system is nothing more than a scheme of measurement in the city plan, except as it forms part of the transportation system. The truth of this assertion becomes clearer if one compares the plan of a city with the plan of a building. If the floor plan of a building were left as an open space, and if its area were then marked off into a series of small squares, the building would be "planned" like most modern cities. A building has an effective plan only when its floor area is divided clearly into separate but related spaces, each carefully arranged and dimensioned to suit the purposes for which the building is used. So, likewise, a city becomes an organized, efficient structure, only when it is arranged by districts, each of which is a carefully defined unit serving a definite purpose. And, since a city cannot be divided into units by walls, its neighborhoods must be set off from one another by law, and by law its character must be prescribed through requiring that all the buildings that are erected within the bounds of each district conform to the standards established for the district. In a word, one may compare this new conception of a city with the older one by saying that older ideas picture the city as a kind of fungus, in which the street and block system are the cells ~ while the new ideal created by the Zoning Resolution conceives it to be a mechanism of related parts, or units, in the shape of neighborhoods.

The break in ideas is evident in the working out of the zoning scheme. The districts were established by classifying them into types. The types were deter- ▶

mined not at all arbitrarily, but only after a long study which, at the time that it was made, impressed people by its breadth, its thoroughness, and its practical and scientific accuracy. As a result of this investigation, the legal neighborhoods which are formed by the Zoning Resolution correspond closely to the physical characteristics of the neighborhoods as they existed—some of them vaguely defined—at the time of passage of the resolution. The physical characteristics of the neighborhoods are chiefly their area of streets and blocks, and types of buildings, and, even more important, their local social and economic organization.

But it should not be thought that the character of these neighborhoods was fixed solely upon their local aspects; the process of zoning also covered the city as a whole and took account of all its many factors of co-ordination. In the resulting scheme, the block system is but the unit of measurement, and recently it is coming to be thought of as the proper unit of housing in apartments. Thus the century-old block sub-division into lots 25 by 100 feet promises to become obsolete. This relationship of housing to city planning was treated in the two preceding issues of the Architectural Record under the title of "Garden Apartments in Cities."

But, important as zoning is, its organization of a city into a mechanism of districts is not the whole of city planning. City planning has come to mean in recent years a multitude of activities, and its field has expanded until it includes most of the aspects of city life. The relationships of these other aspects to zoning

deserve a brief notice.

City planning may be said to have both a mechanical and a non-mechanical side. The mechanical side includes the familiar activities of engineering, sanitation, the street system and transportation. On the non-mechanical side there are the human relationships, taking form in countless ways, but principally in the fields of law, political administration, economics and social organization. Together, all this variety of factors tends to create a tangle of interests, which hitherto has foiled attempts to unravel it. The confusion has bred in some quarters an attitude of hopelessness toward the problems of the modern business city. Many observers have pronounced the task of organizing a city to be impossible, and they can see at best but a method of haphazard day-to-day meeting of difficulties as they arise.

The zoning principle definitely repudiates this muddle-through method of city organization. Zoning is only another factor of the mechanical side of city planning; and housing is still another new department to be added to those of engineering, sanitation and transportation. Now when we view this mechanical side of city planning as a whole, it would seem as if a significant truth in regard to it becomes apparent. That is, the mechanical activities of a city function more efficiently, and reach higher standards than do the non-mechanical activities of political administration and of social and economic relationships. These latter, every one knows, are the dark part of modern business cities. Consequently, in view of the contrast, may not the essential need of a city be to regard it as a structure and as a mechanism of city planning and engineering and of architecture; and then to plan and to construct it soundly on this basis? If that be done, the political and social side of the city, with all its human relationships, might become more wholesome. There might then be less confusion and disagreement and partisanship. It would seem as if many of the troubles of city life were debated on the wrong premises. Energies are wasted in a conflict of isms and ologies, when the real cause may be discomfort, due to faults in the mechanical structure. The civic organization can hardly function properly in a city if the city is not planned to accommodate it, any more than a business organization can be efficient if it operates in a building that has not been planned to suit its needs.

When these broader relationships of zoning in the city plan are thus understood, one will more easily appreciate the technical operation of its principles. It should be said that the

law itself is intricate in its workings, because it deals with the intricate conditions of New York real estate. These in turn reflect both the divided topography of the Port of New York and of the surrounding lands, and also the complex, growing, ever changing character of the modern business city. For these reasons, taking a specific example, the particular technical details of the law which deal with heights of buildings are much more involved than the corresponding building regulations of certain European cities like Paris. Paris is a city of a long history of steady, slow growth, which has been carefully planned and controlled for generations. Also, Paris is not a center of commerce like New York, and it is not to any extent industrial. The Paris restrictions are rigorous and simple in application; and they enforce aesthetic principles, because they recognize that a beatitiful city has value, even commercially.

* * *

The Liggett Building, * as it is coming to be called, is in process of construction on the corner of Madison Avenue and Forty-second Street. The key to the success of this building lies—as in most triumphs of architecture—in its plan. It will be noted that most of these structures illustrated are planned solid, without a center light court. Under the zoning restrictions, such a court would be very large; and, if it made the plan of the building a hollow square, the great area needed for the service features of corridors, lobbies, elevators, stairs, toilets, etc., which bring in no rent, would be subtracted from the desirable space along the outside wall. But, by building the plan solid, these service features are placed in the center, where the space is not well lighted and is hence not rentable for offices. This arrangement makes not only an efficient plan, but, in the upper stories, it has the great merit of facilitating the beautiful setbacks in terraces and towers. In the Liggett Building, for example, the fine central tower—which is the making of the design of the exterior—could never have been constructed over a center court.

The illustration showing the perspective of this structure indicates that it should be one of the most effective buildings in New York. Such distinction in mass, outline and detail, if carried into all architecture, would make the business districts of American cities beautiful not only in respect to individual buildings, but considered from the aspect of each street as a whole. They would furnish an extraordinary picture where the building masses would harmonize by virtue of the cornice line of the first setback coming on the same level, forming thus a vast terrace, above which would rise a wonderful array of minor terraces, pavilions, loggias, roofs, dormers, turrets, towers, all pyramiding into the sky. New York might vie with ancient Rome of the seven hills, but in a different way, in a character entirely its own. Such is the possible effect of the zoning principle, and how different it is from the present collection of crude cubical masses that poke their harsh, gaunt outlines into the sky, without any harmony of one building to another, blunt, angular objects that no skill in design or in details can redeem or else conceal. I believe that the reader will admit that this picture of the ugliness of American cities is not exaggerated. It is true, here and there the imagination of the architect and the appreciation of an owner have created a building that shows artistry in its mass and outline: but such exceptions are rare, and they occur mostly when a building resembles the form of a tower. The beauty of these towers suffers from the proximity of bulkier structures. Even the tower of the Woolworth Building is somewhat marred by the two low, boxlike wings beside it. Had the Woolworth Building been erected after the passage of the Zoning Resolution, Mr. Cass Gilbert would not have let pass the opportunity thus offered of modelling the lower wings in setbacks and terraces, so that their form and outlines would have harmonized better with the design of the tower. On the whole, it is fair to say that most of the tall buildings of New York antedating the Zoning Resolution are failures architecturally, in spite of the ingenuity which their architects have lavished on them, trying vainly to overcome their blocky mass. Such beautiful effects as one sees are due either to isolated towers or to occasional picturesque effects of groupings or perspectives which are purely accidental. Of such is the famous spectacle of the buildings in the financial district of lower Manhattan, where the ugly blocks of the bulky buildings cannot be distinguished from the silhouette of the mass, with outline of the whole group accented here and there by the tall towers of the Woolworth, the Singer and the Bankers' Trust buildings. And if New York is afflicted with many ugly tall buildings, what shall be said of other cities, whose picture shows two or three or a half dozen colossal, crude, block-line structures poking up at intervals above low buildings into the sky, without shape or proportion, unrelated to each other—about as beautiful and as inspiring as a collection of packing cases on a sidewalk. Quantity is not quality, and vast size of itself is not a recipe for beautiful architecture.

On the other hand, one should not make the mistake of concluding that the Zoning Resolution of itself creates beautiful buildings. It merely offers the architect an opportunity to prove his ability. As stated above, the law is based on economic and sanitary factors, and does not directly take account of aesthetic values. If the desire for fine architecture appears to be growing in New York City, that is due to the spirit of the owners of these tall buildings, and to the architects, who are slowly persuading the public of the truth that fine architecture has definite value in a commercial building. Therefore, the effect of the Zoning Resolution is to offer the architect a geometrical shell which is based almost solely on sanitary and financial considerations. If the architect proceeds to fill this shell with a building, he will find that the result has no form or proportion or symmetry of outline. It is his duty to model within the limits of the legal shell a beautiful building. In the process he may even find it necessary to persuade the owner to sacrifice a bit of space here and there in order to achieve his design.

Such was the method employed in the Liggett Building. The fine symmetry of its upper stories is not prescribed by the law, which would enforce only two setbacks, those in the streets. The setbacks have been carried around the other two sides, where a small amount of space was sacrificed beyond the requirement of the law in order to gain the effect. The owners thus viewed the project broadly, carrying the same fine appreciation into details, with concessions here and there to design, yet at the same time mindful of the necessary limitations of cost of a business structure. For instance, they objected to the use of metal spandrels between the windows, which, painted black, made possible the fine vertical lines of the front, but approved the making of these spandrels in black terra cotta. The owners, on their own initiative, installed marble wainscots in the corridors of all floors. I cite these details to show the broad point of view that governs the design of these great buildings, and how even present costs do not prevent people from obtaining fine architecture.

Some further features of the design of this Liggett Building are of interest. In the elevations, factors of design and cost are finely adjusted. Brick was used effectively instead of more expensive materials, and the blending of color promises to be one of the best features of the upper stories. In the two lowest floors, the big motive of glass and metal is a hold device in design, forming a fine, strong base to the whole building, and yielding the maximum space for the show windows of the stores. This is a far better solution than the usual thin, long lines of stone, wide apart, that cover the steel points of support, a very weak looking effect indeed.

* * *

All in all, New York may look forward to the day when these giant structures shall be completed, when they shoulder their tops of terraced and pyloned masses high above the skyline of the city, into the brilliant light of the sky in America. At times, when the wind is from the north and the atmosphere is crystal, these vast shapes will jut up gaunt and stark, every line and detail revealed, as if cut from steel, naked in the cold blinding glare. But on other days, when the wind comes off the sea, from the east or south, tingeing the light with a faint mellowness or mist, then the towers will stand in a thinnest dazzling veil of atmosphere, their soaring outlines melting ever so slightly into the blue sky, their vast flanks streaming with sunshine. In this softer, slightly golden illumination they may have something of the harmony and mystery and illusion that brings the final quality of art into architecture.

These new skyscrapers will be the visible symbols of the Zoning Resolution. But one should not forget that they are but the crowning dramatic feature of the deep-lying new purpose of the modern business city of its new structural organization. The Zoning Resolution is the basic step in city planning; the new city planning that aims to bring order, coherence and coordination into city life. The older conception of a city as a formless, unrelated mass of blocks, growing as it will, tied together by the system of streets, developing haphazardly—this no longer serves the purpose. In New York this idea of a fungus has now given way to an organization of well defined units of districts and neighborhoods, carefully co-ordinated to the plan of the whole city. Such is its theory, and New York came to accept it as a matter of self-preservation. ●

* Liggett-Winchester-Ley Corporation Building (opposite), New York City, Carrère & Hastings, and R.H. Shreve, consulting architects.

7 Lessons Soon Forgotten: The Passing of a Prophet

Louis Sullivan was, and still is, a powerful force to reckon with. He was called a prophet, the only architect to have solved the so-called skyscraper problem. And, as many a prophet before him, he was quickly ignored and soon forgotten. Never by Montgomery Schuyler, incidentally, who wrote in 1912:

"There is no denying that a new work of Louis Sullivan is the most interesting event which can happen in the American architectural world to-day. There has been nothing like the professional interest which his works inspire since Richardson ceased to produce, a quarter of a century ago. The succession of Richardson's works was indeed followed with more of professional attention, and for an obvious reason. The architectural profession meaning a large majority of the active and ambitious practitioners of architecture, attended to the series of works which Richardson produced during the decade to which his professional activity and conspicuousness were confined, for the purpose of imitating, or at least of applying them in their own practice, in so far as they were imitable or applicable, and often further. The interest was thus selfish and practical, as well as disinterested and artistic. But Mr. Sullivan has few imitators. His "school" consists of a few disciples only, of one only whose discipleship has produced very noticeable or memorable works."

Among those who failed to appreciate or had forgotten Sullivan altogether was Claude Bragdon, who notes in his autobiography in 1938:

"I confess to being as unalive to Sullivan's essential rightness as were most of my colleagues, and it is one of the regrets of my life that the perception of it should have come so slowly and so late. In the course of time I came to the realization that he alone of us all was honest, and I said so, in an article I wrote about him in *House and Garden*. This led to an interchange of letters, and thereafter whenever my business or desires took me to Chicago, we met." [see below]

In the last few years before Sullivan's death, Bragdon and co-protegé Frank Lloyd Wright, would take up many of his themes, and by 1922, his public credibility

Wainwright Building, St. Louis
Adler and Sullivan, architects, 1890–92

had revived. Ironically, but not surprising, it was Sullivan's death two years later that finally restored interest in him and his ideas.

Frank Lloyd Wright began his career as "Sullivan's pencil" in the Chicago offices of Adler and Sullivan in 1887. As Wright tells it, the only one with a greater gift of prophecy than Sullivan was himself:

> "When he brought in the board with the motive of the Wainwright Building outlined in profile and in scheme upon it and threw it down on my table, I was perfectly aware of what had happened. This was Louis Sullivan's greatest moment his greatest effort. The "skyscraper," as a new thing beneath the sun, an entity with virtue, individuality and beauty all its own, was born." [56:1 Jul 1924 p 29]

It's hagiography to be sure, but with real impact on the *official story*. In fact, following his death, Sullivan was *resurrected, canonized,* and *enthroned* in the highest place of honor in the history of 20th Century American architecture.

Lewis Mumford meanwhile, took a more sober view of the man. He saw Sullivan as "one of the hardest figures to place in American architecture, though his distinction and his creativity are indisputable." Mumford was particularly disturbed by the strident tone of his writings:

> "Sullivan's *Kindergarten Chats*, which had a long underground reputation before being republished...show him at his best and his worst: the Wagnerian prose is often perfervid and bombastic; his attitude toward his interlocutor, a student, is unpleasantly superior and over-authoritative; nuggets of pure gold in criticism and in interpretation are often buried in rhetorical mud. His *Autobiography of an Idea* holds perhaps the best of his writings; and the student who seeks to come close to him would do well to begin with this work." [*Roots of American Architecture*, ed. Lewis Mumford, 1952, pp.432–3]

The myth aside, what *was* Sullivan's contribution exactly? Claude Bragdon saw stagnation in skyscraper design as early as 1890, where all an architect did "was to divide the façade vertically and horizontally into manageable units by means of columns, pilasters, entablatures, string courses—sometimes squeezing in a pediment for good measure—and to crown the whole with a cornice...

> "Sullivan swept away all these ridiculous conventions at a single stroke. What, he asks, is the dominant characteristic of the tall building? Its *tallness*: the force of altitude must be in it. Let it be therefore 'a proud and soaring thing, without a dissenting line from bottom to top.' Looking further, he discovers that an office building has two functions: that of providing stores,...and above these numberless offices,...well and equally lighted. Each of these functions necessitates a different form, which, rightly determined, will in turn express the function—as in the case of any natural organism. Accordingly, on the ground floor level he provided broad display windows...thrust forward to the very building line. Above this mercantile storey (or storeys) he subdivided the wall into vertical piers separating rows of equal-sized windows. These upward-soaring piers, 'without a dissenting line from bottom to top,' he terminated in an unconventionally designed cornice—for even Sullivan never emancipated himself from the idea that a building must necessarily have a cornice.

> "Sullivan's solution of the design problem of the tall building...was so universally adopted by other architects—even by Sullivan's detractors—that the present generation does not realize the magnitude of his achievement..." [*More Lives Than One*, Claude Bragdon] ■

LOUIS H. SULLIVAN
(1856-1924)
[Obituary by A.N. Rebori]
Vol. 55, No. 6, June 1924, pp. 586-87.

Louis H. Sullivan passed away quietly on Monday, April 14, 1924, after a week's illness, of heart failure. As far as the material world is concerned, he ceased to exist some fifteen years ago. The last years of his life were spent in writing and in executing small commissions for appreciative clients.

His article on the Tribune competition, which appeared in the RECORD, expressed his creed in words which have stirred the souls of dreamers through the ages. "The craving for beauty," said Sullivan, "is imbued with romance; with that high romance, which is the essence, the vital impulse, that inheres in all the great works of man in all places and all times, that vibrates in his loftiest thoughts, his heroic deeds, his otherwise inexplicable sacrifices, and which forms the halo of his great compassions, and of the tragedy within the depths of his sorrows. So deeply seated, so persistent, so perennial in the heart of humanity is this ineffable presence that, suppressed in us, we decay and die. For man is not born to trouble as the sparks fly upward; he is born to hope and to achieve."

For the past two years Sullivan devoted himself almost entirely to writing. ▶

"After Richardson's death there was need of a new prophet in our architectural Israel, and to the eyes of a little circle of devotees in Chicago, he presently appeared in the person of Mr. Sullivan, who early developed a style of his own, which straightway became that of a number of others,...not fettered by too much knowledge—not fettered, indeed, by enough!"

Claude Bragdon Architecture in the United States I: The Birth of the Spirit, *Architectural Record* 1909.

1924

Guaranty Building, Buffalo, New York, Adler and Sullivan, architects, 1894-96

In this, the quintessential "Sullivanesque" skyscraper, the simplest forms are combined with a richness of detail and color. The red of the terra cotta was a marked break from the whiter Beaux Arts structures of the time. Frank Lloyd Wright described Sullivan's use of ornament in this building:

"...Louis H. Sullivan's exuberant, sensuous nature and brilliant imagination took terra-cotta—and it lived. It no longer asked permission of the Styles....In it this master created a grammar of ornament all his own....His ornamentation was the breath of his life. Clay came into his hand, that both might live on forever."
[63:6 Jun 1928 p 556]

The Guaranty Building was the last project of the fourteen-year Adler and Sullivan partnership.

opposite: Getty Tomb, Chicago, Louis H. Sullivan, architect, 1890.

LOUIS SULLIVAN—AN OLD MASTER
Fiske Kimball

. . . For in all their works they proceeded on definite principles of form and in ways derived from the truth of Nature. Thus they reached perfection, approving only those things which, if challenged, can be explained on grounds of truth.—Vitruvius, Book IV. Chap. ii.

IN LOUIS SULLIVAN America had a great master of realism in architecture. His achievement was not merely provincial or parochial—he belongs with a very few thinkers and designers, leaders of the scientific school of the nineteenth century: Ruskin, Viollet-le-Duc, Gottfried Semper, Otto Wagner.[1] More than to any of these, it fell to him to embody their organic theory in a creation of vital originality, deeply rooted in the new soil of modern life. Not since the genesis of Gothic construction had there been a development like that of the steel frame building, the skyscraper, to which he was the first to give artistic form.

The demand for truth and reason in architecture, the appeal to the laws of nature, is as old as Antiquity. Vitruvius,[2] the arch-villain of the modernists, expressed it, we see, in words which Sullivan himself might have written. So, too, Boileau,[3] the high-priest of French classicism, reiterated, as his central doctrine:

Rien n'est beau que par la verité,

and Voltaire wrote of his own Temple du Goût:

Simple en était la noble Architecture;
Chaque ornement á sa place arrêté,
Il semblait mis par la nécessité
L'Art s'y cachoit sous l'air de la nature;
L'oeil satisfait embrassoit sa structure,
Jamais surpris et toujours enchanté.

Each generation has been able to interpret the doctrine of truth, of obedience to nature, as the guiding principle of its own artistic strivings.

It was in the hands of Herder and Goethe[4] that the idea of relation between art and nature began to take on a modern coloring. From a model of ordered unity, for merely rational imitation, nature became the source of romantic inspiration. The artist, filled with its spirit, in impressing form on his material, accepts the practical necessities, and gives chatacteristic beauty:

. . . bis in den kleinsten Theil notwendig schön, wie Baüme Gottes.

The mid-nineteenth century, under the spell of natural science, identified beauty in painting with minute "truth to nature," and, in consonance with its biologic theory of adaptation of organic form to function and environment, emphasized onesidedly the attainment of beauty in architecture through expression of use and structure. Ruskin wrote in 1851:

"Every building presents its own requirements and difficulties; and every good building has peculiar appliances or contrivances to meet them. Understand the laws of structure, and you will feel the special difficulty in every new building which you approach. . . . And an enormous number of buildings, and of styles of buildings, you will be able to cast aside at once, as at variance with these constant laws of structure and therefore unnatural and monstrous."

Semper in 1860 crystallized the organic theory in the formulae:

"Every technical product a resultant of use and material.

"Style is the conformity of an art object with the circumstances of its origin and the conditions and circumstances of its development."

Viollet-le-Duc in his Discourses on Architecture (1863), exalted truth as the supreme merit, and said:

"There are two ways of expressing truth in architecture: it must be true according to the programme of requirements, and true according to the methods and means of construction. . . . fulfil with scrupulous exactness all the conditions imposed by necessity; . . . employ materials with due regard for their qualities and capacities."

Simultaneously, and likewise related to evolutionary theory in biology, came the interpretation of the history of art by Hegel, Taine and Schnaase[5] as a resultant of chang-

"The Autobiography of an Idea" appeared serially in The Journal of the American Institute of Architects, and has only just been published in book form. In addition to this "A System of Architectural Ornament," containing a group of exquisite drawings showing the evolution of that inimitable Sullivanesque ornament. was recently completed, proofs of which were shown to him on his deathbed. Thus, the Ornament and the Life of Sullivan have been left to us as a record for all time.

He lived long enough to see most of his buildings demolished or altered by others. Buildings are for a little while, but the idea remains forever.

In the Museé Des Arts Decoratifs, in Paris, there is a full size plaster cast of his doorway to the famous Getty Tomb. This doorway found its way to Paris as an exhibit in 1900, and was placed in the Museum to form a feature of the permanent collection of the world's works of decorative art. The French were appreciative of Sullivan's genius as far back as the Columbian Exposition, when the medal of honor for the best building at the "Great World's Fair" was awarded the Transportation Building. In Bannister Fletcher's History of Architecture is given a reproduction of the Schiller Building, now known as the Garrick Theatre, Chicago, as an example of American skyscraper architecture.

These few tokens of appreciation, coming as they do from ▶

April
1925

Auditorium Building, Chicago,
Adler & Sullivan, architects,
1887–88.

*Given the large number of references
in this article, only those not mentioned elsewhere are noted.*

1 Gottfried Semper (1803–1879),
German architect.

Otto Wagner (1841–1918),
Austrian architect; his book
Moderne Architecture was
highly influential.

2 Marcus Vitruvius Pollio
(1BC–1AD), Roman writer, engineer, and architect for the
Emperor Augustus.

3 Boileau-Despréaux, Nicola
(1636–1711), French literary critic
and poet.

4 Johann Gottfried von Herder
(1744–1803) German philosopher,
critic, and clergyman.

Johann Wolfgang von Goethe
(1749–1832), German poet,
dramatist, novelist, and scientist.

5 Georg Wilhelm Friedrich Hegel
(1770–1831) German philosopher.

Hippolyte Adolphe Taine
(1828–1893), French critic and
historian.

Carl Schnaase (1798–1875),
German historian wrote pioneering works in art history.

6 *The Innocents Abroad*, Mark
Twain, 1869.

7 Henry Van Brunt (1832–1903)
continued to receive commissions from across the country
after moving to Kansas City in
1887. The firm was chosen to
design the Electricity Building for
the Chicago World's Columbia
Exposition of 1893. He translated
Vol. II of Viollet-le-Duc's
Discourses in 1881.

ing natural and historical conditions.

The predominance of these ideas was fundamentally hostile to every survival or "revival" of historical forms, but the new principles were only gradually driven to their extreme consequences. The classic style, however rationalized, could not justify itself under them as an expression of modern uses. Ruskin still thought the way of salvation lay through Gothic. Viollet-le-Duc, in spite of his enthusiasm for the Middle Ages, came to deny "the propriety of imposing on our age any reproduction of antique or mediaeval art." Semper announced that "the solution of modern problems must be freely developed from the premises given by modernity." He was, himself, however, still content to do his work with historical elements; and Viollet-le-Duc's attempts to deduce new architectural forms from the sporadic employment of iron in construction had little success. They were too purely cerebral, too little felt. We must recognize, also, that the problems and materials currently offered to the designer in 1870 had not yet changed enough from those of previous centuries, or yet crystallized enough, to give sufficient basis for a revolutionary change of forms.

A new continent, a new society, a new community, was needed for the realization of modernist ideas. In America commercialism, industrial society, developed unrestrained. Patriotic motives added the call for in "American style" to the more general demand for a "modern style."

In the eighties, while the East sought to assimilate itself to cultivated Europe, the West gloried in the American "innocence" exaggerated by Mark Twain.[6] A conjunction especially favorable existed in Chicago. The great fire left a tabula rasa—all was to be made new. For once there was an opportunity for young men in that most difficult and responsible of arts, where the "younger men" are usually past fifty. On the active and independent spirits who were attracted to the city, the ideas of Viollet-le-Duc and Semper made a deep impression. Van Brunt[7] of Kansas City had translated the "Dis-

courses"; John Root in 1889 was to publish excerpts from Semper's work. The Western Association of Architects was founded, with pronounced modern tendencies; a new journal, The Western Architect, gave its sponsors a voice and an audience. There was a ferment of discussion, experiment, and emulation.

In the unregulated commercial exploitation of urban land, a new type was just coming into being, the tall office building. It is a common fallacy to suppose that it was evoked by conditions peculiar to New York, by the circumstance that Manhattan is an island. The enormous preponderance of low buildings on Manhattan, even today, teaches us that the cause lay rather in the absence of legal restriction on the development of preferred sites. It could operate even more freely in the rebuilding of Chicago. Out of the Chicago ferment came the decisive structural invention—first used by William Holabird in the Tacoma Building[8]—the riveted steel frame, carrying the enclosing walls as well as the floors. This frame must be encased for protection against fire. How might its indispensable presence be expressed? How might the monstrous, unprecedented pile be given artistic form?

In Louis Sullivan, Chicago found its poet. Half French, half Irish, he had the analytical mind of a scientist, the soul of a dreamer and artist. Overflowing with romantic enthusiasm for Nature, dazzled by the logical splendor of mathematics, fascinated by Taine and Darwin,[9] abased before the titanic creative power of Michelangelo, he had passed rapidly through the discipline of school and of the Beaux-Arts—assimilating, questioning, feeling. At seventeen enamored of Chicago, its energy, its wide horizons of lake and prairie; at twenty-five already established in a position to build his air-castles; at thirty he was a prophet to youth, in lyrical outbursts of rushing words, enveloping an authentic philosophy.

Among the architects of our day, whose expressed notions are apt to be the *disjecta membra*[10] of inconsistent systems, his aesthetic had an intuitive harmony and value, under "the dominant, all-pervading thought that a spontaneous and vital art must come fresh from nature, and can only thus come." The artist is "to arrest and typify in materials the harmonious and interblended rhythms of nature and humanity." To him reason and analysis are not all; structure but the first step.

"It would appear to be a law of artistic growth, that the mind, in its effort toward expression, concentrates first upon matters of technical detail, next upon certain abstractions or theories-for the great part mechanical, and quite plausible as far as they go—and at last upon a gradual relinquishment of these, involving a slow and beautiful blending of all other faculties with the more subtle manifestations of emotion."

Sensitive, passionate, and courageous, he illustrates in his own career that:

"To the master mind . . . imbued with the elemental significance of nature's moods, humbled before the future and the past, keenly aware of the present, art and its outworkings are largely tragic."

Sullivan's early work, like the work of Root,[11] and so many others of less genius, was colored by Richardson's influence. The treatment of the Auditorium Building (1886-90), with its masonry walls and arches, was suggested by Richardson's design for the Field wholesale store, made in 1885. From Richardson also must have come the first suggestion of the foliate ornament which Sullivan afterwards developed so characteristically, and which flowered especially in the Golden Doorway of the Transportation Building at the Chicago Fair and in the Schlesinger and Mayer store. On the completion of the vast auditorium enterprise followed a breakdown, recuperation, a long communing with nature, a gathering of new forces. The return to Chicago in March, 1890, marks the opening of Sullivan's great creative period.

His first problem was the novel one of the steel-frame office building. "He felt at once that the new form of engineering was revolutionary, demanding an equally revolutionary architectural mode. That masonry con-

struction, in so far as tall buildings were concerned, was a thing of the past, to be forgotten, that the mind might be free to face and solve new problems in new functional forms. That the old idea of superimposition must give way before the sense of vertical continuity." So he wrote in his autobiography a generation later. The Wainwright Building in St. Louis, designed before the close of the year, was the perfect embodiment of this idea. With the taller Guaranty (Prudential) Building in Buffalo, completed 1896, in which the same system is developed and perfected, it represents Sullivan's greatest achievement.

His own interpretation, "The Tall Office Building Artistically Considered," appeared in *Lippincott's Magazine* for March, 1896. Here was formulated most briefly and clearly his whole philosophy of art:

"It is my belief that it is of the very essence of every problem that it contains and suggests its own solution. This I believe to be natural law. Let us examine, then, carefully the elements, let us search out this contained suggestion, this essence of the problem.

"The practical conditions are, broadly speaking, these:

"Wanted—First, a story below-ground, containing boilers, engines of various sorts, etc.—in short, the plant for power, heating, lighting, etc. Second, a ground floor, so called, devoted to stores, banks, or other establishments requiring large area, ample spacing, ample light, and great freedom of access. Third, a second story readily accessible by stairways—this space usually in large subdivisions, with corresponding liberality in structural spacing and in expanse of glass and breadth of external openings. Fourth, above this an indefinite number of stories of offices piled tier upon tier, one tier just like another tier, one office just like all the other offices—an office being similar to a cell in a honeycomb, merely a compartment, nothing more. Fifth and last, at the top of this pile is placed a space or a story that, as related to the life and usefulness of the structure, is purely physiological in its nature—namely,

from:
LOUIS H. SULLIVAN—HIS WORK
Frank Lloyd Wright
Vol. 56, No. 1, July 1924, pp. 28-32.

* * *

Until Louis Sullivan showed the way the masses of the tall buildings were never a complete whole in themselves. They were ugly, harsh aggregates with no sense of unity, fighting tallness instead of accepting it. What unity those masses now have, that pile up toward New York and Chicago skies, is due to the Master-mind that first perceived one as a harmonious unit—its height triumphant.

The Wainwright Building cleared the way and to this day remains the master key to the skyscraper as a matter of architecture in the work of the world. The Wainwright and its group were Architecture living again as such in a new age—the Steel Age— living in the work of the world! The Practical therein achieving ▶

Design for a Trust and Savings Bank Building, St. Loius, Adler, Sullivan & Ramsay, architects, 1893–95 (unbuilt).

8 William Holabird (1854-1923), Chicago architect. For the demolition of the Tacoma building, see page 29

9 Charles Robert Darwin (1809-82) English naturalist, firmly established the theory natural selection.

10 *disjecta membra:* Disjunction, Disorder Nonassemblage, dispersion.

11 John Wellborn Root, (1850–1891) Chicago architect.

right: Chicago Stock Exchange Building, Chicago, Addler and Sullivan, architects, 1893–1894 (demolished 1972).

the attic. In this the circulatory system completes itself and makes its grand turn, ascending and descending. The space is filled with tanks, pipes, valves, sheaves, and mechanical etcetera that supplement and complement the force-originating plant hidden below-ground in the cellar. Finally, or at the beginning rather, there must be on the ground-floor a main aperture or entrance common to all the occupants or patrons of the building. . . .

"The practical horizontal and vertical division or office unit is naturally based on a room of comfortable area and height, and the size of this standard office room as naturally predetermines the standard structural unit, and, approximately, the size of window openings. In turn, these purely arbitrary units of structure form in an equally natural way the true basis of the artistic development of the exterior. Of course the structural spacings and openings in the first or mercantile story are required to be the largest of all; those in the second or quasi-mercantile story are of a somewhat similar nature. The spacings and openings in the attic are of no importance whatsoever (the windows have no actual value), for light may be taken from the top, and no recognition of a cellular division is necessary in the structural spacing.

"Hence it follows inevitably, and in the simplest possible way, that if we follow our natural instincts without thought of books, rules, precedents, or any such educational impedimenta to a spontaneous and 'sensible' result, we will in the following manner design the exterior of our tall office building—to wit:

"Beginning with the first story, we give this a main entrance that attracts the eye to its location, and the remainder of the story we treat in a more or less liberal, expansive, sumptuous way—a way based exactly on the practical necessities, but expressed with a sentiment of largeness and freedom. The second story we treat in a similar way but usually with milder pretension. Above this, throughout the indefinite number of typical office tiers, we take our cue from the indi-

vidual cell, which requires a window with its separating pier, its sill and lintel, and we, without more ado, make them look all alike because they are all alike. This brings us to the attic, which, having no division into office cells, and no special requirement for lighting, gives us the power to show by means of its broad expanse of wall and its dominating weight and character, that which is the fact—namely, that the series of office tiers has come definitely to an end. . .

"However, thus far the results are only partial and tentative at best; relatively true, they are but superficial. We are doubtless right in our instinct, but we must seek a fuller justification, a finer sanction, for it. . . . We must now heed the imperative voice of emotion.

"It demands of us, What is the chief characteristic of the tall office building? And at once we answer, it is lofty. This loftiness is to the artist-nature its thrilling aspect. It is the very open organ-tone in its appeal. It must be in turn the dominant chord in his expression of it, the true excitant of his imagination. It must be tall, every inch of it tall. The force and power of altitude must be in it, the glory and pride of exaltation must be in it. It must be every inch a proud and soaring thing, rising in sheer exultation that from bottom to top it is a unit without a single dissenting line—that it is the new, the unexpected, the eloquent peroration of most bald, most sinister, most forbidding conditions.

★   ★   ★

"The true, the immovable philosophy of the architectural art . . . let me now state, for it brings to the solution of the problem a final, comprehensive formula:

"All things in nature have a shape, that is to say, a form, an outward semblance, that tells us what they are, that distinguishes them from ourselves and from each other.

"Unfailingly in nature these shapes express the inner life, the native quality, of the animal, tree, bird, fish, that they present to us; they are so characteristic, so recognizable, that we say, simply, it is 'natural' it should be so. . . .

"Whether it be the sweeping eagle in his flight, or the open apple-blossom, the tolling work-horse, the blithe swan, the branching oak, the winding stream at its base, the drifting clouds, over all the coursing sun, form ever follows function, and this is the law. Where function does not change, form does not change. . . .

"It is the pervading law of all things organic and inorganic, of all things physical and metaphysical, of all things human and all things superhuman, of all true manifestations of the head, of the heart, of the soul, that the life is recognizable in its expression, that form ever follows function. . . .

"Does not this readily, clearly, and conclusively show that the lower one or two stories will take on a special character suited to the special needs, that the tiers of typical offices, having the same unchanging function, shall continue in the same unchanging form, and that as to the attic, specific and conclusive as it is in its very nature, its function shall equally be so in force, in significance, in continuity, in conclusiveness of outward expression? From this results, naturally, spontaneously, unwittingly, a three-part division—not from any theory, symbol, or fancied logic.

"And thus the design of the tall office building takes its place with all other architectural types made when architecture, as has happened once in many years, was a living art. Witness the Greek temple, the Gothic cathedral, the mediaeval fortress.

"And thus, when native instinct and sensibility shall govern the exercise of our beloved art; when the known law, the respected law, shall be that form ever follows function; when our architects shall cease strutting and prattling handcuffed and vainglorious in the asylum of a foreign school; when it is truly felt, cheerfully accepted, that this law opens up the airy sunshine of green fields, and gives to us a freedom that the very beauty and sumptuousness of the outworking of the law itself as exhibited in nature will deter any sane, any sensitive man from changing into license; when it becomes evident that we are merely speaking a foreign language with a noticeable American accent, whereas each and every architect in the land might, under the benign influence of this law, express in the simplest, most modest, most natural way that which it is in him to say: that he might really and would surely develop his own characteristic individuality, and that the architectural art with him would certainly become a living form of speech, a natural form of utterance, giving surcease to him and adding treasures small and great to the growing art of his land; when we know and feel that Nature is our friend, not our implacable enemy, then it may be proclaimed that we are on the highroad to a natural and satisfying art, an architecture that will soon become a fine art in the true, the best sense of the word, an art that will live because it will be of the people, for the people, and by the people."

★   ★   ★

In Sullivan's actual designs, wall surface was abandoned for a system of pier and spandrel. That the terra cotta which gave fire-protection was not self-supporting masonry, but merely a casing, was expressed with particular success in the Guaranty

expression as Beauty. A true service rendered humanity in that here was. proof of the oneness of Spirit and Matter, when both are real-a synthesis the world. awaits as the service of the artist and a benediction it will receive when false ideas as to the nature and limitation of art and- the functions of the artist disappear.

The Transportation Building at the Columbian Exposition cost him most trouble of anything he ever did. He got the great doorway "straight away," but the rest hung fire. I had never seen him anxious before, but anxious he then was. How eventually successful this beautiful contribution to that fine collection of picture-buildings was, itself shows. But the Transportation Building was no solution of the work of the world as was the Wainwright Building. It was a "picture-building"—but one with rhyme and reason and, above all, individuality; a real picture, not a mere pose of the picturesque. It was not architecture in its highest sense, except as a great theme suggested, an idea of violent changes in scale exemplified, noble contrasts effected—meanwhile its excuse for existence being the enclosure of exhibition space devoted to transportation. It was no masterful solution of a practical problem. It was a holiday circumstance and superb entertainment, which is what it was intended to be. It was original, the fresh individual note of vitality at the Fair—inspiring, a thing created but—something in itself, for itself alone. Except that if here—where a mischief was done to architectural America from which it has never recovered, by the introduction of "the classic," so called, in the Fair buildings, as the "Ideal,"—had that note of individual vitality as expressed in the Transportation Building been heeded for what it was worth, that mischief might largely have been averted. Only the Chicago Auditorium, the Transportation ▸

1925

12 Albert Kahn (1869-1942), architect. Kahn was responsible not
only for almost all of the major
industrial plants of the Big Three
and other auto manufacturers in
the US, but also for aviation
industry plants, hospitals, banks,
commercial buildings, public
buildings, temples, libraries, clubs
and over one hundred mansions.
Ernest Wilby partnered with
Albert Kahn.

13 Paul Hankar (1859-1901),
Belgian architect.

Victor Horta (1861-1947) Belgian
architect, one of the leading figures of modern architecture in
Belgium.

14 Refers to *The Wasmuth
Portfolio*, see page 148.

15 Jean-Baptiste Carpeaux (1827-
1875)French Realist Sculptor.

Auguste Rodin, page 194, n.5.

16 Gustave Flaubert (1821-1880)
French novelist.

Emile Zola (1840-1902) French
novelist and critic.

Henrik Ibsen (1828-1906),
Norwegian playwright.

17 Paul Cézanne, (1839—1906)
French painter.

18 Joseph Morrill Wells
(1853–1890). A draughtsman for
McKim, Mead and White, Wells
was spoken of as "McKim's
right-hand man."

Stanford White (1853–1906),
architect.

Charles Follen McKim,
(1847–1909), architect.

19 Charles Adams Platt
(1861–1933), landscape painter
and architect.

opposite: Terra cotta detail from
the façade of National Farmer's
Bank of Owatonna, Minnesota,
Louis H. Sullivan, architect,
1907–08.

Building, by a delicate surface ornament. The height was emphasized by unbroken continuity of the vertical piers, and by their close spacing, between every window, two to each office. Vitally united in a form deeply felt by its creator, the building became indeed "every inch a proud and soaring thing," filled with the "force and power of altitude."

The achievement was widely recognized and acclaimed. Almost without exception, tall buildings from 1897 to 1912 showed its influence by accented vertical lines. This was scarcely more true in the work of consistent "modernists" like Sullivan, who sought to abandon all historical forms, than of their antagonists, the eclectics. They gave at least lip-service to "structural expression," and turned often to Gothic with its soaring lines. Even the most consistent devotees of abstract form did not remain untouched. In their New York Municipal Building (photo page 189), designed in 1908, McKim, Mead & White marked the lines of the steel columns by shallow vertical strips. Thus in the treatment of the skyscraper Sullivan's creative work attained a historical influence corresponding to its artistic significance.

In many other fields the free and functional mode of design which he championed achieved signal triumphs. Ernest Wilby, working with Albert Kahn,[12] established a characteristic physiognomy for American industrial buildings. Frank Lloyd Wright, a disciple of Sullivan, developed a system of domestic design and an idiom of form which had considerable following in Chicago's sphere.

Abroad, the leaders of the movement, developing independently under similar cultural influences, were certainly later than Sullivan in arriving at a system of new forms. The experiments of Hankar and Horta[13] in Belgium, of Otto Wagner in Vienna, were scarcely begun in 1890. The People's Palace at Brussels, the manifesto of l'art nouveau, seems hesitating and inchoate beside the Wainwright building. Indeed the foreign architects have lacked a great novel problem like the skyscraper to give point to their striving for originality. Wagner's church at the Steinhof, for all its novel treatment of materials, remains a child of the Renaissance by its composition of space and mass. On the other hand, nationalism in Germany, by adopting the "secession" movement as its own, gave it a currency which it never attained in America. Thus Sullivan, whose work at the Chicago Fair attracted foreign attention in 1893, and Wright, whose designs were sumptuously published in Germany,[14] have had more influence there than in their own country.

The general victory which Sullivan long prophesied, indeed, has not come to pass. He realized the defeat, and tried to console himself by hope in a coming generation. To him the outcome was a corruption, a national confession of failure, an evidence that the American people of today had proved unworthy to have a modern architecture.

"Modern," however, is a relative term: its meaning changes from generation to generation. The creative nature of art itself determines that no single formula, however cogent, can long prevail. There is not, as in science, a single, "right" way. Art must change to live; and will change, harmoniously in all its manifestations, through every generation.

The coherence of the realistic treatments of the subject matter of modern life by Sullivan and his fellows was with the work of the realistic schools of the nineteenth century in painting and sculpture, in literature and music. Under the domination of science, the painting of Monet and the impressionists, the sculpture of Carpeaux and Rodin,[15] the music-drama of Wagner, the novels and plays of Flaubert, Zola, Tolstoi, and Ibsen,[16] all sought characteristic beauty through truth to nature, rather than abstract beauty through relations of form.

Against this domination of art by science, this equation of beauty with truth, there began a reaction even before 1890. Cézanne[17] let anatomy and photographic foreshortening in painting give way to formal organization; sculpture became "archaic" and geometrical; there was a renaissance of verse, of "absolute" music. The counterpart in architecture has been a renewed interest in unity and simplicity of form, as against a functional or dynamic emphasis. As in previous great periods of abstract composition of mass and space, the fifteenth and eighteenth centuries, there has been a reversion to the classic elements, regarded as a universal language of elementary geometrical simplicity. Beginning in New York in the eighties with Joseph Morrill Wells, White, and McKim,[18] triumphing at the Chicago Fair, the movement, American in its genesis, is now pressing on to foreign conquests.

Even the skyscraper, the last stronghold of functionalism, is yielding. Long ago had come a voice of protest, that "instead of constructing first, without preoccupation with the final appearance, promising oneself to utilize the ingeniousness of the construction as the decoration, one should relegate the ingenuities of structure to a position

among the secondary means, unworthy of appearing in the completed work." Even as to an effect of loftiness it might be argued that a sheer cliff of bedded stone is as impressive in its height as the serried trunks of the forest. By 1912 the leaders of the formalists, Platt[19] and McKim, no longer compromised. In the tall New York apartments east of Central Park, in the Leader-News Building at Cleveland, the steel frame disappeared again behind sheer unbroken walls, the merits of which lay in uniformity and proportion. The zoning law of 1915 has placed a premium on varied compositions of mass, and these possibilities of form are now engaging the designers. For better or worse, the problem of expressing the steel frame, so crucial in the nineties, has become a dead issue.

Instead of the forerunner of the new century, Sullivan, we now see, was the last great leader of the old. He was the Monet; Wells the Cézanne. Like Monet, living on into another age, he was within his life-time already an old master.

In the revaluing which accompanies such a change of ideals as has taken place in the past generation, many a reputation has gone down. In their narrow search for truth to nature, for expression of use and structure, too many of the impressionists and functionalists lost all form. The little men have now only a historical position. The quality of greatness, however, is to survive such changes, by fulfilling the new demands as well as the old. The exaltation of an ideal of form has not dimmed the luster of Sullivan's achievement. We find the Wainwright Building, still more the Guaranty Building, simple, crystalline, cast in one jet. In them Sullivan rose superior to any merely mechanical theory of expression. The steel occurs only at alternate piers, yet all are uniform. A unity of form has been arbitrarily achieved. The artist has felt, not calculated. Louis Sullivan lives not merely as the founder of a great school of the past, but as a master who can speak out of the past to pupils of succeeding generations in the eternal language of form. ∎

Building, the Getty Tomb, the Wainwright Building are necessary to show the great reach of the creative activity, that was Louis Sullivan's genius. The other buildings he did are blossoms, more, or less individual, upon these stems. Some were grafted from one to the other of them, some were grown from them, but all are relatively inferior in point of that quality which we finally associate with the primitive strength of the thing that got itself done regardless and "stark" to the Idea: sheer, significant, vital.

* * *

What does it matter if Tradition's followers fail to see that Louis Sullivan's loyalty to Tradition was wholly complete and utterly profound? His loyalty was greater than theirs, as the Spirit transcends the Letter. What lives in New York architecture is little enough, and in spite of its grammar and far beyond the style-mongering it receives in the Atelier. It is the force of circumstance piling itself inexorably by mere mass into the sky—the darkening canyons that are paths leading into darkness, or to Death! It seems incredible now, but such unity as those tall masses may have is due to the master-mind that first conceived and contributed one as a unit. The Wainwright Building cleared the way for them—and to this day remains the master key to the skyscraper as Architecture the world over. Why is it so difficult for standardization to receive to a greater degree the illumination from within that would mean Life instead of Death? Why is the vision of such a master-mind lost in the competitive confusion of so-called ideas and jostling ambitions? Why is the matter, except for him, still all from the outside—culture nowhere sane nor safe except as the imitation or the innocuous is safe—which it never is, or was. Look backward toward Rome! •

Perspective study—competition entry for the Chicago Tribune Tower, Raymond Hood, of Howells & Hood, 1922.

The architects explained their use of the Gothic Style as a means of expressing the building's steel structural columns. As the piers rise to the summit, these same strong vertical elements terminate in flying buttresses, a design device used to link the structure's lower mass to its ornamental tower. For increased dramatic effect, the architects also proposed that the crown be illuminated at night (photo page 199).

It's no coincidence that the tallest building in the world at the time, the Woolworth Building (photo page 187), also employed the Gothic Style.

opposite: Georgia O'Keefe's *East River from the Shelton*, 1927–28. In 1925, O'Keefe and her photographer husband, Alfred Steiglitz moved into the Shelton Hotel. Inspired by the shapes of the city outside their 28th-floor windows, the dramatic urban views exerted a profound influence over their work.

EVOLUTION *of an* ARCHITECTURAL DESIGN

By
Leon V. Solon

I- *The* TRIBUNE BUILDING TOWER, CHICAGO
John Mead Howells & Raymond M Hood, Architects —

A GENERAL SURVEY of architectural magazines in this country conveys the impression that editorial interest is centered upon structural fact, to the neglect of the creative activity in which it originated: weight of evidence would justify the deduction that the practice of architecture is an accessory to general contracting. Literary comment consists in the aggregate of descriptions of the various parts of which the structure is composed, and of the materials with which it was erected or decorated; the design itself is usually dismissed with perfunctory terms of commendation. The intricate imaginative processes involved in the creative effort, architectonic values and subtleties of stylistic expression, have little place in criticism or are estimated from an angle of perception at which personal enthusiasm or bias is more apparent than the study of Aesthetic. Readers of these magazines who are unfamiliar with the intense stress of creative effort, might conclude that the leaders of the profession produce masterly compositions with that completeness and spontaneity with which a hen lays an egg.

In the average architectural illustration we are impressed primarily with the skill of the photographer, the builder, and the craftsmen; all have prominence save that individual who sweats blood to achieve beauty, and through the success of whose effort opportunity is created for all subsequently involved.

Of recent years American architects have designed structures which have achieved international fame, and have exerted a powerful influence in this country. Each of these has resulted from an intensely interesting imaginative process, the evolution of which must be a subject of the highest professional interest; those endowed with the creative faculty (not forgetting those less fortunate) are invariably intrigued and anxious to follow a trend of thought from its inception to the final issue. The development of such compositions involves a number of experimental stages, and frequently a modification of some feature of minor importance will give a new direction to invention resulting in the dominant motif. In contriving the silhouette of mass, its articulation, and the decorative representation of various factors, many versions are usually essayed previous to the adoption of that finally executed. It appears to us a rare privilege to have the opportunity to observe the workings of resourceful imaginations throughout the creation of remarkable design.

This series starts with the Chicago Tribune Building by architects Howells and Hood, by whose courtesy we are able to reproduce the most important sketches made in the order in which they evolved, beginning with the first vague concept of effect and proceeding to that point at which the scheme was ready for specification.

The achievement of excellence in any form of design depends upon some systematic habit of thought; this varies in its direction and method with the temperament of each gifted practitioner; so far the younger men have had little opportunity to ascertain the nature of those points of view which have controlled the evolution of successfully developed schemes. For this reason we feel that a series such as we are undertaking should be of educational interest, and record data which are too frequently destroyed, despite their high historical value to future generations. ∎

from:

THE EVOLUTION OF AN ARCHITECTURAL DESIGN II:
The Shelton Hotel
Arthur Loomis Harmon, Architect
By Leon V. Solon
Vol. 59, No. 4, April 1926, pp. 367-375.

IT IS PROBABLE that no design produced in recent years has attracted as much attention, or received more commendation than this. By his confrères the architect was awarded the Gold Medals of both the American Institute of Architects and the Architectural League.

Our series unfortunately lacks a number of initial sketches, representing the various versions devised for the solution of this problem which were made tentatively previous to its final state in composition. These, together with numerous other sketches, were destroyed by Harmon (whose notorious modesty caused him to attach no value to these extremely interesting documents), during the customary cleaning-up incidental to change of premises. We hope that if no other benefit is derived from this series, it will awaken those who are engaged upon important structural problems to a realization of the fact that, though preparatory sketches have little significance to their producer, they have a psychological value which is considerable, in revealing the progress of complex mental processes to an important issue.

Last year, a number of foreign architects visited New York in connection with the Convention of the Institute and the Exhibition at the Grand Central Palace. ▸

above: Cathedral of Rouen, "Tower of Butter," Rouen, France.

above: Photograph of a plasticine model of the Shelton Hotel showing the completed design.

right and opposite: Perspective studies for competition entry for the Chicago Tribune Tower, Raymond Hood, of Howells & Hood, 1922.

The writer in discussing New York architecture with a number of these, recorded one impression which was held unanimously, to the effect that the Shelton design was the most remarkable and adequate solution of the old skyscraper problem, an opinion heartily endorsed by the majority of the profession in this country. We doubt that any design has exerted so prompt and beneficial an influence, both as regards silhouette in structural mass and textural quality. The creator of so individual a composition must inevitably be victimized by the appearance of numbers of flagrant imitations; so far these have redounded to his credit through their marked inferiority.

In works such as this we see the aesthetic future of American architecture contained. The simplicity with which mass is conceived, the scale conveyed with subtle proportional adjustment, and the scenic capacity of substance developed, ranks this composition among the few which may be designated as stylistic types. Distinction has not been procured with mannerism, for in spite of its originality it is normal in every respect. One series of developments reproduced shows the manner in which the architect finally arrived at the remarkable treatment of the base of the structure, and the fashion in which the Romanesque influence of the later compositions was readjusted to produce thoroughly individual results without stylistic depreciation. Few American examples demonstrate as successfully the adjustment of stylistic matter to modern effect, made necessary through the difference of conditions in observation that exists between the ancient and modern range of inspection. This proportional adjustment of stylistic detail has become a striking feature in American practice, which in course of time will be appreciated abroad, and our architects absolved of the implication that they are mainly archaeologists. ●

1926

THE PUBLICATION, first in *The Architectural Record* and other periodicals and now in book form,* of Fiske Kimball's studies in American architecture of today, evoked an interchange of letters with some of the leading figures in the world of architecture and of art criticism in America and in Europe. It constitutes a veritable symposium on the neo-classic and progressive trends in modern architecture, and on their great protagonists in the last generation such as Joseph Morrill Wells, McKim and Louis Sullivan. Through the kind consent of the writers we are privileged to present this correspondence to our readers. — EDITOR.

Philadelphia, May 6, 1925
DEAR KIMBALL:
I had hoped to see you in New York and possibly to have a stimulating discussion of your paper on Louis Sullivan. All you write is of interest to me, even though I do not share your views entirely.

To me, Sullivan has the merit of being a pioneer who struggled to open a trail to a barren country. As I do not judge of the value of an effort by its success alone, I have great respect for him. His effort, however, was against the trend of the American architecture of his time with the consequence that he lived to survive his own influence. His main claims to fame are his theory of design of the skyscraper and his system of ornament. The former rests on a conception of steel construction which assumes that in a system of a girder resting on two posts, the posts have a metaphysical nobility which entitles them to a special magnification. His system of ornamentation is, of course, a matter of taste, and we have to admit that its popularity was short lived. In both there was a good deal of "literature," and literary architecture is not worth much more than literary painting.
Sincerely,
PAUL P. CRET

Huntington, L. I., May 8, 1925
DEAR CRET:
...I wonder just a little if you have caught exactly my own view of Sullivan. I do not think for a moment that his work is the last word in American architecture. That was what I meant by calling him an "old master" in the title. I meant he was a great master of a school which is now a thing of the past. The nub of the article was really in the last few paragraphs where I say that his effort to express the steel is now a dead issue and suggest that the vital and really "modern" movement in American architecture is the effort to organize form irrespective of structure. That is what seems to me significant in the work of

McKim, Mead & White, beginning in the 1880's, in which to me the superficial following of classical details is a secondary matter.

It seems also immaterial to me whether this organization of form, which is the artistic element in architecture, is embodied in the spirit of calm uniformity of this neoclassic or the dynamic and dramatic energy of opposite movements as in the Baroque, which we both admire.

On the other hand, it seems to me that as the essence of art is creative originality, any great creative effort, even if contrary to our own ideas, is valid, for its author and for its day, and thus Sullivan is entitled to a sympathetic interpretation on the basis of his own canons of thought, and to admiration even if not imitation. To impose a single universal canon in the hope that it will permanently prevail is to stifle art in its creative essence. Art will continue to change from generation to generation as it has in the past. Happily it is now ceasing to follow the gods of the nineteenth century of whom Sullivan was a worshipper, and is turning to the new (and old) god of beauty of form. . .
Sincerely yours,
FISKE KIMBALL

New York, May 6, 1925
DEAR KIMBALL:
Thanks very much for The Architectural Record with your article on Sullivan. I read it with pleasure and with interest. And though I am going to renew, at least in part, my old objection, I am glad to say I think we are not as far apart as may at first appear.

For I do believe in formalism, if I use the word accurately; at all events in an abstract harmony of proportion. And to attempt to make the evidence of the system of construction replace that, is, in my opinion, to abdicate all title to artistry. That does not mean, however, that the proportions of a Greek building will hold good for a Gothic, a Renaissance or a modern building. Even where the systems of construction are sufficiently similar, there will be difference in the periods that will give any valid work a difference of aspect from those of the earlier time. And where a difference of construction occurs, as with the steel skeleton, there must be difference of aspect. I do not see it, in any essential degree, in the work of Wells and his school.

That may be my insensitiveness. But where I feel sure of my objection is in respect to your comparison with the painters. Monet is, in reality, only at the

slightest of removes from his immediate predecessors. His color analysis is a very slight disguise only the academic simpletons of the '80s and '90s could have failed to see that, and we know what nonentities they were. Sullivan and the steel frame men, on the other hand, made a real break with the past. As the immediate past was mostly bad, I believe their relative position as regards it is different from that of Monet as regards the Corots, Rousseaus, and Daubignys of his youth. The latter were most admirable men, and so Monet could proceed in harmony with their principles, as the architects could not as regards their predecessors.

But what I fall foul of entirely is calling Wells the Cézanne of architecture. Leaving out the question of their greatness (and I cannot believe myself so insensitive as to fail to see something of the grandeur of Cézanne in Wells—if he has it) Cézanne simply carries classical balance and proportion into the vision of the Impressionists (his own in his early days). If something more than an Impressionist in his later period, his last work in no way contradicts his first. Matisse said to me once that Cézanne added nothing to his earlier work, but merely developed what he had at the start. In contradistinction to this, Wells et al. seem to me a revulsion from Sullivan, attempting return to forms once vital but no longer so in their handling of them. But I repeat that I am in accord with the idea of art that they are trying to keep alive....
Yours cordially,
WALTER PACH

Huntington, L. I., May 8, 1925
DEAR PACH:
I am delighted to have a good long letter from you, in the same mail as one from Paul Cret, most intelligent of architects. It is amusing to see how different Cret's point of view is still. I do not think we are really very far apart. Of course, just as you say that Monet was only slightly removed from his immediate predecessors, I would emphasize that the same was true of Sullivan. All the long historical part of my article at the beginning was designed to point this out, by emphasizing his continuity with the thought of Ruskin, Semper, and Viollet-le-Duc. When I spoke of Wells as the Cézanne, I myself left aside the question of their "greatness." What I wish to emphasize is that it was Wells who first reacted against the prevailing realistic or scientific theory that the merit of architecture is to be found in truth to structure, as Cézanne was the first to react against the

realistic theory that the merit of painting was to be found in "truth to nature."

I would quite agree that "there will be a difference of genius in the periods that will give any valid work a difference of aspect from those of the earlier time. " I think this is true of the work of Bramante as compared with the work of the Romans, and I think it is true of the work of Wells and McKim as compared with the work of Rome and of the Renaissance. But I think this difference comes from the inevitable difference of requirements, rather than from a conscious effort to invent a new alphabet of forms. Naturally it will appear most where the requirements are most different, and thus the most notable work of today is in the steel-frame buildings where the essential problem of the moment is the composition of mass. As I recently saw it expressed by a Dutch critic, their merit lies "nicht so viel in ihren Wahrheit, als in ihren Klarheit," but this clarity of organization of form could never have been attained without the reaffirmation of the principle by Wells in buildings of traditional type.

When you write "Where a difference of construction occurs, as with the steel skeleton, there must be a difference of aspect," I think that (so far as this difference of construction does not itself bring new types of mass and space), you are still unconsciously tinged with the old nineteenth century scientific theory of functionalism. We are all together on what Harvey Corbett said to me the other day: "I have only one God, beauty of form."
Faithfully yours,
FiSKE KIMBALL

Philadelphia, December 19, 1927
DEAR KIMBALL:
I have just been reading your "Critical Estimate of Goodhue." If you remember this definition given by an old gentleman, "Mon fils, un journal bien pensant est un journal qui pense comme celui qui le lit," you will understand why I think you are writing the most penetrating criticism.

I have had, and I have, a high regard for Goodhue's talent. I feel, however, that the recent hero-worship has been somewhat far fetched. As a creator of modern forms, he did not go beyond the stage of attempting to conciliate contraries, with the usual result. Starting from Gothic Romanticism, he was attracted to Classicism by that element of the picturesque found in minor works, such as Spanish Colonial architecture, and did not live long enough to come to understand the real greatness of classi-

cal forms. Classicism is a discipline which requires a certain humility, the abandonment of too much personality of the modern exasperated "self expression."

So he remained half way on the road, and his later work is, after all, quite similar to his early productions, if one looks below mere external forms. All this you have admirably shown and you are doing much more for Goodhue's memory by showing his achievements and failures than well meaning but misleading eulogists.
Sincerely,
PAUL P. CRET

Berlin, April 11, 1928
MY DEAR MR. KIMBALL:
...I find your conception of American architecture dual—and therefore rightly seen from the side, as you yourself say, of abstract form and from that of technique. Just such a method distinguishes the historian from the artist: with the historian objectivity is present from the beginning, while the subjectivity of the artist's creative processes can only objectify itself in the completed work. Especially I have read with the greatest pleasure your account of the now-historic struggles which are today clearly to be recognized as far as Wright; struggles to whose effects the supremacy of space over decoration and the purifying of details (even the zoning law, I believe) are to be traced back. I believe also that my "dithyramb" on Wright may stand: that the Old gradually unclothes itself to nakedness, while the New is born naked-naturally not without mutual influence.,

I am happy, too, that you have embodied in your book the impression of Einstein about the Einstein Tower. Einstein's word of praise, "organic," I would interpret as deeply as could be at all possible, for fundamentally one cannot say better of any work of art. I am convinced that Einstein himself meant more by this word than any merely physical significance....
With cordial greetings,
ERICH MENDELSOHN

Phoenix, Arizona, April 30, 1928
DEAR FISKE KIMBALL:
A copy of your attractive new book came to hand, forwarded to me here in the Desert yesterday.

I have been reading my obituaries to a considerable extent the past year or two, and think, with Mark Twain, the reports of my death greatly exaggerated.

You were very kind to me though you used me to point your moral and adorn your tale, and left me in exile. Yours was no donkey's kick at a "dying lion." Nor am I

a lion, nor dying, nor am I in exile.

Sometime let someone come far enough away from Manhattan to mark what the thought-built houses they called the "New School of the Middle West" have done (consciously or unconsciously) to three out of five buildings from Buffalo to Los Angeles, quietening the skyline, broadening and strengthening the mass, ordering the openings, reducing the "fancy-features," marrying all of them to the ground to some extent, and be convinced of the potency in America of those ideas. Those ideas are more potent today than ever before, though their origin is growing obscure in the flood of pseudo-classic. This to offset inevitable abuse.

"A lost cause"? "The Triumph of the Classic"?—Dear man!—The cornice has gone! The Larkin Building, about which you write so well, struck it first.

No cornice, no classic! and Life goes on!

From your honorable niche in the museum in conservative Old Philadelphia, does that ancient dream "The Classic" still possess and obsess you? Or are you merely comforting the abstraction that was lost at the Columbian exposition thirty-two years ago—lost—because it was only again reborn to be commercialized to death. Trying to make it open its lips—eyes it never had—and seem to speak?

...I intend...to enlist your pen in behalf of the nature of the thing—as architecture—whereas the nature of the thing as practised is what you have been talking about —and how!

Meantime my best to you, faithfully. You are a friendly enemy. They make ultimately the best friends.
FRANK LLOYD WRIGHT

Philadelphia, May 25, 1928
DEAR FRANK LLOYD WRIGHT:
I am just back from Europe and find your very kind letter to a "friendly enemy. " I would not even say an enemy at all. The chapter on "The Triumph of the Classic" deals with a past event which I think really did take place, but in the chapter "The Present" you will see, I believe, the feet of the conqueror are crumbling.

Mendelsohn has written me an interesting letter in which he sees the ultimate unity of present trends, by the stripping naked of the old to accord with the new, born naked.
Faithfully yours,
FISKE KIMBALL   ∎

*AMERICAN ARCHITECTURE, Fiske Kimball, Bobbs-Merrill, Company, New York, 1928.

1926

8 Restless Object:
The Search for Something More

Once the severe effects of the Great Depression began to take hold, very little building occurred due to the ruined economy. In 1939, the Second World War broke out in Europe and it wasn't until the 50s that the building industry, and the rest of the country, returned to some degree of normal. Meanwhile, not so strangely perhaps, there was increased promotion of well designed, streamlined, labor saving products that promised to make every life a life of ease and pointed the way to a better future. The ideal was high quality design; standardized, machine-made, mass-produced.

The powerful lure of the machine, gleaming and efficient, was reflected in every object from the automobile, to the streamlined locomotive, to the skyscraper. "The Machine Age" Exhibition of 1927, co-curated by the editors of the *Little Review* was an instant sensation; the first time the public looked at machines, machine parts, and machine products as if they were art. The almost redemptive power that technology held forth, however, was nowhere demonstrated as forcefully than at the opening of "A Century of Progress" Exposition in Chicago in 1933.

The fair opened with a dramatic look towards the future, and a symbolic link to the past—to the World's Columbian Exposition of 1893. During the opening ceremonies, a huge searchlight, trained on the tower of the Hall of Science (left), was illuminated by an electric current which had been ultimately generated by a ray of light from the orange star Arcturus, a ray of light which had left the star forty years earlier.

The architects and designers hoped, along with the Fair's director, that it would stand "as a symbol of the architecture of the future—a very modern expression of architectural ideas." But, for many the Fair was a disappointment; perhaps everyone wished too hard. At the very least it had a purgative effect on past formulas. Forms were planar and as playful as the structures themselves. Color and light were major themes; Joseph

Hall of Science,
'A Century of Progress' Exposition, Chicago
Paul Philippe Cret, architect, 1933

Urban was appointed "director of all exterior color," and lighting consultant. The vertical fins of the Hall of Science were lit at night by neon tubes. There was an increased public awareness of good design. And, there was further impetus given to the style loosely labeled "moderne." (This style, which actually surfaced at the *Eposition International des Arts Décoratifs et Industriels Moderns* in Paris eight years earlier, later took the name Art Deco as a consequence.)

This was a time of vital debate over Modernism, when one picked up *Architecural Record* and found Frank Lloyd Wright, Le Corbusier, Lewis Mumford and Henry-Russell Hitchcock in the same issue. Though the latter two had respect for one another, they held strongly opposing views when it came to the future of architecture. Whereas Hitchcock was the champion of a group of European architects he called "The New Pioneers," particularly Le Corbusier and his "machine for living," Mumford had basically sworn eternal hostility towards the machine, or at least the thoughtless awe in which he felt too many regarded it.

When Henry-Russell Hitchcock reviewed the first English translation of Le Corbusier's 1923 polemical tract, *Vers une Architecture*, for *Architectural Record* (June 1928), he called it "the one great statement of the potentialites of an architecture of the future and a document of vital historical significance." The book's challenge, "Architecture or Revolution" was hard to ignore. As progressive-minded architects seriously contemplated the so-called "International Style," even conservative American designers were beginning to realize that the best European architects had shed the neoclassic forms of Beaux-Arts academicism once and for all.

The general feeling in the United States was that hope lay in the pared-down classicized forms of Bertram Goodhue and Paul Cret, or in the Deco styles of Ralph Walker, Ely Jacques Kahn, and Raymond Hood. Walker's Barclay-Vesey Building in New York (photo 246), completed in 1926, had captured the imagination of architects, critics, even the public,—and Lewis Mumford.

Though Mumford's influence is now thought of as synonymous with his "Sky-line" articles for The New Yorker, he felt a deep attachment to *Architectural Record* where he began writing after publishing *The Brown Decades*. In his collection of essays, *Roots of American Contemporary Architecture*, Mumford says of himself,

> "[I] may be looked upon as one of the few continuators of Montgomery Schuyler; and there is even a slight thread of connection in the fact that Herbert Croly, who had begun his literary life as an editor of Schuyler's paper, the *Architectural Record*, was one of the editors who as early as 1921 opened the pages of his magazine, *The New Republic*, to [my] writings upon modern architecture."

At best Mumford was ambivalent about what had become of the skyscraper. He was dismayed by "the application of a single formula to every problem;" a formula that left people out.

> "It is not for nothing that almost every detail of the mechanized building follows a standard pattern and preserves a studious anonymity. Except for the short run of the entrance, the original architect has no part in its interior development. If the architect himself is largely paralyzed by his problem, what shall we say of the artisans, and of the surviving

Battery City Building, New York City, Churchill & Thompson, architects (unbuilt). Compare this building to Walter Gropius' entry in the *Chicago Tribune* Competition, page 203.

from:
WHAT IS A CITY?
Lewis Mumford
Vol. 82, No. 5, November 1937,
pp. 58-62

Limitations on size, density, and area are absolutely necessary to effective social intercourse; and they are therefore the most important instruments of rational economic and civic planning. The unwillingness in the past to establish such limits has been due mainly to two facts: the assumption that all upward changes in magnitude were signs of progress and automatically "good for business", and the belief that such limitations were essentially arbitrary, in that they proposed to "decrease economic opportunity"—that is, opportunity for profiting by congestion—and to halt the inevitable course of change. Both these objections are superstitious.

Limitations on height are now common in American cities; drastic limitations on density are the rule in all municipal housing ▸

"Does a dynamo need ornament? Does a Diesel engine need color? Our world is essentially a world fit for dynamos, Diesel engines, steamships, a thing of black, gray, white conscientiously utilitarian...we are still human beings, not dynamos or Diesel engines: and there must be something more."

Lewis Mumford The Search For Something More, *1928.*

1927

These photos appear, among others, as examples of new uses for "Glass," by Knud Lönberg-Holm [*AR* 68:4 Oct 1930 pp 327–358]. The photo of the Bauhaus on page 280 is also from this article.

top: Model for Glass Skyscraper, Ludwig Mies van der Rohe, architect, 1920–21.

center: Restaurant, Stockholm Exposition, Sweden, Gunnar Asplund, architect.

bottom: Store Fronts, Hoek van Holland, the Netherlands, J.J.P. Oud, architect.

handicraft workers who still contribute their quota of effort to the laying of bricks and stones, to the joining of pipes, to the plastering of ceilings? Gone are most of their opportunities for the exercise of skilled intelligence, to say nothing of art: they might as well make paper-boxes or pans for all the personal stamp they can give to their work….A great architecture, however, is something to be seen and felt and lived in. By this criterion most of our pretentious buildings are rather pathetic." [*STICKS AND STONES*, P. 171]

The problem, as he saw it, was how to make the skyscraper more humane:

"The four great components of design are site, materials, technical construction, and feeling...In considering the advances made in our commercial and industrial buildings we may leave out site, and put to one side materials...It is by utilizing new methods of construction and embodying a new feeling that our modern architecture lives: but the feeling and the construction are not always in harmony. In Europe modern architects, like Gropius and Le Corbusier, have faced this situation with inexorable logic: they have modified or curbed their feelings so as to fit the construction!" (page 245)

Mumford was sympathetic to architects who, if they had to build tall buildings, used color and texture, particularly at street level, to entice pedestrians to enter what are often formidable spaces, and give people something to experience inside. Among the architects he championed were Ralph Walker, Ely Jacques Kahn, and Raymond Hood.

Walker was known for his 1920s art deco skyscrapers. He was acclaimed in 1957 by the American Institute of Architects as "the architect of the century" and by Frank Lloyd Wright as "the only other architect in America." Of Walker's Barclay-Vesey, Mumford said,

"[Mr. Walker] permits the mass itself to be cold, hard; the building as a whole has a feeling of dark strength; but in the stonework of the lower stories and in the interior the designer introduces a delicate, naturalistic carving, heightened within by the use of gold. When one enters the main hall, one almost forgets its purpose: it is as gaily lighted and decorated as a village street in a strawberry festival. Mr. Walker, in other words, accepts the contrast between structure and feeling: he does not attempt to reconcile them. One remains clear and logical, inflexibly committed to its programme; the other is warm and intimate and a little confused. In Mr. Walker's design decoration is an audacious compensation for the rigor and mechanical fidelity of the rest of the building; like jazz, it interrupts and relieves the tedium of too strenuous mechanical activity."(page 248)

The firm of Buchman and Kahn specialized in loft manufacturing buildings and offices. The colorful decorative vocabulary Ely Jacques Kahn employed was based on an affection for and sound knowledge of Asian and Pre-Columbian arts as well as Art Deco. In addition to frequent decorative exterior treatment, Kahn particularly delighted in unleashing this ornate vocabulary on all the details of the interiors. He said,

"It is interesting to record a growing desire among owners of commercial buildings to break away from ready-made stock designs. The carping critic may suggest that such expenditure is only good as advertising, but it seems that once the major details of the structure are fairly well developed, the architect is allowed a great deal of liberty in the minor details, if he himself has the imaginative ability to visualize the beauty and charm to be derived from specially designed details." ■

from:
The Architect's Library (Book Reviews)
FRANK LLOYD WRIGHT AND THE NEW PIONEERS
By Henry-Russell Hitchcock
Reviewed by Lewis Mumford
Vol. 65, No. 4, April 1929, pp. 414-417.

* * *

To begin at the beginning, Mr. Hitchcock places Mr. Wright at the head of the movement which is represented by Berlage in Holland and by Hoffmann in Austria. This manner of placing Mr. Wright puts him definitely with the past generation, and it serves to bring out Mr. Hitchcock's underlying thesis of a cleavage in form between the generation of Wright and the generation of Le Corbusier and Oud, but it ignores the fact that America has gone through a different architectural and social development from Europe, and that the contemporaries of Berlage and Hoffmann, architecturally speaking, are Richardson and Sullivan. The worship of industrialism, which has become the keynote of the modern movement in Europe today, belongs to an earlier generation in America, that which actually built the grain elevators and the primitive skyscrapers of Chicago. There is, of course, a difference in technical methods between a stone construction like the Monadnock Building and a house by Le Corbusier but the philosophy and method of approach are exactly the same.

* * *

When Mr. Hitchcock observes that Mr. Wright has learned less from the "lesson of Ford" than the European has, he neglects the fact that the Chicago of Mr. Wright's youth was wholly conceived in the image of Ford; business success and mechanical efficiency were the only factors that entered into the architectural problem; and, Mr. Wright's development, instead of being toward the goal of the "building-machine" had this conception, rather, as a starting point.

* * *

The victory of the new pioneers in Chicago was incomplete, partly because of their failure to organize their gains, and partly because, in the hands of Sullivan and Wright, their architecture began to go through a natural and inevitable process of development. With his fundamental education as an engineer, and with that solid acquaintance with utilitarian necessities which the very being of Chicago gives, to a philosopher like Dewey or to a poet like Sandburg quite as much as to the business man or industrialist, Mr. Wright took the next step. This step consisted in the modification of mechanical forms in harmony with the regional environment and with human desires and feelings.

* * *

Success under present conditions demands unhesitating conformity on the part of the engineer to the terms laid down by the banker and investor; the result is sometimes good design and economy, and quite as often it is poor design and deformity and inadequacy to perform the function that the building is supposed to perform. This is not the milieu in which good architecture can become the rule, and if modern architecture flourishes in Europe and lags here, it is because the Europeans have far better conditions under which to work, as a result of the socialized activity of European municipalities, with their comprehensive and financially unremunerative housing programs.

The truth is that Mr. Wright's capital qualities alienate him both from the architects who do not acknowledge a handicap in conforming to the present demands and from the society that ignores the higher values of life if they happen to conflict with the principle of a quick turnover and a maximum profit. Chief among these qualities is Mr. Wright's sense of the natural environment; and here again, I think, Mr. Hitchcock's principles keep him from grasping Mr. Wright's significance. Mr. Hitchcock refers to the "absurdity and the provincialism of the term prairie architecture" to characterize Mr. Wright's early Chicago work. On the contrary, the phrase is not absurd but accurate. Mr. Wright is, definitely, our greatest regional architect; his Chicago houses are prairie houses, as his Pasadena houses are "mediterranean" ones, to harmonize with that climate and milieu. Even machines, as some of our new pioneers forget, differ in design according to the region they are used in: steamers designed for tropical trade have larger ventilating units than the usual North Atlantic liners, and automobiles in England are designed for low power because of the relatively easy contours of the country. The essential form of architecture is of course largely conditioned by the method of construction; but this again is not independent of regional qualifications—as the use of the concrete form instead of the steel frame in Chicago testifies.

* * *

Mr. Wright's architecture is an early witness of what may generally come to happen when our regional cultures absorb the lesson of the machine without losing their roots or renouncing all those elements which give landscapes and men their individualities. The formula which would exclude such a manifestation belongs as little to the future as the five orders. ■

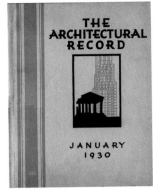

estates in England: that which could not be done has been done. Such limitations do not obviously limit the population itself: they merely give the planner and administrator the opportunity to multiply the number of centers in which the population is housed, instead of permitting a few existing centers to aggrandize themselves on a monopolistic pattern.

These limitations are necessary to break up the functionless, hypertrophied urban masses of the past. Under this mode of planning, the planner proposes to replace the "polynucleated city", as Professor Warren Thompson has called it, with a new type of "polynucleated city" in which a cluster of communities, adequately spaced and bounded, shall do duty for the badly organized mass city. Twenty such cities, in a region whose environment and whose resources were adequately planned, would have all the benefits of a metropolis that held a million people, without its ponderous disabilities: its capital frozen into unprofitable utilities, and its land values congealed at levels that stand in the way of effective adaptation to new needs. •

**Two Park Avenue Building,
New York City,
Buchman & Kahn, architects.**

Leon Victor Solon, (1872-1957)
was responsible for much of the
glazed tile-work outside and
inside Two Park Avenue, which
explains the knowing degree to
which he describes it in his
article.

Solon worked for Minton Potters
(England), 1900–09, designing art
nouveau pottery and later wrote a
classic text, *Architectural Poly-
chrome Decoration: An Analysis
of Fundamental Principles of Polychromed Terra Cotta*. After moving to the United States Solon
worked as a ceramic designer
and interior decorator, often col-
laborating with Ely Jacques Kahn.

THE ARCHITECTURAL RECORD

*An Illustrated Monthly Magazine of Architecture
and The Allied Arts and Crafts*

VOLUME 63   APRIL, 1928   NUMBER 4

THE PARK AVENUE BUILDING, NEW YORK CITY

BUCHMAN & KAHN, ARCHITECTS

BY LEON V. SOLON

THE EVOLUTION OF A STYLE

W E ARE living in a period in which the origination of a new order of aesthetic expression is under way; not as a passing vogue such as from time to time influences professional practice, but as a general movement compelling the direction of progressive activities. The movement designated as "Modernistic," with an unfortunate transitory implication, is exciting a furore for analytical study in all incidental discussion and investigation. When it constitutes the subject for discussion in any assemblage of architects or craftsmen, the common desire of all is to ascertain its aesthetic elements, creative impulses, and physical characteristics. This unusual manifestation of interest may be due to two causes: first, it may result from conviction that professional distinction is assured those who develop capability for sincere expression; or, secondly, it may be indicative of radical alteration in the angle from which aesthetic problems will be approached in future— more in accord with contemporary scientific investigation than that order of procedure which, in the past, attended stylistic evolution.

We experience an obligation to consider this Movement in all seriousness, deriving what guidance we can from investigation of evolution in recognized stylistic species, in order that we may determine significance in

fact. The genesis of stylistic types is definitely attributed to external influences of social or circumstantial character; this fact is established with a measure of certainty which removes it from the field of debate. Those who entrench themselves behind historic prejudice, would assuredly be shaken in their belief in an unsurpassable past by a general summary of social and intellectual conditions today, and would discover ample justification for the advent of an unprecedented aesthetic movement of major dimensions.

Stylistic evolution has invariably been a systematic process of cause and effect. Our analytical and introspective tendencies lead us to investigate the manner in which the creative individual of each stylistic period reacted to those dominating influences which were primarily responsible for the adoption of view points peculiar to each type of expression. So far as we can judge at this early stage of activity, the spirit of this modern movement differs from that of its predecessors. The creative individual of those periods designated as historic, absorbed dominant influences in a state of passive receptivity and there is little reason to believe that systematic analytical activity was incidental to the assimilative process. At the present time we discern a totally different mental attitude in the leaders who, in

from:
THE PASSING OF THE SKYSCRAPER FORMULA FOR DESIGN
Leon V. Solon
Vol. 55, No. 2, February 1924,
pp. 135-144.

THE POPULAR DEFINITION of "Architecture," frequently accepted as currency, is "the artistic expression of structure." By the majority this is conceded to comprise the main function of the art. The general accuracy of this view cannot be gainsaid, but our interest for the moment is to determine whether an esthetic interpretation of structure is the major objective in architectural composition; and if we should estimate the artistic value of unprecedented modes of architectural design, on the basis of their capacity for structural expression; also whether we may appraise certain individual phases of American architecture which depart from the classic, from the same standpoint. In considering the future of American architecture, it is necessary to determine the esthetic relation of design and construction. In former ages the mechanics of construction adapted themselves naturally to expression in artistic terms; there were no contradictory conditions, as they all ▶

 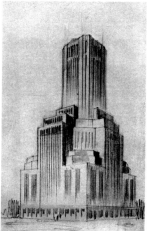  

1 Ely Jacques Kahn (1884–1972), was graduated from Columbia University School of Architecture in 1907. He studied at Ecole de Beaux-Arts, Paris for the next 4 years. In 1915 he joined the architectural firm Buchman and Fox in NYC. Over the years the firm was known as Buchman and Kahn, Ely Jacques Kahn and Kahn and Jacobs. The firm specialized in loft manufacturing buildings and offices, which were different from the set-back style of the commercial skyscraper. His colorful decorative vocabulary was based on knowledge of Asian and Pre-Columbian arts and Art Deco. His book *Design in Art and Industry* was published in 1935.

above: Progress sketches showing Kahn's development of the design: (from left to right) scheme A, scheme B, scheme C, scheme D.

opposite: Ornamental details, Two Park Avenue Building.

full consciousness of a compelling force, embark upon each imaginative excursion equipped with the "why" and the "wherefore," as infallible means for overcoming the leisurely processes of all evolution. We recognize the spirit of our age in this approach, which aspires to reduce the abstract to an elemental basis of cause and effect. We abandon, too, the prejudice that aesthetics should be divorced from logical argument, and that it is more fittingly considered when entangled in the vagaries of individual temperament.

Ely Kahn,[1] of the firm of Buchman and Kahn, is responsible for the design of the Park Avenue Building. In order that the significance of his work may be better grasped, it is advisable to recall certain circumstances common to stylistic evolution in general. When any of the historic types is investigated with the purpose of recognizing physical characteristics, it is found that distinctive techniques have originated in the practice of every art during that period in which it flourished. Though identical media may have been employed in successive periods, each vehicle for expression has been considered from an individual and distinct angle; with the result, that peculiar selective and manipulative processes have developed as part and parcel of each stylistic type. These

modifications in the technique of each art are attributable to a definite cause: when external influences commence to affect creative aspiration, consciousness of nebulous and unprecedented ideals causes the creative faculty to seek qualities and capabilities in expressive media which will be conducive to the materialization of the aesthetic objective. Idea, in the plastic, graphic, and decorative arts, only becomes an actual aesthetic quantity when physically stated in such form that its aesthetic content is transmissible. We consequently find when a new order of expression is in process of formulation, that the creative group has commenced by discerning contributory capabilities in physical media which it will employ in expression. In the productive activity these capabilities are directed to the attainment of the new artistic objective and made available through the origination of a distinctive technique. Technique therefore becomes the practical means for externalizing the aesthetic need.

The stylistic evolution of Gothic architecture is an illuminating illustration of this fact. From inception of the dominant influence novel capabilities were sought in structural material which, when discovered, became the basis for decorative characteristics which identify that manner. If we consider the decorative and structural functions with which stone was invested in that style, we find capacities discovered and brought into general practice which had previously been unsuspected. From the commencement of the movement the dominant aspiration sought a unique quality in silhouette for structural mass, and a new order of fenestration. The origination of tracery represents the perception of unrealized plastic capabilities in stone, which were discovered when that material was viewed under the stress of creative urgency to achieve a specific quality in design. When capability in substance was summarized in technique, imaginative energy achieved freedom, and style was given birth through the association of the new order of adaptability in medium—a fitting manipulative method and a guiding ideal.

There is little evidence in stylistic periods to prove that the discovery of innate capabilities in substance was other than an intuitive process. In such eras, technique, as the physical vehicle for expression, was comparatively slow of development, as are all forms of artistic activity in which the creative individual is actuated mainly by intuitive reaction to abstract and indeterminate influences. In Kahn's work we detect an aggressive and systematic form of pioneering into expressive capability in substance which determines its development and adaptability in terms of effect consistent with the modern ideal. The reduction of physical appearance in structural media to terms of opportunity in design, represents the culmination of a preparatory period from which we have almost emerged, in which texture has been accorded an inordinately high value in the choice of material for all effect purposes. This predilection for texture has been responsible for the vogue for appearances of dilapidation, actual or simulated, which for several years has fascinated the architect and interior decorator.

In the new order of effect values which we see exemplified in this design of Ely Kahn's, there is a complete revision of selective standards: it entirely disregards fictitious values, such as indications of ageing, the fouling of color with so-called "antiquing," the featuring of semi-disintegrated substances, and those accidental surface conditions which have been assumed to realize "quality." In the Park Avenue Building every substance therein incorporated depends for interest and effect upon virile and substantial properties which alone have entered into calculation; the manner in which these have been directed to the performance of decorative and scenic functions reveals a discernment of expressive capabilities akin to that which was active during the inception of historic types.

Brick has been employed as the principal structural material: if we analyze its function in effect we find it employed upon a basis totally different from that recognized by Harmon and so successfully applied by him in the Shelton Hotel. In that building a quality was imparted to structural mass through diversity in local interest throughout its vast superficial area, achieved with intricate craftsmanship in brick-laying and skilled adjustment of color and tonal quantities. This charm in surface, which is ideal in connection with the Romanesque suggestion, would prove an obstacle to the realization of that form of structural breadth for which Kahn strove: austere simplicity in structural mass would have been seriously depreciated by "accidentation" of surface with projecting headers and intricate articulation in assembly of the structural unit.

The brick selected is of a practically uniform hue, but that hue was made the keynote of a tonal gamut deliberately calculated in design. Through contrivance of structural surfaces with regard to conditions in illumination, each tonal denomination of the brick color resulting from those conditions is identified with some important feature. We find what might be termed the normal tone of the brick in the large plain area; of the main masses; another tone of that hue is developed in the long triangular pilasters which traverse the lower mass; other variations exist in the window spandrels, with accents in such details as the cor-

appertained to the tensile strength of like materials employed in building, involving the simple calculation of height to width, controlled by the margin of safety. Similarity in the character of structural materials, so far as weight and resistance were concerned, was productive of certain proportional relations in design to which the eye became accustomed, which were, in course of time, identified with the expression of artistic feeling Rather than with their actual source. Now, the inherent strength of stone or brick no longer restricts the height of a wall in proportion to the width of its base; the steel frame has long rendered such calculation obsolete. Our critical faculty has been developed upon standards which possess historic association; the functions of those standards in modern problems is purely sentimental. To what extent should such standards determine esthetic possibilities in modern problems with which they have merely a traditional relation. Taste is a reflection of the individual's judgment in imaginative selection; in architecture, the standards of taste are based upon types of artistic expression which evolved through intensely practical problems concerning the gravitational force of materials of definite weights. In the architectural forms which resulted, our ▸

A Tikal Temple from "The Architecture of the Ancient Mayas," by S.K. Lothrop, [57:6 Jun 1925 pp 491–509].

A presentation sketch by Hugh Ferriss for the Southwestern Bell Telephone Company Building, St. Louis, Missouri from the same issue as illustration above.

Pre-Columbia America became a rich source of inspiration for architects such as Frank Lloyd Wright as early as 1915. Numbers of artcles appeared in *ARCHITECTURAL RECORD* throughout the 20s on Mayan architecture and its influence including "Kinship Between Maya and the Modernist," [61:1 Jan 1927 pp 87–89].

opposite: Ornamental details, Two Park Avenue Building.

bels upon which the pilasters rest, accentuating through sharp shadow projection the identity of each tonal variant.

The stone employed for the base was obviously chosen for its contributory value to the tonal gamut; in its application in design the same principle in tonal development controlled the profile of the great cyma reversa from which the great triangular pilasters appear to spring. Despite the extreme severity of the main structural mass, insofar as detail of decorative intent is concerned, qualities of great refinement have been realized through systematic determination and regulation of effect capacities in the materials therein combined; with the result that we experience that peculiar and subtle structural impression which we now associate with the modernist manner.

It was decided to treat this building polychromatically, and an entirely new system in ornamental design was evolved, as compared to those previously identified with that form of effect. In place of the ornamental subject silhouetted upon its field forming an individual or segregated feature, the motifs are composed of silhouetted repeating forms, superimposed, each treated with a color. There is a great advantage in this ornamental system, in that each of the component factors of a colored feature possesses continuity in the direction in which it operates architecturally, instead of being subject to the peculiar rhythm of an ornamental composition, operative in the classic motifs. The colors employed are: red of a magenta character, black, ochre, and a peculiar blue with a greenish cast. These are mat in texture, with the exception of the black; this latter glaze being somewhat shiny reflects the light of the sky, depreciating considerably the measure of emphasis originally calculated. The ochre was selected as a liaison color between the color of the brick and the terra cotta group; it performs the function of association principally in corner pylons, where it figures upon deeply recessed ornamental bands.

When the general harmony of glazes was determined and the location of each estab-

lished, a certain amount of practical experimentation was undertaken previous to final acceptance; this was advisable in view of the large dimension of color areas, and the inevitable uncertainty as to how each would endure in distance. Full size models of some of the principal colored features were made in plaster, sprayed with color matching the color of the glazes selected, and set in place upon the roof of the factory workshops at an approximate distance of 250 feet. This proved very instructive, resulting in certain revisions in the original selection. The conventional employment of terra cotta has been considerably departed from, and a new vista of polychromatic possibilities revealed in the superimposed ornamental silhouettes.

The illustrations and studies reproduced give graphic information concerning this unusual building upon which it would be futile to expatiate. The richness in invention, and the pure logic of all argument responsible for each phase of expression is so self-evident and convincing, that we will not insult the reader's perception by describing the obvious; for this reason we have dwelt upon factors which may not be apparent to all, that is to say, its significance, the analytical consideration of substance and subjection of design to the development of intrinsic qualities in structural substance.

The great lobby, which is probably the most impressive in the country, contains a wealth of fascinating invention. The wainscot is of golden grey polished marble, surmounted by a superb frieze of gilt bronze from which gilded vaults spring. The Modernistic feeling has actuated the creation of every detail, and the ornamental principle described in connection with the terra cotta decorations of the façade has controlled practically all composition of plastic features. Probably the most interesting example of its application is found in the main entrance doorways, which are of gilt bronze: the motifs are in silhouette, superimposed in diminishing dimensions, and produce a tonal condition in the gold surfaces, accentuated with high lights on the edges, which achieves great richness. Color is introduced in the flat ceiling of the entrance lobby, and in tympana below the vault penetrations. The latter were designed by the architect for glass mosaic and are extremely original in design and color composition.

Details such as the mail box, building directory tablet, and other minor features are pure examples of this fascinating manner, and will do much to stabilize a form of expression which for the moment has an inherent tendency to the erratic. The lighting fixtures are conspicuous features of the lobby, and are of singular beauty and originality, the source of illumination being concealed without depreciation in efficiency. These were also designed by the architect, and embody new principles in decorative illumination capable of the most interesting and varied development.

On pages 305-325 (see page 240) we further illustrate with working drawings as well as photographs some of the outstanding features of the Park Avenue Building but considerably more space would be necessary than is here available to render justice to this remarkable building. Many features and points of view of vital interest to architects have been passed over in this brief appreciation. After a practically unvaried diet of the scholastic manner to which we have been subjected for so many years, it is more than refreshing to examine a composition in which basic aesthetic principles of varied nature have been formulated, and rigidly adhered to in the minutest detail. ∎

imagination, through force of unquestioning habit, now identifies the architectural feature with its architectonic function, regarding the former as "typical" of the latter. With the advent of the steel frame as the structural means for all that is most important in American architecture, and the consequent alteration in the original mathematical relation of structure to design, are we not confronted with the complex problem of purging the imagination of those automatic optical associations which we have inherited from a bygone condition? The practice of leaning upon tradition in questions of taste, has caused us habitually to accept certain architectural features as symbolic of the function which they were originally created to perform; our analytical sense has become so torpid that we assume a structural condition provided for, if the architectural symbol be logically placed.

When the engineer posed the greatest of all architectural problems to American architects, the shock was entirely without artistic anticipation. In the dire necessity for clothing this unsightly monster, architecture flew to tradition, and hurriedly devised an artistic formula. But the formula was in direct contradiction to the basic axiom of the art—that design must reveal structure ▸

1928

Prudence Building, New York City, Severance & Van Alen, 1924.

Bainbridge Building, New York City, Severance & Van Alen, 1924.

artistically. It was felt that the mere sacrifice of an axiom was a trifle, as compared with the necessity of hiding a method of structure which was without a parent in an art of pedigrees.

Those architectural conventions which influence our visual impressions and artistic judgment, have all originated in structural necessities, which were encountered as normal problems previous to the introduction of steel; the activity of the art depended primarily upon mathematics for those premises which assured stability; mathematics still furnish the premises for structure, but the present quantities have no relation to the original calculation. Proportional relations, as we appreciate them in the historic styles, embody in great measure the artistic solution of dynamic problems in building, and have survived by reason of their thorough adequacy in coping with incidental phenomena; when they cease to be logical, because of their inapplicability to actual conditions, they are doomed; American design is seething with insurgency, seeking to establish new proportional standards and forms of articulation, which will admit the steel frame as a palpable fact and a controlling factor in design.

The typical skyscraper design was the outcome of a very definite artistic argument (based upon fraud), which determined its articulation. It was assumed that the structural mass should consist of some form of base, the main body of the building, and an ornamental terminal. This resolved itself into a proposition of suspended weight, its architectural support, and an embellishment to top all. The orders in their various guises were the accepted emblems for architectural support, and it was assumed that nothing could be devised to furnish the imaginative requirement more completely. The wide variance in the proportion of the main body of the building from all accepted types seemed to demand the elimination of any possible interest from that part that might attract the eye to a feature considered abnormal. The result in effect was a contradictory weakening of the base, through the large areas of its penetrations, and a consequent increase in the apparent weight of the superimposed mass. The shocking effect of cornices which appeared in many cases around one side of the building only, is too familiar to discuss.

By some strange species of professional prudery, or that tenacity of precedent which constituted the architectural insurance against bad form, structural steel, when used as a concealed sup-

port, was considered the equivalent of malpractice. For the first time in the history of architecture, a deliberate line of separation was drawn between construction and artistic effect, with the deliberate intent to create an impression which would deceive the observer as to actual circumstances. The effort to maintain traditional impressions in the solution of the high building involved architectural design in serious complications, affecting elemental points of view and the logic of procedure. In every type of architectural expression which preceded the introduction of structural steel, design and construction were inseparable, each in a measure a consequence of the other. Their sudden separation, with the creation of the new method, was responsible for the vogue of the structural emblem; for when it was considered expedient to fabricate an artificial impression of structural support, the eye demanded an imaginative equivalent, and architecture descended to the subterfuge of devising scenery.

We are now arriving at a stage in progress at which an imperative need is recognized for the complete readjustment of architectural calculation, and the establishment of new optical standards in effect. We are about to bid a glad farewell to the standard formula for the skyscraper design, with its Graeco-Roman or Byzantine feet, its geometrically punctured torso, and its Renaissance top-gear. With the inevitable revision in optical standards, many architectural extravaganzas which the formula brought about, will be sources of professional wonder; and it is probable that the business-like mezzanine windows which make the best of so many classic porticos, will be classed with the architectural indigestions of other periods.

The fundamental of an adequate solution, must be the recognition of the steel frame in design, as the structural factor of which we are intuitively cognizant in the contemplation of modern American architecture. We are so aware of this structural means, that our imagination is most activated by its presence, in precisely those buildings of the formula type which now energetically deny its existence. An end must be put to a phase of artistic activity which aims to perpetrate an optical fraud, particularly when it has involved its practitioners in a maze of contradiction without artistic compensation.

Among those architects who show the greatest energy in shaking off the shackles of purposeless convention are Severance and Van Alen. The designer of the firm, William Van Alen, started in practice with a high saturation in Beaux-Arts tradition; he demonstrates the value of classic study as imaginative ballast, when individual points of view rebel against standard solutions for architectural problems. On his return from Paris he began to experience the urge to solve these complexities and architectural contradictions which had evolved with American structural methods; it was then that the admirable training of the Beaux-Arts asserted itself in his conception of planning, and in a hypersensitive feeling, for ornamental scale. The incongruities in design which arise through ignoring the steel frame seemed to offer the most promising field for imaginative effort, and he threw himself energetically into a careful and logical analysis of conditions. He determined that the recognition of engineering was no barrier to the realization of structural interest; and that design must state conditions as they are, without decorative subterfuge; namely, a metal skeleton with a veneer of structural material. All misleading impressions were carefully avoided; his aim was to convey to the observer, that walls are merely the enclosures of the steel subdivisions, and that there was no necessity for pretending that the lower part of the walls are responsible for the support of the upper. The deep embrasures which are contrived in the standard solution, with the purpose of giving the building a fortress-like rigidity, were abandoned as deceptive and superfluous, and the minimum reveal designed for openings on all floors, which reacts curiously upon the imagination, as we become conscious of the rigid and enduring strength of the frame. This deliberate intention to lighten the walls was in complete opposition to the standard solution, which attempted by every means to give them the maximum appearance of substantiality, regardless of the fact that they were actually supported features in the structural system, not the supporters. The impression thus contrived brought a natural consequence in the treatment of ornamentation; as the walls had to appear as thin as possible, to reduce their weight upon the steel frame, heavy sculptural ornamentation would have been illogical; he devised a type of ornamental treatment which clearly showed that the thinness of the stone veneer controlled relief. In this feature we gain another reflex impression of strength—the strength of the rigid frame, through the entire absence of intention to endow the stone with a predominant structural signifi-

cance. His solution of this architectural problem is most satisfying by reason of the sound logic of his premises, the accurate surmise of imaginative reaction, and the skill with which he states convictions in artistic terms.

In his last design for a business building on West 57th Street, New York, which we reproduce, we see an admirable solution of the great American problem; despite its deliberate lightness in treatment there is no sense of structural inadequacy; on the contrary, we are conscious of the presence of a structural factor of extreme rigidity and homogeneity, in the structural mass; it is a most interesting study in architectural reactions of an unprecedented order.

In studying the fenestration of this façade we can appreciate the enormous advantages which are offered when the high building is considered from this new angle. Decorative interest ranges from sidewalk to roof, and we feel enormous relief in finding that it is not really essential that the major area of a skyscraper should be architecturally negligible. A sky-line of a logical order is developed with considerable ingenuity and skill; a novel type of roof crowns the structure in place of the slice of cornice.

Our space does not permit enumeration of the concrete advantages which this form of design is capable of achieveing [sic] in terms of cubic feet; but the figures which the writer has examined, as compared with the standard type of plan, are truly astonishing. At no period has architecture been so absolutely controlled by economic considerations as it is today. The relation of design to investment is a vital factor in architectural calculation, and a principle of design which shows decided advantages in floor areas and cubic capacity is economically important: such advantages are too frequently procured at the sacrifice of artistry.

With designs such as those which illustrate this article, we will rapidly form new mental standards for the basic relation of design to steel structure; the outer covering could have the same relation to its frame that the epidermis has to the human frame, with a corresponding range of variety in external appearance. As our imagination accustoms itself to a new conception of decorative and structural relations, the old type of skyscraper, with its attempt to simulate a self-supporting skin, will be as unattractive as a human equivalent. In William Van Alen's work we welcome the identification of design with structure in the skyscraper after its long architectural dissociation. ●

A book review by
Henry-Russell Hitchcock, Jr.
HOW AMERICA BUILDS
By Richard J. Neutra
Vol. 63, No. 6, June 1928, pp. 594-95.
[Wie Baut Amerika? 4to–105 abb. 77
pp. Hoffinarin, Stuttgart: 1927.
Paper. $2.50.]

* * *

Mr. Neutra goes further than his programme perhaps implies, and discusses the traffic question which is so closely related to the question of our building methods; and in this discussion he offers suggestions with regard to automobiles for handling both the matter of distribution and of garaging, and with regard to trains for railroad stations devoted to commuting traffic. His scheme for a large commuting station is interesting and ingenious both in plan and in design and his "Rush City" would be fortunate to be so well provided.

He further considers the relation between the almost universal use of taxis and private automobiles and the zoning question both as regards New York and Chicago; and proposes essentially a scheme (such as neither New York nor Chicago approach, but rather Cleveland, Detroit or Hartford), with a business center of rather high buildings surrounded by a wide-spreading low building zone for residences, apartments and the necessary adjuncts, theatres and so forth, to large city life. Thus the first third of his book is of a theoretical but not utopian nature, outlining the conditions which control American building, how they are regulated and how they might well be further regulated to give to our cities something of the logical organism which, with somewhat less advanced traffic conditions, the newer Central European city planners have sought—as for example in the enlargement of Cologne or Vicuna. * * * ●

Two Park Avenue Building, New York City, Buchman & Kahn, architects, 1926-27.

Prevailing fashion not only affected architecture, but how it was rendered and photographed. This photo owes as much to the etchings of Piranesi (photo page 240) as it does to the renderings of Hugh Ferriss (photo page 234, 260). Conversely, images of this kind affected the look of architecture. In his book, *The Frozen Fountain*, Claude Bragdon says, *"Ferriss served his masters so well that he himself enslaved some of them, judging by the increasing tendency to make skyscrapers look as much as possible like his imaginative drawings."*

Lewis Mumford thought Ferriss' drawings less than human. He felt the *"artist has the privilege of bringing out only the aesthetically desirable results."*

opposite: Electrical Building, the Exhibits of the Electrical Industries, "A Century of Progress" Exposition, Raymond Hood, architect, 1933. The structure seems to be a fantasy woven around Assyrian gates of some kind.

ECONOMICS OF THE SKYSCRAPER

Ely Jacques Kahn

It is presumably a bold step for an architect to speak of architecture in terms of economics; he risks betraying his ignorance of the sacred mysteries of business, or possibly raises the brow of the aesthete at something which smacks of the commercial. Neither reaction can worry him; the expert is right under any circumstance, if only to himself.

Contemporary architecture has contributed much that is unusual to a public that in a short space of years has accepted the steel framed building as a commonplace; that has seen so many startling structural developments that it has almost lost the faculty of being startled. It is difficult to realize that in twenty years the plan of the office building, loft building, the hotel, apartment house and factory has changed as rapidly as new equipment has been devised. Modern living conditions in a luxurious atmosphere—no servants, kitchenettes and dining alcoves—evolved the apartment hotel. Industrial competition, efficiency, economy of space sponsored the tall factory buildings. Whether the demand brought these buildings or the result stimulated the demand is not pertinent. What is clear, however, is that an entirely new set of standards has developed, in which the manifold requirements of a mechanical age have been met. The architect has not only accepted the precepts of municipal authorities in regard to building regulations, zoning laws, fire protection rules, labor department restrictions, but the demands of the fire underwriters and building managers suggestions as well.

Another quite vital factor in the development of property is the study of the building from the angle of investment and return —the checking of structural merchandise as accurately as any other major capital outlay. Intense competition has forced the most careful analysis of plan, the financial interests in the operation further accentuating the need of economy and the utmost return for effort expended. The location of the property would determine the degree to which appearance, material, glass area and the like, should be accentuated.

In the approach to the actual problem, the design of the Park Avenue Building for instance, one was faced with a site in a section long neglected due to the nearness of car barns that for years covered the property directly opposite. The old Park Avenue Hotel had been run down to such a point that it had affected the entire neighborhood, and when it was wrecked the occupancy of the new structure was somewhat dubious. A series of plan studies were made, among which the 200 foot square plot was cut into by deep indentations on the street frontages. The additional light obtained by this arrangement could not offset the loss of space and the lack of flexibility of plan where a study of the location indicated that large floor areas would probably be desired; and as a result the square block with a substantial court in the rear was adopted.

The height of the building was determined through a table of calculations largely affected by the number of passenger and freight elevators serving the various floors. The set-back conditions, column centers, standpipe regulations, stairways, toilets, and the like, fixed the extent of the service portions, and the relation of usable space to the unproductive area determined reasonably soon at what floor to stop.

It is interesting to note that the financing of the enterprise was coincident with its planning and that the bankers responsible for the successful development of the enterprise were represented by a technical staff that checked and rechecked the vital service elements, as well as the areas and their square foot values.

In the presentation of preliminary information to the bankers it is essential that the facts be reduced to an outline that can be immediately translated, through cubic contents, net and gross floor areas, to the simple statement of cost and return. The variations of plan, height or type of construction can seriously change the calculations, and the

SURFACE AND MASS,—AGAIN!
Frank Lloyd Wright
from: NOTES AND COMMENTS
Vol. 66, No. 1, July 1929, pp. 92-94

A TRUE announcement of the law of creation, if a man were found worthy to declare it, would carry Art up into the Kingdom of Nature and destroy its separate and contrasted existence.

A wise and noble countryman of mine said that.

I listened before entering an Architect's office and have faithfully worked to be worthy to make that declaration here where Architecture was the game of a rude and youthful people and not the labor of a wise and spirited Nation.

That effort now only well begun, Nature allows me to look in on many "post-mortems," in honor of those foregathered for the purpose. "History" proceeds to repeat itself, as ever,—oblique surmise.

Edificer Cram quotes, ''No one who begins a cause is ever allowed to finish it," calling upon that same History as witness. It seemed to comfort him.

He was discussing with Artificer Tallmadge the fate of the "Modern,"—really modern-"ism." The Artificer lightly underwrote it for the next thirty years as a joke on Oak Park, if New York and Paris came in." The Edificer said it was dead already, he understood, and fervently hoped it was. ▸

April

1928

G.B. Piranesi, from the series,
Capricci de Carceri, etching, 1743.

Lobby, Two Park Avenue Building.

right: Working drawing (top) for
bronze letterbox (bottom) for Two
Park Avenue, Buchman & Kahn,
architects.

bankers, through extensive experience, will
be on the watch for variations that will tend
to increase the cost or decrease the earning
power of their capital.

Flexibility of plan is the keynote of success of the new building. Whether or not it
be designed for some particular individual
or concern, or entirely for prospective tenants of a type merely anticipated, it is vital
that almost any variation of usage can be
accommodated. The Park Avenue Building,
in a zone that permitted manufacturing to
an extent of 25% of its area, was planned to
meet the requirements of the Building,
Labor and Fire Departments in this regard.
As the renting programme developed, it
became evident that more desirable tenants
with no manufacturing privilege would be
available and the leases promptly prohibited
labor of any kind. Where large areas were
required, the lower floors to the first setback
were offered. Above, smaller offices on
divided floors were available and were so
rented. Some day, whether it be ten years or
twenty, if there is a tendency to change the
occupancy, it will be found that the floors
are adapted for normal manufacturing loads
and areas; combination elevators may be
converted to freight elevators and the framing provides for additional cars. This adaptability of plan, the attempt to cover the possibilities of location and the extremely rapid
shift of population and business concentration is a reasonable guarantee of a sound
investment.

In a preliminary study of the building soil
conditions have been investigated—test bor-
ings obtained. The cost of sinking foundations in certain areas of New York, particularly in the lower part of Manhattan, will
have a serious bearing on the height of the
new building. Water conditions, quicksand,
old streams, ancient shore lines become
annoying realities. Surveys of existing and
neighboring buildings will determine
encroachments; continuity of lot possessions; need for underpinning; flues adjacent
which must be elevated; sewer levels and

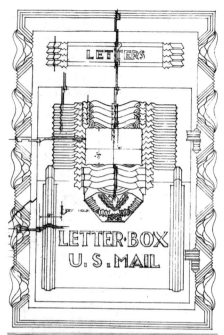

locations; water mains. Some of these obvious details may have a bearing on occupancy where, for instance, bank vaults, subcellars or deep basements are suggested and where the additional cost of their preparation may be quite out of line with the corresponding income.

Location will have determined the character of the building, whether apartment house, apartment hotel, transient hotel, building, loft building, factory. In certain instances none of these categories will be possible. On the site of the Vanderbilt home, long occupying the Fifth Avenue block from 57th Street to 58th Street, it was determined that the very unusual neighborhood facing the open square and Central Park, demanded something different from the average hotel or office building.

A group of eight individual buildings was designed; an arcade arranged to connect 57th and 58th Streets. The units were restricted to six stories in the main; one on 58th Street, rented at the outset, was raised to eight with an apartment on its roof as additional area. In spite of the fact that experts had gathered at weekly meetings and in these carefully organized conferences were realty figures of note—the builders, attorneys, engineers, architects' representatives, owners—the problem was so difficult that when the actual buildings were finished there was still the question as to whether the development was entirely what the circumstance warranted. Curiously enough, a tenant did arrive who rented three buildings of the group, representing over 50% of the unrented balance, and before the elevators in the completed structures have been used, or a single citizen used the arcade, already lined with its marble and bronze, the entire group is being rebuilt to meet the economic conditions requested by this particular tenant. In this instance the matter of design, though important, was definitely secondary to the treatment of a plot of land of great value subject to further enhancement by reason of

its development. The additional cost of the changes, time of execution, (which includes loss of rent during such periods,) when compared with the type of tenant, rent, and the length of lease, obviously substantiated the owners' alteration of the original plan.

The time element is another vital consideration in the analysis of the project. The rental periods, February, October, May, are peculiarly set for the particular types that demand these dates. The buildings, therefore, must be scheduled to start at a precise moment where the minimum of time need be expended and moreover completion at the required day will not be missed. The renting agents will have maintained a close watch on the details of the plans and prepared their renting plans simultaneously so that as the building rises, leases are signed and such changes as may be advisable are promptly executed.

It is obvious that in the preliminary consideration of the building venture the design of the façade plays an extremely important part. The degree to which the owner will concern himself is quite obviously a varying factor. Unfortunately, a large proportion of investment structures are fathered by men whose judgment is more valuable in finance than in design, with correspondingly desperate results. They find available a group of architects who have attained a certain fluency or quasi efficiency and as these men hold as their main qualifications lower fee basis, the temptation is obvious. In this situation lies strength and weakness. Many an owner through honest ignorance and avowed respect for professional skill will study and experiment to an unusual degree. On the other hand, with the advent of something new in architecture, the second flight of practitioners, having absorbed a large proportion of the actual work of the day, seize upon the new forms and with natural economy of brain power jangle forms together that can only have the merit of being different. ■

Nature will surprise and disgust both with that consummation we notice in her for both have betrayed her.

At the moment she has her eye on Douglas Haskell and Russell Hitchcock. Here come, eventually, valuable critics?

Yet, by way of the former, last November, I learn that by "weight" I am satisfactorily betrayed into the long grasp of Tradition. Well—insofar as Architecture may not be divested of the weight of organic nature, I plead guilty,—the trees are guilty likewise.

Useless weight and ornament are sins.

I have sinned. Sometimes for a holiday. Sometimes betrayed by a happy disposition. Week days I seek lightness, toughness, sheerness, preferring them. Week ends I fall from grace.

Has machinery already made exuberance a sin?—poverty a virtue?

Meantime, my critics, although a pupil of Louis Sullivan, never have I been his disciple. He has himself gratefully acknowledged this publicly. Had I been his disciple I should have envied him and in the end have betrayed him.

Unjust then as untrue to quote from his Autobiography,—"The search for the rule so broad as to admit of no exception—as mine when the "exception" still, as always, interests me most, as necessary to prove any rule both useful and useless. That trait enables most critics to fail to penetrate the variegated surface of what I've tried to do.

Do I make excursion into the feeling of an oriental race and, no lessening grasp upon organic Architecture,build their building by means of their own handicraft, dedicate the building to them as oriental symphony? ▸

1928

above: Charles L. Morgan, "Rainbow Bridge," 1927. Morgan was a delineator who worked for D.H. Burnham & Co, Chicago.

Numbers of architects proposed skyscraper bridges in the 1920s and 30s, including Raymond Hood.

right: Skyscraper Bridge, Hugh Ferriss, delineator, 1926.

Proposed Skyscraper Bridge for San Francisco, Louis Mulgardt, architect, 1924.

opposite: Aline Barnsdall "Hollyhock" House, Los Angeles, Frank Lloyd Wright, architect, 1919-21.

A SKYSCRAPER BRIDGE PROPOSED FOR CHICAGO
Vol. 63, No. 4, April 1928, pg. 383.

A monumental skyscraper bridge has been proposed to span the mouth of the Chicago River linking the north and south boulevards. The scheme presented here was conceived by Charles L. Morgan and accomplishes a novel combination of bridge and skyscraper construction.

The bridge would be carried aloft on skyscraper piers twenty-five or more stories in height. These piers would afford valuable office space which could be rented at a considerable profit. The bridge spans would be so high above the river as to permit unobstructed river traffic. The alternate arches between the skyscrapers would span streets and alleys, with the central arch of greater width crossing the river. Tenants and employees would enter the offices by elevators from the upper boulevard or from the street level below. Huge trusses would occupy much of the mass at the crown of the arches but there would be sufficient space to provide two stories for garage purposes. ∎

A SKYSCRAPER BRIDGE FOR SAN FRANCISCO
Vol. 63, No. 6, July 1928, pp.162-163.

THE ARCHITECTURAL RECORD for April showed us A Skyscraper Bridge for Chicago. High-flung arches leapt between piers which were nothing less than huge office buildings. And the accompanying note told us that "the scheme presented here was conceived by Charles L. Morgan."

Yet, on reflection, it was surely several years back that Louis Christian Mullgardt gave to the San Francisco press a skyscraper bridge for San Francisco. Where are the newspapers of yester-year? Ah, here it is—Architect Offers Daring Plan to Connect San Francisco and Oakland with Huge Bridge. Such prolixity in a headline would alone date it in the dim past of three or four years ago. No modern headline writer would think of exceeding Architect Bay Span Looms. The yellowing paper bespeaks its antiquity, too.

Now looked at with philosophical dispassionateness, questions of priority may make little difference. If an idea is worth while, who thought of it first is certainly not the most important thing about it. For all that, we do like to see credit go where it is due, particularly when involving ourselves or our friends. Yet even so, I would scarcely presume to importune Architectural Record readers with Mr. Mullgardt's project solely because it preceded Mr. Morgan's by three and a half years. I feel that it has an intrinsic interest over and above the matter of who saw it first. And it is quite probable that it never went beyond the local newspapers into the architectural press. You can trust Mr. Mullgardt for such negligence in pushing his wares.

Let me intrude just enough statistics to put an outsider in possession of the problem.

The city of San Francisco lies on a peninsula on the west side of San Francisco Bay. On the east side stretch a half dozen continuous cities, of which Oakland is the largest. Despite the divisions of these several municipal governments, the two sides of the bay constitute a united community of close to a million and a half people. Transbay communication to date has been by ferry only—the shortest land route around the end of the bay is a good seventy miles. It will readily be appreciated that under these circumstances the agitation for a bridge becomes daily more insistent. At the point chosen by Mr. Mullgardt—substantially the same point, be it noted, recently recommended by a commission of engineers appointed by the city of San Francisco to make a preliminary Survey of the problem—the distance from shore to shore is five miles.

With this prefatory information out of the way, I can let Mr. Mullgardt offer a few words for himself. This he does just as he designs-with gusto.

"This plan envisions a bridge over San Francisco Bay whereby the East and West Bay communities become as a single unit; ...providing adequate docking harbors, especially for the East Bay communities; aviation landings and jump-offs for government, state and corporations; housing for air mail, wireless stations, naval stations, air and ocean passenger stations, hotels, auditorium, offices, factories, hangars, Zeppelin towers, etc....

"For the present, an adequate bridge will consist of two highways, one above the other, designedly separated for freight and passenger traffic....

"Imagine yourself seated in a motor car, coming up one of the several approaches, all of which lead on to the bridge from different directions and at easy gradients. Immediately you enter on a very wide boulevard which extends more than two miles, at an elevation of only 5o feet above the bay. That is the causeway of the bridge.

"Having traversed the causeway, your car continues upward on a gentle curvature to a maximum elevation of over 200 feet. That is the bridge! You are now crossing the bridge which arches the main channel of the bay,

the arches being sufficiently high to clear the loftiest ships.

"To right and left you look down upon masts and funnels. In the distance you see Goat Island, Alcatraz, Angel Island, Golden Gate, Mount Tamalpais. Ahead is...San Francisco.... "Now your car glides down the opposite gradient; soon it will be on the west causeway, where you perchance see a Zeppelin anchored to its bridge tower, discharging passengers who have come across the continent and elsewhere …

"Alongside the causeway you see inclines. You see rows of motor cars laden with steamship passengers and their luggage. Below you see ocean steamers docked to wide platforms flanking the causeway.

"You see crowds of people coming and going through doors of pavilions as you are traversing the bridge gradients. They have come up on elevators or are going down to the pier landings.

"The pier buildings support the bridge, also, being great structures, splendidly located, to serve a great variety of requirements, greater even than do buildings on shore. Their main entrances are on a level with the surface of the bridge highway. . . .

"You have observed aeroplanes alighting and departing from long concrete floats which project at right angles to the causeways. Those planes carry passengers and mail. The government has a branch post office within the bridge....

"Those taxicabs and busses which you saw going down inclines Nos. 44, 55, and 66 are now parked in their respective garages waiting for telephone calls. These garages are located in the causeways, where cars may give prompt service to the enormous business which the bridge affords at all hours, day and night."

But hold! While Mr. Mullgardt has been slowing down to point out these numerous features, I have overtaken him with a bucket of cold water. It will not do to make this bridge too attractive. Already we seem on the verge of rendering the cities themselves useless. And without the cities, what need would there be for a bridge?

— Irving F. Morrow ■

A wail! I have been false to the mode of the Machine I had proclaimed and championed.

Should I have proclaimed that "Mode,"—now of Paris,—from Tokio house-tops by means of oriental handicraft no matter how false the circumstances? Not for a moment the Machine forgotten, but in abeyance while I took off my hat to the Japanese and destructive force, was conquered by integral building:—Showing that Architecture may be "symphonic" in more sound senses than one.

This exception proved many rules, but broke more and still confounds the critics.

I design a negro schoolhouse in the South—make it theirs, in point of life and color,—form too, departing, nowise, from integral building. The mode of the machine deserted, again, to be humane. This is license?

I build a home for myself in Southern Wisconsin,—a stone, wood and plaster building, make it as much a part of my grandfather's ground as the rocks and trees and hills there are.

This Architect has "lapsed into the picturesque."

On Midwestern prairies I build, in three dimensions, houses that proclaim the prairie's quiet level, —the third dimension evident as unbroken roof-planes likewise lying in similar repose,—as human shelter.

The floor-planes too in evidence to give scale to the whole.

Well,—"The Gothic has been put to bed on its side!" ▶

***Drawing for Two Park Avenue
Building, New York City,
Buchman & Kahn, architects,
1926-27.***

Since he was involved in designing the polychromed tiles for this
building, this unsigned drawing
could very well be by Leon V.
Solon (see page 230).

opposite: Rendering of brick patterns for Barclay-Vesey Building,
Voorhees, Gmelin & Walker,
architects, 1930.

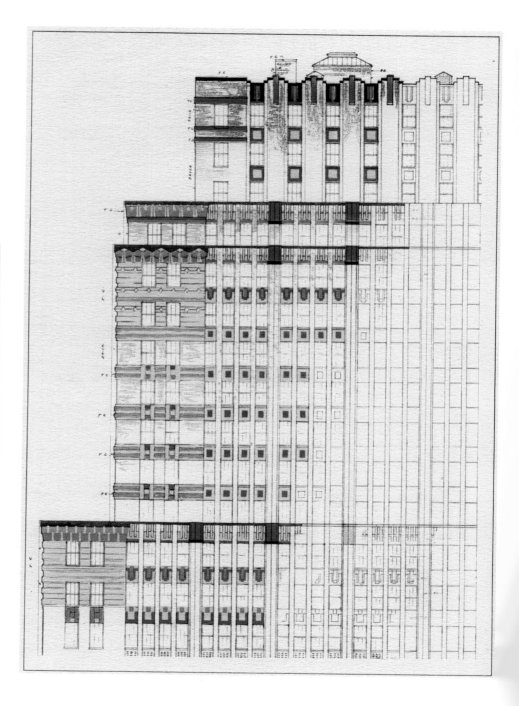

AMERICAN ARCHITECTURE TODAY
Part I: The Search for "Something More"
Lewis Mumford

FOR a whole generation, from 1890 to 1920, the energies of American architecture worked under the surface. When one looked about the scene, it seemed that the American architect, like the child of the colonial settler described by Thomas Hardy, had been born old. Here and there the active energies of architecture broke volcanically through some fissure: the train-hall of the Pennsylvania Station or the concourse of the Grand Central lived by its own naive virtues, in spite of every effort of the architect to ignore or belittle these qualities; but the mask of American architecture was frozen: the face was dead. The very skyscrapers were born old. "If," I wrote in 1924, "there has been any unique efflorescence of style about the entrance or the elevator doors, I have been unable to discover it."

In five years, the entire picture has changed. The energies that worked below the ground so long are now erupting in a hundred unsuspected places; and once more the American architect has begun to attack the problems of design with the audacity and exuberance of a Root, a Sullivan, a Wright. In a sense, we have at last caught up with 1890; but in another sense we have passed far beyond these early pioneers, for the steel cage is no longer an experimental form; the processes of reinforcing and casting concrete are no longer a mystery; and, during the years when, on the surface, little was being accomplished in design, the plans for specific types of building—the loft, the office, the theatre—were being worked out and refined. The economical width of bays, the minimum cubage per floor for light and ventilation, the whole arrangement of a house, a hospital, or a hotel as a working plant all these things were progressively mastered. I do not say that there is not much more to learn; on the contrary, a good part of our knowledge consists in tricks to meet very specific conditions, like Mr. Andrew Thomas's plans for apartment-houses, which

are admirable to the last degree provided one must respect lot lines and provided one does not change the depth of the block.

But the point is that the major technical difficulties are, for the moment, mastered. The proof of this is that the architect has become tired of his Corinthian columns, his acanthuses, or his ogives, of all the clichés that once served instead of the sterling mark on American architecture; and though the elder men, who worked through this period of "refinement," "taste," rectitude, may not be as ready to work out of it as was the late Mr. Goodhue, there is no doubt that the able young men who are following on their heels are in revolt. They are nauseated by acanthus leaves, and they know that if they pull down the stone columns the modern building, unlike the temple of the Philistines that Samson destroyed, will remain standing. One sees this spirit even more clearly in the good architectural schools. In the class in design at Michigan I saw strong designs and weak designs, but I saw no stale designs: the feeling was clear, frank, confident. No one thought that an airplane terminus was a place for displaying archaeological knowledge.

What has been gained during the last five years? What general characteristics emerge in this new American architecture? What have we learned about the treatment of materials, the use of site, the handling of the structural forms? In abandoning the battle of the styles, have we solved the problem of decoration, or must we now face a more genuine issue and experimentally work to a conclusion? Finally: what are our weak points and where do we lag? I have posed these questions in the abstract; but I do not pretend I can give satisfactory answer to them; rather, I shall attempt to show the concrete forms in which the solutions present themselves.

II

The four great components of design are site, materials, technical construction, and feeling. All of these have been modified by the conditions of modern life; but they have been altered in different ways: if the archi-

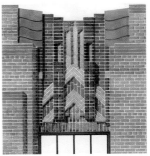

The effort in California and Arizona? Harassed by vexation of industrial confusion, forced lying, hand-sore and heart-sick with makeshift tools, I finally found simple mechanical means to produce a complete building that looks the way the Machine made it,—as much so at least as any woven fabric need look. Tough, light but not "thin," imperishable, plastic, no necessary lie about it anywhere and yet, Machine-made, mechanically perfect. Standardization as the soul of the Machine here, for the first time may be seen in the hand of the Architect, put squarely up to Imagination, the limitations of imagination the only limitation of building.

Unhappily, my critics, having seen, must continue to see Egyptian, Mayan, Chinese, Japanese, Persian, Moorish. Not one motif of the sort can they fairly fix in these buildings for such were never in my mind. Only because these desert buildings too are naturally elemental in form can they verify resemblance.

Did I prefer them lean,—sun-defiant,—ascetic? They might be so, honestly, and please my critics.

Here, in principle,—as servant, not as master is the Machine.

But why should the product look like machinery?

* * * ▶

[first published in the periodical Architecture, which was combined with ARCHITECTURAL RECORD in 1937]

1928

above: Barclay-Vesey Building, New York City, Vorhees, Gmelin & Walker, architects, 1930.

A interesting kind of "family tree" exists between Leopold Eidlitz (page 72), who was in practice with his son Cyrus for a brief while in the 1880s (designer of the New York Times Building), and Ralph Walker (designer of the Barclay-Vesey Building).

CYRUS L. W. EIDLITZ, 1885

EIDLITZ AND MCKENZIE, 1900
Cyrus L. W. Eidlitz - Andrew C. McKenzie

MCKENZIE VOORHEES AND GMELIN, 1910
Andrew C. McKenzie - Stephen F. Voorhees
Paul Gmelin

VOORHEES GMELIN AND WALKER, 1926
Stephen F. Voorhees - Paul Gmelin
Ralph Walker

VOORHEES WALKER FOLEY AND SMITH, 1938
Stephen F. Voorhees - Ralph Walker
Max H. Foley - Perry Coke Smith
Benjamin Lane Smith, 1945

VOORHEES WALKER SMITH AND SMITH, 1955
Stephen F. Voorhees - Ralph Walker
Perry Coke Smith - Benjamin Lane Smith
Charles Haines, 1957

tect has gained freedom in construction, he has, in our big cities, lost a great deal in the treatment of site. Let us see how these elements tend to work out.

In the rectangular plan of the usual American city, the site has become a passive factor: the vast majority of sites are blind sites, without sufficient direct approach, without the possibility of constructing a four-sided building, and without any opportunity to register the façade as a whole. This fact has affected the design of the great mass of buildings in the crowded parts of our cities: both the façade and the cubical mass have become negligible. I am aware that there are exceptions to this generalization: Chicago's lake front is an unrivalled approach, and there are similar points about squares or parks in New York: but within the central district of any city, even a small one like Grand Rapids or Providence, the architect cannot take advantage of his site. This is a genuine misfortune, but not all the results of it have been disastrous, for it has made the architect more ready to scrape off ornamental forms which have no relation to either the structure or the feeling of a modern building. During the last five years the clean façade, devoid of columns, pediments, balconies, cornices, has come back into architecture: the fronts of our better buildings are now as direct and simple as the backs and sardonic observers of the American scene, like Mr. Erich Mendelsohn, need no longer confine their photographic studies of our tall buildings to the rear views.

This gain is indeed a negative one: the absence of a spurious note, the stripping down of design to elemental relationships, and the casting overboard of vestigial ornaments that do not register; but one has only to compare the unbroken planes of the Barclay-Vesey Building with the fussiness, the exaggeration of the vertical, the contemporary ornamental tricks of the older skyscrapers like the Woolworth Tower or the Singer Tower to see the advantage in design. In this negative gain, a great many buildings have shared: the Bronx tenement, the Park Avenue apartment-house, the Seventh

Avenue loft building, have this common quality. This seems to me a real advance. Buildings should be distinguished, if possible, by their site, and by their expression of function and purpose: that a building should express the aims of the client or the personality of the designer is inevitable; but these things should never be the aim of architecture. We need a direct, simple, inevitable vernacular architecture as a setting for our great buildings; indeed, before we can have any tolerable modern ornament, we must first learn to erase every distracting vestige of earlier forms. The earlier skyscrapers in Chicago did this: they were as stark as the Pyramids—and our present efforts here mean, I think, that we are again at a hopeful point of departure.

In the dropping of the cornice and the improvement of the silhouette of our bigger buildings, the zoning and setback restrictions have been given a good deal of credit: but the current advance in architecture owes less to these legal aids than many people have supposed. As a matter of fact, between the "zoning envelope" as defined by law, and the best aesthetic treatment of a building on any particular site, there is no essential relation. The notion that any setback building is better than any cubical one is absurd: when the architect is handicapped by a narrow lot and by the demand of the owner to enclose every possible cubic foot, the setback restrictions frequently create curious deformities. When people think of the architectural triumphs of zoning they think of Mr. Hugh Ferriss's ideal cities, or of one or two great buildings that have been produced on sites sufficiently large to build up into a great mass. This does credit, perhaps, to their hopes and their imaginations; but it has no actual relation to the buildings in our cities. Except for what little light and air the setbacks have introduced—and it is still precious little—it makes absolutely no aesthetic difference whether the great mass of crowded buildings are above ground or below, set up or set back. The architect realizes this quite well: he knows where the shoe pinches. As a result, since 1924, he has gone in for decoration in the few visible parts that remain; and my dictum that there has been no efflorescence of design about the entrance or the elevators no longer holds in 1928. It is precisely in this department that a revolution is going on; and before it is over it will influence many other things besides the vestibules of skyscrapers. Here there have been a dozen brave attempts at fresh designs: the Barclay-Vesey Building, the Radiator Building, the Alabama Power Company's Building, the Fur Capitol, the Graybar Building; and out of a great welter of fine effort, at least one almost complete success: Mr. Ely Kahn's entrance and corridor in the Park Avenue Building.

III

In considering the advances made in our commercial and industrial buildings we may leave out site, and put to one side materials: for the necessities of fireproof construction leave us with steel, concrete, brick, and terra-cotta, with glass still too dubious under sudden changes in temperature to play a big part, except in its conventional form. It is by utilizing new methods of construction and embodying a new feeling that our modern architecture lives: but the feeling and the construction are not always in harmony. In Europe modern architects, like Gropius and Le Corbusier, have faced this situation with inexorable logic: they have modified or curbed their feelings so as to fit the construction! To them, ornament is a snare; color is a smear. Does a dynamo need ornament? Does a Diesel engine need color? Our world is essentially a world fit for dynamos, Diesel engines, steamships, a thing of black, gray, white, conscientiously utilitarian.

Now, this is an extreme position; but it emphasizes a reality. One part of the modern feeling for form, the thing that distinguishes us from the Baroque or the Gothic, is a positive pleasure that we take in the elemental structure of an object. We do not paint pansies on our typewriters or griffons on our automobiles, nor are our office files covered with decorative plaster; and if we conceived the rest of our environment as freshly as we

have conceived these new additions to it, We should strip it similarly to its last essential. To realize form-in-function, by its clear, lucid expression, is what constitutes the modern feeling: it is what unites the Brooklyn Bridge, the paintings of Cézanne, the Sculpture of a Brancusi, a Despiau, an Eric Gill, the structure of a grain elevator, or a piece of clean engineering like the ventilator buildings of the Hudson Tubes. That feeling must exist in our architecture: Le Corbusier is right; at least that much must be there. But we are still human beings, not dynamos or Diesel engines; and there must be something more.

It is over the question of what this "something more" must consist of that the new battle of the styles will be fought. Let us admit as a foundation that an office-building, a factory, a garage, a church, a school, a home will, in any tolerable modern conception, begin at the same point: they will use similar materials and similar methods of construction—what we may now loosely call the vernacular of the machine. Their primary feeling—the tone and attitude produced in the spectator—will be the same: a factory like the Sloane linoleum plant near Trenton, a hotel like the Allerton House at 57th Street, a warehouse like the Detroit Evening News Building, garages and houses like those at Sunnyside Gardens, though they were designed by different architects for different places and purposes, all have a common signature. They are the direct, economical expression of material and plan. If any large part of our buildings approached this simplicity and directness, the outlook for our architecture would be a happy one: such a foundation could not be shaken by archaism, stylicism, or the fake picturesque derived from the latest foreign sketches and snapshots added to the architect's files. The demand for "something more" can only be met by those who have had the courage to go as far as this.

How shall the final expression take place, once we have simple and direct forms to work with? The two opposing answers to this question are typified in the work of

Fountains of aesthetic invention and beauty in our Utopia are all but dried up. If, now, we make gospel of any "mode" whatsoever,—they are gone! Irrationally bound by cruel provincial judgments of Ismtown and Istville, we have known no freedom in Creative Art.

Are we so hide-bound to this bondage that Mode can destroy in Architecture the very principle of Liberty proudly declared in our cherished Jeffersonian charter as essential to Life?

The Modern is. Was always, must always be. At this critical juncture it is at least thirty-two years old.

The New is ever Old,—all shallow pretense aside, and will, repeatedly, seek to become the prison-house of a "mode," beginning with the young.

Therefore, nothing is more vital in America at this psychological moment in her Architecture than active realization of what living, and that means organic architecture, would bring.

We've had little. Until yesterday we were insultingly careless of that little.

Europeans, only, valued and conserved it or we should now be helplessly prone to the "Modern" imported as French Fashion and be, soon, sterile again for another thirty years.

We show signs of pique at such European conservation inclined to disprove the case rather than render thanks. Here is Douglas Haskell,—Russell Hitchcock no less,—in this ungracious act.

These young critics, I believe, love Architecture as a mysterious essence intrigued by the science and philosophy of the great Art.

They see in "surface and mass" abstractions of great and gifted Europeans "inspired by French painting,"—the Truth. But I know these abstractions repudiate the third dimension, ignoring depth of matter to get surface-effects ▸

above: Detail of ornament, Barclay-Vesey Building, New York City.

right: Outer vestibule, Film Center Building, New York City, Buchman & Kahn, architects, 1928–29.

opposite: Columbia Presbyterian Medical Centre, New York City, James Gamble Rogers, architect, 1927.

Messrs. Ralph Walker and Ely Kahn. In the Barclay-Vesey Building Mr. Walker, like Mr. Rogers in the Medical Centre Building, permits the mass itself to be cold, hard; the building as a whole has a feeling of dark strength; but in the stonework of the lower stories and in the interior the designer introduces a delicate, naturalistic carving, heightened within by the use of gold. When one enters the main hall, one almost forgets its purpose: it is as gaily lighted and decorated as a village street in a strawberry festival. Mr. Walker, in other words, accepts the contrast between structure and feeling: he does not attempt to reconcile them. One remains clear and logical, inflexibly committed to its programme; the other is warm and intimate and a little confused. In Mr. Walker's design decoration is an audacious compensation for the rigor and mechanical fidelity of the rest of the building; like jazz, it interrupts and relieves the tedium of too strenuous mechanical activity.

Mr. Kahn's decoration is the exact opposite of this. In the building that strikes the boldest and clearest not among all our recent achievements in skyscraper architecture, the Park Avenue Building, he has kept the exterior and the interior in unity: the first has become more warm, the second has become more rigorous and geometrical and handsome. With a warm buff brick as a foundation, the Park Avenue Building works up into bands of sunny terra-cotta, broken and accentuated with red, green, bright sky-blue. The pattern is abstract; and every part, down to the lighting fixtures, has the same finish, rigor, swiftness, perfection. In this building, structure and feeling are at last one: the directness and simplicity of the first have not been forfeited in the decoration; the warmth and human satisfaction of the decorative forms have not been overpowered in the structure itself, for they are expressed there, too. This building seems to me an answer both to the European who, despairing of synthesis, have sought to enjoy the grimness and inflexibility of modern forms by sitting hard on their organic feelings, and to those who, equally despairing of

synthesis, have permitted the human, sensuous note to break out irrelevantly—either in stale archaeology, in fussy handicraft, or in unrelated bursts of modern decoration.

One swallow may not make a summer; but one building like this, which faces the entire problem of design, and has a clean, unflinching answer for each question, may well serve to crystallize all the fumbling and uncertain elements in present-day architecture. The success of the Park Avenue Building is not due to the fact that it is a tall tower or that it is a setback building. It is not a tower and the setback is trifling. Its success is due to its unique synthesis of the constructive and the feeling elements: its method is as applicable to a two-story building as to one of twenty stories: it is in the line of that rule Louis Sullivan was seeking—which would admit of no exceptions. The Park Avenue Building shows the limit of the architect's skill, to date, under urban conditions, where the programme is inflexibly laid down by the business man and the engineer, and where the site is too costly to be played with. With the part of American architecture that has been favored by more sufficient sites, a more flexible programme, and a broader schedule of resources, I shall deal in another article. ■

characteristic of canvas and pigment as painting and not of Architecture,—no, no matter howsoever stark begot with gas pipe, thin slabs and naked steel work. These "materials" may now be used as "decoration" too. Witness the concoctions of "wire, lead-pipe, plumbing-fittings, brass-keys, bits of glass and wood,—of this school? Sophisticated, ingenious, cleverly curious,—they smell of the dissecting room,—affect me as a morgue.

These artificially thin walls like card-board, bent, folded and glued together, are frankly, likewise dedicated not to the Machine but to machinery! Therefore they do not live.

The "lines" not the spirit of mechanical "mobilization," inspire their dry sophistication with a new "Aesthetic" and for the moment a new Simplicity—lie charms us afresh.

But why strive to divest organic-nature of wholesome natural "weight" in vain endeavor or to make houses seem to "fly" anywhere,—even into the face of poverty?

Dear boys,—do not spend too much too freely, that might be better kept did you make it yours.

We have here, no stranger,—only a familiar in another guise with more guile than the folly we slept with yesterday,-as much pose but with better breeding,—a gesture of the right sort.

But a gesture seeking to ignore steps already faithfully, painfully and soundly taken to establish here the reality thus begestured abroad. In order to prefer French painting as more convenient parent?

Is this because it seeks to be a "movement," always, in Art, a damnable agency, and, that it may move as such must ignore too much?

"Poverty" is no Messiah, needs no prophets. Poverty is disease.

. . . .

Know that at the very center of every true form of human-use or aesthetic-worth, whatsoever, stands Nature. The third dimension naturally distinguishes Architecture from Painting. By it we know, the one mind from the other.

Instead of this inner mastery of method and materials of sound-construction, with scientific surrender to utility, in behalf of plastic-simplicity—these "surface-and-mass" effects are no more organic than the "American Classic" of New-York-City or Los-Angeles Tudor-Spanish.

Moreover, stark boxes blister the eyes by refusing the sun-acceptance trees, rocks, and flowers love.

Is this ignorance,—impotence? Or merely empirical endeavor to force issue upon Nature?

Gracious, grateful, sun-acceptance comes by way of texture, pattern-integration, by way of human Imagination. To the eye it is what music is to the ear.

Buildings not knowing this, or, knowing, refusing it, as does a concrete sidewalk, are no more architecture than are buildings using ornament the way the "New" architects use surface and mass,—that is to say superficially, for itself alone.

Such are the edifices of the Artificer, or the artifice of the Edificers,—not radical work of the Architect.

The nature of true Architectural ornament should not be foolishly mistaken and the abuse of the thing taken for the thing,—preferring "Art and Decoration" per se, to come in commercially triumphant as substitute.

. . . . . .

Handicapped by depth of organic-endeavor and happy disposition I know well how difficult simple, integral-things are in Architecture and believe in none otherwise.

I am seeking plastic-simplicity as Architect, not as Painter. No. Nor believing that because of the Machine the Architect has now become mere agent providing for Art and Decoration.

Therein seems the basis for radical difference between myself and the so called card-board house as "New." Were this vital element of the third dimension deducted from my work, what is now seen in the buildings endorsed by our critics as New would be found to be at least as Old as that work itself.

Nor could the varied group of buildings I have created have been produced by a "mannerist." The matter is too deep, the range too wide.

My concern here is not with the Asceticism of superficial surface and mass effects. That I respect as I would a monk's. Nor with its "Aesthetic,"—which is legitimately mine. And we have in this "New" a "picture-house" more to my "taste" than any before. Were the country to choose it before those of our Edificer's, Artificer's and Fashion mongers, it would choose well, but would have to choose again in course of time and have only its labor for its pains over another period of thirty years.

Poverty might get along with it. "Aristocracy" might, too, for a time,—it lives on gestures of the sort from New York and Paris.

But we have a better choice.

In America, realizing Democracy implies organic architecture,—buildings implicit with the same organic-integrity the aeroplane seeks and has not yet found and our great industrial endeavor seeks, mostly in vain. This quality is nearer in Architecture than in anything else if we will only seek it.

It is a surviving virtue of the skyscraper that it prepared us to see it.

Thirty years, at least, of performance has piled on sound precept until now this country need ask none how to build, from within, its own great buildings in noble, sane, sure way with all the joy of freedom from the prison house of any Mode. No longer creatively sterile but potent beyond anything ever known in this world, America would become, practicing principles of Organic-Architecture, Art be carried up into the Kingdom of Nature and its separate and contrasted existence destroyed. ●

FRANK LLOYD WRIGHT
Chandler, Arizona, April 5, 1929

Page 250

Proposal drawing for National Insurance Company Building, Chicago, Frank Lloyd Wright, 1923.

This is the first of three versions of a project designed, but never built, for AM Johnson in 1923–24. Though composed almost entirely in glass, the towers are related to the concrete "textile blocks" Wright was using in his houses at this time. The only photograph Wright included with the article is a detail of the blocks used in the Millard House pictured on page 252.

opposite: "Voisin Plan" for the development of Central Paris, Le Corbusier, architect, 1925.

IN THE CAUSE OF ARCHITECTURE *VII*
SHEET METAL AND
THE MODERN INSTANCE
Frank Lloyd Wright

THE MACHINE is at its best when rolling, cutting, stamping or folding whatever may be fed into it.

Mechanical movements are narrowly limited unless built up like the timer of a Corliss engine or like a linotype.

The movements easiest of all are rotary, next, the press or hammer, and the lift and slide works together with either or both. In these we have pretty much the powers of the "Brute." But infinite are the combinations and divisions of these powers until we have something very like a brain in action —the Robot itself, a relevant dramatic conception.

The consequences may well be terrifying when man's volition is added to these brute powers. This volition of man's, deprived of soul, may drive these powers to the limit of human endurance, yes—to the ultimate extinction of the humanity of the race.

Commerce, as we have reason to know, has no soul.

Commercial interests left to themselves would soon write their own doom in the exploitation of their own social life. They would soon cease to reproduce. They would fail to reproduce because the elements of commerce are those of the machine—they lack the divine spark necessary for giving life. The margin of profit, piling up into residue, is inert, inept, impotent.

The Machine itself represents this margin of profit in the physical body of our modern world: a profit, inept, inert, impotent.

The question propounded in these papers and the continual haunting reference in all of them—"What is this interpreter of life, the Architect, going to do about it,"—is again insistent here. For in sheet metal there is opportunity to give life to something the Architect seems to despise while forced to use it because it is cheap. He avails himself of it as a degraded material. In the building trade, we find cornices, gutters, downspouts, water-sheds, in lead, zinc and tin, iron and copper, everywhere. Imitations too in these materials, of every other material, are everywhere.

But where may sheet metal be seen used as a fine material for its own sake?

Oh yes, occasionally. But why not everywhere? It is the one "best thing" in modern economy of materials brought by the Machine. Building trades aside, we now make anything at all of sheet metal kitchen utensils, furniture, automobiles and Pullman coaches. And in flashings or counter flashings or roofing it is keeping nearly all the citizens of America dry in their homes at the present moment.

Copper is easily king of this field and what is true of copper will be true also of the other metals in some degree, with certain special aptitudes and properties added or subtracted in the case of each.

Back of this sheet metal tribe, literally, we have the light rolled steel section for stiffening any particular sheet metal area in all particular cases whatsoever. All "spread" materials need reinforcement. Metal sheets no less than concrete slabs.

In the building trades we have had recourse to these metal fabrics in the cheapest and most insulting fashion, in buildings where the architect has either never been seen, or has been set aside. Sheet metal is prime makeshift to his highness the American Jerry-builder.

Roofs seem to be the building problem naturally solved by sheet metal, as it may be stamped into any desired form, lock seamed, and made into a light, decorative and permanent water-shed. It is possible to double the thicknesses in long panels or channels, sliding non-conducting material between them and lock-seaming together the continuous slabs thus made so that they lie together like planks on the roof framing, finished from below as from above. Each slab is a natural water channel.

The machinery at work in the sheet metal trades easily crimps, folds, trims and stamps sheets of metal as an ingenious child might his sheets of paper. The finished prod-

from:
ARCHITECTURE, THE EXPRESSION OF THE MATERIALS AND METHODS OF OUR TIMES
By Le Corbusier
Vol. 66, No. 2, August 1929,
pp. 123-128.

LET US not confuse outward show, however impressive, with an essential truth which is still indistinct in the whirlpool of an epoch in the full tide of evolution.

By "impressive outward show," it is implied that the architecture of today appears to be dictated in the eloquence of its form by modern materials and methods. "Essential truth" suggests an architecture that results from the state of mind of an epoch and that an architecture exists, takes form and is expressed only at that very moment when a general evolution of mind is accomplished. It is at that moment alone when mind has recognized and admitted a system of thought which, above all, represents in every field a profound modification of previous states. There is no architecture during periods of crisis; architecture comes after periods of crisis.

* * *

Meanwhile, shallow spirits of limited vision cried out: "The world is being wrecked, all is lost." And in desperation, like shipwrecked sailors grasping at floating debris, we clung to the past. Never before had so much archaeology been done as during those heroic times when science was pushing us, each day more insistently, along the adventurous paths that lead towards the unknown.

Is not architecture determined ▸

Price Tower, Bartlesville, Oklahoma, Frank Lloyd Wright, architect, 1956 (see page 256).

Alice Millard House, Pasadena, California, Frank Lloyd Wright, architect, 1923.

Part of the Nunnery at Uxmal, from "The Architecture of the Ancient Mayas," by S.K. Lothrop [57:6: Jun 1925 pp 500].

1 Jane Addams (1860–1935), social reformer and pacifist who founded Hull House in Chicago in 1889.

right & opposite: Floor plans for the proposed National Insurance Company Building, Chicago, Frank Lloyd Wright, architect, 1923.

uct may have the color brought up in sur-face treatment, or be enameled with other durable substances as in enamel color glaz-ing or plating, or by galvanizing the finished work may be dipped and coated entire. But copper is the only sheet metal that has yet entered into architecture as a beautiful, per-manent material. Its verdigris is always a great beauty in connection with stone or brick or wood, and copper is more nearly permanent than anything we have at hand as an architect's medium.

But now that all metals may be rolled into sheets and manipulated so cheaply combina-tions of various metals may be made as any other combination of materials may be. And will be.

The Japanese sword-guard shows how

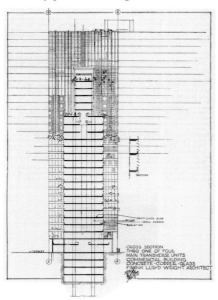

delightful these properties of metal become when contrasted and harmonized in the hands of a master-artist. A collection of these mighty little things in art and craft should be the vade-mecum of every metal student or worker. In fact it seems that upon metals the Japanese, and before them the Chinese, have lavished much of their genius and have

excelled from the making of a keen cut-ting-blade that would hold its edge against blows on steel to inventing subtle texture-treatments in iron for all decorative purposes.

Leaving the precious metals in a category by themselves, these sympathetic treatments of various humble metals are most signifi-cant for us who, as masters of metal production, are committed to it in our industries, though we have developed the beauty of it in use not at all.

In previous ages, beyond the roofer's use of lead in roofing and water-leads and the blacksmith's wrought-iron as seen in gates and lanterns, there has been little use made of metal by architects excepting such occa-sional use of bronze as Ghiberti made in his famous doors. But Ghiberti was a sculptor, not an architect, or his doors would, proba-bly, have been wood elaborately ironed in the mode.

I believe the time is ready for a building of sheet copper wherein the copper may be appropriate carriage for glass only. What would such a building be good for and what would it be like?

Why should we have such buildings? This architect will try to answer in his own fash-ion.

Since first meeting, thirty years ago, James A. Miller, a sheet-metal worker of Chicago, who had intelligent pride in his material and a sentiment concerning it (designing a house for himself at one time he demanded a tin-floored balcony outside his bedroom window in order that he might hear the rain patter upon it), I have had respect for his sheet-metal medium.

At that time I designed some sheet cop-per bowls, slender flower holders and such things, for him, and fell in love with sheet copper as a building material. I had always liked lead, despised tin, wondered about zinc, and revolted against galvanized iron as it was then used in Chicago quite generally as a substitute for granite.

Miller Brothers in addition to other offices of that factory were then interested in sheet metal window-sash and frames especially in skylights and metal doors.

We had contempt for them because they were made to imitate wooden sash. The doors too were made up in wood and covered with metal, the result being an imitation in metal of a wood paneled door. It was usually "grained" to complete the ruse.

No one thought much about it one way or another the city demanded these mongrels as fire-stops in certain places under certain conditions and that was that.

They were not cheap enough in those days—forcing the material as it was forced in this imitation work—to offer much incentive to bother with the problem.

But see how the matter has since grown up! We need no statistics to add to the evidence of our eyes wherever we go, which may see that what is left of the architectural framework of the modern world after concrete and steel have done with it will be in some form or other, sheet metal.

Twenty-seven years ago, under the auspices of Jane Addams, at Hull House, Chicago, an arts and crafts society was formed, and I then wanted to make a study of the Machine as a tool at work in modern materials. I invited Mr. Miller, Mr. Bagley, Mr. Wagner to come to the tentative meeting to represent respectively sheet metal,

machined marble work and terra cotta. I wanted them there with us to tell us what we as artists might do to help them. At that time, to put the matter before the proposed society, I wrote (and read) the "Art and Craft of the Machine" since translated into many languages.

It was useless. As I look back upon it, I smile, because the society was made up of cultured, artistic people, encouraged by University of Chicago professors who were ardent disciples of Ruskin and Morris. What would they want to see, if they could see it in such a programme as mine?

It all came to nothing then—although next day's Tribune, in an editorial, spoke of "the first word said, by an artist, for the Machine." I suspect Miss Addams[1] of writing it herself. Ever since my stand taken there, however, the matter has grown for me, and, if not for them, it is all about them now in nearly everything they use or touch or see, still needing interpretation to-day as much as it was needed then. But to get back from this reflection to this sheet-copper and glass building which has eventually resulted from it.

I have designed such a building.

It is properly a tall building.

It is a practical solution of the skyscraper problem because the advantages offered by

by new materials and new methods? (It is high time I were defining what architecture is.) Indeed to all in America belong the new materials, with you modern methods are in use. But for a hundred years your architecture has not evolved. Alone your programs have changed. And you construct your skyscrapers in the manner of students of the Ecole des Beaux-Arts building a private house. I repeat: a hundred years of new materials and new methods have made no change whatsoever in your architectural viewpoint.

* * *

What, then, is the direction of its progress today?

Industrialism has stated the postulate of economy: to attain the maximum of result at the minimum of expense.

Science, mathematics, analysis and hypothesis, have all created an authentic machinery of thought. An imperative need of clarity, the search for the solution. It is for that which the mathematicians term the "elegant solution."

A hundred years of a mechanical era have brought forth an entirely new spectacle. Geometry is supreme. Precision is everywhere. The right angle prevails. There no longer exists any object that does not tend to severity.

* * *

Has not this all pervading precision, exactness and accuracy definitely annihilated the imperceptible distance and mystery? Miraculously, quite the contrary is the case. This century has officially opened to us gates yawning on the infinite, on majesty, silence and mystery. More than ever before, man's soul is pathetically brought face to face with itself. Never was there an epoch so powerfully, so unanimously inspired. Poetry is everywhere, constant, immanent.

* * * ▶

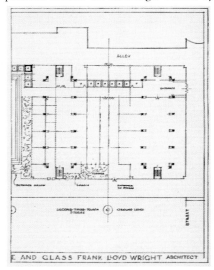

COMMERCIAL BUILDING IN COPPER, CONCRETE AND GLASS   FRANK LLOYD WRIGHT ARCHITECT

1928

Palmolive Building, Chicago, Holabird & Root, architects, 1928–29.

Majestic Apartments, New York City, Irwin Chanin, Jacques Delamarre and Sloan & Robertson, architects, 1930.

the material and method add up most heavily in their own favor where they can go farthest—either up or crosswise.

Standardization here may come completely into its own, for standardization is in the nature of both sheet-metal process and material. It may be again seen that the life of the imagination awakens its very limitations to life.

The exterior walls, as such, disappear—instead are suspended, standardized sheet-copper screens. The walls themselves cease to exist as either weight or thickness. Windows become in this fabrication a matter of a unit in the screen fabric, opening singly or in groups at the will of the occupant. All windows may be cleaned from the inside with neither bother nor risk. The vertical mullions (copper shells filled with non-conducting material), are large and strong enough only to carry from floor to floor and project much or little as shadow on the glass may or may not be wanted. Much projection enriches the shadow. Less projection dispels the shadows and brightens the interior. These protecting blades of copper act in the sun like the blades of a blind.

The unit of two feet both ways is, in this instance, emphasized on every alternate vertical with additional emphasis on every fifth. There is no emphasis on the horizontal units. The edge of the various floors being beveled to the same section as is used between the windows, it appears in the screen as such horizontal division occurring naturally on the two-foot unit lines. The floors themselves, however, do appear, at intervals, in the recessions of the screen in order to bring the concrete structure itself into relief in relation to the screen as well as in connection with it.

Thus the outer building surfaces become opalescent, iridescent copper-bound glass. To avoid all interference with the fabrication of the light-giving exterior screen the supporting pylons are set back from the lot line, the floors carried by them thus becoming cantilever slabs. The extent of the cantilever is determined by the use for which the building is designed. These pylons are continuous through all floors and in this instance exposed as pylons at the top. They are enlarged to carry electrical, plumbing, and heating conduits, which branch from the shafts, not in the floor slabs, but into piping designed into visible fixtures extending beneath each ceiling to where the outlets are needed in the office arrangement. All electrical or plumbing appliances may thus be disconnected and relocated at short notice with no waste at all in time or material.

Being likewise fabricated on a perfect unit system, the interior partitions may all be made up in sections, complete with doors, ready to set in place and designed to match the general style of the outer wall screen.

These interior partition-units thus fabricated may be stored ready to use, and any changes to suit tenants made over night with no waste of time and material.

The increase of glass area over the usual skyscraper fenestration is only about ten per cent (the margin could be increased or diminished by expanding or contracting the copper members in which it is set), so the expense of heating is not materially increased. Inasmuch as the copper mullions are filled with insulating material and the window openings are tight, being mechanical units in a mechanical screen, this excess of glass is compensated.

The radiators are cast as a railing set in front of the lower glass unit of this outer screen wall, free enough to make cleaning easy.

The walls of the first two stories, or more, may be unobstructed glass—the dreams of the shop-keeper in this connection fully realized.

The connecting stairways necessary between floors are here arranged as a practical fire-escape forming the central feature, as may be seen at the front and rear of each section of the whole mass, and though cut off by fire-proof doors at each floor, the continuous stairway thus made discharges upon the sidewalk below without obstruction.

The construction of such a building as this would be at least one-third lighter than anything in the way of a tall building yet built—and three times stronger in any disturbance, the construction being balanced as the body on the legs, the walls hanging as the arms from the shoulders, the whole, heavy where weight insures stability.

But of chief value as I see it is the fact that the scheme as a whole would legitimately eliminate the matter of "architecture," that now vexes all such buildings, from field construction, all such elements of architecture "exterior" or interior becoming a complete shop-fabrication—assembled only in the field.

The shop in our mechanical era is ten to one, economically efficient over the field, and will always increase over the field in economy and craftsmanship.

The mere physical concrete construction of pylons and floors is here non-involved with any interior or exterior, is easily rendered indestructible, and is made entirely independent of anything hitherto mixed up with it in our country as "Architecture." In the skyscraper as practiced at present the "Architecture" is expensively involved but is entirely irrelevant. But here it is entirely relevant but uninvolved.

Also the piping and conduits of all appurtenance-systems may be cut in the shop, the labor in the field reduced to assembling only, "fitting" or screwing up the joints being all that is necessary.

Thus we have, literally, a shop-made building all but the interior supporting posts and floors, which may be reinforced concrete or concrete-masked steel. In this design, architecture has been frankly, profitably and artistically taken from the field to the factory—standardized as might be any mechanical thing whatsoever, from a penny-whistle to a piano.

There is no unsalable floor space in this building created "for effect," as may be observed.

There are no "features" manufactured "for effect."

There is nothing added to the whole merely for this desired "effect."

To gratify the landlord, his lot area is now salable to the very lot-line and on every floor, where ordinances do not interfere and demand that they be reduced in area as the building soars.

What architecture there is in evidence here is a light, trim, practical commercial fabric—every inch and pound of which is in service." There is every reason why it should be beautiful. But it is best to say nothing about that, as things are now.

The present design was worked out for a lot three hundred feet by one hundred feet, the courts being open to the south.

There is nothing of importance to mention in the general disposition of the other necessary parts of the plan. All may be quite as customary.

My aim in this fabrication employing the cantilever system of construction which proved so effective in preserving the Imperial Hotel at Tokyo, was to achieve absolute scientific utility by means of the Machine—to accomplish—first of all—a true standardization which would not only serve as a basis for keeping the life of the building true as architecture, but enable me to project the whole, as an expression of a valuable principle involved, into a genuine living-architecture of the present.

I began work upon this study in Los Angeles in the winter of 192–3 having had the main features of it in mind for many years. I had the good fortune to explain it in detail to "Lieber-meister" Louis H. Sullivan, some months before he died.

Gratefully I remember—and proudly too—"I have had faith that it would come," he said. "This Architecture of Democracy—I see it in this building of yours, a genuine, beautiful thing. I knew what I was talking about all these years—you see. I never could have done this building myself, but I believe that, but for me, you could never have done it."

I am sure I should never have reached it, but for what he was and what he did.

This design is dedicated to him. ∎

St. Marks Tower, New York City, Frank Lloyd Wright, architect, 1921, unbuilt project.

Wright waited 35 years to realize a smaller version of just one of these towers for Harold Price, in Bartlesville, Oklahoma, in 1956 (photo page 252). In his "Notes on the Building of the H.C. Price Company," Wright said:

"Has the country meantime grown up to skyscraper status or has the skyscraper adventured on its own afield? I believe this type of structure, weighing about one tenth of say the Rockefeller Center structure, will become a desirable institution everywhere there are men and companies like the one this building tells us about...

"I wonder now where the next quadruple sky garden pent house duplex residence and office building will rise in our nation. Look for them, presently, all over these United States. It was for this the vertical street was born. To the concrete and steel construction of our modern times this type is natural."

Price Tower was published by _Architectural Record_ in February 1956.

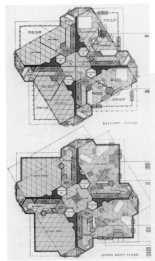

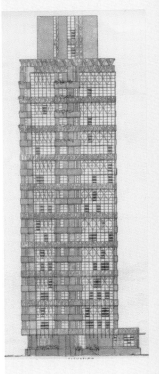

ST. MARK'S TOWER · ST.MARK'S IN THE BOUWERIE · NEW YORK CITY.

IN THIS PROJECT, Frank Lloyd Wright realizes some of the most advanced aims professed by European architects, without attendant anomalies. The uninterrupted glass window is achieved without either unprotected steel, or rooms cluttered with interior posts. The apartments are given a high degree of privacy, plenty of daylight and utilizable space. Located in a park on church property these towers will always stand free.

The whole building is hung on a core of concrete retaining walls, shown projecting at the top in the rendering above, and in section (brown) in the plans (upper right). The network upon which the plan is developed is that of the reinforcing system.

Every apartment is a duplex. The living room carries through both floors. It is marked by the copper parapets (perspective, opposite.) The bedroom stories (projecting in concrete balconies, see same) are set in a continuous steel truss cantilevered at an angle so that on the inside this story forms a balcony across the living room. Openings follow the struts of the truss.

To avoid torrents of water on the glass in heavy rains, every successive apartment projects out slightly beyond that below it, making the building somewhat larger at the top.

The conveniences of internal arrangement can be read from the plan. A noteworthy feature is that though every apartment has two useable balconies each is cut off from direct view of the neighbors. ∎

9 Advantage in Magnitude: Apotheosis of the Tall Building

The Woolworth Building reigned supreme as the world's tallest building for seventeen years until the Chrysler Building took its place in 1930. By then a fierce competition for height reflected just one of the many changes that had taken place in the intervening years. The skyscraper problem had become complex and manifold.

Conservative designers continued to insist that towers carry Roman temples or Greek mausoleums at their summits (photo page 184). Some labored to find regional interpretations of ornament, while others developed the implications of the anthropomorphically-topped pilasters that Eliel Saarinen had worked into his Chicago Tribune competition entry. By the mid 1920s, there was little agreement as to what a tall building should look like, though most architects were conforming to an idea that was circulating—it should have a setback silhouette, be massive and sculptured.

A visual comparison of the buildings in the first two-thirds of this book, with those in the last third, reveals a striking difference in their form. The catalyst for this difference was the New York Zoning Law of 1916. It had a profound impact on the shape of the nation's skyline, starting with New York and rippling across the country. The change shows how the pressures of the marketplace can be met by good design.

Harvey Wiley Corbett was a great champion of the new "set-back style." After a talk he delivered before New York's Architectural League in 1921, Leon V. Solon reported:

> "Indeed, a new and revolutionary factor has entered the whole problem of architectural design. The square-topped flat-roofed packing box building is a thing of the past (fortunately), and we now have the step-back sky line, the intriguing silhouette, the something above and beyond, the play of masses, shadows, forms and lines where formerly only the hard line of a projecting cornice served to stop the composition. Buildings in the future will not be designed merely as "fronts" but will be stud-

Preliminary Perspective Sketch,
Empire State Building, New York City
Shreve Lamb and Harmon, architects, 1931

ied from all angles, even that of the aviator. Architectural design has moved from a two-dimension stage (where it never should have been) to a three-dimension stage (where real design always was). Forward looking designers are now anticipating the arrival of the 'fourth' dimension stage."

Mayan forms had long impressed American architects, notably Frank Lloyd Wright, whose textile-block houses in Pasadena owed a great deal to Mayan inspiration (photos pages 243, 252, 287). Within no time, a fashion fueled by a popular interest in archaeology, spawned buildings with Mayan ornament from The Sears Roebuck Store in Los Angeles to the Telephone Office in Houston, Texas.

Architects soon looked beyond the decorative side of Central American architecture to its massive contours. Alfred C. Bossom (page xiv), an English engineer working in the United States, called the 230-foot pyramid at Tikal, Guatemala (page 234), "the original American Skyscraper," and he proposed a 35-story modern building with a similar form and decoration.

All this was amplified through popular design and decoration, fashion, photography (photo page 261), films and books. Hugh Ferriss published a collection of his moody drawings (pages 234, 260) as THE METROPOLIS OF TOMORROW in 1929. Some of the images resemble Mayan ziggurats loosely mixed with those of Babylonia. Modernists described Pueblo buildings as America's first examples of cubism. The comparison impressed Richard J. Neutra. In his book *Amerika*, published in Vienna in 1930, he placed photographs of Pueblo architecture next to modern skyscrapers, factories, and industrial products. An interest in eclecticism and archaeology joined momentarily with a modern taste for cubism.

Buildings became cliff-like, massive, almost monolithic. Windows alone gave relief to wall surfaces, but they were played down. Piers of broad vertical bands, and solid stone covered much of the space which the early skyscrapers had given to glass. There were no belt courses—all divisions were accomplished by major setbacks and projections. The new fashion appeared in Chicago's Palmolive Building (photo 254) by Holabird and Root. The same spirit moved Raymond Hood to create one of the best examples of the new mode, the Daily News Building in New York City. The tall thin slabs on the building's exterior emphasize the building's verticality; at night, the lighted offices reveal horizontal bands (photo page 273).

The field was now open. L. Andrew Reinhard describes the tension between consideration of horizontal treatment over vertical, with his tongue firmly planted in his cheek. He and Corbett and Hood were working on Rockefeller Center:

"What materials will be used for the exterior walls? This is still an open question. Much study has yet to be given to the external appearance of the buildings. The model, as it stands, represents the rentable cubage. It does not attempt to show any architectural treatment, which is another problem in itself. Four studies have already been made of the exterior of the central tower: one shows a horizontal treatment (to satisfy the "horizontalists"), another a vertical treatment (to satisfy the "verticalists"), the third a wall pattern arrangement (to satisfy the decoratively inclined), and the fourth an unadorned arrangement (to satisfy the functionally minded). Any one of the four schemes can be selected—the rentals will not be affected." (page 274). ■

"Mere size has, indeed, under all disadvantage, some definite value; and so has mere splendor. Disappointed as you may be, or at least ought to be, at first by St. Peter's, in the end you will feel its size—and its brightness. These are all you can feel in it,...but the bigness tells at last."

John Ruskin Mornings in Florence, "The Fourth Morning," 1875–77, p. 72.

from:
BUILDING OR SCULPTURE?
The Architecture of 'Mass'
Douglas Haskell*
Vol. 67, No. 4, April 1930, pp. 366-368.

"Mass" is the word of the street for the prevailing style of American architecture, particularly as applied to the office building; and it is a good word. The rhythms of our tall buildings are free, now, of McKim and his orders quite as much as of Louis Sullivan and his "steel frame." What do they serve? The designer's conception of the stroke and heft of the building—in short, its mass.
* * *
Why do architects so often feel constrained to talk about "structure and construction methods as the basis from which design is developed," when these are almost ignored in their plans and renderings—which could be executed almost interchangeably in brick, limestone, marble, concrete, or even aluminum—and when the thing these architects are really after is plainly something else? Particularly in the steel frame building, structure is now so standardized as to offer, for the moment, no major problems; the face is of no structural interest, being pure veneer,—the basic factor, however, as any architect will recognize, is rentable cubage.
* * *
Since construction is standardized, and the determining factor in our architecture of "mass" is ►

1930

top: An ad for the Herman Nelson Corporation, Moline, Ill., makers of radiators. The caption reads, "Our contribution to the art of heating and ventilation."

above: Crayon drawing and design by Hugh Ferriss, from a January 1931 article on architect's renderings.

opposite: 137 East 57th Street Loft Building, New York City, Thompson & Churchill, architects, 1930 (demolished). Some American architects looked towards Europe for inspiration. Columns were recessed 9 feet behind a façade hung from the roof girders by steel straps.

opposite upper right: One of six photographic studies by Walker Evans published in *RECORD* in September 1930.

---

* Douglas Putnam Haskell (1899–1979) was an associate editor at *ARCHITECTURAL RECORD* from 1929 to 1930 and a senior editor from 1942 to 1949.

Embedded within the article on page 263, much like the letters themselves, which were found in a time capsule, is the following commentary by the author, Richmond Shreve:

"Nearly forty years ago John M. Carrère placed in the corner stone of the Mail and Express Building then being erected in New York under the direction of Carrère and Hastings, the architects, a letter which throws the light of an earlier day on the subject of our discussion. The letter is of the year 1891, and is addressed 'to whom it may concern, be it known:

'That at a time when architecture has become a mere investment—its quality being rated by the income-producing capacity—at a time when no expense which can be avoided is tolerated to beautify a building, whether by architectural effect of treatment or by the use of fine materials, when even reveals and depths of walls, projections of cornices, etc., requisite for effect of light and shadow, are sacrificed for the sake of obtaining a few more feet of rentable floor space in the building, it is due to the encouragement which we have received from [the owner] in the most generous and public spirited way that we have been able to attempt to produce an architectural work in contrast to the 19th century business investment building pure and simple. We hope that our effort may prove a success for the sake of our profession and of our patron.'"

neither the frame nor the material with which it is faced, but the cubage inside for which it was built, the shell itself has come to have little importance save as decoration.

* * *

But the mere fact that in our architecture of mass the openings have become little more than a note on the surface is in itself portentous. This is a condition that has seldom existed above ground before. Even in the dim religious light of the cathedrals there was a better relation to the fenestration. The large office building is a radical departure from the great architectural tradition.

* * *

To compare the skyscraper with sculpture—carved, so to speak, out of the zoning envelope—is an exaggeration for the sake of truth. The practical exigencies are often exceedingly well met. But even when they are, the expression clings stubbornly to "mass." (The idea of mass persists even when a row of store windows at the bottom makes the pyramid as an analogy most embarrassing. The idea of weight, material, dead tonnage. But is not this the age of the airplane and the suspension bridge? Is there no concept that would permit the designer to catch off his space lightly and deftly, and to face it with a mere veil? ●

1930

Reynolds Tobacco Company Building, Winston-Salem, N.C. Shreve, Lamb and Harmon, architects, 1927–29

Including the flagpole, this 21-story structure was the tallest office building south of Baltimore when completed. Used as the model for the offices of the Empire State Building (by the same architects), these art deco headquarters were designated *Office Building of the Year* in 1929 by the National Association of Architects.

opposite: Chrysler Building, New York City, William van Alen, architect, 1930.

THE ECONOMIC DESIGN OF OFFICE BUILDINGS

By R. H. Shreve,
of Shreve, Lamb and Harmon, Architects

THERE are now in existence or in course of construction in New York at least ten buildings fifty stories or more in height and many others approaching this measure.

One of these, the Empire State Building at Fifth Avenue and 34th Street, is to be the largest of its kind in the world. Six months ago the working drawings for this building had not been begun; one year from now it will have been completed, ready for the 10,000 tenants which it is capable of accommodating! A project involving a cost of fifty millions of dollars, containing over two million square feet of usable area in a cube of thirty-five million feet, sustained by a frame composed of fifty thousand tons of steel rising nearly a quarter of a mile above the foundations, is to be designed, erected and completed for occupancy in a brief eighteen months.

Stone from Maine and Indiana, steel from Pittsburgh and Elmira, cement from Pennsylvania and New York, timber from Oregon or the Carolinas, brick from the Hudson River Valley or from the clay pits of Connecticut, glass from Ohio, marble from Vermont or Georgia or Italy, sand from the shores, stone from the hills, materials from all the world must come together and fit together with accuracy of measurement and precision of time if the procession of construction is not to be thrown into confusion, carrying the dollars away in the ruin. One may well believe that with its organized cooperation in the labor of men and the fabrication and placing of materials, its precision of performance to match the timing of a trunkline railroad and connecting services, almost the powers of Aladdin's genii harnessed for a building project, none of all the ancient world wonders in any way matched the amazing assembly of skilled craft and fashioned materials which with uncanny accuracy find their places in the daily wrought miracle of a modern skyscraper.

"Why and how is all this made possible" is the question asked by students of the moving forces of our architectural growth. Even among those most closely identified with the development of the city there are wide differences of opinion as to the place of the skyscraper in any sound scheme of planning. That gracious critic, Mr. Cortissoz, granting that "it is magnificent," asks dubiously "Is it architecture?" Others still are resentful of the intrusion of a cold Martian calculation of values in the field of aesthetic study, and deplore the dominance of these giants of business in one corner of the world of art. Neither these queries nor these protests are new.

Nearly forty years ago John M. Carrère placed in the corner stone of the Mail and Express Building then being erected in New York under the direction of Carrère and Hastings, the architects, a letter which throws the light of an earlier day on the subject of our discussion. The letter is of the year 1891, and is addressed "to whom it may concern, be it known"—

"That at a time when architecture has become a mere investment—its quality being rated by the income-producing capacity—at a time when no expense which can be avoided is tolerated to beautify a building, whether by architectural effect of treatment or by the use of fine materials, when even reveals and depths of walls, projections of cornices, etc., requisite for effect of light and shadow, are sacrificed for the sake of obtaining a few more feet of rentable floor space in the building, it is due to the encouragement which we have received from [the owner] in the most generous and public spirited way that we have been able to attempt to produce an architectural work in contrast to the 19th century business investment pure and simple. We hope that our effort may prove a success for the sake of our profession and our patron."

Whatever may have been the measure of his success, Mr. Carrère's protest was unavailing. Soon after the letter was written, when the building whose birth it signalized was at the age of 25 years, it was torn down

from:
WHERE ENGLAND LOOKS TO AMERICA
By Herbert Read
Vol. 81, No. 3, March 1937, pp. 45-46

FOR the average Englishman, American industry means Ford cars and skyscrapers, and there has not been much disposition on his part to treat these phenomena philosophically, to find a new canon of beauty in them. Indeed, the Englishman prefers to confine his philosophy to the cloistered precincts of the universities (where, incidentally, the existence of a philosophy of art is not recognized), and he does not even indulge in those genial moralizations which, I believe, characterize the American businessman in his leisure moments. The growth of any consciousness for the need of a new aesthetic has been very slow in our country; what uneasiness there has been during the last hundred years has always avoided the issue, turning away from the problems presented by the machine and yearning for the return of an idealized guild system of handworkers. This tendency which was rarely, if ever, the practical policy of industrialists themselves, was nevertheless taken seriously in some quarters; a movement was ▸

from:
HERBERT CROLY, 1869-1930
Editor of Architectural Record,
1900-1906

"It is the idea in a work of art that is striven after," was one of his convictions, and it was this feeling of his for the true, organic meaning of architecture that made him a useful interpreter of it. He had a way of making himself thoroughly familiar with the various categories in this art, and could write with equal effectiveness about city or country houses, clubs and all sorts of public buildings, excluding theaters.

He had ceased to contribute regularly articles on architecture when the skyscraper and the various exigencies of the zoning laws were producing their astonishing effect on the aspect of the modern city. These things I know excited him and he was filled with the hope that some great good to architecture would come of these economic necessities.

My concern at the present time, however, is as to his writings at earlier times. Then he wrote generously, and understandingly and with a clear recognition of historic standards. In the domain of sociology he was a progressive, as we all know. . . . Addressing an audience that embraced the professional and the layman, he appealed to both in favor of good taste. Writing at a period in which American architecture was being transformed he held fast to tried principles and urged discrimination. I come to think of my old friend as having made a most valuable contribution to the highest ideals of architecture.

— CHARLES A. PLATT
(Reprinted by courtesy of the New Republic, of which Mr. Croly had been editor since its foundation in 1914.)

to make way for an addition to one of its commercial neighbors requiring more floor space. And today, less than 40 years after the writing of this letter, New York owns many business structures of unquestioned dignity, of "fine materials" and beauty of treatment, and at least one of them will be without "reveals or depths of walls, projections of cornice" or other of the lamented traditions, but with a charm and logic of design marking a distinct advance in art and structure,- at once not a "contrast" but a combination of "an architectural work" and "a business investment building."

If, as Mr. Cortissoz suggests, it may "be necessary some day to invent a new word to designate the new style, a word drawn from the terminology of engineering, with aid from that of the mechanics rather than the art of building," the dominant expression of that word should be borrowed from the principles of sound design and ordered thought.

For so successful has been the effort of the more modern American architects to interpret the demands of economics and to characterize utility and structural form, that we have today in our modern business buildings an expression in architectural style most encouraging to the fine art of building. These structures are the response to business standards and business demands, and they must meet certain established tests if they are to be considered successful, and are to survive either as individual buildings or as a type.

Today, as in Carrère's day, the modern office building presents a challenge to architecture in the problem of enclosing usable space-attractively, promptly, economically and with sound logical construction. And the office building deserves not alone a high quality of architectural design, but skillful economic planning which means such treatment of the site and the structural elements as will produce an arrangement of space and equipment capable of earning income in excess of expense. It is with such economic planning that these notes are chiefly concerned, not through the presentation of the

detail of the design of a single building but through the review of certain fundamental principles underlying the correct study of such buildings as a type. To set up properly an income-producing building the control of its design and construction should be in the hands of a Board on which sit Owner, Banker, Builder, Architect, Engineers, and Real Estate Men. The record of their decisions finds place in plans, specifications and contracts, financial transactions and leases, and the outcome of their work, if it is to be successful, must have been foreseen far in advance of its realization.

The program starts with the selection of a site; many may be considered, but for each there must be made an analysis of cost of land and building, method of financing, total and net investment and total and net income. For the production of income (or its equivalent) is the primary purpose of building, and whether the structure is to be the home of a great business, such as a public service corporation or a life insurance company, or the abode of numerous tenants constituting a mixed occupancy, it is necessary, if it is to be income-producing and not income consuming, that it should meet the test of the economic and legislative factors which affect every business building project.

One of these factors, and a most important one, is the the element, the answer to the questions "When?" and "Within what time?"

In order that invested capital may be kept to the lowest possible figure and income produced at the earliest possible date, the work must be done in the least possible time consistent with comparative economy.

It is because of this principle that New York has witnessed the erection in one year of the Bank of Manhattan Building at 40 Wall Street, requiring the demolition of existing stone and steel buildings covering a site over 40,000 feet in area, and the creation of a sixty-odd story structure, now the tallest in the world, all of the work including demolition and foundations being done in the twelve months between May 1, 1929 and May 1, 1930.

It is for this reason, too, that a greater construction program is being developed in the case of the Empire State Building, requiring feats of organization in some respects never before attempted. Excavation in rock far below the street goes on for twenty-four hours a day; foundations are placed at one side of the property as the steam-shovels and drills carry on the other; steel columns, some weighing a ton to the linear foot, and girders and beams finished to a sixteenth of an inch, are in various stages of progress at mill and shop or stored ready for delivery in the New Jersey yard, with some truck loads crossing the river, others toiling to reach the site through New York's one-way traffic system, while still others stand at the building unloading, and high above the street great bundles of metal at the ends of cobweb cables swing onto the working platform where steel members lie in orderly arrangement to be set in place by the erecting gang. The prompt delivery and precise erection of 50,000 tons of steel in five months is an essential of the completion of the program. Just below the topmost steel, as it is set, are the riveters securing the lower members in place; alongside and through the frame rise the stairs taking the place of ladders, and at many points are visible the main lines of the pipe trades, the veins and arteries attaching to the steel skeleton. Floor arches, exterior walls and windows, elevator hatchways, finished floors, marble halls, and all the finishing trades follow in such a rapidly moving but orderly parade that the plaster may appear in the lower floors before the roof many stories above has been made tight.

The demands of such a program necessitate the employment of every practical means for shortening the elapsed time required for all construction operations in an effort first to reduce that part of the cost which is known as carrying charges during construction, including interest on investment, taxes, etc., and second to avoid loss of rent through completion later than May first, which is the date as of which most business space leases begin, just as dwelling space leases date from the first of October.

For this reason the time for beginning building operations should be so calculated that the structure, completed in the shortest possible period consistent with relative economy, shall be ready for occupancy before the first of May, for otherwise the loss of income for the period through which the rentable space is unoccupied must be added to the loss due to fixed charges on capital invested and the outlay necessary to operate and maintain the building. This time element enters into our economic study as a variable factor measurably under control; a second influence, land cost is less flexible and, indeed, at present in New York appears as a most compelling influence.

The Waldorf-Astoria Hotel site, upon which the Empire State Building is to be placed, is reported to have cost $16,000,000 something over $8,000,000 an acre. The plot at the corner of Fifth Avenue and 43rd Street was a few years ago sold at a price approximately $340 a square foot, or $15,000,000 an acre. Land at No. 1 Wall Street facing Broadway, now being built upon, is reported to have cost the present owners between $700 and $800 for each square foot, at which rate an acre would reach a price of $35,000,000 or $40,000,000.

There is a difference of opinion as to whether this high land cost is the reason for the intensive building development, or whether permitting the intensive development is what causes the high land cost, but the fact is that with these and even lower land prices, which prevail in most of those sections of New York in which office buildings are built, the structures erected are designed to be of such a nature, extent and arrangement as to justify and support by income production the high cost of the site. It is therefore a prime requisite that the design shall distribute the cost of the land over the largest practical area of usable floor surface set up in accordance with building cost, building laws and profitable use; all influences which must be given our consideration.

Building cost is both a result of the study

created, if only by poets, which forced the aesthetic problem of industrial production into some sort of international prominence.

What in England remained the practice of a few cranks became, on the Continent, a movement affecting industry as a whole. Dr. Nikolaus Pevsner in his recent book, Pioneers of the Modern Movement, has shown exactly by what steps, and through what agencies, all this happened-how it is possible that the logical outcome of William Morris was Walter Gropius. It is perhaps too early to claim that in its developed form this industrial aesthetic has hit England fair and square; but in many obscure and indirect ways the practical ideals of the Bauhaus have penetrated into this country. At least it would be fair to say that in architecture and the related industrial arts (furniture, lighting equipment, domestic utensils, etc.) we have learned more from Germany, Scandinavia, and France than from America. This is not to claim that we have learned much; we have so much more to unlearn than most countries. Nor does it exclude the possibility that in what we have absorbed from the Continent there is already an element which the Continent took from America.

I am not much given to defending the so-called common sense of my countrymen; it is but a polite name for a widespread inability to perform any mental operation involving intellectual abstraction. I need not point out the advantages of this attitude in the field of politics. "Trust in God but keep your powder dry" is our national motto, and it implies that combination of blind faith and practical cunning which has made the British Empire what it is. It is true that we may on occasions change our faith, but not as a result of intellectual persuasion; we change our faith, like our clothes because we have grown out of them, and they begin to pinch. A change of heart is not ▶

500 Fifth Avenue, New York City, Shreve, Lamb and Harmon, architects, 1930.

upper right: Excavation for the foundation of the Empire State Building, New York City, Shreve, Lamb and Harmon, architects, 1931.

below: Diagram of Elevator Service, Empire State Building, New York City, Shreve, Lamb and Harmon, architects, 1931.

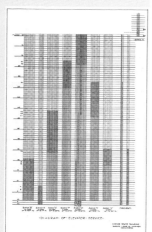

of the design of the building and a factor influencing that design through determination of the methods of construction, selection of materials, and arrangement of structural elements which make up the occasion of the total expenditure for the building itself, and which, later, will enter into the analysis of the design from the economic viewpoint.

But municipal and state laws and the Economic Law have a greater effect than building cost or structural problems in governing the production of floor space, or the height and bulk of business buildings, in the City of New York, so we shall need to see how these two forces, municipal and Economic Law, operate.

Zoning. The Building Zone Resolution of the City of New York divides the entire city into Areas or Zones classified under three heads and dealing with:

1. The use of the property and buildings;
2. The area of the site built over;
3. The height to which the building may be carried.

The use we are considering is that of the office building; the area permitted to be built over will be considered as unlimited (save as courts are required to permit legal subdivision of larger spaces); we may then give our attention entirely to the law controlling the height.

Upon the street lines or building lines of a given property the exterior walls may be carried only to the height fixed by law. This limit is related to the width of the street in front of the site, the permitted height in different districts being from 1/4 to 2 1/2 times the street width. Thus in a 2-times district and on a site facing a street 100 feet wide, the wall on the building line may not be carried more than 200 feet above grade, while on a 60 foot street a height of only 120 feet would be allowed. These limits may be extended through excess height allowances, permitted where neighboring buildings exceed the standard lawful height.

Above this street wall height limit the bulk of the building must be kept within sloping lines setting back from the street

front one foot horizontally for each unit of height this setback height unit factor being twice the factor used in fixing the street wall height; thus, in a "2-times" district the slope is one in four, in a "2 1/2-times " district one in five.

Different rates of setbacks govern the walls on yards or courts; dormers, so-called, are permitted under certain conditions; special rules govern in special circumstances quite too complicated to permit discussion at this time; but finally, the tapering structure having been reduced by a series of setbacks to a building area equal to one quarter of the site area, the tower condition is arrived at. Above this level the building, that is the tower, may lawfully extend to any height, but the study of the mass to determine this height is governed more by the Economic Law and structural problem than by man-made codes.

This maximum permitted envelope, a geometrical form consisting of a base enclosed by vertical walls, an intermediate section defined by sloping limits, and a tower, must be analyzed to determine how most profitably to place within it practical usable office floor area, supported and enclosed by structural forms, served by mechanical equipment, and reached through public spaces which are not directly sources of revenue. This problem which includes fixing the height of the tower is solved by study of the floor plans of the building, by the application of the Economic Law to the form evolved under the Zoning Ordinance. The important floors requiring attention are the ground or first floor, the typical office floor—that is, one of the large number of floors occupying the base of the building, the setback floors and the tower floor.

The most important of these is the typical floor, first because from it generally is derived a great part of the rental income, but more especially because its plan governs the plan of the ground floor below and the tower floor above. There are buildings in which the ground floor plan has been permitted to control the balance of the building. The result is not often fortunate and is frequently disastrous, but in some cases such as use of the ground floor by a bank, may be justified. In order that we shall not complicate our analysis, we may make an assumption quite common in the study of an office building in its preliminary form, that the floors below the third are likely to be of special nature, involving special planning and producing income at special rates; and so we may proceed to the study of the body of the building, beginning with the arrangement of the typical floor.

Office space as distinguished from loft space is built upon a basic office unit, the cell which multiplied around the central group of building "utilities" may be said to make up the floor plans and so produce the total structure.

In New York this office unit is approximately twenty feet wide, measured between columns along the line of the exterior wall, and is from twenty-five to thirty feet deep from the plaster line. Two windows, each perhaps 4'6" or 5'0" wide, provide natural (or legal) light and air. It is possible and practical to form within this larger unit two small offices, each nine to ten feet wide, each having a window and each providing room for one tenant. Two such small offices may have for common use an anteroom or work space opening to the office corridor of the building.

If this office unit is duplicated across the corridor, we shall have established a standard arrangement for a section of an office building containing a corridor six or seven feet wide, with a series of offices on each side

about twenty-eight feet deep, a total width including walls and partitions of say sixty six feet over all. This type is illustrated by the plan of the Graybar Building.

On the other hand, if such standard office units be placed about an arrangement of elevators, stairs, toilets, and a general group of smaller utilities, such as vents, shafts, slop sinks and meter closets, we shall increase largely the width of the building between outside walls, as in the General Motors Building. But in any case, when we speak of the design of office buildings we must have in mind primarily the arrangement of the basic unit spaces with their structural members, their service utilities, and their intercommunication or circulation. In this way we can produce on each floor, and so in the entire building, the greatest practical amount of usable office floor space.

To serve this space, to permit its legal and comfortable use, and to make it the source of income, the other essential elements of an office building must be provided.

Elevators take first place in this group. They, more than any other feature of common use by tenants, fix the standard of the building. The determination of the right elevator installation is therefore of the utmost importance. When a building under the so-called "old law" had a uniform floor area and floor arrangement throughout its modest height, it was common practice to approximate the number of cars by providing one car for each 25,000 square feet of floor area. Today, with buildings carried to greater heights or made up of floors of varying arrangement and area and with the sharper demand for better and more rapid elevator service, more accurate calculation of the elevator installation is necessary.

In considering the elevators we must, therefore, first determine the type of building in the present case an office building; then the type of tenancy, which may be single use occupancy as that of the New York Telephone Company's building, or a mixed occupancy as in the standard commercial structure. It is necessary then to establish the probable number of occupants and the

Chimes Building, Syracuse, New York, Shreve, Lamb and Harmon, architects.

below: Three typical floor plans, Empire State Building, New York City, Shreve, Lamb and Harmon, architects, 1931.

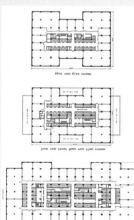

proportion of these people who come and leave at one time as at nine in the morning, or five in the afternoon, or at the lunch hour, these constituting the periods of peak load. It is usual practice to assume as peak load that one eighth or one ninth of the entire building population must be taken care of in five minutes. Further steps in the calculation become more technical but involve the number of floors served as affecting the number of stops, the areas of these floors and their occupancy, and the interval at which cars leave the entrance floor, 20 seconds for excellent service, certainly not over 30 seconds for good service, and not over 40 seconds for fair service. With these conditions known or assumed, we must consider the length of hatchway travel, the speed of the cars, their capacity expressed in number of passengers, the size of cars and number in each bank, the method of controlling the starting and stopping, the control of opening and shutting car gates and hatchway doors; we must allow for a certain number of bad stops or count on mechanical leveling of cars, and must take into account the type of signals; and, allowing for all these and even other factors, we set up our elevator layout. The importance of doing this correctly may be judged from the fact that the existence of an insurance company in a building not designed for such a tenancy has upset the service of an elevator installation otherwise quite adequate to meet normal demands; and the introduction of a stock brokerage house and the use of the elevators by numerous runners incident to its business has destroyed all possibility of satisfactory elevator service.

The position in the building of the elevator hatchways extending vertically through all floors imposes on each other floor from top to bottom of the building a condition practically fixing circulation and plan arrangement. The elevator problem is therefore of importance in any high building, but becomes a vital matter where there are installations of 30, 40, and even 50 elevators, of which there are not a few in New York.

In the design of the Empire State Build-

ing every effort was made to concentrate elevator equipment and eliminate unnecessary hatchways; careful study was given to the possibility of operating two cars in one shaft, thus combining the low and high rise banks, and saving floor space and extra construction cost; plans were made also for a transfer floor near the fiftieth story to which high speed express elevators automatically controlled would run from the ground floor. At some near future date such projects will be carried out but for this building no scheme of elevator installation now available was considered more likely to be satisfactory to tenants and landlord than that shown on the diagram presented with these notes.

To meet the requirements of the Building Code of the City of New York adequate exit facilities for all buildings must be provided. While there are several types of exits, the most common in office buildings is the fireproof enclosed stairway. For each floor there must be one, and an additional one when the floor area is in excess of 2,500 square feet. For still larger floor areas there must be added stair capacity proportional to the floor's population. This occupancy is to be taken as one person to every 50 square feet of floor surface in office buildings, or such other number of persons as may have been stated in the application for permit to construct the building and approved by the Superintendent of the Bureau of Buildings.

In office buildings exceeding certain stated heights, at least one stairway shall be a firetower; that is, the stair shall be enclosed in brick or reinforced concrete and be reached only by an entrance opening to a street front, or the wall of the yard or court, which must be not less than 100 square feet in area.

The capacity of a stairway is required to be calculated on the basis of one person for each full 22" of width and 1 1/2 treads of the stairway, and one person for each 3 1/2 square feet of floor area on the landings and halls within the stairway.

It is the intention of these provisions that the stairways leading down from a floor shall have capacity, measured on the basis just stated, to accommodate the total number of persons permitted to occupy the area which the stairs serve without the necessity of these persons intruding on stairways below or above.

No point on a floor shall be over 100 feet from a stair, nor, if the floor be divided into offices, shall the door of an office be more than 125 feet distant, along an unobstructed hallway, from a stairway.

All of these stairs must have proper exit connections to street or other approved spaces, and at least one stair must be carried to the roof.

It is in accordance with requirements as detailed as these, and covering also the handrails, treads and risers, landings and openings, that the stairs are fitted into the structure under the provisions of the present Building Code of the City of New York. In the course of the work on the proposed revision of this Code much study has been given to the adequacy of such provisions, especially in relation to very tall buildings. In case of fire or other emergency occasion for use of exit facilities, would the stairs be practically useful? How few persons, even those in normal health and unaffected by emergency exit conditions, could make their way down a thousand steps or more in safety, and how much more difficult would the problem be were there many among them overcome by intolerable conditions or aroused by unusual stress? What assurance can we have as to the movement of smoke under the influence of the chimney effect of a high structure?

It is possible that refuge areas, especially protected from fire and cut off from the rest of the building may, with the aid of the modern elevator and its closed hatchway, prove to be the safer and more effective first means of exit. Should this or some other variation of the present plan develop, our use and arrangement of floor space would be subject to such revisions.

Where floors are not occupied by a single tenant but are subdivided, passages affording circulation must give tenants access to each stairway, to the elevators and to the toilet rooms; the building service staff must be able to reach the slop sink closet or porter's work room, and the metering closet for electric service control. These passages or corridors, where essential to public or service circulation, should not be considered a part of income-producing space. It is true that where a floor is leased to one tenant, corridors may not always be partitioned off, and the space may be directly useful and under semiprivate control; but in principle the ultimate income should not thereby be modified, nor the study of the economic setup changed.

On each floor provision must be made for the passage of vent ducts or the smoke stack, if there is to be one, for the shafts in which plumbing and other pipes or conduits are carried up through the building, for basin lines at columns and for sprinklers if these are to be used (though this is not customary in office buildings), for electric feeders and telephone and messenger call connections, sometimes for watchman's connections or for fire alarm service lines and stations, and for a mail chute so placed as to meet the requirements of the Federal Government.

The several typical office building floor plans reproduced on these pages serve to show arrangements of open or divided office spaces extending from the perimeter or outer wall into the corridor leading to or built around the elevators, stairs, toilets and other utilities.

Examples varying in plan system have been selected. The General Motors Building, New York, facing four streets, has an internal utility group placed midway between the outer walls and filling the dark corners of the plan. The second office building is a corner property fronting two streets, with all the mechanical and service elements bunched in the inner angle of the plot. One of the most efficient plans is that of the Standard Building, Albany, lighted from three streets, with the utilities grouped on the inner property line, on which also a small court is placed to light the part of the floor space lying near the second stairway. Two of the three façades of the Reynolds

complete distinction between the vital and organic elements of his inherited concept of beauty and the purely mechanistic elements of machine production; and not being by nature a dialectician, he does not believe in the synthetic resolution of such contradictions.

Since I do not know America at first-hand, I cannot assume that it already offers us the completed synthesis. I only know that in a work like "Technics and Civilization" Mr. Mumford, an American, has clearly shown to us the way which we must all go. I also know that it is impossible that there should exist in America the formidable obstacles that face the English architect and designer whichever way he turns—the obstacle of intrenched and subsidized academic prejudice, and the still greater obstacle of prevailing traditionalism and conservatism. It is the presence of these obstacles which must determine our critical tactics. Here the struggle is primarily an ideological one. We have to break down an old concept of beauty before we can establish a new one. If in support of our theories we appeal to the evidence of the facts, the facts on which we rely are everywhere dominated by the residues of ancient civilizations. Conceive, if you can, the probability of an architect being allowed to build a vitally modern building within the sacred precincts of Oxford or Cambridge! But that is precisely the kind of difficulty which faces the industrial artist in England whichever way lie turns. It may be that a not inconsiderable snobbery operates against the modern artist and architect in America, but snobbery can always be ridiculed and shaken. In the Old World we need the faith to move, if not mountains, at least monuments.

The new aesthetic must be based on the fundamentally new factor in modern civilization: large-scale machine production. It is here that we look to America...

* * * ●

1930

Empire State Building, New York City, Shreve, Lamb and Harmon, architects, 1931.

Tobacco Company's Building (photo page 262) have been set back from the street line to secure better light and air conditions, and a large court has been placed on the inner property line. Utility units are in the darker inner corners of the plan. The fifth plan (photo page 268), that of the Chimes Building, Syracuse, shows an inner core of compactly placed service and mechanical elements, securing a maximum amount of floor space well lighted by the two streets and the court in the inner property corner.

All story-heights of these illustrative plans are alike (11'3" floor to floor) except that the Reynolds building has a greater height (12'6") affording better light and air conditions, but somewhat increasing the cubical content without increasing the floor area.

The analysis of the several typical floors is noted in the table comparing site areas, building areas, usable space and cubical contents; and the ratios existing between these comparable data.

In the study of the building and the selection of the best of several floor arrangements, the plan arrived at for the typical floor fixes the fundamental conditions of the ground floor and the tower floor plans. The next major question is to determine the number of tower floors, the answer to the question,

"How high shall the building be carried?"

Up to a certain height added floors give the advantage of the distribution of the land cost over the added floor space. But as height increases this gain is offset more and more by the need of heavier steel columns and foundations, additional elevators, increasingly disproportionate demands for space for utilities, extreme wind-bracing, and all-round increased construction cost at the higher levels. Extra stories must be thought of as being added at the bottom of the steel frame instead of at the top, just as if the lower building were lifted and the extra stories put under it, or, otherwise the load of the added upper space must be provided for by strengthening the steel carried down through the building. Extra elevators are required to serve the added stories, but these cars must run up through the height of the building before they reach the zone which they are intended to serve, and in each story through which an idle hatchway passes 60 to 80 square feet of floor area are given up to the passing car.

In the higher buildings, at present elevator speeds, a car may be 3/4 of a minute or a minute or more in travel before making a stop. This may mean 3 or 4 minutes to a car round trip; and in order to maintain the elevator service interval at the ground floor after the first car leaves and before it returns, many more cars must be added to serve these upper floors than would be required to serve an equivalent space at a lower level.

Today in New York ten buildings have a height of 50 stories or more. Higher buildings are being considered. Water supply, house and fire pumps, steam supply, ventilation, all must be especially arranged for service through such a height. Heavy wind pressures on such buildings would produce an actual sway of flexible towers not sufficiently wind-braced, and full wind-bracing adds to steel cost.

Taking into account all of these and other conditions, it is evident that in the case of such buildings there is a point where the balance begins to swing back and the rate of return on capital investment begins to diminish as the building goes higher, unless the owner gets a markedly greater unit return for the higher space, or charges the decrease in the direct net return to "advertising."

From such an analysis we may determine if the business outlook is good, and, with the economic problem solved, approach the refinement of the architectural design which has been kept in mind through the survey of the determining factors. The demands of time, cost and practicability need not be hostile to the aesthetic side of the work. Indeed, may it not be fairly said that character is improved and greater success of pure design assured if sound reasoning as to value, and honest recognition of function, accompany and guide our struggle to attain architectural beauty? ■

THE PRIZE-WINNING BUILDINGS OF 1931

REVIEWED BY TALBOT FAULKNER HAMLIN,
Architect
Vol. 71, No. 1, January 1932, pp. 11-23

If anyone doubted the underlying roman-ticism of Americans, a little study of this album of photographs of recent prize-winning buildings in the United States should convert him at once.

It is strange to see even Eliel Saarinen, the creator of the Helsingfors Railway Station and the Second Prize Design in the Chicago Tribune Competition, falling, so soon under the spell. In the Boys' School at Cranbrook, Michigan, awarded a gold medal by the New York Architec-tural League, romanticism achieves an expression of the most ingenious clever-ness. Charm is always a dangerous architectural ideal: here it has led even Saarinen to use that old friend, decora-tive half-timber!

Architects as well as laymen, we are all still romantic, and if we all do "go func-tional," it will not be because of sound basic rational thinking, or any desire for a deep economy, but because we may develop a new romanticism of the machine, and worship it instead of life. Architects and laymen, both; for it is impossible to distinguish the awards made by architects as a class, from those made by Chambers of Commerce and similar bodies. Are the architects merely more sensitive to popular taste than other artists ? Can one imagine the Author's League giving a prize to Harold Bell Wright or Zane Grey, or even Edgar Wallace? Surely architectural bodies in awarding prizes should not only demand high standards, but should, in prefer-ence, strive to encourage the new, the young, the creative rather than the merely tasteful. The judgment of archi-tects should lead, not follow, popular demand. Even commercially it might not be a disadvantage to their own pocket-books to do so, for the true artistic cre-ative advance cannot be copyrighted; it soon becomes common property.

Obviously, the amount of available material limits these awards; and no out-side critic can realize the complex tangle of psychologies filling even the most triv-ial jury room. The result is bound to be a compromise. And no one can cavil at the awards to the Empire State Building (Shreve, Lamb and Harmon), the Hollan-der Building (Shreve, Lamb and Har-mon), or the Adler Planetarium (Ernest Grunsfeld). Yet taken as a class the whole group of commended buildings—judging largely from the photographs—seems strangely and discouragingly dull. Surely, one hopes, they do not com-pletely represent the sum total of Ameri-ca's architectural development for the year.

If these buildings are not representa-tive of American architecture, they may have a value in representing American average taste, and an examination of them all may give some general idea of the direction in which our taste is mov-ing.

* * *

The Buildings Themselves

Four buildings stand out from the mass as exceptional: the Empire State and the Hollander Building, New York, both by Shreve, Lamb and Harmon; the Adler Planetarium by Ernest Grunsfeld; and the Grand Street Apartments by Spring-steen and Goldhammer.

The tower of the Empire State Building is obviously an artistic creation of high value. Its acceptance by the people as a whole is remarkably unanimous and complete, and such expressions of pop-ular approval, when so strikingly univer-sal, are seldom far wrong. It uses masonry, but obviously as a skin, not as a support. The proportions of the set-backs are fine; there is strength and dig-nity in them. The verticals of bright metal

45   EMPIRE STATE BUILDING AT NIGHT, NEW YORK CITY

are superb; the manner in which they pick up the color of the sky, or flash back the brilliance of the sun, as though the whole tower were hung on a frame-work of light itself, has not only, that feeling of delicacy which is peculiarly the spirit of steel construction, but also a deeper quality, an authentic beauty that is a new note, a new creation.

But this tower supports a question, and is supported on an anticlimax. Surely the so-called mooring mast—a pure extrava-gance, perhaps for publicity's sake, which can never be used effectively for its avowed purpose, and which the designers must have realized could not be so used—surely that does not belong with the sureness, the definiteness below it. Rich and interesting as the detail is, there is something inconclusive and soft in the silhouette that expresses this dubiousness of function. By day or night, under sun or cloud or ringed with electric lights, the mast seems unreal.

And the street and avenue façades are a disappointment. As in the case in so many high buildings, a soaring and care-fully composed grandeur above disinte-grates near the ground level. Great tower scale and pleasant street scale seem difficult to reconcile. The Empire State Building architects recognized this inevitable discrepancy, and by placing the tower as it is, freed it from the build-ing around its base. They created thus a great street façade of pleasing height, a whole block long on Fifth Avenue, and several hundred feet on each of the side streets: apparently, an ideal problem for any architect. And then, apparently the creative drive faded; perhaps speed in designing—the curse of American com-mercial architecture—prevented ade-quate study; perhaps the tower absorbed the designers' interest over-much. In any case, there lay the oppor-tunity, and it was lost. Superficial and obvious, its generally merely satisfactory proportions, its rich materials cannot redeem its heavy-handed detail, its basic lack of that creative imagination that dis-tinguishes the tower. To the thousands passing, it brings no lift, no "kick"—it is just another building to walk past—ade-quate perhaps, but humdrum. ●

1930

Proposal drawing for Rockefeller Center, Associated Architects, 1932–33.

L. Andrew Reinhard and Henry Hofmeister are credited with the basic scheme of Rockefeller Center, with Raymond Hood contributing significantly later on. Together with Harvey Wiley Corbett and four others, they called themselves the *Associated Architects.*

The complex originally centered around a new Metropolitan Opera House (the hatbox-shaped structure seen here at lower right). At the height of the Depression, the opera house was dropped from the plan and the city-within-a-city was reconceived as a center for popular entertainment.

opposite: Daily News Building, New York City, Howells & Hood, architects, 1929.

WHAT IS THE ROCKEFELLER RADIO CITY?

Comments By L. Andrew Reinhard, Architect[1]

Ground area: 550,000 square feet. Rentable floor area: 5,000,000 square feet. Estimated cost of construction: $100,000,000. Construction begins June 1931. Central tower and two theaters will be completed in autumn of 1932.

from:
WINDOWS
By A. Lawrence Kocher and Albert Frey
Vol. 69, N0 2, February 1931,
pp. 126-137

*W*as project designed for 1931 or 1951? The whole scheme was studied with an eye to future earnings. To justify its existence as a forerunner of group planning, the project must be as sound economically for the period between 1931 and 1951 (and beyond) as for either of these years.

The vast size of the enterprise made calculations on the expected income from the investment a most important consideration in determining the plan. In the past the architect has had to deal with plots of 25' x 100', then 50' x 100', and gradually increasing until the average city block of 200' x 200' or 200' x 300' became economically desirable. A ground area of 40,000 to 60,000 square feet is considered a large plot. In the Radio City project the ground area is 550,000 square feet. This is equivalent to approximately 10 Graybar Building sites or 13 Chrysler Building sites!

One must realize that what might look like a small change in the plan or arrangement of buildings would throw the income of the enterprise anywhere from $750,000 in the red to $750,000 in the black–a difference of $1,500,000 in the annual revenue. This is not unreasonable-imagine a change in a building the size of the Graybar Building which would show a difference of $150,000 in the rent roll; multiple this figure by ten and you will have the magnitude of the Radio City project. The importance of these income producing considerations cannot be stressed too much. Should the enterprise, as an example of group planning, prove a financial failure, the banking interests, mortgage and realty companies and others who are watching the venture closely would be discouraged as to the professional abilities of architects, and the group planning of commercial structures would go back to the days of 1931 to remain there for a long time to come.

Did neighboring structures affect the design? No: on the contrary, the values of neighboring properties will in very short order be increased to such an extent as to demand future development and improvement of existing structures. These will then be brought along in the spirit of the Rockefeller project.

In what way did the problem of traffic influence the planning? Traffic is an unsolved problem in New York—it was, however, given much thought in the planning of this group. With the theaters and studios of the radio companies, as well as the shops and business offices, attracting each day a moving population of 2,000,000-equivalent to the population of a city like Hartford-some means of facilitating traffic movements had to be found.

Forty-ninth and Fiftieth Streets have been widened 15 feet, each being made a roadway 75 feet wide (approximately the width of Lexington Avenue). Forty-eighth and Fifty-first Streets could not be altered since some of the property fronting on these streets was not under control.

The central plaza with the two new streets parallel to Fifth Avenue likewise opens up the ground plan. This park, from the economic point of view, is not lost space. A new shopping center is created

Good architecture is not dependent upon window shapes. Windows should be given sizes and proportions that are suitable to daylighting needs.

The primary purpose of windows is to provide daylight and ventilation to building interiors. Windows should also permit unobstructed view of surroundings. To aid requirements of view the glazed area should he without division bars unless structurally necessary.

Physicians and illumination engineers have consistently called attention to the value of daylight, particularly of sunlight, but "how it really acts and how its benefits can most practically be secured we are just beginning to comprehend." The Metropolitan Life Insurance Company in its Statistical Bulletin has made a tabulation of data regarding deaths found in a random selection of records of the 40,000,000 risks with it has carried . . . "and found that death rates are higher during the darker winter months than at any other time of the year and that the low death rates are found during the summer months."

Windows should be designed to make usable a maximum of   ►

The magazine's caption for the above images reads:
"Hanging Gardens of Radio City
—The roof terraces of the
$250,000,000 amusement center
now being built by John D.
Rockefeller, Jr. and the
Metropolitan Square Corporation
in New York City will be land-
scaped with pools, fountains,
tiled paths, flower mosaics, trees
and shrubs. The architects are
Reinhard and Hofmeister;
Corbett, Harrison & MacMurray;
Raymond Hood and Fouilhoux."

1 The *Associated Architects* were:
Reinhard & Hofmeister; Corbett,
Harrison & MacMurray; Raymond
Hood, Godley & Fouilhoux.

within the group of buildings. A constant flow of traffic from early in the morning until late at night because of the studios and theaters-practically twice the normal shopping day-permits relatively high ground rentals which compensate the loss of revenue from the plaza itself. Parking space for 663 automobiles is provided on two underground levels running through to all the buildings and united for easy access.

How was the grouping of buildings determined? The office towers are staggered in plan so that one building will not obstruct the others in light or vision. The theaters and studios are kept low as intermediate structures not requiring light.

Why does the bank on the Fifth Avenue site take an elliptical shape? In contrast with the gridiron plan of the city an oval building will be a distinct marker, it is felt. Some feature had to be developed to attract the attention of the passing public on the avenue. Since the property between Forty-eighth and Forty-ninth Streets was not controlled, the middle block alone could be developed with this purpose in view. The oval structure was evolved consequently as a readily recognizable marker. It also opens

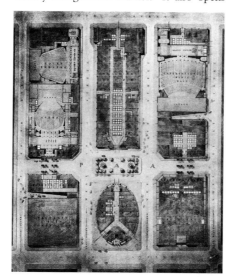

up the line of vision into the plaza and shopping center, which otherwise could not be seen easily from Fifth Avenue.

What determined the tower height? Figures cost and return! The central tower shaft has 2,000,000 square feet of floor area between the second and sixty-fifth stories, or twice the area of the Graybar Building. The tower could of course go higher, but this is not economically necessary.

How was window spacing determined? Purely from a renting standpoint. The fenestration was a natural development from the plan, inasmuch as the service and elevator areas and steel framing were all definitely determined. The steel span of 27' 6" working thus became the working unit. By using four windows to a bay the most flexible subdivision of space was secured. Units of two, three or four offices can be easily provided as the tenants may desire. At the same time there is plenty of window area for large working space.

What materials will be used for the exterior walls? This is still an open question. Much study has yet to be given to the external appearance of the buildings. The model, as it stands, represents the rentable cubage. It does not attempt to show any architectural treatment, which is another problem in itself. Four studies have already been made of the exterior of the central tower: one shows a horizontal treatment (to satisfy the "horizontalists"), another a vertical treatment (to satisfy the "verticalists"), the third a wall pattern arrangement (to satisfy the decoratively inclined), and the fourth an unadorned arrangement (to satisfy the functionally minded). Any one of the four schemes can be selected—the rentals will not be affected.

How far did the planning affect the renting schedule? At all times the owners' interest-that is, the renting schedule-was paramount. A sound plan, like a machine, can always be made beautiful! ∎

floor space with evenly distributed daylight. Light needs are the
basis for determining window
sizes and their placement. These
needs can be determined by the
use to which floor space is put.
Thoughtful investigation by the
architect with advice of technical
illumination experts is essential.
It is obvious, as an example, that
the laboratory where microscopic
work is carried on requires more
light than the room for library
book storage, where light is injuri-
ous to bindings. Light for general
office work requires approximately ten foot candles of intensity at
a desk level, thirty inches above
the door. We are informed by
experience tests that our "seeing
improves with increase in illumination. Speed of vision and accuracy of sight increases. Ocular
fatigue decreases."

One of the most astonishing
discoveries of lighting experts is
the fact that the room flooded
with daylight from an entire wall
of glass is more satisfactory for
working and less disturbing to
the eye than the room with light
from a single moderate size window. In other words, the greater
the glass area the more favorable
the working conditions will be.
This phenomenon is checked by
daily experience. There is no significant eye strain in reading on a
porch that is open on three sides
but there is eye strain in typing or
reading in a room with light from
a single window that is surrounded by dark wall areas. It is essential, therefore, to seek daylight
intensity that is evenly distributed, without excessively bright
or dark spots. Lighting engineers
offer the rule, "The brightest spot
in any building should not have
more than about three times the
illumination of the dimmest spot
in the same building." * * * ●

1931

North Building, Metropolitan Life Insurance Company Building, New York City, Harvey Wiley Corbett and D. Everett Waid, architects, 1929–33

Taking up an entire city block, huge loggias mark each of the building's four corners. The sheer size of this building was its salient feature; it boasted a full 23 acres of floor space. During the Depression the firm made loans to finance the construction of the Empire State Building and Rockefeller Center.

METROPOLITAN LIFE INSURANCE COMPANY
NEW HOME OFFICE BUILDING IN NEW YORK

D. Everett Waid and Harvey Wiley Corbett, Associated Architects

The new home office building for the Metropolitan Life Insurance Company is in no sense "just another building." It could not be characterized, despite its title, as an office building although it contains offices. It could hardly be called a factory although Mr. Ecker, the president of the company, sometimes refers to it as such. It could not be classified as a loft building although it contains many spaces which are in the nature of lofts. It could hardly be thought of as a restaurant although it feeds 8,000 persons daily, prepares meals for over 12,000 and has a kitchen plant capacity of 25,000. It is not yet a completed building, having been planned initially to cover the entire block between Twenty-fourth and Twenty-fifth Streets, Madison Avenue and Fourth Avenue, in New York City; it now covers only the eastern half of this block. It is not a public building except in a minor sense. It is not a show building from the general public's point of view. In fact, it is *a highly specialized building designed primarily as a machine to do as efficiently as possible the particular headquarters' work of our largest insurance company.*

The owners desired adequate working conditions, structural permanence and a cleanliness of aspect which would key with their recognized policy of health, happiness and well-being for their vast staff of employees, a very large percentage of whom are women. The limitations placed upon the architects by the necessity of creating at the present time only half of an ultimately unified building and yet making the present structure a completed working unit; the restrictions of the city's zoning ordinance controlling permissible bulk; the introduction of the latest ideas in ventilation, air conditioning, sound deadening, artificial lighting, intercommunicating pneumatic tubes, telephones, call bells, unit operating clock systems, special elevator and escalator installations to meet on a staggered time schedule the enormous flow of employees, the serving of meals at noon each working day to all of these employees, the receiving and distribution of many truckloads of mail, and many other technical operating problems —all of these were factors influencing plan and design.

—*HARVEY WILEY CORBETT*

The original plan, shown in this early ad for the company, called for a telescoping tower of 80 to 100 stories that would have dwarfed the original Metropolitan Life Tower (page 126).

The chief architectural points of interest lie in the unusual form of the building exterior, the great arcades and public spaces at the street level, the restaurants and lounge rooms in the second and third basements below the street level and the large assembly room and gymnasium on the 27th floor.

The major portion of the building space is used for clerks who work in large groups under the supervision of a group manager. The ordinary normal office depth of 27 to 30 feet from the outer wall was not sufficient. The problem in space arrangement required the largest bulk of building which the restrictions of the zoning ordinances would permit. The first step in design was therefore to determine the possible "enve-lope" by taking full advantage of the "dormer permit" and then to arrange the setbacks so as to gain every possible foot of floor area consistent with structural economy. The form of the building in its upper stories is the result. It is not merely a striving on the part of the designers for a peculiar or bizarre architectural effect.

The arcades and lobbies on the main floor are generously planned for width and height and have the aspect of a public building, but the general public is not drawn to this building except through curiosity. The reason for planning the ground floor on what appears to be so monumental a scale was to provide adequate circulation facilities for the vast working population in the building itself.

North Building, Metropolitan Life Insurance Company Building, New York City, Harvey Wiley Corbett and D. Everett Waid, architects, 1929–33. The building was only completed to its first phase (compare with the drawing on page 277). The Depression halted completion of the final phases. The planar shifts in the building's upper stories are highly unusual.

right, top to bottom: One of several employee lounges, an employee gymnasium, an interoffice pneumatic tube communication system.

Since this building has a daily population of over 8,000 and in its completed form will contain a working population of over 25,000, space must be provided on the ground floor to meet this flow adequately. The employees are taken by elevators from the different departments throughout the building to the dining rooms in the second and third basements, returning after luncheon to the main floor by means of escalators. This allows the elevator system to operate local and express service starting always at the main floor. The employees make use of the remaining time of their luncheon recess to promenade through these lobbies and in pleasant weather to go outdoors in the great corner loggias or on the sidewalks surrounding the building. Store fronts were not required at street line since there are no shops in the building. The arcades were placed parallel to the sidewalks so that all portions of the lower floor are naturally lighted, a feature which is unusually pleasant compared with most city buildings.

Above the ground floor are four floors of filing space where natural light was not as necessary as in the other floors. This gave the architects an opportunity to treat the lower portions of the building as a mass of masonry that adds materially to its monumental aspect.

The restaurants in the second and third basements are unique features not only in their size and plan arrangement but in the scheme of decoration. The desire was to provide a dining space which would not carry the impression of being far under ground, but would be as attractive as possible. These spaces are treated simply and architecturally. The necessary plainness of the walls is relieved by murals which are handled in a manner to retain the sense of wall surface and yet add an air of gaiety and light which would interest and amuse the diners. Conditioned air or "manufactured weather" makes this a very pleasant space at all seasons.

On the twenty-seventh floor is an auditorium which occupies the entire top story. It is used as a meeting place for company managers and agents in their various conventions and also for various conferences and gatherings necessary for transacting company business. Complete motion picture equipment and stage is provided, in addition to a gallery. The space serves also as a gymnasium for company employees outside of business hours.

The building has a floor space of more than twenty-three acres. ■

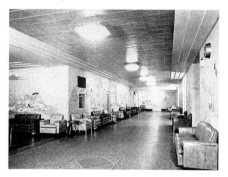

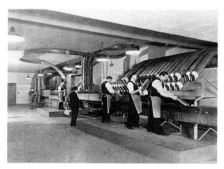

Before the 47-year-old Home Insurance Building was razed to make way for the new Field Building (page 100), a committee was appointed by the Marshall Field Estate to decide if it was entitled to the distinction of being the world's first skyscraper. After a thorough investigation, the committee handed down a verdict that it was unquestionably the first building of skeleton construction (see page 7).The committee's decision, however, was challenged by Chicago architect Irving K. Pond, who had first-hand experience in the construction work of that period.

from:
**NEITHER A SKYSCRAPER
NOR OF SKELETON CONSTRUCTION**
Irving K. Pond
Vol. 76, No. 2, August 1934, pp. 118–119.

NO 8-story structure—which the Home Insurance Building, designed by Major W. L. B. Jenney in 1884, really was as involving metal supports in outer walls—can by any stretching of the term be called a skyscraper. For centuries, probably, 8 and 10-story buildings were commonplace the world over and attracted no attention by their height. When one realizes that the 21-story Masonic Temple (Capitol Building), the first of Chicago skyscrapers, or the completed 12-story Home Insurance Building, doubled in height, would rattle inside the dome of St. Peter's in Rome, one can understand how minor an affair a mere 8- or 10-story building would be to the traveled or knowing.

In the masonry-walled water tower designed by S. S. Beman for the town of Pullman, and which might well fall in the category of skyscraper, Phoenix rolled shapes were used in braced columns some two

hundred feet in height; these and the walls supporting an iron tank 40 feet in depth and of the same diameter! This tower antedated by about two years the Pullman Building in Chicago, on which construction was begun in the spring of 1883 and which is 10 stories in part. As I had charge of the structural design of both edifices, I am fairly conversant with the matter.

Now as to the "skeleton frame" of the Home Insurance Building: All vertical supports, in walls or otherwise, were, as in the Pullman Building, of cast iron and beams and girders of rolled iron. The wall verticals, which occurred in the Home Insurance Building only, and there in but eight stories, from the third to the tenth inclusive, were bolted at the joints. These verticals rested upon a plinth consisting of two stories of massive granite masonry which are ignored in this discussion as having "nothing to do with the case" except to confine the metal of the street fronts to eight stories. Up to and including the third floor system floor beams and girders were wall-bearing on the two street fronts as were the beams and girders of all floor and roof systems on the massive alley and dividing line walls; and floor systems could not be installed until walls were up and ready to receive them. At the fourth, sixth and ninth floors and at the roof on the street fronts, rolled spandrel beams rested on brackets and were loosely bolted to lugs cast on the posts. At the fifth, seventh, eighth and tenth floors no lateral bracing was provided for the verticals and we have the condition, in two vertical units of a bay, of one post standing on an unbraced post beneath, and in one unit, of three superimposed posts with two contiguous unbraced joints. Where is the stability?

In point of fact the frame could not have maintained itself in an upright position had it not been for the massive alley and line walls; and the posts in the street fronts could not have maintained themselves laterally had not the masonry of the piers been carried up simultaneously with the iron to brace the verticals and to take the wide cast-iron lintels which occurred, unbolted to the frame, at the fifth, seventh, eighth and tenth floors. Nor did the metal structure sustain the masonry piers of the street fronts (and only incidentally did they sustain three of the eight spandrel walls in each bay). When once the masonry had "set" an entire story of it on the street fronts might have been removed with small damage to the remain-

der; but no masonry pier could have been installed until that immediately beneath was in place or, as the Engineering Society's report notes, "unless a temporary support had been provided." Major Jenney's notion, expressed later, that he used iron to lighten the load on the Chicago soil must have come as an afterthought. It must have been the need of light which influenced him for it would not take as great a dead load of masonry to serve as piers in his street fronts as he used in his line wall on the same lot with the same soil conditions.

When it comes down to a matter of priority there is absolutely no first "skeleton frame," as we know it, in the world. The most nearly perfected of recent types contains some element appearing in the rudimentary structures; but the elements are so numerous that not all appear in any one design. So far as I now know, Holabird and Roche were new and bold in their application of terra cotta as an envelope to the iron in the street fronts, especially as to the spandrels, of the Tacoma Building which followed the Home Insurance Building by two or three years. But in that building, as in the other, the metal structure could not have maintained itself without the assistance of masonry walls. I know that in the middle of the nineteenth century in Europe the builders were translating half timber construction into terms of rolled shapes; and I saw in benighted Spain (though one could hardly call Barcelona benighted even then) tall buildings, taller than ours, under construction with thoroughly braced frames of rolled iron to which the masonry in which the metal was embedded was applied when and as the builder wished. This phenomenon I described in a letter written in 1883 to the Inland Architect.

Major Jenney was a great student of Viollet-le-Duc but was timid about putting that author's ideas, except as to style, into effect—that is, if he even sensed their implications. That Chicago was alive to progress in construction and design in the early eighties, her buildings, as well as a brochure by Architect Frederick Baumann, which I have in my possession, fully attest. However, it may be set down with a fair amount of assurance that the structure of the original Home Insurance Building had very little or nothing in common with the modern skeleton construction and had little or no influence on "Skyscraper" design. ●

Bauhaus School Workshops, Dessau, Germany, Walter Gropius, architect, 1926.

In their catalogue to the International Style Exhibition (1932), Hitchcock and Johnson wrote,

"the workshops have entirely transparent walls. A good illustration of glass panes as a surfacing material. The projection of the roof cap is unfortunate, especially over the entrance at left."

This photograph was originally published in *Architectural Record* in October 1930.

epilogue

THE INTERNATIONAL STYLE TWENTY YEARS AFTER

Henry-Russell Hitchcock

In the spring of 1928, the building boom of the Twenties was already past its national peak by several years, but the wave of skyscraper production was still rising in New York. Certainly America's faith in her own architectural achievement had never been higher, even though her greatest architect Frank Lloyd Wright was, in those halcyon years, more active at writing articles for magazines than at building. Concurrently with the series "In the Cause of Architecture" by Wright, which began in the January number of the RECORD, there appeared in the April and May numbers two articles, advance samples from my book on Modern Architecture which was published the following year. The second article, "The New Pioneers," presented very briefly, but perhaps for the first time to many Americans, the thesis that the work of a group of young European architects, some part of it actually executed in the previous five or six years, but much of it merely in the form of projects, proposed and illustrated a drastic and unified architectural revolution.

In 1931, the Museum of Modern Art, a new institution in New York devoted primarily to the presentation of the work of modern painters, planned an ambitious venture. Dissatisfied with the selections from contemporary architectural production then being shown in the Architectural League's annual exhibitions and convinced that modern architecture was at least as signifi-

cant as modern painting, the director of the Museum, Alfred Barr, asked Philip Johnson and me to organize an International Exhibition of Modern Architecture to be held at the Museum early the next year. The exhibition emphasized the work of four European architects, Gropius, Le Corbusier, J.J.P. Oud, and Mies van der Rohe, and of five Americans, Wright, Raymond Hood, Howe and Lescaze, Neutra, and the Bowman Brothers (about whom very little has been heard since). But it also included a section devoted to the "Extent of Modern Architecture" in which work from 15 countries and by some 40 architects was included.

At the same time, Philip Johnson and I prepared a book, The International Style: Architecture Since 1922. *In that we attempted to set down the characteristics of the new architecture of the previous decade as it had first been developed, largely by the four Europeans whose work was stressed in the Exhibition, and as it had already been extended by so many others to various countries throughout the world.*

This article takes the form of a series of quotations from the 1932 book with comments made in the light of what has happened since. Typographic differentiation indicates which are the passages quoted from the text of the book prepared in 1931 (and published in 1932) and which are remarks of 20 years later.

—H.-R. H.

T HE INTERNATIONAL STYLE was prefaced by a statement by Alfred Barr, the Director of the Museum of Modem Art. In his first paragraph he made a claim which the authors themselves might well have considered immodest:

. . . They have proven beyond any reasonable doubt, I believe, that there exists today a modem style as original, as consistent, as logical, and as widely distributed as any in the past. The authors have called it the International Style.

To many this assertion of a new style will seem arbitrary and dogmatic . . .

And how! A quarter century after Gropius's Bauhaus at Dessau[1] and Le Corbusier's Pavillon de l'Esprit Nouveau[2] at the Paris Exposition of Decorative Arts of 1925 first made evident that something like a concerted program for a new architecture existed, it is still by no means necessary to conclude that the "International Style" (which they and other European architects were then maturing) should be considered the only proper pattern or program for modem architecture.

The work of many architects of distinc-

1 Bauhaus (opposite).

2 Esprit Nouveau Pavilion (above), The Arts Decoratifs Exhibition, Paris, Charles-Edouard and Pierre Jeanneret, architects, 1925. Charles-Edouard would soon make a reputation for himself under the name of Le Corbusier. Hardly noticed at the time, their simple, unadorned pavilion went on to become, in retrospect, the most influential of all the exhibits.

In 1932, Henry–Russell Hitchcock and Philip Johnson curated a ground-breaking exhibition for New York's Museum of Modern Art called "The International Style: Architecture since 1922." The only hi-rise structures included in the exhibition and the accompanying catalogue were the McGraw-Hill Building (p. 283) and the PSFS Building (p.285).

3 Russell House, Twitchell and Rudolf, architects, 1949.

4 Hitchcock here refers to Gropius who was the Chair of Harvard's Architecture Schoolfrom 1938–1952.

5 Victor Horta (1861–1947), Belgian architect. The Tassel House in Brussels (1892–93), his first mature work, was the earliest monument of art nouveau. It was excelled only by his later works, such as the Baron von Eetvelde house (1895) and the demolished Maison du Peuple (1896–99), both in Brussels. The houses are especially significant for their interior architecture. The irregularly shaped rooms open freely onto one another at different levels. The plantlike design of the iron balustrade is echoed in the curving decorative lines of the mosaic floors, plaster walls, and other surfaces. Horta later reverted to a more traditional mode of architectural expression.

6 William Wurster (1895–1973), was Dean of the Architecture School of the University of California at Berkeley.

tion such as Frank Lloyd Wright, who make no bones about their opposition to the supposed tenets of an International Style, certainly belongs to modern architecture as much as does the work of Gropius and Le Corbusier. Yet the particular concepts of a new modem style which date from the Twenties do conveniently define that crystallization—that convergence of long immanent ideas—which then took place in France and Germany and Holland, and which a quarter century later has spread throughout the civilized world. (Only, I believe, in Russia are the forms of the International Style unpopular—to put outright official proscription rather mildly!)

In general, it has been the concept of "style" itself, as implying restraint or discipline according to a priori rules of one sort or another, which has been hardest for architects, as distinguished from critics and writers, to accept. The introduction of the 1932 book was therefore devoted to defending "The Idea of Style" and this defense is still relevant—even if its validity is also still debatable—today:

The chaos of eclecticism served to give the very idea of style a bad name in the estimation of the first modern architects of the end of the nineteenth and the beginning of the twentieth century.

The most distinguished older modern architects, notably Wright and Gropius, are still perhaps the most perturbed by the idea that anything that can property be called a style, in the historic sense of that word, can have any worthwhile part to play in the architecture of the 20th century. Yet Wright himself obviously has a highly individualistic style—several, for that matter—and it is also obvious that that personal style (or those styles) of his could be utilized as a framework of architectural advance, if his precepts for "Organic Architecture" were widely accepted and conscientiously followed.

Gropius is proud of the fact that it is difficult to tell the work of one of his pupils from that of another—a difficulty that he in fact rather exaggerates. (For the work of Paul Rudolph,[3] for example, differs a great deal from that of the members of what might be called the Boston Suburban School.) But what is this anonymity that the Chairman of the Harvard Department of Architecture[4] admires in his pupils' work but a common style? It is not the "Gropius" or the "Bauhaus" style, moreover, but merely an important part of the broader International Style, as that is practiced by the third generation of modern architects in the North Eastern United States.

The individualistic revolt of the first modern architects destroyed the prestige of the [historic] "styles," but it did not remove the implication that there was a possibility of choice between one aesthetic conception of design and another.

To refuse a comparable liberty of choice today, merely because 25 years ago the development of modern architecture began to be notably convergent, is certainly a form of academicism. This is already only too evident in just the places one would expect to find it, that is, in prominent architectural schools and in large highly institutionalized offices. Modern architecture in the 1950s should have room again for a range of effects as diverse, if not as divergent, as Victor Horta's[5] Maison du Peuple in Brussels of 1897, an early modern building largely of metal and glass that is too often forgotten now, and Wright's River Forest Golf Club (as first built in 1898), of ordinary wooden-frame construction, in which most of the concepts of his now "classic" prairie houses of the next decade were already almost fully mature.

The individualists decried submission to fixed aesthetic principles as the imposition of a dead hand upon the living material of architecture, holding the failure of the [stylistic] revivals [of the 19th century] as a proof that the very idea of style was an unhealthy delusion.

Much of what Dean Wurster[6] has called "Drugstore Modern" suggests that the "individualists" were less completely in the wrong than we admitted 20 years ago. Certainly too rigid a concept of what is stylistically "permissible" is always stultifying.

But throughout most of the intervening period our contention that:

The idea of style, which began to degenerate when the revivals destroyed the disciplines of the Baroque, has become real and fertile again.

has been supported by what has occurred.

The idea of modern style should remain, as it presently is in fact, somewhat loose rather than too closely defined. There will, however, always be some sort of style in the arts of self-conscious periods, whether it is so recognized, and so called, or not. Since it is impossible to return, under the circumstances of advanced civilization, to the unselfconscious production of supposedly styleless "folk arts," it is well to be aware that there is a problem of style. To attempt to dismiss style altogether is culturally ingenuous; it is also Utopian, or more accurately, millennial (in one sense at least, there were no "styles" in the Garden of Eden!).

The unconscious and halting architectural developments of the nineteenth century, the confused and contradictory experimentation of the beginning of the twentieth, have been succeeded by a directed evolution. There is now a single body of discipline, fixed enough to integrate contemporary style as a reality and yet elastic enough to permit individual interpretation and to encourage general growth.

Today that "fixing" is resented, just because it has been so successful. Yet the establishment of a fixed body of discipline in architecture is probably the major achievement of the 20th century, not any technical developments in building production that have become universally accepted; modern technical developments have recurrently disappointed the optimists and they have failed, perhaps even more conspicuously, to live up to the bolder prophecies of 19th century critics.

After 25 years, it is the "elasticity" and the possibility of "general growth" within the International Style which should be emphasized. That was already beginning to be evident to Philip Johnson and myself 20 years ago. Few of our readers, alas, seem to have given us credit for what were then readily dismissed as mere "escape-clauses."

The idea of style as the frame of potential growth, rather than as a fixed and crushing mould, has developed with the recognition of underlying principles such as archaeologists discern in the great styles of the past. The principles are few and broad.

Too few and too narrow, I would say in 1951 of the principles that were enunciated so firmly in 1932:

There is, first, a new conception of architecture as volume rather than as mass. Secondly, regularity rather than axial symmetry serves as the chief means of ordering design. These two principles, with a third proscribing arbitrary applied decoration, mark the productions of the international style.

Today I should certainly add articulation of structure, probably making it the third principle; and I would also omit the reference to ornament, which is a matter of taste rather than of principle. The concept of regularity is obviously too negative to explain very much about the best contemporary design; but I can still find no phrase that explains in an all-inclusive way the more positive qualities of modern design.

In opposition to those who claim that a new style of architecture is impossible or undesirable, it is necessary to stress the coherence of the results obtained within the range of possibilities thus far explored. For the international style already exists in the present; it is not merely something the future holds in store. Architecture is always a set of actual monuments, not a vague corpus of theory.

After twenty years there are many, many more "actual monuments" in existence; the results are still coherent, but the "corpus of theory" is both firmer and broader, if also harder to define. The mistake made by many readers of "The International Style" was—and if any one reads the book now, instead of depending on his memory or on second-hand reports of its contents, still is I fear—to assume that what the authors offered as a diagnosis and a prognosis was intended to be

McGraw-Hill Building, New York, Hood & Fouilhoux, architects, 1931

The catalogue entry for the McGraw-Hill Building reads:
"The lightness, simplicity and lack of applied verticalism mark this skyscraper as an advance over other New York skyscrapers and bring it within the limits of the International Style. The spandrels are sheathed with blue-green tiles . The metal covering of the supports is painted dark green. The set-backs are handled more frankly than in other skyscrapers, though still reminiscent of the pyramidal shape of traditional towers. The regularity approaches monotony except for these set-backs which are determine by legal requirements rather than by considerations of design. The heavy, ornamental crown is an illogical and unhappy break in the general system of regularity and weighs down the whole design."

1951

SC Johnson Company
Administative Building,1939, and
Research Tower, 1949, Racine,
Wisconsin, Frank Lloyd Wright,
architect.

7 Otto Wagner (1841–1918),
Peter Behrens (1868–1940),
Auguste Perret (1874–1954).

8 Notre Dame, LeRaincy (photo
page 286)

9 SC Johnson Company Buildings
(above).

used as an academic rulebook.

It is an old story now, on the other hand, that Wright came very close indeed to the International Style in certain projects of the late 1920s, such as that for an apartment house for Elizabeth Noble in Los Angeles, and that many of his most famous later works, such as Falling Water, seem to include definitely "international" ideas. The architects of the San Francisco Bay Region, whom some critics have wished to build up as the protagonists of a more humanistic school opposed to the International Style, have also frequently followed its principles almost to the point of parody—although admittedly not in their best and most characteristic country-house work. Between these extremes of loose interpretation by one of the original definers of the International Style and of partial, or even at times complete, acceptance of its tenets by those theoretically most opposed to it, lies the great bulk of current architectural production.

Following the section devoted to "The Idea of Style" in the 1932 book came one on the "History" of modern architecture. We said then (rather condescendingly) of the architects active from 1890 to 1920:

Today it seems more accurate to describe the work of the older generation as half-modern.

In 1951 there seems no reason at all not to claim that the work of the older generation of modern architects was "early modern," not "half-modern." The achievements of the earlier men seem much greater today in retrospect, moreover, than they did 20 years ago. Without Wright's work of the last 20 years, it is hard to believe now that the full scope of his greatness could have been appreciated as it certainly had been in 1932 by many architects and critics for almost a generation. Yet it still seems a true enough historical statement to say that:

There was no real stylistic integration until after the war [of 1914-18].

The crystallization of what will perhaps in historical terms some day be called the

"high" phase of modern architecture came in the 1920s. Now I suspect we are entering the "late" phase. Leaving that prognosis aside, much of what we wrote twenty years ago about the "early modern" architects still seems true.

Wright was the first to conceive of architectural design in terms of planes existing freely in three dimensions rather than in terms of enclosed blocks. Wagner, Behrens and Perret[7] lightened the solid massiveness of traditional architecture, Wright dynamited it.

Such things as the interior of Otto Wagner's Postal Savings Bank in Vienna, of [1904–06], or Behrens's German General Electric turbine factory in Berlin, of [1909-10], appear today more extraordinary, in relation to what had preceded them in the previous century, than they did then.

Wright from the beginning was radical in his aesthetic experimentation.

Wright's Yahara Boat Club [Project], [for] Madison, Wisconsin, prefigured, well before Cubism reached maturity, most of the plastic innovations that contact with abstract painting and sculpture were to suggest, [many] years later, to the young European architects who initiated the International Style. The plan Wright prepared for a house to be built for himself in 1903, incorporating all the living areas except the kitchen in one articulated flow, is obviously an early prototype of the one-room houses that are frequently supposed to be a post-war development of the last five years.

Perret was, perhaps, a more important innovator in construction.

Perret's church at LeRaincy[8] outside Paris, of 1923, remains more striking than much of the shell-concrete construction of the last decade. But Perret's later work has seemed less bold, both structurally and aesthetically, and he belongs in the main to the early 20th century. Wright's Johnson Wax Building in Racine,[9] of [1937–39], particularly with the addition of the new laboratory tower completed last year, reveals on the other hand that the American architect's feats as an innovator in construction had not even reached their peak in 1932. If such buildings as Notre Dame du Raincy [sic] and the Racine structures are not prime examples of modern architecture, the word "modern" has no meaning. On the other hand, they certainly do not fit conveniently into the frame of the International Style as it was envisaged between 1922 and 1932.

With regard to the moment of stylistic crystallization in the 1920s I think it is still true to say, as we wrote in 1931:

. . . the man who first made the world aware that a new style was being born was Le Corbusier.

Furthermore, no one has done more than Le Corbusier ever since to extend and loosen the sanctions of the International Style. That was already apparent in 1932 in his house for Mme. de Mandrot at Le Pradet, of 1931, and in his Errazuris house of the same date in Chile. It is in some respects perhaps less evident today, at least in New York, since the UN office building (in whose design he played some part) may be considered "early" Le Corbusier—like his Paris projects of the Twenties-rather than post-War Le Corbusier, at least in the form in which it has been executed.

In [Le Corbusier's] Citrohan house models of [1919–] 1921 . . . the enormous window area and the terraces made possible by the use of ferro-concrete, together with the asymmetry of the composition, undoubtedly produced a design more thoroughly infused with new spirit, more completely freed from the conventions of the past, than any thus far projected.

It is interesting to compare the Citrohan house with Wright's Millard house in Pasadena, designed a year [or two] later. Note the similarity of the volume-concept of the interior, with the two-story living-area in front opening on a balcony, and the bedrooms and services on two levels behind. In 1931 it was hard to appreciate the originality in concept and in structure of the Millard house, because the patterned surface produced with the concrete blocks was so

different from the smooth rendered surfaces which were still the sign-manual of the International Style, particularly as illustrated in the work of the Le Corbusier before 1930. Now, I think it is evident that such surface-patterning is a perfectly legitimate expression of the casting process by which Wright's blocks were made. Above all, 30 years have proved that patterned concrete surfaces, like Wright's of the 1920s, generally weather rather agreeably. The rendered surfaces of the early "International" buildings of the same period too often cracked and grew stained, thus losing all that quality of platonic abstraction which made them so striking.

[Le Corbusier] was not the only innovator nor was the style as it came generally into being after 1922 peculiarly his own. He crystallized; he dramatized; but he was not alone in creating.

Le Corbusier was certainly a good deal responsible for there being a recognizable international style. Yet Gropius's work and the work of his pupils is doubtless more typical of the style; and he has always been an equally effective proponent, even if he does continue to disown the idea of style at every opportunity.

It was in Mies's projects of 1922 that his true significance as an aesthetic innovator first appeared. In a design for a country house he broke with the conception of the wall as a continuous plane surrounding the plan and built up his composition of intersecting planes. Thus he achieved, still with the use of supporting walls, a greater openness even than Le Corbusier with his ferro-concrete skeleton construction.

Mies's country-house project of 1922, with its bearing walls of brick and its van Doesburg-like plan, seems even more significant today than it did twenty years ago. It very evidently does not fit either the principle of enclosed volume or the principle of regularity. (This serious critical dilemma seems hardly to have been noted in 1931.)

The next section of the book was concerned with "Functionalism." For in 1932 The International Style was conceived as a

PSFS Building, Philadelphia, Howe and Lescaze, architects, 1932.

Hitchcock and Johnson said of the PSFS Building:
"The building will not be completed until the summer of 1932. The entire front is cantilevered. The relation of the base with its curved corner to the tower is awkward. The different parts of the building are distinguished by different surfacing materials: the base, housing the bank, of granite slabs; two intermediate storeys of limestone; the spandrels of the tower of brick."

Notre Dame at LeRaincy, near Paris. Auguste Perret, architect, 1922-23.

11 Herbert Hoover (1874–1964), President of the US from 1929 to 1933, was a world-famous mining engineer long before taking office.

opposite: Dining room bay, Innes House, Los Angeles, Frank Lloyd Wright, architect. Pictured in Architectural Record, August 1928.

counterblast to functionalism, at least as we then understood that term.

Some modern critics and groups of architects both in Europe and in America deny that the aesthetic element in architecture is important, or even that it exists. All aesthetic principles of style are to them meaningless and unreal.

There are still those who insist that architecture ought to be entirely a matter of technics and that architects should therefore hand over the whole field of building to engineers. But the glorification of engineering is a less popular critical gambit than it was earlier. (Then it will perhaps be recalled there was even a "Great Engineer" in the White House!)[11] Yet, looking back over the building production of the last two generations, it is evident that the really great engineers have frequently built edifices which were more monumental and in many ways more visually effective than what most architects were able to achieve. The grain elevators of the Great Lakes ports stimulated Le Corbusier's ideas of what the new architecture might be like quite as much as did the "Tubism" of his friend the painter Léger. The engineer Freyssinet's hangar at Orly, of [1916], is still something that architects have been unable to rival for grandeur and clarity of form. The Goodyear Airship Dock at Akron is almost as impressive. What this really means is that some engineers are very good architects!

. . . [It is] nearly impossible to organize and execute a complicated building without making some choices not wholly determined by technics and economics. . . . Consciously or unconsciously the designer must make free choices before his design is completed.

Some sort of architectural style inevitably arises from the characteristic ways in which those free choices are made. Thus functionalism, even in the drastic terms of the Twenties, could have turned into a style, and to some Europeans it seems to have become one-the International Style, in fact! It is not necessary, of course, that engineers, or those architects who prefer to think of themselves as "pure" functionalists, should be able to explain in words their principles of design. (Some engineers at least, such as Arup and Samuely in England, can do so, however, and often very ably.)

. . . Critics should be articulate about problems of design; but architects, whose training is more technical than intellectual, can afford to be unconscious of the effects they produce. So, it may be assumed, were many of the great builders of the past.

As I have already noted, Mr. Johnson has given the most effective evidence of his own broad interpretation of the International Style in the buildings he has designed, rather than in writing. My own writing of the last 20 years, and perhaps particularly the book on Frank Lloyd Wright, *In the Nature of Materials* (1942), indicates—sometimes implicitly, sometimes explicitly—how my own ideas have been modified. It is worthwhile, none the less, to consider here a particular principle of the International Style as we saw it in 1932, notably the one concerning "Architecture as Volume." That was at best an ambiguous phrase, since volume is properly "contained space," while we were then chiefly concerned with the avoidance of effects of mass in the treatment of the exteriors of buildings.

Contemporary methods of construction provide a cage or skeleton of supports. Now the walls are merely subordinate elements fitted like screens between the supports or carried like a shell outside them.

The particular relationship of skeleton and shell which we then considered most characteristic of the International Style can best be illustrated, paradoxically, by the plan of a building that has never been accepted as representative of the style, Perret's church at LeRaincy, of 1923.

It is true that supporting wall sections are still sometimes used in combination with skeleton structure.

An early example of this, by one of the recognized leaders of the International Style, is illustrated in the plan of Le

Corbusier's de Mandrot house of 1931. We considered that rather an exception. But today a very large number of modern American houses include (often quite arbitrarily it would seem) sections of supporting masonry, sometimes of brick, sometimes of rustic stonework, and very frequently of cinder or other concrete blocks introduced for effects of contrast and also because of their suitability in certain functional and structural situations. The idea may be abused but it can no longer be considered exceptional or reactionary.

The effect of mass, of static solidity, hitherto the prime quality of architecture, has all but disappeared; in its place there is an effect of volume, or more accurately, of surface planes bounding a volume. The prime architectural symbol is no longer the dense brick but the open box.

Certainly this statement is even truer, in a general way, than it was twenty years ago. Yet my fellow-author, Mr. Johnson, not only used a tower-like cylinder inside his house of glass in New Canaan, but contrasted the ultimate openness of the main house with a guest house of brick, almost as solid in appearance as if it had no interior whatsoever!

The most dramatic illustrations of the

various methods of expressing interior skeletons still remain the American skyscrapers; but there are now rather more of them than there were in 1932, so that the character of their construction is better understood by the general public.

The McGraw-Hill Building comes nearest to achieving aesthestically the expression of the enclosed steel cage, but it is still partially distorted into the old silhouette of a massive tower.... Yet the architect, Raymond Hood, in the Daily News Building which is in other ways less pure in expression, handled the setbacks so that they did not suggest steps and brought his building to a clean stop without decorative or terminal features.

It has too often been forgotten—and apparently was by us when writing in 1931—that long before Raymond Hood's day the Bayard or Conduit [sic] Building, of 1897, in New York, by Louis Sullivan, or better still his Gage Building, of the next year, at 18 South Michigan Avenue in Chicago, illustrated more clearly than Hood's skyscrapers, then newly completed, the proper architectural expression of steel-skeleton construction in the external cladding of a tall edifice. The later New York skyscrapers (and particularly those since the War that seem most literally to follow the precepts of the International Style in their design) are certainly not more expressive than these 50-year-old buildings. It is also interesting to note that Mies van der Rohe, in his Chicago apartment houses of the last few years, has moved closer and closer to Sullivan in the exterior treatment, whether the skeleton inside be of ferro-concrete or of steel. Even 20 years ago it was very difficult, apparently, to see the grandeur of the Sullivanian forest through the lush foliage of the ornament.

Style is character, style is expression; but even character must be displayed, and expression may be conscious and clear or muddled and deceptive. The architect who builds in the international style seeks to display the true character of his construction and to express clearly his provision for function. He prefers such an organization of his general composition, such a use of available surface

Holabird & Roche/Sullivan, Millinery Buildings for the McCormick Estate, with a façade for the Gage Building by Louis Sullivan, Chicago, 1898–99. Notice how the piers are treated as the stems of flowers that appear beneath the cornice. Also, compare the entrance with that of the Bayard Building (page 61).

materials, and such a handling of detail as will increase rather than contradict the prime effect of surface of volume.

The articulation of visible supports should also have been mentioned, whether isolated (as for example in the Johnson glass house or Mies's Farnsworth house on the Des Plaines river near Chicago) or actual sections of bearing wall (as in Le Corbusier's Le Pradet house or his [project for] Chile). A very striking example of vigorous articulation, in a quite sculptural way, of interior supports was in fact illustrated in the book—Aalto's Turun Sanomat Building at [Turku] in Finland, of 1930.

The flat roof was almost the sign-manual of the International Style in the early days. A loophole which proved very prophetic was left (fortunately) in the text on this subject:

Roofs with a single slant, however, have occasionally been used with success. Flat roofs are so much more useful that slanting or rounded roofs are only exceptionally justified.

The last sentence certainly represented a puristic and also a pseudofunctional position. But roofs are certainly of great importance in determining the character of the architecture of any period, particularly as regards small structures such as houses. Many architects have now swung so far from the belief that roofs must be flat that there is a tendency to over-exploit elaboration of the skyplane.

Since the roof was expected 20 years ago to be invisible, a great deal of space was given to the surfacing of exterior walls in the 1932 book.

The spirit of the principle of [continuous] surface covers many exceptions to its letter. The type of construction represented by Mies van der Rohe's Barcelona pavilion, as well as that represented in Le Corbusier's house at Le Pradet, leads to a treatment of surfaces sensibly different from that which has been primarily stressed here.

Obviously these exceptions should have been a warning that the aesthetic "necessity" for the treatment of exterior walls as contin-

uous surface was being much exaggerated. Curiously enough, California architects, working mostly with wood, have of late years been more faithful to the principle of continuity of surface than the European architects who were originally the most devoted to rendered and painted surfaces of cement.

The general statement with which this section concluded had its sound points:

The principle of surface of volume intelligently understood will always lead to special applications where the construction is not the typical cage or skeleton of supports surrounded by a protecting screen. The apparent exception may not prove the validity of the general principle, but it undoubtedly indicates its elasticity. Rigid rules of design are easily broken once and for all; elastic principles of architecture grow and flourish.

Rather than proceed with so detailed a commentary, it may be well to lead into a conclusion to this article by quoting a few of the more general remarks of 20 years ago which seem to remain valid still.

The second principle of contemporary style in architecture has to do with regularity. The supports in skeleton construction are normally and typically spaced at equal distances. Thus most buildings have an underlying regular rhythm which is clearly seen before the outside surfaces are applied. Moreover, economic considerations tend to favor the use of standardized parts throughout. Good modern architecture expresses in its design this characteristic orderliness of structure and this similarity of parts by an aesthetic ordering which emphasizes the underlying regularity. Bad modern design contradicts this regularity. Regularity is, however, relative and not absolute in architecture.

. . . the nearer approaches to absolute regularity are also approaches to monotony.... The principle of regularity refers to a means of organization, a way of giving definite form to an architectural design, rather than to an end which is sought for itself. ...The avoidance of symmetry should not be arbitrary or distorted.

... The mark of the bad modern architect is the positive cultivation of asymmetry for decorative reasons. For that can only be done in the majority of cases at the expense of common consistency and common sense. The mark of the good modern architect, on the other hand, is that the regularity of his designs approaches bilateral symmetry.

Exceptions to general rectangularity are only occasionally demanded by function and they may introduce complications in the regular skeleton of the structure. Non-rectangular shapes, particularly if they occur infrequently, introduce an aesthetic element of the highest positive interest.... They need seldom occur in ordinary building, but in monuments where the architect feels justified in seeking for a strongly personal expression, curves will be among the elements which give most surely extreme positive or negative aesthetic value. Curved and oblique forms seldom find a place in the cheapest solution of a given problem. But, if they can be afforded, they succeed, as they fail, on aesthetic grounds alone.

Aalto's Senior House at the Massachusetts Institute of Technology, of 1948, is obviously the most striking illustration of the increased use of curved and oblique forms. Whether most people approve of this prominent building or not, they tend to assume that Aalto was here consciously breaking with the rigidities of the International Style. Actually, as the paragraph above makes evident, even this notable post-War structure, though it may be at the extreme limit of the International Style as we understood it 20 years ago, is still in actual opposition to its sanctions only in the expressive irregularity of the plan and a few rather minor details, such as the willful roughness of the brickwork and the excessive clumsiness of some of the membering. Aalto was really reacting here, not against the International Style, but against that vulgar parodying of its more obvious aspects—the "Drugstore Modern"—which had become ubiquitous in the previous decade.

It was naturally to be expected, as the International Style became more widely accepted, that more and more weak and imitative architects would attempt to exploit its characteristic features. In 1932 we were amazingly optimistic and full of faith. We wrote:

Anyone who follows the rules, who accepts the implications of an architecture that is not mass but volume, and who conforms to the principle of regularity can produce buildings which are at least aesthetically sound. If these principles seem more negative than positive, it is because architecture has suffered chiefly in the last century and a half from the extension of the sanctions of genius to all who have called themselves architects.

But it has not, of course, worked out that way. Many docile architects, and even builders outside the profession, have followed the rules dutifully enough, but their buildings can hardly be considered aesthetically sound. Doubtless the principles educed twenty years ago were too negative, and now we are ready, probably too ready, to extend the sanctions of genius very widely once more. If my tentative prognosis be correct, that we stand now at another change of phase in modern architecture between a "high" and a "late" period, we must expect many vagaries in reaction against the too literal interpretation of the International Style. We may also expect—and indeed already have with us—an academic current which is encouraging the repetition of established formulas without creative modulation. If the next 25 years are less disturbed by depressions and wars than the last have been, I suspect that our architecture will grow more diverse in kind. But I doubt if we will, for the next generation or more, lose contact altogether with the International Style, if that be interpreted as broadly as it was meant to be in 1932.

The International Style was not presented, in the 1932 book which first gave currency to the phrase, as a closed system; nor was it intended to be the whole of modern architecture, past, present, and future. Perhaps it has become convenient now to use the phrase chiefly to condemn the literal and unimaginative application of the design clichés of 25 years ago; if that is really the case, the term had better be forgotten. The "traditional architecture," which still bulked so large in 1932, is all but dead by now. The living architecture of the twentieth century may well be called merely "modern." ∎

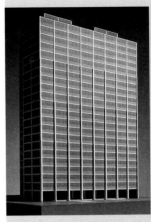

Model, Promontory Apartments, Chicago, 1946–1949, Mies van der Rohe, architect. The building was executed in concrete rather than steel (Mies's preference), due to postwar shortages.

1951

Recommended Reading

Burchard, John and Albert Bush-Brown, *The Architecture of America: A Social and Cultural History*, Boston:Little, Brown and Company, 1961.

Charernbhak, Wichit, *Chicago School Architects and Their Critics*, Michigan:UMI Research Press, 1981.

Condit, Carl W., *The Chicago School of Architecture*, Chicago:The University of Chicago Press, 1964.

Ford, Larry, *Cities and Buildings: Skyscrapers, Skid Rows, and Suburbs*, Baltimore:The Johns Hopkins University Press, 1994.

Gifford, Don, ed., *The Literature of Architecture: The Evolution of Architectural Theory and Practice in Nineteenth Century America*, New York:E.P. Dutton & Co., Inc, 1966.

Hitchcock, Henry-Russell, Jr., *Modern Architecture: Romanticism and Reintegration*, New York:DaCapo Press, 1993.

Huxtable, Ada Louise, *The Tall Building Artistically Reconsidered: The Search for a Skyscraper Style*, Berrkeley:University of California Press, 1982.

Jordy, William H. and Coe, Ralph, ed., *Montgomery Schuyler: American Architecture and Other Writings, Volume I and II*, Cambridge:The Belknap Press of Harvard University Press, 1961.

Kimball, Fiske, *American Architecture*, New York:The Bobbs-Merrill Company, 1928.

Kostof, Spiro, ed., *The Architect: Chapters in the History of the Profession*, Berkeley, Los Angeles and London:University of California Press, 1977.

Landau, Sarah Bradford and Carl W. Condit, *Rise of the New York Skyscraper, 1865-1913*, New Haven:Yale University Press, 1996.

Marston Fitch, James, *American Building: The Historical Forces that Shaped It*, Boston:Houghton Mifflin Company, 1966.

Mumford, Lewis, *Sticks and Stones: A Study of American Architecture and Civilization*, New York:Dover Publications, Inc., 1955.

_____ , *The Brown Decades: A Study of the Arts in America, 1865-1895*, New York:Dover Publications, Inc., 1971.

Pokinski, Deborah Frances, *The Development of the American Modern Style*, Michigan:UMI Research Press, 1984.

Roth, Leland M., ed. *America Builds: Source Documents in American Planning*, New York:Harper & Row, 1983.

Stern, Robert A.M., Gregory Gilmartin, and John Massengale. *New York 1900: Metropolitan Architecture and Urbanism, 1890-1915*, New York:Rizzoli International Publications, Inc., 1983.

_____ , *New York 1930: Architecture and Urbanism Between the Two World Wars*, New York:Rizzoli International Publications, Inc., 1987.

van Leeuwen, Thomas A.P., *The Skyward Trend of Thought: The Metaphysics of the American Skyscraper*, Cambridge:The MIT Press, 1986.

Willis, Carol, *Form Follows Finance: Skyscrapers and Skylines in New York and Chicago*, Princeton:Princeton Architectural Press, 1995.

Zukowsky, John, ed., *Chicago Architecture, 1872-1922: Birth of a Metropolis*, New York:Prestel Verlag, 2000.

Roman face denotes reference in main text.
Italic denotes reference in a side article.
Bold denotes a photograph.

Photo Credits

l. = left; **r.** = right; **t.** = top

cover Collection of The New-York Historical Society, 43502; **xii** Collection of The New-York Historical Society, 48509;
xx t. Keystone-Mast Collection, UCR/California Museum of Photography, University of California, Riverside; **8** Museum
of the City of New York; **30, 37, 40** Avery Architectural and Fine Arts Library Columbia University in the City of New
York; **33r.** J. S. Johnston/ Museum of the City of New York, 91.69.89; **50** Collection of The New-York Historical Society,
56603; **55, 61** Wurts Collection/ Museum of the City of New York; **56** Collection of The New-York Historical Society,
59347; **70** Collection of The New-York Historical Society, 61226; **74** Bettmann/Corbis; **124b.** Chicago Historical Society;
127 Smithsonian American Art Museum/Washington D. C. / Art Resource, New York; **130t.** Charles Garnier/Bridgeman
Giraudon; **180** AT&T.